# PANTHER VISION

*Essential Party Writings and Art of Kevin "Rashid" Johnson*

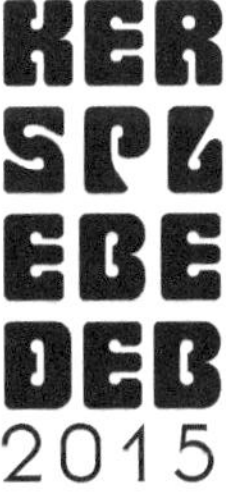

Panther Vision:
Essential Party Writings and Art of Kevin "Rashid" Johnson

ISBN 978-1-894946-76-6
Published in 2015 by Kersplebedeb

Cover artwork by Rashid
Cover and interior design by Kersplebedeb

To order copies of the book, contact:

Kersplebedeb
CP 63560, CCCP Van Horne
Montreal, Quebec
Canada
H3W 3H8

www.kersplebedeb.com
www.leftwingbooks.net

**Since 1998 Kersplebedeb has been an important source of radical literature and agit prop materials.**

**The project has a non-exclusive focus on anti-patriarchal and anti-imperialist politics, framed within an anticapitalist perspective. A special priority is given to writings regarding armed struggle in the metropole, and the continuing struggles of political prisoners and prisoners of war.**

*For the rising youth who see the bankruptcy of what today passes as Black leadership. As a blueprint and inspiration for you in creating the needed leading organization to achieve liberation for us and all oppressed peoples. With eyes wide open, I dedicate these writings.*

*Dare to Struggle, Dare to Win!*
*All Power to the People!*

On December 29, 2020, there was a split in the New Afrikan Black Panther Party and all of the organization's members separated from Shaka Zulu aka Zulu Sharod and Tom Watts and reconstituted as the Revolutionary Intercommunal Black Panther Party. The RIBPP still maintains all of the line and ideology of the NABPP; the only change is in the name of the organization and in separating from those two members. The United Panther Movement was the principal mass org of the NABPP. After the split most of the national UPM joined the RIBPP in separating from the NABPP. The National UPM reconstituted as the Panther Solidarity Organization, which is now the principal mass organization of the RIBPP.

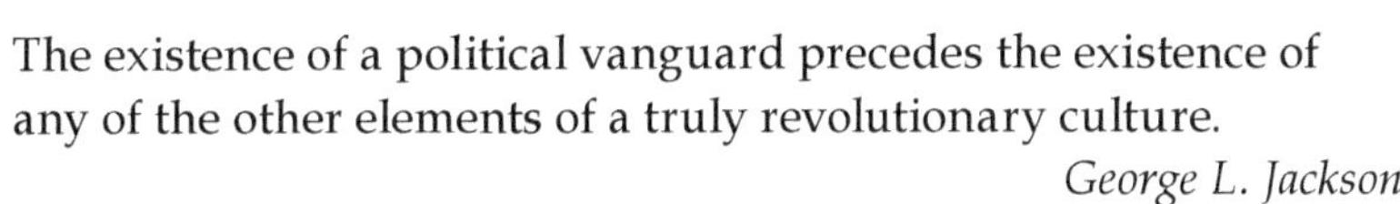

The existence of a political vanguard precedes the existence of any of the other elements of a truly revolutionary culture.

*George L. Jackson*

The vanguard party must provide leadership for the people. It must teach the correct strategic methods of prolonged resistance through literature and activities.

*Huey P. Newton*

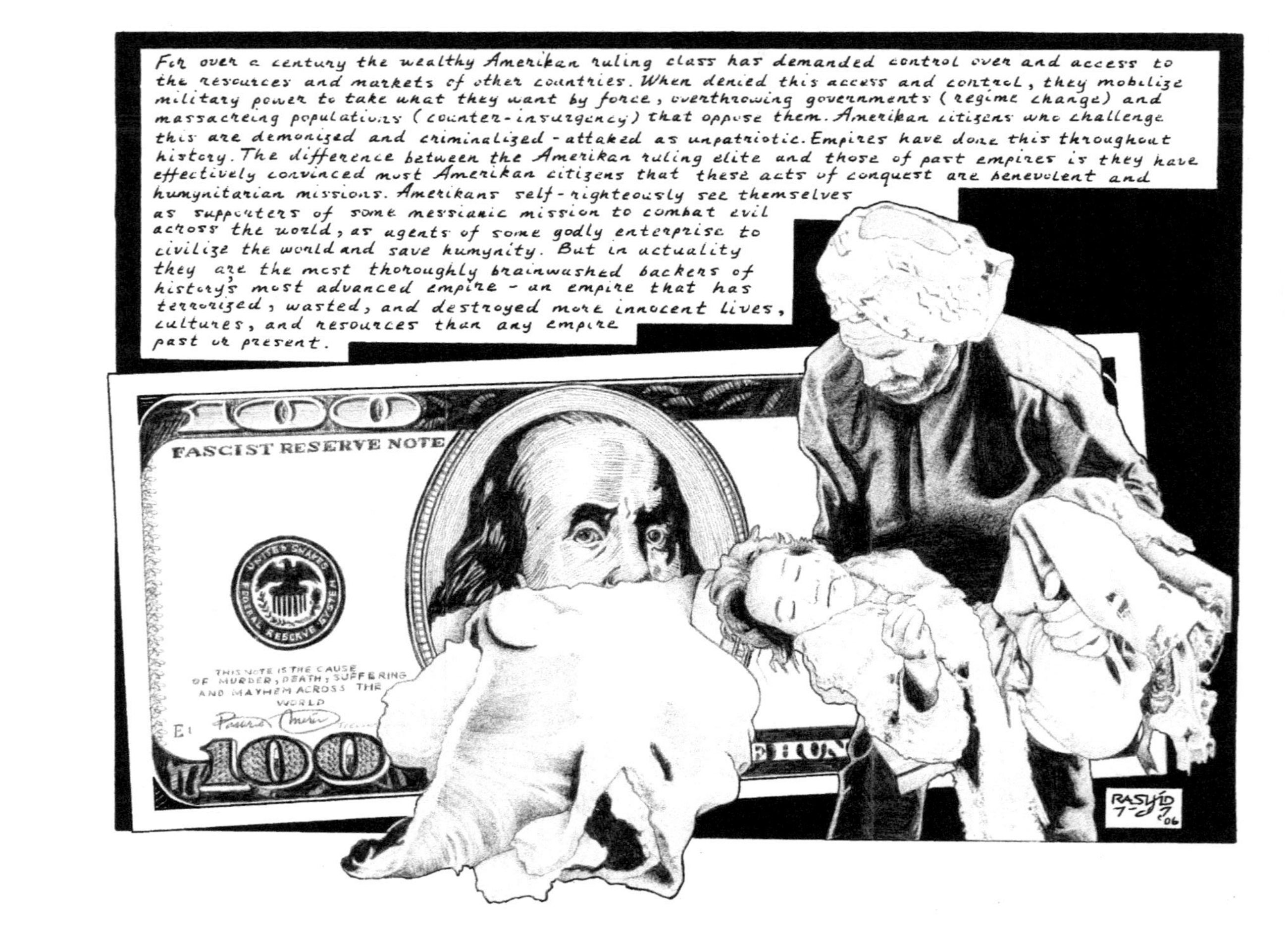

For over a century the wealthy Amerikan ruling class has demanded control over and access to the resources and markets of other countries. When denied this access and control, they mobilize military power to take what they want by force, overthrowing governments (regime change) and massacreing populations (counter-insurgency) that oppose them. Amerikan citizens who challenge this are demonized and criminalized - attaked as unpatriotic. Empires have done this throughout history. The difference between the Amerikan ruling elite and those of past empires is they have effectively convinced most Amerikan citizens that these acts of conquest are benevolent and humynitarian missions. Amerikans self-righteously see themselves as supporters of some messianic mission to combat evil across the world, as agents of some godly enterprise to civilize the world and save humynity. But in actuality they are the most thoroughly brainwashed backers of history's most advanced empire - an empire that has terrorized, wasted, and destroyed more innocent lives, cultures, and resources than any empire past or present.
FASCIST RESERVE NOTE
THIS NOTE IS THE CAUSE OF MURDER, DEATH, SUFFERING AND MAYHEM ACROSS THE WORLD
100
RASHID 7-7 '06

# TABLE OF CONTENTS



## PART I: INTERVIEWS



## PART II: BURNING QUESTIONS

## PART III: PHILOSOPHY



## PART IV: ORGANIZATION

## PART V: ARTICLES AND ANALYSES

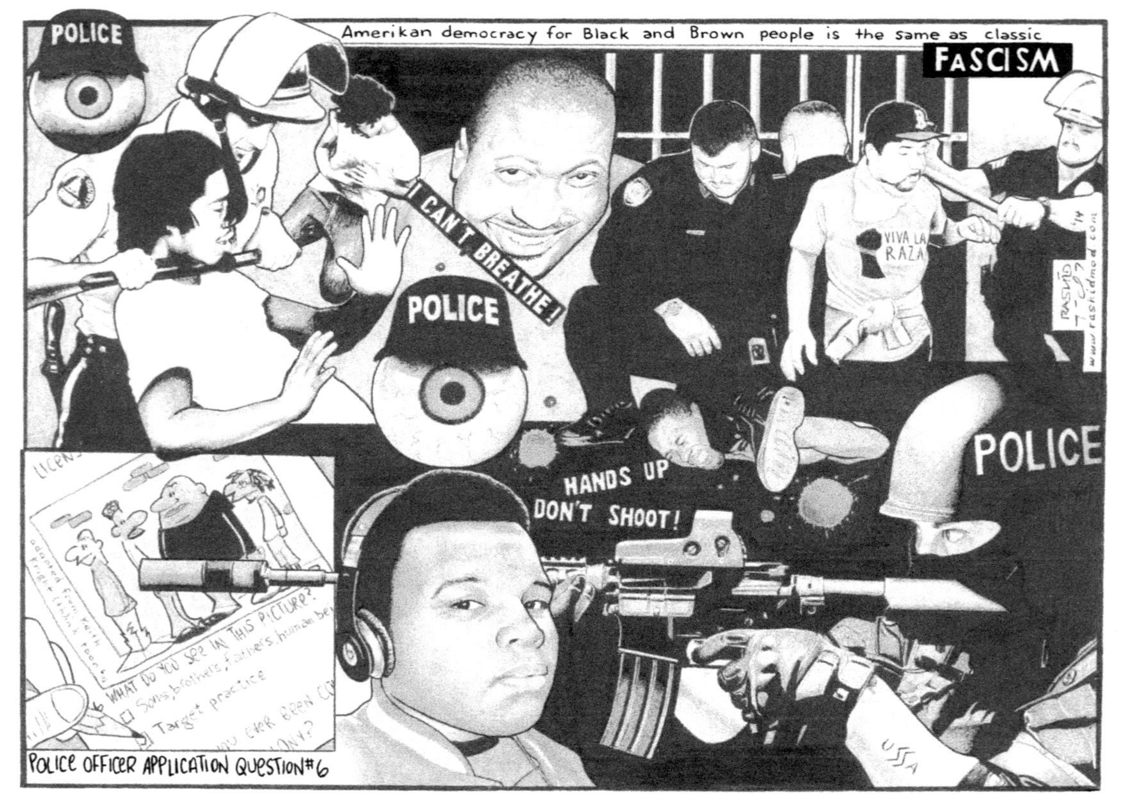

Amerikan democracy for Black and Brown people is the same as classic
FASCISM
POLICE
I CAN'T BREATHE!
POLICE
VIVA LA RAZA
www.rashidmod.com
HANDS UP
DON'T SHOOT!
POLICE
WHAT DO YOU SEE IN THIS PICTURE?
Sons, brothers, fathers, human be
Target practice
adapted from Keith
POLICE OFFICER APPLICATION QUESTION#6

# HANDS UP DON'T SHOOT!

Contrary to the refrain from the tragic Ferguson, MO shooting of Michael Brown, we know that keeping your hands up does not mean you will not be shot. Assata Shakur had her hands up when she was shot on a New Jersey turnpike by a State Trooper, Oscar Brown was laying flat on a subway platform when he was shot by a Bay Area Transit cop, Sean Bell was executed in a hail of bullets by a half dozen cops on the New York city streets, and Trayvon Martin fought to defend himself when he was murdered by a wanna-be cop just yards from his home. Obviously, I find this plea for mercy sorely insufficient, in fact, indefensible when a trained killer has a weapon pointed at you under the guise of Blue authority. Needless to say, this passive posture generally supports the inferior and superior paradigm, creating a social environment in which Black lives do not matter. Brooke Reynolds, in an essay titled *Policing Race*, informed:

> "This 'order' was created and protected by U.S. law. From slavery to today's militarized ghettos, it is clear that racial violence has almost always occurred explicitly or implicitly in cooperation with the law. William and Murphy trace the relationship between the law and social order: 'The fact that the legal order not only countenanced but sustained slavery, segregation, and discrimination for most of our nation's history and the fact that the police were bound to uphold that order set a pattern for police behavior and attitudes toward minority communities that has persisted until the present day' (Parenti). In terms of the relationship to the police themselves, 'Government-sponsored racial discrimination and segregation have deeply affected the organizing ethos and practices of U.S. policing.' (Parenti)—thus, it becomes clear that ' ... relationship between police violence and social institution of policing is structural, rather than incidental or contingent' (Martinot, Sexton). Wielding an arsenal of moralist rhetoric and trained over hundreds of years of historical practice, the police work in conjunction with white society and its government to keep white lawlessness understood as nothing other than 'public order,' enforcing 'the law of white supremacist attack' with determination and fervor."

In response to this reality, Robert Williams wrote the book *Negroes With Guns*, reflecting on the institutionalization of state violence and the inherent human right of Black people to defend themselves, that was also practiced by the Deacons for Defense opposing Klu Klux Klan violence.

Reynolds continues:

> "By conflating the perpetration of police racial violence with the maintenance of social order, it is rendered unidentifiable, ignorable, and inarticulable. Having been so deeply written into our very conception of social organization and policing, police brutality and racism becomes invisible to white society (who also has an investment in denying the reality of racial violence). Shocked by stories of police violence and unmoved by the dehumanization of racial profiling, white people simultaneously reveal their ignorance of and investment in the violence inherent in the protection of white supremacy."

Furthermore, Reynolds states:

> "The ignorability and inarticulability of racist police violence to white society is directly related to its historical and current impunity. Authorized by the government and white society as a whole, the police are given the freedoms necessary in order to guarantee the stability of white supremacy and to continue constructing racialized identities. Within this system, injustices done to people of color are not classified as injustices, if they are recognized at all. Police murders, abuses, and terrorization of people of color, no matter how gratuitous, are more often than not met with legal indifference, public support, and are virtually bereft of consequences. Martinot notes the relationship between modern day police impunity, slave patrols, and white supremacist law:
>
> "'Both the police and the impunity of slave masters belong to the same paradigm of dual systems of law, sanctioned by the law, in producing the subjection of people of color. What contemporary juridicial procedure has done, by valorizing police impunity, is regenerated the doubled system of law of the slave system ... Thus, both manifest the component elements of white racialized identity paranoia ... , violence ... , and white solidarity ... ' (Martinot)
>
> "The racist police violence which pervades the landscape of U.S. society today is not incidental, 'nor [is it] the work of "rogue cops." [It is] an essential part of the larger campaign of social re-racialization' (Martinot). Historically rooted in a very real desire to subjugate and control people of color in America, and operating in a way which inscribes and deepens whiteness as an identity and a value, today's police forces operate along the same paradigm as their predecessors."

These lengthy quotes from Reynolds' *Policing Race* serve to establish the lens through which we are to view Rashid's writings.

As had the original Black Panther Party, Rashid and the New Afrikan Black Panther Party work to defend the struggle of national liberation and independence of Black people (New Afrikans). In this defense, it is extremely important to know the relationship between the government, a system of institutionalized white supremacy, and Black people. I believe Rashid capsulizes this antagonistic relationship, a struggle that has been waged for over 400 years, and in so doing, Rashid immortalizes the heroes of our struggle such as Huey Newton, George Jackson and Malcolm X by seeking to synthesize their ideological thinking into a pragmatic theoretical determination of historical relevance to today's struggle.

The original Black Panther Party for Self-Defense challenged the prevailing socio-political and economic relationship between the government and Black people. The New Afrikan Black Panther Party is building on that foundation, and Rashid's writings embrace the need for a national organization in place of that which had been destroyed by COINTELPRO and racist repression. We can only hope this book reaches many, and serves to herald and light a means for the next generation of revolutionaries to succeed in building a mass and popular movement.

But let us be absolutely clear, "Hands Up Don't Shoot" is a passive plea for mercy, and at best a neurotic concept perpetuated by the misguided belief that We too are Americans.

# GOING BEYOND "REVOLUTIONARY BUT GANGSTA" TO "ALL-THE-WAY REVOLUTIONARY"

The New Afrikan Black Panther Party-Prison Chapter (NABPP-PC) originated as a faction within the prison-based Black Brigade. Comrade Samuel "Angel" Coley, who'd been an original Black Panther Party (BPP) member and was the founder of the Party's Free Breakfast for Children program in Philly, had been the prime mover in organizing the Black Brigade and had convinced me to publish its newsletter, but he was dying from a severe case of hepatitis he had contracted from infected handcuffs breaking his skin. So, leadership fell to another Pennsylvania prisoner named Nathaniel Lee, who was very influenced by Hobbesian philosophy, and he named the Brigade's newsletter *Leviathan* as homage to Hobbes.

Lee styled himself as the "Commander" of the Black Brigade, and was opposed to developing any sort of democratic structure to the Brigade, but he didn't mind it being politically eclectic or the formation of a faction inspired by George Jackson's BPP Prison Chapter (originally called the "New BPP Prison Chapter") of which Kevin "Rashid" Johnson, (a Virginia prisoner), Shaka S. Zulu (a prisoner in NJ) and Hasan Shakur, (a prisoner on "Death Row" in Texas) were the leading members. At least he didn't at first, but as their influence over the Brigade's membership grew (via their newsletter *Right On!*), he tried to expel them. What happened instead was the members followed them in reforming the Black Brigade as the New Afrikan Service Organization (NASO) led by the NABPP-PC and based on agreement with their Ten Point Program (which was the same as the original BPP). NASO's newsletter was called *Serve The People!*

This was not simply a clash of egos, however, but an ideological-political struggle between bourgeois and proletarian worldviews. Thomas Hobbes (1588–1679) was one of the founders of modern political philosophy and political science. He lived in the time of the English Civil War, and he had a foot in both camps, switching from the royalists to the rising bourgeoisie led by Oliver Cromwell. On the one hand, he was a defender of absolutism and vesting unlimited power in the sovereign, and on the other, he laid out the rationale for bourgeois liberalism.

The Panther faction, led by Rashid, countered with the view of revolutionary nationalism, or national liberation leading to socialist revolution. So the nature of the divide was on whether the question of the oppression of Black people in Amerika was one of failure of capitalism to be consistent in its application of the principles of bourgeois liberalism or whether racism and inequality were built into the capitalist system and could only be overcome by socialist revolution. In this epoch, the worldview of the bourgeoisie is dominant, but it is not the same as it was when capitalism was rising. Capitalism has reached its highest and final stage and is in decline. The aspirations of the oppressed nations to be independent are crushed under the weight of global imperialism. Time and again, bourgeois neo-liberalism reveals itself to be disguised fascism. Appeals to professed beliefs in the high-sounding phrases of "Equality before the Law" and "Liberty and Justice for All!" fall on deaf ears. As Lenin correctly observed, "Fascism is capitalism in decline," and whether open or concealed, it has but one rationale, and that is to serve the absolutism of monopoly capital.

The decline of capitalism is also the epoch of proletarian socialist revolution. Revolution advances in waves, and the high-water mark of the last great wave was in the late-60s and early-70s. This was a time when thousands of young Blacks surged to join the BPP, and the Party itself was out in front illuminating the path forward for oppressed people in Amerika and around the world. But the past weighs heavily on the present, and breaking free of it is not easy to do. Old ideas and habits are hard to break and when challenged summon forth waves of reaction and retrogression pulling society backwards. The high tide of struggle that saw U.S. imperialism defeated in Vietnam and "Jim Crow" segregation defeated at home was followed by decades of intensified oppression, concentration of wealth and power, generalization of poverty, and globalization of capitalist-imperialist domination, with the defeat of the socialist countries in the "Cold War."

Black cultural nationalism, which the original BPP had rejected and struggled against, and the FBI's COINTELPRO counter-insurgency program had promoted, rose to dominance in the Black liberation movement after the demise of the BPP. The New Black Panther Party (NBPP), which was founded in 1989 as a split from the Nation of Islam (NOI), was the antithesis of the original BPP. They adopted the Party's name and symbols but promoted a diametrically opposite ideological-political line.

Cultural nationalism takes on different forms, for like all idealism it is not rooted in objective reality but in subjective beliefs. Basically, it is the belief that shared culture alone is sufficient to constitute a nation, an example being the constitution of the Zionist state of Israel in Palestine. Black cultural nationalism opposes itself to class unity and socialist revolution.

Sorting out the legacy and rebuilding the BPP on the foundation of the original Party at its most revolutionary was the task that the core of the NABPP-PC set out for itself at its founding in 2005. Comrades Rashid, Shaka Zulu and Hasan Shakur constituted the original central committee. Each of them had come from the "gangsta life" that had followed the suppression of the original BPP in ghettos across Amerika, and each had been reborn as revolutionaries in prison.

Politically and ideologically, the original BPP had started as a Black nationalist organization strongly influenced by the teachings of Malcolm X, but they soon evolved into revolutionary nationalism through fierce and constant struggle with Black cultural nationalists like Ron Karenga. Indeed, Malcolm X himself was making this leap prior to his assassination. From there, they evolved into proletarian internationalists allying themselves with socialist countries and national liberation movements around the world. By 1970, the BPP had become officially Marxist-Leninists, and with Huey P. Newton's "Theory of Revolutionary Intercommunalism," they began to break new ground in applying the revolutionary science of dialectical materialism to the concrete conditions then emerging. This advance was not consolidated, however, and the Party soon split apart into reformist and adventurist factions and steadily declined. Picking up the pieces 35 years later and applying revolutionary science to the current situation, the core group of NABPP-PC again waged a concerted struggle against cultural nationalism as well as against right and left opportunist tendencies. At every step, there were "nay-sayers" and even veteran comrades who said it couldn't be done and shouldn't even be attempted. The only encouragement that could be found was in Mao's teaching that even if all you've got is a basically correct ideological-political line, and you persevere, everything else you need will come to you. So the comrades put their focus on developing as correct an ideological-political line as possible and propagating it through the newsletters we were publishing, which were made available free to prisoners wherever we could get them past the prison mail room censors. Those that got through were passed from prisoner to prisoner, and around them were formed study circles and Panther collectives.

Everywhere, the comrades were subjected to harassment and repression, and no one more intensely than Rashid, who was subjected to actual torture and constant threats upon his life by guards and their stooges. Instead of "dumbing down" our line, as many critics advised, we strove to make it sharper and more "all-the-way revolutionary." What follows is a selection of Comrade Rashid's writings which were originally published in newsletters from Rising Sun Press that are still being passed hand to hand in the "slave pens of Amerika" and read and discussed by serious revolutionaries around the world.

*THE FUTURE IS UNWRITTEN!*
*DARE TO STRUGGLE, DARE TO WIN!*
*ALL POWER TO THE PEOPLE! PANTHER LOVE!*

*Tom "Big Warrior" Watts was born in 1951 and grew up in the industrial city of Allentown, PA. He hooked up with the White Panther Party at the protests outside the Democratic Party's national convention in Chicago in 1968, and returned to Pennsylvania where he became a regional coordinator for the White Panthers, working alongside Black Panthers and Young Lords.*

*Over the years, Tom has been involved in many struggles as a workers and social activist, and also as a member of the United Eastern Lenape Nation. In the mid '90s, he founded Rising Sun Press to publish the newsletter of the UELN, and in 2000, he founded the Red Heart Warriors Society for Native American prisoners. At the request of Black prisoners, he helped to create the Black Brigade as a fraternal organization to RHWS. In 2005, he helped to create the New Afrikan Black Panther Party-Prison Chapter, which started as a faction within the Black Brigade.*

*He also helped to found the White Panther Party Organization as an arm of NABPP-PC and the Brown Panther Organizing Committee. For many years, Rising Sun Press published quarterly newsletters for all these prison-based organizations that were available free to prisoners. Presently, Tom administers the United Panther Study Group on facebook, and he is working to establish a national newspaper for the United Panther Movement.*

INTRODUCTION BY JARED BALL

# THE POLITICS AND ART OF KEVIN "RASHID" JOHNSON: THE RETURN OF THE REPRESSED

> "The settler's work is to make even dreams of liberty impossible for the native. The native's work is to imagine all possible methods for destroying the settler."
>
> *Frantz Fanon*

> "[Revolutionary thought is] invisibilized within the logic of our present order of discourse and its symbolic representations."
>
> *Sylvia Wynter*

In so many ways the devolving state of our material conditions must be seen in association with limitations imposed on our governing ideas. Our inability to truly and fully extricate ourselves from long-ago set in motion patterns of relationships is directly linked to largely successful efforts to powerfully limit what we consider possible. Even our ability to dream of liberty, of permanently dismantling the colonial binds that hold us, have been among many of us, if not erased entirely, at best reduced to fantasies of Black presidents and Tyler Perry movies.

Thankfully, not for all of us. The process of erasure is not now nor can it really ever be total. The persistent attempt to scrub us of our critical memory, to remove from us any consciousness of radical traditions or appropriate calls for their implementation today in the form of political organization is not yet total. As evidence we have the example of Kevin Rashid Johnson and his comrades. At minimum, what Rashid and they represent is an attempt to restore some of that suppressed critical memory and to develop for us a far more appropriate point of departure for analyzing the world and our place in it. His is a painful reminder to the state and its minions that their work is necessary and still incomplete.

I say their work is necessary only insofar as the desire among an increasingly powerful and insulating elite to maintain their distinction requires tremendous effort. Rashid and the New Afrikan Black Panther Party-Prison Chapter (NABPP-PC) he co-founded extends a tradition of resistance that offers sound analysis and programmatic backing that reminds the enemy of the reasons for its sprawling apparatus, its desire for what is often described as "full spectrum dominance." This is understood as a need to dominate media and communication of all kinds just as the military aspires to the control of land, sea and air (including outer space). Radical intervention in the process of limiting, if not arranging, ranges of thought must be addressed, one way or another.

Persistent and intergenerational exploitation requires systems of spirituality, education and media that define critical thought and its attendant behavior as aberrant, unnecessary or plain crazy. Rashid represents a logic that has been under attack ever since the first person consciously looked to take permanent advantage of another and his treatment physically is analogous to the treatment of his ideas in the broader so-called "marketplace." Schools, prisons and their logic-extending and supportive mass media have ever only been designed as mirror images, partners in their reflection of dominant and normative patterns of thought. In short, social order. Rashid openly calling for these "razor wire plantations" to be turned into centers of "liberation" along with his consciously political and brilliant art assaults/insults these institutions and their political necessity.

Rashid's treatment—isolation, relocation, institutional violence, etc.—then is the material equivalent to what is systematically done to an entire coterie of ideas with which he works or represents. If, as Marshall McLuhan once asserted, media are extensions of consciousness just as tools extend physical capabilities then what occurs in our public sphere is isolation, relocation and violent erasure of radical perspectives in favor of those of our oppressive elite. The FBI's Counter Intelligence Program (COINTELPRO), so expertly dealt with in the text that follows, called explicitly for methods to be devised that would assure Black youth never positively associate with revolutionary nationalism. For centuries before that the state had seen fit to disassociate Black people from any positive identification with Africa. And today, hip-hop, the most vibrant and potentially revolutionary cultural expression ever created has seen the imperial reach of now just three corporations—themselves bit pieces of larger international conglomerates and private equity holdings—impose on its most popular form an absence of any engagement with a radicalism that all its elements had and continue to demonstrate when unfettered.

The study and journalistic coverage of hip-hop has also seen its radicalism forcibly subdued by a creeping commercialism as capitalism adjusted itself over the last several decades. Rather than continue to dismiss hip-hop as fad or anti-musical nonsense as was done initially, much of the first wave hip-hop analysis that obliterated those myths and demonstrated the genius and radical nature of the varied elemental art form has been replaced by well-funded and promoted narratives that allow American empire to take credit and reap ultimate material/immaterial benefit. Hip-hop can now generate billions annually for a variety of major industries and can also be exported in various ways to both falsely define its African captives while cleansing the U.S.'s own national contradictions. Yes, of course, Black people do indeed continue to suffer all forms of increasing inequality but mostly as a result of their own doing considering how so many can clearly become famous rappers, entertainers and even presidents.

Much like earlier dominant cultural expressions created from the internal Black colony hip-hop, as was previously the case with jazz, has selected for it State Department ambassadors who are sent as national emissaries to carry the "America really isn't that bad" message to the world. Similarly, silly linear narratives of hip-hop which parallel those imposed on Black history, attempt to describe a singular upward trajectory toward (at least near) freedom. Hip-hop, like the origins of its progenitors' rise from plantations, arose from the ravages of the Bronx eventually paving new avenues of wealth and power all, again matching the mythic tale of its broader history, preparing the country for the eventual culminating act of liberation; the election of Barack Obama. All of this is meant to pummel our consciousness into submission, to weaken our ability to reconnect with our own radical traditions and those of the rest of the world, to assure we never ask the right questions or achieve the right answers.

In comes Rashid, with Marx, Lenin, Mao, Huey and George. Not only are Black people to assume a revolutionary relationship with Africa but they are themselves to become New Afrikan and revolutionarily intercommunal. Rashid represents the fear expressed by COINTELPRO's fearful question: What happens if this radicalism reaches successive generations and then explicitly calls for the same and more in their time? He both articulates to his contemporaries and those coming behind him the context in which their art exists, the shifts in the landscape that take us from African medallion hip-hop to the bling era. He can also demonstrate with wondrous skill the power artists have in articulating those same ideas, critiques and concepts of revolution. Rashid in this sense becomes the problem he has himself warned is necessary.

In another sense Rashid becomes also the perfect embodiment of the concerns voiced long ago in a critique of William Styron's Nat Turner by John Oliver Killens. Killens noted how Styron could give interviews praising Turner during the late 1960s while being sure not to support the then contemporary struggle of Turner's collective Black revolutionary descendants. That is, while it was fine to speak well of Nat Turner whose actions were so old and so obviously justifiable, it was not acceptable to apply that logic to Styron's contemporaries. In our moment Rashid is both Turner then and now. He is the one whose ideas can only be considered—if at all—as history.

So Rashid is correct to note as he does that in the very year he and his comrade Shaka Sanfoka Zulu founded the NABPP-PC the then governor of California Arnold Schwarzenegger had Stanley "Tookie" Williams put to death specifically for the ideas associated with the dedication in Williams' book to dangerous people and the ideas they represent, most notable among them George Jackson. Jackson, among others, remains the nightmare he was in his life. Even recalling his memory can be a capital offense. We are not meant to even dream of liberty much less engage the thinkers whose ideas might teach us to achieve it.

We need not all fully agree. We need not simply accept each and every idea Rashid offers as unquestionably correct or applied. However, our survival, our only hope, is in engaging these ideas, studying them, challenging them and ourselves. At minimum, those who would spend even a moment critiquing MSNBC, CNN or FOX News, must take at least that much time to struggle with our brightest thinkers, artists, organizers. This book is an essential addition to our revolutionary canon and deserves every bit of our attention, study and implementation. For it is indeed still true, as Fred Hampton once said, genuine peace can only come to those who fight for it.

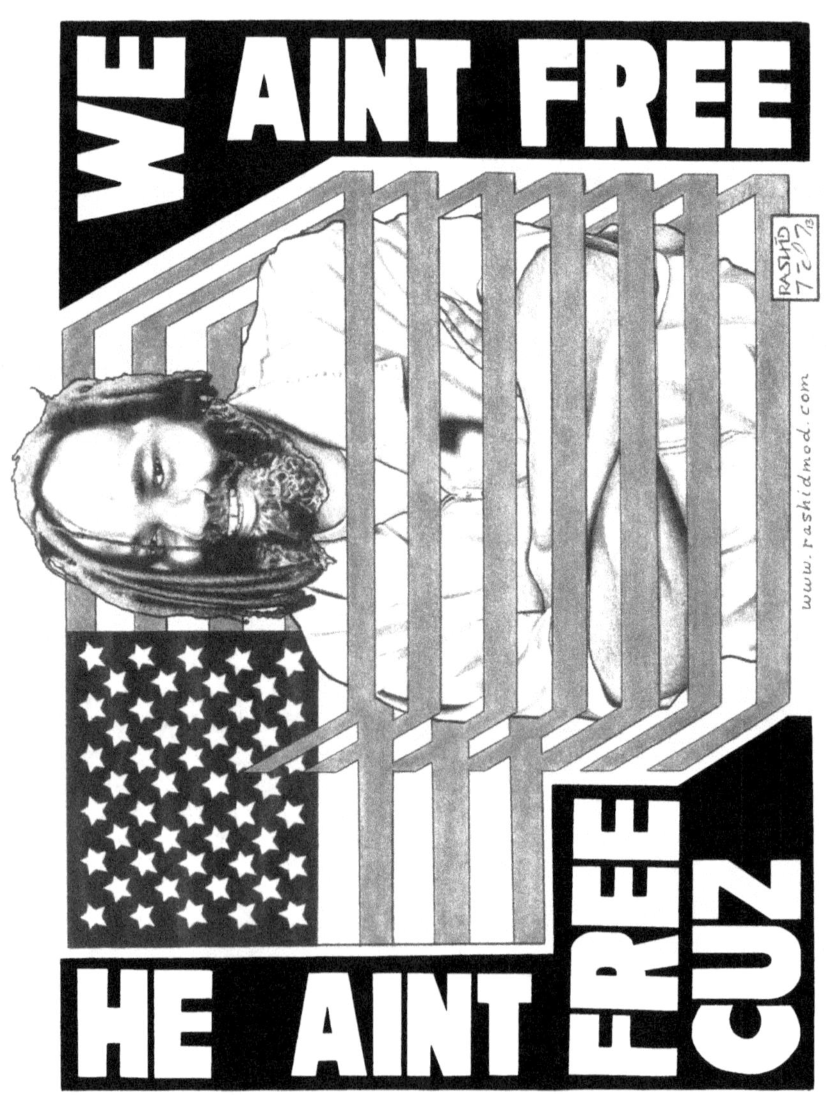
WE AINT FREE
HE AINT FREE CUZ
RASHID 7-27-13
www.rashidmod.com

# 1. FORTY YEARS AFTER: THE BLACK PANTHER PARTY 2006

*By Mumia Abu-Jamal*

Amazingly, it has been 40 years since the Black Panther Party was founded.

Some sticklers to detail will point to the fact that it was in October, not May, of 1966, that the Black Panther Party was founded by two young men in Oakland, California, named Huey P. Newton and Bobby Seale.

That's true; but that's not the end of the story.

The late African nationalist, Kwame Ture (formerly known as Stokely Carmichael), when a leader of SNCC (or Student Non-Violent Coordinating Committee), published a month before Huey and Bobby joined together, an article detailing SNCC's efforts to organize both in the South and the Northeast. In a September, 1966 article published in the *New York Review of Books*, Ture wrote:

> "SNCC today is working in both North and South on programs of voter registration and independent political organizing. In some places, such as Alabama, Los Angeles, New York, Philadelphia, and New Jersey, independent organizing under the black panther symbol is in progress. The creation of a national 'black panther party' must come about; it will take time to build, and it is much too early to predict its success. We have no infallible master plan and we make no claim to exclusive knowledge of how to end racism; different groups will work in their own different ways. SNCC cannot spell out the full logistics of self-determination, but it can address itself to the problem by helping black communities define their needs, realize their strength, and go into action along a variety of lines which they must choose for themselves. Without knowing all the answers, it can address itself to the basic problem of poverty, to the fact that in Lowndes County 86 white families own 90 per cent of the land. What are black people in that county going to do for jobs; where are they going to get money? There must be reallocation of land, of money."
>
> Stokely Carmichael, *Stokely Speaks: Black Power Back to Pan-Africanism* (New York: Vintage, 1965/1971), p. 22

It was in fact, SNCC's efforts in Lowndes County, Alabama, that inspired Huey to use the name "Black Panther Party."

But, it's been 40 years. It's safe to say that much of the history of Huey's Party remains hidden history. This isn't rhetoric—it's fact.

One year ago, I received a wealth of letters from college students who read my book, *We Want Freedom: A Life in the Black Panther Party* (Boston: South End, 2004). Here, scores of letters, from a wide variety of students from various racial and ethnic groups, almost all of whom expressed shock and surprise, not just at the unknown history of the Party, but of the history of Black history overall. One writer, Shanara P. noted, "... most of the facts you wrote in your book were never taught in the schools I went to."

Wayne S. wrote: "'The Beginnings of the Black Panther Party and the History it Sprang From' and 'The Deep Roots of the Struggle for Black Liberation' should become amendments to the history books which choose to leave out the violent uprisings against slavery. If I had not read these chapters, I could have been a graduate-level student about to get a masters degree but would have absolutely no idea of one of the catalysts of the Civil War, such as the Christiana rebellion. This is just one example of the pseudo factual history books which are being implanted around our schools."

Another student, Jon M., wrote: "I feel cheated because this is the first time I have heard such stories."

As a writer and historian, I was, of course, delighted by such letters. But as a former member of the Party, it was eye-opening at how invisible the Party has become with the passage of time.

But why should we be surprised? What did we expect?

The Party played a major role, in its time, to organize our People into resistance to the state. For many millions of youth, Black History means reading about (or hearing boring lectures about) Frederick Douglass, Martin Luther King, Jr., and perhaps Malcolm X. It rarely goes deeper than that.

Before this generation goes on to its ancestors, we should, we must, do our level best to pass on our lessons, so that they live in our people's minds and lives.

There is, already, a new formation that has arisen, which calls itself New Afrikan Black Panther Party, which has prison chapters in several states. Unlike other formations which have used the BPP name, these youngsters actually read and study the works of Huey P. Newton, George Jackson, and other leading Party members. The struggle continues!

# PART I

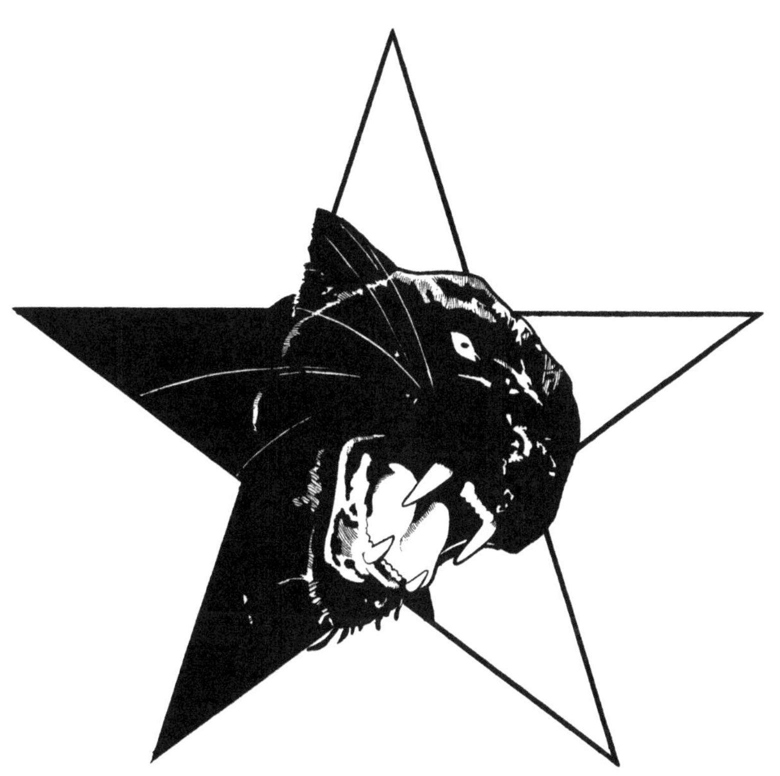

# INTERVIEWS

*Generally, when you do an interview, the interviewer and the interviewee sit down together and the interviewee spontaneously responds to the questions of the interviewer, who may or may not have a prepared list of questions. Usually, afterwards, you think of all sorts of responses you wish you had said, but of course it's too late. Under the circumstances of Rashid's confinement, this sort of interview was impossible, so when Anthony Rayson proposed doing an interview with Comrade Rashid, it necessarily had to be done by correspondence. But I think this was actually better, because it gave Rashid time to reflect upon his answers, and even discuss them with comrades, leading to a very full exposition of the line of NABPP-PC as it was evolving at that time.*

*Comrade Rayson is an Anarchist, whom Comrade Rashid has known and corresponded with for many years, and there is mutual respect between them, and this afforded an opportunity to contrast the line of NABPP-PC with a different ideological and political tendency on the Left, and, indeed, with the current Amerikan Left in general. Rashid also took the opportunity to sum up the history of the Black movement in the U.S. and its two main tendencies leading up to the formation of the original Black Panther Party (BPP), with particular attention to the evolution of the political thought of Dr. Martin Luther King, Jr. and Malcolm X, both of whom had been cut down by political assassination as they began to evolve into socialist revolutionaries.*

*By attempting to go beyond the options of integration into or separation from the white-dominated political-economic system, they were targeted for destruction by the powers that be. This was where the BPP started, and dared to advance along a revolutionary path, despite the danger, and it is in their footsteps that the NABPP-PC has followed, with the full intention of continuing to advance to liberation through socialist revolution. This is the only viable option for Black liberation in Amerika and for the oppressed peoples throughout the world.*

*Tom Watts*

# 2. ON THE PRESENT STATE OF NEW AFRIKAN/BLACK CRISIS IN AMERIKA; REVOLUTIONARY ART; THE UNITED PANTHER MOVEMENT; AND COMMUNISM VS. ANARCHISM: AN INTERVIEW WITH COMRADE RASHID BY ANTHONY RAYSON 2010

**Anthony Rayson**: As you know Amerika does not want people to know what you know and are busy articulating. We're told the "civil rights struggle" of the 1960s took care of racism and that Blacks are cool with capitalism (Snoop Doggism). Tell us what the deal really is and the place the vast gulag system plays in society today—particularly with Black people.

**Rashid**: We both recognize that the last major wave of New Afrikan/Black struggle against this imperialist (monopoly capitalist) system, racism and national oppression here in Amerika, occurred in the 1960s and 1970s. This struggle took place on two fronts, reflecting the aspirations of two *opposite* class poles in Black Amerika. The first was the pro-monopoly capitalist pole (these elements sought an accommodation with and integration into the U.S. capitalist system). The second was the revolutionary national liberation pole (these elements sought independence and separation from the Amerikan capitalist system or fundamental socialist reconstruction of Amerika's political-economy as a condition to Black integration).

The first tendency was most strongly represented in the Civil Rights Movement. The second tendency by the Black Power/Liberation Movement. Because the second tendency represented a direct challenge to the U.S. imperialist system, it was feared the most by the Establishment.

Dr. Martin Luther King, Jr. began as an accommodationist and pro-integrationist. His major gripe with Amerika was that white racism was a major obstacle to Black integration. That the U.S. government in openly fostering racism was not living up to the rhetoric of all people being equal as expressed in its founding creed—the Declaration of Independence.

As a middle class (petty bourgeois) Black, MLK initially held the same class values as the U.S. capitalist ruling class (big bourgeoisie), so he had no beef with capitalism itself, only with the conditions of white racism which prevented Black integration into capitalist Amerika. But

MLK became more class conscious toward the end of his life, and ultimately came to realize that the wealth-worshiping capitalist system was the very cause of social inequalities and exploitation, including white racism. At this point he became an advocate of socialism. But initially, he was an advocate of capitalism. MLK's major presence as a civil rights leader spanned from the late 1950s until his assassination in 1968.

Now at the opposite Black Liberation pole were revolutionary thinkers like Malcolm X. Malcolm's early political understanding was stifled by what I call "reverse racism"—the subjective idea that Blacks are by nature superior to whites and whites are the embodiment of "evil." This view was initially behind his support for Blacks to separate from Amerika. But he wasn't exactly anti-capitalist. In fact, as a leading member of the Nation of Islam, he belonged to an organization that itself promoted Black capitalism. Despite this, his voice was a beacon to New Afrikans who opposed integration into Amerika and accommodation with its white ruling class.

The power structure repeatedly maneuvered to block *both* trends of our movement, prompting New Afrikans to fight back physically against both racial oppression and enforced poverty, and a broad grassroots movement of poor Blacks spontaneously organized to March on Washington, D.C. in 1963, with the intention of shutting the capital down—stopping all movement in D.C. Including shutting down government operations, traffic, airports, commerce, etc.

This is when President John F. Kennedy decided to open up the Democratic Party to Blacks as a "supporter" of us getting basic civil rights and "equality" within the capitalist system, Kennedy and his big money backers financed King, (who was not broadly known then, but was a prominent pacifist civil rights leader in the South), and used him to rein-in and control Black militancy, and the spontaneously-planned 1963 march, which initially MLK had nothing to do with. He became the face and the voice Kennedy and Co. used in the mainstream media, the churches and elsewhere to speak to the riled-up Black masses and contain their festering rage that was threatening to militantly besiege the U.S. capital.

The U.S. government was compelled to use King and the Democratic Party—which was previously rabidly opposed to racial integration and Black civil rights—to avert what would have been a major political and economic crisis that would have shattered its world image. At that time, I believe that MLK, confused by his pro-capitalist class interests, naïve faith in the federal government, and his avowed pacifism, was sincerely opposed to Black racial oppression and felt he was doing the right thing.

So King was used as a political pawn to convert what was going to be an angry Black militant siege of D.C. into a government-controlled, passive, one-day march where Blacks—manipulated into a pacifist spirit with "things will get better someday" speeches—marched, sang, and cried out their frustrations, pain and misery, with a few white sympathizers on the fringes. It was a general repeat of what we'd done for centuries during and since slavery in the Black churches.

Now Malcolm X witnessed this entire farce, saw it for the trick it was, and bitterly criticized King and his allies. Malcolm pointed out that Amerika had repeatedly stifled, subverted, tricked and infiltrated every Black struggle for genuine freedom from oppressive conditions, government brutality and neglect, endemic poverty and white racism; and that the 1963 march was just another example of this. He predicted that the Black masses recognized this too, were fed up, and as a result Amerika was in for a "long hot summer" of Black revolt. And just as he predicted, beginning in 1964, (just months after the 1963 march), and continuing through 1968, Black ghettos across the U.S. exploded in continual revolt.

Meantime, after being excommunicated from the NOI by Elijah Muhammad, Malcolm began traveling across Afrika, studying their liberation struggles, working to build Pan-Afrikan ties between the oppressed New Afrikan masses in Amerika and the newly liberated Afrikan nations. From the 1950s through the 1960s, Afrikans were fighting for and winning political independence from European colonialism, and establishing new formally independent Afrikan-led nations. With the European colonizers being expelled from Afrika, and Afrikans taking over the governments, Amerika sought to establish ties with the new heads of the Afrikan countries, so it could secure access to and control over Afrika's abundant natural wealth. However, racism in Amerika presented an image problem that could prevent the U.S. ruling class from winning the "hearts and minds" of Afrika's new Black leaders, and their diplomats who were visiting or living in Amerika. This was actually the motive behind federal government efforts to outlaw segregation in the southern states, beginning with the landmark ruling in *Brown v. Board of Education* in the mid-1950s.

Even during the most rabid periods of racial oppression, Amerika always projected a patently false international image of the U.S. being a racial and cultural "melting pot" where all people lived and were treated equally. Malcolm's efforts threatened U.S. imperialist ambitions in Afrika, as he was actually exposing the true racist face of Amerika to Afrikans and showing them that their own sistas and brothas were just as brutally oppressed in Amerika, as they had been under the European colonial systems they had just struggled to break free of in Afrika.

Unlike MLK, Malcolm X at this stage was a strong advocate of our right to struggle for political independence and separation from Euro-Amerikan rule—as Afrikans were doing in Afrika—and to defend ourselves against racist violence, "by any means necessary," which included by use of arms. Malcolm's views became more and more revolutionary and less rooted in reverse racism, as a result of his international travels. His pilgrimage to Mecca exposed him to the reality that whites were not inherently "evil," but that the brutal racism that he witnessed in Amerika was the result of conditions created by those who ran and "owned" society.

His closer study of U.S. imperialism led him to reject capitalism. The major government fear of Malcolm was that he was winning the support of the nations of color in Afrika and Asia, who were coming to identify Amerika as an imperialist power that was colonizing the Blacks within its own borders, and Malcolm was seen by Afrikan and Asian leaders as the legitimate leader and representative of the oppressed New Afrikans. This threatened to win international support for our right to struggle for national independence from Amerika, just as Afrikans and Asians were doing against European colonialism. Malcolm was also maneuvering to formally present the grievances of New Afrikans against Amerika, including charges of genocide, before the United Nations through a petition he'd drafted. But before all the pieces could come together, the CIA had him assassinated in 1965.

Inspired by Malcolm's revolutionary nationalist and Pan-Afrikan internationalist visions, Huey P. Newton and Bobby Seale founded the Black Panther Party (BPP) the next year to lead this struggle. The BPP openly adopted an anti-capitalist and pro-socialist platform, and implemented socialist [Serve The People/Survival] programs in the ghettos to organize and serve the needs of the people free of dependence on the imperialist system. This quickly earned the Panthers—and the Young Communist Movement they helped inspire—the label of being *the* major threat to the U.S. capitalist system.

Meantime, King became more and more exposed to the fundamental contradictions in capitalism and became disillusioned with it, and blind faith in the U.S. government, and the idea of Black integration into the U.S. Empire as it existed. He thus broke ranks with the middle class, pro-capitalist, civil rights agenda and came out in support of the poor and working-class, and bitterly opposed the war in Vietnam as an adventure in imperial conquest against Asian people struggling for liberation from imperialism.

King became a closet socialist, knowing he'd be killed if he openly championed socialism. But as a devout pacifist he had no concrete ideas on how to pursue a struggle to empower the oppressed poor and working-class people to transition Amerika into a socialist society.

Realizing that he'd been used by the U.S. imperialists in 1963 to stifle the Black movement for fundamental change, MLK planned a new march on Washington to occur in 1968 as a Poor People's Encampment. This campaign would lay siege to the capital as planned in 1963 until subverted, but this time on behalf of all of Amerika's poor and oppressed peoples. King's "betrayal" of capitalism and radical change of politics could not be tolerated by the imperialists, who'd made him a widely recognized leader whom they knew multitudes of Black people across the nation respected and would follow. Therefore, the U.S. government had him assassinated just months before the Poor People's Encampment was set to occur.

Another factor in his assassination was that, beginning in late 1967, MLK became increasingly vocal that he was losing faith in passive resistance and growing tired of being repeatedly brutalized and arrested by the government. The FBI admitted its aim to "neutralize" (government-speak for murder) King for fear he would ultimately abandon his views on passive resistance and openly embrace a genuinely revolutionary line that included the right of the oppressed masses to defend themselves against official violence and pursue fundamental change through methods that included armed struggle.

When, in latter 1967, he began expressing the need to "fashion new tactics which do not count on government good will, but instead serve to *compel* unwilling authorities to yield to the mandates of justice," I believe Dr. King was beginning to struggle—even if only unconsciously—with the inherent contradictions of pacifism as a political strategy. I think he was coming to realize as well that he was not really a pacifist at all. Since, for example, he had embraced the government's use of violence as "legitimate," while rejecting that of the people acting in self-defense as "illegitimate." Indeed, while he counselled the people to practice pacifism in the face of racist and oppressive violence, he'd long looked to the federal government to provide *armed protection* to him, his colleagues, and their followers during southern marches and protests.

He came to realize that it was Amerika's "very own government" that was actually "the greatest purveyor of violence in the world," which left him with the realization that no such power could be looked to by the people to genuinely provide protection and that he was likely to meet a violent end himself at the hands of the government—and he did. Hence his fear to openly promote and lead a mass movement for socialism in Amerika.

A thorough investigation into the role played by the various U.S. government agencies in King's murder in 1968, and the cover-ups that followed, can be found in William Pepper's *An Act of State: The Execution of Martin Luther King* (2003).

After MLK's death, the liberal wing of the U.S. capitalist ruling class's political vanguard (namely the Democratic Party), used the 1963 pro-capitalist, integrationist version of MLK and Black-capitalist civil rights leaders like Jesse Jackson, Sr., (in his final years King was opposed to Jackson's Black capitalism), to project the Democratic Party as Black Amerika's friend and champion, and the channel through which we should pursue social justice. "Black capitalism" was promoted by the imperialists as the key to Black progress. In fact, a plan was promoted, since 1967 by FBI assistant director William E. Sullivan, to destroy MLK and other influential, independent, Black political leaders and activists, and then handpick a "new national Negro leader" to replace them. Sullivan wrote of his plan to destroy such Black leaders:

> "When this is done, and it can *and will be done*, obviously much confusion will reign, particularly among the Negro people .... The Negroes will be left without a national leader of sufficiently compelling personality to steer them in the proper direction."

He promoted that Samuel R. Pierce, Jr., a Black, capitalist, corporate lawyer, be groomed to replace the destroyed Black leadership. However, a new leadership emerged from amongst the people to fill the void, before the imperialist scheme could take root.

This new leadership, namely the BPP, came under all-out attack by the U.S. government at all levels. Its key members were openly assassinated by police and/or jailed on obvious frame-ups, the government attempted to manipulate and even financed violence-prone street gangs and street-level Black capitalist groups into "gang-warfare" against the Panthers. Government agents and "friendlies" inside the media were used to publish articles and air reports slandering and demonizing the Panthers to the Amerikan public. Agent provocateurs were infiltrated into the BPP to incite and carry out acts of violence that would make government counter-violence appear justified. BPP supporters were harassed, slandered, attacked and arrested, Panther community service programs were disrupted, and so on, all carried out as a counter-intelligence program (COINTELPRO) of the FBI.

Because of a flawed internal organizational structure, and because it came to be wrongly "commanded" by Huey instead of correctly led collectively by genuine democratic-centralism, the BPP rank and file were unprepared to handle and to counter government instigations that caused the Panthers to split into two factions; one wing adopted a rightist-accommodationist, liberal-reformist line [like running Bobby Seale for mayor of Oakland as the Democratic Party candidate], while the other wing adopted an adventurist, ultra-leftist, militarist line. Under continued government attack, while pursuing these flawed and incorrect political lines, the Panthers were unable to combat the government's campaign, and the Panthers ultimately self-destructed, with no suitable leadership in the Black community to replace them.

Although several attempts have been made to regroup and rebuild a revolutionary party to lead and organize the Black masses in our struggles, each has failed or disintegrated because none have correctly summed up the lessons of our previous failures and applied this knowledge. So in this void, the Empire has been able to push Black capitalism on the people free of opposition, challenge or alternative, as the *only viable solution* to our oppressed condition—but capitalism is the very *cause* of our oppression and all of our problems. Indeed, it was the lust for profits and the dollar that was behind the kidnapping and enslavement of our Afrikan ancestors to begin with: Capitalism is the enemy!

The cities, where New Afrikans and other oppressed nationalities are concentrated in large numbers, were and are seen as an area of continual threat by the Empire. Deep-seated mass insecurity and desperation still lie just under the surface. Therefore, if ever organized and united in struggle for fundamental change, the U.S. ghettos and barrios could easily transform into revolutionary fronts and base areas here inside the "Belly of the Beast."

But this cannot happen spontaneously. It demands a conscious and committed revolutionary leadership. The Establishment realizes this, and this is why it has remained committed to undermining and destroying every persyn or organization that threatens to take up the torch of the original BPP and lead our people in this direction. To stifle urban revolutionary potential, the system has implemented policies to foster and perpetuate instability in the urban centers, flooding them with narcotics (first heroin and then also crack cocaine, PCP and other addictive and deadly drugs) and military-grade weapons (like AK-47s and Uzis) which generated severe social degeneration, fratricidal gang wars and genocidal implosion.

Stripped of revolutionary leadership and organization, the urban youth have only had their neighborhood gangs (which have been manipulated and used by the oppressor). In place of political purpose and cultural pride, and the self-respect the revolutionary leadership gave the urban youth—which united them in struggle against oppression and for liberation—the Empire and its entertainment media have promoted a self-destructive subculture of "gangsterism," (Black and Brown imitations of earlier movie images of expensively-dressed, luxury car-driving, Italian Mafioso and other white hoodlums devoid of social consciousness), vulgar materialism, crass consumerism, moral depravity, rampant individualism, self-gratification at the expense of the community, nihilism and an illegal, ghetto version of Black capitalism in general.

Under these government-created conditions, the youth turned their poverty-driven frustration and potentially revolutionary rage against themselves, with inner-community violence, street crime and drug-peddling. The Establishment then used these conditions they had created and facilitated to justify increasing their own violent repression of the urban communities under their declared "War on Drugs," "War on Crime," and "War on Gangs." The result has been enhancing of the militarization of the police occupation of these communities and incarceration of the cream of our potentially-revolutionary youth inside the massive, and ever-expanding prison-industrial complex.

In a 2006 report entitled *Cracks in the System: Twenty years of the Unjust Federal Crack Cocaine Law*, even the ACLU admitted that the "Drug War" is targeted at Blacks and has in effect turned U.S. prisons into mass disposal sites for Black people. We can see this scheme was greatly enhanced with the added "War on Gangs." And make no mistake about it, Black youth are the principal targets. The CIA has acknowledged that the largely, youthful, urbanized ethnic populations present a danger of "regime-threatening unrest." A 1984 CIA report stated:

> "The youth of a growing population may very well play a major role in pressing for change. They are among those who are usually disproportionately disadvantaged: They have less at stake in the existing structure of authority, more idealism, more impatience, and in a society with a steady or rising rate of growth their proportion to the total population increases. The density of the number of youth relative to the total population may thus be a clue to strength of pressure for change."

Malcolm X also observed that it was the youth who made up the greater portion of the rank and file forces leading the struggles against colonial oppression in Afrika and Asia. And it was the New Afrikan youth who rose up in revolt against neo-colonial oppression in the urban centers here in Amerika from 1964 to 1968. It is this dense, growing population of urban ethnic youth that the strategy of mass incarceration is designed to deplete. The U.S. prison-industrial complex is a fascist tool of social containment, a weapon evolved to a level of sophistication that makes the concentration camps of Nazi Germany appear crude and amateurish by comparison.

The Establishment fears nothing else as much as it fears these disadvantaged and oppressed youth developing a revolutionary consciousness. California governor Arnold Schwarzenegger made this quite clear when he refused to commute Stanley "Tookie" Williams' death sentence in 2006, not because "Tookie" was a founding member of one of Amerika's largest urban youth gangs, but because he dedicated his book—*Life in Prison*—to New Afrikan revolutionary leaders of the 1960s and '70s, specifically George Jackson—the founder of the original BPP prison chapter—who was assassinated at San Quentin by prison guards in 1971.

The prisons were a major front in our liberation struggle in the '60s and '70s. It was in an effort to crush this aspect of our movement and the outside support for our movement after George Jackson's murder and the Attica Uprising that followed, that the system began the proliferation of "control units" and "supermax" prisons, beginning with the Marion control unit established in 1972. The strategy was to weed-out and isolate potential leaders while the remainder were pitted against each other with instigated racial and gang violence.

They *want* us to be divided by racial hatred and to kill each other off with "gang-bangin'," to shoot-up and peddle dope in our neighborhoods to weaken and harm ourselves and our communities—just as they used alcohol to destabilize the Native American tribes and imported opium to undermine the Chinese in the 1800s. They *want* us engaged in and degraded by a pimp-ho subculture, objectifying our sistas as commodities and selling their bodies on the block like we were sold into slavery, and catching and spreading deadly sexually-transmitted diseases, like the HIV/AIDS and hepatitis, furthering the strategy of genocidal disposal of our youth. That's how much they *fear* us becoming revolutionaries and uniting and struggling for liberation and to pull down this predatory capitalist system that is the *cause* of our poverty, insecurity and misery.

Another component of urban population control is "spatial deconcentration," a policy implemented since the '60s revolts of breaking up large concentrations of poor Blacks, which includes "urban gentrification" of neighborhoods, closing down housing projects, and pushing poor people into the suburbs, smaller cities and towns. It also includes integrating other ethnic poor into formerly all-Black neighborhoods.

Our conditions of poverty, lack of job availability, security and accessible basic services that are essential to survival for urban people, are worse today than they were back in the '60s. So we exist as a perpetually threatening (to the Empire) dependent population with little value to the wealthy elite. Therefore, we face a very real and ever more intense official policy of genocide calculated to spread us thin and pick us off by increasing our death rate, decreasing our birth rate and lowering our life expectancy.

There is a deeply-rooted capitalist logic behind this policy. If we look back to capitalism's early development out of European feudalism, we find capitalist economic theorists like Thomas Malthus and David

Ricardo openly advocating the need to mass exterminate populations who couldn't be put to profitable use by the rising capitalists. In his 1798 treatise *An Essay on the Principle of Population*, Malthus suggested that if surplus population groups couldn't "go somewhere else," they should be killed off through artificially-created famines, wars and plagues.

Under the feudal system that preceded capitalism, government policies recognized the need for supporting and providing the poor with basic necessities in order to maintain stability and avoid rebellions. Yet the monarchs still found it necessary to seal themselves away from the masses whom they plundered from inside walled and fortified palaces. Under capitalism, however, Malthus and others held that providing for the poor would cause an unacceptable loss of profits for the rich, therefore the poor should be removed to "somewhere else" or exterminated. These "Malthusian" concepts were and remain a basic tenet of capitalist logic in a system that puts profits over people.

It could be no other way in a system that turns on taking and hoarding the wealth produced by the labor of workers, with the result of rendering them dependent and poor, making mass revolt inevitable. So those in power must contain or deplete this potentially rebellious population to prevent their coming together to pull down the system that exploits them and put things under their own control. This is the hidden logic behind the schemes of displacement and depopulation that threaten Black people and poor and oppressed people everywhere and are most apparent in the 3rd World. From imperialist-instigated tribal, ethnic and gang wars through which we are induced to kill each other; to economically-induced famines, such as the one devastating the Sub-Saharan region; to the unchecked spread of the HIV/AIDS virus that is destroying millions of Black lives on every continent; to flooding our communities with narcotics; to mass incarceration of our young men and wimyn in prisons where they cannot reproduce, we are under genocidal attack!

The latter condition basically replicates the same system of using armed lower-class whites to guard and dominate masses of enslaved Blacks that we were subjected to under chattel slavery before the Civil War. The "New Slavery" of the prison-industrial complex shows that "history repeats itself," but as it was then motivated by a shortage of necessary labor to work the land, it is today motivated by a surplus of labor that cannot be profitably exploited by the capitalists. Because we have no value today—as we did on the old plantations—we find ourselves facing genocidal policies much like those historically aimed at the Native Americans.

Also, our conditions become more desperate by the day: with growing mass urban concentrations, and a continuing "Great Migration" of industrial and manufacturing jobs away from the cities, the working class is shrinking fast and Black workers everywhere are being marginalized, even as the urban proletariat keeps growing. They can't find full-time jobs at decent wages, and here in the U.S. there is a cap on welfare. The ghettos have become dead ends leading only to early graves or prisons.

So the power structure has had to feed us false hopes in the form of a "Black" President—a hand-picked Black capitalist-serving President—to mislead us in the face of a genuine leadership vacuum. They now have us chasing dreams of Black capitalism, while we are caught in a crisis of deadly competition with each other and other poor folks for five minutes of fame and a temporary shopping spree, through channels that have destroyed our culture, destroyed our history and collective memory, destroyed our communities, and are ultimately destroying us.

And it is no grand conspiracy. It is the simple logic of the globalized capitalist system which operates only to enrich a tiny, super-rich elite class at the expense of everybody else. Just like the dopeman on the block who doesn't care whose lives he destroys or who he uses to turn a profit and gratify his wants. *This* is the logic we've learned from the capitalists.

The first to get the axe are those the capitalists value least—those considered most expendable—and those least able to defend themselves. In other words: ***us***. That is our situation today.

**Anthony Rayson**: I am astounded by the complexity and subtlety of your artwork. Seeing one of your originals, one cannot but be amazed—especially as you are accorded such rudimentary materials. Can you explain to us how you developed as such an accomplished artist (and what your driving motivation is)?

**Rashid**: In your introduction to this interview you mentioned that my drawing tools consist of pen and pencil. Actually, the only tools I use are five inch long ballpoint pen and standard typing paper.

While I appreciate the compliments I often receive on my art, (which acknowledges that it reaches people on more than a superficial level), I think we all have particular skills and talents—or can develop them—and if driven by a certain level of determination, we can evolve them to exceptional levels.

My art is driven by my determination to contribute what I can towards educating and inspiring the common people to collectively build the struggle to crush imperialist oppression, which is the cause of all other forms of social oppression. A major front in this struggle, as I've already pointed out, is the cultural front. This front—which relates directly to raising the consciousness and resolve of the masses—must directly challenge and counter the dominant bourgeois culture, which reflects and promotes the corrupt values of capitalism and conceals and stifles mass culture. Art (imagery and sound) is a major form of cultural expression. With my art, I aspire to produce images whose quality is both aesthetically pleasing (to capture and hold the eye and emotions) while educating (even if only initially on a subconscious level).

The vast majority of people are affective decision makers rather than cognitive decision makers. Meaning, they base decisions more on emotion than calculated reason. This is especially the case in a society like this where the reasoning faculties of the masses are kept in suspended animation. This is a reality that seems to be lost to most academic "Marxists" and Anarchists alike, and it is why they fail to reach and inspire the masses. (They spend most of their time talking to themselves and going over the common people's heads).

The ruling class realizes this and in fact promotes forms of "education" that basically train the people to function on the spontaneous emotional level rather than cognitively. The masses of Amerikans function without thinking much at all. This is why the capitalists are so successful at manipulating public opinion through media that is targeted almost exclusively at the basest and most primitive emotional levels. They don't call their communications media an *entertainment* industry for nothing. So a big part of our struggle is, as George Jackson recognized, to teach people *how* to think instead of *what* to think. This is a struggle carried out in the ideological and educational fields, and is targeted at *awakening* the conscious mind.

Whereas artistic imagery both captures and informs the emotions, many may be unwilling or unable as yet to grasp the ideas in print or spoken word form. Artistic imagery reaches another, deeper, level of the psyche—often involuntarily and unconsciously. Therefore I try to educate using both words and imagery and reach both the rational and emotional levels of the mind. This allows a dialectical balance in consciousness raising, reaching large numbers of people despite the limitations of my physical surroundings and availability of materials. In fact my art has been copied, circulated and seen by people on a vastly larger scale than my writings. Art makes knowledge accessible across class, race, gender, educational and state boundaries.

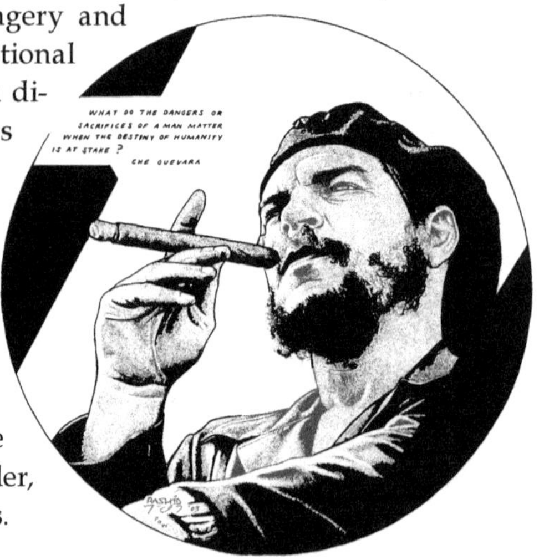

I'm also a particularly determined persyn. When I commit to something, I invest my all into it, often to the point of exhaustion or injury. We all have that capacity, it's just where our interests lie and where we are motivated to invest our energies. I'm no different from anyone else. I'm really not exceptional. Most people's limitations are self-imposed: The result of self-doubt or lack of interest. The same factors I believe are behind New Afrikans and other oppressed peoples having remained oppressed for so long. We've been conditioned to doubt ourselves and our ability to overthrow our oppressors, or we're distracted to the point of lack of interest in pursuing liberation.

I don't doubt myself, although I often question myself and self-criticize (and by extension I don't doubt the masses), because I know that we/I have the same capacity to do what anyone else can. It just requires correctly analyzing problems and devising correct solutions. This awareness is what often allows me to devise ways to counter or overcome adversity and maneuver around external restraints.

We've been so conditioned to self-doubt and therefore have become so consumed with idolizing others that we forget we can each become or do the same things. For example, since 2006, and as part of a campaign of repression, I've been indicted on some sixteen criminal charges—3 times for attempted capital murder of a prison guard. In each case I represented myself and got the charges either withdrawn or dismissed. That's pretty much unheard of, but I didn't approach these cases with self-doubt. I know I have just as much sense as any lawyer, and with the right tools and time can do just as well defending myself. Plus, I planned ahead. Before all this came down, I'd already spent years collecting pertinent legal materials and learning law. This is how I approach most problems.

I study, critically analyze material conditions and evaluate what others have done, and what I've done. I investigate mistakes and successes, looking at things from both sides, pro and con, and I search for play in the joints. I use what tools I have at hand and I improvise. I've done this for so long that it's become natural. In this regard, I was a Marxist—a practiced dialectical-materialist—long before I ever heard of Marx, Engels, Lenin or Mao. Studying them just gave me more clarity and a philosophical and ideological explanation of my practice. And my practice, like *genuine* Marxism-Leninism-Maoism, is anything but dogmatic and mechanical.

As you recognize, I get results. It all boils down to applying practical judgment, determination, flexibility and also audacity (the will to act) to change material conditions. It's the scientific approach to solving problems and is why Mao called Dialectical Materialism a "living science." This is why "intellectuals" and "academics" who've become conditioned to trying to solve problems inside their heads instead of in the real world don't comprehend Marxist theory and can only perceive it mechanically as a dogma.

And I'm determined. This struggle means a great deal to me, so I will find ways to contribute my best to it. Period. Until I stop breathing, that's what I'll do.

I suppose I've always had an inclination towards art, but never much pursued it. As a child, I used to draw, although infrequently. While I was never consistent with it, I could just do it at will, unlike a lot of "natural" artists I've known who have to be in a certain mood. Between 1990, when I began my present term of imprisonment, and 2001, I probably drew no more than about 15 pictures total. It wasn't until I began studying the struggle that I really set into drawing regularly, creating images that expressed and depicted themes of struggle and oppression and those who organized against oppression, which continues to develop, as does—I feel—the quality of my art.

**Anthony Rayson**: You've poured a lot of your energies lately into building up your Panther Prison Chapter. Can you tell us what the main tenets are, who the principal activists are, what you hope to achieve, and how it relates to other Panther formations and other anti-imperialists?

**Rashid**: Yeah, the New Afrikan Black Panther Party-Prison Chapter (NABPP-PC) has been my main energy focus since Comrade Shaka Sankofa Zulu and I co-founded it in 2005.

The major tenet is "Pantherism" as elaborated by the original Black Panther Party (BPP) during its most revolutionary stages. Specifically, Pantherism is revolutionary New Afrikan/Black nationalism, pan-Afrikanism and proletarian internationalism illuminated by the "Science of Revolution" (Historical and Dialectical Materialism). We identify with the BPP because in our analysis it *was*, when at its best, the most revolutionary and successful organization on Amerika's Left, and made the greatest all-round gains for New Afrikans in our struggle against national oppression and white supremacy.

Before the BPP was split into two factions by government attacks that left each pursuing opposite erroneous lines, (one of ultra-leftist militant reaction and the other of rightist-reformism), the BPP was breaking new ground in building the struggle for revolution in Amerika. Through applying HDM, we aspire to rebuild the BPP, learning from and applying the lessons of its advances and mistakes and learning from the lessons of the struggles of today. Especially we are focused on studying and correcting its errors, because we are determined that this time we shall win.

Our work is at this time focused on transforming the "Razor wire

Plantations" into "Schools of Liberation," to educate, uplift and organize those within the prisons and convert these humyn warehouses into revolutionary universities which will produce Panther cadres and activists of all nationalities and races. 85% of all those incarcerated in the U.S. will eventually return to society. Our goal is to see many of them empowered to return to their oppressed and poor communities and play a role in transforming them into revolutionary base areas. The next step is to replicate this process on an international level.

At this point in time we have Party collectives in many U.S. prisons. But unlike other formations people can't just join our Party, but are instead recruited based upon *proven* commitment to the struggle, and they must adopt and adhere to our Rules of Discipline and Ten Point Program. This is required because we fully understand that talk is cheap, and many folks who claim aspirations and dedication to push the struggle forward don't have a full understanding of or the resolve to sustain the difficulties of the work, the hardships and self-sacrifice that is required. Some who approach us will be working for the enemy.

So we are setting it up so that commitment and sincerity must be proven through service in a mass organization like the New Afrikan Service Organization (NASO) before a candidate is recruited into the Party. NASO operates under the leadership of our Party and has as its basis of unity support for the Ten Point Program, but it is building its own leadership structure under a National Steering Committee. Folks *can* join or start new NASO chapters very easily. NASO operates on democratic principles (as opposed to democratic centralism), and we seek to include a wide spectrum of ideological and political orientations within this organization.

Contrary to bourgeois propaganda and bourgeois "leadership style," a genuine vanguard party, such as we aspire to become, doesn't lead the people by compulsion or "commandism." Its leadership must be voluntarily accepted by the masses based on its proven commitment to serving their genuine welfare and interests, and demonstrated ability to organize and lead the people in solving their own problems. As Mao pointed out:

> "Every comrade ... should help the masses to organize themselves step by step and on a voluntary basis to unfold gradually struggles that are necessary and permissible under the external and internal conditions obtaining at a particular time and place. Whatever we do, authoritarianism is always erroneous because, as a result of our impetuosity, it makes us go beyond the degree of the masses awakening and violates the principle of voluntary action on the part of the masses."

In its practical application, this style of leadership is based exclusively on the principle "from the masses to the masses," which means we take the ideas of the masses (raw, unorganized and scattered ideas) and concentrate them (through study and transform them into organized systematic ideas) and return them to the masses in the form of slogans and programs. And we rely upon collective leadership.

As an illustration, take for example a mass of people confined to a barren land. The overall group doesn't know how to work the land so it will become productive and produce food or sustain livestock and are therefore on the verge of starvation. There can be no doubt that the masses *want* to produce sufficient food to eat and survive. Problem is *they don't know how.* Now there are a couple of their members who have managed to study the ecological factors of their given environment and learned techniques to transform the barren land into a virtual paradise of production. So they go about showing the people by example how to do it and organize their collective power to produce this result.

Now they don't force their leadership on the people, the people embrace them voluntarily because of their proven example and ability to help them help themselves, and because they are themselves *of the people.* Instead of standing *above* the people giving orders and punishing their errors, the comrades work alongside the people and share their knowledge freely, encouraging collective leadership, so that ultimately the leaders and the people become one in understanding and practice. In essence, this is how a mass-based vanguard leadership works—though my example may be a bit oversimplified. And this is what the Chinese Communist Party under Mao's leadership strove for during China's revolutionary years, contrary to bourgeois lies and propaganda—that are often uncritically parroted by many "Leftists."

Under this leadership style, the masses' disorganized and unsystematic ideas are organized and systematized, returned to them as programs, explained and popularized until they embrace and implement them. Then they are tested and refined through summing up practice. This process is repeated over and over in an ongoing spiral of practice–summation–practice. The ideas thereby become more and more correct and useful—connected to life and productive.

This is the scientific method which reflects the Marxist-Leninist-Maoist Theory of Knowledge. Through *proof* of its correctness in theory by practice in serving the people, the Party continuously *earns* the support and confidence of the masses. It makes no claim to leadership except by the consent of the masses it serves.

It takes an organization of people who share a certain level of consciousness, commitment and discipline to provide this sort of leadership, and an organizational structure that facilitates the maximum degree of inner-party discussion with the maximum degree of unity in action. It requires constant struggle to check corrupting influences and tendencies. In this context, the New Afrikan masses and the Party must be able to expect a high degree of commitment and dedication to the cause of revolution and social justice—even unto death.

We Panthers must put the highest interests of humynity above self-interest and endure hardships and self-sacrifices when they are called for. The oppressed masses have a right to expect us to be consistent and not vacillate or sell them out—no matter what—to build strength and not weakness, to be honest and humble and never dishonor ourselves or the Party. Our duties as revolutionaries are many, among which I think are:

- To embrace Historical Materialism (HM) and Dialectical Materialism (DM) and not sentimentalism, romanticism or any kind of idealism.
- To proletarianize ourselves and be loyal to the class of the future (the proletariat) and not the petty bourgeoisie and their petty (and less than revolutionary) concerns over bourgeois rights and privileges.
- To be all-the-way revolutionary thinkers and leaders in the fight against all oppression, all forms and manifestations of racism, sexism, ageism and any other divisive prejudices harmful to uniting all who can be united to overthrow capitalist-imperialism and build socialism.
- To reject sectarianism while at the same time standing firm for proletarian ideology and struggling for a correct ideological and political line to lead our movement forward.
- To combine unity with struggle and be principled and aboveboard.
- To oppose liberalism (see Mao's Sept. 7, 1937, essay *Combat Liberalism*) and rectify incorrect styles of thinking, work and conduct.
- To be open to criticism by comrades and the masses and to practice self-criticism.
- To struggle for objectivity, seek truth from facts and learn from the masses and the struggle.
- To be fair-minded, to listen to the people's concerns and suggestions and apply HDM to deepen their understanding and raise their level of consciousness and ability to solve problems.
- To be loyal to the Party and regard its life as your own, to defend it, build its strength and influence and strive to perfect it as the vanguard of the people's struggle.

- To respect, uphold, build and defend the democratic centralism of the Party, the subordination of lower bodies to higher bodies, the minority to the majority and the whole Party to the Central Committee or a sitting Party Congress.
- To be united in spirit and action and to speak with one voice and act as one body.
- To be self-disciplined, to live by the Party's Rules of Discipline, uphold proletarian morality and represent the bright future in the struggles of today, striving always to be the people's pride and a credit to the Party.
- To have courage and dare to struggle and dare to win all power to the people, to die for the people if necessary and endure any oppression as a true red-hearted revolutionary.
- To practice and promote revolution and not reformism, Pantherism and not cultural nationalism, and revolutionary optimism and not cynical defeatism.
- To uphold and defend and work to extend revolutionary intercommunalism and unite all the people in all the oppressed communities on the planet through the United Panther Movement.

I think these sixteen points should be kept in mind at all times and serve as a basis for further discussion throughout the Party and our movement.

Now, there are a *lot* of misconceptions and distortions about democratic centralism, some of which I addressed in *On the Roles and Characteristics of the Panther Vanguard Party and Mass Organizations.* These misconceptions are largely the result of bourgeois-propagated disinformation about the role and character of communist parties, but also they reflect historical misapplications of the concept by groups on the Left where *commandism* was substituted for the *mass line* while claiming to be practicing democratic centralism either out of ignorance or revisionism. Also many critics have seized one-sidedly on errors made by various organizations on the Left and presented those errors (while ignoring their correct aspects) as the essence of these organizational forms and practices. [I explain and discuss DC in greater depth in "On the Vanguard Party, Once Again" and "The New Afrikan Black Panther Party's Organizational Principles, Policy and Practice: The 3-P's"]

As Dialectical Materialists, we recognize and understand that nothing proceeds in a straight line, that every positive has a negative side (and vice versa), and that humyn error is inherent in life. We simply aspire to honestly evaluate things from both sides, to identify and correct errors instead of throwing out the baby with the bath water. If we fail to act for fear of making mistakes then we give victory to our oppressors by default.

The NABPP-PC includes the White Panther Organization (WPO) and the Brown Panther Organizing Committee (BPOC), which are arms of our Party being set up to represent our Party among and give ideological and political leadership to oppressed white and all other people in the prisons and oppressed communities. Our Party unites with all anti-imperialist forces, including other Panther formations—such as the Black Riders Liberation Party, the National Alliance of Black Panthers, the New Panther Vanguard Movement, the Anarchist Panthers, etc.—even if we have disagreements with their line and practice.

There have been some inquiries and assumptions made regarding ties or similarities we might have with the New Black Panther Party (NBPP) which came out of the Nation of Islam (NOI) in the 1980s. We began as an autonomous chapter of NBPP aspiring to change the orientation of the outside NBPP into that of a genuine vanguard party in the New Afrikan communities, however, we soon realized it was better to separate ourselves from NBPP's narrow nationalism and reverse racism. We also changed our name to the New Afrikan BPP-Prison Chapter to further distinguish ourselves and reflect our orientation towards revolutionary New Afrikan nationalism.

Information and some of our publications can also be obtained through the Anarchist Black Cross (ABC) network.

Lastly, we feel the U.S. prisons are an important front in the struggle against imperialism. Prisoners are among the most oppressed sectors of the U.S. population, and because many have a good deal of time and opportunity to read and study, we stand to be potentially one of the most advanced sections of the people. This is why prisons are sometimes called the "poor man's universities." Comrade George Jackson once stated that only two types of people ever leave these concentration camps—the rebels and the broken. But there's one other type he overlooked, namely the revolutionaries. The oppression inherent in these expanding humyn warehouses by nature breeds rebels, but infused with proletarian revolutionary theory, prisoners can make the qualitative leap from rebels to revolutionaries.

Comrade Lenin said, "Without revolutionary theory there can be no revolutionary movement." And it is these revolutionary prisoners who, upon their release, can hit the streets like paratroopers, joining and building the outside movement to educate, organize and lead the less advanced masses in determined struggle to deal this dying capitalist-imperialist system the *coup de grace*.

We don't plan to build our Panther movement just in the U.S. but wherever poor and oppressed Black people (and all oppressed people) are concentrated throughout the world. We plan to build WPO wherever there are concentrations of poor whites and BPOC where all other poor and oppressed brown people are concentrated. Half the world's people now live in urban settings, jammed together in urban slums or shanty-towns, and we aspire to transform these into revolutionary Panther base areas throughout the global capitalist empire.

We aim to create and build people's power from the grassroots up, and to organize Serve the People (STP) survival programs, People's security forces and liberation schools. And we aim to link these urban revolutionary base areas into an inter-communal network through the Party and our own media and United Panther Movement. Between our work in the prisons and the oppressed communities, we aim to raise up a revolutionary generation schooled in the Science of Revolution, trained and tested in class struggle through the Party and the mass organizations, so that we will not be dependent upon petty-bourgeois intellectuals to lead our revolutionary movement. There will of course be a role for these types who are willing to commit "class suicide" and dedicate themselves to becoming all-the-way revolutionaries and remold themselves to adopt the class stand of the revolutionary proletariat.

**Anthony Rayson**: As you know, I am a serious Anarchist, as you are a dedicated Communist. At this point, we are on the same side of the barricades. The fundamental difference of course, is the Communists want to take state power, as the "leader" of the oppressed, and the Anarchists have as their goal the elimination of oppressive state power altogether. As international capitalism, led by the voraciously murderous U.S., gets more and more desperate to retain its empire, the world's people will suffer through more hellacious wars, occupations, enslavements, lack of life's basics such as food, water, health, safety, etc. People will become more and more politically polarized. Some will be suckered-in as fascist dupes (or outright agents and killers of the criminal state). Others will look for truth, protection, and involvement in revolutionary opposition—Communist, anarchist, New Afrikan, or otherwise.

Anarchists believe that state power is the epitome of evil—the ultimate corrupter. Now let's assume that through a worldwide effort we are able once-and-for-all to destroy the centuries' old nightmare of capitalism. Let's also assume we were also able to stop them from dragging all life on earth down with them.

So, there's a chance at "Socialism." Anarchists believe in the equitable distribution along anti-authoritarian principles. Communists want to assume state power and orchestrate it all from a "Central Committee." Every other time Communists have attained power, they've repressed Anarchists, other revolutionaries, etc. What would be different this time?

**Rashid**: I think this question offers the opportunity for an important discussion in the ongoing debate between Anarchism and Communism. Also, it exposes a common tendency I've observed of critics of Communism, namely that their critiques are often pretty inaccurate and just repeat charges based on superficial stereotypes. In fact, when one pushes Anarchists to the wall, and compels them to give concrete answers to concrete problems, instead of abstract criticisms, they begin to sound a lot like genuine Communists. Otherwise, they don't go deeply and thoroughly into solving the real problems that arise in struggling to defeat an oppressive class system such as capitalism. But many of their criticisms are valid and worthy of consideration.

You begin with placing emphasis on the fact that Anarchists want an equitable distribution of social wealth and to abolish the state, but, by implication, you suggest Communists do not. Even the "mainstream" recognizes these implications to be untrue. Take for example this definition of "Communism" given by the *Merriam Webster Collegiate Encyclopedia* (2000):

> "Communism: Political theory advocating community ownership of all property, the benefits of which are to be shared by all according to the needs of each. The theory was principally the work of Karl Marx and Frederick Engels. Their *Communist Manifesto* (1848) further specified a 'dictatorship of the proletariat,' a transitional stage Marx called socialism; communism was the final stage of which not only class division but even the organized state—seen by Marx as inevitably an instrument of oppression—would be transcended. That distinction was lost and 'communism' began to apply to a specific party rather than a final goal ..."

This summary of the nature and goals of Communism sounds pretty similar to what you state are the goals of Anarchism: equitable distribution of property and abolition of the state. Indeed, both Communists and Anarchists agree that the state is an "instrument of oppression." But it seems, just as the mainstream reference book points out, you've embraced the erroneous view that Communism is a "specific party" rather than a "final goal." Can it be that the imperialists have a more accurate and fair understanding of what Communism is than the modern Anarchists?

However, prominent Anarchists of the past have conceded that the goals of Anarchism and Communism are much the same. Indeed, Alexander Berkman in his *ABC of Anarchism* (1929) saw the goals of Communism and Anarchism as synonymous. In fact, he used the term "Anarchism" to describe Communism:

> "The greatest teachers of socialism—Karl Marx and Frederick Engels—had taught that anarchism would come from socialism. They said that we must first have socialism [the dictatorship of the proletariat], but that after socialism there will be anarchism, and that it would be a freer and more beautiful condition of society to live in than socialism."

So the "fundamental difference" between Anarchism and Communism is *not* in their views on equal distribution of wealth and abolishing the state. The fundamental difference is on *how* to go about achieving these ends and their class basis. Anarchism promotes an *idealistic* approach rooted in a petty-bourgeois class perspective, while Marxist Communism promotes a materialist and dialectical approach rooted in a working-class perspective.

Now Communists and most Anarchists agree that armed struggle will be required to compel and wrest control of property relations from the bourgeoisie (or capitalist ruling class) and to overthrow and smash the state it rules through—because the essence of state power is a specialized armed force of men (and now also wimyn). The capitalists aren't going to relinquish their power and wealth without a fight—never have, never will!

So essentially, it is a question of what to do after the bourgeois class is overthrown, and when do we lay down our arms? Because that is what *state power* is all about. So by resorting to arms in the first place, the Anarchists *are* taking part in *the exercise of dictatorial power* and the use of *authoritarian* means to repress the bourgeois class. Here's how Frederick Engels made the point:

> "The anti-authoritarians demand that the political state be abolished at one stroke, even before the social relations that gave birth to it have been destroyed. They demand that the first act of the social revolution shall be the abolition of authority.
>
> "Have these gentlemen ever seen a revolution? A revolution is certainly the most authoritarian thing there is; it is an act whereby one part of the population imposes its will upon the other part by means of rifles, bayonets and cannon, all of which are highly authoritarian means. And the victorious party must maintain its rule by means of the terror which its arms inspire in the reactionaries. Would the Paris Commune have lasted more than a day if it had not used the authority of the armed people against the bourgeoisie? Cannot we, on the contrary, blame it for having made too little use of that authority? Therefore one of two things; either the anti-authoritarians don't know what they are talking about, in which

> case they are creating nothing but confusion, or they do know, and in that case they are betraying the cause of the proletariat. In either case, they serve only reaction."

So we see an inherent contradiction in Anarchism that renders it fundamentally either pro- or counter-revolutionary, namely, whether it supports or opposes the armed struggle of the proletariat and consolidation of people's power. In either event, overthrowing the state power of the bourgeoisie won't in one stroke abolish the bourgeois class and its aspirations to regain state power. The Communists' goal is to smash the state power of the capitalists *right away*; to do away with their army, their police, their courts and their prisons. *But*, we cannot get rid of the bourgeois class so easily, nor the petty bourgeoisie, nor the bourgeoisified workers and lumpen proletarians.

If we were to put down our guns at this point—if we did not maintain our own army, police, courts and prisons—these elements would turn right around and rig up a new bourgeois state. They would rig up a bourgeois state and use it to repress us—everyone connected with the revolution and the masses. This is exactly what happened in the Mexican Revolution when Emiliano Zapata listened to his Amerikan Anarchist advisors and gave up state power after victory and went home. The new reconstituted bourgeois state quickly hunted him down and murdered him like a dog—and Mexico has been under a bourgeois dictatorship and U.S. imperialist domination ever since.

This is also what happened in the very short-lived Spanish Revolution, the revolution the Anarchists claim to have been successful at. The bourgeoisie overthrew it overnight and immediately reasserted their rule. This occurred because the Anarchists opposed establishing a workers' state and the Communists who were trying to create one. The Fascists reaped the victory and ruled Spain with an iron fist for decades after.

In *Homage to Catalonia*, George Orwell's memoir of the Spanish Revolution, he gave an account of how instantly and completely bourgeois rule reasserted itself in Barcelona only months after it had been overthrown by the working class. In the beginning of his memoir, Orwell gives a glorious account of Barcelona when the popular revolution was still underway in latter 1936. He then contrasts how only months later the revolutionary successes had vanished without a trace. Here is his description of conditions in April 1937:

> "Everyone who has made two visits, at intervals of months, to Barcelona during the war has remarked upon the extraordinary changes that took place in it. And curiously enough, whether they went there first in August and again in January, or, like myself, first

in December and again in April, the thing they said was always the same: that the revolutionary atmosphere had vanished. No doubt to anyone who had been there in August, when the blood was scarcely dry in the streets and the militia was quartered in the small hotels, Barcelona in December would have seemed bourgeois, to me, fresh from England, it was liker to a worker's city than anything I had conceived possible. Now the tide had rolled back. Once again it was an ordinary city, a little pinched and chipped by war, but with no outward sign of working-class predominance … . The officers of the new Popular Army, a type that had scarcely existed when I left Barcelona, swarmed in surprising numbers … [wearing] an elegant khaki uniform with a tight waist, like a British officer's uniform, only a little more so. I do not suppose that more than one in twenty of them had yet been to the front, but all of them had an automatic pistol strapped to their belts; we, at the front, could not get pistols for love or money …

"A deep change had come over the town. There were two facts that were the keynote of all else. One was that the people—the civil population—had lost much of their interest in the war; the other was that the normal division of society into rich and poor, upper class and lower class, was reasserting itself."

Communists simply recognize the state for what it is—namely an instrument by which one class asserts its power over another. Unless the proletariat overthrows the bourgeois capitalist state and replaces it with a proletarian socialist state, the bourgeoisie will maintain its dominance. Only under working-class state rule can massive Cultural Revolutions take place to purge bourgeois thinking and practices, which, once this process succeeds, will bring about the egalitarian stateless social order. So our object is to create a proletarian state with our own special bodies of armed wimyn and men, our own courts and our own prisons for those who commit crimes against the people. Under this system the armed workers will defend the revolution and use their power to transform all of society to eliminate classes and lay the basis for advancing to the kind of society both the Anarchists and Communists want.

It is at this point, *and not a moment sooner,* that we will lay down our guns and move forward to advance the stateless society, because only then will it be *possible* to do so. Any other approach is just pipe-dreaming idealism. We believe in the principle of from each according to their ability and to each according to their needs—that is, doing away with the whole concept of commodity exchange. In short: abolishing money. But there has to be a whole lot of cultural revolution and transforming of society to make that possible. There has to be basic changes in how production and distribution of goods are organized. People have to be willing to participate in socialized production without being forced to by economic necessity, and we have to produce enough of everything for everybody to be able to get what they need to survive and be happy.

Another factor is that you've got to do it in such a way as to preserve and protect the natural environment so future generations will be able to get what they need and be able to keep society running. This calls for revolution in the cultural, social and political realms and also in science, production and ecology. This all has to be planned, organized and done on a global scale as well as regionally and locally. A stateless society must by definition be a global society without borders. And we can't have one section of humynity hogging all the world's resources, like we do now, which is just what would happen if we didn't start with a worldwide dictatorship of the proletariat.

As to who will get repressed along the way, well, that's up to the proletariat, isn't it? We advocate a step by step, planned transformation of society rather than anarchy. We believe the masses can be won to understand the logic of this and support it. In this way, repression can be kept to a minimum and democratic methods of persuasion will be the primary focus and means of the struggle. But counter-revolutionaries will be repressed at every stage, and the proletariat will decide how and when and who—no matter what the counter-revolutionaries call themselves—through the organs of people's power and the people's courts.

One thing we've learned from past revolutions is that the greatest threat of capitalist restoration will come from within the upper ranks of the Party and state from those who betray the class stand of the proletariat and assume that of the bourgeoisie. As socialism is a stage of transition from capitalism to communism, it is relatively easy for those at the top to rig up a state capitalist system under the cover of building socialism and take the country back down the capitalist road. This is what happened in the Soviet Union after Stalin, when Khrushchev came to power, and in People's China after Mao died in 1976.

The lesson here is for the proletariat to keep a firm grip on its Party and to exercise all round dictatorship over the bourgeoisie—and especially on those in leadership positions in the Party and the workers' state. Cultural Revolution is the weapon to prevent capitalist restoration and to keep moving society down the path of socialist revolution.

The working class must arm itself with a thorough understanding of the *Science of Revolution* and increasingly take power into its own hands directly to revolutionize every aspect of society. When we say "All Power to the People!," we mean that literally in an ever deepening and all-round way. So long as classes exist, it is the proletariat who will be exploited and oppressed, and it is the proletariat who must play the leading role in waging class struggle to overcome it. The class struggle leads inevitably to the elimination of classes and communist society. But at every step it will be a struggle—against idealism and those who would sidetrack and derail the class struggle to preserve and enhance their own privileged positions and keep on exploiting the masses of people.

There is no way to avoid this protracted struggle, and certainly not by disarming the proletariat as soon as the old bourgeois order is overthrown. It certainly can't be done by substituting anarchy for a rational strategy. Only the petty bourgeoisie—anxious to replace the old bourgeoisie—would intentionally propose such a short-sighted "solution." The true solution is for the petty bourgeoisie—*including those who become upwardly mobile through the revolution*—to be won to a position of *committing class suicide* and aligning themselves with the oppressed and exploited masses struggling to end all oppression and exploitation by revolutionizing every aspect of society—in a planned, organized and disciplined way through the application of the *mass line* and the illumination of the *Science of Revolution*.

Do we see the contradiction between ourselves and the Anarchists as inherently antagonistic? No, we do not. We believe that it can be resolved non-antagonistically so long as it remains a contradiction within the people. We do not want to repeat the Stalinist errors of treating contradictions within the people the same as contradictions with the enemy.

For many people, as it was with me, Anarchism is a starting place, because it is fundamentally an *emotional* response to the evils of capitalist-imperialism. This was the case with Mao Tse-tung, who self-identified as an Anarchist before becoming a Communist. Throughout his political career he was accused of still being an anarchist by both dogmatists and revisionists alike. Three times he was kicked off the Central Committee of the Chinese Communist Party (CCP), but he maintained that it was a Marxist-Leninist principle to go against the tide and stand firm for revolution. At the Lushan Conference, he threatened to quit his post as Chairman and go back to the mountains and start a new CCP and People's Liberation Army if it was necessary.

As Chairman of the CCP Mao was not the Head of State and was constantly at odds with the state bureaucracy. During the Great Proletarian Cultural Revolution, he suspended the democratic centralism of the Party so that lower bodies were no longer subordinated to higher bodies and he issued the call to the youth, workers and peasants to "bombard the Headquarters!"

Does this mean he was not really a Communist? No, it does not! It means that as a Communist his first and foremost loyalty was to proletarian socialist revolution and the class struggle. "A revolution is not a dinner party," he said, "it is the violent overthrow of one class by another." "By any means necessary!" was the way Malcolm X put it.

Many of the criticisms of the Communist movement made by Anarchists or others are right on. But they are also usually non-dialectical and one-sided. Often they obscure the criticisms of the proletariat who look at the same problems differently. Mao was a firm believer that Communists should openly reveal, criticize and struggle against their "dark side."

We can't do without a proletarian state any more than we can do without smashing the bourgeois state. Does this mean we love violence or love authority? No! It means we are serious enough about ending wage slavery, and all of the evils of capitalist-imperialism, that we are willing to be scientific about revolution and go beyond an emotional response.

As a New Afrikan and a condemned slave of the state, I can't afford not to be serious and scientific about the liberation of my people—and all oppressed people everywhere—through socialist revolution. Our fates are intertwined. Only by carrying the class struggle all the way to Communism will there be a bright future for our posterity. For us, there is only slavery or liberation, so we can have no hesitation when it comes to applying Brother Malcolm's dictum to our struggle. Step by step, stage by stage, we shall advance the revolution through all the twists and turns, setbacks and victories until full liberation is won.

As I said, we can't do without a proletarian state, but there is a tendency for it to turn into its opposite—and we are wise to it. Power does corrupt, and the inevitable continuation of old class relations—particularly in the lower stages of socialism—and the deeply-rooted ideology of the past will nurture the tendency for capitalist restoration. Commodity relations—even under socialist state control—do regenerate capitalism and bourgeois ideas. Non-proletarian class forces—who are necessary to keep the economy and social services going—are going to demand concessions, such as higher wages, personal power and retention of bourgeois rights.

Technicians and professionals in all spheres will defend their privileged position in society and resist the encroachment of the common people in their *business*. And only when the proletariat can do without them can we move from the lower to the higher stage of socialism. The struggle between "Reds" and "Experts" was a major aspect of the Great Proletarian Cultural Revolution in China. We all know that after Mao's death, the "Reds" were defeated and that the "Experts" now live "high on the hog" in China and the so-called "Communist Party" has become a fascist party of "Experts" and capitalists.

Mao predicted that this outcome was "very possible," but he also predicted that their rule would be short-lived and that they "would know no peace," and we see that today there is a resurgence of Maoism in China and internationally, and we see that China's masses are waging sharp class struggle against their exploitation and oppression.

We also see a resurgence of Anarchism today, and particularly among the youth of the imperialist countries. I *should* say among the *white petty-bourgeois* youth and students, because there is a class and race basis to this resurgence. Anarchy extols the supremacy of the individual and individual freedom, which is also a way to separate oneself from identifying with one's *skin* and *class privileges*. One can say, "I am not responsible for racist and class oppression or for global imperialism. I reject all that. I am an Anarchist." But that neither threatens the ruling class nor helps the oppressed class. It's merely a lifestyle choice, a fashion. You can dress up for it, dye your hair black and get a "bad" haircut, eat vegan food, ride a bicycle, pierce your nose, nipples or tongue, dumpster dive and make the scene.

Then there are the Anarchist careerists, which brings to mind admissions made and the example set by Greg Wells, an Anarchist journalist out of Richmond, Virginia, with whom I was corresponding a few years back. At a time when I was facing a high-point of repression from prison officials, I proposed a few ideas to him about consolidating discrete activists into a practical support network for prisoner activists and other oppressed individuals. He replied that my proposals definitely needed doing, and that "as much as" he'd "love to" help he was "simply too comfortable to do any such thing." He added, "I'll tell you something that other Anarchists won't admit, but it's true. You know that most Anarchists are comfortable white middle-class and aren't going to do much more than a little protesting and critical writing."

Greg is a prolific writer who has made a career out of railing at capitalism, racial and gender oppression, U.S. imperialist wars, etc., yet he concedes his unwillingness to jeopardize his status and comfort level by allying himself in practice with the oppressed. As he confessed, this is typical of most of the milieu of petty bourgeois Anarchists. Indeed, I would say it is typical of most radical intellectuals on the Amerikan Left. As I stated in a previous unpublished article:

> "99% of the radicals are divorced from the masses. They attend rallies and protests but lock their doors when driving through oppressed neighborhoods. They don't know how to do mass work, how to agitate and organize. They think it's their opinions that matter, that they fulfill their political duty by expressing them. Whereas, they need to create a presence on the street, amongst the oppressed workers and nationalities, and time is of the essence."

Of course, there are some Anarchists like ABC, whom we consider to be comrades, who actually do play a role in assisting the struggle in the prisons and are groping with the question of making revolution. We are, as you say, "on the same side of the barricades." The question is can we build a *higher* level of unity and what would that take? Well, we've created the White Panther Organization (WPO) as an arm of the New Afrikan Black Panther Party-Prison Chapter (NABPP-PC), so white comrades can fully unite with us and represent our Party among the oppressed white people. They do have to accept the democratic-centralism of the Party and its rules of discipline, the same as the Black Panthers. They have to study and apply the Science of Revolution and commit to being all-the-way revolutionaries.

NABPP-PC is not a Communist Party per se. We are revolutionary nationalists and internationalists. Our ideological and political line, "Pantherism," is illuminated by Marxism-Leninism-Maoism, and we are committed to fighting for proletarian socialist revolution. We see the key alliance in the United Front Against Capitalist-Imperialism to be between the oppressed nations and nationalities and the multi-ethnic, multi-national working class.

For New Afrikans, the solution to our national oppression is socialist revolution. As long as Black people are oppressed *because* we are Black, there needs to be a Black Panther Party to lead the Black Liberation Struggle. We need to stand together as a Nation under the leadership of our proletarian vanguard. To fight most effectively against white racism, we need white comrades to stand with us—as fellow Panthers or as supporters. We also need to stand in solidarity with all other oppressed peoples and have them stand with us. This is the basis of the United Panther Movement. We believe that the Nation of New Afrikans in Amerika must play a vanguard role in this revolution because of our historical oppression and because we are in a position to do so.

We live in the "Belly of the Beast." We are concentrated in the urban centers of the sole imperialist superpower, and we are infiltrated throughout the oppressor's military and political-economic infrastructure. We are everywhere, even if only pushing a broom or a mop.

We are also part of the Third World, and we are kindred to all other sons and daughters of Afrikan descent. Everywhere we are oppressed because of our black skin under white world domination. As Mao said:

> "The evil system of colonialism and imperialism arose and throve with the enslavement of Negroes and the trade in Negroes, and it will surely come to its end with the complete emancipation of the Black people."

He said, "The Afro-American struggle is not only a struggle waged by the exploited and oppressed Black people for freedom and emancipation" but that it is a "clarion call" to all the oppressed peoples. This history and this positioning gives us the opportunity to play a vanguard role in the world revolution, not exclusive of others but in dialectical relationship to all people of color and all who suffer oppression. This does not negate the leading role that must be played by the international proletariat as the class of the future, for it is the ideology and worldview of this class that guides our struggle for liberation.

The New Afrikan Nation is primarily a proletarian nation—on the whole, we own nothing and are forced to sell our labor power to survive or otherwise to survive by any means necessary. Even most of our lumpen proletariat has an on again off again relationship with wage slavery. Our Party must work ceaselessly to ground our cadre and comrades in a thorough-going proletarian class stand and struggle resolutely against lumpen and petty-bourgeois influences and tendencies.

For several decades now the ruling class has been pursuing a strategy of criminalization of the poor and our mass incarceration—particularly of our Black youth—and we must counter this with proletarianizing and revolutionizing our young wimyn and men by teaching "Pantherism" and raising up a generation of revolutionary warriors.

But let me return to your question and your point about Anarchists wanting nothing to do with state power and their accepting nothing short of its instant abolition. Well, *the* foremost modern Anarchist intellectual, Noam Chomsky—affectionately known in Anarchist circles as "Uncle Noam"—is both a proponent of using state power (and *bourgeois state power* at that) to address social ills, and he conceded that Anarchism is not an instantly attainable social order. Were it not for his speaking in support of *bourgeois* state power, instead of promoting *proletarian* state power, one would think Chomsky was a Communist espousing the need for the rational use of state power to transform society. "Uncle Noam" put it like this:

> "Well it's true that the Anarchist vision in just about all its varieties has looked forward to dismantling state power—and I personally share that vision. But right now it runs directly counter to my goals: My immediate goals have been, and now very much are, to defend and even strengthen certain elements of state authority that are now under severe attack. And I don't think there's any contradiction there—none at all, really.
>
> "For example, take the so-called 'welfare state.' What's called the 'welfare state' is essentially a recognition that every child has a

right to have food, and to have health care and so on—and as I've been saying, those programs were set up in the nation-state system after a century of very hard struggle, by the labor movement, and the socialist movement, and so on. Well, according to the new spirit of the age, in the case of a fourteen-year-old girl who got raped and had a child, her child has to learn 'personal responsibility' by not accepting state welfare handouts, meaning by not having enough to eat. Alright, I don't agree with that at any level. In fact I think it is grotesque at any level. I think those children should be saved. And in today's world, *that's going to involve working through the state system*, it's not the only case.

"So despite the anarchist 'vision,' I think aspects of the state system, like the one that makes sure children eat, have to be defended—in fact, defended very vigorously. And given the accelerated effort that's being made these days to roll back the victories for justice and human rights which have been won through long and often extremely bitter struggles in the West, in my opinion the immediate goal of even committed anarchists should be to defend some state institutions, while helping to pry them open to more meaningful public participation, and ultimately to dismantle them in a much more free society.

"There are practical problems of tomorrow on which people's lives very much depend, and while defending these kinds of programs is by no means the ultimate end we should be pursuing, in my view we still have to face the problems that are right on the horizon, and which seriously affect human lives. I don't think those things can simply be forgotten because they might not fit with some radical slogan that reflects a *deeper vision of a future society*. The deeper vision should be maintained, they're important—but *dismantling the state system is a goal that is a lot further away*, and you want to deal first with what's at hand and nearby, I think … .

"So I think it's completely realistic and rational to work within structures to which you are opposed, because by doing so can help to move to a situation where then you can challenge these structures."

Chomsky's proposing that radicals work within bourgeois state institutions to address social needs actually conforms to a strategy of absorbing and controlling dissidents and activists within government structures, which was proposed by the U.S. National Security Council in the late 1970s. This reflects how the confused class stand of the petty bourgeoisie leads to erroneous approaches to opposing imperialist oppression. But, *that* Chomsky recognized the need to use state power along the road to ultimately abolishing the state shows that Communist and Anarchist theory is not so irreconcilable. Anarchists must simply recognize the role of the proletariat as preeminent in the struggle against capitalist-imperialism and the advance to a classless society.

I want to add that we reject the nihilism that is so often associated with both Anarchism and gangsterism. We base ourselves on *Panther Love*. As both Che Guevara and Mao pointed out, love is the motivation of a true revolutionary. Our love for the people, for liberty and justice, and for the unborn generations for whom we stand ready to sacrifice our lives, is manifested in everything we do and say.

On the question of who should legitimately coordinate the application of state power and lead society in general, again "Uncle Noam" promotes the need and role for a leading structure very similar to our concept of a genuine vanguard party operating with committee structures and democratic centralism. He opposed the ultra-democratic approach to running even a basic community as impossible. Indeed there has never existed a society without some form of leadership. Here again is Chomsky:

> "No, I don't think [a large mass of people could actively participate in all the decisions that need to be made in a complex modern society]. I think you've got to delegate some of those responsibilities. But the question is, where does authority ultimately lie? I mean, since the very beginnings of the modern democratic revolutions in the seventeenth and eighteenth centuries, it's always been recognized that people have to be represented—the question is, are we represented by, as they put it, 'countrymen like ourselves,' or are we represented by 'our betters'?
>
> "For example, suppose this was our community, and we wanted to enter into some kind of agreement with the community down the road—if we were fairly big, we'd have to delegate the right to negotiate things to representatives. But then the question is, who has the power to ultimately authorize those decisions? Well, if it's a democracy, that power ought to lie not just *formally* in the population, but *actually* in the population—meaning the representatives can be recalled, they're answerable back to their community, they can be replaced. In fact, there should be as much as possible in the way of constant replacement, so that political participation just becomes a part of everybody's life.
>
> "But I agree, I don't think it's possible to have large masses of people get together to decide every topic—it would be unfeasible and pointless. You'd want to pick committees to look into things and

> report back, and so on and so forth. But the real question is, where does authority lie."

Now compare Chomsky's emphasis on the legitimacy of representative committee structures lying in the election and recall by votes of leading members and such organizations being accountable to the masses by full exposure of their activities, with this 1905 Bolshevik summary of democratic centralism:

> "Recognizing as indisputable the principle of democratic centralism, the Conference considers the broad implementation of the elective principle necessary, and while granting elected centers full powers in matters of ideological and political leadership, they are at the same time subject to recall, their actions are given broad publicity, and they are strictly accountable for these activities."

Also, consistent with Chomsky's point that political power should be vested in the common people and not with "our betters," the struggle which Mao initiated during the Great Proletarian Cultural Revolution between the "Reds" and the "Experts" was to displace political power from those who by virtue of their technical expertise considered themselves the "betters" of the common laboring people, and to have that power spread broadly amongst the working people.

This is one of the reasons why the petty bourgeoisie cannot lead all-the-way revolution—or even the struggle to defend the humyn and democratic civil rights of the oppressed—as their class conditioning has them seeing themselves as the intellectual "betters" of the masses towards whom they have a "superior" attitude. George Jackson demonstrated that you don't have to be middle class or attend a university to become a *revolutionary intellectual*—a "Red" who is also armed with intellectual expertise. Some would say that I demonstrate this myself.

Those of us who have nothing to lose but our chains, who have no reason to hesitate or vacillate and every reason to be serious, dedicated, all-the-way revolutionaries have a responsibility to be in the vanguard and to struggle relentlessly against every form of oppression to build the mass-based revolutionary vanguard party to unite and lead the masses of oppressed people to rise up and end oppression at its source through proletarian socialist revolution and proletarian cultural revolution.

*Dare to Struggle, Dare to Win!*
*All Power to the People!*

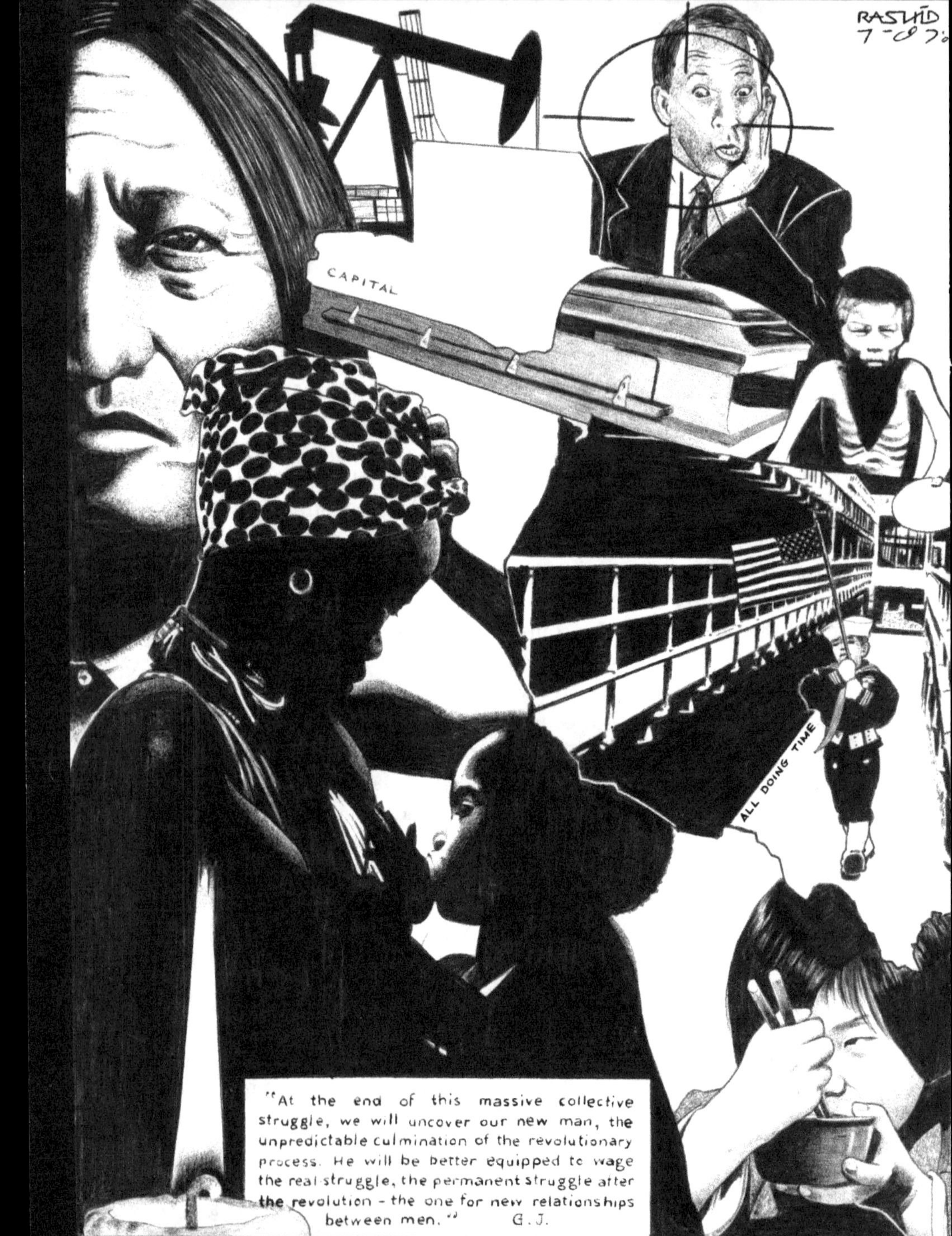
RASHID
7-07
CAPITAL
ALL DOING TIME
"At the end of this massive collective struggle, we will uncover our new man, the unpredictable culmination of the revolutionary process. He will be better equipped to wage the real struggle, the permanent struggle after the revolution - the one for new relationships between men." G.J.

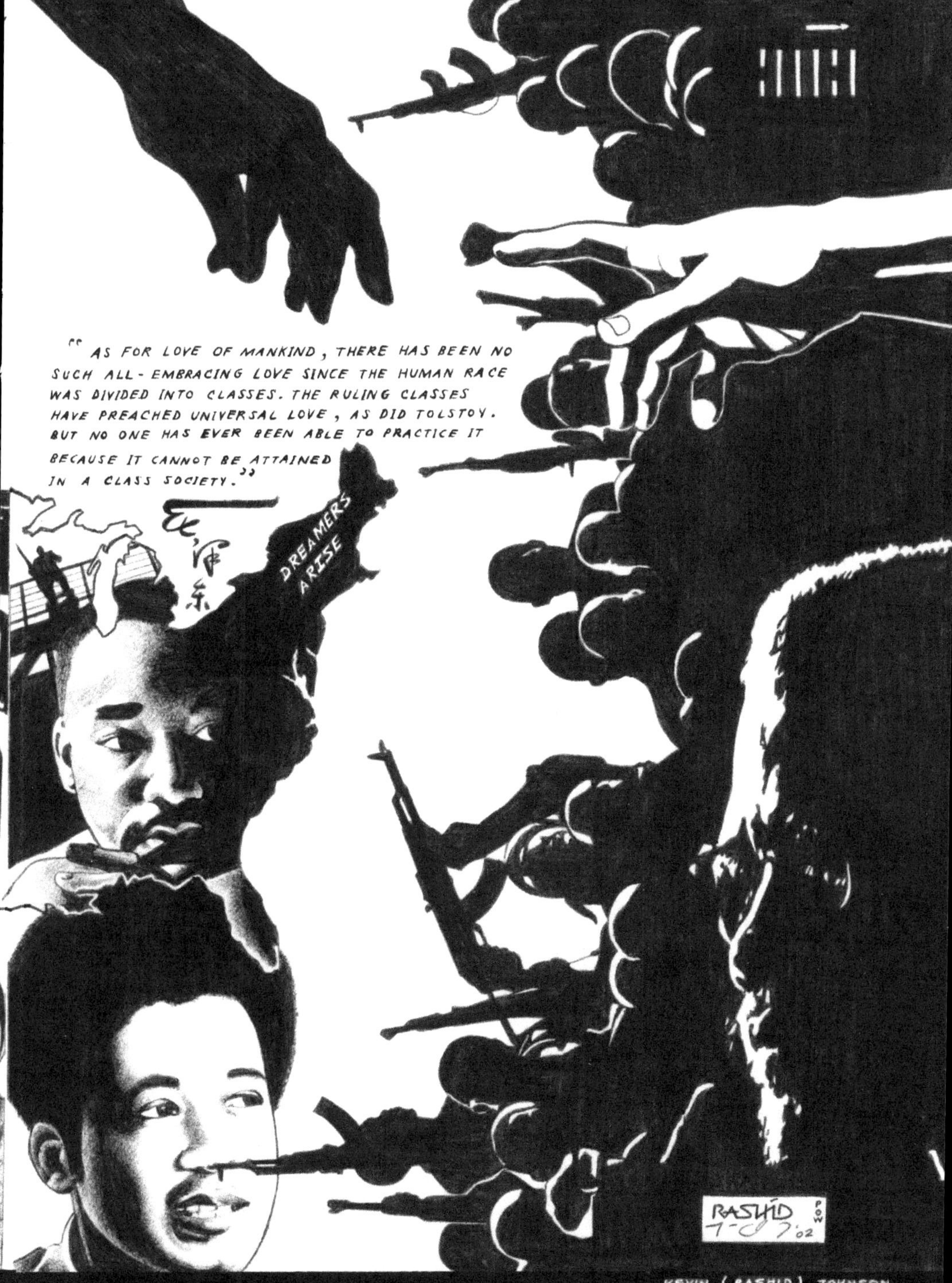
"AS FOR LOVE OF MANKIND, THERE HAS BEEN NO SUCH ALL-EMBRACING LOVE SINCE THE HUMAN RACE WAS DIVIDED INTO CLASSES. THE RULING CLASSES HAVE PREACHED UNIVERSAL LOVE, AS DID TOLSTOY. BUT NO ONE HAS EVER BEEN ABLE TO PRACTICE IT BECAUSE IT CANNOT BE ATTAINED IN A CLASS SOCIETY."
DREAMERS ARISE
RASHID POW
7-07-'02
KEVIN (RASHID) JOHNSON

# 3. ON THE VANGUARD PARTY, ONCE AGAIN 2012

**Anthony Rayson:** You've expressed admiration for Hamas, the revolutionary Palestinian group.[1] They've managed to build popular support and established social/survival programs, even under horrific conditions of occupation—extreme violence, poverty, etc.—yet they are not an explicitly Marxist-Leninist group, but rather a national liberation organization, with a strong religious (Muslim) component. These popular organizations have come in many flavors, including Communist and anarchist. Why do you believe so strongly in the traditional Leninist model (Vanguard Party/Democratic Centralism, etc.) in this uniquely racialist, consumerist, extreme capitalist country, with such a moribund, marginalized and subservient (to Moscow) Marxist tradition?

**Rashid:** Why in today's struggle do I promote the need for a Marxist-Leninist-Maoist (MLM) style party leadership? This is a question asked often of and by many avowed Communists, which many can't answer. Many also reject the "Vanguard" party concept as you do because it's been frequently misapplied and misunderstood. But to me, the answer seems pretty simple—common sense really—once you get past rhetoric and stereotypes, and face the concrete realities and needs of revolutionary struggle. I'll begin with this question, then move on to your other points.

## Why the Vanguard Party?

Once you understand that class lies at the center of any genuine struggle against capitalism, namely the struggle between the working class (proletariat) and the capitalist class (bourgeoisie), then it becomes clear that there's a need to awaken the consciousness of workers (as a common class) to the fact and cause of their exploitation and oppression, and the criminal rule of the bourgeoisie. Also, the working class needs to be united and organized to challenge their oppression. Furthermore they need to understand that overcoming their exploitation compels coordinated struggle on many fronts, beyond merely seeking better wages/work conditions, job security/benefits, etc., which is the typical extent of what workers struggle for when left to their own spontaneous activism. They must realize that it is a broad political struggle, and the bourgeoisie oppresses many sectors other than just the working class. To accomplish this, and uniting them with other oppressed sectors against the bourgeoisie, requires a proletarian-based leadership structure.

But the critical problem which opponents of the vanguard party have never answered in over 100 years of debate is the theoretical and practical question of how to unify the broad and fragmented working class into a united movement wherein it is *conscious of itself (and its interests) as a class.* Only genuine ML and MLM parties have solved this problem, and been able to awaken and maintain working-class consciousness and unity, and on a level of struggle higher than mere trade union politics (what Lenin called "economism").

Many on the "Left," (including anarchists and avowed Communists) because they *can't* resolve this problem, avoid, downplay, distort or have altogether abandoned the question of class struggle and its central role in any genuine anti-capitalist revolutionary movement, or they otherwise endlessly speculate how working-class success might be achieved.

Karl Marx expressed early on that capitalism could be destroyed and a free and equal society ultimately achieved, only by the proletariat first overthrowing the bourgeois class, and then exercising its own (economic, political, military and cultural) dictatorship over the bourgeoisie. Failure to suppress the bourgeoisie after its power was overthrown would only result in its regaining state power. This he witnessed first hand.

Because proletarian struggle was only in its infant stages during his day, Marx was unable to answer *how* it could effectively defeat and exercise its dictatorship over the bourgeoisie. But his studies of those early workers' struggles, specifically the Paris Commune of 1871, gave him some ideas on the methods that the workers were in the *process* of discovering. He did recognize, although he supported the commune as a heroic effort, that it could not successfully hold onto its power because the French proletariat was not yet sufficiently class conscious, united and organized.

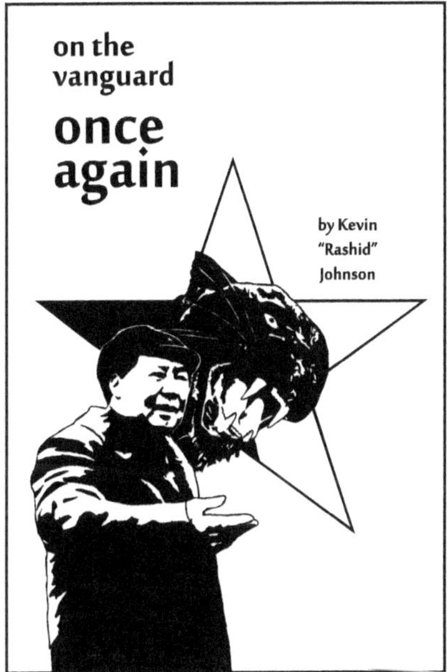


Subsequently, Lenin, who analyzed and actively participated in the day to day fight against the even more advanced, consolidated and powerful capitalist system (monopoly capitalism or imperialism) of his era, furthered Marx's analyses and was able to devise and apply a definite organizational form and tactics with which to unite and organize the proletarian struggle. He realized that a disciplined party, committed explicitly to the interests and philosophy of the working class, was needed to awaken the proletariat on a nationwide scale to their common class identity and interests, to unite and organize them upon this common class stand against and to overthrow the bourgeoisie, and to hold onto that power and repress the bourgeoisie.

And his method—the ML party—above all others, worked. In fact, it achieved the first working-class socialist state (in Russia in 1917), which doesn't discount the fact that in the process many mistakes were made alongside the achievements. And errors were to be expected, since it *was* the first successful struggle of its type, and met with determined resistance from the capitalist class in Russia and the major imperialist powers, all of whom promptly invaded Russia attempting to overthrow the new socialist state.

Unlike much of today's academic and petty bourgeois "Left," Lenin and company did not refuse to take the lead for fear of failure or a fight, nor get bogged down in moral dithering. Instead they stoutly took the lead, defied and endured the severest state repression, applied theory to practice, refined their tactics, and gave the world and those to follow an invaluable standard of leadership and struggle to learn from and build upon.

In China, Mao Tse-Tung, studying and observing Marx's, Lenin's and Russia's examples, further advanced the ML party concept, and adapted it to his own people's struggles against multiple advanced imperialist powers and the internal class enemies of the Chinese masses. From this experience Mao discovered that even after a proletarian revolution succeeds in defeating the bourgeoisie and achieving a socialist society, the class struggle continues—often in forms more complicated than the initial struggle to overthrow capitalist state power. This because, although overthrown, the bourgeoisie and its influences still exist within the new society, and they will struggle *unceasingly* to regain power. To combat this tendency he found that a series of revolutions in culture had to be waged to wipe out bourgeois influences and values, and that class struggle had to continue especially *within the vanguard party* itself and upper levels of the socialist state, to keep the party loyal to the proletariat and ensure it wasn't subverted by aspiring and regenerated bourgeois elements into their own vanguard. This required giving the masses greater oversight and control over the party and state, and active power to combat bureaucratic degeneration. He thus enhanced party democracy.

But in any event, the party structure is indispensable. The key issue is what class's interests it serves and is loyal to. It's ironic that many people ask why the working class—which is infinitely larger and thus more difficult to organize than the bourgeoisie—(or oppressed nationalities of people) needs a leading party to unite and organize it in struggle against the imperialist class and system. Yet no one *ever* questions—nor even recognizes—that the capitalist class also has and needs its own political organizations to successfully exercise and organize *its own* unity and dictatorship over the working class and everyone else. Lest we forget, bourgeois political structures and leaders preceded, and led, every movement where capitalism and imperialism overthrew feudal, slave-owning, etc. political economies (especially here in Amerika ... what indeed were the Whigs, Democrats, Republicans, Tories, etc. but parties of the existing or aspiring ruling classes?) And it is these parties that rule in capitalist societies in the interests of the bourgeoisie.

In case you didn't notice, it's the wealthy minority who the entire political system and its parties serve in capitalist society, and it's *against* the working class, poor and other marginalized groups that their laws, courts, police, military, prisons, etc. exert control. *This* is why you have no genuine ML parties (I should say MLM parties) operating legally in any capitalist country.

The bourgeoisie *everywhere* is *very* class conscious; and remains vigilant in keeping the workers atomized; divided against each other along racial, gender, national, religious and other lines; and focused on immediate individual survival needs.

To counter this, to awaken, unite, organize and coordinate the proletariat *as a common class* against bourgeois rule, requires a leading organization that is totally committed in theory and practice to, and is rooted in, the working class. *This* is what the MLM revolutionary vanguard party is all about and why it's needed.

## What is a Vanguard?

Since we both use the term to refer to the MLM party, and because in many circles the term has taken on a distorted meaning equivalent to a four letter word, I want to comment on what a "vanguard" actually is.

As any dictionary will tell you, vanguard simply means "leadership," whether of a class, society, army, movement or opinion. Essentially it is an advanced sector or group that unites, informs, organizes and guides a larger sector or group. Just like the Central Nervous System (CNS) unites, informs, organizes and guides the activities of the body's organs and major muscle groups, while it also remains an organic part of and draws information from the very body it serves. Only when the vanguard or leadership is unhealthy or represents the interests of a body other than the one it directs, does it become an oppressive thing. *Keep this in mind.*

Societies, movements, armies, etc. are complex social structures that require a centralized leadership to unite, coordinate, draw practical lessons from, organize and guide them. In fact there has *never* existed a society without a centralized leadership, whether you're looking at communal pre-state band or village, or slave-owning, or state level feudal or capitalist societies, they all had a centralized leading body: from clan mothers and head matrons, to big men, head men, chiefs and elders' councils, from monarchs to political parties with legislative, executive and judicial branches or a combination of these.

Even esteemed anarchists like Noam Chomsky agree that it's impossible to organize a society without leaders. Again, the key question turns on *whose* interests the leaders serve. Are they leaders who exist as an organic part of the society and movement they lead, or are they representatives of a small specialized group that aims to impose its own will and values upon everyone else? (Whether by force, fraud or otherwise). And in *all* cases of leadership, a combination of democracy and centralism is used. The question is whether it is democracy exercised by and among the masses and their genuine leadership, or by and among a select minority acting *against* the masses. Which brings me to the concept of Democratic Centralism (DC), which you imply is something unique to MLM Parties.

## On Criticism and DC

Let's look at communal pre-colonial Afrikan villages for example, which many anti-authoritarians and anti-"vanguardists" hail as genuine models of social equality and democracy. It may be relevant to point out to some of our readers that many Afrikans kidnapped and brought to the Amerikas in chains came from such societies. Consequently, many of the escaped slave societies here in the western hemisphere, known as the Maroons, modeled their more egalitarian societies after those precolonial communal villages.

In those Afrikan societies there existed a very centralized authority which resided in an elders' council that spoke through a head elder. This council was composed of respected elders who presided over various traditional social and civil functions in the village. The head elder was appointed and could be removed or replaced by vote. Many people confuse the terms *chief* and *head elder,* or think they denote the same type of leadership, which I should distinguish. Unlike the head elder, the chief rules over a patriarchal clan society, he inherits his position by heredity (instead of by vote), and he can only be deposed by defeat in war. Many Maroon societies were also ruled by such chiefs. The chief also had command over a specialized body of warriors. Unlike the chief, the head elder had no power to force her/his will on the village because s/he had no special army or police. Instead, a decision announced by her/him had greater force (moral authority) because it was actually the decision reached by collective agreement of the village's most respected members (the elders' council), with participation and input from the society as a whole.

Once a decision was reached by the council in a dispute, or in selecting a head elder, or other matters, it was binding on everyone, including those who disagreed with it. Those who bucked the social will were also taken before the village council and masses if the offense were serious enough. If found guilty in the mass hearing they were punished accordingly, which could include banishment from the village. This is in essence DC. In fact it is duplicated almost exactly in the model of organization and decision-making used by the MLM party, which I'll demonstrate momentarily.

But first I'd like to give actual examples of such centralized authority (a vanguard) in the communal Afrikan village and how they applied internal popular democracy, or what many MLM'ists call "self-criticism." Ojinga Odinga described the head elders' role in his pre-colonial Luo village in Kenya:

> "A [head elder] did not issue orders, he sounded out the elders, met them in consultation and when he said 'this is my decision,' he was announcing not his personal verdict but an agreed upon point of view. His function was not to lay down the law, but to consult and arbitrate to learn the consensus of opinion and to keep unity of his people. Elders were men of substance and integrity, and recognized as outstanding individuals. Even when they came from leading lineages they did not inherit leadership but had to earn it … ."[2]

Frantz Fanon described the internal public democracy practiced by Afrikan societies as "tradition," a process used by MLM Parties, which communists call criticism and self-criticism. He furthermore observed that this practice counteracts the anti-communal mental habits of the western intellectual types:

> "Self-criticism has been much talked about of late, but few people realize that it is an African institution. Whether in the djeemas of North Africa or in the meetings of Western Africa, tradition demands that the quarrels which occur in a village should be settled

in public. It is a communal self-criticism, of course, and with a note of humor, because everybody is relaxed, and because in the last resort we all want the same things. But the more the intellectual imbibes the atmosphere of the people, the more completely he abandons the habits of calculation, of unwonted silence, of mental reservations, and shakes off the spirit of concealment. And it is true that already at that level we can say that the community triumphs, and that it spreads its own light and its own reason."[3]

So we see a centralized leadership structure, a vanguard, in Afrikan communal society, and the combination of public democracy and centralized enforcement of the collective will in their decision-making and dispute resolution processes. But these are concepts rejected by anti-authoritarians because they don't really understand them. Just as they don't understand, or otherwise tend to stereotype, or idealize, many things, due to failing to objectively search out and draw truth from facts instead of opinions, or responding to the oppressive system with emotion rather than reason.

Now allow me to show you the parallels between the DC of communal societies as described above and that of the genuine MLM parties, by quoting none other than Mao himself critically explaining DC to his own party comrades, who failed to grasp and apply what he called "unity of the leadership and the masses," or simply the "mass line method":

> "It seems that some of our comrades still do not understand the democratic centralism which Marx and Lenin talked of ... They are afraid of the masses, afraid of the masses talking about them, afraid of the masses criticizing them. What sense does it make for Marxist-Leninists to be afraid of the masses? When they have made mistakes they don't talk about themselves, and they are afraid of the masses talking about them. The more frightened they are, the more haunted they become. I think one should not be afraid. What is there to be afraid of? Our attitude is to hold fast to the truth and be ready at any time to correct our mistakes. The question of right or wrong, correct or incorrect in our work has to do with contradictions among the people. To resolve contradictions among the people we can't use curses or fists, still less guns or knives. We can only use the method of discussion, reasoning, criticism and self-criticism. In short, we can only use democratic methods, the method of letting the masses speak out.
>
> "Both inside and outside the Party there must be a full democratic life, which means conscientiously putting democratic centralism

> into effect. We must conscientiously bring questions out into the open, and let the masses speak out. Even at the risk of being cursed we should still let them speak out. The result of their curses at the worst will be that we are thrown out and cannot go on doing this kind of work—demoted or transferred. What is so impossible about that? Why should a person go up and never go down? Why should one only work in one place and never be transferred to another? I think that demotion and transfer, whether it is justified or not, does good to people. They thereby strengthen their revolutionary will, are able to investigate and study a variety of new conditions and increase their useful knowledge. I myself have had experience in this respect and gained a great deal of benefit."[4]

Having thus explained that party democracy is a process of decision-making that compels openness, and draws upon and implements the collective will of party cadre and the masses, Mao went on to explain party centralism as all party cadre being bound by the decisions reached collectively through the democratic process,[5] just like in the communal village.

Furthermore, the MLM Party's central committee (CC) is organized horizontally much like the elders' council. Like the council, the CC consists of elected group members who preside over specifically defined social and civil functions (ministries). As you're aware I preside over the Defense Ministry of our NABPP-PC. The democratically elected chairpersyn or secretary corresponds to the head elder. The party's general membership is drawn from the proletarian class of the people it leads and represents, or its members must have developed the proletarian class stand and integrated themselves with the people. Leadership positions are democratically bestowed, based upon proven ability and commitment, and are subject to revocation by vote. Party leaders and their practices are to be openly scrutinized by party members *and the masses* it proposes to lead. There is thus "unity of the leadership and the masses" in purpose and practice, just as the bourgeoisie and their parties are linked together. Indeed the party is directly connected to the masses by party organs and mass organizations, just like the CNS is connected to the body's organs and muscles by the peripheral nervous system.

## It's a Class Struggle

As I've noted, a vanguard becomes problematic when it represents and pursues the interests of those other than it leads. What recommends the MLM party is its ideological orientation to countering such subversion.

It first of all emphasizes its proletarian orientation, and recognizes that so long as there is class society and class struggle (which continues even under socialism), there is always and in all places going to be struggle for domination between the classes. In capitalist societies where the bourgeoisie rules, its values and its own vanguard dominate the society, economy, culture and institutions. And it will maneuver and strive ceaselessly to prevent the development and rise of a genuine vanguard of the proletariat, subjecting the masses to the rule and influences of its own vanguard. In socialist societies where the proletariat is in power, the overthrown bourgeoisie will struggle at every turn to subvert the proletarian party and state, and to regain power. This is what class struggle means. It is because many don't understand class struggle, that they've witnessed reversals of socialist gains, the overthrow of socialist parties and states and their reversion to capitalist systems, and splits and struggles within revolutionary parties, yet failed to recognize these were the product of ongoing struggle between the bourgeoisie and the proletariat. What we Communists call the "two line struggle."

Therefore, any aspiring revolutionary vanguard must be conscious to resist being infected, influenced and infiltrated by the class values of the enemy. This means the party must be uncompromisingly committed to the working class. It is impossible to prevent elements that share, harbor or develop enemy class values from creeping into or cropping up within a revolutionary party. This is why Lenin promoted splits as the health of the party and Mao promoted cultural revolutions arousing the masses to rise up against bourgeois influence and elements within the revolutionary party and state.

Attempts to maintain unprincipled unity between genuine revolutionaries and bourgeois elements within such parties have led time and again to their being subverted by counter-revolutionaries, such as occurred in Afrika—in the African National Congress when Winnie Mandela was purged and Chris Hani assassinated in the early 1990s and power was "given" to capitalist turncoat Nelson Mandela; in the PAIGC when Amilcar Cabral was assassinated in 1972 and his brother Luis was purged, and so on.

## Answer to Comrade "Maroon"

There was an article written a few years ago by Comrade Russell "Maroon" Shoatz, called "The Dragon and the Hydra,"[6] which was a response to my own earlier article on the role and need of vanguard parties.[7] In that article Comrade Maroon levelled charges against ML parties, claiming they have a legacy of internal factionalism, sterile practice and betraying the very people they are supposed to lead in struggle against oppression. Since these charges are relevant to this discussion, and I haven't had the opportunity to finish my formal reply,[8] I want to briefly respond here.

I've just answered the point on factionalism, to which I might add that Maroon's article completely overlooks the role of class in revolutionary struggle; and even proposed that anarchists, anti-authoritarians and proponents of ultra-democratic movements, share organizational concepts with the Maroon societies that had elders and chiefs and were *in no form* ultra-democratic or decentralized. But to further illustrate my point, imagine that several committed conscious prisoners came together to form a leadership group to educate and unite others to struggle against the administration and guards' abuses. So they develop a solid line of theory and tactics to achieve this end. And it meets with initial success in winning over and organizing other prisoners. This group answers to and is committed to its prisoner base and grows as they educate more prisoners into their class line.

As soon as the pigs see their authority and monopoly on influence and power challenged, they're going to try and repress the leadership group in various ways, including by trying to "turn" its supporters and members, using both the carrot and the stick. Inevitably you're going to have some driven by their own power agendas, pig inducements, or other motives to become agents, infiltrators and turncoats. These subversives will maneuver to increase and consolidate their influence and numbers, and to subvert and sabotage the gains and goals of the genuinely committed cadre. So what do you do? Do you go along with them? Do you maintain an unprincipled unity with them inside your organization or movement where they are privy to your plans, identities, etc. enabling them to subvert the entire group and movement? Of course not! What you do is expose them and distinguish yourself and your position from them before the people. If they are enemy agents you "correct" them, if they are not but persist in their reactionary aims you purge them from your ranks (if their numbers are not so great), or (if their numbers are substantial) you and the serious cadre split off from them into a separate organization. This is all done within the structure of democratic centralism of course and distinguishing your commitment to the masses from their opportunism, self-interest, or reactionary politics.

This isn't mere factionalism. It is part of the *class struggle*. Part of the struggle to keep the people's vanguard loyal to the class it represents and not subverted by the enemy of that class. That's how the enemy controls us right now. Using Judases who look, talk and/or act like us, but who really aspire toward and serve them, or have other ulterior interests at heart. To counter this, only the MLM party specifically and explicitly adheres to the ideological and political lines of the proletariat *and no other.*

As Lenin observed, Marx warned that when communists unite with others in struggle, "they enter into agreements to satisfy the practical aims of the movement, but *do not allow any bargaining over principles, do not make theoretical 'concessions'.*"[9] In other words, while we may compromise and adapt our tactics to align ourselves with allies, we must never compromise our class stand. Our commitment is to the ideological and political line of the revolutionary proletariat and no other. This is why Mao emphasized that political and ideological line determines everything, particularly the success or failure of revolutionary struggle. The moment we allow influences of the bourgeoisie, petty bourgeoisie, lumpen and other less than revolutionary sectors to seep in and sway us, we betray the working class. Not adhering to the proletarian class line as Marx cautioned, is how many revolutionaries have been turned from the course of revolutionary class struggle to one of reaction.

As for "sterile" practice. This critique doesn't apply to genuine MLM elements, because as with the elders' councils, a vanguard isn't a vanguard simply because it calls itself one, or because it forces its leadership on the people. It becomes a vanguard because a substantial part of the people *voluntarily accepts* and follows its leadership, which it earns through correct analysis, practice and example. If it ain't doing nothing and the people don't recognize it, it ain't *their* vanguard. Like with the NABPP-PC. We aren't a New Afrikan vanguard yet, only the nucleus of one. But we definitely aspire to this.

So you see this is complicated.

Before turning to the next issue, I should make a few final points regarding Comrade Maroons's article. The Maroon societies which he promotes as model revolutionary organizations never attempted to nor were capable of overthrowing the slave system—a system much weaker and less organized than today's imperialist one. Furthermore, they coexisted with the slave system, fed off it, and many became its agents and slave catchers, and were often manipulated into fighting each other by the planters.

The Maroons were not revolutionaries but rebels who merely fled and defied the slave societies, but left them intact to oppress others. So in relation to the masses of slaves left behind, one could say the Maroons had a legacy of betrayal of the oppressed masses, sterile practice, and of being factionalized among themselves. Exactly like the hydra that comrade Maroon uses to symbolize the rebel Maroon societies, they amounted to a common class of oppressed peoples but composed of many contending heads, unorganized, uncoordinated, often bickering, fighting, and contending with each other, and thus unable to lead the collective body in struggle to defeat the common enemy. A task which the one-headed dragon—the MLM party—once awakened, has proven eminently capable of leading its collective body in achieving. Consider also, how easily the European imperialist powers overran Afrika's separate village societies, instituting colonialism across the entire continent, during the late 1800s and early 1900s, exactly *because* those societies lacked a unifying leadership. Yet, Comrade Maroon promotes such localized forms of social organization as *models of resistance* against today's even more advanced imperialism?! Then contrast this with the fact that the *only* time a society of many separate communal villages held their own and ultimately defeated imperialist forces was when they were united, organized and coordinated by an ML or MLM party: the Chinese defeated multiple imperialist powers under the leadership of the Chinese Communist Party, the Vietnamese defeated the French in 1954 and then the U.S. in the Vietnam War under the leadership of the Vietnamese Communist Party, etc.

It also speaks volumes that the only slave uprising that actually overthrew a slave system, was organized under a conscious class leadership, albeit that of an aspiring bourgeois one (the Haitian Revolution, 1791–1803).

This last point answers the comrade's point about betrayals of the masses. Again, any group that does this is not a mass-based vanguard, or it has been subverted, which is what happens when you *don't* struggle against, purge and/or ultimately split from subversive influences and elements to maintain the health and class integrity of the party.

## Speaking admirably of Hamas

Speaking of a party's remaining true to its base, this brings me to Hamas. Yes, I've spoken admiringly of Hamas on this very basis. Which is not to say that I agree with their politics or tactics per se. Hamas, as you pointed out, is not a working-class party. Actually, it wasn't initially a Palestinian national liberation group either. In fact Hamas began as an Islamist organization that clashed not only with the Israeli occupation forces, but with secular nationalists and communists as well. It actually rejected the concept of Palestinian nationalism, promoting instead an abstract Islamic theocracy. Secular politics were left to other groups like the Palestine Liberation Organization (PLO)—later becoming coopted by the U.S. and Israel and changing its name to the Palestinian Authority (PA). Hamas's focus was instead on spreading its Islamist ideology and responding to the immediate needs of the Palestinian people, particularly their physical need of basic services, and psychological need to resist Israel's brutal and racist military occupation of Gaza and the West Bank.

Hamas *became* a political structure because the Palestinian people made it that, choosing Hamas over the corrupt PLO that outright sold out their struggle for national liberation by signing the Oslo agreement with Israel in 1993. The people put their might behind Hamas, electing its functionaries into positions of local leadership, then ultimately as their overall national leadership. To its credit, Hamas's leadership and membership always remained indigenous to its operational bases in Gaza. Only members of its political bureau lived in exile and thereby interfaced with other Arab states and regional actors, where Hamas got most of its funding from. It also has a leadership branch within Israeli prisons, where more than 10,000 Palestinian resistance leaders are confined. Therefore Hamas remained free of pressures and influences of outside forces, and was always able to keep informed of the needs, interests and desires of the Palestinian people.

It was the will of the Palestinian people that made Hamas their national liberation organization and moved Hamas's military arm to take up arms against Israel and its illegal settlements that have been mass murdering Palestinians—especially children—and increasingly stealing their land. It was the Palestinian will that moved Hamas to set up social support programs to help provide for basic needs like food, medical care, etc. that Israel is blocking. And it was the Palestinian will that elected Hamas in 2006 as their national political leadership in place of the PA despite knowing the U.S. and Israel would retaliate by cutting all funding they were giving to prop up the neo-colonial PA, and crumbs they were tossing to the already ruined Gaza economy. So Hamas is a reflection of Palestinian spontaneity. But remaining confined to Gaza with its mass base, it evolved to reflect their developing political consciousness in response to desperately oppressive conditions, and a thriving culture based in keeping alive the Palestinian historical memory—something that New Afrikans have been robbed of because we do not have a vanguard party to keep alive and unite us around our own collective historical experiences, struggles, and consciousness. We are therefore like a people suffering historical amnesia or Alzheimer's.

So here again we see the confirmed role and need of organized leadership, to unite an oppressed people around a collective identity, consciousness, and resistance, even without revolution being the organization's explicit aim.

And in case you didn't realize, Hamas has—or at least it had—an organizational structure similar to an ML party's. They practice DC, although with less open mass participation and publicity due to their operating under Israeli military occupation. And as noted they are mass-based and generally responsive to the will of the people. Its organizational structure has always distinguished Hamas as the most disciplined and organized—and therefore most feared—Palestinian organization. While I don't suppose it has changed drastically since 2004, I'm most familiar with the structure Hamas had under its founder Sheikh Ahmad Yasin, who was assassinated that same year by the Israeli military.

Hamas relied on group leadership and consensus decision-making, with Yasin as the spokesman or chairman. Although he did have plenary power to make unilateral decisions, he seldom exercised it. To make collective decisions reflecting the popular will under the extreme conditions of military occupation, the organization would circulate written policy options among activists for discussion and decision, who would then give their feedback to "knowledgeable people in [their] area." This way the group could "make a decision acceptable to the widest possible base of our ranks which, at the same time, would preserve the movement's achievements and remain faithful to its goals and principles"[10]

As already mentioned, like a communist party, Hamas has a politburo. But having some of the same organizational features of an MLM party doesn't make Hamas the equivalent of one. In fact not only is Hamas not specifically a working-class group, it isn't opposed to capitalism. No Islamist group is, despite the formal rejection of secular politics by many of them. As I noted, most of Hamas's funding came from capitalist Arab states, organizations and individuals. Indeed, Islamism, or "Political Islam," has been used by the U.S. as an agency of imperialist expansion and intervention in the Middle East. As Samir Amin observed:

> "We should not be surprised that the U.S. is pleased by the services that Political Islam renders to its project of world hegemony. With the exception of Hamas in Palestine and Hizbollah in Lebanon (pre-911), no movement of Political Islam is designated as an enemy by Washington. The pre-911 designation of Hamas and Hizbollah as 'terrorist organizations' was clearly an accident of political geography, since both are opposed to the state of Israel, which evidently takes precedence in U.S. considerations over everything else. Hamas and Hizbollah are the only manifestations of Political Islam fighting foreign military occupation, whereas the others direct their violence only at their compatriots. Double standards and hypocrisy—can we expect anything else from the imperialists?"[11]

Akin to Hamas is another modern Middle East organization, just mentioned, that single-handedly repelled a pretty vicious Israeli invasion of southern Lebanon in 2006. Namely, Hizbollah. It too has an organizational structure similar to the model you reject as moribund and marginalized. Hizbollah has, in fact, proven almost impossible to penetrate and monitor, yet it too has won broad popular support and sunk deep roots within Lebanese civil society.

Hizbollah also has a politburo that interfaces with an Executive Council which mirrors a central committee. The Executive Council members preside over specific social and civil functions like civil defense, health care, regional offices, education, labor unions, etc. Even the commander of Hizbollah's resistance fighters is elected to his position. But because it combines both a military and political structure, the organization is a bit more centralized in its decision-making than Hamas. However, instead of a general chairman, the group is presided over by a seven-member consultative council, which does have a chairman. There is then a special security branch that reliably protects the leadership and acts as security via liaison committees in Hizbollah base areas.

Although concentrated along Israel's northern border, Hizbollah kept such a low profile that Israel believed it could successfully invade southern Lebanon and seize valuable territory and waterways it had been plotting on for decades. In the summer of 2006, the Israeli army invaded, and was swiftly corrected by Hizbollah and made to retreat empty-handed back into Israel.

Because Hamas and Hizbollah generally trail behind mass spontaneity, and represent patriarchal and bourgeois class interests, they do not unify and raise the consciousness of the masses above immediate needs, nor empower them through class struggle to seize power from their class enemies and imperialist domination. This distinguishes them from an MLM party. Moreover, their mass bases have forced them to become national liberation groups to a greater or lesser degree.

Now I *can't* agree that there are or have been any popular-based anarchist organizations. Actually that's a sort of oxymoron. I've never heard of nor seen anarchists "organize" and coordinate anyone other than a handful of people, and certainly not in any sort of organized leadership structure.

Which is not to invalidate the invaluable help and support that quite a few anarchists, especially the ABCs (Anarchist Black Cross) have given to oppressed groups within the USA, particularly to prisoners—and including me. You all have been genuine comrades and I recognize and regard you as such. But, you cannot deny—in fact you've *often* complained to me—that these groups and their memberships have remained small in number. Also, as a principle, they reject the role and responsibilities of leadership, although by working to influence the ideas and actions of prisoners through the literature and line they spread, they are in fact acting as leaders. Thus they leave those they "lead" without the needed guidance and organization to apply those ideas and change their oppressed condition. I talk about this a bit in a recent article: "Unity-Struggle-Transformation: On Revolutionary Organization, Leadership and Cadre Development."

### A Moribund and Marginalized Method?

Other reasons I promote the MLM party model … well, because it works, it is infinitely adaptable and it is the most effective model of political leadership in mass-based revolutionary movements. Even the imperialists admit this. It can't be so "moribund" and "marginalized" as you allege since a Maoist movement just a couple of years ago toppled the oppressive monarchy in Nepal. A Maoist people's war presently controls most of rural India, and Maoists are giving the neo-colonial puppet governments of the Philippines and Peru nightmares. And lets not forget that despite Colombia's being the hemisphere's largest recipient of U.S. financial and military aid, the FARC-EP, an ML party, has won broad popular support and is holding its own against the Colombian military and multitudes of U.S. and Colombian government-backed deaths squads.

Somehow you seem to overlook that today there are millions being led in active resistance against imperialism by ML and MLM parties, and billions supporting or influenced by such struggles. *That's a large portion* of the world's population being led by such parties. To call such a vast number of people "marginal" smacks of imperialist country chauvinism, since most of these numbers are in the Third World, and I can't find anything that anti-authoritarians have contributed to their livelihoods and struggles.

Indeed, contrast this all with the fact that the last *and only* revolutionary victory that anarchists claim responsibility for (and that was with communist help that they turned on) was in Spain, way back in 1936. And that was localized and very brief—lasting only a few months—and furthermore paved the way for Francisco Franco's decades-long fascist dictatorship. Whereas in the former Soviet Union and China, it took decades to dismantle socialism and reinstate capitalism after their revolutions.

With only one revolutionary victory to its name occurring almost a century ago, and being a small counter-cultural trend among white middle-class folks and youth, what would you call anarchism if not "moribund" and "marginalized"?

Again, even the imperialists acknowledge that the Maoist strategy is still, above all others past and present, very relevant, very much alive, and the most revolutionary, political and threatening to their class, because it appeals to and mobilizes *the entire population* (how's that for "marginal") against a common class enemy. Meaning it provides a class conscious leadership that remains true to its base. At West Point, the U.S. Army's "distinguished" war college, Mao's works are mandatory study, and they still admit inability to contend with the Maoist strategy. Similarly here's what the imperialist hired guns, the U.S. Army, says of that strategy, led by an MLM party, in its Army Field Manual #100-20:

> "Peoples war is the invention of Mao Tse-tung and the Chinese Communist Party. Although the era of Communist-sponsored wars of national liberation has apparently ended, any serious insurgent would be advised to consider carefully the effectiveness of People's War, the most political of all insurgent strategies. The Maoist or Mass Strategy attempts to mobilize a whole people against their government. The most sophisticated of insurgent strategies, it emphasized organization and its relationship with the entire population. It is also the most military in its latter stages as it attempts to raise an army within the affected country and to challenge the government on the field of battle. The Maoist mass strategy has many imitators. The Vietnamese Communists used it to great effect, and it has been emulated in Peru, the Philippines and elsewhere. Thus the mass strategy deserves special attention."

It was Mao who made clear that the MLM party's leadership was the key to waging any successful revolutionary mass struggle, including the one he successfully led in China.

> "A well-disciplined Party armed with the theory of Marxism-Leninism, using the method of self-criticism and linked with the masses of people; an army under the leadership of such a party; a united front of all revolutionary classes and all revolutionary groups under the leadership of such a party—these are the three main weapons with which we have defeated the enemy."[12]

> "If there is to be a revolution, there must be a revolutionary party. Without a revolutionary party, without a party built on the Marxist-Leninist revolutionary style, it is impossible to lead the working class and the broad masses of people in defeating imperialism and its running dogs."[13]

And as I pointed out elsewhere:

"Mao's vanguard party walked its talk. Not only did it repel a Japanese imperialist invasion, defeat the imperialist-backed KMT army and seize power in 1949, empowering and improving the living conditions of China's millions, but with a peasant army—and fresh from a civil war—it repelled the world's most powerful combined military forces, the U.S. and UN, from its borders in the Korean War (1950–1953)"[14]

And we're talking about a party that united, organized and led a nation of multiple distinct nationalities and "races" of people, that composed fully one fifth of the world's entire population. Mao was fond of pointing out that China was so vast that when the sun was setting on the western border of China, it was rising on the eastern border. Is *that* marginal?!

## Subservient to Moscow?

As for MLM Parties being "subservient to Moscow," because the concept was first developed by Lenin in Russia; that sounds a lot like the rhetoric of cultural nationalists and subjective reverse racists who reject the vanguard party concept because Lenin was "white." James and Grace Lee Boggs long ago answered such arguments:

"In the United States, as the Black movement struggles to define its goals and true means to achieve them, the question of what constitutes a Black revolutionary party is going to become increasingly the center of discussion and controversy. In order for this discussion and controversy to be meaningful, the Black movement will have to make a serious study of the concept of the vanguard party as developed and practiced by its originator. To believe that the Black revolutionary movement can evade such a study because Lenin was white and a European would be just as ridiculous as for an African freedom fighter to forego to fly an airplane because the Wright brothers were white Americans. Blacks don't refuse to drive Cadillacs because they are made by General Motors or to watch television because Philco (Ford) manufactures TV sets. What has been achieved in human history, whether technological or political, Blacks have a right to inherit. The very high development of the theory and practice of the vanguard party as originated by Lenin in Russia, and subsequently developed by Mao and Ho in Asia and Amilcar Cabral in Africa, belongs to all oppressed people of the world, providing those who seek to end the domination of man by man with guidelines which they ignore at their peril. It must be borne in mind at the same time that these guidelines can be applied only in relation to the specific conditions of a particular country and only by an organization that has developed out of indigenous forces and is not totally dependent upon external or foreign aid for is existence."[15]

They went on to point out:

"Until the Black revolutionary movement is ready to take seriously the scientific approach to revolution developed by Marx, Lenin, Ho and Giap, it will still be depending upon mystical or external guidance to achieve the power which can only be achieved by the most rigorous scientific appraisal of social forces. Mao, Ho and Cabral did not reject the necessity for a scientific approach to revolution because the founders of the approach were white. They used the method of Marx and Lenin, being careful at the same time to distinguish between the specific conditions of their own countries and those of Europe and Russia."[16]

Not only were the various revolutionary movements under ML-style Parties also not "subservient to Moscow" in the sense of trying to duplicate what occurred in Russia in their own countries, but, although he upheld Stalin's achievements while criticizing his errors, Mao explicitly refused to allow the Soviet Union and Stalin to direct the struggle in China. I'll let Mao tell you about it:

"The Chinese revolution won victory by acting contrary to Stalin's will ... During the quarrel with Wang Ming from 1937 to August 1938, we put forward ten great policies; while Wang Ming produced sixty policies. If we had followed Wang Ming's, or in other words Stalin's, methods the Chinese revolution couldn't have succeeded. When our revolution succeeded, Stalin said it was a fake. We did not argue with him, and as soon as we fought the war to resist America and aid Korea, our revolution became a genuine one [in his eyes]. But when we brought out 'On the Correct Handling of Contradictions Among the People' we talked about this question but they didn't. And what's more they said we were going in for liberalism, so it seems we were not genuine again. When this report of ours was published, the *New York Times* printed it complete, and also carried an article which claimed that China was being 'liberalized'. It is quite natural for the bourgeoisie to clutch at straws when drowning. But bourgeois politicians are not altogether without discernment. For example when Dulles heard about our report he said he wanted to see it. Within a couple of weeks he had come up with a conclusion: China was bad through and through; the Soviet Union was a little better. But the Soviet Union couldn't see it, and sent us a memorandum because they feared we were moving to the right. When the Anti-rightist movement started, naturally our 'liberalization' vanished.

"In short, our basic line is universal truth, but details differ. This applies to each country and to each province. There is unity and there are also contradictions. The Soviet Union stressed unity, but doesn't talk about contradictions, especially the contradictions between the leaders and the led."[17]

On the latter point Mao was criticizing Stalin for deviating from the principles of DC and the "Mass Line Method" in the practice of the Communist Party of the Soviet Union. An error which led to the alienation of the party from its mass base, the regeneration and concentration of aspiring bourgeois elements within the upper ranks of the party and state of the USSR, and a capitalist clique seizing power upon Stalin's death. Unlike Mao, Stalin had not come to terms with the reality that class struggle continues even under socialism, and within the revolutionary party itself. So it's clear Mao's party line was not "subservient to Moscow."

## Without a Head the Body Will Fall

A revolutionary mass struggle needs an MLM party-style leadership, like the body needs a healthy central nervous system. The masses without their own revolutionary party is like a body without a healthy CNS, in that they only react spontaneously (reflexively) to their pain and discomfort and look to outside forces to think for them and control their choices and actions. They can't effectively unite, organize and coordinate their activities or even be conscious of themselves as a common organism (class), nor intelligently analyze, judge and solve their problems, especially more complex ones that require deeper study and analysis.

How many of us, because of being controlled by external forces and/or not thinking beyond reflex, emotion, impulse, prejudice and rhetoric, cause ourselves pain, injury and even death, or readily attack and destroy others for little or nothing? This is because at the class, national and individual levels, we lack a healthy CNS (mass-based leadership) that genuinely and organically recognizes and serves our bosom interests.

Just as a centralized leadership is needed in the communal village to organize and "keep the unity of the people," so too do we as vastly larger and more complex oppressed classes and nationalities need the same. Only the MLM party structure has *proven* able to do this.

You can have an anarchist bookstore or bakery, and be quite successful. But we're not talking about something so localized, simple and basic. We're talking about overthrowing the monopoly capitalist ruling class and transforming the political economy and social relations of the whole world to end all oppression and exploitation. This is not so simple and cannot be done in an anarchistic fashion.

Taken together, these are the reasons I promote the MLM-style party leadership.

*Dare To Struggle, Dare to Win!*
*All Power to the People!*

## END NOTES

1. My prior discussions of Hamas can be found in Kevin "Rashid" Johnson, *Defying the Tomb: Selected Prison Writings and Art of Kevin "Rashid Johnson," Featuring Exchanges With an Outlaw*, (Montreal: Kersplebedeb, 2010), pp. 49–50, 135–136.

2. Ojinga Odinga, *Not Yet Uhuru: The Autobiography of Ojinga Odinga* (New York: Hill and Wang, 1967), p. 12.

3. Frantz Fanon, *The Wretched of the Earth* (1966).

4. Mao Tse-Tung, "Talk At An Enlarged Working Conference Convened By The Central Committee Of The Communist Party Of China," January 30, 1962. http://www.marxists.org/reference/archive/mao/selected-works/volume-8/mswv8_62.htm

5. Ibid.

6. This essay is included in the recent compilation of Maroon's writings, *Maroon the Implacable*, edited by Quincy Saul and Fred Ho and published by PM Press in 2013.

7. Johnson op cit., p. 351, note 1.

8. The discussion between Comrade Maroon and me was disrupted by the untimely illness and hospitalization of the persyn who was facilitating the exchange. I remained out of touch with that persyn for several years afterward, and found no one to fill in for them and supply desired reference materials, to fully prepare a reply to Maroon.

9. V.I. Lenin, *Introduction to Marx, Engels, Marxism* (NY: International Publishers, 1987) (1988, edition), p. 20 (emphasis added).

10. Shaul Mishal, et al., *The Palestinian Hamas: Vision, Violence and Coexistence* (NY: Columbia University Press, 2000), pp. 121–131.

11. Samir Amin, "Political Islam," *Covert Action Quarterly*, No. 71, Winter 2001, pp. 3–6.

12. Mao Tse-Tung, "On the People's Democratic Dictatorship" June 30, 1949. http://www.marxists.org/reference/archive/mao/selected-works/volume-4/mswv4_65.htm

13. Mao Tse-Tung, "Revolutionary forces of the world unite, fight against imperialist Aggression!" November 1948. http://www.marxists.org/reference/archive/mao/selected-works/volume-4/mswv4_44.htm

14. Johnson, op. cit., p. 367, n1.

15. James and Grace Lee Boggs, "The Role of the Vanguard Party," *Monthly Review*, April 1970, pp. 10–11.

16. Ibid., p. 12f.

17. Mao Tse-Tung, "Talks at the Chengdu Conference," March 1958. http://www.marxists.org/reference/archive/mao/selected-works/volume-8/swv8_06.htm

# PART II

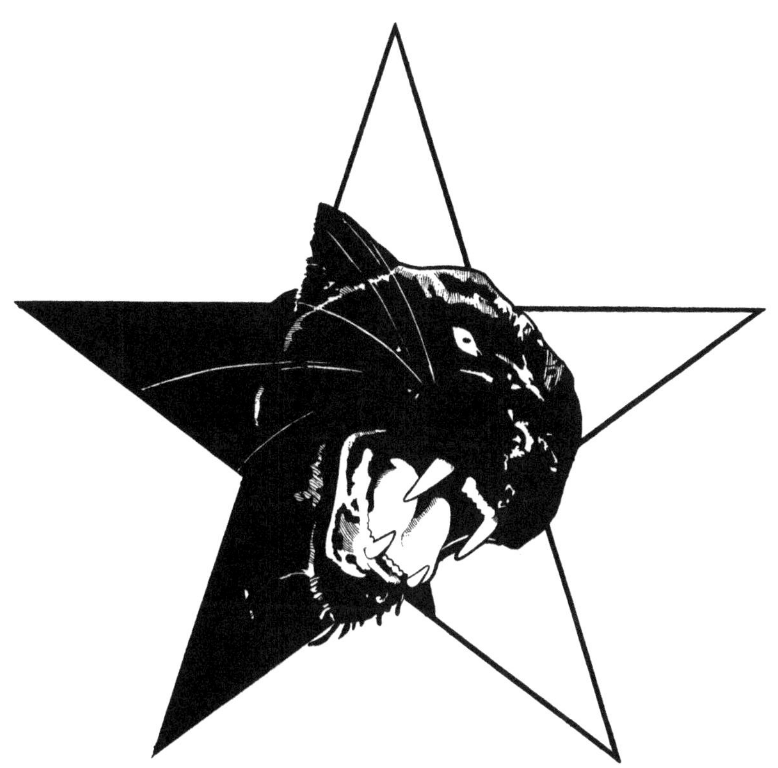

# BURNING QUESTIONS

*Having resolved that Historical Dialectical Materialism was the correct method to employ to develop a revolutionary ideological and political line to guide the struggle, and having rejected the method of subjective idealism characterized by Anarchism and various other ideological and political tendencies, the next step was to apply this method to the burning questions of our time; the problems of racism, sexism, gang violence, imperialist wars, and so on: And in particular to the task of transforming the prisons into "Schools of Liberation" and the oppressed communities into "Base Areas of Cultural, Social and Political Revolution."*

*Within the prisons, there are three primary divisions based on ethnicity; Blacks, Browns and Whites. To overcome these divisions, it was necessary to go deeply into the question of "race" and racism and develop a scientific understanding of it. That white prisoners were at that time coming forward seeking to ally with NABPP-PC made it an urgent question. When Huey Newton was asked what white people could do to support the original BPP, he suggested they could form their own White Panther Party (WPP), which they did along with numerous other formations based in working-class white communities that were allied with the BPP, like the Young Patriot Party (YPP), based in Chicago's Hillbilly ghetto. NABPP-PC made the same suggestion to the white prisoners.*

*Studying up on the history of the WPP, YPP and other BPP-affiliated white organizations, it was decided that the White Panther Organization (WPO) should be built as an arm of NABPP-PC under the leadership and democratic centralism of its central committee. That is, it was decided that NABPP-PC should remain an all-Black political party with Brown and White arms to represent the Party among the Brown and White prisoners. All Panthers would be equal comrades, but with a division of labor to apply the Party's line to organize among their own ethnic communities, working together to uplift and unite the whole prisoner population.*

*Understanding that the concept of "race" was a social construct invented and engineered by the exploiting class to accomplish their "divide and rule" strategy to control the oppressed and exploited masses, it was still undeniable that these divisions were real among the masses, and the Party needed to integrate itself with each group to work at building a common class consciousness. Further, it was recognized that the WPO must be more than just a white support group for the Black Panthers, they must be revolutionaries in their own right, working to organize and build anti-capitalist, anti-imperialist, anti-fascist, anti-racist and anti-sexist consensus among the poor whites, who also suffer under class oppression.*

*Another way the prisoners and oppressed masses are divided is into rival gangs (lumpen street organizations), and this too had to be analyzed and a correct line formulated using historical dialectical materialism. It was reasoned that the gang members themselves must be won to not only support a gang truce to end the fratricidal violence but to actively work to build an inter-gang alliance as part of the overall United Panther Movement (UPM), transforming themselves into proletarian formations oriented to serving the people and uplifting their communities.*

*The "Willie Lynch Speech," it turns out, is an urban legend no older than the late 1960s, and has been debunked by historians in its particulars, but it is based in historical truth: Truth that must be grasped and built upon, and truth as old as the division of society into classes. Classes arose with the invention of private property and the division of society into master and slave classes. "Divide and Rule" is the way the exploiting class maintains the status quo of inequality. Lots of things can be used to divide us, but we must struggle to unite ourselves around what will change things for the better—and that is revolution! All the burning questions we must deal with have a common solution in proletarian socialist revolution!*

*Tom Watts*

# 4. ON THE QUESTIONS OF RACE AND RACISM: REVOLUTIONARY NATIONAL LIBERATION AND BUILDING THE UNITED FRONT AGAINST IMPERIALISM: A STATEMENT IN SUPPORT OF THE WHITE PANTHER ORGANIZATION 2006

> "The economic nature of racism is not simply an aside ... Racism is a fundamental characteristic of monopoly capitalism."
>
> *George L. Jackson, 1971*

## Introduction

Many people believe that racism—indeed the very concept of race itself—develops automatically when groups of people with different complexions, hair, and body types are brought together. This is not so! Actually, the concept of race is barely 500 years old. The common people have been programmed into accepting "race" as a normal and natural thing, to prevent them from questioning, investigating, and challenging the ideas and roots of race and racism. Race and racism are the inventions of a specific social class, and devised to serve a specific social purpose. The creators are the oppressor capitalist ruling class, and the purpose is to divide the laboring class that the capitalists exploit against themselves. This is because, if united, the workers pose the single greatest threat to the capitalist class monopoly over social wealth, power, and control. A dispassionate study will show that in every situation where race has arisen to become a sharp dividing social factor, the hands of the capitalists can be seen pulling the strings, and it is only they who benefit from the conflicts.

George Jackson clearly recognized this. He pointed out that while white racism, the dominant form of racism in Amerika, expresses itself as:

> "... the morbid traditional fear of Blacks, Indians, Mexicans, [and] the desire to inflict pain on them when they began to compete in the industrial sectors. The resentment and the seedbed of fear are patterned into every modern capitalist society. It grows out of a

> sense of insecurity and insignificance that is inculcated into the workers by the conditions of life and work under capitalism. This sense of vulnerability is the breeding ground of racism. At the same time, the ruling class actively promotes racism against the Blacks of the lower classes. This programmed racism has always served to distract the huge numbers of people who subsist at just a slightly higher level than those in a more debased condition (in the 1870s the strikes frequently ended in anti-Chinese or anti-Black lynchings) ... Racism has served always in the U.S. as a pressure release ..."

The sole concern of the capitalist class is to secure and increase their profits and power. They do not care whom or what they damage or destroy to accomplish this, nor do they care what nationality or complexion the people are whom they exploit, only that they keep the exploited workers unable to unite and mobilize against their conditions of exploitation. Racism has been the capitalists' most effective method of accomplishing this. Here in North Amerika, the game began in the late 1600s.

### The Creation of the White Race and Racism

The first laborers exploited in North Amerika under British colonialism consisted of Afrikan, European, and Indian slaves and indentured servants. The concept of "race" did not exist then. The laborers were all equally oppressed and exploited of their wealth-producing labor by the capitalist plantation owners and thus saw each other as equals. They lived, labored, loved, suffered, bred, bled, escaped, and died together. They also repeatedly rebelled and revolted together. But because they lacked a unifying leadership and vision or control over resources, they were unable to come together en masse to wage a united revolution to overthrow the plantation elite and the British colonial government that served and backed the elite. This all changed in 1676 when Bacon's Rebellion occurred.

The leader of the rebellion, Nathaniel Bacon, was a young plantation owner. He had left England to settle in the British colonies in 1673, and was appointed to the Council of British Colonial Governor William Berkeley. The colonial government's principal concern (as with any capitalist government) was to maintain stability in the colonies while protecting and expanding the holdings and wealth of the ruling class. To achieve this, Berkeley promoted developing trade relations and peace with the Indians who lived on surrounding lands. Bacon, however, promoted running the Indians off their land to expand the colonial settlements. In defiance of Berkeley's policies, Bacon independently organized and led poor farmers who lived on the outskirts of the colonies (most of whom were recently freed indentured servants), on murderous terror raids against nearby Indian communities. But instead of fleeing, the Natives responded with counter-raids against their attackers. Bacon, unable to match the Indian counter-attacks, sought but was denied military support from Berkeley.

Bacon then turned on the established colonial ruling class and Berkeley's government. He armed and organized the colony's Afrikan and English slaves with promises of freedom, and in 1676 led them in revolt against the colonial rulers. The revolt succeeded in overthrowing the colonial ruling class and government, and captured the capitol at Jamestown, Virginia.

However, six months into the revolt, and at the height of his power, Bacon died of influenza. Bacon's Rebellion, deprived of its leader and organizer, collapsed, and the colonial ruling class and Council quickly regained control, though not without a determined last stand by the core group of rebels, principally composed of Afrikan slaves. It was at this point that the plantation elite and their reinstated government realized the immense danger and power of a unified working class. Consequently they decided to ensure that no united revolt like Bacon's Rebellion occurred again. Their solution was to split the lower class by permanently enslaving one sector while winning the loyalty of another sector, inciting its fear and contempt against and using it to police the enslaved sector. To divide, agitate, and rule was the plan. This they accomplished by inventing the concept of race and dividing the lower class along racial lines.

Laws were immediately passed that established the categories of "negro" (Spanish for "black"), and "white" as distinct racialized social statuses. In 1682 legislation was enacted that made slavery a permanent and hereditary status for all "Blacks," and over the next several decades slavery and indentured servitude of "whites" were phased out. Further laws were passed that forbade and penalized positive social interactions between the races, particularly escapes, marriages, and procreation.

The poor white men made up the body of the colonial militias and, beginning in 1727, were conscripted into manning slave patrols under fines and other penalties if they refused. This plantation police force was the forerunner and grandparent of today's urban police forces that continue to be concentrated against people of color to repress them across Amerika with violence and terror. In most areas, the slave patrols came to outnumber the black slaves. A variety of minor privileges were also granted to the poor whites, including tiny plots of land to live on—at the Indians' expense—a musket, the authority to kill rebellious Blacks, tax exemptions, and other benefits for manning slave patrols, greater leniency in the eyes of the law than Blacks, voting privileges, etc.

By inventing the social category of "white," and granting the lower class Europeans a share in power over the super-exploited and enslaved Afrikans, the capitalists created a scheme that caused the poor Europeans a false sense of privileged class unity with, and a confused loyalty toward the ruling class which was the source of all of the lower classes' poverty and misery. By selling out their own class interests to the elite, the poor whites made a deal with the devil that saw them focus their frustrations on Blacks instead of the capitalists, and thus ensured that they would remain an impoverished and exploited class, just a step above the Blacks.

To ensure the dedication of the slave patrols, and whites in general, in repressing and containing the black slaves, the ruling class generated a paranoid fear of slave revolts and especially of "Negroes with guns." From every pulpit, and every center of white social gathering and influence, Blacks were depicted as always plotting to revolt with the aim of murdering all whites indiscriminately (men, wimyn, and children), molesting white wimyn, and subverting "good" white Christian civilization with Black "heathenism." Both the political and religious institutions were, and remain today, proponents of racism and white fear of Black revolt.

The church hierarchy, which was tied in with the ruling elite, also added fuel to the fire of racism by theologizing the myth of white racial superiority over all other races, claiming that whites were the Creator's "chosen people" destined to rule over all others as a divine right, and that slavery was a punishment ordained by the creator for Blacks as the "Curse of Canaan." It was through these combined methods that "white supremacy" and the very concept of the "white" and "black" races were born and spread, and remain today normalized concepts that divide the lower class to further the interests of the wealthy elite.

The capitalists found race and racism such effective tools for manipulating and undermining the working class that appeals to race and racism, (overtly and subliminally), have been their generalized method of subverting working-class struggles and manipulating workers to serve as mercenaries and mindless cannon fodder in fighting capitalist wars. To solidify lower class support, the capitalists who were struggling to break free of British control appealed to poor whites to fight the Amerikan Revolutionary War (1775–1783), to achieve an independent "white nation." The Declaration of Independence expresses this in its statement "When … it becomes necessary for one people to dissolve the political bonds which have connected them with another." Because of the racialized identity of "whiteness," the colonists had come to identify themselves as a different "people" than the English.

From such wealthy elite notables and "Founding Fathers" as Benjamin Franklin (in 1751 to John Jay), James Madison, Jedediah Morse (to Andrew Johnson in 1864), they all emphasized in public and in private letters that Amerika was to be a "white nation." (See Steve Martinot, *The Rule of Racialization: Class, Identity, Governance* [PA: Temple University Press, 2003]). This was specified in one of the first legislative acts of the independent Amerikan government—the Naturalization Act of 1790—that stated that the U.S. was to be a "white republic." The "White" racialized identity which had its origins in the Virginia colony, was subsequently adopted into European thinking and served as it had in North Amerika, to rationalize European colonization of people of color in Asia, Afrika, Australia, and elsewhere, and to alienate the European working class from uniting with the super-oppressed peoples of color.

The Amerikan capitalists used the same device to justify their brutal and genocidal seizure of Indian and Mexican lands to expand their agricultural empire. They won the allegiance of the poor whites by promoting these actions as white "Manifest Destiny," as the duty and calling of whites to conquer "inferior" peoples, and by giving out free land grants. These same appeals are used today in pursuit of U.S. conquest and repression of people of color, only the concept of white supremacy and "Manifest Destiny" have become so ingrained and normalized in the collective white Amerikan mind, that they need not be explicitly stated. Moreover, to do so is politically incorrect and unwise in today's world where people of color have proven unwilling to accept overtly expressed racist oppression, (witness the national independence struggles of the 20th century against European colonialism that swept Asia and Afrika; the urban uprisings, civil rights, and New Afrikan, First Nation, Mexican, and Puerto Rican liberation struggles in Amerika, the worldwide opposition to South Afrikan Apartheid, etc.).

Therefore, the white supremacist appeal today is made and pursued more clandestinely and with greater sophistication, using such code words as "spreading democracy," "fighting terrorism," "fighting crime," "preventing the spread of Communism," etc. But any objective analysis quickly reveals that these policies, backed by extreme state violence, and demonizing labels such as "criminal," "terrorist," etc., are consistently applied to non-white peoples, and it's the white U.S. population that's appealed to in order to back these policies. That the national identity of Amerika remains that of a white nation is revealed by its population being still classified by race, with panic arising anytime the elites claim some "other" race like Latin Amerikan migrants are threatening to overrun the "white majority," or that Blacks are a danger to the stability and moral integrity of Amerika.

White racism caused many whites, (especially of the lower class), to become so consumed and intoxicated with the myth of their racial superiority, their right to repress and contain Blacks and others' ambitions, and the idea that their own poverty and lack of power was somehow the fault of Blacks, that they've resorted to confused, fundamentalist reactionary violence to subvert every effort of Blacks to improve or challenge their own conditions. Thus, Black political and economic struggles and gains have frequently been followed by reactionary white violence, or the rise of far right-wing white terrorist groups, like the Ku Klux Klan and Knights of White Camellia for example, the white mobs that attacked Blacks in Massachusetts (1850) and Philadelphia, Boston, and Cincinnati (1830s) to repress the Black vote; the frequent lynchings during Reconstruction (1865–77), white riots against Blacks communities when Blacks moved in large numbers to Northern and Western cities to fill industrial jobs in the early 1900s, mob attacks and violence to repress civil rights struggles in the south during the 1950s and '60s, etc. This reactionary fanatical racial violence and conflict occurs always upon incitement of the ruling elite, to divert and neutralize the danger of revolt of any sector of the working class against their class exploitation and political impotence.

## Division Created Within Racial Ranks

The divide and rule scheme was further refined based upon the claimed proposals of a Caribbean slave owner, Willie Lynch, to a gathering of plantation owners in Virginia in 1712. Lynch proposed not only instigating sharp division between Blacks and whites, but among the Black slaves as well, by playing on minor differences between them to generate envy, fear and distrust. He proposed that the slaves should trust no one except the plantation elite. That they should be hostile toward themselves and that hostility should be maintained between them and the lower class whites. Lynch put it this way:

> "Gentlemen, I greet you here on the banks of the James River in the year of our Lord 1712. First, I shall thank you, the gentlemen of the Colony of Virginia for bringing me here. I am here to help you solve some of your problems with slaves. Your invitation reached me on my modest plantation in the West Indies where I have experimented with some of the newest and still the oldest methods for control of slaves. Ancient Rome would envy us if my program was implemented. As our boat sailed south on the James River, named for our illustrious King, whose version of the Bible we cherish, I

saw enough to know that your problem is not unique. While Rome used cords of wood as crosses for standing human bodies along its old highway in great numbers, you are here using the tree and the rope on occasion.

"I caught the whiff of a dead slave hanging from a tree a couple of miles back. You are not only losing valuable stock by hangings, you are having uprisings, slaves are running away. Your crops are sometimes left in the fields too long for maximum profit, you suffer occasional fires, your animals are killed. Gentlemen, you know what your problems are; I do not need to elaborate. I am not here to enumerate your problems, however, I am here to introduce you to methods of solving them.

"In my bag here, I have outlined a number of DIFFERENCES among the slaves, and I take their differences and make them bigger. I use FEAR, DISTRUST, and ENVY for control purposes. These methods have worked on my modest plantation in the West Indies and it will work throughout the South. Take this simple little list of differences, and think about them. On top of my list is 'AGE,' but it is there because it starts with an 'A'; the second is 'COLOR' or 'SHADE', there is INTELLIGENCE, SIZE, SEX, STATUS ON PLANTATION, ATTITUDE OF OWNERS, WHETHER THE SLAVES LIVE IN THE VALLEY, ON THE HILL, EAST, WEST, NORTH or SOUTH, HAVE FINE HAIR or COARSE HAIR, or is TALL or SHORT. Now that you have a list of differences, I shall give you an outline of ACTION—but before that I shall assure you that distrust is stronger than trust, and envy is stronger than adulation, respect or admiration.

"The Black slave after receiving this indoctrination shall carry on and will become self-refuelling and self-generating for hundreds of years, maybe thousands.

"Don't forget you must pitch the OLD BLACK MALE vs. the YOUNG BLACK MALE, and the YOUNG BLACK MALE vs. the OLD BLACK MALE. You must use the DARK SKIN SLAVE vs. the LIGHT SKIN SLAVE and the LIGHT SKIN SLAVE vs. the DARK SKIN SLAVE. You must use the FEMALE vs. the MALE and the MALE vs. the FEMALE.

"You must also have your white servants and overseers distrust all Blacks, but it is necessary that your slaves trust and depend on us. They must love, respect, and trust ONLY US.

"Gentlemen, these kits are your keys to control. Use them. Have your wives and children use them. Never miss an opportunity—if used intensively for one year, the slaves themselves will remain perpetually distrustful. Thank you, gentlemen."

These methods of dividing slaves and Blacks versus poor whites can clearly be seen still in operation today, and the effects still remain with us—the distrust, fear, and envy. While the lower classes have come to love, emulate, and depend on the predatory capitalist class, its wealth, luxury, and artificial prestige, are all obtained through the labor, powerlessness, and poverty of the working class. Yesterday's chattel slaves are today's wage slaves: only the slave class today has grown to include all races and nationalities.

## Capitalism Creates Racism Abroad

Kwame Nkrumah observed that the same game of racial divide and rule was played when capitalism took root in Afrika:

> "The close links between class and race developed in Africa alongside capitalist exploitation. Slavery, the master-servant relationship, and cheap labor were basic to it. The classic example is South Africa, where Africans experience a double exploitation—both on grounds of color and of class. Similar conditions exist in the USA, the Caribbean, in Latin America, and in other parts of the world where the nature of the development of productive forces has resulted in a racist class structure. In these areas, even shades of color count—the degree of blackness being a yardstick by which social status is measured.
>
> "... [A] racist social structure ... is inseparable from capitalist economic development. For race is inextricably linked with class exploitation; in a racist-capitalist power structure, capitalist exploitation and race oppression are complementary; the removal of one ensures the removal of the other ...
>
> "The effects of industrialization in Africa as elsewhere, has been to foster the growth of the bourgeoisie, and at the same time the growth of a politically-conscious proletariat. The acquisition of property and political power on the part of the bourgeoisie, and the growing socialist and African nationalist aspirations of the working class, both strike at the root of the racist class structure, though each is aiming at different objectives. The bourgeoisie supports capitalist development while the proletariat—the oppressed class—is striving towards socialism.

"In South Africa, where the basis of ethnic relationships is class and color, the bourgeoisie comprises about one-fifth of the population. The British and the Boers, having joined forces to maintain their positions of privilege, have split up the remaining four-fifths of the population into 'Blacks', 'Coloreds', and 'Indians'. The Colored and Indians are minority groups, which act as buffers to protect the minority whites against the increasingly militant and revolutionary Black majority. In the other settled areas of Africa, a similar class-race struggle is being waged.

"A non-racial society can only be achieved by socialist revolutionary action of the masses. It will never come as a gift from the minority ruling class. For it is impossible to separate race relations from the capitalist class relationships in which they have their roots.

"South Africa again provides a typical example ... It was only with capitalist economic penetration that the master–servant relationship emerged, and with it, racism, color prejudice and apartheid ...

"Slavery and the master–servant relationship were therefore the cause, rather than the result of racism. The position was crystallized and reinforced with the discovery of gold and diamonds in South Africa, and the employment of cheap African labor in the mines. As time passed, and it was thought necessary to justify the exploitation and oppression of African workers, the myth of racial inferiority was developed and spread.

"In the era of neocolonialism, 'underdevelopment' is still attributed not to exploitation but to inferiority, and racial undertones remain closely interwoven with the class struggle.

"It is only the ending of capitalism, colonialism, imperialism and neocolonialism and the attainment of world communism that can provide the conditions under which the race question can finally be abolished and eliminated."

Kwame Nkrumah, *Class Struggle in Africa,* 1970

### An Example of Racism Incited to Divert Working Class Struggle

World War I (1914–1918) was a competition between the European imperialist countries for access to and control over the abundant natural resources and markets of the Third World colonies. The war generated a boom for the war industrialists, particularly the Amerikan steel and manufacturing industries that were producing and selling weapons, machinery, and spare parts needed by the European elite to supply their armies, (which were manned by the working class of course). When the U.S. entered the war in 1917, the mandatory draft created a large shortage of white industrial workers. Laborers were needed. With promises of plenty, southern Blacks were drawn by the industrialists' job recruiters into the Northern and Western cities to fill the vacant jobs. The poor migrant Blacks were also a welcome replacement, since they would accept work at much lower wages than the white workers would tolerate, thus increasing the capitalists' profits by lowering labor costs.

The war's end in 1918 saw the return of the whites in need of employment. A strong working-class movement was already underway in the U.S., which had the capitalists in a panic. They feared working-class revolution, like the one that had just succeeded in overthrowing the capitalist class in Russia in 1917. To offset a united radical struggle of the working-class poor, capitalist agents within the trade union movement incited the whites against the Blacks, diverting their attention away from challenging capitalist class oppression and toward the Blacks who'd "stolen" their jobs and were driving down wages.

This appeal to reactionary race hate to channel the anger of white workers away from challenging working-class exploitation provoked racial violence against Blacks, which culminated in widespread white race riots in the "Red Summer" of 1919. These riots saw over 20 incidents of white mobs converging on Black neighborhoods to gang rape Black wimyn and girls, and murder and maim Black men, wimyn, children and the elderly indiscriminately.

Fast-forwarding to today, we now see an identical situation of competition over jobs along racial lines taking place between Blacks versus Mexican and Latin Amerikan migrants. Under centuries of colonial and neo-colonial policies, U.S. capitalists with government backing have robbed the fertile land and resources and crushed the economies of their countries, imposing imperialist policies that have violently driven millions upon millions off their native lands and into complete insecurity, poverty and beggary. In desperate need of jobs to provide for their families, many are forced to migrate to Amerika, to fill jobs that pay starvation wages or deprive them of benefits enjoyed by "legal" workers. Their predicament duplicates that of Blacks who were forced to migrate to the northern and western cities from the south in search of employment upon being pushed off the land by Klan terror, and being otherwise compelled to live in impoverished servitude.

But instead of struggling alongside these migrant workers today, Blacks have been incited by imperialist agents and propaganda to assume much the same repressive role as the white workers during the early 1900s. We perceive these migrants to be "stealing" "our" scarce jobs, government benefits and housing, and driving down wages. Consequently a virtual war has been taking place of Black versus Mexicans and Latin Amerikans on the streets and inside U.S. prisons. Much of the violence, which begins inside the prisons where these "races" are forcibly confined in miserable close quarter, spills over into society.

In just 2005, over 300 race riots occurred in the California prison system alone, mostly between Black versus Mexican and Latin Amerikan prisoners. These conflicts have been exposed repeatedly as incited by the imperialist controlled prison guard unions. So, once again, the capitalists, whose greedy ambitions are the cause of massive poverty, job shortages, land theft, and forced migrations of both Blacks and the Native peoples of this region of the world, (who must risk their lives to cross borders created by the capitalists and white racism), have the commonly oppressed people, who are all victims of class and national oppression, warring amongst themselves.

### The Race Game Played Between Whites

The game of racism was not only created and used to play working-class whites against people of color. It was also used between whites, and with the same purpose of undermining working-class struggles against capitalist class exploitation. Indeed it was the principal method of whipping up mass hysteria in support of fascism in Western Europe during the early 1900s. And contrary to popular deception, the U.S. capitalist elite and government supported its purpose and function, which was to suppress working-class revolution. There is an extensive although repressed record in proof of this.

The tendency in mainstream circles and of the ruling class propaganda industry has been to paint German Nazism, for example, as a sort of odd latent German anti-Semitism, which was brought to the surface by a "mad" leader (Hitler), who by luck and guile found himself in power. This, however, runs counter to the actual fact that the German and Amerikan capitalists consciously and deliberately financed and pushed Hitler into power to suppress a working-class revolution that was threatening to take power. The capitalist Great Depression had disillusioned the workers across Europe about the promises of capitalism, and they were looking with hope to the example of Russia, (Socialist Russia being independent of the imperialist countries was not affected by the Depression). The capitalists also feared that the destabilized middle class would join forces with the lower class workers to overthrow their economic and political control. They opted to play the race card.

By inciting "Aryan" racism—blaming non-Aryans for Germany's economic crisis, which was actually caused by the capitalists—the Nazis won over the confused German middle and lower class and youth to subvert the working-class movement and re-channel its momentum toward attacking sectors of German society that were classified as non-Aryan ("inferiors" and "degenerates"). Violent repression was thus targeted against the German Communists and radical youth, who were leading and organizing the workers' struggle, and the Jews, Slavs, Poles, Gypsies, gay and disabled people. Overt fascism, like pure racism, was a desperate political strategy of capitalist class control.

Just as the method of allying the majority white Amerikan working class to back the capitalist class's designs has been, by rallying them under the banner of a racialized "white nation," so too did the German capitalists do the same using the Nazis to rally the German workers' support under the banner of a racialized "Aryan nation." And as intended, this incitement of racist sentiments divided a once united working class against itself, whipped up hysterical and irrational mass support for the ruling class's designs to smash working-class struggle and to back the capitalists' aims to expand and colonize other nations, in this case not only nations of colored people but Europeans as well. Under the spell of a purely invented racism, the German masses proceeded to back the Nazi war machine that saw them kill and die by the millions and carry out acts of the most savage brutality recorded in history—and all by and against white working-class people. As said, the U.S. government and business community supported Hitler and Mussolini before World War II. See for example:

- Christopher Simpson, *The Splendid Blonde Beast: Money, Law and Genocide in the Twentieth Century*. Monroe, ME: Common Courage Press, 1995. pp. 46–64;
- David Schmitz, *Thank God They're On Our Side: The United States and Right Wing Dictatorships, 1921–1965*. Chapel Hill, NC: University of North Carolina Press, 1999, Chapters 1 and 3;
- David Schmitz, *The United States and Fascist Italy, 1922–1940*. Chapel Hill, NC: University of North Carolina Press, 1988;
- John P. Diggins. *Mussolini and Fascism: The View from America*. Princeton, NJ: Princeton University Press, 1972.

U.S. government internal documents explain the class-based reasons for the warm Amerikan business support for fascism that is detailed in these books. In 1937, for example, a report of the U.S. State Department's European Division described the rise of fascism as a natural and commendable response of "the rich and middle class, in self-defense" when the "dissatisfied masses, with the example of the Russian revolution before them, swing to the Left." Fascism, thus, "must succeed or the masses, this time reinforced by the disillusioned middle classes, will again turn to the Left." The report also stated that "if Fascism cannot succeed by persuasion [in Germany], it must succeed by force." (See Schmitz, *The United States and Fascist Italy, 1922–1940,* p. 140). U.S. Ambassador to Russia, William Bullitt "believed that only Nazi Germany could stay the advance of Soviet Bolshevism in Europe." (Daniel Yergin, *Shattered Peace: The Origins of the Cold War and the National Security State,* Boston, MA: Houghton-Mifflin, 1977, p. 26).

The Amerikan charge d'affaires in Berlin wrote to Washington in 1933 that Amerika should back the Nazi Party as the hope for Germany. He stated that Nazi policies "appeal to all civilized and reasonable people." Amerikan Ambassador Frederic Sackett noted that "it is perhaps well that Hitler is now in a position to wield unprecedented power." (See Schmitz, *The United States and Fascist Italy, 1922–1940,* pp. 174, 133, and Chapter 9).

U.S. corporations like Ford Motor Company were totally approving of fascism; financed and profited from the Fascist states, and participated in plundering Jewish assets under Hitler's Aryanization programs.

> "Many U.S. companies bought substantial interests in established German companies, which in turn plowed the new money into Aryanizations or into arms productions banned under the Versailles Treaty. According to a 1936 report from Ambassador William Dodd to President Roosevelt, a half-dozen key U.S. companies—International Harvester, Ford, General Motors, Standard Oil of New Jersey, and DuPont—had become deeply involved in German weapons production …
>
> "U.S. investment in Germany accelerated rapidly after Hitler came to power, despite the Depression and Germany's default on virtually all of its government and commercial loans. Commerce Department reports show that U.S. investment in Germany increased some 48.5 percent between 1929 and 1940, while declining sharply everywhere else in continental Europe. U.S. investment in Great Britain … barely held steady over the decade, increasing only 2.6 percent."
>
> Christopher Simpson, *The Splendid Blonde Beast: Money, Law and Genocide in the Twentieth Century,* supra, p. 64

The U.S. government did not in fact unanimously declare European fascism an avowed enemy until it attacked U.S. interests. And even then Amerikan business interests still backed the Fascists. In fact, Prescott

Bush, (grandfather of George W. Bush), and his father-in-law, George Herbert Walker, were the Nazis' financers and traders through periods of the Jewish Holocaust, after their attacks on Britain and France, and even after the bombings of Pearl Harbor in 1941. It took the seizure of their Union Banking Corporation by the U.S. government in October 1942, under the Trading with the Enemies Act, to stop Bush and Walker.

Prior to WWII U.S. support for Italian Fascism was much the same. In December 1917, the Wilson administration expressed that the rising labor movement posed, "the obvious danger of social revolution and disorganization." Mussolini's Black Shirts solved the problem with violence. Referring to Mussolini's October 1922 march on Rome, which smashed Italian democracy, the U.S. Ambassador noted with approval that the Fascists carried out "a fine young revolution." With government backing, the racist thugs bloodily repressed working-class agitation. The U.S. embassy noted, Fascism was "perhaps the most potent factor in the suppression of Bolshevism in Italy." In a February 1925 report, the embassy also approvingly observed that the Fascists had smashed the workers struggle through "restricting the right of free assembly, in abolishing freedom of the press and in having at its command a large military organization." It was also stated that "between Mussolini and Fascism and Giolliti and Socialism, between strong internal peace and prosperity and return to free speech, loose administration and general disorganization, Peace and Prosperity were preferred." (See Schmitz, *The United States and Fascist Italy, 1922–1940*, pp. 76–77). These approving pronouncements are as undemocratic as one could get. It should also be remembered that when these official champions of capitalism talk about "disorder," and "peace" and "prosperity," they're speaking about these things from the perspective of their capitalist bosses in containing, repressing, and controlling the exploited workers, and against the workers' struggles to gain control over the society's economic and political institutions and power.

The U.S. business press spoke openly in support of Fascism. *Fortune* magazine, for example, devoted a special issue to Fascism in July 1934. And in its article "The State: Fascist and Total," it commented approvingly that "the purpose and effect of Fascism is to un wop the wops," and any views by Amerikan people that the Italians should resent Fascism, "is a confusion, and we can only get over it if we anesthetize for the moment our ingrained idea that democracy is the only right and just conception of government."

The rise of counter-revolutionary racist Fascism in Europe was accompanied by an attendant rise of far right-wing racist counterrevolutionary elements in Amerika. The Klan for example saw a resurgence, and its membership swelled as never before in the 1920s.

Clearly when any struggle arises from within the ranks of the working class, the capitalists incite a corresponding rise of racist elements to divide and counter the up-thrusting masses and their challenge to capitalist domination. In essence, racism, and its most fundamentalist political and military form (namely fascism) are purely counter-revolutionary tools of the capitalist class used to sabotage working-class struggle by dividing, inciting and turning the working class against itself.

### The Race Game Played Between Blacks

Racism has also been used to divide exploited Blacks against themselves to further imperialist interests. One outstanding example occurred among the people of Rwanda and resulted in the genocidal war of 1994, which saw hundreds of thousands murdered while the imperialists sat by and watched. Until the Belgians entered Rwanda with imperialist aims in 1916, the Rwandans were a united people. The various ethnic groups shared the same language and had for centuries cooperated, supported, and sustained each other. The Hutu were 85%, the Tutsis 14%, and the Twa 1% of the population. The Hutu raised crops, the Tutsis tended herds. Economic relations between them were based upon the Hutu exchanging their surplus of vegetables for surplus Tutsi livestock. Their economies also sustained each other in that the Hutus set aside land for the Tutsis to graze their animals on. The manure of the animals in turn provided fertilizer for the Hutu crops.

In 1918 the European imperialist League of Nations "awarded" Rwanda to Belgium as a colony. This Afrikan country presented a source of great wealth to the Belgian King Leopold, in the form of vast forests of rubber trees. Rubber was in high demand in the industrial countries due to the recent invention of the inflatable tire. Like the agricultural capitalists of Amerika, the Belgians needed a local slave class to work the rubber plantations and a local middle level force to police them. The colonial Belgian government, along with the Catholic Church played the race game to produce the desired result. They opened mission schools to only the Tutsi and forbade the Hutu from receiving an education. In the schools, Rwandan history was rewritten to project the Tutsi as the racial superior of the Hutus. The myth was taught that the Tutsi were a partly Caucasian Hamitic people because of their having taller statures, thinner features, and lighter complexions than the Hutu. Identity cards were issued which classified the entire society as Hutu, Tutsi, or Twa.

The Belgians treated the Hutu with the most savage brutality to enforce their submission. Millions upon millions resisted and were massacred, while millions more had ears, noses, and limbs cut off. Tutsi chiefs were appointed by the Belgians over the Hutu to serve as agents to this brutality. The Tutsi, like whites in Amerika, were pleased to be identified as allies of the ruling powers and to believe the myth of their racial superiority. Consequently, the Tutsi also lived in perpetual fear of Hutu revenge if the Hutu ever came together in revolt.

When the national independence struggles against European imperialism began to sweep across Afrika in the 1950s and 1960s, the educated Tutsis took notice and agitated for Rwandan independence. In turn the Belgians backed the Hutu to repress the Tutsi. Rwanda still won independence from Belgium in 1962, but this saw the Hutu take control of the upper levels of government. The Tutsi remained in the lower ranks, continuing to control the educational system, church, and livestock. The Hutu however took much of the Tutsi land upon taking power. Many of the Tutsi fled.

A 1973 coup saw a new Hutu government take power which changed the status of the Hutu, Tutsi, and Twa from racial to ethnic groupings, and sought to democratically restructure the ethnic groups within social institutions according to their numbers. This meant a larger share for the Hutu in the economy, church, and educational institutions. Thousands of Tutsi lost their jobs and fled the country. A few years later the government turned sour, state property was privatized, and the economy collapsed. In addition to droughts and famines, the imperialist International Monetary Fund imposed a neo-liberal structural adjustment program that totally devastated the country. The Tutsi were repressed and another wave fled Rwanda, to refugee camps in Uganda.

The genocidal war of 1994 was the result of the exiled Tutsis returning and seeking to regain power in Rwanda. The imperialists, including Amerika, were fully aware of preparations for the genocide before it began, but sat by as events unfolded. This "race" war, like many other race-based conflicts, saw "respectable" people engaged in the murderous frenzy: teachers, doctors, nurses, journalists, and clergy. Husbands killed wives, friends killed each other, gang rapes were frequent, etc. Such is the result of race hate, racism, and the violence they spawn. Over 500,000 were killed in a matter of just a few months.

The entire "racial" division in Rwanda was, like that here in Amerika, created by a ruling capitalist elite, whose power and profits were served by dividing a previously united people along racial lines, granting one sector a share of relative power and elevated social status, and a sense of racial connection to the ruling elite, so to use it to repress and control the other sector that is super-exploited by the ruling capitalist class. While in reality the entire divided people are collectively exploited by the ruling capitalist class.

## Racism in Reverse

For a people, like Blacks in Amerika, who have endured centuries of brutality, degradation, disrespect, indignity, powerlessness, and being labeled "inferiors" based solely upon skin color, the desire for respect became and remains very strong. This desire for respect has left many Blacks vulnerable to the appeals of reverse racism. Reverse racism is here defined as a belief in Black superiority and white inferiority. But, for Blacks in Amerika, who have no independent access to or control over any institutions of power or productive wealth, the features of reverse racism take place primarily in their minds, as they lack the means to exercise any dominant or comparable power over those they claim to be their inferiors, namely whites.

Reverse racism first took root on a large scale with the teachings of Marcus Garvey, who preached the beauty and high culture of Blacks. In colonizing Afrika, beginning in the late 1800s, the European imperialists used racism to alienate their country's own oppressed working class from the super-exploited Afrikans, and to rationalize their brutal colonial oppression of Afrikans. To give a scientific gloss to their racist doctrines, the imperialists commissioned novelists and intellectuals to develop theories to support their claims of European racial superiority and African racial inferiority. These European and Amerikan writers claimed that Afrika, when discovered by the white man, was a land of backward, ignorant savages upon whom they had bestowed the benefits and blessings of Christianity and white civilization. Garvey reversed these false and degrading European histories and views of Afrikans. He countered that ignorant, murderous, pillaging European savages attacked Afrika out of jealousy over our power, prosperity, and having achieved the highest level of civilization yet known. Neither version was objectively true. However, Garvey's teachings had an electrifying effect on Amerikan Blacks. In only a few years millions of Blacks joined his Universal Negro Improvement Association, supporting his "back to Afrika" movement. Garvey's teachings offered Blacks a new basis for pride, self-esteem, self-confidence, and respect, all tied into a messianic notion of Black racial superiority. By turning the teaching of white supremacy on its head, Garvey brought together the largest Black organization in U.S. history.

Following his arrest and exile, and the collapse of his UNIA, Garvey's doctrine and its Black capitalist underpinnings became the common doctrine of Black organizations that sought a large following. Most notable was the Nation of Islam, which was founded three years after Garvey's deportation. Indeed, the NOI absorbed many who came under Garveyite influences, including some of the NOI's most influential leaders like Malcolm X whose parents were Garveyites. The NOI, however, enhanced and gave a theological twist to Garvey's doctrine, (much as the white church had done with white racism), by posing Blacks as the Creator's chosen people and whites as spawns of the Devil. The NOI's teachings were enhanced even further by its excommunicated member Clarence 13X, in his youth-based Nation of Gods and Earths, (formerly the 5% Nation), which promotes the Black man as god and whites as the actual devil.

Another proponent of subjective reverse racism was Dr. Khalid Muhammad, another excommunicated member of the NOI, who led the New Black Panther Party (NBPP) up until his death in 2001. Dr. Muhammad steered the NBPP far away from the class-based ideological and political line of the original BPP and in the direction of race-based anti-white politics, the NBPP's present path.

The New Afrikan Black Panther Party-Prison Chapter (NABPP-PC) distinguishes itself from such race-based politics as promoted by the NBPP, as we are proponents of class struggle and the revolutionary nationalist liberation struggles of those oppressed by imperialism. We recognize that the capitalists created and use race divisions to perpetuate conflict within the oppressed lower class sectors, and that racism and the race blame game serves the interests of the oppressor class and undermines the interests of the oppressed. This is proven historical fact. Furthermore, as revolutionary New Afrikan nationalists, we realize that there is a contradiction between race and nationalism, and moreover, that there is no nation composed of a single race. All existing nations, like the Indian Nations here in North Amerika, include whites and mixed bloods, even though there are contradictions. It was the policies of white colonialism created by the ruling class that produced these contradictions, and indeed the New Afrikan Nation. In this regard, we say all people of Afrikan heritage, regardless of skin tone, are part of a single Afrikan-New Afrikan Nation … A Pan-Afrikan Nation. Indeed most "Blacks" in Amerika are mixed bloods, mixed with white and/or Indian bloodlines.

We therefore move beyond the black and white dogmatism—Native Americans have always done this in adopting any "race" of people into their nations who embrace and respect their heritage and culture. All non-chauvinistic nations have done this. We also accept that nationalities can overlap and are not merely an either/or situation. People the world over embrace multiple nationalities, and so can New Afrikans. One can be Venezuelan and New Afrikan, or Lenape and New Afrikan, etc. This concept becomes practical revolutionary internationalism that has all oppressed nationalities struggling for both national self-determination and united multi-national anti-imperialist cooperation.

In the context of national liberation, we must remember that nationality is itself a temporary form of social organization and identity. It is a means to an end and not an end in itself. The nation is a product of social-historical development, and will wither away in time. Our orientation as genuine revolutionaries is to the whole of humynity and the future classless and nation-stateless society. Getting from here to there involves national liberation struggles and security issues. As Mao Tsetung observed, "Proletarian nationalism is applied proletarian internationalism." It involves uniting all who can be united at each stage of the struggle. From our point of view, the key question is building alliances between the oppressed nations within the U.S. and abroad and the multi-national proletariat.

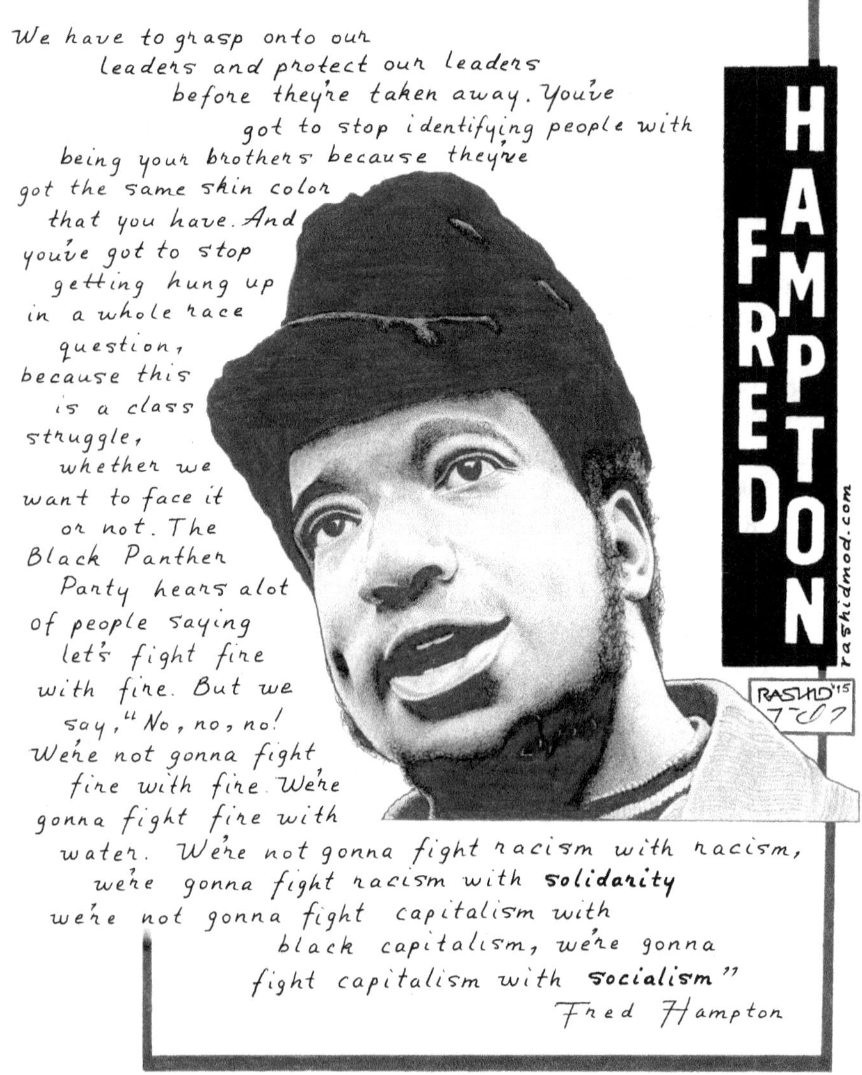

## Rising Above Race to Build Class-Based Alliances

World suffering and oppression, poverty, and want are not caused by race, but by national and class exploitation and oppression at the hands of the monopoly capitalist class. However, as repeatedly pointed out above, race and racism have been a principal tool and weapon of this class used to keep the oppressed workers of the world divided and warring among themselves, to divide, agitate, and rule. Toward the end of their lives, both Malcolm X and Martin Luther King, Jr. came to realize that basing struggle against oppression on race without challenging capitalist economic exploitation was a losing battle. And it was at that point when they began to agitate to have their followers struggle against capitalism, imperialism, and colonial oppression instead of exclusively focusing on race, (merely struggling against white oppression), that they were murdered. George Jackson pointed this out:

> "It's no coincidence that Malcolm X and M.L. King died when they did. Malcolm X had just put it together ... You remember what was on his lips when he died, Vietnam and economics, political economy. The professional killers could have murdered him long before they did. They let Malcolm rage on Muslim nationalism for a number of years because they knew it was an empty ideal, but the second he got his feet on the ground, they murdered him."

Fred Hampton, Sr. summed it up perfectly in his November 1969 speech delivered at the University of Northern Illinois and aptly entitled "It's a Class Struggle Goddammit!" Fred stated:

> "You know a lot of people have hang-ups with the [Black Panther] Party because the Party talks about a class struggle. And the people that have those hang-ups are opportunists, and cowards, and individualists and everything that's anything but revolutionary. And they use these things as an excuse to justify and to alibi and to bonify their lack of participation in the real revolutionary struggle. So they say, 'Well, I can't dig the Panther Party because the Panthers they are engrossed with dealing with oppressor country radicals, or white people, or hunkies, or what have you.' They say, these are some of the [reasons] why I am not in the struggle. We got a lot of answers for these people. First of all, we say primarily that the priority of this struggle is class. That Marx, and Lenin, and Che Guevara, and Mao Tse-Tung and anybody else that has ever said or knew or practiced anything about revolution, always said that a revolution is a class struggle. It was one class—the

oppressed—against the other class, the oppressor. And it's got to be a universal fact. Those that don't admit to that are those that don't want to get involved in a revolution, because they know as long as they're dealing with a race thing, they'll never be involved in a revolution. They can talk about numbers; they can hang you up in many, many ways …

"[We] never negated the fact that there was racism in Amerika, but we said … the by-product, what comes off of capitalism, that happens to be racism. That capitalism comes first and next is racism. That when they brought slaves over here, it was to make money. So first the idea came that we want to make money, then the slaves came in order to make that money. That means that through historical fact, racism had to come from capitalism. It had to be capitalism first and racism was a by-product of that."

Like Malcolm X and MLK, and not even a month after giving this speech, Fred Hampton was assassinated, shot in the head while asleep in bed, by Chicago police (in collaboration with the FBI), in a well-orchestrated hit. Coincidence?

The imperialists' hired guns made no pretences about murdering Fred. No attempts were made to conceal their involvement by using puppets or agents. They used forces in government uniform, and a Black cop pulled the trigger at that. So what made Fred so threatening that the capitalists' hired guns would go to such open extremes to neutralize him? It was because Fred proved to be a much greater danger to the ruling class than all other leaders of the Black Movement combined. He was not only an exceptional organizer and inspirational leader and teacher of New Afrikans, but he could turn the most reactionary of white workers into revolutionaries.

It was Fred's work that led to the formation of the Young Patriot Party (YPP), a revolutionary party of poor redneck white Appalachian youth whose symbol was a confederate flag with a red star emblazoned on it. Fred's approach was to appeal to class instead of being sidetracked by race. He walked into a redneck Hillbilly bar in Chicago when they asked, "What are you doing here?" he said, "I'm here to organize the Niggers." They said, "No Niggers come in here," and were ready to fight. He said, "Oh yeah? Well the way I see it, they work y'all like Niggers, treat y'all like Niggers, and make y'all live like Niggers. So that makes y'all niggers in my book, and I say it's time to get organized and deal with this shit!"

In another 1969 speech Fred pointed out:

"We got to face some facts. That the masses are poor, that the masses belong to what you call the lower class, and when I talk about the masses, I'm talking about the white masses, I'm talking about the Black masses, and the Brown masses, and the Yellow masses, too. We've got to face the fact that some people say you fight fire best with fire, but we say you put fire out best with water. We say you don't fight racism with racism—we're gonna fight racism with solidarity. We say you don't fight capitalism with no Black capitalism; you fight capitalism with socialism ...

"We have to understand very clearly that there's a man in our community called a capitalist. Sometimes he's Black and sometimes he's white. But that man has to be driven out of our community, because anybody who comes into the community to make profit off the people by exploiting them can be defined as a capitalist. And we don't care how many programs they have, how long a dashiki they have. Because political power does not flow from the sleeve of a dashiki ..."

From within the Chicago chapter of the BPP, Fred was the leader of a growing multi-racial, multi-national, anti-imperialist united front that included the BPP, the Puerto Rican Young Lords Party, the Students for a Democratic Society (before the Weathermen faction took over), and the Revolutionary Youth Movement II. He even worked to politically develop apolitical street gangs. The imperialists realized, as did the southern plantation owners in the wake of Bacon's Rebellion, that the greatest threat to their power is the united resistance of all elements of the oppressed laboring class. "In order for capitalism to continue to rule, any action that threatens the right of a few individuals to own and control public property must be prohibited and curtailed whatever the cost in resources ... whatever the cost in blood ... The national repressive institutions (police, National Guard, army, etc.), are no less determined." (George Jackson). It was because of the genuine threat that Fred's revolutionary practice posed in bringing together the divided "races" into a united movement to combat imperialism that he had to be liquidated.

### New Afrikan Liberation and the Race Question

The position on race presented here is not to say that New Afrikans or "Blacks" should abandon or hand over our liberation struggle to the initiative or control of whites, nor that our struggle in this regard should depend or wait upon the cooperation of those who identify as "white." Quite the opposite: We are our own liberators!

New Afrikans are an oppressed and colonized nation within Amerika. As such, reforms cannot secure racial and social equality for us. Nor can whites identify with and recognize the conditions we suffer under—no one knows our oppression, the forms it takes and the liberation we desire like we do. We are a people with a history, a culture, and an identity that is our own, and was forged over centuries of common experience and oppression. It is therefore our place and no one else's to claim those things as uniquely our own and develop them to their highest potential as a people. In order to have any security as a people and not be dependent upon the whims of any other sectors, we must control the basic means of our survival and governance. If we are not able to defend our own destiny and selves, we are not free. And if we do not break free from the conditions of our colonization, we leave ourselves open to further colonization under any number of reformed conditions and methods.

Merely joining up with Amerikan whites cannot ensure this because our oppression exceeds theirs. We must be able to assert and protect our economic and political rights whether whites support us or not. Self-determination is the essence of our achieving liberation, and it is our right and duty to run our own organizations and liberation struggle. As the victims of racism only we know best how to resist it. But overall, we are oppressed as a nation and must free ourselves as a nation. In doing so we will destroy the basis of our colonized condition within the Amerikan Empire.

In aid of our struggle, the advanced sectors of white Amerika should work to destroy the notion of white skin privilege and white national chauvinism, which are the underlying national identity of Amerika. They must aid us in protecting our democratic rights and the democratic right of all peoples, including their own. In turn, we must join up with the entire multi-ethnic, multi-national, and multi-racial working class, radical youth, and progressive elements in a United Front Against Imperialism, to smash the overall imperialist system.

Imperialism is capitalism is colonialism. The defeat of imperialism requires the liberation of the colonized and neo-colonized nations on which imperialism feeds. But we must also remember that imperialism is capitalism, capitalism on a global scale that enslaves and profits off not only the workers of the non-industrialized nations and oppressed nationalities across the world, but also the workers of the industrially advanced capitalist countries. To defeat capitalism we must join together in a united struggle of the entire working class of all nations, ethnicities, and "races" in a United Front Against Imperialism, and to ultimately overthrow the capitalist political economy and its ruling class's power, privilege, and domination over social labor and wealth. Without a repressed working class under its thumb, capitalism cannot exist. Therefore, the entire working class must deny the capitalists its labor power.

Political forms of organization to lead the whole working class are necessary, and we support them. The advanced and anti-imperialist whites must also struggle against the fanatical and backward white supremacist elements like the Klan, Neo-Nazis, etc. These elements represent overt fascism in embryonic form, who will be backed by or handed state power to suppress and divide any working-class and national independence struggle that arises to challenge monopoly capitalism, as the elite are wont to do, (and Western Europe in the early 1900s stands as a glaring example), when their power is threatened from below. They will move the most rabid racists into positions of political and military power to attack and smash revolutionary and progressive elements and incite and engage in a divisive race war. They will certainly also incite the fanatical Black reverse racists to turn on and attack Black revolutionary elements. The reverse racists will justify such actions with claims that those who collaborate with any whites are "sell-outs." To them all whites are the enemy, as they have no concept of class struggle and will back dictators and sub-fascists like Haiti's Papa Doc Duvalier and the Congo's Joseph Mobutu, so long as they have black skin.

To the reverse racists it's all about a racial contest, and their backward thinking enables them to be used as imperialist agents to attack and kill the revolutionary elements. This is how Amilcar Cabral was assassinated in 1973. Cabral was Afrika's leading revolutionary, a Pan-Afrikan and anti-imperialist theorist and fighter of the 1960s and 1970s. He effectively led the people of Guinea-Bissau against the greatest odds, in a successful national independence struggle against Portugal's colonialism.

Cabral emphasized that race must not be the basis of his country's independence struggle; that he did not confuse imperialism and colonialism with the color of people's skins, but desired to see economic, political, and military power in the hands of the working people so to free his country of all oppressive forces, be they white or black. In fact, his position and showing of solidarity with the white workers of Portugal generated a general uprising of the lower classes in Portugal that nearly saw a revolutionary overthrow of power there. He was also able to turn other white nations against Portugal's colonial policies in his country. It was this uprising and international support coupled with the political and armed liberation struggle of the people of Guinea-Bissau that ultimately forced the Portuguese military and colonial administration to abandon Guinea-Bissau and return to Portugal to suppress the revolt there.

In turn, Portuguese agents inside of Cabral's party assassinated him. Those Black agents, Cabral's fellow countrymen, were opponents of his class-based struggle and were incited to murder Cabral because of his collaboration with "whites" and his being of mixed Afrikan and Portuguese blood. The Portuguese imperialists used proponents of reverse racism to kill the man who had led Afrika's greatest national independence struggle, freed his people from a savage and brutal colonial existence, and even offered his country's support to the struggles of New

Afrikans here in Amerika. There are valuable lessons to be learned here.

The imperialists have used reverse racists many times in attempts to derail many other revolutionary movements of people of color and to assassinate key leaders. Such racialist elements were used to murder Malcolm X. The FBI used such elements as the US Organization to assassinate key members of the BPP, Alprentice "Bunchy" Carter and Jon Huggins in January 1969. Indeed in many cases, such as during the national independence struggles in Africa during the 1960s and 1970s, the elements who promoted anti-white ideology ended up becoming open collaborators with and agents of the very "white" imperialist powers they were supposed to be fighting. For example, Holden Roberto's UPA/FNLA (União das Populações de Angola/Frente Nacional de Libertação de Angola) and Jonas Savimbi's UNITA became open agents of South Africa and U.S. imperialism in Angola. These groups became agents of their imperialist sponsors and turned their arms away from fighting the colonial forces and declared war for them against their own people's revolutionary forces, namely the MPLA (Popular Movement for the Liberation of Angola).

At no time and in no place has playing the race card or the racial blame game ever won any people freedom from oppression. But what it has done is generate most every known major genocidal war that has occurred over the past several centuries, from the genocidal extermination of tens of millions of Native Amerikans to the genocidal attacks on Afrikans by Arabs in Southern Sudan today. The racial game produces only a back and forth cycle of bloodshed, carnage, and misery between competing racial groups. For its blind participants, racism offers nothing positive except a subjective and superficial sense of belonging to a group which professes to be "superior" to another group and the destruction of the natural compassion and sanity that would otherwise prevent humyns from brutalizing and massacring innocent people. And it's a double-edged sword: one "race" victimizes another and is in turn victimized, or another "race" becomes the target of the victim. The complicity of many Jews today in Anglo-Zionist race-oriented genocidal policies against Palestinians and other Arabs is an outstanding example of a people who were once victims of racial violence in turn victimizing another innocent people in the name of race and claims of "God-given" right. And all to advance the wealth and power interests of a capitalist elite.

For white and Black supremacists here in Amerika, a race war would not prove beneficial to either "race"! It would only produce a cycle of mutual slaughter of members of both races. No one would be "liberated" as a result, but multitudes of loved ones, friends, and colleagues on both sides would be brutalized, butchered, maimed, massacred, and displaced. In the race hate game no one wins—there is simply no way for a sane mind to romanticize it. But in a unified struggle of the oppressed classes and nationalities against imperialism, the very source of world suffering, misery, and racism itself can be uprooted and power turned over to those who can be trusted to use it properly, namely the oppressed masses.

In the fevered minds of racists, their fanatical howlings about violent repression or annihilation of "inferior races" sounds like fun: that is until the bloodshed begins and they find themselves on the receiving end of counter-violence that quickly spins out of control. To many racist southern whites, the brutal enslavement of New Afrikans seemed like a fun enterprise: that is until revolts like Nat Turner's turned the guns back on them. At that point a massive Black and white abolitionist movement sprang to life to end slavery. There are simply no superior and inferior races. Indeed the very concept of race is an invention. A comrade put it this way in a letter to me:

> "Racism is the spawn of colonialism and is based on lies. The technological edge the Europeans took advantage of came late in the game. Much of it was borrowed from other cultures like gunpowder from China, or the lanteen sail from Afrika, and potatoes from South Amerika. The combination of these elements and the ability to use them to establish global hegemony created the illusion of white supremacy.
>
> "In reality, we're all pretty damn equal. Even the difference between smart and dumb people is not so great. No one of us is really all that smart. Is capitalism smart? We let the nastiest men run the show by the nastiest means and hope that it will work out alright for the rest of us. Is that smart? We've got all these gadgets running, but the sum of it is we've burned a hole in the atmosphere and the ice caps are melting.
>
> "Even the idea of Communism is not so brilliant. It is just common sense. Ants work together for their common welfare. The genius lies in overcoming our own stupidity to do what is necessary to survive, and this will be a big struggle and one we could lose. There is a time factor in our getting our collective act together.
>
> "The good news is that all the elements necessary for our survival as a species are present. We just have to sort out our political-social organization, and deal with the nasty men."

Even mainstream sources now admit that the concept of race is today a scientifically unsustainable concept. That the "theories" invented centuries ago to validate the idea are invalidated by today's science. The *Merriam Webster Collegiate Encyclopedia* (2000) defines and dismisses the notion of race thusly:

> "Race: Term once commonly used in physical anthropology to denote a division of humankind possessing traits that are transmissible by descent and sufficient to characterize it as a distinct human type (e.g. Caucasoid, Mongoloid, Negroid). Today the term has little scientific standing, as older methods of differentiation, including hair form and body measurement, have given way to the comparative analysis of DNA and gene frequencies relating to such factors as blood type, the excretion of amino acids, and inherited enzyme deficiencies. Because all human populations today are extremely similar genetically, most researchers have abandoned the concept of race for the concept of the cline, a graded series of differences occurring along a line of environmental or geographical transition. This reflects the recognition that human populations have always been in a state of flux, with genes constantly flowing from one gene pool to another, impeded only by physical and ecological boundaries. While relative isolation does preserve genetic differences and allow populations to maximally adapt to climatic and disease factors over long periods of time, all groups currently existing are thoroughly 'mixed' genetically, and such differences as still exist do not lend themselves to simple typologizing. 'Race' is today primarily a social designation, identifying a class sharing some outward physical characteristics and some commonalities of culture and history."

This same text goes on to admit that racism is a creation and tool of colonialism:

> "Racism: Belief that race is the primary determinant of human traits and capacities and that some races are inherently superior to others. More broadly, the term refers to any racial prejudice or discrimination. Throughout the era of European colonialism, the British viewed imperialism as a noble activity ('the white man's burden') destined to bring civilization to the benighted races, while the French invoked the notion of mission civilistrace, their duty to bring civilization to backward peoples. An influential modern proponent was the Comte de Gobineau, who held that the so-called Aryan was the supreme race. His most important follower was Houston Stewart Chamberlain, whom Adolf Hitler credited with supplying the 'scientific' basis of the Nazi's racialist philosophy, used to justify the persecution of Jews and other non-Aryans.

> South African society was built on the principle of apartheid, or racial 'separateness.' Today the general trend is away from racism, though the problem of racist thinking remains intractable."

Although this mainstream reference work totally avoids pointing out what social-economic class invented the entire racial concept and its birth and role here in North Amerika, it does make clear that both "race" and "racism" are today proven to be scientifically baseless and live on solely as psycho-social concepts. So why then do the Amerikan political and economic rulers still classify Amerikan citizens by race? It is obviously because they desire to maintain its role as a divisive undercurrent to be appealed to and whipped into hysteria when their power and privilege are threatened from below. Thus, the national identity of Amerika remains that of a "white nation."

The concepts of race and racism, like a deeply ingrained backward superstition, are so deeply embedded in the social psyche and are so deeply influential on social attitudes and behaviors, that they cannot be simply ignored. The oppressed "races" must collectively struggle against racial oppression and domination, while the conscious members of the oppressor races must struggle to conquer the myth of racial superiority within their own "racial" groups. Reverse racism must also be countered. In confronting racism we must be aware of its counterrevolutionary nature and the forms it takes in the minds of those who embrace it consciously or subconsciously. George Jackson gave an insightful analysis on this point. He stated:

> "Racism is a matter of ingrained traditional attitudes conditioned through institutions. For some, it is as natural a reflex as breathing. The psychosocial effects of segregated environments compounded by bitter class repression have served in the past to render the progressive movement almost totally impotent.
>
> "The major obstacle to a united left in this country is white racism. There are three categories of white racists: the overt, self-satisfied racist who doesn't attempt to hide his antipathy; the self-interdicting racist who harbors and nurtures racism in spite of his best efforts; and the unconscious racist, who has no awareness of his racist preconceptions.
>
> "As Black partisans, we must recognize and allow for the existence of all three types of racists. We must understand their presence as an effect of the system. It is the system that must be crushed, for it continues to manufacture new and deeper contradictions of both class and race. Once it is destroyed, we may be able to address the

problems of racism at an even more basic level. But we must also combat racism while we are in the process of destroying the system.

> "The self-interdicting racist, no matter what his acquired conviction or ideology, will seldom be able to contribute with his actions in any really concrete way. His role in revolution, barring a change of basic character, will be minimal throughout. Whether the basic character of a man can be changed at all is still a question."

As Comrade George pointed out, our struggle demands that we acknowledge and recognize the three categories of racists. However, we must also acknowledge and recognize that the reverse racists also fit into these three categories. And in answer to George's question whether there is a possibility of changing the basic character of the "self-interdicting racist," we think yes. The Marxist recognizes that there is a dialectical relationship between our social practice and how we think. That reactionary thinking can be corrected through revolutionary social practice. But that practice must also in turn be guided by and committed to correct ideology.

Our Comrade Tom Big Warrior analyzed the process very well in a discussion we had some time ago concerning a New Afrikan brother with whom I was struggling to break out of a deeply ingrained hatred of whites. This brother's views had been imbedded in him at a very young age by a now deceased grandfather, whose memory he held with the highest respect. While he could not refute my arguments against race-based hatreds, he also felt powerless to change his feelings. Here is Tom:

> "I understand what you're talking about with the brother who has deeply rooted hatred of whites. I've got brothers in my nation who have the same issues regarding Blacks, particularly among the hillbillies of mixed white-Native heritage. It was bred into them from a very young age and reinforced by their social practice (or lack of it) with Black folks.
>
> "Hell, everybody in Amerika has been brainwashed on race. I know I have been affected by it, but I've got the advantage of both a theoretical understanding and a lifetime of positive social interaction with people of all ethnic backgrounds (and particularly Black Comrades), so I can identify and throw away feelings that come from racist programming as they come up.
>
> "I think the key with this brother is to get him to see that his feelings are part of the slave mentality he (and his grandfather) were programmed to have to keep Black people from throwing off their oppression. If you can't inspire meek submission and self-deprecation,

you can inspire hate and fear, (which is the next best thing), and this leads to alienation and division.

"The greatest threat in the South was unity between the Blacks and poor whites, who had common class interests. So the big landlords played them against each other by promoting blind hatred and racism.

"If he can grasp that his feelings are chains upon him causing him to act against the interests of Black people and working people in general, (that he is falling into the role of a 'Nigger' set for him by 'Mr. Charlie'), he will see that it must be overcome so he can be a 'true Black Warrior' and a genuine revolutionary.

"We feel the way we feel because we think the way we think. Changing our thinking changes how we feel. In fact our feelings expose how we think at the deepest levels. Sometimes we think we have something all sorted out and understood, but then a feeling pops up to show us that we are still in process, and we have to keep struggling to grasp the idea more firmly.

"If the brother wants to be a revolutionary, he can't be liberal with himself. He has to recognize that white people must be won to support Black liberation and make proletarian revolution. Unless this is done, Black people will continue to be oppressed, and the imperialists will keep running the show.

"He has to decide if he wants to be part of the problem or part of the solution. The MC5, the house band of the White Panther Party, had a song where the singer shouts out, 'It takes 5 seconds to decide and determine your purpose here on the planet, 5 seconds to decide if you are going to be a part of the problem or you are going to be a part of the solution—KICK OUT THE JAMS MOTHERFUCKER!'

"This is just what they were talking about—this mental/emotional programming that jams up our ability to make revolution. Ain't nothing to do but kick it out, get rid of it, to get to what needs to be done.

"When you reason with him he says, 'Yeah, yeah you're right, Brother,' because you can't reasonably argue for racism. But he's not willing to let go and backslides right back into it. As if counter-revolution was his purpose on the planet.

"It's time to invoke the 5 second rule. Time for him to make a commitment and stop being liberal with himself. The world can't wait for us to get serious about revolution.

"If he really wants to honor his grandfather's memory, he shouldn't let the wounding that was done to him and other Blacks go on another generation. You can't play the blame game and win.

"The pigs didn't kill Fred Hampton because he was good at organizing Black people, but because he could turn redneck Hillbilly crackers into Red revolutionaries, which he did with the Young Patriot Party—that's true history.

"He was a better revolutionary than Huey Newton, Bobby Seale and Eldridge Cleaver put together, and he is the one we should measure ourselves and our praxis by.

"It is our practice that determines our thinking, but there is a dialectic between theory and practice called praxis, in which theory becomes the determining factor.

"This is different than idealism, which Marx was struggling against. This is what Mao was talking about when he said ideological and political line will determine everything. It is the difference between Utopian socialism and our Scientific socialism.

"We begin with a concrete analysis of concrete conditions and from this developed theory, then apply our theory to practice, then sum up our practice to strengthen and advance our theory, then go back to practice, over and over getting sharper and sharper. That's praxis.

"That's how a bush-wah intellectual, or a peasant or a lumpen can transform into a proletarian revolutionary without working in a factory or even ever seeing one. It doesn't happen spontaneously, it takes struggle."

When we truly recognize that the capitalists are at the root of racism, that it is a tool and weapon invented and used by them to preserve their power and privilege and to keep the lower classes divided, oppressed, miserable, and powerless, then we must also recognize our revolutionary duty to rise above racist and reverse racist programming. This is a difficult task that demands concrete practice. It is because of the depth of race-conditioning that the liberation struggle of New Afrikans and other oppressed nationalities cannot be dependent upon white cooperation, however, that cooperation should be sought and developed in process to build a United Front Against Imperialism. True liberation from national oppression compels destruction of the imperialist system. Otherwise, the monopoly capitalists will continue to derail independence struggles by allying themselves with racialist and comprador elements within the bodies of the oppressed nationalities and races, push them into positions of power, and then use them to subvert the liberation struggles and bring the masses back under imperialist control. This is the essence of neocolonialism and the method used by the imperialists to undermine most all of the national independence struggles of the last century.

In that it's the capitalist institutions that create, perpetuate, and benefit from racism, (indeed they need to preserve it to maintain their elevated power and status), they will assuredly mobilize resistance against all genuine efforts to build class-based racial solidarity. They will use the most rabid of white racists, and incite many New Afrikans, Natives and other people of color to fall out on the reactionary side, and the more intelligent reactionary, (reverse racist and comprador), leaders will encourage this. Our movement must be prepared to confront and counter such measures. We must set an example of promoting class unity and solidarity. It will also occur that some people will vacillate between the revolutionary and reactionary sides and that the dividing line won't be static and clear-cut. The task of winning people politically will ultimately decide victory.

## Conclusion

It should be clear by now that those of us who play into racism act as agents of our own imperialist oppressors, (whether consciously or not), and we aid in continuing our own oppression and want. In fact, we increase and intensify our own oppression and misery by inciting and perpetuating hatred, humiliation, insensitivity, and violence not only against the other race(s), but also in turn against our "own" race. It's a cycle that no one benefits from except the oppressor class that sits at the top laughing at what fools we are, while their power and wealth remain secure from any real challenge. It is on this basis that the New Afrikan Black Panther Party-Prison Chapter promotes, unites with, and supports the White Panther Organization and all anti-imperialists of all nationalities and all oppressed peoples in a common struggle against imperialism. We welcome the WPO as fellow comrades and Panthers within the democratic centralism of our aspiring Vanguard Party.

*Dare to Struggle, Dare to Win!*
*All Power to the People!*

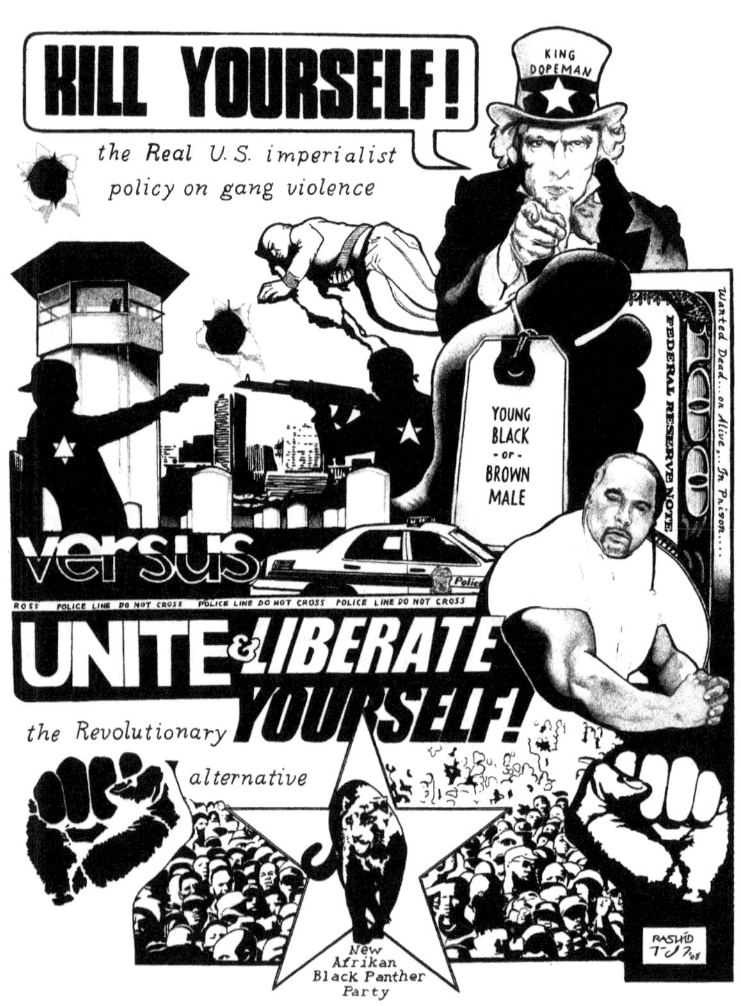

KILL YOURSELF!
the Real U.S. imperialist policy on gang violence
KING DOPEMAN
YOUNG BLACK -or- BROWN MALE
FEDERAL RESERVE NOTE
Wanted Dead... or Alive... In Prison....
versus
POLICE LINE DO NOT CROSS POLICE LINE DO NOT CROSS POLICE LINE DO NOT CROSS
Police
UNITE & LIBERATE YOURSELF!
the Revolutionary alternative
New Afrikan Black Panther Party
RASHID

# 5. KILL YOURSELF OR LIBERATE YOURSELF: THE REAL U.S. IMPERIALIST POLICY ON GANG VIOLENCE VS. THE REVOLUTIONARY ALTERNATIVE 2010

> "Look into the matter of your enemy's alliances and cause them to be split and dissolved. If an enemy has alliances, the problem is grave and the enemy's position is strong; if he has no alliances the problem is minor and the enemy is weak."
>
> *Chinese military proverb*

> "Approximately 28% of the [FBI's domestic covert action] efforts were designed to weaken groups by setting members against each other or to separate groups which might otherwise be allies and convert them into mutual enemies. The techniques used included ... encouraging hostility up to and including gang warfare between rival groups ..."
>
> Church Committee, *U.S. Congressional Report: Intelligence Activities and the Rights of Americans,* 94th Congress, 2nd Session, Report No. 94-755 (1976)

There are some one million youth gang members in Amerika today. No wonder the popular image of a young Black male, or a youth of color is that of a violent "gang banger." While no one can deny that gang violence is a common occurrence in the oppressed communities, what is seldom mentioned is that the U.S. government has been behind instigating and spreading this violence and creating the conditions that gave rise to it.

The official response to gang warfare is to demonize and violently attack gang formations while refusing to discuss or address the social and economic problems that contribute to gang activity. Moreover, no effort has ever been made to resolve the conflict of gang rivalries, because deliberate government policies are at the root.

Many of the groups labeled as youth "gangs" actually began with missions to serve, uplift and defend the poor and oppressed communities. But government policies directed at destroying grassroots political leadership that was a strong influence attempting to steer these groups in a positive direction pushed them in a negative and criminal direction to prey upon and destabilize their own communities.

After the government destroyed such organizations as the original Black Panther Party, the Puerto Rican Young Lords Party, the Chicano Brown Berets and Alianza, and the Appalachian white Young Patriots Party in the 1970s, it moved to destroy the political consciousness and unity of the oppressed urban communities—especially the New Afrikan communities. In 1978, the National Security Council decided to implement a policy set out in National Security Council Memorandum No. 46 (NSC-46) the purpose of which was to ensure the continued demise of the Black civil rights and liberation movements.

Among the "policy options" proposed in NSC-46 was preventing the rise of any genuine Black leader who could unite the New Afrikan people in the U.S. and link the struggle here with the liberation struggles in Afrika, and to cause splits and internal conflicts within the movement and the communities. These things were proposed in the interests of "national security." Here are some of the proposals in NSC-46:

> "The concern for the future security of the United States makes necessary the range of policy options. Arranged without intent to imply priority they are:
>
> "... (b) to elaborate and bring into effect a special program designed to *perpetuate division* in the Black movement and *neutralize the most active groups* of leftist radical organizations representing different social strata of the Black community; to *encourage* division in Black circles;
>
> "(c) to preserve the present climate which *inhibits the emergence* from within the Black leadership *of a person capable of exerting nationwide appeal;*
>
> "... (e) to support actions designed to sharpen *social stratification* in the Black community—*giving rise to growing antagonisms between different Black groups and a weakening of the movement as a whole ...*"

The motive and goal is plainly stated: to destroy our genuine leadership and divide the people against themselves. It is the old Roman dictum *"Divide and Rule."*

With these stated intentions in mind, the facts and considerations set out below should be given *serious* thought by *every* critic, victim and member of the youth gang subculture. The reader needs first and foremost to recognize that the violence, crime, lost lives, and suffering that is taking place within and between the various "gang" formations of every "race" and ethnicity are the result of an *officially orchestrated scheme of divide and rule* in the context of a system of class exploitation and a policy of deliberate genocide.

The cycle of violence that has caused the deaths and injury of countless "homies" and the consequent chaos that is wrecking our communities is not the "fault" of the youths caught up in the culture of "gang bangin'," rather the blame belongs with the government so many Amerikans blindly trust and hold in uncritical awe. The New Afrikan Black Panther Party-Prison Chapter (NABPP-PC) calls upon *all* of the brothers and sisters in the street "tribes" to critically examine the truth, end the fratricide, and unite in a *clenched fist alliance* to serve, uplift, protect and defend our home communities and join in the struggle for our common liberation from this capitalist imperialist system that is at the root of *all* our problems.

### The Art of Divide and Rule

In understanding the imperialist game behind spreading and perpetuating gang warfare, two things should be kept in mind:

- Divide and Rule (or Agitate, Indoctrinate and Divide), and
- Self-Inflicted Genocide

Divide and Rule is a strategy of containing and controlling populations that are of profitable use to those in power, but represent a threat if allowed to unite. Genocide is a strategy employed to dispose of a population seen to be of little or no profitable use to those in power. Self-Inflicted Genocide is the strategy of Divide and Rule *taken to the extreme.*

Within this framework two trends in Amerikan history are relevant. The first is described in the autobiography of Frederick Douglass, an escaped and self-educated Black slave. Douglass observed that when groups of slaves from different plantations came together, they would often fight each other over whose "owner" was "superior." As absurd as this sounds, even though *all* of them hated being enslaved, they would brawl over what amounted to claims of territorial supremacy and identification with their hated masters and the plantation he put them on. None of them *owned anything,* and all were oppressed and exploited, yet they felt compelled to "rep" their masters and their status and fight each other. Sound familiar?

The second trend relates to the extermination of the Indians and the theft of their lands. This "Indian removal" and genocide (which reduced them to less than 1% of the population of their native land), was accomplished in large part by the Europeans playing different Indian nations against each other and getting them to kill each other—*the equivalent of gang warfare*. Think about that!

On the plantations, (which were built upon the Indian's stolen land), the labor of the Black slaves was the source of the plantation system's wealth. They cleared the fields, planted, tended and harvested the tobacco, sugar cane, cotton and other crops and performed other useful labor. They were therefore "highly valued *property*," so with the slaves, the strategy of Divide and Rule was employed—(recall the Willie Lynch process). But because the Indians proved too difficult to enslave profitably and they stood in the way of expansion of the plantation system, genocide was the strategy employed against them.

But since the abolition of chattel slavery, the value of Blacks has gone down to the capitalist rulers and genocide has been employed proportionately. Following the Civil War, lynchings, KKK terror and the "chain gang" were employed to force the freed slaves back to work for the landowners as "sharecroppers" and to deprive them of newly won civil rights. During World War I masses of Blacks were pushed to migrate to the industrial centers to replace white workers called to war, then in the '20s, another wave of KKK terror, lynchings and bloody "race riots" were instigated to push them down into the lowest paying jobs in segregated ghettos.

Following the uprisings in the '60s and '70s and the emergence of the Black Panther Party and Black Liberation Movement, an even more serious plan of genocide and marginalization was hatched involving flooding the ghettos with drugs and criminalization and mass incarceration of the poor, and promotion of self-genocide in the form of gang warfare. The "War on Drugs" is in reality a war on the poor—and in particular the Black youth.

Sun Tzu, the ancient sage of the "Art of War," recognized that unity is essential in war. He also pointed out that *"all warfare is based on deception."* It is on this basis that the very imperialist system that is waging this war hides itself and its true intentions behind a cover of "serving and protecting" us, in the guise of "Law and Order," keeping us passive and ignorant victims. But to actually conquer a foe, Sun Tzu proposed three stages:

The first stage, which he gave top priority, is to *"stop the enemy's plans."* That is, defeat the enemy's strategy with one of your own, or in other words, prevent him from making and executing successful plans against you. One effective way to do this is to identify and neutralize his strategic thinkers and leaders. Another method is to confuse his plans and prevent his being able to execute them.

The second stage, if the enemy's plans cannot be stopped, is to *"disrupt his alliances."* This is, in essence, the principle behind *"Agitate, Indoctrinate and Divide."* But methods of dividing the enemy are not only to be applied between the enemy and his potential allies, but also *within the enemy's own ranks.* As long as his ranks are divided (by jealousy, fear, ambition, anger, hate, etc.), he cannot move against you with full effect. Therefore you must keep your enemies divided—this is common sense.

The third stage proposed by Sun Tzu is *"attack and defeat the enemy"* with armed force. At this point, if the enemy has good leadership and you can't divide his ranks or him from his allies, success then turns on your military skills in formulating and executing battle plans.

So in simple terms the three stages are: 1) ATTACK THE HEAD (and the body will remain disorganized, confused and vulnerable), 2) DIVIDE THE BODY (so it cannot function together to carry out the will of the head), and 3) FIGHT THE BODY (to destroy or cripple it with armed force).

> "If you cannot nip his plans in the bud, or disrupt his alliances when they are about to be consummated, sharpen your weapons to gain victory."
>
> *Chang Yu, Chinese military historian and annalist*

## The Combined Method of Imperialist Conquest

The U.S. ruling elite recognizes that the body of the oppressed masses is amorphous and adaptive. Like a salamander, its severed limbs are capable of growing back, and new leaders will emerge to replace the fallen. The imperialists therefore combine and apply all three stages of military conquest to contain and defeat the mass resistance of poor and working-class people, both without and within Amerika.

In "Protect Our Leaders Defend Our People," we discuss the U.S. government's persistent efforts to pinpoint and destroy every genuine leader and leading organization that has arisen from amongst our oppressed ranks. Then they replace our fallen or isolated leaders with ones they pick and approve to mislead us. In this way they "ATTACK THE HEAD."

They also "DIVIDE THE BODY," and this is where promoting division and sectarian violence between the youth gangs (the major focus of this discussion) comes in. Furthermore, they "FIGHT THE BODY" by engaging the gangs—and whole communities—in low intensity warfare through the increasingly militarized police forces.

But because the people are kept leaderless, divided and confused, they generally don't realize that they are under constant enemy attack. The government sanctioned misleaders deceive the people into thinking that their real enemy is their protector, therefore we don't quite detect the real meanings behind such plainly declared Establishment terms as the *"War on Drugs,"* the *"War on Crime,"* and more precisely, the *"War on Gangs,"* which are in effect and reality declarations of war on the poor and people of color.

The U.S. government (as the armed protectors and enforcers of the U.S. monopoly capitalist ruling class), destroys our leaders and leading organizations, divides and destabilizes our communities with crime, violence and drugs (that they covertly promote), and then it uses the chaotic conditions to vilify the poor and people of color, and justify targeting us with its own armed attacks and incarceration. Therefore, we can see that U.S. imperialist policy combines Sun Tzu's methods of attacking the head, dividing the body and fighting the body's scattered parts.

Let's examine the features and evidence of each of these methods more closely:

### 1. Attack The Head

Comrade George Jackson, who was a product of the inner cities, developed into one of the most prominent strategic thinkers of our liberation movement in the 1960s and '70s. He understood that capitalist imperialism was and is the real enemy and the cause of our overall suffering, oppression and exploitation. He was keenly aware of the oppressed people's need for leaders to unite and organize against and overcome their oppressed condition. More to the point, he recognized that the imperialists also recognize this need and the Establishment remains alert and vigilant in identifying and neutralizing potential leaders as part of a well-developed policy of containing and keeping the oppressed leaderless.

Here is how Comrade George broke it down:

> "Capitalism is the enemy. It must be destroyed. There is no other recourse. The system is not workable in view of the modern industrial city-based society. Men are born disenfranchised. The contract between ruler and ruled perpetuates this disenfranchisement.
>
> "Men in positions of trust owe an equitable distribution of wealth and privilege to the men who have trusted them. Each individual born in these Amerikan cities should be born with those things that are necessary to survival. Meaningful social roles, education, medical care, food, shelter, and understanding should be guaranteed at birth. They have been part of all civilized human societies until this one. Why else do men allow other men to govern? To

what purpose is a Department of Health, Education, and Welfare, of Housing and Urban Development, etc.? Why do we give these men power over us? Why do we give them taxes? For nothing? So they can say the world owes our children nothing? The world owes each of us a living the very day we are born. If not we can make no claims to civilization, and we can stop recognizing the power of any administrator. Evolution of the large city-based society has made our dependence upon government complete. Individually, we cannot feed ourselves and our children. We cannot, by ourselves, train and educate them at home. We cannot organize our own work inside the city structure by ourselves. Consequently, we must allow men to specialize in coordinating these activities. We pay them, honor them, and surrender control of certain aspects of our lives to them so that they will in return take each new helpless entry into the social group and work on him until he is no longer helpless, until he can start to support himself and make his contribution to the continuity of society …

"What is it that has been working against my generation from the day we were born through every day to this one?

"Capitalism and capitalist man, wrecker of worlds, scourge of the people. It cannot address itself to our needs, it cannot and will not change itself to adapt to natural changes within the social structure.

"To the Black male the losses were most tragic of all. It will do us no good to linger over the fatalities, they're numberless and beyond our reach. But we who have survived must eventually look at ourselves and wonder why. The competition at the bottom of the social spectrum is for symbols, honors, and objects; Black against itself, Black against lower class whites and Browns, virulent, cutthroat, backstabbing competition, the Amerikan way of life. But the fascists cooperate … This competition has destroyed trust. Among the Black males a premium has been placed on distrust. Every other Black male is viewed as the competition; the wise and practical Black is the one who cares nothing for any living ass, the cynic who has gotten over any principles he may have picked up by mistake. We can't express love on the supposition that the recipient will automatically use it against us as a weapon. We're going to have to start all over again. This next time around we'll let it all hang out, we'll stop betraying ourselves, and we'll add some trust and love.

"Recall the stories you've read about the other herd animals. the great Amerikan bison, the Caribou or Amerikan reindeer.

"The great Amerikan bison or buffalo—he's a herd animal, or social animal ... just like us ... we're social animals, we need others of our general kind about us to feel secure. Few men would enjoy total isolation. To be alone constantly is torture for normal men. The buffalo, cattle, caribou, and some others are like folks in that they need company most of the time. They need to butt shoulders and butt butts. They like to rub noses. We shake hands, slap backs, and rub lips. Of all the world's people we Blacks love the company of others most, we are the most socialistic. Social animals eat, sleep, and travel in company. They need this company to feel secure. This fact means that socialistic animals also need leaders. It follows logically that if the buffalo is going to eat, sleep, and travel in groups some coordinating factor is needed or some will be sleeping when others are traveling without the leader–follower complex, in a crisis the company would roar off in a hundred different directions. But the buffalo did evolve the leader–follower complex as did the other social animals; if the leader of the herd of caribou loses his footing and slips to his death from some high place, it is very likely that the whole herd will die behind.

"The leader–follower complex. The hunter understood this. Predatory man learned of the natural occurrence of leadership in all of the social animals, that each will by nature produce a group leader, and to these natural leaders fall the responsibility for coordination of the group's activity, organizing them for survival. The buffalo hunter knew that if he could isolate and identify the leader of the herd and kill him first, the rest of the herd would be helpless, at his mercy, to be killed off as he saw fit.

"We Blacks have the same problem the buffalo had; we have the same weakness also and predatory man understands this weakness well.

"Huey Newton, Ahmed Evans, Bobby Seale, and the hundreds of others [of our genuine leaders] will be murdered according to this fascist scheme.

"A sort of schematic natural selection in reverse. Medgar Evers, Malcolm X, Bobby Hutton, Brother Booker, W.L. Noland, M.L. King, Featherstone, Mark Clark, and Fred Hampton—just a few who've gone the way of the buffalo.

"The potential Black leadership looks at the pitiable condition of the [leaderless, confused and scattered] Black herd: the corruption, the preoccupation with irrelevance, the apparent ineptitude concerning matters of survival. He knows that were he to give the average brother an M-16, this brother wouldn't have anything but a club for a week. He weighs this thing that he sees in the herd against the possible risks he'll be taking at the hands of the fascist monster and naturally he decides to go for himself, feeling that he can't help us because we are beyond help, that he may as well go get something out of existence. These are the 'successful Negroes,' the opposite of 'failures.' You find them on the ball courts and fields, the stage, pretending and playing children's games. And looking for all the world just as pitiable as the so-called failures.

"We were colonized by the white predatory fascist economy. It was from them that we evolved our freak subculture and the attitudes that perpetuate our conditions. These attitudes cause us to give each other up to the klan pigs. We even on occasion work gun in hand right with them. A Black killed Fred Hampton; Blacks working with the CIA killed Malcolm X; Blacks are plentiful on the payroll of the many police forces that fascism must employ to protect itself from the people. These fascist subcultural attitudes have sent us to Europe, Asia … and even Afrika [to kill] … and die for nothing … We are so confused, so foolishly simple that we not only fail to distinguish what is generally right and what is wrong, but we also fail to appreciate what is good and not good for us in very personal matters concerning the Black colony and its liberation. The ominous government economic agency whose only clear motive is to further enslave, number, and spy on us; the Black agency subsidized by the government to infiltrate us and retard liberation, is accepted and by some even invited and welcomed, while the Black Panther is avoided and hard-pressed to find protection among the people … If we allow the fascist machine to destroy [the Black Panther Party], our dream of eventual self-determination and control over the factors surrounding our survival is going to die with them …

"The young Panther party member, our vanguard, must be embraced, protected, allowed to develop … our communion in perfect harmony and there'll never, never be another Fred Hampton affair."

But the BPP was identified as a herd leader. It was labeled as "the greatest threat to U.S. national security" by the FBI, and it was destroyed by the U.S. government. The leadership was not protected as Comrade George pointed out was essential to advancing our struggle. Indeed, only a year after writing the above words he was himself assassinated by San Quentin prison guards. Our herd leaders were identified and neutralized. And just as Comrade George predicted, the masses scattered in confusion and have since remained vulnerable to enemy attack.

The youth, deprived of the strategic leadership of the BPP and similar formations, saw these revolutionary structures replaced with a rise of sectarian gang formations that were devoid of revolutionary guidance and vision. These groups fell under the spell of gangsterism that was glamorized by Hollywood. As Comrade Russell "Maroon" Shoats noted, the youth went from representing the leading force in our liberation struggle to promoting "expensively dressed big hat wearing, Cadillac driving, imitations of the Italian Mafia." Furthermore, Maroon observed, they were converted from "fighting oppression into pawns who were used to further destroy their own communities." Even worse, these formations fell into the old slave mentality of fighting each other over turf that none of them owned, but with violence on the level of Self-Inflicted Genocide.

Other BPP leaders predicted this counter-revolutionary outcome, that it was what the government planned in its efforts to destroy the revolutionary leadership, leaving the urban masses confused, helpless, and easily divided and played against themselves. Black Panther Comrade ji-Jaga expressed as much in a 1993 interview:

> "Huey Newton [the BPP's Minister of Defense] gave a lecture on that one time and we had foreseen that this was gonna happen. After the leadership of the BPP was attacked at the end of the '60s and the early '70s, throughout the Black and other oppressed communities, the role models for up-coming generations became the pimps, drug dealers, etc. This is what the government wanted to happen. The next result was that the gangs were being formed, coming together with a gangster mentality, as opposed to the revolutionary progressive mentality we would have given them."
>
> Quoted in Mumia Abu-Jamal's *We Want Freedom: A Life in the Black Panther Party* (2004), pp. 237–238

Another BPP veteran, Comrade Dhoruba Bin-Wahad, made a similar observation in a recent article on the execution of Stanley "Tookie" Williams, cofounder of the Crips street gang:

> "[I]t was the destruction of militant groups such as the Black Panthers that left a social, political and ideological void in Afrikan Amerika to be filled by street gangs ... Although law enforcement experts are anxious to dispel and distort the social and political roots of street gangs such as the Crips, the fact of the matter is that

> gangs like the Crips were in part a consequence of the success of [the U.S. government's] devastation of the militant Black liberation movement in Amerika."
>
> *The Ethics of Black Atonement in Racist America: The Execution of Stanley Tookie Williams*

Even today the imperialist U.S. government opposes oppressed people admiring the leadership example set by the BPP. Because Tookie dedicated his book *Life in Prison* to Black Panthers (specifically Comrade George), California's Governor Arnold Schwarzenegger rejected the plea to spare Tookie's life. He said that the dedication "defies reason and is a significant indicator that Williams is not reformed."

The imperialists remain ready and willing to identify and "Attack the Head" of the oppressed to defeat our attempting to resist our oppression. Having accomplished their intentions, the body was left leaderless and deprived of revolutionary vision. Their next step was to divide the body.

## 2. Divide The Body

As part of the strategy to keep the oppressed communities, and particularly their youth, divided, the Establishment has continuously kept the politically leaderless street gangs locked in a cycle of fratricidal violence. While some Amerikans may be fooled, most of the aware people realize the U.S. government has no wish to resolve sectarian gang violence. Certainly no "gang bangers" believe it does. Within gang circles it is widely believed that the government murdered Bobby Lander, an OG Blood in Watts in 1989, staging the killing to appear as though the Crips were responsible to destroy a peace treaty established in 1986 between the groups.

This predictably set off a wave of back and forth revenge killings. Furthermore, most youth involved in the gang subculture have personally experienced or witnessed police "gang units," "narcotics squads," "gang task forces," etc. deliberately instigate violence between youth from rival groups or neighborhoods.

Here is a typical scenario I've heard over and over. The cops pick up one or several young males under the pretext of arresting them, but instead they're driven to a rival neighborhood and kicked out of the police vehicle. The pigs then draw the attention of a group of rival youth to the "marks" and quickly drive off leaving the unarmed targets to fight and/or flee for their lives. Whatever the immediate outcome, the objective and ultimate outcome is to provoke or continue a cycle of retaliatory violence.

Plainclothes police driving unmarked, often confiscated, cars and wearing clothes bearing gang colors and making identifying gang signs have been identified, or suspected, of shooting and killing leaders and members of rival gangs to undermine alliances and truces and spark wider-scale gang wars. The 1989 murder of Bobby Lander and the murder of OG Crip Raymond Washington, (which was blamed on Piru Bloods), are two such examples.

In his book, *Blue Rage, Black Redemption* (2004), Tookie bore witness to the role of the police in inciting and escalating gang wars:

> "Yes America, as unbelievable as it may seem, 'hood cops, with impunity, commit drive-bys and other lawless acts. It was common practice for them to abduct a Crip or Bounty Hunter and drop him off in hostile territory, and then broadcast it over a loudspeaker. The predictable outcome was that the rival was either beaten or killed on the spot, which resulted in a cycle of payback. Cops would also inform opposing gangs where to find and attack a rival gang, and then say, 'Go handle your business.' Like slaves, the gang did exactly what their master commanded. Had they not been fueled by self-hatred, neither Crips, Bounty Hunters, nor any other Black gang, would have been duped.
>
> "The 'hood cops were pledged to protect and serve, but for us they were not there to help, but to exploit us—and they were effective. With the cops' Machiavellian presence, the gang epidemic escalated. When gang warfare is fed and fueled by law enforcement, funds are generated for the so-called anti-gang units. Without gangs, these units would no longer exist."

The 1976 Church Committee report of the U.S. Congress found that the FBI and local police were repeatedly involved in inciting gang wars, and in fact took pride in their roles in the resulting carnage they'd caused. In the words of that report:

> "This report does demonstrate ... that the chief investigative branch of the Federal Government, which was charged by law with investigating crimes and preventing criminal conduct, itself engaged in lawless tactics and responded to deep-seated social problems by fomenting violence and unrest ...
>
> "The select committee's staff investigation has disclosed a number of instances in which the FBI [manipulated] violence prone organizations ... in an effort to aggravate 'gang warfare' ... equally disturbing is the pride which these officials took in claiming credit for the bloodshed that occurred."

This ongoing policy of officials inciting violence between various youth groups and races is especially played out inside U.S. prisons. Many of the rivalries begin in the prisons and carry over to the street. Indeed prison officials even admit to such schemes. California, where the U.S. gang sub-culture has its deepest roots, provides a clear example.

The 1997 documentary film "Maximum Security University" exposed the "gladiator fights" set up from 1989 to 1994 between rival prisoners at California's Corcoran State Prison. Many of the involved prisoners were seriously injured or murdered by rival prisoners and guards, who shot them with rifles for fun under the pretext of breaking up the fights they'd arranged. These were not isolated occurrences. In fact, in 1999, California's Department of Corrections (CDCR) officials admitted facilitating and manipulating violence between rival prisoner groups allegedly to keep control of their prisons.

In response to a prisoner hunger strike at the New Folsom Prison, where prisoners were protesting to receive yard time with prisoners they got along with instead of with rival groups, CDCR Ombudsman Ken Hurdle refused to negotiate, stating: "Then you'd have two groups normally aligned on the yard at the same time. They would have only the staff as their enemy." (Quoted from the *Sacramento Bee*, Dec. 8, 1999.) The motive of "Divide and Rule" couldn't have been stated plainer.

Further reports followed, culminating in a February 23, 2000, melee involving 200 prisoners. The summer 2000 issue of *California Prison Focus* (CPF) newsletter found that these riots resulted from CDCR officials deliberately fostering tension between rival racial groups at Pelican Bay State Prison and their arranging a number of smaller fights between members of rival groups. CPF stated:

> "At the center of this [violence] is the longstanding CDCR policy of forcing warring prisoner groups onto the yard together while, at the same time, refusing to provide any means of for these rival factions to negotiate peaceful resolutions to their disputes."

CPF went on to add:

> "The February 23 incident [which resulted in guards firing 24 rounds from their assault rifles, killing one prisoner and injuring 15 others], occurred on only the second day since the August incident that the entire population was placed on the yard. In the months between these two full scale melees, instead of moving to lessen hostilities, prison officials appear to have made matters worse by instigating a long series of smaller fights. Either Pelican Bay officials have lost control of their institution or we are witnessing a return of the 'gladiator days' of early 1990s Corcoran."

Of course the CDCR wasn't losing control of its prisons. As Ken Hurdle admitted, keeping prisoners violently divided and at each other's necks is a policy calculated to maintain control and keep the prisoners' focus off of the officials who are oppressing them all. As CPF concluded: "CDCR officials have a long history of promoting and instigating violence among prisoners. This has been documented in legal proceedings ..."

The officially instigated violent cycle grew to the point that, according to Taxpayers for Improving Public Safety, there were 315 prisoner-on-prisoner riots in 2005 alone. Furthermore, California's prison guard's unions have been involved in inciting the "gang wars" to promote building more prisons in California. As Comrade Tom Big Warrior noted:

> "Complicity between neo-Nazi white inmates and guards and Southern Hispanic gangs is becoming more evident in all these 'spontaneous' race riots. Governor Schwarzenegger has clearly failed in his attempt to gain control over the California prison system and institute reforms. His predecessor, Governor Davis, virtually handed over the prison system to the notoriously corrupt guards union, and Schwarzenegger's attempt to reassert control has collapsed under pressure from the special interest groups, as cited by prison chief Roderick Hickman in his resignation last month.
>
> "Though the majority of California's 170,000 prisoners are Black, and the politically conscious Chicano, Indigenous, and Northern Mexican prisoners are struggling to build unity between all prisoners, the white Aryan Nation and other neo-Nazi factions have found willing allies among the Southern Hispanic gangs who are the instigators in the racial violence with the complicity of the guard union. The goal is to polarize and drive a wedge between the prisoners along racial lines, to put a halt to reform efforts that would interfere with the construction of new prisons.
>
> "In 2004, Hickman announced a bold new change in policy that would highlight drug rehabilitation, halfway houses, and home detention for minor parole violators as an alternative to sending them back to prison. This was attacked in a media campaign sponsored by the guards union and a victim's rights group, and Schwarzenegger got 'cold feet' and backed down."
>
> *Anatomy of a Spontaneous Prison Riot*

So the reality boils down to government instigated racial and group violence which it exploits to generate public alarm and consequent support for building more prisons, (which benefits only the industries, corporations and special interest groups whose profits are tied in with prison expansion), and intensifying the nationwide "War on Gangs"—all under the pretext of responding to the very death and bloodshed officials themselves incite and spread. These "Divide the Body" tactics are applied everywhere in U.S. prisons. Virginia, for example, has been on a prison building binge in economically strapped rural white communities since the late 1990s, building them at a pace far faster than the state can fill, despite abolishing parole, revoking "good time," enacting "three strikes" laws in the mid-1990s, and having one of the nation's highest conviction rates.

When those prisons, especially Virginia's two "supermaxes," were repeatedly exposed as unneeded and the justifications used to promote building them were exposed as lies, Virginia officials had to keep crafting new rationales for continuing its prison expansions. The latest "justification" being promoted is to "curb gang violence." In reality, the officials have been working overtime to instigate and spread prisoner-on-prisoner gang-related violence.

For example, at Red Onion State Prison (ROSP), the remote supermax where I am confined, prisoners identified as members of rival ethnic gangs, (particularly leaders and the most territorial individuals), are concentrated in two select segregation units called "gang pods," to keep hostilities festering between them. Because the foul motives behind the use of such units are obvious, ROSP officials deny the existence of these units.

These rival prisoners are then released piecemeal from the "gang pods" into the general population units. The intent is to see the festering conflicts erupt into group violence in the larger open population setting. Any resulting (deliberately manufactured) situations then validate official claims of "problems" with gang violence, justifying their demonizing labels and pre-designed intentions to enhance measures of repression and official violence against ethnic youth, demands for increased public funding for crime and "gang" control, expanding the prison and militarized police structures, and overall: *Keeping the body divided, confused, and warring with itself.*

So these systems operate to provoke and increase gang violence (*divide the body*) and in turn *respond* to the violence they have created with official counter-violence (*fight the body*). This is a general imperialist offensive military strategy applied in both "*Low Intensity*" wars (like the war on youth in the oppressed communities) and "*High Intensity*" wars (as in Iraq).

Indeed, we see it being applied to divide the Shiite and Sunni Muslims in Iraq, and justify the continued U.S. military occupation. From the very beginning of the U.S. invasion in 2003, the plan was to seize control through winning the allegiance of the majority Shiite population, (in whose territory most of the oil reserves are located), by playing them off the Sunni minority, (just like the U.S. ruling class keeps power in Amerika by playing the white "majority" against the Black and other ethnic "minorities").

The overthrow of Saddam Hussein and his Sunni-dominated Baathist government was essentially intended to win over the Shiites. But as with all wars of imperialist occupation, overreaching U.S. military violence against Iraqi resistance to foreign invasion prompted a nationalist response from both Sunni and Shiite ethnic populations. This led increasingly to united resistance against the common enemy, despite the persistent efforts of the U.S. imperialists to drive a wedge between them. By 2005, calls by Shiite clerics and resistance groups for a formal Shiite-Sunni alliance and increasing armed resistance compelled drastic measures to divide the Iraqi people as U.S. casualties shot up and morale plummeted.

On February 22, 2006, the Golden Mosque, the holiest Shiite shrine, (which is in Samara), was bombed while full of worshipers, killing scores of Shiites and destroying its golden dome. U.S. intelligence agencies and media assets quickly spread the word that the Sunnis were responsible, but many observers suspected that U.S. and British forces were the culprits. In fact video footage of British troops dressed as Arabs packing explosives surfaced. However, nothing could stop the rage generated by the attack from sparking a wave of back and forth sectarian revenge killings, which diverted some of the heat off the occupying U.S. and U.K. forces. Just like the government-instigated gang wars in the U.S.

During June 2007, Nuri al-Maliki, the U.S. hand-picked, puppet, Shiite Prime Minister of Iraq, told U.S. Deputy Secretary of State John Negroponte in a phone conversation, "We've eliminated the danger of sectarian war," indicating that Sunni–Shiite hostilities were winding down. The *very next day* the Golden Mosque was bombed again, bringing down its minarets. You do the math!

The main cry of the U.S. officials is that Shiite–Sunni hostilities present a danger of all out civil war in Iraq if U.S. forces are withdrawn. Therefore, it is argued, the military occupation must go on and on indefinitely.

On a similar note, there is a lesson that can be drawn from Amerikan history. It is a little known fact that originally Black, white and Indian forced labor worked side by side on the early plantations. That is until 1676 when white and Black slaves rose in rebellion in the Virginia colony, overthrew the colonial government, and burned down the capitol at Jamestown. The leader and organizer of the rebellion was Nathaniel Bacon, a white man, who became ill and died at the height of the revolt. By losing its head, (Bacon), the body of rebelling slaves and servants lost cohesion and became vulnerable to counter-attack and defeat by colonial forces.

Upon regaining control, the Virginia Company implemented a plan to permanently *divide the body* of the poor masses that set the pattern of racist division that has continued until today. In 1682, the colonial government passed laws that made slavery a permanent and inherited status for Afrikans. The enslavement of Europeans was phased out and the colonial society was divided along racial lines of "white" and "negro" (Afrikan).

The line was further established and underscored in 1705 by a law that classified as "negro" anyone having "one drop" of Afrikan blood. The poor whites were given a sense of social privilege, even though many were poorer than the slaves, and a belief in "racial superiority," as well as license to lord it over and brutalize the "negroes" in the role of overseers. Whites were culturally conditioned to hate and fear Blacks (and vice versa), and to strive to make sure the slaves never united in numbers except to labor under close supervision of overseers. Some Blacks were also chosen to be overseers, and all were encouraged to be "snitches" and spies for their white masters—AGITATE, INDOCTRINATE AND DIVIDE—DIVIDE AND RULE!!

Returning to the present and the gang wars, the sectarian violence generated by the U.S. government—attended by the flooding of the oppressed communities with drugs—also imperialist-generated—has in turn been used to justify open warfare against the divided body of the oppressed masses. What's worse is that these tactics have turned the oppressed communities against their own youth. The anti-social behavior of the gangs invokes fear and turning to the police for protection. Desperate to contain the gang violence and predatory behavior that threatens their security, the people in the oppressed communities turn to their oppressors to increase and enhance the militarized police occupation of their communities, only to be further outraged when these occupiers kill innocent people and act no different than the gangs.

### 3. Fight The Body

Under the cover of waging a "War on Drugs" and a "War on Gangs," the U.S. government has increasingly enhanced its militarization of the police in the inner cities and stepped up its violence against the youth and oppressed communities. Since 9-11, this has been increasingly incorporated with the government's "War on Terrorism." The steady erosion of civil rights and civil liberties parallels the widening divide between the incomes and lifestyles of the rich minority and those of the poor and working-class majority. Youth gangs, and youth of color generally, feature as principal targets of each of these "Wars." In a 1984 report of the Central Intelligence Agency (CIA), the imperialist's fear of the youth is explained:

> "The youth of a growing population may very well play a major role in pressing for change. They are among those who are usually disproportionately disadvantaged: they have less at stake in the existing structure of authority, more idealism, more impatience, and in a society with a steady or rising rate of growth their proportion of the total population increases. The density of the number of youth relative to the total population may thus be one clue to the strength of the pressure for change."

This sheds light on their focus on youth gangs. But let's trace the sequence of the domestic "War on Drugs" to the "War on Gangs" and how in each of them urban youth gangs have been the major targets of official violence. First though, a little history of how the youth gangs became so prominent is in order. As already noted, in the late 1960s and early '70s the imperialists moved to suppress and destroy all revolutionary political consciousness within the oppressed urban communities. These actions were rationalized under the cover of preventing and containing violence—the same rationale promoted today.

California features largely in the history of this repression, which is not surprising as it was in California that the original Black Panther Party was formed in 1966. It was also in California that two of the major youth gangs, the Crips and the Bloods were formed. According to the Establishment's National Gang History website:

> "In 1969, a Los Angeles youth named Raymond Washington, 15, organized a group of other neighborhood youths and started a gang called the Baby Avenues. The Baby Avenues wanted to emulate a gang of older youths who had been involved in gang activity since 1964 and provided minor crimes for the Black Panthers of Los Angeles. This gang was called the Avenue Boys since they claimed their turf on Central Avenue in East Los Angeles. Raymond Washington, along with Stanley 'Tookie' Williams and several other gang members from the Baby Avenues Gang were fascinated with the hype of the Black Panthers and they wanted to develop the Baby Avenues gang into a larger force. The Baby Avenues Gang

began using the name Avenues Cribs since members lived on the avenue (Central Avenue). Crib members would wear blue scarves (now called bandanas) around their necks or heads. The color blue became their representative color.

"In 1971, the use of the word 'Crip' had become so common among the Avenues Cribs that it became an acceptable name for the gang. Meanwhile, Raymond Washington and his collection of young gang members influenced other area youth gangs resulting in the formation of many Crip sets. Some of these sets included Avalon Garden Crips, Eastside Crips, Inglewood Crips and Westside Crips. Crips gangs were violent and constantly expanded their turf. Because of their aggression, several rival gangs joined forces as a gang collective called the Bloods. They adopted the color Red as their representative color. A fierce rivalry between these two gangs existed throughout the 1970s and '80s. By the early 1980s, Crips gangs were heavily involved in the drug trade that they commenced an expansion throughout the United States to sell a new drug product called 'Crack.' Throughout the 1980s and 1990s the Crips developed intricate networks and a respected reputation with other gangs across America and neighboring countries."

In August 1965, the South Central Los Angeles ghetto of Watts erupted in violent rebellion. The six-day uprising was driven by the outrage of Black youth to the racist status quo, to police brutality and murder of Black youth, systematic discrimination and poverty, and the government's repeatedly subverting and suppressing attempts to peacefully organize and effect change.

These conditions, which prevailed in Black ghettos across the country, attended by the ideas of Malcolm X, who was assassinated that same year, inspired Huey P. Newton and Bobby Seale to form the Black Panther Party for Self-Defense in Oakland, California. The series of urban uprisings that swept across Amerika from 1964 to 1968, (which included the 1965 Watts Rebellion), and the subsequent rise of political activism and consciousness of the urban youth, prompted the federal government to finance and undertake various studies designed to contain the Black rebellion. In 1973, Ronald Reagan, (who was then governor of California), announced in his State of the State address a planned biomedical facility—the Center for the Study of the Reduction of Violence—to be set up at the University of California in Los Angeles (UCLA). Louis "Jolly" West, a controversial psychiatrist who had long worked with the CIA, was to run the facility.

West proposed to focus on Mexican and Black neighborhoods to screen residents for "genetic defects" and proposed implanting electrodes in their brains as a "cure." Broad public opposition to this plan prevented it from getting off the ground. West then sought to set up a laboratory for humyn experimentation at a former U.S. missile base in Santa Monica, California.

Following the Watts Rebellion, West proposed mass sterilizations of youth of color to render them passive eunuchs. In 1972, he proposed chemical sterilization of U.S. prisoners. Protests across California in 1974 against West's proposals, and plans to implement them, led to cuts in government funding for his Nazi-like projects. But he still remained on the government's payroll.

The next year (1975), in a book he edited entitled *Hallucinations: Behavior, Experience and Theory,* West revealed that use of narcotics was being considered as a weapon of social control against select "minority" and political groups. He wrote:

> "The role of drugs in the exercise of political control is also coming under increased discussion. Control can be imposed either through prohibition or supply. The total or even partial prohibition of drugs gives government considerable leverage for other types of control. An example would be the selective application of drug laws against selected components of the population such as members of certain minority groups or political organizations."

This revelation has great relevance to the "War on Drugs" that would be declared only a few years later—which has focused almost exclusively on people of color. It was also in this time period (1978) that NSC-46 was developed by the White House with the expressed intent of forever destroying the Black political movements in the U.S.

Throughout the 1970s, the BPP came under vicious attack by the government—led by the FBI—and it was destroyed. The Bloods and Crips, although then relatively small factions, became locked in conflict over turf, respect and other grievances—with both accusing the other of harming the communities under their control.

In the early 1980s, events occurred that pushed these and other urban youth gangs into prominence, namely the introduction of crack cocaine into the inner cities—starting with Los Angeles—by the CIA, under President Ronald Reagan. Reagan's Vice-President, George Bush, Sr.—a prior CIA director—was appointed to be head of Reagan's National Narcotics Border Interdiction System and immediately expanded the CIA's role in drug operations. Under the Reagan-Bush administration, the CIA channelled tons of cocaine into the hands of the Bloods and Crips in LA through a local dealer named "Freeway" Rick Ross, (who processed it into crack). Crack, which is both cheap and highly addictive, proved to be a very effective weapon in the government's *attack against the divided body.*

The cocaine was being shipped to LA from Colombia by Nicaraguan exiles—and the CIA itself—and was sold to the Crips and Bloods to finance a mercenary army (the Contras) that the CIA had organized to overthrow the revolutionary Sandinista government in Nicaragua.

> "Reagan came into office just after a revolution had taken place in Nicaragua, in which a popular Sandinista movement (named after the 1920s revolutionary hero Augusto Sandino) overthrew the corrupt Somoza dynasty (long supported by the United States). The Sandinistas, a coalition of Marxists, left-wing priests, and assorted nationalists, set about to give more land to the peasants and to spread education and health care among the poor.
>
> "The Reagan administration, seeing in this a 'Communist' threat, but even more important, a challenge to the long U.S. control over governments in Central America, began immediately to work to overthrow the Sandinista government. It waged a secret war by having the CIA organize a counter-revolutionary force (the 'contras'), many of whose leaders were former leaders of the hated National Guard under Somoza.
>
> "The contras seemed to have no popular support base inside Nicaragua and so were based next door in Honduras, a very poor country dominated by the United States. From Honduras they moved across the border, raiding farms and villages, killing men, women, and children, committing atrocities. A former colonel with the contras, Edgar Chamorro, testified before the World Court:
>
> "'We were told that the only way to defeat the Sandinistas was to use the tactics the agency [the CIA] attributed to Communist insurgencies everywhere: kill, kidnap, rob, and torture ... Many civilians were killed in cold blood. Many others were tortured, mutilated, raped, robbed, or otherwise abused ... When I agreed to join ... I had hoped that it would be an organization of Nicaraguans ... [I]t turned out to be an instrument of the U.S. government ... '
>
> "There was a reason for the secrecy of the U.S. actions in Nicaragua: public opinion surveys showed that the American public was opposed to military involvement there. In 1984, the CIA, using Latin American agents to conceal its involvement, put mines in the harbors of Nicaragua to blow up ships. When information leaked out, Secretary of Defense Weinberger told ABC news: 'The United States is not mining the harbors of Nicaragua.'

> "Later that year Congress, responding perhaps to public opinion and the memory of Vietnam, made it illegal for the United States to support 'directly or indirectly, military or paramilitary operations in Nicaragua.' The Reagan administration decided to ignore this law and to find ways to fund the contras secretly, looking for 'third-party support.' Reagan himself solicited funds from Saudi Arabia, at least $32 million. The friendly dictatorship in Guatemala was used to get arms surreptitiously to the contras. Israel, dependent on U.S. aid and always dependable for support, was also used."
>
> Howard Zinn, *A People's History of the United States* (NY: Harper Collins, 1999), pp. 585–586

The U.S. also pursued two other channels for funding the illegal Contra War: one by selling weapons to Iran in exchange for the release of U.S. hostages held in Lebanon, and giving the profits from those sales to the Contras (the Iran-Contra scandal), and the second by allowing the Contras to raise money by dumping tons of cheap crack cocaine into the U.S. inner cities—starting and spreading the "crack epidemic." The Contras not only flooded the inner cities with crack through the gangs, but also sold the gangs military weapons to enforce their power against each other and over disputed drug turfs. This sudden access to wealth and weapons enhanced the power and prestige of the gangs and membership flourished inside the poor ghettos. As Mike Davis observed:

> "With 75,000 unemployed youth in the Watts-Willowbrook area, it is not surprising that there are now 145 branches of the rival Crips and Bloods gangs in South LA, or that the jobless resort to the opportunities of the burgeoning 'crack economy.'"
>
> "Chinatown Part Two? The 'Internationalization' of Downtown Los Angeles" *New Left Review*, Vol. 164 (1987), p. 75

These were the government-created conditions that produced the crack explosion and gang wars beginning in the early 1980s.

The CIA's role in the whole affair was first exposed by a series of front page articles, written by journalist Gary Webb, from August 18–20, 1996, in the *San Jose Mercury News* under the heading "Dark Alliance," and subtitled "The Story Behind the Crack Explosion." The series prompted a major outcry from LA residents whose communities had long suffered the ills of the crack infestation and attendant gang warfare. The CIA first denied any involvement and used its power to destroy Webb's career. On December 10, 2004, Webb was found dead from two gunshot wounds to the face. His death was dismissed by officials as a "suicide."

Black Congresswomyn Maxine Waters, who was the Representative for LA, received a flood of complaints from LA residents in response to Webb's 1996 articles. In turn she pressed for Congressional and CIA investigations and herself conducted an independent investigation. She found Webb's story fully validated. She later recalled:

> "In South Central Los Angeles we wondered where these guns were coming from. They were not simply handguns, they were Uzis and AK-47's, sophisticated weapons brought in by the same CIA operatives who were selling the cocaine because they had to enforce bringing the profits back in. It was at this time when you saw all these guns coming into the community that you saw more and more killing, more and more violence. Now we know what was going on. The drugs were put in our communities on consignment, out to the gangs and others. If they did not bring the profits back, the guns were brought in so they could enforce their control. The killing just mounted and people said, 'What are they fighting about? What are all these drive-by shootings about? What is this gang warfare?' And the press they said, 'Oh, it's the colors. Some like red, some like blue.' Well, you know it was about the drugs, it was about the crack cocaine, introduced into our communities by people who brought it in with a purpose."
>
> quoted in Alexander Cockburn, et al.,
> *Whiteout: The CIA, Drugs and the Press* (NY: Verso, 1998), p. 65

Her efforts to get Congress to conduct public hearings and for mainstream media coverage ran into brick walls, leading her to spread the word independently. The CIA conducted an internal investigation of itself, not digging too deep. Its final report revealed clear known connections between the CIA and the Contras' drug trafficking. Yet the report concluded by denying CIA knowledge or involvement. Waters responded that the report "lacks credibility and its conclusions should be dismissed." Under mounting pressure the CIA finally revealed in October 1998 that it had concealed from Congress and other agencies its knowledge and support of the Contras smuggling drugs into the U.S. to fund their operations. Further revealed was that the CIA had clearance from Reagan's Justice Department in 1982 to keep the CIA's knowledge and role in these activities secret.

But CIA involvement in drug-running is nothing new. In fact, throughout its existence the CIA has been the central facilitator of the international drug trade, in pursuit of financing its many illegal foreign and even domestic operations. Indeed, the CIA was behind the heroin epidemic that shattered Black communities in the 1960s and 1970s, prompting Richard Nixon's first "War on Drugs."

"What cannot be denied is that U.S. intelligence agencies arranged for the release from prison of the world's preeminent drug lord [Charles 'Lucky' Luciano on February 9, 1946], allowed him to rebuild his narcotics empire, watched the flow of drugs into the largely black ghettoes of New York and Washington D.C. escalate, and then lied about what they had done. This founding saga of the relationship between American spies and gangsters set patterns that would be replicated from Laos and Burma to Marseilles and Panama …

"A few weeks before he died [in 1962] Luciano gave an interview to an Associated Press reporter who asked him why he had been released from prison. 'I got my pardon because of the great services I rendered to the United States,' Luciano said …

"From the moment of its inception the CIA has held to the same policies of its progenitors in keeping gangster organizations in business. By 1947 the Agency was backing heroin producers in Marseilles, Burma, Lebanon and western Sicily."

*Whiteout*, p. 134

Those who don't recognize the genocidal implications of the U.S. imperialists flooding the oppressed communities with narcotics should pay close heed to the words of Professor Yusuf Nuruddin, who narrowly survived the heroin epidemic of the 1960s and '70s:

"I estimate that circa 1967–1972 roughly two-thirds of the males between 16 and 35 in my [Bedford-Stuyvesant] neighborhood [in Brooklyn, NY] were [using] heroin. Decades before the so-called 'paranoid' accusations of the CIA involvement in distribution of crack-cocaine in Los Angeles surfaced, many folks in my generation had surmised that local police were involved in heroin distribution … Those who didn't die of overdoses or simple long-term neglect of basic health which characterizes hard core addiction, found themselves victim of shared 'dirty' needles … [T]he AIDS epidemic wiped them out. Between the ages of 35 and 39 they were dropping like flies. Few brothers in my neighborhood from [my] generation reached the age of 40. Ninety percent of the generation was wiped out. It was genocide."

"Brothas Gonna Work it Out!" *Socialism and Democracy*, Vol. 18, No.2, July–Dec. 2004, p. 246–47

Worse still he has witnessed a repeat of history with the crack epidemic, but on a more destructive level due to the role of armed gang warfare, and how this process has served the imperialists.

"Shying away from needles ... the early Hip Hop generation ... turned to smokable crack-cocaine as a drug of 'choice.' I watched the whole cycle of generational genocide re-occur in the mid-to-late '80s and '90s, as the violence of the drug trade escalated to unprecedented levels (heroin junkies were known for theft, but not for violence). This time the powers that be pumped not only drugs into our communities, but drugs and guns. Hold ups for cash, jewelry, and shearling leather coats by crack junkies frequently ended up in violence and death. While the heroin trade had been controlled by middle-aged whites in organized crime cartels like the Mafia (increasingly challenged by rising adult Blacks in cartels such as the Nicky Barnes outfit), the trade in crack-cocaine was controlled by ... rival gangs of young Blacks who regularly engaged in gun battles for control of turf. Held in a grip of rampant drug abuse and narco-terrorism, the inner cities imploded. The anger that had triggered 'social explosions' (inner city insurrections, urban uprisings, civil disturbances, 'riots') in the past had now been channelled by the powers-that-be into 'social implosions'—violent inward collapsings of community life. This was all part and parcel of a socially engineered policy of containment—containment of the revolutionary potential of the Black masses via the transformation of latent guerrilla warriors into thugs and addicts. Who's really in charge?"

Ibid. p. 247

After creating the crack epidemic, the U.S. government declared a "War on Drugs," which was soon merged with a declared "War on Gangs." To win public support for these "wars" the Empire pushed a major media campaign against drugs.

"In early September 1989, a major government-media blitz was launched by the President. That month the [Associated Press] wires carried more stories about drugs than about Latin America, Asia, the Middle East and Africa combined. If you looked at television, every news program had a big section on how drugs were destroying our society, becoming the greatest threat to our existence, etc.

"The effect on public opinion was immediate. When Bush won the 1988 election, people said the budget deficit was the biggest problem facing the country. Only about 3% named drugs. After the media blitz, concern over the budget was way down and drugs had soared to about 40% to 45%, which is highly unusual for an open question (where no specific answers are suggested).

"Now when some client state complains that the U.S. government isn't sending it enough money, they no longer say, 'we need it to stop the Russians'—rather, 'we need it to stop drug trafficking.' Like the Soviet threat, this enemy provides a good excuse for a military presence where there's rebel activity or other unrest.

"So internationally, 'the war on drugs' provides a cover for intervention. Domestically, it has little to do with drugs but a lot to do with distracting the population, increasing repression in the inner cities, and building support for the attack on civil liberties."

Noam Chomsky, *What Uncle Sam Really Wants*
(Berkeley, CA: Odonian Press, 1999), pp. 82–83

Under cover of the War on Drugs, the CIA-generated crack-cocaine epidemic was used to enact the Anti-Drug Abuse Act of 1986, a law targeted selectively, (as "Jolly" West had proposed a decade earlier), at crack-cocaine—the form of cocaine sold cheaply to inner city people of color. This law made mandatory criminal penalties for crack 100 times more severe than penalties for powder cocaine—the drug of choice in white suburbia. Likewise, under cover of the "War on Gangs," the sectarian gang violence over drug turf was used to validate violent occupation of the inner cities by militarized police, the creation of gang databases, and police conducting massive gang sweeps indiscriminately targeting males of color—most having no gang affiliations.

As Christian Parenti described in *The Soft Cage*:

"During the late eighties, before terrorism eclipsed communism as official enemy number one, the media and political class became almost delusionally obsessed with gangs. The moral panic had some basis in truth; after all, deindustrialization, increased economic inequality and the ready money of the new and chaotic crack trade did create an explosion of gang warfare in cities both large and small."

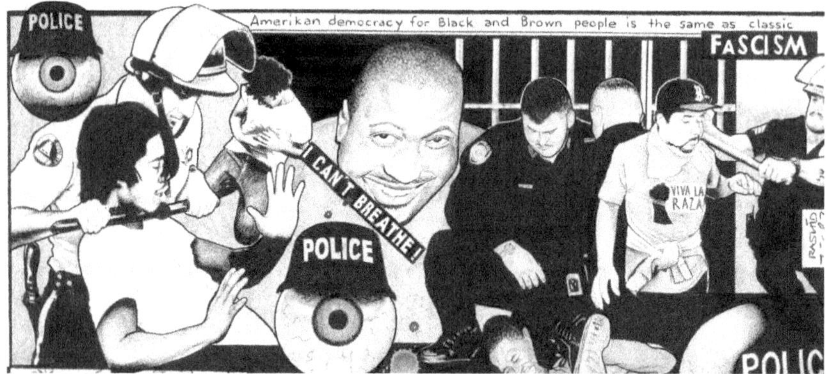

A major byproduct of the "war on gangs" has been the creation of huge computerized gang databases designed to identify and track gang members, suspected gang members and their associates.

The impact of the War on Drugs on the Black communities was to exacerbate crises.

> "It would be difficult to find any documentary evidence that this war on drugs had anything other than a deleterious effect. By 1990 Black youth unemployment in the greater Los Angeles area was 45 percent. Nearly half of all black males under the age of twenty-five had been in the criminal justice system. Life expectancy for blacks was falling for the first time in this [20th] century, and infant mortality in the city was rising. Some 40 percent of black children were born into poverty."
>
> *Whiteout*, p. 78

Not only has the drug war seen the U.S. prison population quadruple since the 1970s but militarized police have become a growing norm. In his *New York Times* article "Crack's Legacy: Soldiers of the Drug War Remain on Duty," Timothy Egan describes the situation:

> "... what started out as a response to the violent front of the war on drugs has evolved, here and in cities across the nation, into a new world of policing.
>
> "Special Weapon and Tactics Squads, once used exclusively for the rare urban terrorist incident or shootout, transformed themselves through the crack years into everyday parts of city life ...
>
> "Encouraged by federal grants, surplus equipment handed out by the military and seizure laws that allow police departments to keep much of what their units take in raids, the Kevlar helmeted brigades have grown dramatically, even in the face of plummeting crime figures.
>
> "'It is the militarization of Mayberry,' said Dr. Peter Kraska, a professor of criminal justice at Eastern Kentucky University, who surveyed police departments nationwide and found that their deployment of paramilitary units had grown tenfold since the early 1980s.
>
> "'This is unprecedented in American policing and you have to ask yourself: What are the unintended consequences?'"

Here are two accounts on how this all plays out at the street level against urban youth of color (for those who don't live in the 'hood and see it everyday):

> "Members of the NYPD's street Crime Unit are known as 'the Commandos of the NYPD.' In existence since 1971, the unit has undergone a 300 percent buildup since 1997. Former NYC Police Commissioner William Bratton encouraged the men to 'become far more aggressive.' Currently made up of roughly 400 mostly white officers, this unit, along with the 7,000 strong Narcotics Unit, represent the front line in Mayor Giuliani's 'Quality of life' crackdown on—and criminalization of—people of color, especially young, poor and homeless people. They wear (and peddle) tee shirts that say 'Certainly There is No Hunting Like the Hunting of Men.' And their slogan is, 'We Own the Night.'"
>
> Frank Morales, "The Militarization of the Police,"
> *Covert Action Quarterly*, Spring–Summer 1999

> "[R]ecently, there have been some very interesting studies of urban police behavior done at George Washington University, by a rather well-known criminologist named William Chambliss. For the last couple of years he's been running projects in cooperation with Washington D.C. police, in which he has law students and sociology students ride with the police in their patrol cars to take transcripts of what happens. I mean, you've got to read this stuff: it is all targeted against the black and Hispanic populations, almost entirely. And they are not treated like a criminal population, because criminals have Constitutional rights—they're treated like populations under military occupation. So the effective laws are, the police go to somebody's house, they smash in the door, they beat the people up, they grab some kid they want, and they throw him in jail. And the police aren't doing it because they're all bad people, you know—that's what they're being told to do."
>
> Noam Chomsky, *Understanding Power:*
> *The Indispensable Chomsky* (NY: New Press, 2002)

Even the ACLU has pointed out the destructive impact of the "Drug War" on Black communities and families and its targeting of Blacks:

> "The collateral consequences of the nation's drug policies, racially targeted prosecutions, mandatory minimums, and crack sentencing disparities have had a devastating effect on African American (sic) men, women, and families. Recent data indicates that African Americans (sic) make up only 15% of the country's drug users, yet they comprise 37% of those arrested for drug violations, 59% of those convicted, and 74% of those sentenced to prison for a drug

offense. As law enforcement focused its efforts on crack offenses, especially those committed by African Americans (sic), a dramatic shift occurred in the overall incarceration trends for African Americans (sic), relative to the rest of the nation, transforming federal prisons into institutions increasingly dedicated to the African American (sic) community. The effects of mandatory minimums not only contribute to these disproportionately high incarceration rates, but also separate fathers from families, separate mothers with sentences for minor possession crimes from their children, leave children behind in the child welfare system, create massive disenfranchisement of those with felony convictions, and prohibit previously incarcerated people from receiving social services such as welfare, food stamps, and access to public housing."

American Civil Liberties Union, "Cracks in the System: Twenty Years of the Unjust Federal Crack Cocaine Law," October 2006

Not only is this war on the oppressed communities seen to be a mass disposal project to sweep our youth into prisons where they cease to be able to reproduce, but also as a move to ultimately dispose of the urban Black communities. For example, residents and representatives from several projects in Watts, and California professors, saw these implications in federal efforts to learn from residents the whereabouts of young Black men, under claims of conducting hypertension research:

"The representatives from Watts saw sinister implications. At best, they believed the hypertension study was a cover story for violence initiative research [like that proposed by 'Jolly' West in the '70s]. At worst, the aim was to make a list of black resisters in preparation for future police or army invasion of the projects, leading to their ultimate destruction. They feared that the iron fences erected around the project would ultimately be used to pen them in rather than protect them.

"Contrary to the public and media images, the project representatives felt grateful for where they are living. As fearful as they were about neighborhood violence, they were more afraid of the outside white community's intentions toward their homes and children. (Similarly, many black parents are more afraid of their children being hurt by the police than by neighborhood youth. Time and again, as I have traveled, mothers and fathers have told me stories about their teenage sons being arbitrarily arrested and brutalized by police officers). The bad publicity about the projects, describing them as nightmarish jungles did not fit with their experience of community and their gratitude for an affordable place to live. The uniformly negative public images of the projects among whites, they feared, are aimed at preparing the city to accept the demise of these communities. They felt sure that many white-owned businesses hunger to demolish the projects to make way for 'progress' through economic encroachment. They also saw hints of genocide through the dismantling of yet another established black community and the possibility of the ultimate extermination of the project population. They uniformly believed that government policies are purposely fostering the lethal environment of drugs, guns and gangs."

Dr. Peter and Ginger Breggin,
*The War Against Children of Color: Psychiatry Targets Inner City Youth*
(ME: Common Courage, 1998)

Many of these concerns have come to pass, as we see massive gentrification taking place in the inner-cities, demolition of projects, and even mass displacement, as occurred in New Orleans in the wake of Hurricane Katrina, with white businesses moving in to "redevelop" Black neighborhoods. And we should be reminded that the Louisiana governor used the patently false claim that "Black gang-bangers" had fired on the U.S. Army Corps of Engineers as a pretext for declaring "War" (martial law) against a starving, dehydrating, drowning, stranded Black population in New Orleans during the Katrina crisis. The power structure uses the "gang" label as justification for any level of violence and abuse against people of color and our communities.

"So take a significant question you never hear asked despite this supposed 'Drug War' which has been going on for years and years: how many bankers and chemical corporation executives are in prison in the United States for drug-related offenses? Well, there was recently an O.E.C.D. [Organization for Economic Cooperation and Development] study of the international drug racket, and they estimated that about a half-trillion dollars of drug money gets laundered internationally every year—more than half of it through American banks. I mean, everybody talks about Colombia as the center of drug-money laundering, but they're a small player: they have about $10 billion going through, U.S. banks have about $260 billion. Okay, that's serious crime—it's not like robbing a grocery store. So American bankers are laundering huge amounts of drug money, everybody knows it: how many bankers are in jail? None. But if a Black kid gets caught with a joint, he goes to jail.

"And actually, it would be pretty easy to trace drug-money laundering if you were serious about it—because the Federal Reserve requires that banks give notification of all cash deposits made of over $10,000, which means that if enough effort were put into monitoring them, you could see where all the money's flowing. Well, the Republicans deregulated in the 1980s, so now they don't check. In fact, when George Bush was running the 'Drug War' under Reagan, he actually cancelled the one federal program for this which did exist, a project called 'Operation Greenback.' It was a pretty tiny thing anyway, and the whole Reagan/Bush program was basically designed to let this thing go on—but as Reagan's 'Drug Czar,' Bush nevertheless cancelled it.

"Or why not ask another question—how many U.S. chemical corporation executives are in jail? Well, in the 1980s, the CIA was asked to do a study on chemical exports to Latin America, and what they estimated was that more than 90 percent of them are not being used for industrial production at all—and if you look at the kinds of chemical they are, it's obvious that what they're being used for is drug production. Okay, how many chemical corporation executives are in jail in the United States? Again, none—because social policy is not directed against the rich, it's directed against the poor."

*Understanding Power*, p. 372

Chomsky then described the Drug War for exactly what it is—a race/class war against people of color in Amerika and the poor:

"[I]f you just look at the composition of the prison population, you'll find that the crime control policy that's been developed is very finely honed to target select populations. So for example, what's called the 'War on Drugs,' which has very little to do with stopping the flow of drugs, has a lot to do with controlling the inner-city populations, and poor people in general. In fact, by now over half the prisoners in federal prisons are there on drug charges—and it's largely for possession offenses, meaning victimless crimes, about a third just for marijuana. Moreover, the 'Drug War' specifically has been targeted on the black and Hispanic populations—that's one of its most striking features, so for instance, the drug of choice in the ghetto happens to be crack cocaine, and you get huge mandatory sentences for it: the drug of choice in the white suburbs, like where I live, happens to be powder cocaine, and you don't get anywhere near the same penalties for it. In fact, the sentence ratio for those drugs in federal court is 100 to 1 ..."

Ibid., p. 371

So whether most "gang-bangers" want to face it or not, you're being used like those before you, by the very forces that are oppressing us all (fascist U.S. imperialism) to destroy yourselves, your "homies," your communities, killing and injuring each other and poor people in general, only to be killed, injured or imprisoned in turn—a losing cycle for all except the powers that be who're profiting off your actions and misery and keeping your focus on other victims. Consequently, you give the imperialists the pretext to justify waging open war against you, your "homies," and us all. Attack the head, divide the body, fight and destroy the divided body: An imperialist recipe for genocide.

### Reverse Their Game

The Establishment recognizes the potential of the street formations to become revolutionary organizations. This is the main reason they are a major focus of official attack and disruption, and their potentially revolutionary leaders systematically purged. Remember it was Tookie's paying tribute to Black revolutionaries that sealed his fate. As the FBI stated in a memo dated March 9, 1968: "The Negro youths and moderates must be made to understand that *if* they succumb to revolutionary teaching, they will be dead revolutionaries."

Well, they're killing us anyway, purging and destroying our genuine leaders, dividing us against each other, manipulating us to kill each other, and warehousing us in concentration camps. So what we got to lose? Nothing but our chains! But, like the slaves on the old plantations, that *ain't* gonna happen by set tripping and bangin' against other slaves.

We need to pay heed to Sun Tzu and throw his book of war right back at them. Build alliances and defeat their strategy and plans. Their plan has been to destroy our leaders, to divide the people and the street *organizations*, to infest our *communities* with crime and drugs—let's unite: their plan has been to attack our divided numbers—let's *organize* for collective *community* defense!

### Toward A Clenched Fist Alliance

Looking to history and the future, the street formations can and should formally unite in a common revolutionary alliance: A Clenched Fist and Red Front Alliance. The various formations' colors and flags wouldn't change, but as Clenched Fist and Red Front allies, they'd have the opportunity to explain and distinguish their changes in *orientation*, to present a revolutionary option for other sets and gangs to follow their example and lead.

This is the only eventuality that could free all our oppressed peoples, communities and nationals from oppression and suffering. Each formation must realize that divided, their potential for power is sorely limited, and as such they will be continually played *against* each other with violence. And none have a monopoly on violence. When one formation or set attacks another, they in turn invite violent retaliation against themselves. Kill a rival and in turn they kill one of your own. The cycle repeats endlessly, the pigs are entertained by the result and our real need and struggle for liberation from imperialist oppression is neglected.

Before their leaders were picked off (killed or imprisoned), the Vice Lords became revolutionary. They styled themselves after the BPP, wore brown berets, etc. The Young Lords (NYC, Chicago, Philly) evolved into the Young Lords Party and became full allies of the BPP. They wore purple berets and later morphed into the Puerto Rican Revolutionary Workers Organization. In 1968 the Blackstone Rangers were paid to attack the anti-war demonstrations at the Democratic National Convention, but instead joined with revolutionary demonstrators in fighting the pigs, who attacked the demonstration.

Large contingents of the Almighty Latin Kings y Queens Nation turned out at demonstrations in NYC, including against the bombing of Iraq. In the 1940s the ALKQN began as a group that assisted Puerto Ricans immigrating into the U.S. and Chicago, and soon spread to the Mexican barrios providing the same support services.

In 1992, following the LA uprising, Bloods and Crips leaders in LA worked out a truce that included an economic plan for improving the communities. The pact lasted two years during which gang related killings declined immensely. The Establishment targeted the leaders and ultimately sabotaged the alliance.

The Gangster Disciples was founded in the early 1980s with a program of community support in Chicago influenced by the past example of the BPP.

Most all the prominent U.S. street formations began or at some point aspired to serve as assets to their communities. All were derailed by pig incitement and instigation and media glamorization of violent "gangsterism" into fighting other formations. All were driven off the revolutionary path and into illegitimate capitalism (criminal activities) to survive, many after witnessing the destruction of the BPP by the U.S. government. The hatred and anger over lost lives and injuries are focused on the wrong "enemies." We are all victims of the same oppressive system—victims played against victims.

As pointed out, the violence of the youth street formations is what the imperialist system creates and then uses to justify its own counter violence against them and us all. A major tactic used to destroy the BPP was the U.S. government's creating a violent image of the party which it used in turn to isolate and violently attack it.

> "[R]ecently a reporter's Freedom of Information Act investigation in [the FBI's] COINTELPRO files found that the American government had done everything possible to infiltrate the Black Panthers and other lesser-known activist groups, then had its 'agents' lead the groups into violent gestures that would divide them, undermine their credibility and bring down the full weight of the state on the leader's heads. The lethal effects of ultra-left actions by misled people's movements have proved disastrous over and over again."
>
> William Hinton, *Through a Glass Darkly: U.S. Views of the Chinese Revolution* (NY: Monthly Review, 2006)

The crimes of our oppressed class pale by comparison to those of the oppressor ruling class. Indeed our "crimes" are a direct product of the conditions of poverty and exploitation imposed upon us by those in control—and as has been demonstrated throughout this paper many of our crimes are the result of the direct manipulations and entrapments of the U.S. government itself. It is against these forces and system that we must struggle, and win the criminalized poor elements over to serving the people as revolutionaries.

The Clenched Fist Alliance would lead and organize our urban youth whose job would be to defend the communities and back up striking workers or rent strikers, discourage drug dealing and street crime. It would promote and enforce a gang truce and channel youth's energies into productive activities and community service programs, lead in conducting political education and train in the methods of community defense, martial arts and urban combat.

### A Concluding Statement

As a young brotha on the inside of a street formation pointed out to me in a recent discussion between us about this Self-Inflicted Genocide:

> "Killing ourselves is exactly what the poor Blacks, Brown, and even whites are doing. I believe the most incriminating evidence against the known ruling class and government promoters and instigators of this self-inflicted genocide is that everything in this society glamorizes such behavior. Especially the mainstream media that is owned, controlled, and regulated not by poor people but by the

ruling class and government. But any movie, rap video, newspaper, school of thought, etc. which opposes this rotten system is anti-self hatred, promotes community independence and even hints of being politically conscious and pro-revolutionary is immediately criticized, neutralized, and its orchestrators destroyed. There is no mainstream conscious rap, all conscious musicians are forced to operate 'underground' unless they camouflage and water their message down to the point of swimming in contradictions. But the rappers who talk about selling drugs, bangin' and killing and other self-destructive, self-hating and frivolous shit are promoted far and wide by mainstream producers and record labels. It's the system that's teaching us, promoting and glamorizing this shit day in and day out! I'm in total agreement with you—we're being played right into the graveyard and prisons, while the real enemy (the real gangsters) are making bank off our suffering, doing shit to us that we'd never tolerate from each other (Who killed Tookie? Who runs our families out of the 'hoods at will? Who kidnaps us and throws us in jail at will? Who has us fighting over a slice of bread—while they own the whole wheat field?), and keeping our focus off of him. Yeah, our priorities are backwards … just like the broken slaves back in the day!"

Looking back to the near total extermination of the Native Americans and then considering the predicament of people of color and the poor in Amerika today, we see the undeniable truth of the old cliché that "those who don't learn from history are doomed to repeat it." But we can break the cycle of slavery and genocide and our chains, by uniting in revolutionary struggle. Otherwise we only play into the plans of this imperialist system and our own Self-Inflicted Genocide.

The key to victory as Sun Tzu pointed out is good planners (correct leaderships), strong alliances that can't be broken or weakened by enemy schemes, and highly skilled defense forces.

If we must rep anything let it be the united struggle for liberation from the chains of imperialism, and not for empty claims to turf owned by the imperialists—turf we cannot even defend from pig attacks, and that we are readily swept off of into prisons or barred from or run off of when they desire to seize entire neighborhoods for capitalist "redevelopment" plans. If we must die, let it be in struggle for freedom and not as pawns manipulated into fighting other slaves.

*Dare to Struggle, Dare to Win!*
*All Power to the People!*

# 6. WHAT IS A "COMRADE" AND WHY WE USE THE TERM 2012

The concept of "Comrade" has a special meaning and significance in revolutionary struggle. We have often been asked to explain our use of this term, especially by our peers who are new to the struggle, instead of more familiar terms like "brother," "homie," "cousin," "dog," nigga," etc.

Foremost, is that we aspire to build a society based upon equality and a culture of revolutionary transformation, so we need to purge ourselves of the tendency to use terms of address that connote cliques and exclusive relationships. A comrade can be a man or a womyn of any color or ethnicity, but definitely a fellow fighter in the struggle against all oppression.

Terms like "mister" or "youngster" imply a difference of social status, entitlement to greater or lesser respect and built-in concepts of superiority or inferiority. Terms like "bitch," "dog," nigga," "ho," etc., are degrading and disrespectful—even when used affectionately—as some do to dull the edge of their general usage in a world that disrespects us.

"Comrade," however, connotes equality and respect. It implies "I've got your back," and "we are one." Comrades stand united unconditionally, and if need be, to the death. It implies a relationship that is inclusive, not exclusive, and not based on any triviality but revolutionary class solidarity. It represents the socialist future we seek to represent in the struggles of today, and the eventual triumph of classless communist society.

Most forms of address used by New Afrikans carry subtle implications of differing status and worth, or were originally meant to insult and dehumanize us. Embracing these terms has led to our subconsciously embracing these roles, and feeling and believing we are inferior and treating each other as worth less than others. So it is definitely important that we remind ourselves constantly that we are equal to and as good as anyone else and address each other accordingly. As Malcolm X put it in an interview with the *Village Voice* in 1965:

"The greatest mistake of the movement has been trying to organize a sleeping people around specific goals. You have to wake the people up first, then you'll get action." "Wake them up to their exploitation?" the interviewer asked.

"No," Malcolm replied, "to their humanity, to their own worth."

Conscious use of the term "Comrade" instead of the many disparaging terms of address popular today, explicitly connects all people up as humans and equals. It reminds us of our interdependence for survival; promotes relations of equality, friendship and camaraderie between all oppressed and exploited people; it expresses the unified outlook of the proletariat; and it will promote a change in people's outlook and thinking. Its use identifies those committed to the revolutionary struggle and represents the future in the struggles of today.

As Amilcar Cabral expressed in "Our People are Our Mountains": "I call you 'comrades' rather than 'brothers and sisters' because if we are brothers and sisters it's not from choice, it's no commitment; but if you are my comrade, I am your comrade too, and that's a commitment and a responsibility. This is the political meaning of 'comrade'."

In the interpyrsonal sense, camaraderie binds people by respect, mutual support and trust, making organizations cohesive and stable. It builds and cements unity in the process of struggle, generating mutual confidence between people, affirming that we can rely upon each other regardless of the dangers that come from standing for the people and social justice for all.

Examples of genuine camaraderie are inspirational to the people and build their willingness to make a commitment to the struggle. The development and maintenance of organizational structure depends on the close and genuine camaraderie of the revolutionaries—what we call Panther Love!

# 7. CAPITALISM + AIDS = GENOCIDE

2006

No people can wage a struggle for self-determination and independence if they are wiped out of existence. The imperialists realize this and so should we. This is the concrete reality that makes survival programs key organizing work for New Afrikan and Afrikan people everywhere. In addressing our survival needs, in Afrika, Amerika and elsewhere, we must have correct leadership and draw upon the broadest international support as well as practice self-reliance.

Our unmet needs growing out of imperialist and neo-colonial domination and oppression are many; lack of adequate basic nutrition and health care, support of prisoners and their families, providing relief to the multitudes of refugees and orphans produced by imperialist-instigated, armed tribal conflicts and people being forced off their ancestral lands for economic reasons in various parts of Afrika, the ravages of West Nile Virus, Malaria and other diseases—but the greatest single crisis facing Afrikan people worldwide is HIV/AIDS.

Many of us prefer to ignore this issue and rely on the governments and the World Health Organization to properly address it. But that's not happening. What is happening is genocide! In 2002, of the 3 million people who lost their lives to AIDS in that year, 2.2 million were Afrikans, and that's not counting the New Afrikans in the Diaspora. In the interest of survival, we had better pay attention to this issue.

Five million people contract AIDS each year. Three million or more die from it each year. Nearly 90% of these are people in the 3rd World. Every day, 1,600 children die from AIDS. Two thirds of those infected with HIV/AIDS live in Afrika, where some six to eight thousand people die from it every day. That's like two 9-11s every day! If this were happening to white people, you would hear about it every day! In some Afrikan countries, like Lesotho, a full one third of the adult population is testing positive for HIV. Between 1992 and 2000, the HIV-positive rate rose from 7 million to 22 million. In 2005, one million Afrikan school children lost their teachers to AIDS. In Sub-Saharan Afrika alone, there are now 12 million AIDS orphans.

The disease is spreading in the New Afrikan Nation within Amerika too. It's now estimated that 1 in 50 Black men in Amerika are AIDS infected, while 50% of all newly detected HIV/AIDS cases are Black wimyn. In 1998, Blacks accounted for 49% of AIDS deaths in the U.S. Although we are but 13% of the U.S. population, we account for 51% of the newly diagnosed HIV cases. Black men are 7 times more likely to contract the HIV virus than white men. And Black wimyn are 20 times more likely to contract it than white wimyn. Clearly this disease that is devastating Afrika is beginning to impact New Afrikans as well. HIV/AIDS statistics for Haiti now mirror those of the most hard-hit areas of Mother Afrika.

According to the United Nations, some 25 million have died so far from AIDS. This number will rise dramatically as those who are infected succumb to this killer disease. An estimated 40 million people are HIV infected worldwide, and only 20% of them are receiving any treatment to slow the infection, while less than 1.3 million people with AIDS are receiving necessary medications. Moreover, testing is limited, and probably 90% who are HIV positive don't know it. No one knows how bad the situation really is.

Because the first AIDS cases detected in Amerika were male homosexuals, the media and religious right quickly hyped it as a "gay disease," and even as "God's punishment." This stigma has left a continuing impression on public opinion in this country that runs contrary to facts. At least 75% of wimyn who are infected contracted the disease through heterosexual sexual intercourse. IV drug use is another cause, but the "moral majority" continue to frustrate free needle exchanges for drug addicts, as if their spreading the virus did not spill over into the general population.

Some will look at these statistics and say, "Good! Let it kill off the nigg*rs, queers and junkies!" There can be no doubt that racism, bigotry and homophobia have retarded social and governmental response to this crisis. But even more significant is the fact that from the monopoly capitalists' perspective there is a surplus of labor that can't be profitably exploited and too many poor people who can't afford to consume the products they're selling. This is genocide—for real—and it is up to us to put a stop to it!

None of the existing policies on HIV/AIDS awareness, prevention and treatment reflect or address the real world needs and crisis of this global epidemic, which for Afrikan and New Afrikan people is becoming a pandemic with genocidal overtones. Activism around this issue must be built beyond the ranks of those who have already fallen victim and are dedicating what remains of their strength to serving the people. These sisters and brothers deserve our respect and support, but a much bigger effort must be mounted and one that is not afraid to point out the political realities from a revolutionary New Afrikan perspective.

The building of the New Afrikan Black Panther Party (NABPP) must take place in the thick of struggle around the most important issues affecting our people. Survival issues are of highest priority. We must survive in order to resist—in order to overcome—and in order to create a brighter future for future generations.

Tens of millions have died already, and many more are dying and will die, and literally billions are in danger. While the big name imperialist foundations and governments drag their feet and procrastinate, the infection is spreading. Action is needed! It is time to build the survival programs our people need with our own hands and resources, mobilizing and unleashing the power of the people to act in their own interest.

A vanguard party and mass organizations are needed to lead and organize the people's struggle. These won't fall from the sky. We have to build them in the course of struggle!

*Dare to Struggle, Dare to Win! All Power to the People!*

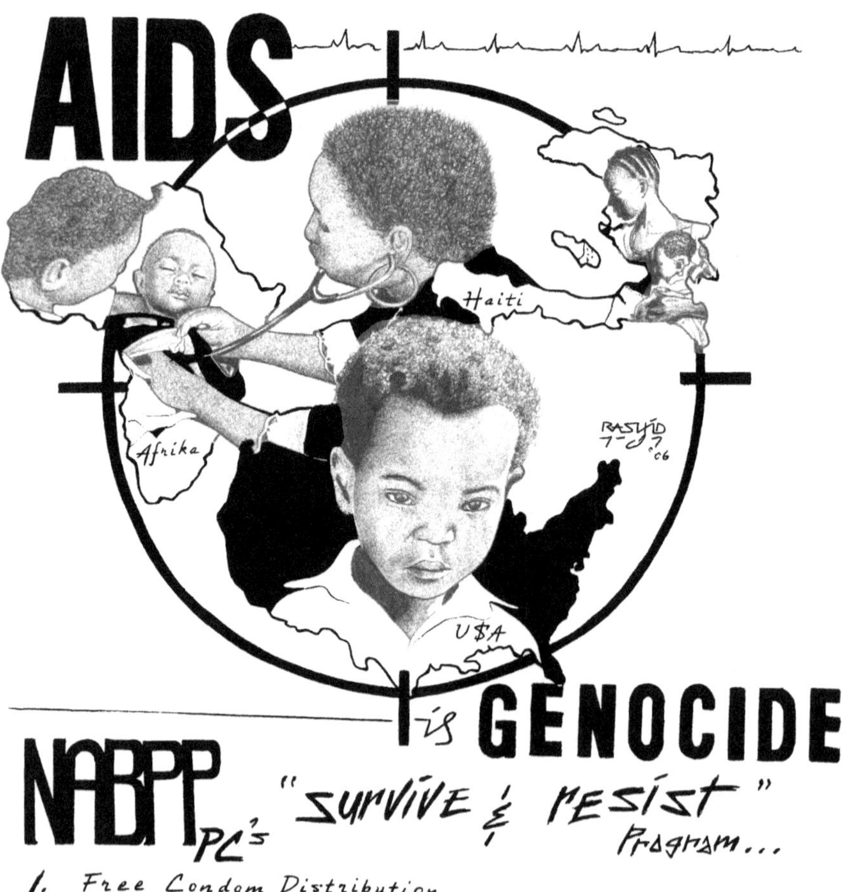

# 8. WIMYN HOLD UP HALF THE SKY! ON THE QUESTIONS OF WIMYN'S OPPRESSION AND REVOLUTIONARY WIMYN'S LIBERATION VERSUS FEMINISM 2008

> "Women comprise one half of the population. The economic status of working women and the fact of their being specially oppressed proves not only that women urgently need revolution, but also that they are a decisive force in the success or failure of the revolution."
>
> Mao Tse-tung, *Peking Review*, 1974

We acknowledge that presently, the New Afrikan Black Panther Party-Prison Chapter (NABPP-PC) lacks a substantial femyl membership. Because of this situation some mistaken views have developed concerning our position on the questions of wimyn's oppression and liberation. That we lack a femyl presence right now *in no way* reflect our views on these *fundamental* questions. Actually the *major* cause of this predicament is the uncommon circumstances under which our Party was founded, namely, by brothas who are isolated away from sistas by their confinement in various U.S. prisons. Another contributing factor is that unfortunately very few prison activists have maintained active ties with wimyn prisoners, with the result that these sistas' ideological and political educations and active involvements in social justice struggle has been minimal. However, we are in the process of taking affirmative measures to remedy these situations. And along with these efforts it is also imperative that we set out our line and position on wimyn's oppression and liberation with special attention given to the plight of New Afrikan wimyn.

We recognize, as one revolutionary New Afrikan writer expressed:

> "We can't generate [mass-based struggle] if we continue to think and act as if all the people are men, and as if all the children are boys.
>
> "We can't build a mass movement if we fail to educate and organize on the basis of the particular needs of women, who 'hold up half the sky.'
>
> "We can't shout 'Black workers take the lead!' while failing to address ourselves to the particular interests of those workers who are women.

"ALL problems facing the nation and ALL of its citizens are interrelated and interdependent, and the policies and programs of the new movement must base themselves on this reality. We must address ALL issues, and then coordinate the many struggles and fronts of war."

But to the question, are we, the NABPP-PC, "feminists," we answer, "No, we are not feminists. We are proponents of Revolutionary Wimyn's Liberation (RWL)." To some this position may sound contradictory and confusing. Some will ask: "What is the difference between feminism and Revolutionary Wimyn's Liberation? Aren't they the same thing?" We answer that there's a big difference between them, and no, they are

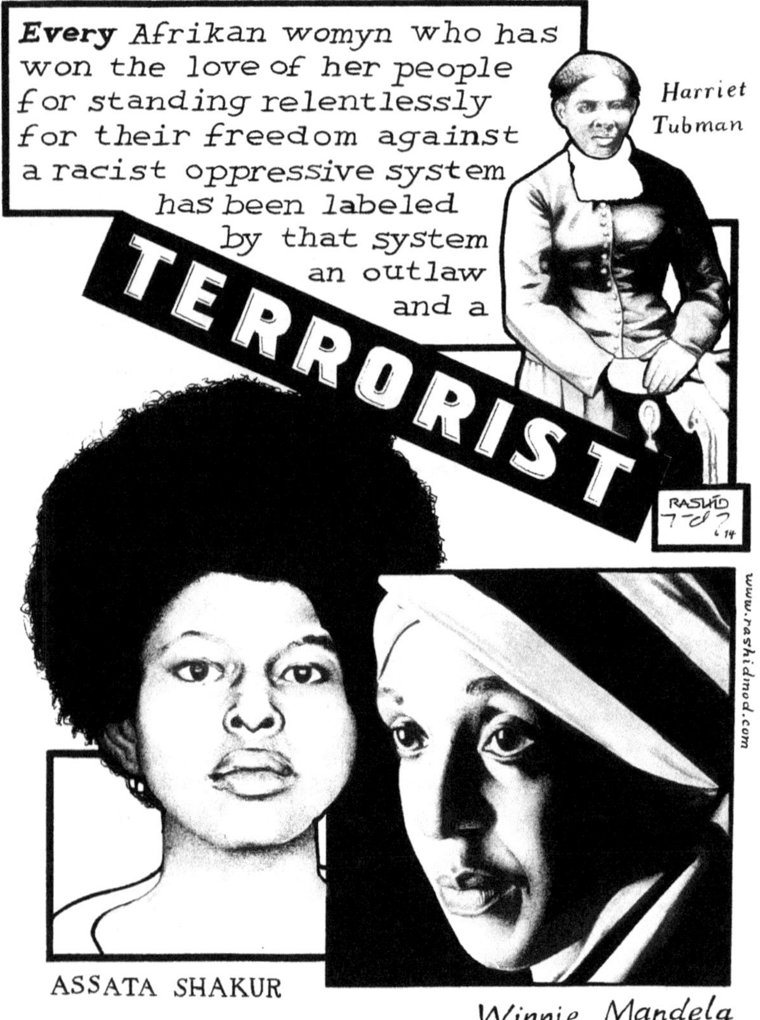

not the same thing. Although both perspectives developed in response to wimyn's oppression in patriarchal class society, they represent two opposite class perspectives on the womyn question: one bourgeois and reactionary (feminism), the other proletarian and revolutionary (RWL).

The oppression of wimyn predates bourgeois capitalist society and goes back to the beginning of class society and patriarchal slavery. To a certain extent, the bourgeoisie needed to accommodate the liberation of wimyn in order to exploit their labor power as proletarians and their brains and organizational abilities as managers, professionals and even as executives. For these reasons capitalist society has granted wimyn certain limited "freedoms" and "advances" from the binds of feudalist and slave-owning societies. But class society will always prevent wimyn from achieving full liberation.

"We understand that wimyn's oppression is tied in with the general bourgeois oppression of the working class, and that genuine and full emancipation of wimyn can only be accomplished with the total destruction of class society. "Genuine equality between the sexes can only be realized in the process of the socialist transformation of society as a whole." (Mao Tse-tung). Bourgeois society cannot eliminate gender oppression, because inherent in its divisive culture is the tendency to divide and play various social sectors against each other and to elevate ranks of essentially equal people above one another to perpetuate its "divide, agitate, miseducate and rule" schemes. Only the struggle of the international working class against capitalist-imperialist domination seeks to fully eliminate the artificial differences and prejudices that sustain bourgeois-dominated class society.

As Lenin noted, proletarian wimyn must firmly lead the struggle for wimyn's liberation and this struggle must be tied in with the broad working-class revolutionary movement. This is because there is an:

> "... unbreakable connection between woman's human and social position and [emphasizing this] will draw a strong, ineradicable line against the bourgeois movement for the 'emancipation of women.' This will also give us a basis for examining the woman question as part of the social, working-class questions and to bind it firmly with the proletarian class struggle and the revolution. The communist women's movement itself must be a mass movement, a part of the general mass movements; and not only of the proletarians, but of all the exploited and oppressed, of all victims of capitalism, or of the dominant class. Therein, too, lies the significance of the women's movement for the class struggle of the proletariat ..."
>
> Lenin, 1920, quoted in *My Recollections of Lenin*, "An Interview on the Woman Question," Clara Zetkin

Our distinction between feminism and RWL is based in our Party's ideology of Historical and Dialectical Materialism (HDM), which rejects uncritical idealism and instead demands that we make concrete analyses of concrete conditions and understand things in their motion and development. "Social Democrat" and "Communist" used to be used as interchangeable terms, but the consolidation of a deviationist Social Democratic tendency required genuine Communists to distinguish themselves from this revisionism. So too must we distinguish ourselves from the feminist movement. There are liberal feminists and radical feminists, but a Communist is a Communist and by definition holds a Marxist view on the womyn question.

## Feminism as a Deviationist Tendency

In analyzing the womyn question using HDM and recognizing that wimyn's oppression is tied in with and generated by class oppression, it becomes clear that feminism embraces bourgeois ideology and is thus a deviationist tendency. Feminism elevates above class and essentializes gender much like cultural nationalists elevate and essentialize race, whereas both gender and racial oppression are the outgrowths of class contradictions and oppression. In this light, we bear in mind that sexism is not merely male chauvinism any more than racism is simply white supremacy.

Indeed mainstream feminism is just as much a blatant manifestation of bourgeois ideology as male chauvinism. And while male chauvinism is "politically incorrect," despite that it is still practiced everywhere in capitalist society, (just like racism), one cannot oppose or criticize feminism without risking being called "sexist." The same with one who opposes reverse racism; if the critic is white s/he'll be labeled a "racist," if a persyn of color, s/he'll be labeled an "integrationist" or "racist collaborator."

The prevailing feminist tendency of "male-bashing" is no more revolutionary and liberationist than Blacks playing the racial blame game. Wimyn's oppression by men is definitely real, as is the racial oppression of people of color. But gender oppression and racial oppression, must be understood not as things unto themselves, but as manifestations of the oppressive and divisive conditions and culture of class society.

Most single issue movements against oppression, like feminism, don't focus on class. They therefore are or become infused with bourgeois ideology and openly embrace such reactionary and equally divisive tendencies as men-bashing and reverse racism. And much of the Left, in adopting revisionist politics, openly embraces and fears to criticize feminism and male-bashing, in fact they tail behind it. However, we in the NABPP-PC oppose these tendencies and do not fear to expose or criticize such deviations, (whatever the consequences, whatever the attacks), being conscious that the most dangerous deviation is always that which is not being struggled against.

As proponents of RWL, the NABPP-PC promotes full gender equality and opposes all forms of discrimination and oppression against wimyn, and we are committed to the struggle for wimyn's equality. But we also understand that gender equality can only be genuinely achieved in the process of building, and as a result of, socialist reconstruction of society. That is, by socializing both productive and reproductive relations and making both these social relations gender neutral. While many past socialist struggles have failed to fully implement socializing not only productive but also reproductive social relations, (child care, household work and unwaged production), and in gender neutral fashions, feminism does not seek or pursue these objectives at all. In reality feminism has served to advance the bourgeois aspirations of petty-bourgeois white wimyn while stifling the genuine liberation struggles and culture of the broad masses of wimyn of the lower classes, and replaced them with the psycho-emotional feel-good sub-culture of men-bashing and a counter-culture of wimyn's separatism and gender antagonism. These tendencies run counter to building gender neutral social relations and achieving gender equality.

By gender neutral reproductive relations we mean both parents being fully involved in the responsibilities of housekeeping, baby care and child rearing and sharing the necessary labor and time investment. As much as possible this should also be facilitated by socialized caregiving, freeing wimyn to play a full and active role politically, socially, culturally and in the struggle for production.

## Applying Dialectical Materialism to the Womyn Question

As Dialectical Materialists, we recognize that every existing thing, including social phenomena, relations and conditions, is in a constant state of motion and change. Nothing is stagnant, nothing remains the same. The cause and source of this continuous motion and change is the presence of contradictory forces within all existing things, phenomena and conditions. These contradictory forces constantly act together and against each other, contending and competing for dominance, exchanging and replacing positions. This "unity of opposites" is universal and absolute; however, it expresses itself differently in various particular phenomena based upon the nature of the contradictions and the conditions under which they operate. What must also be understood is that all contradictions do not take on antagonistic forms, but open antagonisms can and do develop at particular stages and under certain conditions of the struggle of opposites.

On this point Mao gives this illustration:

> "Before it explodes, a bomb is a single entity in which opposites coexist in given conditions. The explosion takes place only when a new condition, ignition, is present. An analogous situation arises in all those natural phenomena which finally assume the form of open conflict to resolve old contradictions and produce new things."

While some controversialists would likely contend otherwise, it is a simple matter to recognize that within the complex reproductive biology of the humyn species, wimyn and men are physiological opposites. This is not to say that either sex is superior or inferior to the other. In fact concepts of superior/inferior play no part since wimyn and men are equal and interdependent opposites. They are essential to each others' very existence. Indeed they are essential to the very existence of humyn beings as a species. The point is simply that wimyn and men, like all existing things, exist as a unity of opposites. They exist in contradiction and struggle as well as unity and accord:

> "Contradiction and struggle are universal and absolute, but the methods of resolving contradictions, that is, the forms of struggle, differ according to the differences in the nature of the contradictions. Some contradictions are characterized by open antagonism, others are not. In accordance with the concrete development of things, some contradictions which were originally non-antagonistic develop into antagonistic ones, while others which were originally antagonistic develop into non-antagonistic ones."
>
> Mao Tse-tung, "On Contradiction," *Selected Works*, Vol. I, p. 311

The social oppression of wimyn is not a condition that has always existed, and it did not just drop from the sky. It is a condition that developed in humyn societies at a definite stage of social-economic development. It therefore has definite historical features and points of origin, and definite prevailing social-economic conditions allow it to continue or support its elimination.

Until certain changes came about in humyn society, wimyn and men originally existed in relative equality. Definite change within society created the antagonistic social relations between the sexes which expressed themselves in the structuring of social relations, institutions, and traditions which oppress wimyn and exalt men. Before classes developed, the contradiction between the sexes was non-antagonistic. Unity of interest prevailed because both genders shared relatively equal roles in both the productive and reproductive life of society, and although productive and reproductive roles were gender-specific, they were also social activities that involved the entire community. Indeed, the root causes of wimyn's oppression are clearly found on investigating the changing gender roles in societies as they evolved from the early egalitarian, ("primitive communal"), structures to the more technologically advanced and stratified stages of class-divided society.

Only by making such a historical materialist examination of social development can the roots of wimyn's oppression be unearthed. And with this knowledge it becomes evident why the liberation of wimyn from oppression can be fully achieved only with socialist reconstruction of humyn society and the ultimate abolition of classes. But we must not only reconstruct humyn productive relations in this socialist struggle. We must also reconstruct our reproductive relations and eliminate gender-specific roles in these relations. Unlike the conditions of "primitive communalism," modern post-industrial society allows virtually every job to be performed equally well by men or wimyn. Proletarian is a gender neutral term describing a class of equals, and this equality must extend to the rearing of the next generation.

Wimyn's oppression is rooted in class oppression and developed roughly along these lines; classes (rich/poor, rulers/ruled, etc.) developed as a result of social production, means of production and social wealth becoming concentrated more and more into private hands; with the development of pastoral (animal raising) societies, slavery and private property, men came to increasingly dominate and control productive relations, the means of production and social wealth; reproductive relations in society became less and less a public, community-oriented and gender neutral activity, but become more and more confined to individual wimyn whose roles and lives became increasingly confined to a "private" sector, (i.e. the domestic home), and like cattle and other productive "possessions," they came to be regarded as the "property" of the male who "ruled" the domestic household. With men dominating control, acquisition and distribution of social wealth and tools of producing social wealth, and wimyn and children therefore compelled to "depend" on men to provide for the basic needs of the "household," gender relations took on the form of domination, (men), and dependence, (wimyn), which has come to be "normalized" and expressed in innumerable oppressive forms against wimyn. These forms of social-economic development are clearly seen through historical materialist analysis of social development.

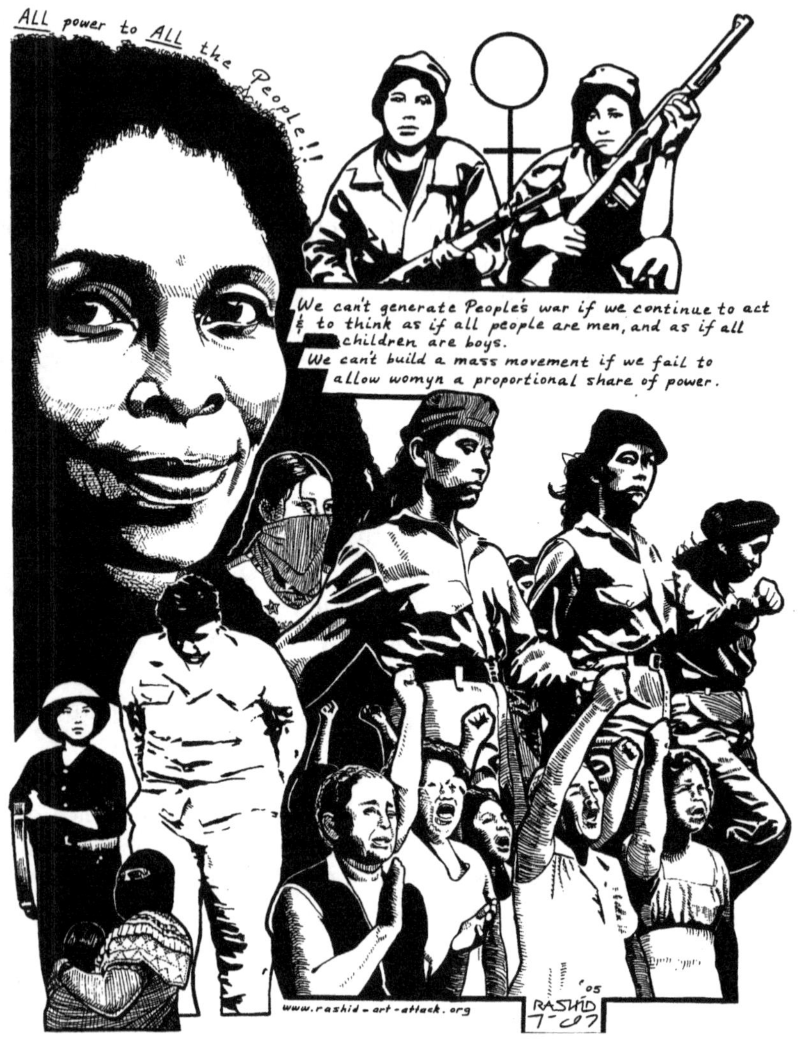


## Historical Materialist Analysis of the Development of Gender Oppression

Outside of Historical Materialist analysis, (namely the analysis of social development by applying Dialectical Materialism); attempts to understand history are confusing at best. Historical Materialism understands that the basic underlying reality of humyn existence is the struggle of humyns to survive and continue their existence from one generation to the next. History is the process of social development. This process compels people to produce the basic material necessities of life, and indeed to reproduce humyn life, to develop and advance technologies to serve these purposes and pass on survival and social skills to their offspring.

These are the economic and reproductive conditions of humyn society. And like all social conditions, the source of wimyn's oppression is rooted in economic conditions, (namely how people act on nature and with or against each other to survive), past and present. A society's culture, political and spiritual institutions and traditions, forms of play, etc. form its superstructure and merely reflect the nature of its members' economic relations, which form its basic infrastructure (foundation).

With men having come to dominate the economic life of society, they thus came to control the society's political power, armed force, culture, ideology and religious institutions. This domination of the political economy in class societies by wealthy males was duplicated at all levels of society high and low. In fact the tiny male-dominated ruling classes have always been able to exert greater controls over class-divided societies by perpetuating and preserving cultures and traditions that gave men a preferential status of social superiority and domination over wimyn. Therefore, if the poor and working-class men couldn't share in ruling over society, they could at least rule over their own wimyn and domestic life. In fact, domination over wimyn became expressed as the social "duty" of men to "protect" wimyn and came to essentially define "manhood." And when societies clashed, the rallying cry of the men was that of protecting their wimyn and children, who were deemed and socialized to be helpless, passive weaklings.

But let's examine how these notions and developments came to be. In the older social systems beginning in Afrika, which anthropologists call "hunter-gather" societies, there was equal participation of both sexes in acquiring and providing for the basic needs of their societies' members; Wimyn foraged, men hunted. In fact, as foragers who harvested wild fruits, vegetables, nuts, berries, etc. from the land and forests, wimyn were these societies' principal producers. These foods formed the staple of the societies' nourishment.

But in the oldest societies also beginning in Afrika, which were based completely on gathering, there was no particular bond between males and femyls at all, only a taboo against incest. These societies were organized into clans where wimyn and children remained in groups that consisted of the mother's blood relatives. In some cases, all the males of one clan were "married" to all the femyls of another clan and vice versa. Men had no obligation towards their offspring at all. The children belonged to the clan of their mother. In these small roaming societies, gathering of plant life was the staple food, supplemented by the occasional scavenging of animal carcasses—or what was left of them—for protein to augment a principally carbohydrate diet. It was the competition with animal scavengers that prompted the development of weapons (sharpened sticks and throwing rocks).

Being unencumbered by pregnancy, nursing and attending to young children, males could roam farther in search of food and were thus more likely to find meat, and with their upper body strength were more able to fight for it. This practice led to hunting and further development of weaponry and the evolution of "hunter-gatherer" societies. Although humyns have no fangs or claws, they do have forward-looking eyes like a predator as opposed to sideways-looking eyes like a game animal. "Sharpened sticks and stones" became our "fangs and claws." As hunting is not a reliable food source, (particularly in its most primitive state), the femyls supported the males with the fruits of their gathering to get them to specialize in hunting. This established the basis for pair-bonding. Wimyn wanted meat and were willing to bond with a man to get it. The man also provided a degree of protection, (when he was around). But wimyn were in the central position as primary providers and society was matrilocal as she was living with her clan. Within the clan children were raised in common. Because of the nature of these productive and reproductive relations and overall gender equality, there existed no concepts of dominant and subordinate sexes.

The bonding between mothers and their offspring determined the reckoning of kinship relations through the mother's line. As wimyn enjoyed sexual freedom, one could only be certain of who one's mother was. Kinship-based society thus developed around a matrilineal clan structure. These relationships could be biological or adoptive. In either case, the taboo on incest extended to all members of one's clan, and thus a few or several clans allied to form a band or village. As children belonged to their mother's clan, the Clan Mother had overall responsibility for their welfare, and maternal uncles played a significant role in their upbringing.

A handful of these societies exist today in Afrika, South Amerika and a few Pacific Islands, although most have been affected by contact with "modern" societies. But recorded accounts of such societies, even those that existed in this region of the world and were transitioning to more "settled" stages, (such as the Arawak Indians of Hispanola and Cuba), give testament to the gender relations of the now nearly extinct Indians of Cuba as found by the Spanish who destroyed them:

> "Marriage laws are non-existent: men and women alike choose their mates and leave them as they please, without offense, jealousy, or anger. They multiply in great abundance; pregnant women work to the last minute and give birth almost painlessly; up the next day, they bathe in the river and are as clean and healthy as before giving birth. If they tire of their men, they give themselves abortions with herbs that force stillbirths, covering their shameful parts

> with leaves or cotton cloth: although on the whole, Indian men and women look upon total nakedness with as much casualness as we look upon a man's head or at his hands."
>
> Bartolome de las Casas, *History of the Indies*, (NY: Harper & Row, 1971)

As the tools and technologies of these "primitive" societies developed, people no longer had to exclusively forage and hunt for foods, but learned how to grow their own crops. Therefore, societies become relatively stationary as villages. Meat was still acquired by hunting and fish by fishing, and these were male responsibilities. In these "transitional communal" societies the people still cooperated in their relations of producing and providing for the society's basic needs, and their spiritual and cultural relationships reflected this. All labor was based upon "natural" division between both sexes, adult and child. Thus all members of the society shared equal rights and duties within the society. Children were often raised in common by men and wimyn, hence the Afrikan proverb "It takes a village to raise a child." The entire village took equal care and responsibility for the upbringing of the children. Therefore, there was no artificial division between anything called public life and domestic life. Productive and reproductive life were genuinely communal. These social systems were based on extended kinship, (which saw the entire community as "family"), because everyone recognized everyone else as necessary and equal contributors to the survival of the entire community and each of its members. In that all adults performed the productive labor needed to feed and sustain the society and collectively "owned" the wealth that their collective labor produced, all adults, (wimyn and men), equally participated in decision making matters that affected the community.

These societies were based upon humyn production of primitive agriculture without the use of domesticated animals for fertilizer and cultivation, but many advanced into use of tamed animals, upon development of metal tools and other technologies and handicrafts. Some, like the Bantu speaking tribes of Afrika, pushed out from forest lands into grasslands seeking greener pastures for their growing herds. These pastoral tribes were centered around a headman who owned the cattle. Like the head bull, he took many wives and concubines, as many sons served to tend and defend his herd.

With the development of pastoral societies, animals were tamed and bred by men; (men took over tending animals from their prior role as the societies' principal hunters), and in turn were used to fertilize and help cultivate the crops. The role of men came to dominate this aspect of the society's economic life, while land ownership and agricultural labor remained vested in wimyn. The domesticated animals became like tools, a "means of production," as well as part of production (sources of milk and meat).

The development of cattle and settled agriculture produced larger crops and the attendant need for more laborers to plant, cultivate and harvest crops. Cattle and settled agriculture allowed societies to produce greater surplus product, which in turn was traded between the village societies.

With the development of surplus wealth, the opportunity presented itself for stronger groups to raid and take the herds or harvest of weaker groups including their wimyn, (for reproductive purposes), and in general to make slaves of those captured by warfare or those who fell into debt. The role of war leader became enhanced and dominated over the formerly democratic decision making of the people.

In the agricultural-based societies of Afrika where wimyn were predominant in land ownership and agricultural labor, patriarchy was built on top of the matriarchal system where wimyn still retained a great deal of power, including over the mostly femyl slaves who worked the land under the direction of the tribes' free wimyn. The Patriarch (chief) was basically a warlord whose power base was command of the warriors. He had wives and concubines but power in the villages of his domain rested in the matrons whom he was obliged to supply with slaves. It was thus an economic impetus that led to the development of slave-owning societies and pushed men into roles where their power was concentrated in the arena of exercising physical force.

A similar set-up can be observed amongst the Iroquois Indians of North Amerika, where the clan mothers can make or break chiefs and have veto power over the village and tribal councils. One of the reasons the Iroquois were always at war is because the wimyn could demand replacements for lost loved ones or slaves or torture victims to ease their grief—the war chiefs were compelled to honor these demands. Concrete class divisions had not as yet taken place but we can see where it was headed.

Trade and barter of surplus production was enhanced by uses of developed technologies—irrigation, the plow, diverse forms of specialized labor, etc.—which ended in productive work being performed not merely to meet the needs of the society's own population, but for purposes of exchange. This trend of production for exchange enhanced the practice of greater concentrations of social wealth into the hands of individual headmen and led to the patriarchal domination of society.

The great civilizations of antiquity, from Egypt to Rome, were based upon slavery. At the top of society was a land-owning aristocracy and at the bottom masses of slaves. In between was a middle strata, that was free, but subservient to the Aristos. In these pre-Christian civilizations, sexuality was more open, and marriage was primarily for establishing heirs.

Feminism confuses the basic reality of class society, which is that it was built upon the foundation of class exploitation not gender oppression. The switch from matrilineal to patrilineal society, (the overthrow of "mother right"), had principally to do with inheritance of property and position. To make this work, wimyn's sexual freedom had to be repressed. To determine who would inherit the patriarch's wealth and position his eldest son needed to be apparent along with a line of succession of heirs. Ultimately power rested upon might. Rulers had to fear being deposed by their sons or younger brothers, but if there was no clear heir apparent, a potentially devastating struggle for succession could ensue in which neighbors were tempted to intervene.

Feudalism arose to overthrow the slave-owning political-economies with monogamous feudal marriage instituted to compel wimyn to be married off to the male and forced to live with the family of the male. It differed essentially in that the peasants belonged to the land and the land to the monarch. This system of monarchy was devised to preserve the monarch's power of control and inheritance of control over land and surplus social wealth, and religious doctrines assured this privilege by declaring his bloodline to have been ordained by God. This claim gave the monarch and his "royal" bloodline a claimed "divine right" to dominate society and social wealth. Feudal marriage preserved the inheritance of wealth and power within the noble patriarch's bloodline and further fragmented the pre-feudal remnants of the clan system and communal ownership of property. Agricultural land which was the private property of kings was farmed out to feudal overlords and nobles, who paid taxes from crops produced by peasants, who were compelled to turn over their surplus produce as taxes or "land rent" to the nobility. Feudal society was organized into estates where the monarch's power was preserved by specialized armies of paid mercenaries and the knights and retainers of landed lesser nobles, who owed allegiance to the king.

Royal and noble marriages were arranged to cement alliances between houses. Wimyn had the duty of producing male heirs for their husbands. Expensive dowries were paid by the bride's family to lure prospective husbands. Under feudalism the sense of community and kinship remained strong amongst the peasants, only the role of the male came to dominate the household, while the role of the "wife" was one of subservience to the husband's family and the lord. The noble lord had the right to take sexual liberties.

With the development of classes under feudalism the oppression of wimyn became absolute. Whereas under systems of primitive society wimyn freely chose their mates, under patriarchy and feudalism femyls were married off by force to males whose families "chose" them and in effect became lifelong domestic house slaves to the husband and his family. The wife was expected to produce male children to inherit the family wealth and household power. Femyl children were looked down on, and groomed to be good servants and attractive to males with the hopes of bringing her family a good marriage or concubinage to a wealthy feudal lord.

Further technological advances gave birth to capitalism which overthrew the old feudal political-economies. Under capitalism proletarians are compelled to sell their labor power in manufacturing and service industries to the factory, land and corporation-owning bourgeois class. In the capitalist political economy, marriage serves specific interests of the particular classes—the bourgeois marriage has as its purpose maintaining class division and domination, and cementing family alliances. As with previous class systems, romantic notions of love can be entertained but are not confined by the bonds of matrimony. Essentially there was little change from feudalism.

Petty bourgeois marriage is just a scaled down version of the same, but proletarian marriage took on more of the characteristics of primitive communal pair bonding—as it is often not formalized and in any case either party can break it off at will. Love and marriage are more connected.

Under the capitalist system organized religion has sought to preserve and enforce monogamy and restrict freedom of divorce and choice in childbirth, however, as men and wimyn achieve equality in pay, (or come close to it), there is a natural tendency towards equality in status, decision-making power, and right of divorce. Organized religion, which reflects feudal and patriarchal ideology, has resisted these trends, but the separation of church and state, (which were united under feudalism), has established both civil marriage, civil divorce, and legalized abortion. Many couples simply apply the principles of pair-bonding by living together without either a church or civil marriage.

The bourgeoisie still try to use marriage as a means of preserving their class status, inheritance of wealth and building alliances between families of their class, as the nobility did, but the pull of spontaneity is towards the proletariat's tendency towards freedom of choice.

Part of the feminist reaction is that this freedom often leaves wimyn in the position of being single parents. While New Afrikan and other proletarian wimyn often seek to remedy this situation by persuading men to be more family-oriented and to bond with their children and themselves, the feminist response is to be anti-men and anti-family. In the past pair-bonding was functional because the mother's clan provided a primary support system for mothers and children, which the mother's male relatives contributed to.

In countries like Sweden wimyn are heard to say that they are free to choose and leave men because they are not compelled to try to trap them into marriage. If Swedish wimyn want to have a child the government supplies them all needed support. This is not the case with the conservative Christian-run government in the U.S. If a womyn can't afford daycare or a maid and a nanny, it's pretty tough to be a single parent.

Concentration of wealth and power increased along with the enhancement of productive technologies as class societies advanced from slave-owning to feudal, to capitalism and its highest stage, capitalist-imperialism, (monopoly capitalism). In each of these stages of political-economic development, men dominated the economic infrastructure and thus also the political, military, cultural, ideological, and religious superstructure of the state.

In the pre-state communal societies, warriors were made up of the basic members of the society, essentially the hunters. However, with the development of classes, those who privatized and hoarded social wealth created a separate caste of specialized armed forces, whose role was and remains that of protecting their property holdings and preserving a social arrangement where their balance of power as non-laboring haves over the laboring have-nots is not upset by either internal or external challengers. This specialized armed military/police structure is the foundation of the state.

So, in essence, wimyn's oppression grew out of the overthrow of the matrilineal kinship system, through the political-economic displacement of wimyn as major producers and societal center in kinship-based society, and the attendant separation of the smaller family unit from the greater community, making the nuclear family, (instead of the community), the source of child-rearing, (which becomes confined to wimyn), and the man, (instead of the collective community), the source of providing for the basic needs of the family. Wimyn became confined to domestic, (reproductive), private life and men came to control political-economic, (productive), "public" life. From this economic arrangement grew various cultural, political and religious forms in various state societies which oppress and subjugate wimyn. And it has been against such forms of economic, political, social, military and cultural repression that wimyn have risen up and rebelled, in class societies and even in pre-state structures that have been influenced by the oppressive traditions, ideologies and religious institutions of class societies.

It must be pointed out also that the Western Europeans and many of the Afrikans who fell victim to the trans-Atlantic slave trade existed at different stages of economic development. Feudalist class society had taken deep root in West Europe, particularly within those states which were actively involved in the slave trade, whereas the Afrikan victims of the slave trade came from societies where clan relations or remnants of them were still strong. Unlike the West European wimyn, (who were constrained and subjugated by feudalist Anglo-Christian culture), Afrikan wimyn still played a major role in the public life of many of their tribal societies.

During chattel slavery in the Amerikas, Afrikan wimyn were compelled to labor just as hard and resolutely and were brutalized just as harshly as their men (indeed more so in the form of routine rapes by white "owners" and overseers), and white wimyn, although oppressed by their males, shared in the domination over and oppression of the Black slaves—especially those slaves (principally femyls and children) who labored inside the "big houses" of the plantation estates. These differing conditions and extremes of oppression made the aspirations of the struggles of New Afrikan versus white wimyn very different in many ways. Their views of wimyn's liberation were therefore often perceived, expressed, and pursued quite differently.

Professor and historian Howard Zinn offers an accurate summary of the different characters of economic relations and treatment of wimyn between the West European societies and the communal Native American and Afrikan societies which they overran:

> "Societies based on private property and competition, in which monogamous families became practical units for work and socialization, found it especially useful to establish [a] special status of women, something akin to a house slave in the matter of intimacy and oppression, and yet requiring, because of that intimacy, a long-term connection with children, a special patronization, which on occasion, especially in the face of a show of strength, could slip over into treatment as an equal. An oppression so private would turn out hard to uproot.
>
> "Earlier societies—in America and elsewhere—in which property was held in common and families were extensive and complicated, with aunts and uncles and grandmothers and grandfathers all living together, seemed to treat women more as equals than did the white societies that later overran them, bringing 'civilization' and 'private property'."
>
> *A People's History of the United States*
> (NY: Harper Collins, 1999)

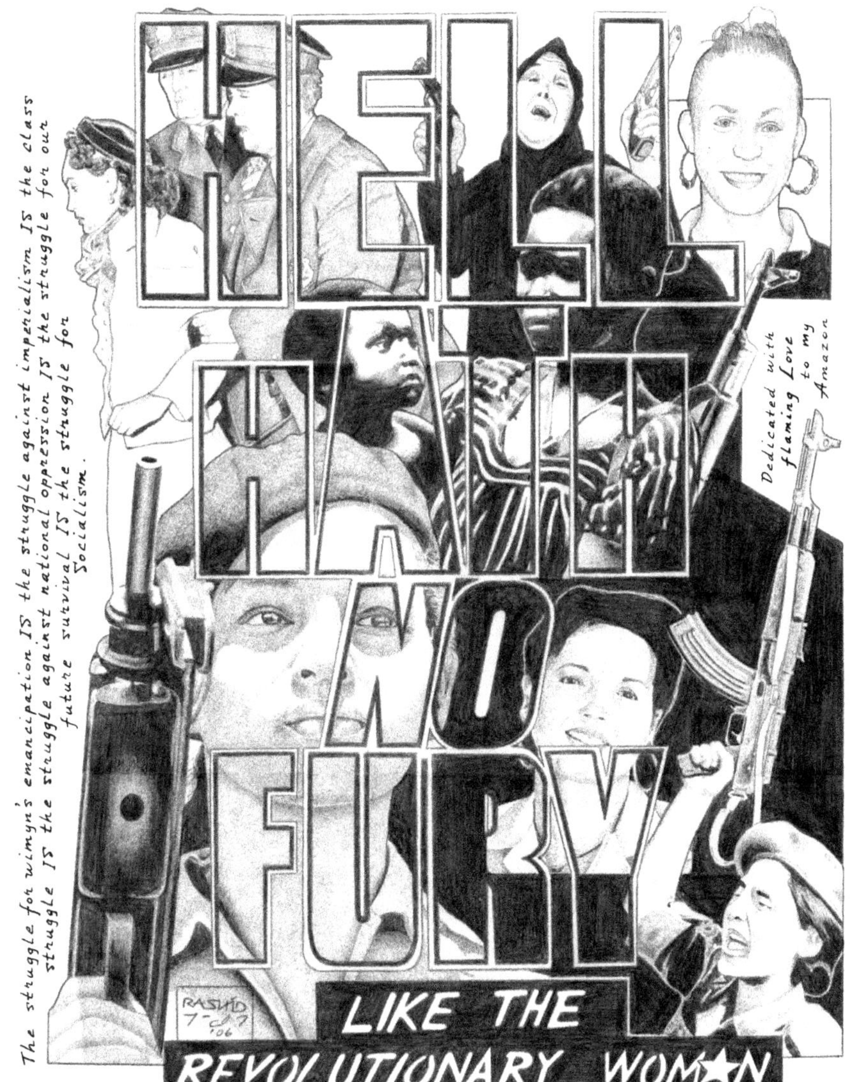
HELL HATH NO FURY
LIKE THE
REVOLUTIONARY WOMAN
The struggle for wimyn's emancipation IS the struggle against imperialism IS the class struggle IS the struggle against national oppression IS the struggle for our future survival IS the struggle for Socialism.
Dedicated with flaming Love to my Amazon

## Differing Gender Oppression of New Afrikan versus White Wimyn

The oppression of New Afrikan versus white wimyn in Amerika assumed different forms based upon the roles assigned to or demanded of them in the society's economic and public life. White wimyn, like New Afrikan wimyn, were considered as powerless property objects of the white man, but their terms of servitude were very different.

Through most of early Amerikan history, white wimyn were confined primarily to a status of domestic slaves to their male counterparts. Like Blacks they had no political rights, but in addition they were subjected to various restraints in manners of dress, speech, and conduct in public. As Howard Zinn pointed out, they were a "convenience for men who could use, exploit, and cherish someone who was at the same time servant, sex mate, companion, and bearer-teacher-warden of his children."

As pointed out earlier, under such class-divided patriarchal systems as existed, (and still exists), here in Amerika, "manhood" was/is defined by the passion, zeal, willingness and ability of the male to "protect" his sheltered femyl. "Womanhood" was/is defined by a "ladylike" performance of feeble and helpless dependence on men. These concepts of "manhood" and "womanhood" inherently grew out of the economic-based oppression and exclusion of wimyn, and they were used as formidable and brutal weapons of subjugation against New Afrikans.

Indeed the most brutal and frenzied white violence against Blacks was often incited by typically false accusations of Black males making sexual advances toward or attacks on white wimyn. Throughout U.S. history Black struggles for economic and political gains often lost white support under charges by opponents that economic and political equality for Blacks would end with Black men coupling with white wimyn. This was intolerable because the white males deemed the white womyn as exclusively their own property.

For example the wave of southern lynchings of Black men following the abolition of slavery in 1865 through the early 1900s, was repeatedly attributed to Black men raping white wimyn. Ida B. Wells and Frederick Douglass exposed such accusations to be false and the lynchings to have been actually prompted by poor whites who feared and opposed political and economic competition and displacement in the South by Blacks. In 1923 the predominantly Black town of Rosewood, Florida was burned down and depopulated by mobs of whites following the false accusations of Fannie Taylor, a young white womyn, that she'd been sexually assaulted by a Black man. It was later discovered that she'd lied, that her attacker was actually a white Mason who was able to escape scrutiny by relying on the society's code of requiring members to conceal one another's crimes.

On August 28, 1955, 15-year-old Emmett Louis Till was kidnapped, bludgeoned and shot point-blank in the head by two white men for allegedly whistling at a white womyn in a store in Sumner County, Mississippi. Indeed, throughout the South, every opponent of Black equality equated racial equality seekers with Black rapists and efforts to "rape" the rights of southern power holders. FBI Director J. Edgar Hoover wrote to the Selective Services director during World War II that white wimyn were in increased danger by the number of Black men not inducted into the military.

In his book *Mind of the South*, Wilbur J. Cash described the southern white mentality thusly, "... any assertion of any kind on the part of the Negro constituted in a perfectly real manner an attack on the Southern [white] woman." Dixiecrats used rape as a common metaphor to attack all proposals to change southern race relations. Noted segregationist Strom Thurmond wrote that efforts to change race relations in the South were attempts to "rape the rights of the states." As Jaquelyn Dowd Hall aptly summed it up in her *Southern Exposure* article "The Mind That Burns in Each Body": "As absolutely inaccessible sexual property, white women became the most potent symbol of white male supremacy."

Conversely, white men were free to routinely rape Black wimyn. W.E.B. DuBois rebutted repeated Dixiecrat uses of rape as metaphors for challenges to the Southern white racist status quo in stating, "The rape which your gentlemen have done against helpless black women in defiance of your own laws is written on the foreheads of millions of mulattoes and written in ineffaceable blood." In the same light, James Baldwin answered those whites who depicted Blacks' struggles for justice and equality as nothing but Black men aspiring to marry the sisters and daughters of white men with an unrebuttable observation, "You're not worried about me marrying your daughter. You're worried about me marrying your wife's daughter. I've been marrying your daughter since the days of slavery." The system of routine rapes of New Afrikan wimyn by white men served as a gendered form of psychological warfare against Blacks to reinforce the dominant status of the white male, (Black men were not deemed to be "men" at all but "boys" because they had no power to protect "their" wimyn), and to repress the Black womyn whose prominent role in productive work and attendant hardships of slave life conditioned her to be quite strong and independent—immensely so in comparison to the "sheltered" white womyn—and the conditioned equal of any man. Rape of Black wimyn was also practiced as a rite of passage into "manhood" by young white males. The actual practice of routine rapes of Black wimyn by white men is a feature of slavery and U.S. history that mainstream historians and modern criminologists unanimously evade and gloss over. Here's Angela Davis's assessment:

"Black women were equal to their men in the oppression they suffered; they were their men's social equal within the slave community; and they resisted slavery with a passion equal to their men's. This was one of the greatest ironies of the slave system, for in subjecting women to the most ruthless exploitation conceivable, exploitation which knew no sex distinctions, the groundwork was created not only for Black women to assert their equality through their social relations, but also to express it through their acts of resistance. This must have been a terrifying revelation for the slave owners, for it seems that they were trying to break this chain of equality through the especially brutal repression they reserved for the women. Again, it is important to remember that the punishment inflicted on women exceeded in intensity the punishment suffered by their men, for women were not only whipped and mutilated, they were also raped.

"... Rape was a weapon of domination, a weapon of repression, whose covert goal was to extinguish the slave woman's will to resist, and in the process to demoralize their men. These observations on the rape of women during the Vietnam War could also apply to slavery: 'In Vietnam, the U.S. military command made rape "socially acceptable"; in fact, it was unwritten, but clear policy.' When GI's were encouraged to rape Vietnamese women and girls, (and they were sometimes advised to 'search women' with their penises), a weapon of mass political terrorism was forged. Since the Vietnamese women were distinguished by their heroic contributions to their people's liberation struggle, the military retaliation specifically suited for them was rape. While women were hardly immune to the violence inflicted on men, they were especially singled out as victims of terrorism by a sexist military force governed by the principle that war was exclusively a man's affair.

"In the same way that rape was an institutionalized ingredient of the aggression carried out against the Vietnamese people, designed to intimidate and terrorize the women, slave owners encouraged the terroristic use of rape in order to put Black women in their place. If Black women had achieved a sense of their own strength and a strong urge to resist, then violent sexual assaults ... would remind the women of their essential and inalterable femaleness. In the male supremacist vision of the period, this meant passivity, acquiescence, and weakness.

"Virtually all the slave narratives of the nineteenth century contain accounts of slave women's sexual victimization at the hands of masters and overseers ...

"Despite the testimony of slaves about the high incidence of rape and sexual coercion, the issue of sexual abuse has been all but glossed over in the traditional literature on slavery."

Davis went on to add:

"One of racism's salient historical features has always been the assumption that white men—especially those who wield economic power—possess an incontestable right of access to Black women's bodies.

"Slavery relied as much on routine sexual abuse as it relied on the whip and the lash. Excessive sexual urges, whether they existed among individual white men or not, had nothing to do with this virtual institutionalization of rape. Sexual coercion was, rather, an essential dimension of the social relations between slave master and slave. In other words, the right claimed by slave owners and their agents over the bodies of female slaves was a direct expression of their presumed property rights over Black people as a whole. The license to rape emanated from and facilitated the ruthless economic domination that was the gruesome hallmark of slavery.

"The pattern of institutionalized sexual abuse of Black women became so powerful that it managed to survive the abolition of slavery. Group rape, perpetrated by the Ku Klux Klan and other terrorist organizations of the post-Civil War period became an uncamouflaged political weapon in the drive to thwart the movement for Black equality."

*Women, Race and Class* (NY: Vintage Books, 1983)

The role, experience, suffering, resistance and survival of slavery by New Afrikan wimyn alongside their men demonstrated in lived reality that wimyn are the equals of men. It is therefore no wonder that the early feminist movement found and still finds its greatest inspiration in the image of a slave womyn—Sojourner Truth. Unlike the middle class white wimyn who have dominated the feminist movement, Sojourner had not lived a sheltered life, so unlike those wimyn she could rebut as living proof the claims made by white men that womyn is innately weak and inferior to man. This she did in her famous "Ain't I a Woman?" speech delivered at the 1851 Women's Rights Convention in Akron, Ohio.

An emancipated slave, Sojourner walked uninvited into the church where the convention was being held, took a seat on the steps in the corner of the pulpit and listened quietly for several days first to the timid arguments of the white wimyn in favor of equal rights, then to the fiery arguments of white male ministers who argued that men were by right to enjoy superior privileges and rights on account of claimed "superior intellect," because of the "manhood of Christ" and the cardinal "sin of our first mother."

At this Sojourner rose and approached the pulpit to address the crowd that filled the church and stood outside listening at the windows and doors. Members of the white crowd—wimyn and men—protested but were hushed by Frances Gage, the convention's organizer, who announced Sojourner Truth.

Sojourner began "Well children," fixing her intent gaze on the crowd, "where there is so much racket, there must be something out of kilter. I think that between the Negroes of the South and the women of the North all talking about rights, the white men will be in a fix pretty soon. But what's all this talking about?" She continued:

> "That man over there says that women need to be helped into carriages, and lifted over ditches, and to have the best place everywhere. Nobody ever helps me into carriages, or over mud-puddles, or gives me any best place! And ain't I a woman? Look at me! Look at my arm."

And she bared her muscular arm for all to see.

> "I have plowed and planted and gathered into barns and no man could head me! And ain't I a woman? I could work as much and eat as much as a man—when I could get it—and bear the lash just as well! And ain't I a woman? I have borne thirteen children, and seen most all of them sold off to slavery, and when I cried with my mother's grief, none but Jesus heard me! And ain't I a woman?"
>
> "Then they talk about this thing in the head; what's this they call it?"

An audience member whispered "intellect."

> "That's it, honey. What that got to do with women's rights and Negroes' rights? If my cup won't hold but a pint, and yours holds a quart, wouldn't you be mean not to let me have my little half measure full? Then that little man in black there [she said pointing and looking intensely at the man who'd made the argument], he says women can't have as much rights as men 'cause Christ wasn't a woman! Where did your Christ come from? From God and a woman! Man had nothing to do with him. If the first woman God ever made was strong enough to turn the world upside down all alone, these women together ought to be able to turn it back and get it right side up again! And now they asking to do it. The

men better let them. Obliged to you for hearing me, and now old Sojourner ain't got nothing more to say."

With this and to the tune of applause and tears of gratitude on the faces of many of the white wimyn in attendance, Sojourner returned to her seat in the corner. Gage recalled, "She had taken us up in her strong arms and carried us safely over the slough of difficulty turning the whole tide in our favor. I have never in my life seen anything like the magical influence that subdued the mobbish spirit of the day, and turned the sneers and jeers of an excited crowd into notes of respect and admiration. Hundreds rushed up to shake hands with her and congratulate the glorious old mother, and bid her Godspeed on her mission of 'testifying' again concerning the wickedness of this here people."

The hardships of slavery and racism produced of New Afrikan wimyn some of the most outstanding examples that wimyn are not only equals, but in many instances have shown strength and fortitude surpassing that of the typical man. Our ancestor Harriet Tubman was such a womyn, of much smaller stature than Sojourner Truth. Harriet Tubman personally led multitudes of slaves on daring escapes and flights to freedom over miles and miles of woodland, roads, fields, and hills on the Underground Railroad; in her own words she stated "I freed thousands of slaves. I could have freed thousands more if they had known they were slaves."

Even today, Harriet Tubman bears the distinction of being the only womyn in U.S. history to lead Amerikan soldiers in battle, (during the Civil War). What made her exceptional? Nothing except her harsh lived experience in slavery and skills given by her father that enabled her to hunt, forage, and survive off the land. This combined to give her both the fortitude and ability, fueled by outrage and devotion to her oppressed people, to struggle for freedom. How many New Afrikan men today could hold a candle to this sista?

Time and again, hardship and necessity have brought the noble and fierce fighting spirit of wimyn to the surface, demonstrating over and over that wimyn are no less witty, strong, able and passionate than men. Unlike their white counterparts, New Afrikan wimyn have endured brutal oppression not only because of their gender, but because of their race and repressed nationality as well. Her struggle is therefore against three levels of oppression, whereas that of the Amerikan white womyn's is but one or two. However, genuine liberation for either or both of them can only be achieved by the successful overthrow of the monopoly capitalist political economy, and wimyn must march at the head of such a revolutionary struggle under the banner of revolutionary wimyn's liberation.

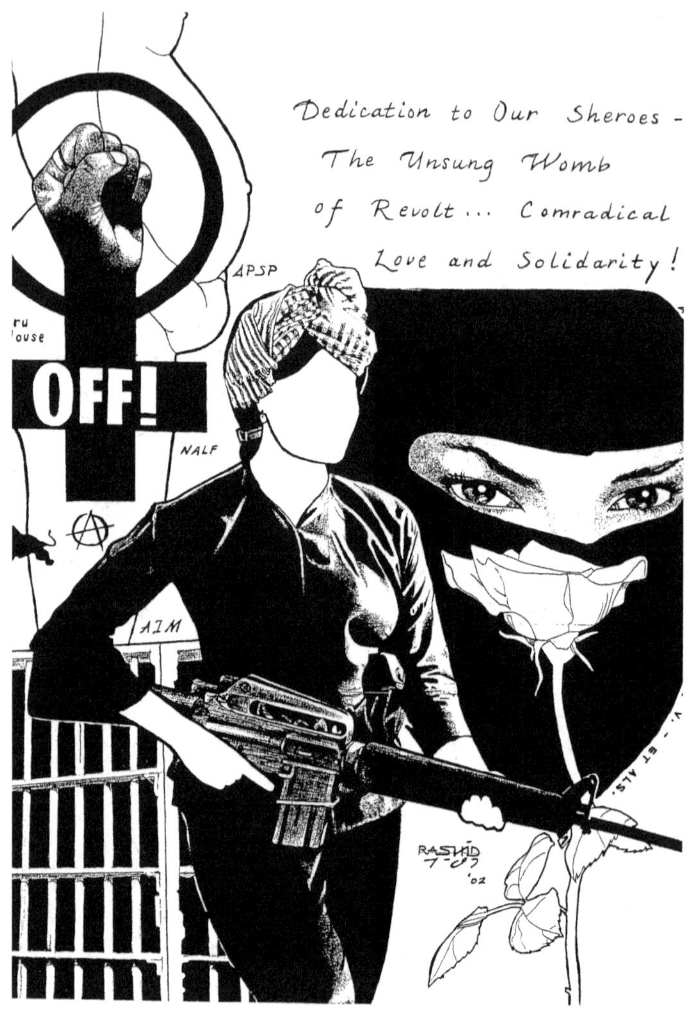


## Wimyn's Liberation Cannot be Achieved Through Feminism

It was the survival, fortitude, and fearless struggles of wimyn like Sojourner Truth and Harriet Tubman, and also many working-class white wimyn like Margaret Corin ("Dirty Kate"), "Molly Pitcher," Deborah Garnet, Mother Jones, Gurley Flynn, the wimyn of the Lowell (Massachusetts) Textile Mills and others, that gave the greatest impetus to the progressive aspirations of feminism. However, lacking a revolutionary working-class perspective, feminism has repeatedly been subverted and contained by the bourgeois enemies of working-class wimyn.

Indeed, feminism has always been a movement based in the middle and upper class of privileged white wimyn, a movement that essentially seeks equality of such wimyn with their men in sharing bourgeois privileges in capitalist society.

As Howard Zinn observed, "When feminist impulses are recorded, they are almost always the writings of privileged women who had some status from which to speak freely, more opportunity to write and have their writings recorded."

The sham movement for "women's liberation" has each time co-opted and used the image of wimyn who stood firmly opposed to oppression as tools to subvert and marginalize the radical working-class and oppressed nationality elements within the wimyn's liberation movement. It has in turn merely expanded the ranks of the bourgeois class to include wimyn willing to share in the class oppression of the poor working-class people, (wimyn included), and preserved the very system that is at the root of wimyn's oppression.

Even today "radical feminists" attempt to coopt the image of New Afrikan slave wimyn like Harriet Tubman, proclaiming her to have been a "radical feminist," when in fact the feminists were part of the class sector that oppressed Blacks, and the illiterate Harriet Tubman had no connection to this toothless white wimyn's movement at all.

Moreover, even the radical wing of feminists distorts or avoids the hystorical roots of wimyn's oppression which began with the development of and continues to be based upon the preservation of class society. They fail to recognize the historic reality that wimyn's oppression grows out of the property relations and economic mode of production of class-divided societies, and instead substitute a non-historical "patriarchy" in its place.

This is in essence why we oppose feminism and instead promote a struggle for wimyn's liberation explicitly led by working-class wimyn and illuminated by revolutionary class ideology. For lack of a clear working-class and anti-imperialist perspective, the feminist movement has served as a platform for and opened its ranks to every foul element and trend of thought that exists across and indeed sustains imperialist and class society; from the eugenicists of the early 1900s like Margaret Sanger, who promoted the genocidal extermination of all Blacks in Amerika through mass sterilization and proposed using Black preachers to influence Black wimyn to submit to sterilization; to the daughter of the late billionaire H.L. Hunt who finances various "feminist" foundations; to Laura Bush speaking on the November 17, 2001, presidential radio address in support of the imperialist massacre of Afghanistan in the name of feminist concerns for the Taliban's oppression of wimyn.

As a movement that has been reduced to a rhetorical culture of "political correctness" that talks wimyn's equality and places the issue of sexism above class, the feminist movement functions as a toothless, vacillating and reformist melting pot that brings wimyn of exactly opposite and irreconcilable classes together in an artificial alliance under a rhetorical banner of seeking equality of wimyn. Acting under the pretense of being the "collective" voice of oppressed wimyn, mainstream feminism has served only to advance the perspectives and the material interests of privileged wimyn and those who aspire to achieve bourgeois privilege, while leaving the poor working-class and oppressed nationality wimyn marginalized, voiceless, and still oppressed.

Some radical elements within the feminist movement have attempted to give voice and recognition to the concerns and issues of working-class, poor, and oppressed nationality wimyn, but their voices are largely muted by the dominating voices of middle and upper class wimyn in the movement. Indeed the two great waves of the wimyn's liberation movement in Amerika were brought to an end as a result of reforms and bourgeois concessions made by the male-dominated ruling class to the opportunist collaborating sectors of the movement, thereby preserving the imperialist system of working-class, national, racial, and gender oppression.

We stand adamantly opposed to the repression of wimyn and the enforced inequalities imposed upon them by patriarchal class society; but because we also recognize that wimyn are indeed the equals of men in every respect, (this is a dialectical reality), we know that an imperialist is an imperialist, a jingoist is a jingoist, a racist is a racist and a class enemy is a class enemy whether they wear pants or a skirt. So our struggle for wimyn's equality, while it opposes many of the gender oppressions that even bourgeois wimyn suffer, is guided by principles of class and oppressed nationality liberation. We therefore promote a principled alliance with the oppressed class/national and advanced elements of the feminist movement, and beseech them to approach the struggle against wimyn's oppression from the perspective of class and not merely gender struggle.

Class society has succeeded to a great extent in conditioning many wimyn of all sectors to embrace individualism, which is deeply rooted in bourgeois culture, inculcating in them, as in many men, a "me first" mentality. This mentality is at the root of the trend in feminism of placing wimyn above class. Whereas class is the principal contradiction, while gender oppression is secondary, in reality nowhere in society have wimyn been more successful in gaining leadership positions than in movements on the Left, but the anti-class tendency toward individualism which such feminist-influenced wimyn have brought with them has aided in the Left's break-up into factional single issue groups with reformist agendas and a lot of well-feathered nests. The Left is much to blame on account of uncritically embracing feminism for fear of being criticized as male chauvinist.

Bourgeois society breeds divisiveness and individualism and is ideal for wimyn who aspire to upper class achievements. They are freed from many of the pre-capitalist feudal restraints and able to rise in power. The feminist movement has opened the door for this, and we therefore see a growing number of wimyn rising in business and government to high positions, like Condoleeza Rice, Hillary Clinton, and Nancy Pelosi. Many companies now have femyl CEO's and top executives. In fact there has been much more of an opening for wimyn than for Black men into the middle class and the bourgeoisie. Even wimyn of the oppressed class are pulled towards a feminist ideological and political line to some degree. But what about proletarian ideology and politics? In its correct application, it stands in contradiction to both male chauvinism and feminism.

And at the same time, we have seen dramatic cutbacks in social services and masses of poor wimyn with children cut from welfare roles. We've seen a rise in sweatshops and in the number of wimyn going to prison and becoming homeless, all without an outcry from the feminists.

What about children's rights and their need to be loved and nurtured and raised with strong proletarian values and morality? We must apply Panther Love to them, because a gendered ideology and political line cannot resolve these issues. Solving these problems demands that we introduce all-sided collectivism in a pragmatic way to draw together wimyn, men, and children in the oppressed communities—wimyn and men who are down for this proletarian line are worthy of recruiting and training as warriors of the vanguard. To watch out for feminism as well as male chauvinism, we must promote proletarian ideology and egalitarianism among comrades.

Social and economic support bases for single New Afrikan mothers need to be established, such as Party-organized free daycare and free meals for children, liberation schools, etc. But our men must also be encouraged to be good fathers and help to build strong proletarian families.

Sisterhood is a good thing, and wimyn's inner-party and mass organizations are essential to the struggle of wimyn, but partnerships between men and wimyn to have and raise children is more basic and necessary to humyn society. Statistics show that children of single parents are in the highest risk categories at double the rate of two parent families. Most New Afrikan males in U.S. prisons have no father figure in their lives, and many no mother either. The bourgeoisie of course wants to smash up the families of the oppressed and thus weaken the Black nation and the poor.

Feminism helps this attack on families of the oppressed. It vilifies men (and particularly white men) as if the problem of wimyn's oppression is one of genetics. We see the result of this trend in a competition between white petty-bourgeois feminists and black wimyn for the attention of Black men. These feminists often claim an ability to better relate to Black men than white men because they are equally "oppressed," which begs the question: "How many middle class white wimyn are getting beat up by cops and railroaded into prison?"

It's almost a status thing—(rooted in white middle class privilege)—"Look what I got!" But in most cases there's no intention of having a family, which is what Black wimyn want and our New Afrikan Nation needs.

Radical feminism borrows much from Marxism, indeed all feminism does, but with a critical revision rendering it counter-revolutionary. Whereas Marxism reveals that the oppression of wimyn is rooted in the creation of private property and the division of society into classes, and thus wimyn's oppression can only be fully eradicated with the abolition of classes and private property, feminists attempt to create the illusion that wimyn's oppression is the primary source of all other oppression and exists outside of class exploitation, and therefore the class struggle is irrelevant or a side issue to the struggle against wimyn's oppression.

Patriarchy begins to break down with the rise of the bourgeoisie and liberal democracy. The main cultural prop of patriarchy is organized religion, which reflects the pre-capitalist (principally the feudalist) mode of production. As liberalism gives way to overt fascism and resurrects many of the oppressive cultural norms of feudalism, it gives patriarchy a new shot in the arm, but it is class oppression that is at the heart of fascism. Fascism arises as the bourgeoisie grows desperate to maintain its dominance over the working class due to the decline in capitalism. This is why Lenin terms fascism as "capitalism in decline."

Just as they do with Blacks and immigrants, the capitalists summon wimyn into the work force not only to exploit their labor as proletarians, but also to attack the price of the male proletarians' labor power. Wimyn's wages are set lower to pull down the wages of men. But the feminists blame men in general (and particularly the male proletarians) for these conditions which are created by the bourgeoisie. Much like backward white workers blame Blacks and immigrants for taking their jobs and driving down their wages, and backward Blacks and immigrants counter with blaming white workers for keeping them out of better salaried jobs and limiting them to "non-white work." The workers are thus divided against themselves and diverted from uniting against the bourgeoisie in class struggle.

Indeed, instead of encouraging wimyn to be active in class struggle, feminists dub it as a "men's movement" and proletarian revolution as a "men's revolution." They encourage wimyn to sabotage and not take part in it.

Feminists make an issue of the percentage of wimyn in leadership positions, as if this and not the ideological and political line that is leading is important. By this logic, Margaret Thatcher, Indira Gandhi, or Condoleeza Rice would be better than Lenin, Mao Tse-tung or Amilcar Cabral. The role of wimyn is not more important than the role of the proletariat in the class struggle and ending the oppression of wimyn. Wimyn are not and never have been a class nor do they share a common class interest nor an overall common interest in ending all oppression—including the oppression of wimyn.

Bourgeois wimyn share in and benefit from the general bourgeois oppression of proletarian wimyn, and while they will pretend to back proletarian wimyn in their struggle against gender oppression, their goal will not be to achieve total abolition of all forms of oppression of wimyn, but to add numbers to the ranks of their own movement to achieve greater equality with bourgeois men in reaping the spoils and privileges of capitalist society: A society whose political economy thrives upon the oppression and exploitation of working-class wimyn and dividing the working class against itself.

These goals of gaining status and privileges enjoyed by upper class men instead of abolishing class privileges and classes themselves are the root aspirations of the feminist movement, and will remain so long as this movement is led by elements that do not place class struggle foremost and allows middle and upper class wimyn to mold its line. Has the growth of wimyn bosses changed the reality of class oppression for wimyn workers or their particular oppression as wimyn? Of course not!

The struggle for wimyn's liberation will necessarily be protracted, but even in the early stages of socialism significant advances have been made. These are most evident in the post-socialist countries where capitalism has been restored and these advances have been lost. The fall of the Socialist Bloc has also led to concessions being lost in the western capitalist countries as well.

Yet radical feminists still deny the connection between the class struggle and wimyn's rights. There are now many wimyn CEO's and wimyn in high places in government and business. We may even have a womyn president soon (as has occurred in India, the Philippines and other countries), but what does this mean for the masses, for wimyn workers and welfare mothers?

Wimyn are integrated into the armed forces and the police, but what effect has this had on imperialist wars or police state oppression? Have wimyn guards made prisons more humane? Have wimyn judges made the courts more just? Of course not—no more so than the neo-colonial policies of raising Blacks to high political and business positions has changed the economic and national oppression and subjugation of New Afrikan workers or masses in general.

"Divide and Conquer, Divide and Rule," has forever been the exploiters' game—the "Golden Rule" of the "Willie Lynch School of Subjugation." Get the poor whites to blame the Blacks and the Blacks to blame the poor whites. Get immigrants and native workers against each other and wimyn against men, and so on ...

Unity is what is called for—unity behind the leadership of the international proletariat! It alone has the class perspective to lead the fight against all oppression. Narrow nationalism, reverse racism, feminism, religious sectarianism, etc., all objectively serve the ruling class and reflect bourgeois ideology. Feminists can rant about the "male-dominated Left," but this doesn't absolve the bourgeois-dominated wimyn's movement or its class collaboration and counter-revolutionary role.

"Marxist Feminists" are those who eclectically confuse the two worldviews. The fundamental contradiction is not between men and wimyn but between the socialized character of production and the privatized ownership of its means. To promote clarity, Communists must create and lead their own wimyn's movement. It must stand up to the bourgeois feminist movement in its liberal and radical variants, and it must uphold that "women hold up half the sky," and "workers must unite to lead the fight against all oppression."

### Two Waves of Feminism's Rise and Decline in Amerika

As pointed out above, the Amerikan feminist movement saw two waves—the initial broad impetus of which came from working-class wimyn—but was both times co-opted and subverted into reformism by middle class and bourgeois elements. Similar methods of using opportunists and middle class collaborators within the oppressed group were applied to undermine our own New Afrikan liberation movements, (the tactic of neo-colonialism), and to undermine the early working-class movement of the early 1900s in Amerika, (buying off labor leaders and making token political and economic concessions to workers).

The first wave of the Amerikan feminist movement was sparked by the resistance of working-class white wimyn in textile mills, like the working wimyn of Lowell Massachusetts, and sweatshops, like in the Garment District in NYC. An attendant impetus was driven by the rising anti-slavery movement in the early 1840s. White wimyn in general came to see their conditions of domestic servitude to white men as not unlike the chattel enslavement of Blacks. This rise in consciousness gave rise to a broad movement for wimyn's equality. However, towards the end of the 19th century and into the early 20th century this movement was co-opted, reduced and channelled into one to win wimyn's suffrage.

Emma Goldman, a radical feminist who was deported from Amerika in 1919, recognized this reformist trend in feminism of merely seeking wimyn's suffrage for what it was. She stated of feminism:

> "Our modern fetish is universal suffrage ... The women of Australia and New Zealand can vote and help make laws. Are the labor conditions better there? ..."

In a similar vein, in 1911 Helen Keller, an avowed socialist, criticized the same trend in England thusly:

> "Our democracy is but a name. We vote? What does that mean? It means that we choose between two bodies of real, though not avowed autocrats, Tweedledum and Tweedledee ...
>
> "You ask for votes for women. What good can votes do when ten-elevenths of the land of Great Britain belongs to 200,000 and only one-eleventh to the rest of the 40,000,000. Have your men with their millions of votes freed themselves from this injustice?"

Lacking a clear revolutionary working-class leadership, this first wave of feminism was corralled into a narrow movement of wimyn's suffrage. When the wimyn's vote was granted, the movement petered out.

Although based primarily amongst white wimyn, the second resurgence of feminism found its inspiration in the struggles of the 1960s, especially by the activism of Black working-class wimyn and college students, centered largely in the Student National Coordinating Committee—formerly the Student Non-Violent Coordinating Committee. SNCC was itself founded by Ella Baker—a sista who performed much of the behind the scenes work to push the Black Civil Rights movement to the forefront of U.S. politics. Wimyn members of the various radical social movements of the '60s—anti-war groups, civil rights groups, student organizations, etc.—began coming together to organize against gender oppression.

Wimyn were especially prominent within the Black Liberation Movement; many came to link gender oppression up with class and racial oppression. Indeed the most advanced Black political formation of that era—the Black Panther Party—came to be in fact, (despite its popularized male image), largely a wimyn's party. But the movements of the 1960s and '70s were brutally repressed, co-opted and/or bought off by the power structure, and by the influence of feminism—again lacking a consolidated revolutionary working-class leadership and ideology, and based largely amongst middle class white wimyn—the Women's Movement was effectively neutralized as a movement for social justice for wimyn.

The activism of this second wave was diverted—again—by civil reforms, (affirmative action), and the entry of greater numbers of white wimyn into the middle and upper classes, thanks in large part to the restructuring of the U.S. economy, (from factory to service-based), and the "general prosperity" of the time. Today, feminism is proclaimed by its mainstream voices to have "succeeded" on account of wimyn today enjoying more positions as corporate CEO's and directors, in high political offices, and in other prominent careers and positions. Yet for wimyn of color and working-class wimyn in Amerika, conditions of poverty and male chauvinist oppression prevail.

Overall, the broader entry of wimyn into the U.S. work force and expanding their roles in the public sector of capitalist society has not won them equality, nor working-class liberation. Violence against wimyn continues; wimyn are still largely kept out of traditionally male fields, they still earn less than men, and amongst the poor and oppressed nationalities and races single wimyn with children predominate. As with the proclamations of racial equality, wimyn's equality is promoted as a publicly accepted principle, yet in reality these are empty "politically correct" pronouncements which do not actually exist. So while wimyn's aspirations and consciousness concerning gender equality are an existing cultural trend, their struggle for genuine liberation has been subverted and has petered out.

## Our Line on Revolutionary Wimyn's Liberation

We are no more "feminists" than we are "masculinists." We are social egalitarians who oppose placing either gender above the other. But as an oppressed group, wimyn definitely have the right and duty to organize and struggle against their oppressive conditions, against all stereotyped social roles and exploitation by men. Male revolutionaries must commit to aiding our sistas and ensuring that all forms of oppression against them are ended.

However, we must keep our class perspective foremost. It is only through class struggle, through materially changing and eliminating gendered categories in the process of socializing productive and reproductive life that we can change how people think. We need to gain the power to effect these changes.

Some feminists, (and even some comrades), propose ending gender oppression by simply eliminating the social categories of gender by ceasing to classify people as femyl and male. This idea reverses materialist principles; and supposes that simply by changing how people think we can change material reality. Whereas, it is our social practice that determines our thinking. Furthermore, how is it possible not to recognize that the sexes exist as a unity of opposites? This becomes apparent as soon as we stand naked side by side, as soon as we carry out our respective functions in the reproductive processes, which are at the very root of our existence and survival.

Moreover, the mere fact of gender differences is no more the basis of gender oppression than attempting to ignore them could eliminate gender oppression. It is the material relationships within societies that brought the contradictions between the sexes into a stage of antagonism which expresses itself as gender oppression and consequent struggles against it. These are material conditions that developed organically alongside the development of class society. In order to eliminate wimyn's oppression, we must eliminate the material social conditions that cause this condition. We must eliminate class society and consciously socialize all social relations. Wimyn must participate equally with men in economic, political, military, cultural, and social life. And these activities must be public activities, mass-based and not monopolized by or centralized into the hands of a small wealthy elite, male or femyl.

These changes cannot happen overnight. In the process of working towards them, we will definitely persist in certain gendered practices and thoughts. This is inevitable, since we are the products of a gendered society and have inherited certain behaviors and perceptions over our lifetimes, (and over thousands of years in some cases), that will demand continuous and difficult struggle to overcome. We are not idealists. But our path forward is illuminated by the examples, successes, and errors of those who've gone before, and it is our duty to study and learn from, apply and advance the lessons of those advances and mistakes.

Our struggle as New Afrikans must begin with the understanding that cultural imperialism has imposed bourgeois concepts of "manhood" and "womanhood" on us, yet these definitions have never fit our lived reality. This bourgeois warp defines the gender role of the "man" as that of protecting the womyn, whose role as a "lady" is that of being helpless, subservient, passive, and incapable of contributing to the administration and defense of our communities.

Our lived experience contradicts these concepts for several reasons. First, during and since chattel slavery, our men have been largely prevented from defending our wimyn and communities from violence. Second, New Afrikan wimyn—because of their prominent role in productive and reproductive life—have endured the "authority" of the husband much less than white wimyn. Her role throughout U.S. history, (in slavery, domestic service, as a general service-trade wage-earner, etc.), has thrust her into a position of doing manual labor and thereby providing for the productive needs of family and community. Therefore she has generally exercised greater decision making power in matters of family and community than her white counterpart.

Finally, attempts by New Afrikan men to live up to the bourgeois image of "manhood" often expresses itself in a subculture of exaggerated violence, (directed against ourselves and other poor and powerless social groups), and preoccupation with one's sexual potency. The former tendency has our males routinely engaging in irrational, often stupid acts of violence and feigned bravado to "impress" femyls and "prove" manhood. Yet we've never been able to defend ourselves, much less our communities, from the oppression and abuses of the power structure and its violent enforcers. The latter tendency is in large part a carry over from the degraded role of our men on the old slave plantations. Particularly after the abolition of the transport of slaves from Afrika, breeding of slaves to increase stock became all-important. Consequently strong and sexually potent "studs"—like bulls—became among the most prized slaves.

So, as opposed to bourgeois culture, "manhood" for the slave was merely an expression of sexual potency, (how many wimyn the male could sexually use and impregnate). We see traits of this today in Black communities: young males boast about how many "baby mamas" they have while being unable or unwilling to assume responsibility for the welfare and upbringing of the children they have produced. There is also the frequent practice of young males holding their crotches to emphasize or exaggerate the size and potency of their sex organ.

Class society socialized its members to believe that the man should be the principal provider. Much of the disrespect and exploitation of wimyn by the poor, unemployed lumpen comes from feelings of emasculation at not being able to assume the role of working-class breadwinner due to the high unemployment of young Black males. In turn the males assume such funky patriarchal roles of pimps in the "Daddy/Baby" relationship to the "Ho," reflecting the master and slave relationship that is the essence of patriarchy. The pimp as the owner, the prostitute as his property.

Bourgeois concepts of "womanhood" also do not apply to Black wimyn. As Sojourner Truth pointed out, our sistas have never enjoyed the general "privilege" of being sheltered, pampered, and protected. Nor have they been passive, submissive and deferential in their domestic life. Domination over Black wimyn by their men has remained relatively weak. Still, the pervasive imperialist-manufactured urban youth subculture encourages our males to denigrate our sistas. They are projected as sex objects, concubines and prostitutes, to be used and depreciated by men, not to be loved, appreciated, and respected as the other half of our Nation, as producers, reproducers, and indeed as the source of our very existence. In fact it has been the almost super-humyn strength and struggle of our wimyn that has allowed us to survive as long as we have.

Since the close of chattel slavery in 1865, (excluding prisoners), New Afrikan wimyn have remained prominent in performing the hard productive and reproductive work necessary to sustain our communities both in the rural and urban sectors. From planting and harvesting, to working as domestic servants, to doing factory work, to now struggling to maintain employment within the service trades, our wimyn have always assumed a major role in the productive work to pay the bills and put food on the table. What's more, our sistas' burden in sustaining our communities and families is attended by combined gender, racial and class oppression. Indeed, our males, acting under the influence of bourgeois concepts of "manhood" while excluded from participation in bourgeois society, have supported and aided in the oppression of our wimyn. As George Jackson observed in a letter to his mother:

> "The Black woman has in the past few hundred years been the only force holding us together and holding us up. She has absorbed the biggest part of the many shocks and strains of existence under a slave order. The men can think of nothing more effective than pimping, gambling or petty theft. I've heard men brag about being pimps of Black women and taking money from black women who are on relief. Things like this I find odious, disgusting–You are right, the Black men have proven themselves to be utterly detestable and repulsive in the past. Before I would succumb to such subterfuge I would scratch my living from the ground on hands and knees, or die in a hail of bullets! My hat goes off to every one of you. You have my profoundest respect … The men of our group have developed as a result of living under a ruthless system a set of mannerisms that numb the soul. We have been made the floor mat of the world, but the world has yet to see what can be done by men of our nature, by men who have walked the path of disparity, of repression, of abortion, and yet come out whole. There will be a special page in the book of life for the men who have crawled back from the grave. This page will tell of utter defeat, ruin, passivity, and subjection in one breath, and in the next, overwhelming victory and fulfillment."

In order to take our place in history as men, as revolutionary men, and not to be defined by and ape bourgeois culture, we must join with our sistas in the collective process of building, nurturing, and sustaining our communities and nation. Wimyn and men together must assume equal roles in our cultural, social, political, productive and reproductive life. Neither our brothas, nor our sistas, are slaves or property, and we must cease relating to ourselves as such! These twisted concepts have us treating our wimyn and sex as commodities, (articles of property), to be given to men in exchange for material gifts and "protection."

In building and serving our communities and nation, material equality for our wimyn must be developed and practiced. Only in this way will we undermine the prevailing subjective advantages our men have been conditioned to believe they have over our sistas, entitling them to demean, marginalize, use, abuse, and oppress them. And only in this way will we survive as a people and be strong enough to end our oppression.

Our men's very concept of social significance and their warped notions of "manhood" will be challenged by sistas who actively and effectively take the lead in a collective unified and organized manner to advance our Nation's struggle for survival and against imperialist oppression. With wimyn taking the lead, shoulder to shoulder with our revolutionary brothas, (our "New Men"), and youth, the other so-called "men" will be compelled to either recognize sistas as their equals and unite with their mothers, daughters, sisters, aunts, grandmothers, lovers, and wives in support of our struggle, or be widely recognized as less than the men they claim and define themselves to be.

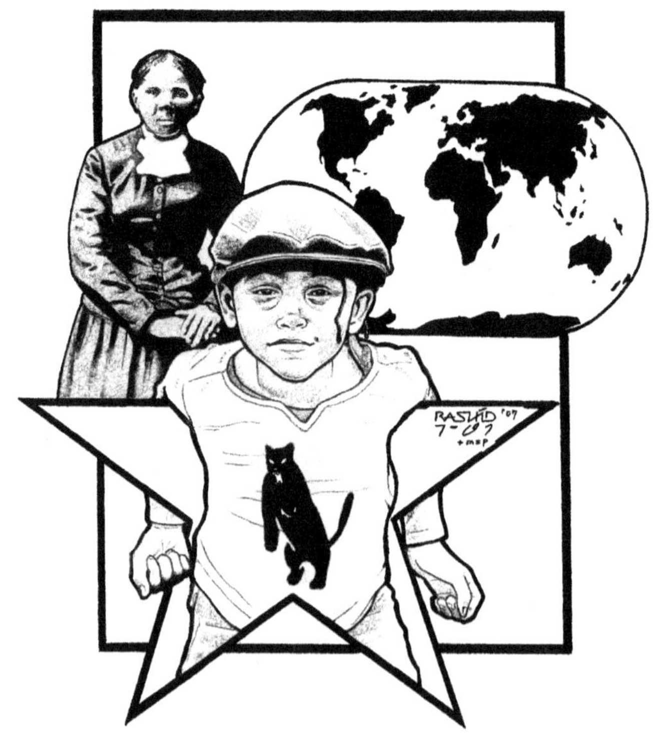

## Lessons to be Drawn from the Black Panther Party

In this struggle, important lessons can be taken from the practical work of the original BPP, its effects on gender relations in the New Afrikan communities it served, and its broader implications within revolutionary struggle. In this context it is important to point out that rural peasant-based societies typically retain strong communal ties, (remnants of kinship), at least subjectively. All of the successful revolutionary struggles of the last century occurred in societies where peasants were the majority: in Russia, China, Vietnam, Guinea-Bissau, Angola, Mozambique, Cuba, etc. This is because, as a people accustomed to relating to social members in a sense of kinship and community, peasants are more readily able to unite in a community-wide struggle against oppressive forces once they become organized and conscious of being oppressed, of who is oppressing them, and the methods by which that oppression is imposed. In this regard, rural people are more ready to accept political discipline.

However, in the case of oppressed urban folk in developed capitalist societies in particular, senses of kinship and community have been largely destroyed through their constant experiences of having to hustle, compete, and scramble on an individualized basis against their peers to survive. This is especially reinforced by the division of communities into small nuclear families which do not see themselves as dependent on each other for overall survival and protection of the community and each other. The imperialist system has conditioned them to look to outside forces—the imperialist corporate workplace, government and police—for these things—forces that prey upon and oppress rather than serve the interests and needs of these communities.

Furthermore, in the urban New Afrikan communities the sense of kinship in even the small nuclear family has been shattered under our neo-colonial conditions. In our urban communities both wage earning and child care fall largely on the shoulders of our wimyn. Our men have been increasingly alienated from both productive and reproductive life. Dwindling jobs, racist and class-based stereotypes, and massive imprisonment of young Black males have made it increasingly difficult for them to find and maintain work, especially non-degrading work. They are pushed into illegal capitalist pursuits, or chasing remote dreams of brief careers as entertainers or athletes. Moreover, the dominant chauvinist culture has conditioned them to view child-rearing as essentially a womyn's vocation. The socially destructive result is that our children are growing up without positive male role models and examples. It was in its moves toward solving this great social problem that one of the greatest achievements of the BPP can be found.

The BPP was able to transform the competitive and individualistic "lumpenized" (broken), urban mentality in the Black communities it served into a communal one. The key was its focus on mobilizing the entire community around something that its individual members were able to place above their personal interests: their kids.

In the U.S. government's anti-Panther crusade, FBI director J. Edgar Hoover fingered the BPP as the single greatest threat to U.S. domestic "security." The most fearsome thing he said the Panthers were doing was the Free Breakfast for Children Program (FBCP). What made a program that served free wholesome meals to hungry poor Black children such a dangerous activity? It was the program's practical ability to counter the Black communities' conditioned dependence upon the imperialist system.

The FBCP struck at the heart of this system and its values. It brought together in public communal and cooperative productive and reproductive life all ages and groups in the communities, including wimyn, men and youth, and thereby built that sense of unified, community oriented, self-sufficiency and kinship that predominated in our historical communal societies.

The Panthers' FBCP demonstrated by practical example, along with the BPP's other Serve the People programs, that working together in unified, community-based and gender-neutral structures, even the poorest of people can solve their own problems without need of begging for handouts and crumbs from the imperialist system. The FBCP implemented gender-neutral, socialist programs that brought out the collective community to serve and meet its own economic needs and collectively participate in child rearing. This was a move toward revolutionizing urban life. It focused on investing collective energy into the children, as they most clearly reflected the future they were struggling for. The Panthers educated and demonstrated by example and mass participation that socialistic practice was the answer to the problems of the people.

As martyred Panther leader Fred Hampton Sr. observed, it was the Panthers' service to the people that most securely welded the communities to the Party and vice-versa. He noted that when the cops attempted to alienate the Black communities from the Panthers by emphasizing to them that the BPP was a communist and socialist party, the consistent response they got from community members was they didn't care what the Panthers or the FBCP were, because they were feeding their children and providing services for community needs that the government couldn't, wouldn't, and had long ignored. And if the cops touched those programs they would get the communities' collective foot put up their pig asses. In fact on many occasions when the cops laid siege to and threatened to conduct assault raids on BPP offices, the communities came out en masse, surrounded the Panther building, and themselves drove the pigs off.

But what relevance does this all have to the question of and answer to wimyn's oppression? Well, point is, as former Panther Malika Adams expressed, the BPP's community service programs, (which were staffed and implemented on a collective, public and community-based level), engaged in activities that were traditionally viewed as "wimyn's work," such as feeding children, taking care of the sick, etc. They also implemented activities to provide for the basic economic needs of the communities. What's more the Party, which had a largely femyl membership because of this orientation, saw many of the wimyn comrades face armed confrontations with police side by side with men in the Party. Thus, the Panthers brought into public life the work of acquiring survival necessities for the community, nurturing the community, caring for children and community members, passing along moral values, and community defense.

It combined both traditionally male-centered and womyn-centered roles in community service programs, carried out by men and wimyn of various ages. Furthermore, it gave wimyn leadership roles in the Party at a time when wimyn were largely blocked out of leadership positions everywhere else, including within civil rights groups. While the rise of wimyn into leading ranks of the BPP came with considerable struggle against typical male machismo, intolerance, insolence and disrespect early on, the wimyn demonstrated courage, shared brutality at the hands of the pigs and refused to accept male-imposed limitations. This caused much of the resistance to give way. Wimyn held such a dominant position in the BPP that Panther vet Mumia Abu-Jamal referred to the BPP as a "woman's party." In Sista Malika's words, "women ran the BPP pretty much. I don't know how it got to be a male's party or thought of as being a male's party."

These sistas didn't stand on the sidelines huffing and puffing, refusing to join the BPP because it was initially male-dominated. Instead they recognized the overall need of its presence and work in uniting, serving, and uplifting the oppressed New Afrikan communities. From inside the party these revolutionary wimyn struggled against the resistance of the males to advance the leading role of wimyn—they proved their determination, fortitude, equal ability to the males and basically forced equal treatment and respect as comrades. This is how revolutionary work proceeds. Not by folks trailing behind the movement waving and criticizing and refusing to join "men's" parties. They must join the movement and struggle from within to resolve its inner contradictions and strengthen it, recognizing the dialectical relationship between gender and class oppression, thereby enabling it to struggle resolutely to resolve the external contradictions of bourgeois class society.

The BPP in its practice even struck a blow against the bourgeois concept of the nuclear family and marriage. Their members lived in communal houses, and wimyn as well as men selected their partners freely from amongst other Panthers. This is not to say that many Panthers did not function as married couples or live in nuclear families, but in either case there was struggle over gender roles and to put politics in command.

And like our New Afrikan sistas, who struggled alongside our brothas throughout our ordeal of chattel slavery, Panther wimyn were anything but weak. Comrade Mumia has these reminiscences of Panther wimyn:

> "When I read or hear critics employ their projections against the BPP on charges of sexism I can barely conceal a chuckle for my memories of women in the Party were of able, determined and powerful revolutionaries who fought with and for their brothers like lionesses.
>
> "Women in the Party in which I spent several years of my youth were not dainty, shrinking violets. They were, of course, of various backgrounds and, as is common in Black America, of every which hue.
>
> "They were also tough women.
>
> "We lived in spartan, virtually bare 'Panther Pads,' where we fell onto mattresses at the end of a long day's work.
>
> "Whether I was in Philadelphia, the Bronx, or in Berkeley, California, I was under the authority of a female Panther who ran a tight and efficient operation …
>
> "On both coasts, in cities of different rhythms and pace, one found confident, capable, proud and inspiring women who commanded respect, camaraderie, intense loyalty, and sisterly love.
>
> "We knew from experience that they would be treated as viciously as we if they fell into the hands of the enemy, and we loved them all the more for their courage and their sacrifice. We knew, and could recite, the names of our sisters who were political prisoners of the pigs, and their names were like a mantra of resistance: Ericka Huggins, Angela Davis, Afeni Shakur, Joan Bird …
>
> "As for sex, women chose their partners as freely as the men, and many could and did say no …

"To be a Panther meant something extraordinary in 1970, and one felt immensely honored to know, work with, and love these tough, committed women. These were, as Elaine Brown would later recount, 'hard' women who were seen as 'soldiers, comrades—not pretty little things.' They were, to use Eldridge Cleaver's words, our 'other half,' who fought as 'strongly as enthusiastically as we [did] … in the struggle … '

"In the ranks and offices of the Black Panther Party, women were far more than mere appendages of male ego and power. They were valued and respected comrades who demonstrated daily the truth of the adage 'a revolutionary has no gender.'"

Furthermore, at a time when many social justice movements were uncertain how or if to relate the question of the oppression of homosexuals to their own agendas, BPP Minister of Defense Huey P. Newton acknowledged that gays are not enemies of the people and indeed may be the most oppressed social group. He pointed out in his August 1970 statement on "the Women's Liberation and Gay Liberation Movements," that many men's first instinct is "to want to hit a homosexual in the mouth." Not because they've done one any wrong, but because many of us men are insecure about our own manhood. He gave the example that this is a result of social conditioning in class society, which caused him to feel male homosexuality a threat but not femyl homosexuality. Huey took the novel position that we should cease in derogatory and oppressive behaviors toward gays and instead ally with them in the struggle.

In our struggle against imperialism and patriarchy, the BPP offered much that we can learn from, apply and advance. As a genuinely revolutionary program, the Panthers were the first structure to pursue socializing both productive and reproductive humyn relations in a gender neutral fashion, thereby creating a genuinely revolutionary communal culture in one of the most reactionary and competitive of social environments.

In our struggle today people have to be allowed to make lifestyle choices, and the NABPP has to defend that right, whether it is to be single or married, gay or straight, to be interracial in preference or whatever, we don't want to fall into the "racial purity" bullshit. In fact in today's world there are no "pure" races. But we can understand why Black wimyn get pissed off when middle and upper class white wimyn throw themselves at Black (Latino and Indian) males, particularly when the guys leave these sistas with all the child raising responsibilities.

Furthermore, our NABPP must be mindful in denouncing feminism to not replicate internalizing patriarchal values, as other parties on the Left have done. On this point there's much we can learn from the observations of comrade Parvati, head of the Women's Department of the Communist Party of Nepal (Maoist), in her "The Question of Women's Leadership in People's War in Nepal." Comrade Parvati noted:

> "Since the feminist movement is a product of the bourgeois revolution, quite often communist parties tend to become hyper-sensitive to women's issues. As a result they fall prey to patriarchal values even while agreeing in theory to women's liberation. This is manifested in many ways. For example instead of taking women as reliable long-term equal partners in the communist movement it takes women's role as supportive. As a result the Party is often found overemphasizing the class struggle at the cost of gender exploitation forgetting the dialectical relationship between the two. There have been cases of delaying the formation of separate women's organization or even temporarily dismissing existing women's organization within communist parties. In parties where separate women's organization exists, there are cases where the women's mass front is not given the required degree of freedom so as to make their own plans and programmes, thus robbing them of initiative and creative power. This ultimately breeds alienation and tailism in the party. This can also take place by not coordinating the women's programme with the party's programme and as a result the party programme gets priority over the women's programme. Conservativism in the party can also be seen through relegating women cadres to only women related work, thereby robbing them of the chance to develop in party policy matters and other fields.
>
> "In the practical front, this leads to spontaneity whereby women's issues are addressed but not implemented because one leaves it to circumstances, leading to gradualism. Often it is seen that the party does not actively intervene in the existing traditional division of labor between men and women whereby men take to mental work while women are left to do physical labor. This is also manifested in taking men and women as absolute equals by not being sensitive to women's special condition and their special needs. This becomes all the more apparent when women are menstruating or are in the reproductive period."

Because in class society wimyn have been assigned to roles as servants and were long held out of spheres of mental work, they have little experience at leading in political arenas. In a revolutionary party leadership ability is based upon one's command of ideology and its correct application. Hence we must advance our sistas to positions of leadership by developing their political and ideological understanding and application of Historical and Dialectical Materialism, and their practice of class struggle, inner-party struggle and inner-self struggle.

It is also imperative in today's struggle that we develop and implement affirmative programs that will provide for our sistas' independent security and self defense, to act as a brake on 1) tendencies toward male domination and 2) tendencies to stereotype national and community defense as exclusively male functions. In this way we can struggle against male "macho" tendencies which seek to "protect" wimyn or prove oneself, which as a comrade recently pointed out to me is "synonymous most often with stupidity." We must equalize the roles and positions of our sistas in these areas to give them both the means and confidence to defend themselves and our communities and thus pull the carpet from under the very concept of patriarchy that wimyn must be men's passive playthings, subservient, and weak because dependent on males for protection. But even in this endeavor we must keep politics and our class interests in command. All our efforts—economic, political, defense, cultural, and social—must be regulated and illuminated by historical and dialectical materialism.

*A WOMAN'S PLACE IS IN THE REVOLUTION!*
*ALL POWER TO THE PEOPLE!*

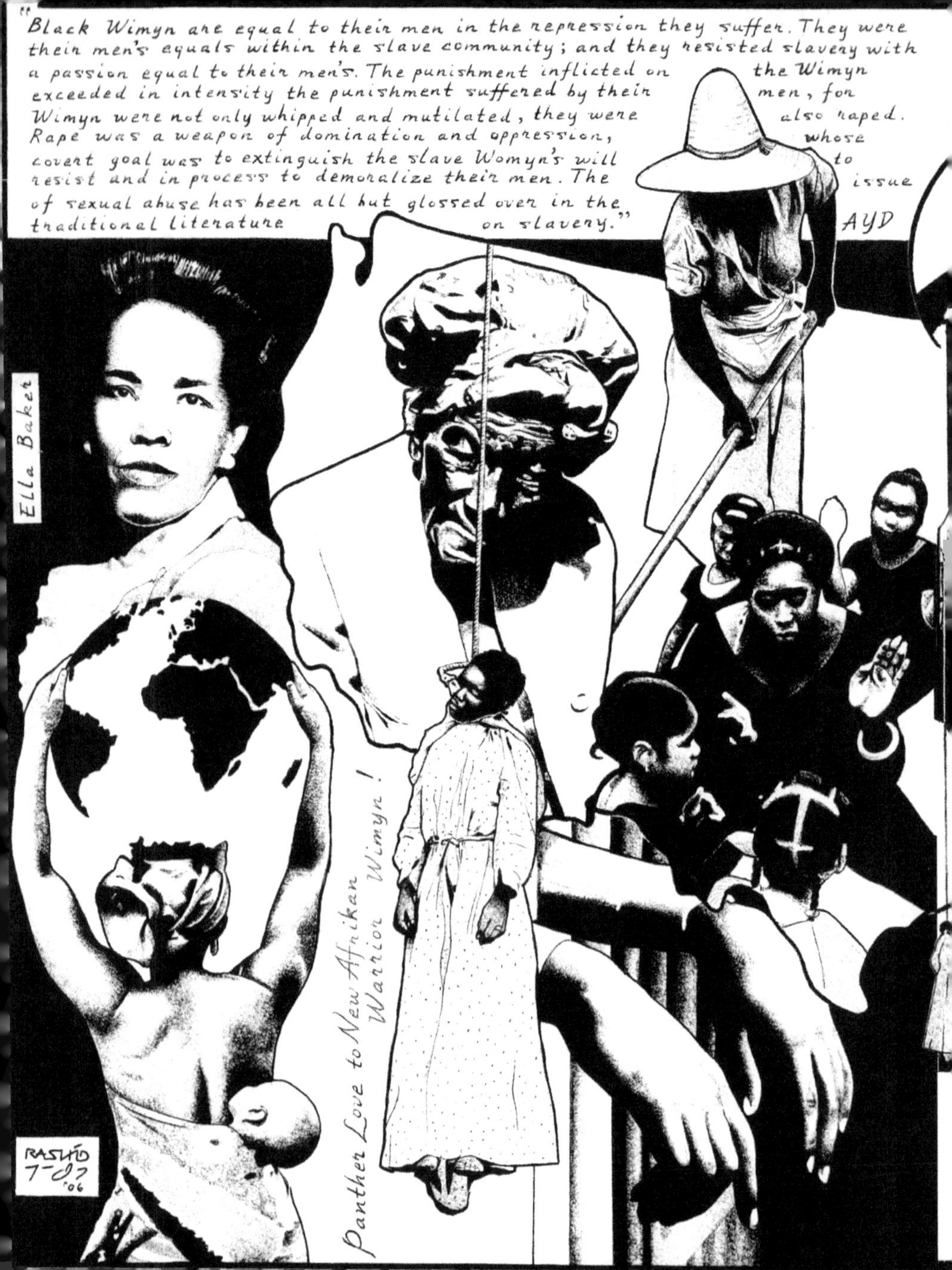
"Black Wimyn are equal to their men in the repression they suffer. They were their men's equals within the slave community; and they resisted slavery with a passion equal to their men's. The punishment inflicted on the Wimyn exceeded in intensity the punishment suffered by their men, for Wimyn were not only whipped and mutilated, they were also raped. Rape was a weapon of domination and oppression, whose covert goal was to extinguish the slave Womyn's will to resist and in process to demoralize their men. The issue of sexual abuse has been all but glossed over in the traditional literature on slavery."
AYD
Ella Baker
Panther Love to New Afrikan Warrior Wimyn!
RASHID

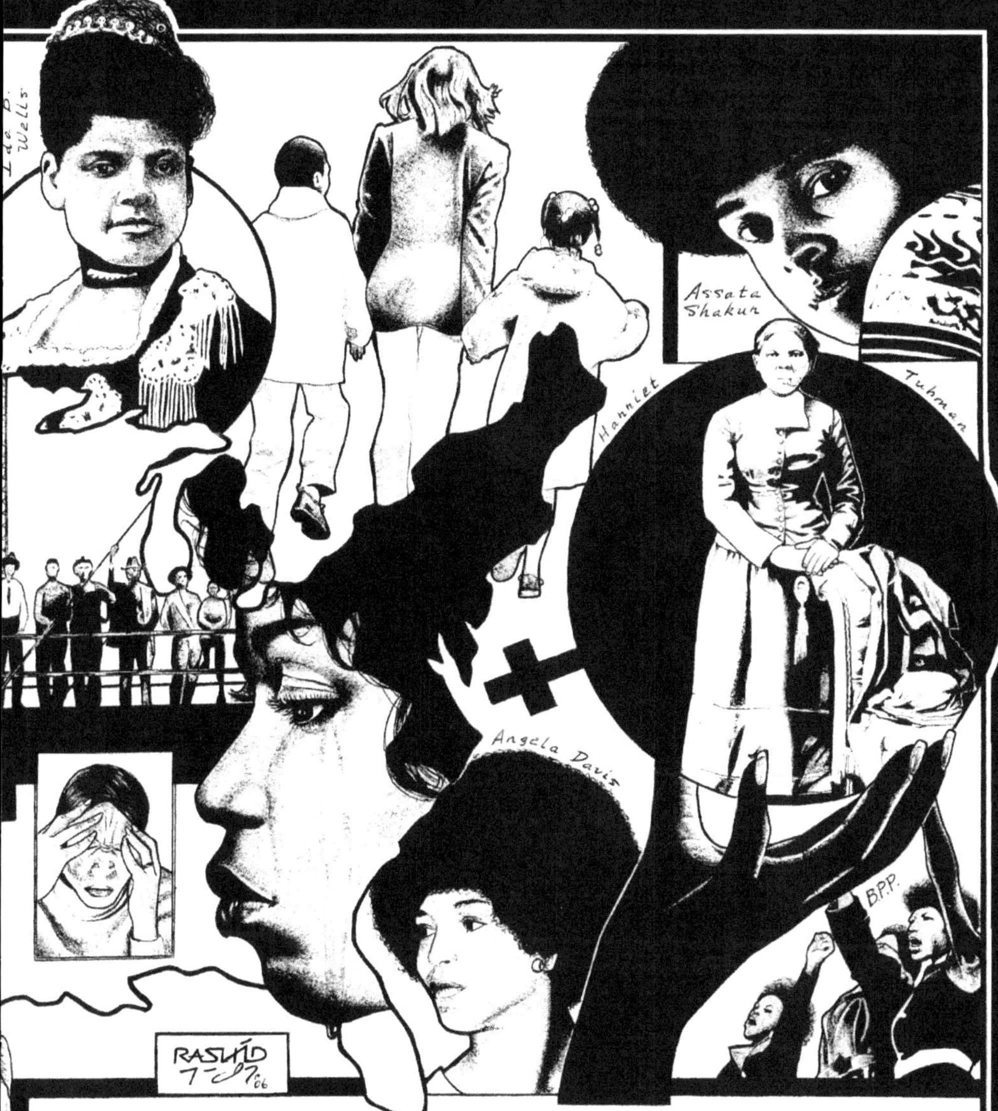


The Black Womyn has in the past few hundred years been the only force holding us together and holding us up. She has absorbed the biggest part of the many shocks and strains of existence under a slave order. The men can think of nothing more effective than dealing drugs, pimping, gambling, or petty theft. I've heard men brag about being pimps of Black Wimyn and taking money from Black Wimyn on relief. Things like this I find odious, disgusting - these Black men have proven themselves to be utterly detestable and repulsive in the past. Before I would succumb to such subterfuge I would scratch my living from the ground on hands and knees, or die in a hail of bullets! My hat goes off to every one of you, you have my profoundest respect."

George L. Jackson

# 9. REPARATIONS OR REVOLUTION?

2007

## Introduction

During the weekend of June 22, 2007, the National Coalition of Blacks for Reparations in America (N'COBRA), sponsored a gathering in Philly. The aim of the conference was to build and channel a broad base of mass energy towards winning reparations for Blacks in Amerika; to repair the ongoing suffering and negative effects we've suffered as a result of slavery, segregation and racism.

In light of the amount of work put into this conference and the overall campaign, we thought it important to say a few words on the question of reparations, to challenge the focus of this energy and to contrast it with working towards revolution. As revolutionary nationalists and internationalists, we feel working towards revolution should be the main focus of the New Afrikan Nation in Amerika.

No one can argue that the past exploitation of Black people in Amerika did not enrich the white capitalists or that it played an insignificant part in making the U.S. today's sole imperialist superpower. Moreover, the capitalist ruling class continues to super-exploit and oppress Black people in the U.S. and internationally. The point and the solution, however, is not to beg for a monetary settlement but to settle accounts by putting an end to the system of capitalist imperialism altogether.

This means revolution, and we believe that this should be the focus of our energy and what we are down with organizing. It is not a simple task, but it is pure idealism to believe that the U.S. government is going to pay out trillions of dollars to Black people simply because we make a compelling moral argument that they should. At best all they will give is a carefully worded apology.

What we see within this talk about keeping money in the Black community is a plea by aspiring Black capitalists to get a bigger piece of the profits made off the exploitation of the Black masses. There is nothing new about a section of the Black community profiting in this way. It is the same old neo-colonial trickery that was used to derail the revolutionary struggles of people of color throughout the 20th century.

Capitalism is the problem, and there were Black people all along who profited from our exploitation going back to our ancestors' enslavement back in Afrika. There were Black overseers on the plantations and even some Black slave-owners. Historically, Black businessmen and gangsters have fronted for white businessmen and gangsters in the Black community, and this is still the case. Black "illegal capitalists" are a big part of the problem in the Black community, but so too are the "respectable" Black bourgeoisie.

We're not saying that there is not some room for making tactical alliances in furtherance of building a united front against capitalist imperialism, but this class cannot lead us to liberation. Their class interests don't go that way. The Black bourgeoisie and bourgeois nationalism cannot lead to the liberation of Black people in Amerika any more than they have in Afrika.

The Nation of New Afrikans in Amerika is in a unique situation. We cannot achieve our national liberation by separating from the white supremacist United States nor by integrating with it—only by overthrowing it and putting an end to capitalist imperialism. So long as this system exists, it will maneuver its money and power and its military force and neo-colonial agents to keep us down and exploited. Divided, the colonized people who have struggled for national liberation could not escape the bonds of neo-colonial economic and political domination.

Much less could we secede from the U.S. and form our own republic in the Black Belt South. Such dreams and schemes are a diversion from what must be done. We must pull the system down. Black people are not the only ones exploited and oppressed by capitalist imperialism—the whole world is! This comes down unevenly—with some people being more oppressed and more exploited than others—but almost everybody stands to gain from proletarian socialist revolution and sweeping capitalist imperialism onto the trash heap of history.

## With the U.S. economy in crisis, where would reparations come from?

The U.S. government and economy is headed towards bankruptcy. In fact it is running on borrowed money now! Whereas the U.S. used to be the #1 lender nation, it is now the #1 debtor nation. As the national debt grows, more and more of the GNP must be channelled towards servicing that debt. The U.S. ruling class is doing to the U.S. economy what it has done to the 3rd World. It is cannibalizing it. How will it get out of the crisis it is creating? It won't.

No wonder leading ruling class figures are talking about the "End Times" and "Revelations." Imperialism is the last stage of capitalism, and globalization has only sped up the decline. So in the face of this growing economic crisis, how can any sane persyn imagine that the U.S. government would borrow trillions more to pay for the past exploitation of Black people? And who would be the caretakers of this vast sum of money? This is just pandering to the Black capitalist element with dollar signs in their eyes.

It's a diversion from the real need of the Black masses to end their exploitation and oppression by organizing to make a revolution when a truly revolutionary situation presents itself—as it will. Since 1987, when N'COBRA was founded, the situation for the masses of Black people in Amerika has steadily declined. Unemployment has risen, and so has incarceration for millions of Black and other oppressed people. Social service programs have been dramatically cut, and social problems have dramatically worsened.

But instead of rebuilding the Vanguard Party and mass movements of the '60s and '70s, many Black activists shifted towards accommodation with capitalist imperialism and the U.S. government. Stripped of its nationalistic rhetoric, that is just what this reparations movement is about.

### Imperialist payoffs as classic neo-colonialism

Whether given out in the name of "economic aid," "debt forgiveness" or "reparations," large sums paid out by the imperialists to "imperialist-approved" leaders of oppressed people is a classic neo-colonialist tactic. It serves a purpose—namely that of propping up their control over the oppressed people and countries. The aspiring capitalists of the oppressed nationalities serve to hold in check and divert the oppressed masses from the struggle for their liberation from all oppression and channel their energy into substituting one master for another—a master through whom the imperialists can rule indirectly.

This has happened across the 3rd World, from Afrika to Palestine, to Latin America, to Native America; from Cape Town to Harlem. The native bourgeois act as front men in the exploitation of "their own" oppressed masses. Is this national liberation? We think not! It is classic neo-colonialism, which is the preferred means of domination by the U.S. Empire. It can then talk about promoting "Democracy" and "Independence," while reserving the "right" to effect "regime changes" whenever it suits its interests, and dollars are more cost efficient and less obvious means of control than colonial administrators.

If the oppressed people choose leaders the U.S. doesn't approve of, it can cut off payments, as the U.S. did when Hamas was elected last year by the Palestinians. And then there is the option of sanctions and U.S. invasion and occupation as in Afghanistan and Iraq.

India under British rule was an early archetype of neo-colonial domination, and the U.S. learned from this model. Under British domination, India was administered by Indians for 200 years. This "Jewel of the British Empire" was primarily administered by an Indian elite and garrisoned by brutal Indian soldiers who oppressed the Indian people.

Even under Apartheid in South Afrika, it was Black soldiers and police who did most of the dirty work of oppressing the people. But more revealing is that after the fall of Apartheid, a native Black elite was substituted for the white colonial settler regime and given a cut of the profits from the exploitation of the still miserably poor Black masses while the local white elite and imperialists continue to control the economy.

This neo-colonial process is how the U.S. keeps Latin America under its thumb and controls its wealth of resources. These countries are run by imperialist agents who receive U.S. "economic aid" and depend upon a military system that props up the local elite and allows U.S. economic exploitation of their oppressed masses. The poor are kept poor and "in line."

The same would be the case with New Afrikans, if we did manage to convince the U.S. Government to pay us reparations. It would go into the hands of the Black bourgeoisie elite for services rendered to the Empire. But they don't need to do that. Not when straight up exploitation and oppression are doing just fine.

There are those who want to protest and seek to reform this rotten system and those who was to end it, overthrow and bury it, and move on to build a new, radically different kind of system based upon serving people's needs through socialist ownership of the basic means of production and people's power. The New Afrikan Black Panther Party-Prison Chapter and our allies are quite clear where we stand and on the absolute need for revolution. That is what our ideological and political orientation—"Pantherism"—is based upon.

Yes, we will and do protest the many outrages perpetrated by this system, and we do demand certain reforms, but not as ends in themselves and not to reach any accommodation with imperialism. We do so only to build a truly revolutionary movement and to create more favorable conditions for struggle. We need to agitate, educate and organize to this end.

To make revolution, we must have a revolutionary vanguard party that is steeled in struggle, a mass movement that builds mass revolutionary consciousness, and a revolutionary united front that is both national and international. The Party must be guided by the most advanced revolutionary theory and organized along tried and proven revolutionary lines to facilitate the maximum amount of democratic discussion and unity in action.

## The Debt We Owe

A nation is a continuum. It includes those who have passed on and those yet to be born. As a nation, the most fundamental question we New Afrikans should be asking is: "What do we owe our ancestors and to future generations?"

To those whose bones lie at the bottom of the Atlantic Ocean and under the black soil of the South, to those who will come after us bearing our DNA, we owe our life's blood. We owe the determination to carry the struggle against exploitation and oppression forward to victory, so that our progeny will not labor for exploiters or suffer cruel oppression because of the color of their skin.

Beyond the Nation, we owe it to our class—to all who labor for their daily bread—here and around the world—to break the chains of servitude and subjugation—to bring to an end the Epoch of Exploitation—and to advance humyn social evolution to a higher stage.

The system of capitalism—which arose with the kidnapping and enslavement of our ancestors from Afrika—will only perish when we New Afrikans rise to lead the world proletarian revolution. Can anyone put a price on that?

Capitalist imperialism is the final stage of capitalism. It is capitalism in its most rotten and decadent form—rotten ripe for revolution. It imposes poverty on the masses worldwide to serve the enrichment of a small class of social parasites. It destroys the natural environment and wastes precious resources. It devalues humyn life, destroys families and communities, and promotes alienation and shallow individualism and consumerism.

It is the final stage of the long Epoch of exploitation that began with the overthrow of Mother Right and the imposition of Patriarchy. Slavery was thousands of years old before it brought our ancestors to Amerika. So who owes the descendants of the slaves of Afrika, Asia and Europe reparations? The evolution of class exploitation with all its suffering—wars, rapes, tortures, hunger and poverty—the suffering of slaves, serfs, tenant farmers and wage slaves—has brought us to this point in time when it can be finally ended once and for all.

The possibility of social justice for all is now a reality if we but dare to SEIZE THE TIME and take history into our own hands. The globalization and socialization of production and advances in technology cry out for liberation from private ownership to serve the needs of all humynity. The possibility of providing everyone on the planet with a decent standard of living, with decent health care and persynal liberty exists now.

All that is needed is the courage and conviction to take the power into our hands to do it. The Nation of New Afrikans in Amerika has the moral responsibility to stand up and lead this revolution. We who live within the "Belly of the Beast," the sole imperialist superpower that was built upon the backs of our ancestors, we owe it to them, to our posterity and to ourselves not to seek accommodation with capitalist imperialism but to dig its grave and bury it!

In the words of our late comrade, Hasan Shakur, an innocent man murdered by the state of Texas because of the color of his skin: "The sooner begun the sooner done!"

*All Power to the People!*
*Dare to Struggle, Dare to Win!*

# 10. BLACK LIBERATION IN THE 21ST CENTURY: A REVOLUTIONARY REASSESSMENT OF BLACK NATIONALISM 2010

> "[T]rue revolutionary leaders must not only be good at correcting their ideas, theories, plans or programs, when errors are discovered ... but when a certain objective process has already progressed and changed from one stage of development to another, they must also be good at making themselves and all their fellow revolutionaries progress and change in their subjective knowledge along with it ..."
>
> Mao Tse-tung, *On Practice*

## Introduction

Some time ago comrades of the New Afrikan Maoist Party (NAMP) expressed a desire to reconcile contradictions between their line and the line of our New Afrikan Black Panther Party-Prison Chapter (NABPP-PC) on the question of Black National Liberation in the 21st Century. On this question, NAMP along with several other organizations—including the New Afrikan People's Organization (NAPO), the Provisional Government of the Republic of New Afrika, the Maoist International Movement (MIM) and others promote the Black Belt Thesis (BBT) as it was set out by the Comintern (Third Communist International) in the 1920s.

The NAMP comrades are correct in pointing out that our respective organizations have a major line contradiction on this question. We have as yet not publicly fleshed out our line on this, in contrast to that of NAMP and others, so it is time we did so in a formal position paper.

In developing our line on the Black National Question in the U.S. we have applied the method of historical and dialectical materialism and deepened the analysis put forward by Huey P. Newton of the original Black Panther Party (BPP). This means we do not hold dogmatically and idealistically to outmoded ideas and formulations that no longer fit the current situation. Instead we base our analysis on the study of concrete conditions in the context of their actual historical development, realizing that everything is in a state of motion and development from a lower to a higher level, and that correct ideas develop in struggle and contradiction with incorrect ones.

### The Black Belt Thesis and the New Class Configuration of the New Afrikan Nation

The BBT was developed by the U.S. "Black Bolshevik," Harry Haywood, in his 1928 and 1930 "Comintern Resolution on the Negro Question," which was adopted by the Comintern and the U.S. Communist Party with support from V.I. Lenin. It holds that Blacks in Amerika (New Afrikans) constitute a nation within the territorial U.S. and that we should establish our own sovereign national territory in Alabama, Mississippi, Georgia, Louisiana and South Carolina (the "Black Belt" also known as the "Cotton Belt"). These states were chosen because we slaved there and developed and evolved as a national group and "internal colony" where Blacks made up the majority. The principal factors which supported the BBT were economic and demographic that existed in the 1920s but no longer exist today.

No one can sensibly deny that Black people were forged into a "nation within a nation" because of their loss of Afrikan national identity under slavery and exclusion from the white Amerikan nation under conditions of "Jim Crow" segregation. Nor can one deny that this nation is bound to its Afrikan origin and defined by the imposed value that a drop of Afrikan blood sets one outside of the "melting pot" of white Amerikan society.

But where the BBT breaks down is that our present situation doesn't fit into the neat definition used by the Comintern in the 1920s. The reality is more complex today.

At the time the BBT was developed, Blacks in the "Black Belt" were a predominantly peasant (sharecropper) nation tied to cotton production. This condition was also shared by many poor whites and some Indians and mixed bloods. The BBT was based on Comrade J.V. Stalin's analysis of the National Question as essentially a peasant question. Unlike the analysis put forward by Lenin, and more fully developed by Mao, Stalin's analysis limited the National Question to essentially a peasantry's struggle for the land they labored on geographically defined by their having a common language, history, culture and economic life together. Hence the slogans "Free the Land!" and "Land to the Tiller!"

Indeed, ALL the national liberation struggles of the 20th Century occurred in peasant-based societies in opposition to colonial or neocolonial domination and feudal or semi-feudal class oppression. Today, however, the Black population within the U.S. is no longer a rural peasantry. It is overwhelmingly a proletarian nation (wage slaves) dispersed across the U.S. and concentrated in and around urban centers in predominantly Black or multi-ethnic oppressed communities.

The trend since World War I has been towards migration away from the "Black Belt" South and from the rural to the urban setting (even within the South). Check this out from "1001 Facts" on Black History:

> "African Americans (sic) continued to move northward and cityward after World War I in 1918. In fact, the migration increased during the 1920s as another million southern African Americans (sic) picked up their bags and left southern living conditions. The migration expanded in the 1930s as the New Deal Agricultural Adjustment Act of 1933 forced many more to migrate once the AAA paid white southern farmers not to produce crops and made it profitable to dispense with Black sharecroppers. Technological advances such as the cotton picker machine made large numbers of unskilled agricultural laborers obsolete in southern agriculture. Then, as World War II began, Black mass migration exploded and nearly 5 million African Americans (sic) left the South for the North from 1940 to 1960 ... [This] Second Migration created huge ghettos in all the major American cities. Whereas in 1890 close to 90 percent of African Americans (sic) lived in the South, by 1960 only 50 percent of African Americans (sic) still resided there. Moreover, the movement north was also a movement toward urban rather than rural living. By 1990 over 84 percent of African Americans (sic) lived in urban areas, making 'African American' (sic) and 'urban' almost synonymous in modem America."

Therefore, without need of pursuing a struggle to achieve a New Afrikan nation state, we have achieved the historical results of bourgeois democracy, at least as far as transforming ourselves from a peasant to a predominantly proletarian national grouping through the "Great Migration."

Of course the Amerikan liberal democratic revolution begun in 1776, which was continued by the Civil War (1861–1865), remains unfinished—in particular as far as Black people are affected. Pre-capitalist forms of exploitation continue to exist, such as the "slave status" of U.S. prisoners, institutionalized torture, legalized "lynching" as embodied in the racist death penalty, and all manifestations of racism, sexism and discrimination that prevent all from enjoying the "life, liberty and pursuit of happiness" promised by liberal democracy.

To complete the liberal democratic revolution and move forward to socialist reconstruction the proletariat must lead the struggle which is stifled by the increasingly antidemocratic, fascistic and reactionary bourgeoisie. The bourgeois are no longer capable of playing a progressive role in history.

### The Revolutionary Advantages of Our Proletarian National Character

That we New Afrikans are now a predominantly proletarian nation—and one without a national territory—is an advantage to the cause of building a multi-ethnic, multiracial socialist Amerika. Indeed, it thrusts us into playing a vanguard role in leading the whole working class and the broad masses in pulling down the capitalist-imperialist system and achieving social justice for all.

This conception of our historical role corresponds with Lenin's and Mao's lines on the National Question which we contrast with Stalin's and dogmatic continuation of the BBT. Lenin and Mao saw the national question primarily as a matter of building the ranks of the proletarian revolution to pull down the system of imperialism. In fact, in all of his writings on Black liberation in the U.S. Mao consistently talks about merging the Black liberation struggle with the proletarian revolutionary struggle in the U.S. He doesn't mention the land issue once. In *A New Storm Against Imperialism*, (April 16, 1968), he stated:

> "Racial discrimination in the United States is a product of the colonialist and imperialist system. The contradiction between the Black masses in the United States and the U.S. ruling circles is a class contradiction. Only by overthrowing the reactionary rule of the U.S. monopoly capitalist class and destroying the colonialist and imperialist system can the Black people in the United States win complete emancipation. The Black masses and the masses of white working people in the United States have common interests and common objectives to struggle for.
>
> "Therefore, the Afro-American struggle is winning sympathy and support from increasing numbers of white working people and progressives in the United States. The struggle of the Black people in the United States is bound to merge with the American workers' movement, and this will eventually end the criminal rule of the U.S. monopoly capitalist class."

In his August 8, 1963, article, *Oppose Racial Discrimination by U.S. Imperialism*, Mao's emphasis is on racial discrimination, not "Free The Land!" He sees Black liberation as driving forward the United Front

Against Capitalist-Imperialism and pulling white workers and other strata towards socialist revolution in the U.S. The issue is not integration versus separation but revolution.

Even Malcolm X came to embrace this position. In fact, every popular, independent Black leader who came to hold this view and actively advanced it was promptly assassinated. Why? Because neither separation nor integration threatens the imperialist system—socialist revolution does!

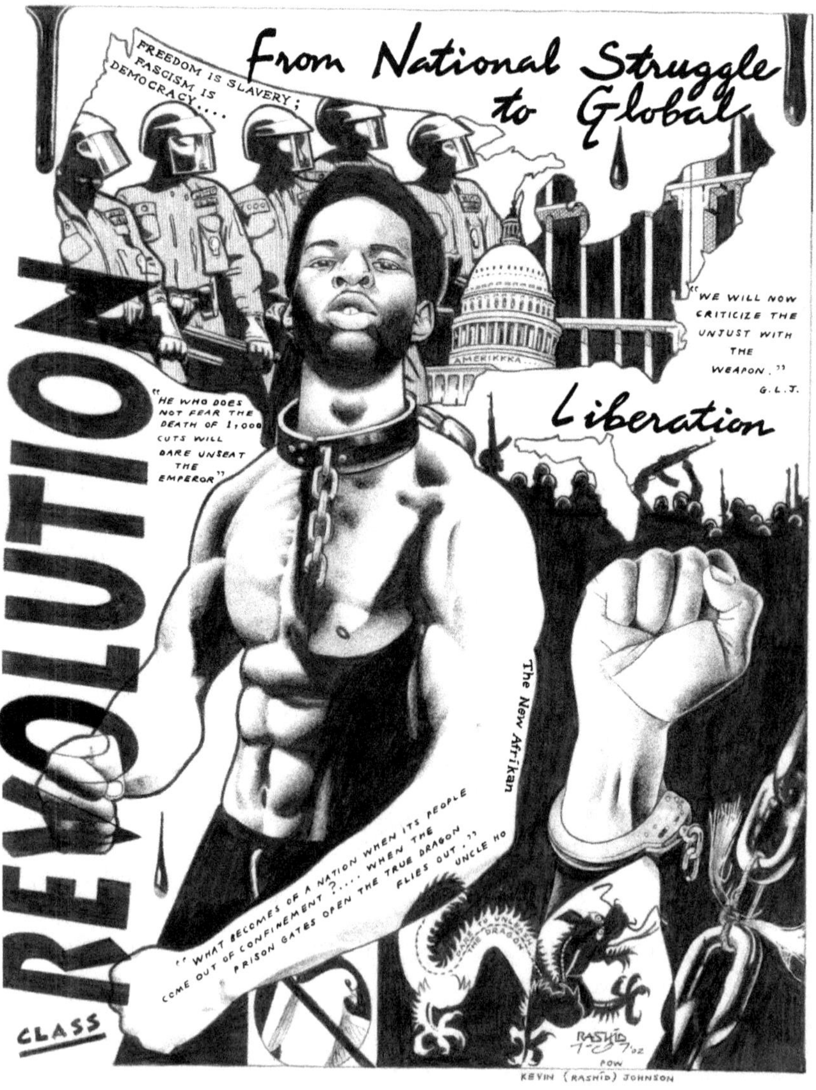

## Separation, Integration or Revolution?

Take Brother Malcolm; in his early stages of political development, he promoted Black separatism. Based upon his observation of independence struggles across the predominantly peasant-based Third World of the 1950s and early 1960s, he adopted the view that revolution was about land, and he embraced the slogan "Free The Land!" which he elaborated on in his Message to the Grassroots speech given in 1963. However, in an April 6, 1964, speech given in Harlem, he expressly rejected both Black separatism and integration, in favor of revolutionary change of Amerika as a whole. He stated:

> "We have to keep in mind at all times that *we are not fighting for integration, nor are we fighting for separation.* We are fighting for recognition ... for the right to live as free humans in this society" [my emphasis]

Malcolm increasingly came to identify capitalism and imperialism as the ultimate enemy—embracing the need of Afrikan people everywhere to consolidate their struggles into a united Pan-Afrikan movement, and for Blacks in Amerika to unite in a common struggle with all the "have-nots", regardless of their skin color, against the common exploiters who try to divide everyone and play us against each other. It was at this crucial stage of his development as a revolutionary that he was silenced by assassins' bullets.

A few months before his assassination, Malcolm X criticized his earlier views on separatist Black Nationalism, finding that:

> "I was alienating people who were true revolutionaries dedicated to overturning the system of exploitation that exists on this earth by any means necessary .... I had to do a lot of thinking and reappraising of my definition of Black Nationalism. Can we sum up the solution to the problems confronting our people as Black Nationalism? And if you notice, I haven't been using the expression for several months. But I would still be hard pressed to give a specific definition of the overall philosophy which I think is necessary for the liberation of Black people in this country."

At the opposite pole, Dr. Martin Luther King, Jr.—who was initially pro-integration and pro-capitalist—also came to identify capitalism and imperialism as the ultimate enemy, expressly rejecting integration and privately promoting socialist revolution in Amerika as the way forward. He stated in November 1967: "Something is wrong with capitalism as it stands here in the U.S. We are not interested in being integrated into this value structure." During later 1967 and 1968, shortly before his assassination, King repeatedly promoted socialism to his inside circle, but he refused to make this stand publicly for fear of government assassination. But his private statements, public opposition to U.S. imperialist wars abroad, and support for the rights of the poor and workers' strikes were enough for the imperialist ruling class to mark him for death.

George Jackson, pursuing the same path and arriving at the same conclusions in a more developed way, was likewise cut down by an assassin's bullet. He observed:

> "It's no coincidence that Malcolm X and M.L. King died when they did. Malcolm X had just put it together .... You remember what was on his lips when he died, Vietnam and economics, political economy. The professional killers could have murdered him long before they did. They let Malcolm rage on Muslim nationalism for a number of years because they knew it was an empty ideal, but the second he got his feet on the ground, they murdered him."

Despite Malcolm X's and even King's clearly-stated revolutionary positions that New Afrikan liberation lies neither in assimilation (accommodation) nor separation (running away), but in fundamentally changing Amerikan society as a whole, so that we can live as a free people right here, the Black Movement, and those purporting to lead it, have remained deadlocked between these two less than revolutionary positions. The original Black Panther Party has been the notable exception.

The Panthers recognized that the New Afrikan Nation can neither effectively separate from nor integrate into capitalist imperialist and white supremist Amerika. Neo-colonialism precludes the former and racist national oppression precludes the later. Our path to liberation—which even the Panthers found a bit difficult to consistently articulate—is to overthrow U.S. imperialism and play a leading role in the global proletarian revolution and socialist reconstruction. We must be the tip of the spear and rally everyone who has contradictions with imperialism to unite with us.

Huey P. Newton and Bobby Seale, who were greatly influenced by Malcolm X, were organizing in this direction, in implementing the BPP's Ten Point Program and Serve The People (STP), survival programs while carrying out revolutionary agitation, education and political organizing to build community-based people's power. Huey saw that Blacks were an oppressed nation inside Amerika, but his ideas on charting our path to liberation took a quantum leap forward when he visited and toured Mao's revolutionary China. There he found that numerous racial and ethnic minorities had attained genuine liberation within China's socialist state, without separating or integrating in the classic sense.

What Huey observed in China gave him a blueprint for organizing Black folks to become self-reliant in the very urban communities where they were concentrated in preparation for revolution in the U.S. The BPP's implementation of these ideas quickly earned it the label of the "greatest threat" to imperialism's security, and the U.S. government concentrated its forces in an all-out campaign to destroy the Panthers. Here's what Huey found in People's China that inspired the BPP's STP survival programs and illuminated his ideas about Black liberation in Amerika:

> "I saw, crystal clear, how we can start to reduce the kinds of conflicts that we're having in [Amerika]. I saw an example of that in China ... what I saw was this: when I went there, I was very unenlightened and I thought I knew something about China. I thought, as it has been said so often, that China would be a homogeneous kind of racial/ethnic territory. Then I found that 50 percent of the Chinese territory is occupied by a 54 percent population of national minorities, large ethnic minorities. They speak different languages, they look very different, and they eat different foods. Yet there is no conflict. I observed one day that each region—we call them cities—is actually controlled by those ethnic minorities, yet they're still Chinese ... . I'm talking about a general condition in China where ethnic minorities I've observed control their whole regions. They have a right to have representation in the Chinese Communist Party. At the same time they have their own principles ... . The cities in this country could be organized like that, with community control. At the same time, not Black control so that no whites can come in, no Chinese can come in. I'm saying there would be democracy in the inner city. The administration should reflect the people who live there."

While Huey proved less than adept at linking together, organizing and leading a multi-racial anti-imperialist united front in Amerika, Fred Hampton, the leader of the BPP in Chicago, successfully pulled together a revolutionary coalition of poor whites (Rising Up Angry and The Young Patriot Party), Puerto Ricans (the Young Lords Organization), Mexicans (the Brown Berets) and various student groups known as the "Rainbow Coalition." He was being considered for promotion to national leadership when he was killed in his bed by FBI and Chicago police in a planned assassination.

Around the country the Black Panthers did inspire and forge alliances with many different ethnically-based groups including the White

Panther Party, I Wor Kuen (Chinese), Ang Katipunan (Filipino), the American Indian Movement (AIM) and many others. This was paving the way for a revolutionary united front against imperialism rooted in the oppressed communities.

The NABPP-PC also finds relevance in Huey's theoretical concept of "Revolutionary Intercommunalism", which recognized that the U.S. no longer fits the classical definition of a nation state nor do the countries under its neo-colonial domination. Using "Dollar Diplomacy", along with covert operations and outright invasions, the U.S. has successfully imposed itself upon all of the former European colonies and overthrown the socialist-oriented governments brought to power by national liberation struggles in the 3rd World. This paved the way for the U.S. becoming the world's sole imperialist superpower. Amerika's consolidation of global power since the collapse of the Soviet Union and the increasingly globalized economic interdependence gives greater credibility to Comrade Newton's theory of "Intercommunalism," but we embrace this theory conditionally, recognizing that nation states still exist in the geopolitical sense under various political and military set ups of "reactionary intercommunalism," although they exist within a system of relative dominant and subservient positions with the U.S. in the position of "Top Dawg." The shackles of bourgeois nationalism still bind the productive forces of the various nations to some degree, from which world proletarian socialist revolution will liberate them, creating the conditions for "revolutionary intercommunalism."

### Reassessing the National Liberation Question

As every national liberation struggle in the 20th Century has demonstrated, genuine national liberation and self-determination have been unattainable. In each case the capitalist-imperialists have created and appealed to aspiring native bourgeois and petty-bourgeois elements within the oppressed national groups and used these puppets to derail their own people's liberation struggles. They have used "Dollar Diplomacy" to forge neo-colonial bonds upon these new republics.

Through their neo-colonial designs, the budding socialist and non-aligned Third World blocs were undermined and overthrown (sweeping the tillers off the land) and their natural resources and productive forces were brought under U.S. imperialist domination (with other imperialist powers getting a share). In this world of U.S. imperialist hegemony, any New Afrikan struggle for independence and separation from the U.S.—along the lines of the BBT—would suffer the same fate in spades. Even if we did manage to reconstitute ourselves as a territorial nation in the "Black Belt," we would only join the ranks of imperialist dominated Third world nations—and with the imperialist U.S. right on our border.

At a time when few within the Third World national liberation struggles foresaw the danger of U.S. neo-colonialism, Amilcar Cabral sounded a warning to other leaders of anti-colonial national liberation movements in the Third World. He questioned whether the national liberation movements were altogether born of the colonial peoples' determination to be free or if they were also to some degree instigated by imperialism to create and "liberate" Third World bourgeois and aspiring petty bourgeois forces to serve as imperialist agents and "front men" to impede and counter the growth of world socialism and create global U.S. imperialist hegemony. Few took heed to his words—then or now. Here is Cabral:

> "In Guinea, as in other countries, the implementation of imperialism by force and the presence of the colonial system considerably altered the historical conditions and aroused a response—the national liberation struggle—which is generally considered a revolutionary trend; but this is something which I think needs further examination. I should like to formulate this question: is the national liberation movement something which has simply emerged from within our country, is it a result of the internal contradictions created by the presence of colonialism, or are there external factors which have determined it? In fact I would even go so far as to ask whether, given the advance of socialism in the world, the national liberation movement is not an imperialist initiative. Is the juridical institution which serves as a reference for the right of all peoples to struggle to free themselves a product of the peoples who are trying to liberate themselves? Was it created by the socialist countries who are our historical associates? Let us not forget that it was the imperialist countries who recognized the right of all people to national independence."

Cabral went on to point out the inherent contradiction in the imperialists "promoting" Third World national independence if indeed such struggles were a threat to imperialism:

> "This is where we think there is something wrong with the simple interpretation of the national liberation movement as a revolutionary trend. The objective of the imperialist countries was to prevent the enlargement of the Socialist Camp, to liberate the reactionary forces in our countries which were stifled by colonialism, and to

enable these forces to ally themselves with the international bourgeoisie. The fundamental objective was to create a bourgeoisie where one did not exist, in order specifically to strengthen the imperialist and the capitalist camp."

> Amilcar Cabral, *The Politics of Struggle* (1964)

Cabral found that "what really interests us here is neocolonialism," which he observed was a new phase of imperialism devised after World War II to replace the old colonial system, by "grant[ing] independence to the occupied countries plus 'aid.'"

Witnessing the failed promises of "national liberation" Cabral recognized that to be genuinely revolutionary and "liberating" the struggles for national independence had to be joined with the struggle of the international proletariat. He concluded:

> "... that imperialism is quite prepared to change both its men and its tactics in order to perpetuate itself. It will make and destroy states and, as we have already seen, it will kill its own puppets when they no longer serve its purposes. If need be, it will even create a kind of socialism, which people may soon start calling 'neosocialism.' if there has been any doubts about the close relations between our struggle [for national liberation] and the struggle of the international working-class movement, neo-colonialism has proved that there need not be any." (Ibid.)

Even the U.S. imperialists admitted using such "new tactics" of neocolonialism as Cabral observed in supporting Afrika and Asia's various national liberation movements. In the words of Vice President Richard Nixon on his return from a 1957 tour of Afrika:

> "American interests in the future are so great as to justify us in not hesitating even to assist the departure of the colonial powers from Africa. If we can win native opinion in this process, the future of America in Africa will be assured."
>
> Quoted in *Dirty Works 2: The CIA in Africa*, edited by Ellen Ray, et al. (Seacaucus: Lyle Stuart, Inc., 1979) p. 58

Accord this statement of the U.S. National Security Council:

> "We must recognize, although we cannot say it publicly, that we need the strong men of Africa on our side. It is important to understand that most of Africa will soon be independent ... . Since we must have the strong men of Africa on our side, perhaps we

should in some cases develop military strong men as an offset to Communist development of the labor unions."

quoted verbatim from the record
of a January 14, 1960, meeting of the NSC

So clearly the U.S. government favored pushing its European rivals and their colonial governments out of Afrika by supporting the Afrikan national liberation struggles, by backing or placing native puppets at the head of those anti-colonial movements. In doing so:

> "The stage was set for the transition to neo-colonialism: formal political independence for the African countries, but continued economic domination by imperialism, with imperialist political control exerted indirectly through bureaucratic African governments more or less subservient to imperialism, and military control exerted indirectly through covert links between imperialist powers and African military/police hierarchies."
>
> Daniel Fogel, *Africa in Struggle: National Liberation and Proletarian Revolution* (CA: ISM Press, 1982), p. 116

National "Liberation" has therefore proved empty of substance to oppressed Third World peoples, absent the defeat of imperialism, just as it would be in a struggle for New Afrikan national "liberation" in the southern U.S. territory absent the defeat of imperialism.

Moreover, any such struggle would almost certainly degenerate into an imperialist-sponsored race war, similar to what went down in the Kosovo conflict (1998–1999), and present day Sudan. In any such struggle, Blacks would be at a decided disadvantage—witness our helplessness in the face of the Hurricane Katrina Crisis and attendant martial law in Louisiana and Mississippi (both "Black Belt" states). And in that crisis we didn't have to contend with angry and desperate whites fighting to keep their land and homes. Or do our proponents of the BBT expect whites in the "Black Belt" to passively concede the territory and leave? Or do they think we will just grab the imperialists by the throat and demand that they give us five states, make all the arrangements, and then let us run the show there without interference?

And what about the white proletarians who live in the "Black Belt"? What stake would they have in this? Or would we want to just push them into the arms of the reactionaries opposing us? Such a plan would only divide the proletarians along racial lines, set them against each other and give the imperialists a free hand to play the "Divide and Rule" game "Willie Lynch"-style.

Furthermore, our migration back to the "Black Belt" would be "a leap from the frying pan into the fire" for how would we survive in the already poor economy of the rural South? "Returning to the Land" may sound romantic, but trying to bust a living out of the depleted soil of the Deep South was a dead end that caused the "Great Migration" in the first place.

And what a loss it would be to the international proletariat for us to give up our strategic positions within the urban centers across Amerika. Of course revolutionary work should be done among the people of the "Black Belt" South (including the poor whites and others) as well, as part of building the revolutionary movement to overthrow capitalist-imperialism.

The BPP did not promote a mass exodus of New Afrikans back to the "Black Belt"; rather they correctly looked to New Afrikan self-determination right in the oppressed urban communities where Black people are concentrated. It really wasn't until Harry Haywood's book *Black Bolshevik* was published in 1978 that the BBT was revived among the New Communist Movement in the U.S. The name New Afrikan was adopted by a convention of 500 Black Nationalist leaders in Detroit in March of 1968 at a Black government conference.

For the NABPP-PC "New Afrikan" is more than the latest in a series of monikers given to Black people in Amerika. Afrika is our common heritage. It (not the "Black Belt") is our common historic homeland. When a Black persyn comes to Amerika from the Caribbean, Brazil or from Afrika they become a part of the New Afrikan Nation in Amerika—and suffer national oppression and discrimination—even though their ancestors never set foot in the "Black Belt."

As proletarians, our relationship to production and the world economy makes us "New" and different from the peasantry of the Third World and our ancestors in the Old South. Even if we could go back it would be a retrogressive step—and we doubt this is what the Black masses want.

### We Have Not Liquidated the National Question

By our pointing out that the shift from peasantry to proletarian and from rural to urban has fundamentally changed the National Question for New Afrikans, we expect some critics will accuse us of having "liquidated" the National Question. For those who dogmatically apply Stalin's analysis, the problem is: "How can we be a nation without a land base?"

We reiterate that the issue is a bit bigger and more complex than that.

If we look at the New Afrikan Nation as being part of a greater Pan-Afrikan Nation, inclusive of the peoples of Afrika and the Afrikan

Diaspora (as Malcolm X did), and this liberation struggle in the context of world proletarian socialist revolution, then we shall see the issue a bit differently. Then we can also see our struggle within the context of a future socialist Amerika that is multi-ethnic and a strong ally of the oppressed peoples internationally.

The proletariat fundamentally has no country and seeks to create a world without boundaries or nation states. So to the proletariat national liberation is not an end in itself but a stage to pass through on the road to World Communism. It is a stepping stone to greater unity and the ending of all oppression.

There are many white comrades (Communists, Socialists, Anarchists, Radicals and Progressives) who are committed to supporting Black liberation because it serves the cause of liberating all of humynity from imperialism and exploitation, and because it strengthens the workers' movement. The cause of uniting the Black liberation struggle with the proletarian class struggle is a step towards the total liberation of humynity and the whole world becoming one people.

Just as the proletariat seeks to abolish itself as a class by abolishing all classes, we must seek to abolish ourselves as a nation by abolishing all nations—all national divisions and all national oppression. But this has to begin with liberating ourselves as nations from the grip of colonialism, neocolonialism and imperialism. Just as the proletariat must rise as a class and "pick up the gun to put down the gun" (what is the state but a special body of armed men and wimyn?), we create nation states only to render them obsolete and allow them to fade away when they are no longer necessary. The transitory nature of nation states under socialism is clear.

## Comparing Racial and National Oppression

We can only speak of New Afrikan national liberation because we suffer from national oppression. National oppression is linked to but not the same as racist oppression. The people of Haiti don't just suffer national oppression as citizens of a Third World nation but also racist oppression because they are Black. Iceland is a small island nation too, but if an Icelander family emigrates to the U.S., they will be accepted as whites. If a Haitian family moves here they will face racial oppression. All people of color, to one degree or another, suffer racist oppression because of the institutionalization of the ideology of white supremacy.

The Haitian family will suffer oppression and discrimination in the U.S. because they are immigrants, because they are Black, and because they are not white. A Korean family will have to face the first and the last but not the specific oppression and discrimination levelled at Blacks (New Afrikans in Amerika). This oppression is rooted in the history of slavery (not just in the "Black Belt" South) and colonialism that spawned the white racist mentality.

Whereas in Amerika, the oppression of the indigenous people is a bit different. People with Indian features ("Skins") suffer from national oppression and so do Indians with black or white-skinned features. Black Indians are also oppressed as New Afrikans. White-skinned Indians (if they are identifiable by their dress) may be subjected to racial slurs and discrimination, but this is really national oppression. There is a difference between "white Indians" and "white people" in Amerika, but the difference is national rather than racial.

Within the Indian nations there are divisions between "Bloods" and those who are perceived as "Black Indians" and "White (or mostly white) Indians." These contradictions (which can be antagonistic) between "Red", "White" and "Black" members of the same oppressed indigenous nations are a reflection of the culture of racism that permeates Amerikan society (a colonial settler state) and projects throughout the world.

We do not (as many Black nationalists do) confuse race with nationality. Nationality is not confined by race. One can change their nationality. One can also have dual or multiple nationalities. One can be a Puerto Rican and a New Afrikan (and also a Taino Indian). One can be a Palestinian, an Arab and a New Yorker all at the same time. National identity is a complex issue.

Do not some New Afrikans identify primarily as Amerikans? What is Obama trying to sell us? Yet look around any prison and what do you see? Look at the statistics on poverty, infant mortality, hunger, unemployment, and violent deaths. These tell a very different story—one of continued (and intensified) national and class oppression for the Black masses in the U.S.

I have written before that:

> "As revolutionary New Afrikan nationalists, we realize that there is a contradiction between race and nationalism, and moreover, that there is no nation composed of a single race. All existing nations, like the Indian nations here in North Amerika, include whites and mixed bloods, even though there are contradictions. It was the policies of white colonialism created by the ruling class that produced these contradictions, and indeed the New Afrikan Nation. In this regard, we say all people of Afrikan heritage, regardless of skin tone, are part of a single New Afrikan Nation ... a Pan-Afrikan Nation. Indeed, most 'Blacks' in Amerika are 'mixed bloods'; mixed with white and/or Indian bloodlines.

"We therefore move beyond black and white dogmatism, Native Americans have always done this in adopting any 'race' of people into their nations who embrace and respect their heritage and culture. All non-chauvinistic nations have done this. We also accept that nationalities can overlap and are not merely an either/or situation. People the world over embrace multiple nationalities, and so can New Afrikans. One can be a Venezuelan and a New Afrikan, or a Lenape and a New Afrikan, etc. This concept becomes practical revolutionary internationalism that has all nationalities struggling for both national self-determination and united multinational, anti-imperialist cooperation ...

"From our point of view, the key question is building alliances between the oppressed nations [and nationalities] within the U.S. and abroad and the multi-national proletariat."

Kevin "Rashid" Johnson, *On the Questions of Race and Racism, Revolutionary National Liberation, and Building the United Front Against Imperialism*, 2007

The success of socialist revolution in the U.S. would "break the back" of global imperialism and create conditions for successful revolution in every other country. This eventuality will create the conditions for a global dictatorship of the proletariat and move the struggle decisively towards rendering nation states obsolete. What then will be the need for national boundaries or militaries?

Could we not then move forward towards classless society at an accelerated pace? Could we not, for example, create a single international currency and globalized planning of production and distribution of goods? Would it not be possible to have a World Health Organization that really provides for people's health needs and a global commission with clout to address the issues of ecological preservation and balance? Could we not standardize wages and prices and ensure a decent standard of living for everyone on the planet—eradicating poverty?

## Conclusion

Most theories on the National Question do not address the dialectical relationship between New Afrikans in the Diaspora and Afrikans in Afrika, the contradictions between Afrikans everywhere and imperialism in the Age of Neo-Colonialism and the Crisis of Capitalist-Imperialism, and between New Afrikans in the U.S. and the white-supremacist, imperialist U.S. ruling class. These questions demand a reanalysis of the BBT and our strategy for Black Liberation.

Kwame Nkrumah's concept of an All-Afrikan (Pan-Afrikan) Revolutionary Party (supported by a military arm) is the correct answer to neo-colonialism. We can take a lesson in this from the struggles going on in South Asia. India contains many nationalities with their own languages and regions, yet they are being led by a united Communist Party of India (Maoist). Likewise we can look to Nepal where the Maoists have won the support of many national minorities and have created autonomous regions. In Afrika, neo-colonialism had an advantage because it was able to play the various budding nation states and tribal groups against each other. Our strength is based on unity and common purpose.

Our concept of Afrika as a Pan-Afrikan nation departs from the Comintern's definition of the National Question which confines the nation to the boundaries already in existence (even though these only reflect the imperialists' carving up of Afrika). We don't expect that the New Afrikan Nation will ever constitute itself again in the "Black Belt," but we can play a significant role in the constitution of a Socialist Afrikan Union, and in the creation of a Socialist USA.

We believe that it is the historic destiny of the nation of New Afrikans in Amerika to play a leading role among the oppressed peoples of the World in overthrowing capitalist imperialism and advancing humynity to a higher stage of political-economic organization based on the principles of social justice and equality.

Our unique history and position within the "Belly of the Beast" gives us the opportunity to deal the coup de grace to U.S. imperialism. Our long-suffering at the hands of white supremacist Amerika gives us a bond with all who have suffered racist and national oppression and enables us to be truly internationalist in outlook.

As Mao predicted:

> "The struggle of the Black people in the United States is bound to merge with the American workers' movement, and this will eventually end the criminal rule of the U.S. monopoly capitalist class."

This is the mission of the New Afrikan Black Panther Party-Prison Chapter and our position on the National Question.

*Dare to Struggle, Dare to Win!*
*All Power to the People!*

# 11. PROMOTING PROLETARIAN CONSCIOUSNESS AS PRISONER REHABILITATION 2007

Since our inception, the NABPP-PC has emphasized the leading role of the proletariat in any genuine revolutionary struggle. In our founding article, "The NABPP-PC: Our Line," we explained this position and contrasted the revolutionary character of the proletariat with the counter-revolutionary character of the lumpen (or "broken") proletariat.

Because lumpen values have been deeply ingrained in the New Afrikan and general urban and prison culture, advancing revolutionary proletarian ideology is essential to building our Party, organizing our mass organizations, revolutionizing prisoners and the oppressed masses in general, and consolidating the struggle against capitalist imperialism.

We promote proletarianizing prisoners through ideologically and politically training them in the principles and practices of class struggle and in the science of Revolution (Historical and Dialectical Materialism). But, there's yet another approach (which can turn a negative into a positive), namely by genuinely transforming prisoners' economic statuses from that of slaves into wage earning proletarians.

This can be done within the prison setting.

Our Party has already taken a firm stand in promoting abolishing prisoners' slave status (including amending the 13th Amendment to strike the clause that legalizes convict slavery) and granting them the right to vote (which is the fundamental component of citizenship), and abolishing the racist death penalty, indefinite solitary confinement, physical and mental torture, and other humyn rights abuses. But an additional step in organizing prisoners, advancing our revolutionary consciousness and ranks, and preparing us for a more stable and productive re-entry into society is to demand prisoners' right to work for minimum wage and to union representation.

As part of and in addition to advancing proletarian consciousness, paying prisoners a real wage for their labor could help them support their families and build up a nest egg for when they get out to get a place to live, a car, survival and therefore greatly reducing recidivism. They could pay off fines and restitutions before they get out and be more likely to sustain relationships on the outside as well as retain legal services.

This would counteract warehousing of prisoners and reducing us to slaves, and instead promote proletarian consciousness and aspirations as a means of rehabilitation, which would include the right to organize and to strike.

This would not be a move to legitimize the prison-industrial complex and the use of convict labor for profit (which the imperialists are already doing). But turning the conditions that they have created against us to our benefit and that of revolutionary organizing.

As Karl Marx pointed out, productive work is essential to womyn and mankind's very existence, that independent of meeting financial needs, people need productive labor—enforced idleness corrupts and deteriorates the humyn character and is itself a humyn rights violation.

The lumpen are distinguished from unemployed workers because they do not look for work and avoid it—it is in this sense that they are "broken." If given a choice, they prefer to steal, deal, hustle or pimp, living as parasites and preying on others—even killing their fellow humyns.

Proletarianizing the lumpen is the highest and only legitimate form of "rehabilitation." Prisoners have a right to be rehabilitated as opposed to the humyn rights violation of being merely warehoused (unless the "criminal justice" system admits its real design and intentions to be that of creating and unleashing predators to prey upon the general society), and this means freedom to sell their labor power and to collectively bargain over the terms of sale.

Enforced slavery contradicts the "inalienable" rights, as declared in the U.S. Declaration of Independence, of all people to life, liberty and the pursuit of happiness. Beyond the security considerations inherent in incarceration, the state cannot be allowed to kill, cannot be allowed to deny the right—the liberty—to be a proletarian or to pursue meaning and purpose in life.

If society accepts that one must do time as punishment for a crime, then it follows that the time must productively serve the needs of the society by promoting the genuine rehabilitation of the incarcerated individual so that s/he will function as productive members of the society upon release.

Enslavement does not teach one how to be free. Abuse does not promote good citizenship or emotional stability. A criminal justice system will still be needed under socialism—to deal with anti-social criminal behavior. But our model must be a "school of liberation." The principles of a genuine correctional system must be articulated and struggled for as part of the overall revolutionary struggle. The question is how should these prisons be run and what rights should the prisoners have that are inalienable and will promote rehabilitation and good citizenship.

Revolution is a birthing process, the new society forming in the womb of the old one. Through struggle we create more favorable conditions for greater struggle. Nothing comes instantly. Changing social and economic relations must proceed and develop from a lower to a higher level.

As revolutionaries we want to transform the prisons into "Schools of Liberation" to provide the revolution with trained cadre and fighters. But on a deeper level we want to revolutionize social relations under capitalism to better enable us to revolutionize social relations under socialism and in the advance to a classless society.

Our goal is not to make acceptance of wage-slavery more palatable and thus prolong the inequality, exploitation and injustice of capitalist-imperialism.

Our goal is to serve and advance the interests of the world proletarian revolution to abolish the system of capitalist-imperialism.

Toward this end we should seek to proletarianize the prisoner population through revolutionary political education, promoting revolutionary culture and as much as possible drawing them into proletarian social relations to the means of production.

Can the system altogether oppose the demand for the right to work and to collective bargaining through union representation? They do want to exploit convict labor. A concession on this issue would force the state to expand work industries bringing more prisoners into the workforce and counter the present model of long-term segregation.

Free world unions could be won to support the prospect of 2.5 million new dues paying members and an equally large electoral voting bloc. It's also possible to win criminologists and people in the criminal justice system to support this program.

Organizations like the National Council on Crime and Delinquency are already actively advocating increasing prisoners' wages to free world levels. The policy statement of the NCCD's Board of Directors reads in part:

> "The present condition of prison industries limits the value of [work programs]. The deficiencies vary from prison to prison ... The pay for inmates employed in prison is too low to be regarded as wages. The average prison laborer receives from ten cents to 65 cents a day. Few institutions pay inmate workers for a day's work what the federal minimum wage law requires for an hour's work. The rate of pay ... is only a token ... a daily rebuke to the inmate, reminding him [or her] of society's power to exploit at will.
>
> "This counterproductive prison labor system must be changed. An inmate receiving equitable payment for work performed will be able to provide some support for his [or her] family, continue payments on social security ... make some payment for room and board, and save money to assist himself [or herself] upon return to society.

"Therefore the National Council on Crime and Delinquency urges the introduction of federal and state legislation requiring that an inmate employed at productive work in a federal, state, or local institution shall be paid no less than the minimum wage operative nationally or in his [or her] state.

"Developing prison labor unions is also a practical goal, as such institutions presently exist with beneficial results in other countries.

"Prison labor unions are not an American invention. The first successful prisoner labor union was organized in Sweden. Since 1966, the union, which represents the vast majority of Swedish prisoners, has carried out a long series of successful negotiations with the government. Every effort has been made to make the prisoners' wages the same as free wages. Prisoners pay rent for their cells and board for their food. They are encouraged to pay their debts in the free community, including restitution to the victims of the crimes. They pay taxes and generally have enough left at the end of the month to save around $50.

"Additional benefits from unionization have been a good working relationship with Swedish industry, widely available vocational training, safer prison factories, eligibility for workmen's compensation and, perhaps most important of all, the democratic involvement of prisoners in forming their own destiny.

"The union is credited with diminishing violence in prisons, lowering recidivism and making prisons more open institutions in Swedish society."

Paul Comeau, *Labor Unions for Prison Inmates*

Amerika's liberal democratic revolution of 1776, of which the Civil War (1861–1865) was a continuation, remains an unfinished revolution. The most glaring examples of this are the U.S. prison system and the continuation of the status of "slave," the racist death penalty (legalized lynching) and the institutionalized racism, sexism and humyn rights abuses that constitute "legally sanctioned torture." Until the inalienable rights of "Life, Liberty, and the pursuit of happiness" is extended to all in Amerika—including those convicted of crimes—the liberal democratic Revolution remains unfinished. To bring this stage to its completion and move forward to socialism the proletariat must lead this struggle. Democracy leads to socialism and democratic revolution leads to Socialist revolution.

The slave emancipates her/himself by becoming a proletarian and the proletarian emancipates her/himself by the abolition of classes.

Recognizing that the bourgeoisie are no longer a progressive and revolutionizing force as they were in 1865 when they overthrew the chattel slave system, in fact they have become reactionary to the core and increasingly fascist and anti-democratic, the proletariat must lead in completing the democratic revolution and carry it forward to make socialist revolution to put an end to the dictatorship of the bourgeoisie.

We are not calling for an all new democratic revolution, but there is unfinished business that clearly falls under liberal democracy, and resolving it moves us forward towards socialist revolution.

Towards this end, the New Afrikan Service Organization (NASO) should outline a comprehensive program for Transforming the Razor Wire Slave Plantations into Schools of Liberation. This program should include amending the 13th Amendment, abolishing the death penalty and life without parole, establishing voting rights for prisoners, job training and the right to work and union representation, education and cultural programs, religious freedom and self-help programs, freedom of correspondence between prisoners, an end to political censorship, etc. It should call for a national task force of humyn rights abuses and institutionalized racism and sexism to investigate the federal, state and local prisons and jails.

The program should be based upon the NABPP-PC's Ten Point Program in its minimal form—ending the slave status for prisoners and establishing our status as proletarians, and from there moving forward to proletarian socialist revolution.

*Dare to Struggle, Dare to Win!*
*All Power to the People!*

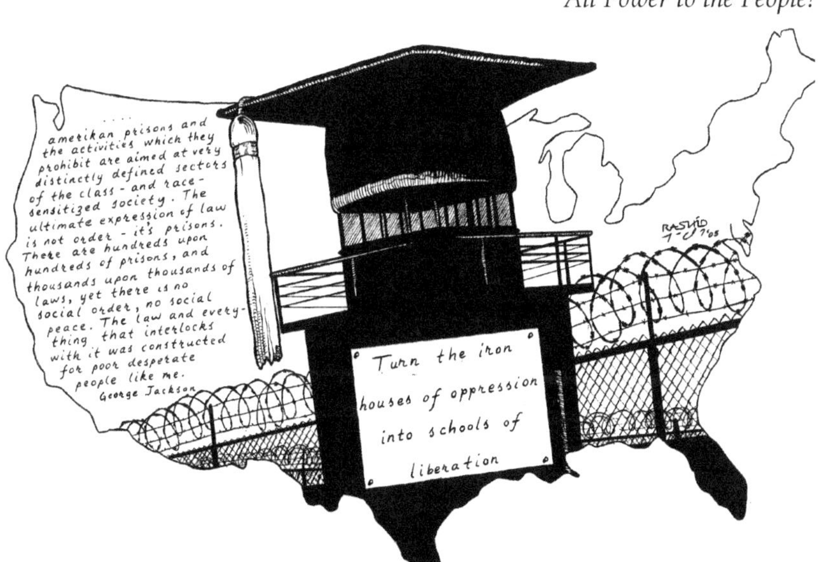

# PART III

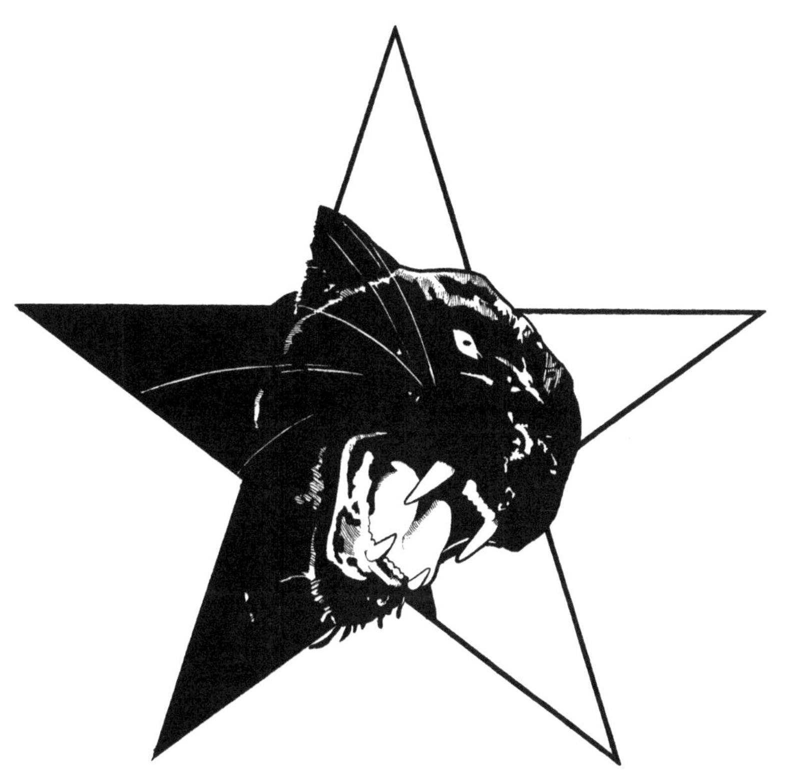

# PHILOSOPHY

*From ideology to politics and back to ideology—ever sharpening our tools—and proving that iron sharpens iron. As Lenin pointed out; "Without Revolutionary Theory, There Can Be No Revolutionary Movement!" Nothing stands still. Everything is in motion and process of transformation, and we must see it as such to correctly analyze and understand. We must see things in their interconnectedness and in their essence. We must see the contradictions that are within everything and determine a thing's development and transformation.*

*Our world has changed since the time of Marx and Engels, and since the time of Lenin, Stalin and Mao, and even since Huey, and we must make fresh analysis of these changing conditions utilizing and further developing the method they used to derive the "Science of Revolution," that is in this period known as Marxism-Leninism-Maoism. Unlike other sciences, like Psychology, Sociology and Anthropology, which can be utilized by either side, MLM is partisan and serves the proletariat in overthrowing capitalist-imperialism, building socialism and advancing to global classless society. Not that they do not study Lenin and Mao at West Point and the Army War College at Carlisle, they do, but only to learn how to attempt to throw us off our game. They freely admit that Mao's strategy of People's War is unstoppable unless the vanguard party deviates from its basic principles. Ideological-political line determines victory or defeat!*

*Tom Watts*

# 12. HISTORICAL & DIALECTICAL MATERIALISM: THE SCIENCE OF REVOLUTION 2006

> "The tool of analysis is for us a further development of the historical materialist method, the dialectical method. We will not even waste our time debating the values of Marxism with those who are essentially hung up on white people—hung up to the point of ideological blindness. We understand the process of revolution, and fundamental to this understanding is this fact: Marxism is developed to a higher level when it is scientifically adapted to a people's unique national condition, becoming a new ideology altogether. Thus was the case in China, Guinea-Bissau, Vietnam, North Korea, the People's Republic of the Congo and many other socialist nations [during the revolutionary era of the 20th century]. For Black [New Afrikan] people here in North Amerika our struggle is not only unique, but it is the most sophisticated and advanced oppression of a racial [and] national minority in the world. We are the true 20th [and now 21st] century slaves, and the use of the dialectical method, class struggle and national liberation, will find its highest development as a result of us. This dialectic holds true not only for Marxism, but for revolutionary nationalism as well; it holds true for concepts of revolutionary Pan-Afrikanism; it is true on the theoretical basis in developing revolutionary [New Afrikan] culture. All of these ideological trends will find their highest expression as a result of our advanced oppression."
>
> *Message to the Black Movement: A Political Statement from the Black Underground*—CC—BLA

### Introduction

Karl Marx developed the scientific method of analysis, which came to be called Dialectical Materialism (DM) by those who came after him. As an analytical tool, DM provides a method for understanding the laws of material existence and for changing material conditions by acting within these laws. Historical Materialism (HM) is the application of DM to the study and understanding of social development and history.

## Marx's Teachings

Marxism developed during an era of struggle between the philosophical schools of rationalist versus materialist thinking. Marx was able to merge the best of both schools, drawing dialectics (study and analysis) from the rationalists and materialism from the materialists.

The most advanced rationalist thinker during Marx's time was George Wilhelm Friedrich Hegel, and the most advanced materialist then was Ludwig Feuerbach. But both schools of thought were tied up in and hindered by traditional idealistic and theological influences.

## Marx's Dialectics

Hegel saw the "idea" as an absolute and as the creator and center of the material world. From Hegel's thinking Marx seized on the pertinent role of the "idea," but found it to be "nothing else than the material world reflected by the human mind, and translated into forms of thought."

Marx understood that the brain—the very medium of our thoughts and ideas—is itself a material construction, it grows and develops with and as a result of material conditions without which it would cease to be and could not generate thoughts. Purged of metaphysical influences, dialectics regards nature as a connected and unified whole, as a combination of organically bound phenomenons that are interdependent and affect each other's development. Therefore, no activity in nature can be understood if it is isolated from surrounding phenomena.

Metaphysics teaches that nature exists in an absolute and unchanging state. The dialectical method teaches that nature remains in a state of constant change, development and renewal. This can be seen through scientific and even general studies of nature and natural processes. Nothing remains the same.

Everything is in a state of either growth, relative equilibrium or decline, but is never stagnant. All matter is in a state of constant motion through increases or decreases in quantity.

But dialectics doesn't merely see things in a state of motion where there is only increase or decrease in quantity without fundamental changes in quality. This means that phenomena moves and develops not in straight lines but in spirals. These qualitative and overlapping changes are seen as leaps. An example of change from quantity to quality can be seen in how all matter changes in quality, according to the quantity (increase or decrease) of temperature, from gas to liquid to solid.

In recognizing the continual growth and development of all material processes, dialectics recognizes that at the root of all motion are internal contradictions—opposite forces operating inside of things, pulling back and forth between their poles for control. Such polar forces can be seen competing, merging and changing positions in everything; negative and positive, light and dark, sickness and health, hot and cold, birth and death, pain and pleasure, advancement and decline, old and new, contraction and expansion, electron and proton and etc.

This is the unity of opposites that operates within all phenomena large and small, known and unknown. Without one, the other could not exist, nor could the matter or phenomenon exist that they combine into. Because of the constant struggle between such opposite forces, everything remains in constant motion. Because of this constant motion and resultant change, dialectics recognizes that that there are no unchangeable absolutes, and therefore continual study and experience of these material processes is the only source of proofs, "truth," and understanding.

Many people today see, in an abstract and unconscious way, the value of studying the history and development of things in order to determine and understand how they reached their present state, in order to attempt to determine what their potential for future change and development might be. But in order to really accomplish these ends, they must understand and practice this method in the comprehensive manner of Marxist dialectics.

Without proper analysis of material conditions and their internal and external contradiction, it is impossible to develop a proper understanding of them. Lenin stated:

> "… in order really to know an object we must embrace, study, all its sides, all connections and 'mediations.' We never achieve this completely, but the demand for all-sidedness is a safeguard against mistakes and rigidity."

This scientific method of all-sided analysis, which is not the method of lazy or idealistic minds, can be applied to all areas of existence; mental, emotional, social, physical, etc. Dialectics "… takes things and their perceptual images essentially in their interconnection, in their concatenation, in their movement, in their rise and disappearance." (Marx and Engels)

The term dialectics comes from *dialego* (Greek) which means to debate or discuss, and was in times past the pastime of philosophers, who would engage in debates to overcome the arguments of their opponents that contradicted their own. The ancient philosophers who practiced this "art" thought such introspection and debate conducted without practice and experiment in the material world was the best method of discovering "truth."

Most social, economic, political, cultural and historic theorists today continue in this tradition to a greater or lesser degree. However, the Marxist approach advanced dialectics as a method of understanding reality in relation to existing phenomena and its internal and external contradictions, allowing "truth" to be determined and proved through the test of material practice. In essence, Marx's dialectical method is the opposite of conjecture, idealism and metaphysics.

> "The philosophers have only interpreted the world in various ways; the point, however, is to change it.
>
> "Hitherto men have constantly made up for themselves false conceptions about themselves, about what they are and what they ought to be. They have arranged their relationships according to their ideas of God, of normal man, etc. The phantoms of their brains have got out of their hands. They, the creators, have bowed down before their creations … .
>
> "One has to 'leave philosophy aside' … one has to leap out of it and devote oneself like an ordinary man to the study of actuality, for which there exists also an enormous amount of literary material, unknown, of course, to the philosophers.
>
> "The question whether objective truth can be attributed to human thinking is not a question of theory but is a practical question. Man must prove the truth, i.e.: the reality and power, the this-sidedness [Diesseitigkeit] of his thinking, in practice. The dispute over the reality or non-reality of thinking which is isolated from practice is a purely scholastic question."
>
> *Karl Marx*

## Marx's Materialism

Feuerbach's materialism, rather than perceiving physical phenomena simply as it is, was, like Hegel's concept of the "idea," marred by traditional metaphysical idealism. But as Engels pointed out, Marxist philosophical materialism "… means nothing more than simply conceiving nature just as it exists, without any foreign admixture."

Idealists claim only our consciousness really exists and the real world, therefore, exists only in our minds. However, Marxist materialism recognizes that the world of matter, nature and being is an actual world that exists independent of our consciousness. Matter is primary, since it is the source of all we know, feel and think, whereas consciousness is secondary, since it is a product of and reflection of matter that actually exists in the physical world. The brain is of material construction. Without it, we'd have no thoughts and no mechanism with which to process thoughts into physical actions—so how can we separate or raise our consciousness above matter? "It is impossible to separate thought from matter *that* thinks. This matter is the substratum of all changes going on in the world."—Marx

On a grander scale, there is a dialectical relationship between universal consciousness and physical matter. In physics, this unity of opposites was proven by the physicist, Albert Einstein, (who was a Marxist), in his famous formula $E=mc^2$, or that energy is matter moving at great speed; light, electricity, magnetic force, etc. are examples of this. Indeed our brain signals, which communicate thoughts or messages—and can transmit them to be acted upon in the physical world—are electrical impulses of matter in motion.

Marxist materialism solved the problem that philosophers had long disputed—the relation of thinking to being, spirit to nature. "Matter is that which, acting upon our sense organs, produces sensations ... Matter, nature, being, the physical—is primary, and spirit, consciousness, sensation, the psychical—is secondary." (Marx)

> "Is there such a thing as objective truth, that is, can human ideas have a content that does not depend on a subject, that does not depend either on a human being, or on humanity? If so, can human ideas, which give expression to objective truth, express it all at one time, as a whole, unconditionally, absolutely, or only approximately, relatively? This second question is a question of the relation of absolute truth to relative truth. ... for dialectical materialism there is no impassable boundary between relative and absolute truth.
>
> "From the standpoint of modern materialism i.e., Marxism, the limits of approximation of our knowledge to objective, absolute truth are historically conditional, but the existence of such truth is unconditional, and the fact that we are approaching nearer to it is also unconditional. The contours of the picture are historically conditional, but the fact that this picture depicts an objectively existing model is unconditional. When and under what circumstances we reached, in our knowledge of the essential nature of things, the discovery of alizarin in coal tar or the discovery of electrons in the atom is historically conditional; but that every such discovery is an advance of 'absolutely objective knowledge' is unconditional. In a word, every ideology is historically conditional, but it is unconditionally true that to every scientific ideology (as distinct, for instance, from religious ideology), there corresponds an objective truth, absolute nature. You will say that this distinction between

> relative and absolute truth is indefinite. And I shall reply: yes, it is sufficiently 'indefinite' to prevent science from becoming a dogma in the bad sense of the term, from becoming something dead, frozen, ossified; but it is at the same time sufficiently 'definite' to enable us to dissociate ourselves in the most emphatic and irrevocable manner from fideism and agnosticism, from philosophical idealism and the sophistry of the followers of Hume and Kant. Here is a boundary, which you have not noticed, and not having noticed it, you have fallen into the swamp of reactionary philosophy. It is the boundary between dialectical materialism and relativism."
>
> *V.I. Lenin*

Holding that thought is a product of matter, Marxist materialism understands that the material world and its laws are fully knowable. That by testing our knowledge of nature by experiment and practice, we can learn and know objective "truth." Nothing is unknowable. There are only things that are as yet unknown, but which we can learn through the scientific approach of dialectical experiment and practice.

Marxist materialism therefore opposes idealism, which believes that the world is beyond our ability to know, and therefore we can never really grasp objective truths or change conditions. This idealist view is non-dialectical and non-materialist. It ignores the proofs of developing physical science and provides only a method of abstractly interpreting the world, but none to change it. It therefore ignores, avoids and fails to understand in worldly social relations the importance of "revolutionary, practical—critical activity."

In essence, idealism leaves people feeling helpless to understand and change conditions. We can see the importance of Marxist dialectical and materialist philosophy to those who aspire to change and improve social conditions. It provides the fundamental approach for developing revolutionary theory based upon physical reality, instead of attempting to interpret the world idealistically, based upon creations of the mind and imagination that are unrelated to material reality.

## Dialectical Materialism

DM is a scientific tool that allows us to consciously understand and change material conditions by coming to "know" the laws governing the physical world, and prove or disprove our knowledge by applying it through practice and experiment. As the scientist knows, it is the result of physical experiment that ultimately proves or disproves the "truth" of his/her theory—"the rat is always right!"

How indeed do scientists approach studying and solving problems in the material world? They begin with using their perceptual senses to observe some phenomenon and its internal properties as it interacts with its environment and other phenomena, and then they analyze the data accumulated from these observations. Through this process of observation, scientists accumulate a quantitative amount of perceptual knowledge about the object(s) of their study, and at some point, a qualitative leap takes place, and they begin to make conceptual connections and develop theories, ideas and predictions about the observed thing(s), its development and its nature.

In order to prove or disprove these theories, ideas and predictions, the scientists begin to design and perform experiments that will add to their conceptual knowledge. It is only by acting out their ideas in practice that "truth" can be determined. The science surrounding particular things or phenomena is then advanced. This is the essence of DM, the scientific approach to study and practice.

Likewise, any genuinely revolutionary people and/or party must base their revolutionary practice on study and application of the laws of social development, and not upon the conjecture, morals, reason or good intention of individuals. This is because social life in this material world is a material thing. And just as with all material phenomena it is knowable and changeable according to correctly understanding and acting within its governing laws and contradictions.

> "Thought proceeding from the concrete to the abstract—provided it is correct— ... does not get away from the truth but comes closer to it. The abstraction of matter, of a law of nature, the abstraction of value, etc., in short, all scientific (correct, serious, not absurd) abstractions reflect nature more deeply, truly and completely."
>
> *V.I. Lenin*

DM realizes that, like all processes, social development repeats stages previously passed through, but on a higher level—in spirals not circles. These leaps in cycles of development are the dialectical transformation of quantity into quality, namely revolution. They are the result of the contradictions within a thing or process that act on and are acted upon by external contradictions. It is the law of motion expressing itself. By understanding this law, we can act upon and within the internal contradictions of a thing—our society—to bring about fundamental changes in its quality—through revolution. As Mao Tse-tung observed: "Marxist philosophy holds that the most important problem does not lie in understanding the laws of the objective world and thus being able to explain it, but in applying the knowledge of these laws actively to change the world ..."

## Historical Materialism

HM is DM applied to the study and understanding of social development and history. Marx saw that the past philosophical approaches to understanding history and social development were not scientific but were inconsistent and incomplete. He therefore applied DM to the study and analysis of society and history. In doing this, Marx saw that the very core of human society is the struggle for survival, which expresses itself in the systems of social production. These are the relations that a given people engage in to work up and extract survival necessities from nature for social consumption and use. In these productive processes, people become involved in definite relations that are necessary and independent of their will. These relations are the economic basis, the foundation, and root of every society. It is upon these economic foundations that the society's social institutions or superstructure (political, legal, religious, ethical, cultural, etc.) are built.

> "The application of materialist dialectics to the reshaping of all political economy from its foundation up, its application to history, natural science, philosophy and to the policy and tactics of the working class—that was what interested Marx and Engels most of all, that is where they contributed what was most essential and new, and that was what constituted the masterly advance they made in the history of revolutionary thought."
>
> *V.I. Lenin*

Based upon advances in the technologies used to extract survival necessities from nature, the quantity of production increases (or has the potential to do so) and this creates a conflict with the existing social institutions, which have become a fetter on further development and represent outmoded social relations. This dialectical relationship (contradiction) between the developing productive forces and decadent relations of production and distribution creates a revolutionary situation.

In other words, when the economic foundation advances and changes while the social institutions and those running them attempt to remain conservative, and rigid, there inevitably develops a social-economic demand for overthrow of these old and outmoded institutions and those running them. New and progressive institutions and leaders are called forth which will be compatible with the changes in the mode of production.

Based upon these processes of social-economic development, HDM holds that humyn societies have developed through several transitional stages, beginning with the primitive communal, to the slave, to the feudal, to the wage-slave or capitalist system. Modern imperialism, or monopoly capitalism, is the highest stage of capitalist development. From here, society is ripe to make the leap to communism, or classless society, by passing through the transitional stage of socialism.

> "[T]he history of one human group or of humanity goes through at least three stages. The first is characterized by a low level of productive forces—of man's [and womyn's] domination over nature; the mode of production is of a rudimentary character, private appropriation of the means of production does not yet exist, there are no classes, nor consequently, is there any class struggle.
>
> "In the second stage, the increased level of productive forces leads to private appropriation of the means of production, progressively complicates the mode of production, provokes conflicts of interest within the socio-economic whole in movement, and makes possible the appearance of the phenomenon 'class' and hence of class struggle, the social expression of the contradiction in the economic field between the mode of production and private appropriation of the means of production.
>
> "In the third stage, once a certain level of productive forces is reached, the elimination of private appropriation of the means of production is made possible, and is carried out, together with the phenomenon 'class,' and hence of class struggle; new and hitherto unknown forces in the historical process of the socio-economic whole are then unleashed.
>
> "In politico-economic language, the first stage would correspond to the communal agricultural and cattle-raising society, in which the social structure is horizontal, without any state; the second to feudal or assimilated agricultural or agro-industrial bourgeois societies, with a vertical social structure and a state; the third to socialist or communist societies, in which the economy is mainly, if not exclusively, industrial (since agriculture itself becomes a form of industry) and in which the state tends to progressively disappear, or actually disappears, and where the social structure returns to horizontality, of a higher level of productive forces, social relations and appreciation of human values."
>
> *Amilcar Cabral*

## Class Struggle

Each of the social-economic systems, after the primitive communal and preceding communism, are distinguished by class divisions, and consequently class struggle.

> "Freeman and slave, patrician and plebian, lord and serf, guild master and journeyman, in a word, oppressor and oppressed, stood in constant opposition to one another, carried on an uninterrupted, now hidden, now open fight, a fight that each time ended, either in a revolutionary reconstruction of society at large, or in the common ruin of the contending classes ...
>
> "The modern bourgeois society that has sprouted from the ruins of feudal society has not done away with class antagonisms. It has but established new classes, new conditions of oppression, new forms of struggle in place of the old ones.
>
> "Our epoch, the epoch of the bourgeoisie, possesses, however, this distinctive feature: It has simplified the class antagonisms. Society as a whole is more and more splitting up into two great hostile camps, into two great classes directly facing each other—bourgeoisie and proletariat."
>
> Marx & Engels, *The Communist Manifesto*

This basic contradiction within the capitalist system, between a small exploiting class that privately owns the socially produced wealth and means of production (land, tools, factories, railroads, natural resources, and the labor power of the workers), and the exploited majority (who must sell their labor power to survive) who are the producers of society's wealth, is the basic contradiction in capitalist society, manifested in the class struggle.

However, as Lenin pointed out, the capitalist class consolidated its forces and began to exploit the whole non-industrialized world to feed the industries of the imperialist countries with cheap raw materials and capture markets for their products, transforming the class contradiction into an international one.

Imperialism, as the highest form of capitalism, represents the concentration of the fundamental contradiction within capitalism; with the people and nations exploited and oppressed by the system at one pole and the monopoly capitalists and their henchmen at the other. Within the 3rd world countries, the struggles against colonialism and neo-colonialism take the form of national or "New Democratic" revolution.

Whereas, in its ascendancy the bourgeoisie (capitalist class) was revolutionary, sweeping away pre-capitalist forms of exploitation and their accompanying superstructure through "Liberal Democratic Revolution," under imperialism the bourgeoisie becomes thoroughly reactionary, promoting fascism and defending the remnants of feudalism, even slavery, under the banner of "Anti-Communism." "Democracy" is no more than a window-dressing to conceal its deeply reactionary essence. Therefore, the proletariat must lead the fight to continue to sweep away feudalism and patriarchy along with imperialist domination in order to set the stage for socialist reconstruction.

This has application as well for the internal colonies and oppressed nations and nationalities within the imperialist countries. Inside Amerika, the struggle against national oppression by New Afrikans, Indigenous People and others, is revolutionary class struggle and part of the international struggle to overthrow imperialism.

But even after socialist revolution, class struggle continues and in fact intensifies. Because socialism is a transitional stage from capitalism to communism, the class struggle can go forward or backwards to capitalist restoration. The continuance of aspects of the bourgeois mode of production and bourgeois social relations and culture regenerate the bourgeoisie, most particularly within the upper ranks of the Party and state.

These elements, together with the overthrown bourgeoisie, will stubbornly resist the advance towards communism as "going too far" and will attempt to rig up a new capitalist system under the cover "socialism." Mao Tse-tung was the first Marxist-Leninist to truly recognize this phenomenon. This is what actually occurred in the post-Stalin Soviet Union, in other socialist countries, and in China after Mao's death in 1976. But, Mao pointed to the Chinese Communist Party headquarters as the place where the most dangerous capitalist-roaders lay hidden and through which they could easily rig up a new capitalist system if not stopped.

This leap in historical and dialectical materialist understanding was the basis of the Great Proletarian Cultural Revolution in which Mao urged the Chinese people, and particularly the youth, to "Bombard the Headquarters!" and continue the march towards communism.

Mao made several advances in Marxism by applying HDM to the particularities of his own country and the struggle of a colonized people against imperialism. While he acknowledged that the contradictions of capitalism made the proletariat the only class capable of leading genuine all-the-way revolution against the bourgeoisie, he saw that China was an overwhelmingly peasant society with only a very small proletariat. Therefore, he reasoned that the peasants must be the main force in the revolution but led by a revolutionary proletarian party. This approach deviated from earlier applications of Marxism-Leninism, which focused solely on organizing the urban workers.

Based upon the material reality of China's prevailing mode of production (broadly semi-feudal with small capitalist enterprises under foreign imperialist domination), he led the Chinese people's struggle for national liberation as a "New Democratic" revolution to achieve national independence and free the peasants from semi-feudal domination. Then with political independence achieved, he led the workers and peasants in the socialist reconstruction of People's China.

Mao's advances of Marxism-Leninism, which included developing the theory and practice of waging "People's War," are still relevant today. In Nepal, India, Peru, and the Philippines and other 3rd World countries, Maoist parties are leading "New Democratic People's Wars" against imperialism, bureaucratic capitalism and the remnants of feudalism. All around the world, anti-revisionist communist parties and organizations basing themselves on Marxism-Leninism-Maoism, as the concrete application of HDM in this epoch, are struggling to develop revolutionary theory and practice as part of a growing international united front against imperialism.

> "The fortunes of the African revolution are closely linked with the world-wide struggle against imperialism. It does not matter where the battle erupts, be it in Africa, Asia or Latin America, the mastermind and master-hand at work are the same. The oppressed and exploited people are striving for their freedom against exploitation and suppression. Ghana must not, Ghana cannot be neutral in the struggle of the oppressed against the oppressor."
>
> *Kwame Nkrumah*

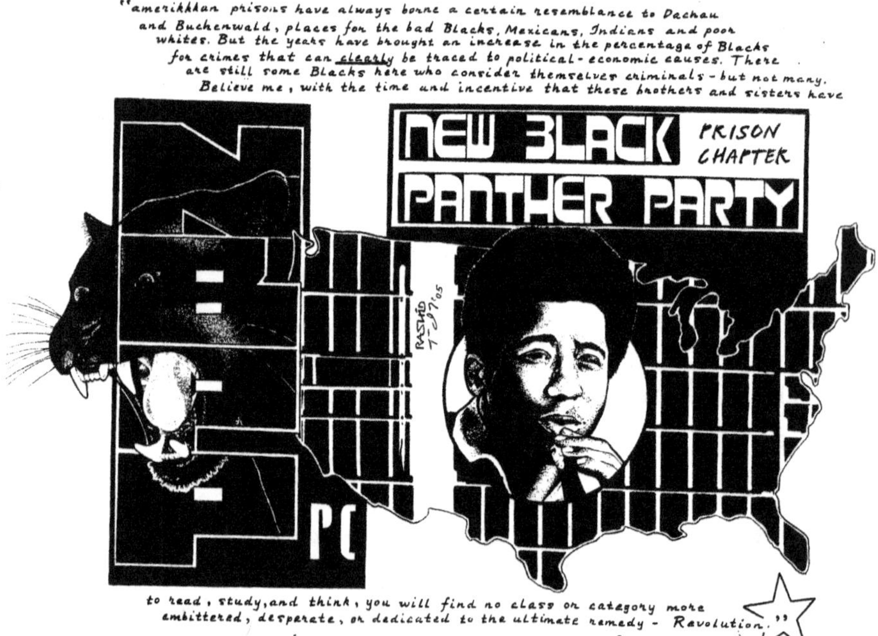

Like every existing thing, imperialism exists as part of and within a dialectical relationship: that relationship being characterized by over-development and underdevelopment, by a new world order and a new level of chaos and disorder. Wealth is drained from the exploited 3rd World countries which lack an autonomous and independent infrastructure and are made dependent through debt to U.S-dominated structures like the World Bank and the International Monetary Fund (IMF). While the U.S. itself has become the world's greatest debtor nation and continues to borrow to finance its military aggression in Afghanistan and Iraq.

Mao characterized this period as one of "Great disorder under Heaven," but he also predicted that "The future shall be bright." Whatever setbacks that have or will occur, revolution is still the main trend in the world today.

We must therefore arm the masses with the correct and scientific method—HDM—so that they can analyze and determine how to arrive at that bright future, becoming the masters of their own destiny. Armed with this knowledge, they will become that conscious social force capable of taking history into their own hands and bringing an end to this epoch of exploitation!

> "Theory becomes a material force as soon as it has gripped the masses!"
>
> *Marx and Engels*

> "Thought without practice is empty—action without thought is blind!"
>
> *Kwame Nkrumah*

*Dare to Struggle, Dare to Win!*
*All Power to the People!*

# PART IV

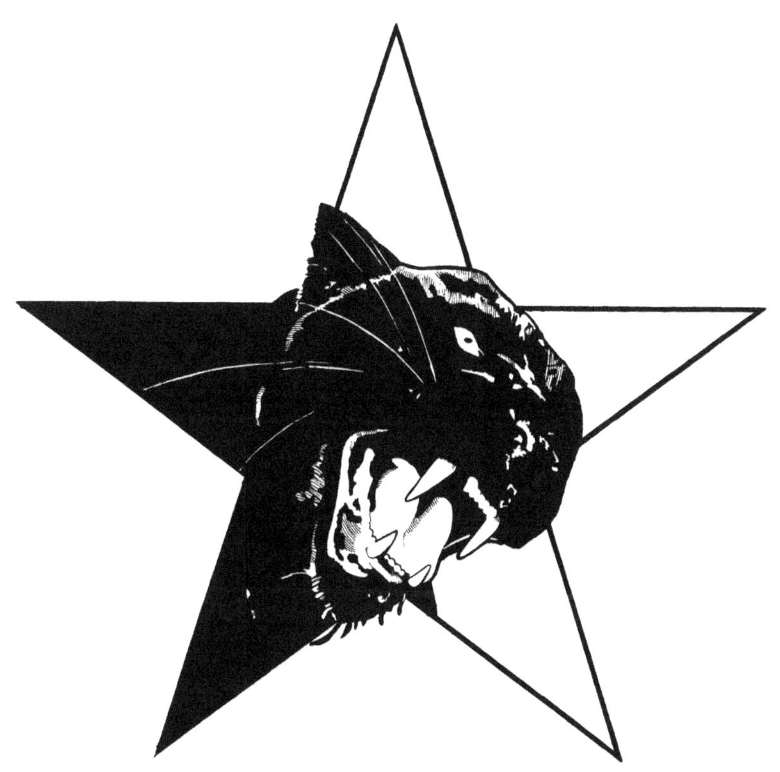

# ORGANIZATION

*The organizational (logistical) problems confronting NABPP-PC and the United Panther Movement were from the start, enormous. Many veteran comrades told us we were setting an impossible task for ourselves—that it was a "fool's errand"—and we shouldn't even attempt it. This brought to our minds Mao's concluding speech to the 7th National Congress of the Communist Party of China in 1945, and the story he told about "The Foolish Old Man Who Removed the Mountains." Mao used this story to illustrate his point that: "We must first raise the political consciousness of the vanguard so that, resolute and unafraid of sacrifice, they will surmount every difficulty to win victory. But that is not enough; we must also arouse the political consciousness of the entire people so that they may willingly and gladly fight together with us for victory."*

*Mao retold the story of the Foolish Old Man of North Mountain, who decided to remove two peaks that blocked his view, so he gathered up his sons and with their hoes they began hacking away at the mountain tops. Along came the Wise Old Man who ridiculed them saying, "How silly of you to do this! It is quite impossible for you few to dig up those two huge mountains!" But the Foolish Old Man was not deterred, he reasoned that if his family worked at it generation after generation, they would succeed. Now in this old story from North China, God was touched by the Foolish Old Man's determination and sent angels to carry away the mountains. Mao's point was that if the masses' hearts were touched by the struggle and sacrifice of the vanguard and they pitched in beside them, the mountains of imperialism and feudalism oppressing the people of China could be removed.*

*From this perspective, it is not foolish at all for a small group of prisoners scattered about in maximum security prisons to dedicate themselves to building a vanguard to lead the struggle to sweep away capitalist-imperialism, racism and police state repression. As the Chinese say, "A journey of a thousand li begins with a single step!" Hopefully, the publication of this book will put it in the hands of many oppressed people, touch their hearts and spur them to action. The firm conviction of the members of NABPP-PC that the masses are the makers of history will then be rewarded!*

*Only when the United Panther Movement has spread to oppressed communities far and wide will it be possible to build a vanguard party that can lead the day to day struggle based on the Mass Line and the principles of democratic centralism. Hopefully, there will be many cadre among them who got their ideological and political training in the NABPP-PC's "School of Liberation"!*

*Tom Watts*

# 13. THE NEW AFRIKAN BLACK PANTHER PARTY-PRISON CHAPTER: OUR LINE 2005

## Introduction

In this paper, we outline the political and ideological line of the New Afrikan Black Panther Party-Prison Chapter.[1] The NABPP-PC, an all-Afrikan people's revolutionary party, proposes through its work and example to spread its line to create the general NABPP on the outside, to unite all revolutionary-minded New Afrikans, and ultimately to expand the Party into a broad international vanguard of all Afrikan people the world over. We are in full accord with the analysis set forward in "The Panther and the Elephant," which this paper intends to further illuminate.

## The Vanguard Party

As a vehicle for coordinating masses of people for action, organization is necessary. Planning is necessary, and so is assigning roles and tasks to those most capable of performing them, and holding them accountable for performing their assigned tasks completely and to the best of their abilities. Coordinating the activities of the active forces of the Afrikan Nation in Amerika towards the achievement of full democracy and national liberation requires a genuine vanguard party based among the masses. No revolutionary or genuine national independence struggle has ever succeeded without a party to organize and coordinate the energy of the struggling people into focused result-oriented action.

"From the People to the People" is the Mass Line—the opposite of top-down organizations. The NABPP-PC practices and promotes the Mass Line. In applying this, the Party workers must go among the People, and, by living with them and struggling along side them, experience and learn their needs, ideas and interests. The Party then—applying the principles of Historical and Dialectical Materialism—returns the People's unorganized ideas to them in a comprehensive form, coordinating their collective actions, resources and abilities around their needs and thereby aids and organizes them in solving their own problems.

As an aspiring revolutionary vanguard party, the NABPP-PC realizes that strategic or tactical inflexibility runs counter to the organic nature of a mass-based leading party. Such a party must operate within the limits of existing concrete conditions as they develop and change, and it cannot attempt to drive people to stick stubbornly and mechanically to methods of struggle, which actual conditions do not support or allow. It has been by failing to exercise flexibility and initiative and practicing "commandism" that many would-be revolutionary movements in the past have failed and have given vanguard parties a bad name.

Our strategic and tactical decision-making process is that of Democratic Centralism, which does not contradict applying the Mass Line. Nor does it go against maintaining flexibility and initiative and being creative in our political work. Democratic Centralism is the method by which our Party determines, through intense internal discussion, debate, and then majority agreement, the Party's overall strategic and tactical line. The basic principle is to raise criticisms and ideas up and to implement down. Once a strategy and tactical approach is decided, the lower bodies of the Party can then exercise a great deal of initiative and creativity in applying the line in practice, adapting to the particularities of local conditions.

At the heart of any democratic process is the need and right to be informed of all issues relevant to making accurate analyses and correct decisions. Therefore, Party cadre must never stop learning, (and teaching the People), and must never hold stubbornly to views not supported by the ongoing experience of the Party. Our sources of learning are our people's life experience, books, and especially our practice. We must never stop learning.

Essential to democratic practice is criticism and self-criticism. All Party members must feel free to criticize other Party members and leaders, line and practice within the context of internal Democratic Centralism. The Party must also be open to listening to the criticisms of the masses. If what is unproductive or harmful cannot be criticized, then how can what is productive and good be determined?

The Party will exercise greater or lesser degrees of centralism, depending upon the freedom and necessity of the struggle in a given time and place. For example, security considerations may restrict the ability to hold discussions and force the leadership to assume more authoritative methods at times, restricting certain information, to protect the cadre or the Party as a whole. But overall, our goal is to promote democracy and collective decision-making. In all cases, we must adjust and adapt new, varied and creative tactics and approaches to maintain the initiative in our work and avoid becoming predictable and thus susceptible to being out maneuvered and defeated.

## Classes and Class Struggle

On the point of classes and class struggle, we adopt the analysis presented in "The Panther and the Elephant," we also add in relation to the

Lumpen Proletariat that the NABPP-PC, as its name implies, is centered within the prisons. The vast majority of prisoners in the U.S. are proletarians, but many come from a lumpen background, and all are influenced by this perspective in the context of prison culture. The lumpen class[2] overlaps with the proletariat, (drifts in and out of employment), but maintains an outlook that opposes a proletarian class outlook. The lumpen's confused and backward values stem from its position of preying upon others and general ignorance, which can be corrected through education and struggle, and through guided practice in a mass organization like the Black Brigade.[3] A minimum condition for the acceptance of lumpen class militants into the Party must be a period of re-education and practice inside a Party-affiliated mass organization like the Black Brigade, where we can observe their practice, and they can remold their class outlook and develop into a full-time, all-the-way revolutionary.

## Contradictions in Proletarian versus Lumpen Perspectives

Many people when presented with the Marxist-Leninist-Maoist idea that only the proletariat can lead in making all-the-way revolutionary class struggle question why this is, and why some other class, (without changing its class perspective), cannot lead such a struggle. One reason is because the proletariat is the only class that has no real stake in preserving the class relations of the capitalist system, but has everything to gain in taking control over the social wealth it has itself created by its labor and the tools it uses to create it. Another reason is that the proletariat, (in contrast to the lumpen), has the conditioning in patient work, social unity and cooperation necessary to wage the protracted class struggle required to abolish all exploitation and oppression. Basically, it is our social practice that determines how we think and not how we think that determines our social practice. But there is also a dialectical relationship between the two where they advance and enrich each other.

The proletariat has a strong sense of family commitment and unity and a sense of respect for and commitment to the community. These values grow out of the routine of going to work each day in the social environment of the workplace to provide for the needs of one's family, and not only maintaining employment but also engaging in domestic labor in the home, rearing children, and taking part in the social life of the community. This requires and instills stability, discipline and responsibility as well as cooperation with one's peers.

The class-conscious worker can be of two sorts, the militant and the revolutionary. The militant worker takes the sense of commitment beyond the family into the workplace and will stand up to the bosses for workers' rights, even to the extent of jeopardizing one's employment, freedom and safety by participating in strikes and job actions. The revolutionary worker takes the sense of commitment even farther and challenges the oppressive social order to change the social relations for all and put an end to class exploitation and oppression once and for all. The revolutionary is inspired by a great love for the people and sense of duty to the masses and to future generations.

The revolutionary worker doesn't swagger or boast and has little sense of ego. He or she is serious-minded and self-disciplined. The revolutionary knows that like a strike, the revolutionary struggle must be a united mass struggle, and that it will take quite some time to succeed. Each contribution is important, and the end result is to benefit the overall society. In contrast to the proletarian's practice and outlook, the lumpen schemes and preys upon others to acquire survival needs and personal wealth, which renders him or her indifferent to the effects visited upon others and society as a whole.

The lumpen mentality mirrors—on a smaller scale and with less sophistication—that of the big gangsters (the monopoly capitalists), and amounts to a ruthless drive for immediate self-gratification, power, control and "respect," (even though their lifestyle is anything but respectable), through deception, corruption, violence and intimidation of others. These tendencies are what lie behind certain lumpen aspiring to be perceived as "crazy" and unpredictably violent.

Translated into the revolutionary movement, the lumpen tendency has some thinking that militant swaggering, posturing, and "talking shit," is acceptable behavior for revolutionaries, which is very wrong and demonstrates political immaturity and lack of a true proletarian outlook. Such posturing leads to actions of a reactionary, adventurist and provocateur nature, that invites enemy attack that the movement is unprepared to deal with and alienates the masses. Comrade Sundiata Acoli, (a member of the old BPP and BLA), observed that just such lumpen tendencies contributed to the downfall of the old BPP and the general Black Liberation Movement in Amerika. (See Sundiata Acoli, "A Brief History of the Black Panther Party and its place in the Black Liberation Movement," [1985], which is posted on the internet and was recently reprinted in the Summer Issue of *Leviathan*, the newsletter of the Black Brigade).

Also, because they are conditioned to seek immediate and short-term benefits in their daily practice, the lumpen generally lack the resolve to pursue and stick with tasks that require hard work and patience. We in the NABPP-PC feel that a major factor that led to the old BPP's destruction was the failure to raise many of the Party members' worldview to that of the revolutionary proletariat and allowing the Party and its leadership to become saturated in lumpen ideology, values and practice.

The motives behind revolutionary violence are fundamentally different from the reactionary violence of the lumpen, who model their violence after that of the big gangsters. Revolutionary violence is rooted in the collective resistance of the masses organized against the violence of the big gangster bourgeoisie system of repression and exploitation. History is made by the collective masses, with the genuine revolutionary vanguard serving to raise their consciousness and organize their force into collective revolutionary struggle. Correct thinking is the catalyst, just as intelligence draws order out of chaos—out of the chaos of noise—music, and out of chaos of images and color—art.

### Raising the Lumpen Outlook to a Revolutionary Proletarian Outlook

To serve in the capacity of a truly revolutionary vanguard, the Party must consist of committed, disciplined people who have the outlook of truly revolutionary workers; people who are committed to work every day in a patient and disciplined way until the conditions for a revolutionary seizure of power by the masses arise. Without remolding their class outlook, the lumpen will pursue ultra-leftist militant acts of exhibitionism and spew forth "Off the Pig!" rhetoric, and when this provokes repression from the Establishment, they will flip-flop to right opportunism, turn rat and become enemy agents, or run for cover. Lacking correct analysis, self-discipline and patience, they will vacillate left to right, and they will confuse one stage of the struggle for another and try to skip the stages that require hard work and tenacity.

These elements disdain to apply the Mass Line, ignore the Democratic Centralism of the Party, fear Criticism and Self-Criticism and lean towards individualism and "commandism," indulging in personal attacks and attempts at intimidation and coercion of other Party members and the masses through threats and force. Their unremolded lumpen ideology is a corrosive to building Party unity and maintaining discipline, and it makes them easy prey for recruitment by the enemy. The lumpen are capable of "the most heroic deeds and the most exalted sacrifices, or of the basest banditry and dirtiest corruption."

A large part of our work in NABPP-PC is to properly educate and reorient the lumpen through ideological and political training and bringing as many of them who are capable of "the most heroic deeds and the most exalted sacrifices" into the active work of the struggle as possible, and thereby expand the Party while struggling against opportunism, both of the "left" and right varieties. We know that in this work, the enemy will unceasingly attempt to infiltrate its agents of repression and seek out the weak links among us to turn them into their snitches and agents provocateurs, and we must be vigilant to guard against this, without becoming paranoid. In the struggle, "ideological and political line determines everything," and we must rely on ideological and political training and commitment to practicing the Mass Line, Criticism and Self-Criticism and the Democratic Centralist method of determining what should be done and how to do it.

We realize that the lumpen are our brothers and sisters, and we do not desire to make war on them, rather we look upon their wrong ideas and lack of understanding as loads upon their backs, and we endeavor to help them cast them off. "Cure the sickness to save the patient," is our goal. However, we are not naive idealists, and we realize that there are those who lack the moral fiber and will to change or courage for the struggle. Some people have no integrity or loyalty, and those who, after struggle, persist in wrong ways must be purged from the ranks of the people's movement.

Before someone is recruited into the Party, they must be tested and prove themselves in the people's mass organizations, like the Black Brigade. They must show proof of both good character and advanced understanding of what needs to be done. Words are cheap. Practice is the measure of commitment and the way consciousness develops.

Our goal is to be more than a prison organization. The struggle of our New Afrikan and Afrikan people worldwide cries out for vanguard leadership. With the Black proletariat concentrated in Amerika and Europe and our peasantry concentrated in Afrika, we have an internationalist duty to provide revolutionary proletarian leadership and to set an inspiring example. Our struggle against imperialism and neo-colonialism is a class struggle of international dimensions. We have much to learn and much to do. We must become good at learning and resolute in struggle.

## END NOTES

1. The NABPP-PC was initially called the New Black Panther Party-Prison Chapter. This was changed to New Afrikan Black Panther Party-Prison Chapter after the first issue of *Right On!* (the newsletter of the NABPP-PC) to avoid confusion with the narrow nationalist New Black Panther Party (NBPP). Reprints of *Right On!* were subsequently amended.

2. The lumpen are not a class in the fullest sense but part of the lower strata of the proletariat. "Lumpen" means "broken". The lumpen proletariat are those who exist by illegal means or hustle.

3. Now the New Afrikan Service Organization (NASO). See Summer 2007 article "Advancing from the Black Brigade to the New Afrikan Service Organization: A Great Leap Forward!"

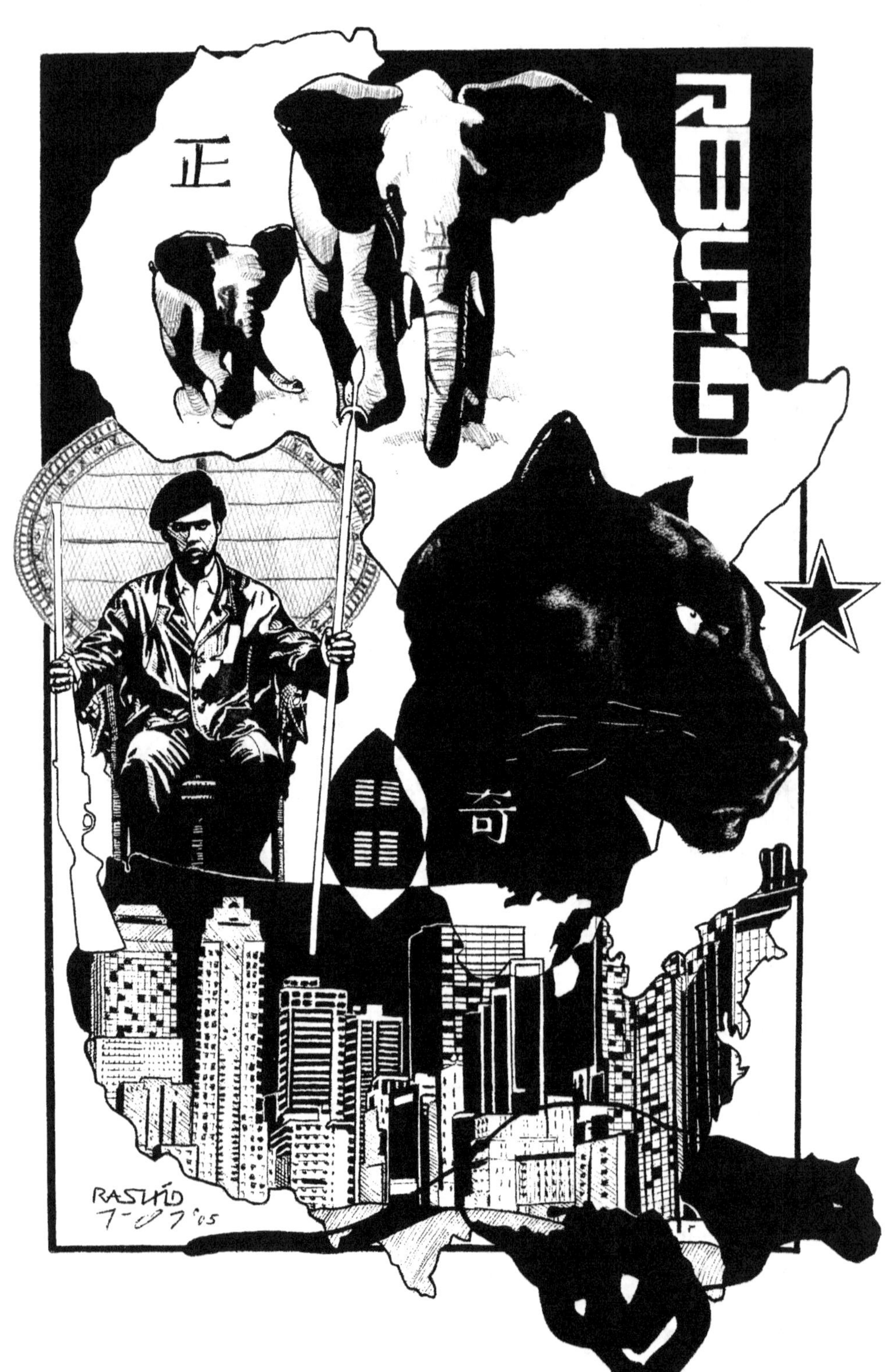

REBUILD!
正
奇
RASHID
7-07'05

# 14. THE PANTHER AND THE ELEPHANT

2005

The elephant is large and powerful and is unsurpassed in direct confrontation. The Panther is agile and stealthy and is unsurpassed in indirect confrontation. The Elephant relies on his size, thick skin and tusks to meet his enemy head on, while the Panther blends into the night, exercises patience, and employs the art of surprise and ambushes his prey. His intelligence and cunning are greater weapons than his formidable fangs and claws.

In the *Art of War*, the ancient Chinese sage, Sun Tzu, proposes that two types of forces and maneuvers are called for. He called these CHENG and CH'I. These would be regular and special forces and direct and indirect maneuvers. The purpose of CHENG forces is to engage the enemy, and the purpose of the CH'I forces is to defeat the enemy.

In advancing the cause of Black Liberation, both types of forces, CHENG and CH'I, are needed. Or to put it another way, both a vanguard and a mass form of organization is needed. The mass form of organization is based upon programmatic unity, and includes people of various political, spiritual and cultural orientations. In the case of the Black Brigade, its basis of unity is service to the Nation of Afrikans in Amerika. The vanguard form of organization is based upon a higher level of unity, application of the Science of Revolution, which is Historical and Dialectical Materialism, and commitment to being a full time revolutionary.

## Classes and Class Struggle

The Proletariat is the class that must sell its labor power to the capitalist class, submitting to exploitation, to survive. In other words, it is the working class, the class of "wage slaves." This is the only class with nothing to lose but its "chains," and thus is the only class capable of leading the United Front Against Imperialism to make all the way revolution and advance society to communism or classless society. Other classes have more or less of a stake in the capitalist division of society, even though they are compelled to resist and to revolt against the Monopoly Capitalist Class dictatorship and the imperialist system to some degree.

In this historical period, the most advanced application of the Science of Revolution is Marxism-Leninism-Maoism, but one need not be a communist with a capital "C" to be part of the Vanguard force. However, one must be a revolutionary nationalist, and as Mao put it: "Revolutionary

Nationalism is applied Proletarian Internationalism." There is a difference between the New Afrikan/Black Nationalist Movement and the Proletarian Internationalist or Communist Movement, but the two are inexorably intertwined.

The Nation of Afrikans in Amerika is divided into classes, though overwhelmingly it is a Proletarian Nation. There is also a Black Bourgeoisie (Bush-wa-zee), which is divided into National and Comprador sections, the latter being those who objectively serve the ruling class of the white colonial-settler regime. Clarence Thomas and Condoleezza Rice are examples of this grouping. The National Bourgeoisie is more independent, and those who got rich through sports or the entertainment industry are examples.

The Petty Bourgeoisie is the stratum in the middle between the rich class and the working class. It includes the professionals, (like doctors, educators and lawyers), small business owners and middle and lower management. Though they may actually make less money than the upper strata of the industrial proletariat, their relationship to production is less direct, and they are more likely to reflect the outlook of the employing class and to nurture hopes of becoming big bourgeois themselves.

Some sections, such as the intellectuals, or the semi-proletarian artisans, can be won to become relatively firm allies of the revolutionary proletariat. On the other hand, sections of the middle class are the historic base of fascism. The upper strata of the industrial proletariat, or "Labor Aristocracy," were the vanguard of the unionization movement, but due to the super profits engendered by imperialism and the exploitation of the Third World countries, the monopoly capitalists were able to bribe these strata with a higher standard of living and middle class aspirations. Their class-consciousness was dulled and the white workers particularly were rallied around U.S. national chauvinism and anti-communism.

Now, as a result of increased globalization, this stratum has been greatly reduced by the outsourcing of their jobs overseas by the multinational corporations and the downsizing of their U.S. workforce. This has greatly reduced the power of the industrial workers and the number of unionized workers overall. The largest section of the Black proletarians are part of the great mass of non-organized workers who have no unions, (and in most cases no health coverage), and live from paycheck to paycheck barely getting by. Linked to them are their dependents and the de-classed poor, welfare and disability recipients, pensioners, the marginally employed, and the jobless and homeless.

There is also the Lumpen Proletariat. "Lumpen" literally means "broken." The Lumpen make their living by illegal means, as petty gangsters, drug dealers, pimps, con artists and thieves. They reflect the mentality of the big gangsters and monopoly capitalists and feed parasitically off the people, but some have the potential to be won to a proletarian outlook and become revolutionaries. Unlike the big parasites, they do not enjoy immunity from prosecution for their crimes and often end up spending most of their lives in prison.

### The Black Nation in Amerika

Black people were forged into a nation in Amerika under conditions of slavery and segregation. Stripped of their national cultures, languages and identities under slavery, they were amalgamated into a new nation based upon their common Afrikan origin and features. Four hundred years of oppression and exploitation shaped the national identity and culture of this nation. Originally centered in the "Black Belt," or "Cotton Belt," of the Deep South, where most Blacks and many poor whites were reduced to a condition of being made sharecropping peasants after the overthrow of slavery, KKK terror and Jim Crow segregation laws denied them a political voice even though they were the majority, and the region was made an internal colony of the U.S. with Third World-like conditions.

Mechanization of cotton picking and the demand for industrial workers in the industrial centers, particularly during WWI and WWII, encouraged a massive exodus of Black people from the South to the North and the West. Huge urban ghettos sprang up and become new internal colonies of the U.S. From Harlem to Compton, these centers defined the faster-paced urbanized culture of Black Amerika in the 20th Century. New music and worldliness replaced the rural lifestyle and outlook.

The national liberation struggles of the people in the former European colonies in Afrika and throughout the Third World were echoed in the civil rights and Black Nationalist movements within the U.S. Revolutionary Black Nationalist groups, like the Black Panther Party, sprang up to challenge both racism and imperialism and begin the struggle for socialist revolution. The high tide of struggle in the U.S. in the '60s and '70s coincided with the Great Proletarian Cultural Revolution in People's China and the Vietnam War and numerous other national liberation struggles and attempts to establish socialism in Afrika, Latin America and Asia.

The U.S. emerged victorious from the Cold War, and the ebb in struggle internationally, (with the right-wing coup in China following Mao's death, the collapse of the former Soviet Union and Socialist Bloc and the defeat of socialist forces in Afrika and elsewhere), was mirrored by a decline in the Black Liberation Struggle here too. But the emergence of the New World Order and sole-superpower domination only served to intensify exploitation and the aggressive and predatory nature of U.S. imperialism.

Neither the Neo-Liberals nor the Neo-Conservatives saw a need to continue the pattern of Cold War Liberalism and concessions to common people. The decline of the Left was more than matched by the rise of the extreme Right. Backing both Islamic and Judeo-Christian religious fundamentalism, the stage was set for the invasion of Afghanistan and Iraq and increased pressure on all the oil-producing countries by U.S.-Anglo imperialism. Under the cover of the "War on Terror," major attacks on the democratic rights and protections of the Amerikan people have been made and steps have been taken to build a more efficient police state.

Since the end of the Cold War, a massive increase in the number of people incarcerated in the U.S. has taken place, (mostly Black and other people of color), so that Amerika now accounts for nearly half the imprisoned people in the world. Affirmative action programs have been cut back and social welfare programs have been dramatically slashed. The ruling class is aggressively waging class struggle against the working-class and poor while the Neo-Cons are aggressively suppressing the Neo-Liberals, characterizing them as the "Radical Left."

The white, capitalist, colonial-settler state was built upon genocide and dispossession of the indigenous nations and the kidnapping, enslavement and exploitation of the Afrikan people, and this oppression continues to this day. Legal desegregation has not altered the condition of super-exploitation of Black people in Amerika or in Afrika. Civil Rights is still an issue. White Racism is still an issue. The right to self-determination and national liberation is still an issue. The Nation of Afrikans living in Amerika has the right, and the necessity, to struggle for solutions to its problems as a nation. This includes the right to define and govern its own territory and to transform the internal colonies of exploitation into base areas of cultural, social and political revolution.

At the same time, it also includes the right to fight for full civil rights for all within the U.S., including prisoners and those convicted of felonies and the so-called "illegal aliens." We say: "NO INCARCERATION WITHOUT REPRESENTATION!" and: "AMEND THE 13TH AMENDMENT TO ABOLISH SLAVERY FOR ALL!" And we say: "IF YOU ARE HERE, YOU HAVE A RIGHT TO VOTE AND TO RESPECT OF YOUR CIVIL RIGHTS!" It is the white-settler colonial regime that are the real illegal aliens. Every bit of this land was stolen from the indigenous nations. These indigenous nations have historically been the main ally of the Afrikan people in Amerika. Long before there was an "Underground Railroad," the path to freedom led to the Indian nations. Many of the so-called "illegal aliens" are in fact Native Americans from south of the border drawn by the whites. The Red-Black Alliance is key to national liberation within the U.S.

### Pan-Afrikanism

Just as Afrikan people were formed into a new nation in Amerika, so too Afrikan people internationally have been formed into a new type of nation by conditions of colonialism, slavery and racism. This Pan-Afrikan movement and nationalism links the primarily proletarian New Afrikans of Amerika and Europe with the primarily peasant Afrikans of Afrika. The Afrikan Diaspora created new conditions for both building All African Unity and advancing World Socialist Revolution.

The anti-colonial wars of national liberation following WWII, led to numerous attempts to build Afrikan socialism in several countries. Undermined by CIA and European-hatched assassinations, coups and tribal conflicts, these were rolled back, and a destabilized condition of neo-colonial domination prevails in Afrika. Dire poverty and conditions exist across Afrika. Famine, AIDS, alcohol and drug addiction, warlordism and religious and inter-tribal strife weigh heavily on the Afrikan peoples. Rich in natural resources, Afrika remains the poorest place on Earth, while everywhere people of Afrikan descent are faced with racial discrimination.

Building Pan-Afrikan Unity is vital to the uplifting of the Afrikan people everywhere and particularly here in the U.S. Conversely, supporting the Black Liberation Movement here is vital to continuing the struggle for liberation and socialism in Afrika. This calls for new forms of organization and struggle as well as the renewal of previous forms. The Black Panther Party needs to be renewed not only in the U.S. but also internationally and the Black Brigade needs to be built both nationally and internationally.

In supporting and building ties with Afrika, it is important to include elements of the national bourgeoisie and all classes in contradiction with imperialism and neocolonialism uniting all who can be united. The principles of New Democratic Revolution need to be applied.

### New Democratic Revolution

National liberation involves a two stage revolutionary process to advance to the building socialism. First you have to liberate the country from imperialist neo-colonial domination and their agents and address the question of: "LAND TO THE TILLERS." Since the emergence of Monopoly Capitalism and modern imperialism, the bourgeoisie has proven incapable of leading democratic revolution against remnants of the old feudal order, and this duty has fallen to the proletariat and its vanguard.

The national bourgeoisie can be a vacillating ally in this struggle, in which the peasantry is the main force, but the ideological and political leadership must come from the proletariat. Even within the internal colonies of the U.S., the principles of New Democratic Revolution have some relevance, particularly in overturning the feudal remnant of the 13th Amendment, which perpetuates the status of slave for those convicted of crimes, and the unfinished civil rights struggle.

In the 3rd World, the New Democratic Revolution is advanced by means of People's War, surrounding the cities from the countryside and creating people's power on a national level before liberating the urban centers and consolidating state power. The people's war in Nepal is a classic example of this strategy.

## Strategy and Tactics

The Black Brigade is needed to confront and engage the colonial-settler power structure frontally creating institutions of people's power locally. The basic unit of people's power must be neighborhood councils composed of the veteran fighters and respected elders of the community. We can then organize programs for the people's security and social welfare under these committees.

Private security firms can be created and licensed to operate under contract to the neighborhood councils, supported by voluntary neighborhood security patrols. These can present offenders with the option of having their cases decided by the people's council instead of being turned over to the municipal authorities. The council can levy fines, order that restitution be paid and/or mandate community service. It can also banish offenders from the community.

The security officers would be armed, equipped and trained to handle this role in a professional manner. Besides dealing with the problem of crime in the neighborhood, the people's security force can also monitor and collect evidence on police complicity and corruption. Over time, it can displace the police as the force most relied upon by the people to handle their security issues, empowering the people's councils to function as a parallel government.

Besides addressing the issue of the people's security, the neighborhood councils would also initiate and coordinate all manner of social service and survival programs taking up the slack of government cutbacks and responsibility to see that the hungry are fed, the homeless are given shelter, the sick and injured are provided with medical care and health services and in general that the needs of the people are addressed. In addition, the councils would work to promote the political economy of the neighborhoods by assisting in the creation of workers' co-ops and consumers' co-ops and in the countryside growers' co-ops.

An important link to be forged is between the urban oppressed communities and the rural communities where most of the prisons are located. Regular transportation and housing for families visiting prisoners need to be established. As part of the drive to extend voter rights to prisoners, uniting with the progressive forces in the communities where the prisons are located is important. These include family members who have relocated to be close to their loved ones.

Our general strategy must be to: "TRANSFORM THE IRON HOUSES OF OPPRESSION INTO SCHOOLS OF LIBERATION, AND TO BUILD THE OPPRESSED COMMUNITIES INTO BASE AREAS OF CULTURAL, SOCIAL AND POLITICAL REVOLUTION." There is a dialectical relationship between these tasks. The more we are able to succeed at one aspect the better we will do at the other.

The vanguard force has the principal task of providing political education to the masses and making them conscious. They must represent the broad and revolutionary viewpoint of the proletariat. They must also act as shock troops and jump in as needed when a highly motivated and disciplined force is called for.

## Conclusion

While a revolutionary situation does not at present exist in the U.S., as Sun Tzu pointed out: "BATTLES AND WARS ARE WON OR LOST BEFORE THEY ARE FOUGHT!" The Panther and the Elephant, the CH'I and CHEN warriors and forces of the people, must be organized now so that when a revolutionary situation does present itself, the people will not be unprepared.

"IT IS RIGHT TO REBEL!" against tyranny and national oppression, and we must "SEIZE THE TIME!" and "DARE TO STRUGGLE AND DARE TO WIN!" Many fine comrades and heroes of the people have sacrificed themselves to illuminate the path forward. We have our duty to the future generation. POWER TO THE PEOPLE!

*Dare to Struggle, Dare to Win!*
*All Power to the People!*

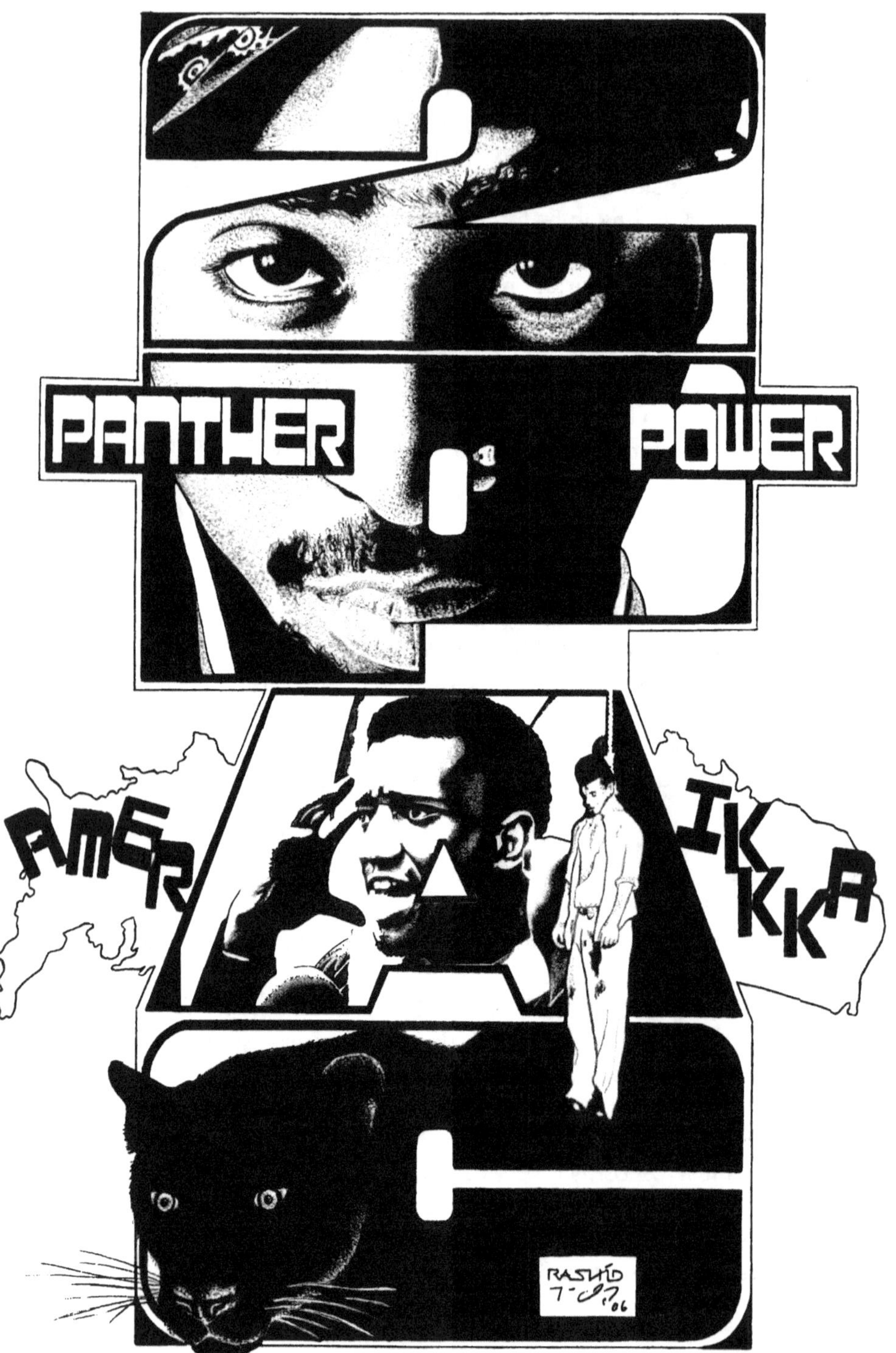
PANTHER
POWER
AMER
IKKA
RASHID
7-'06

# 15. THE NEW AFRIKAN BLACK PANTHER PARTY'S ORGANIZATIONAL PRINCIPLES, POLICY AND PRACTICE: THE 3-P'S 2012

### Organizational Aims

In several past articles we have expressed the need to resolve various questions of Party organization and cadre development and training. We want to begin now working on resolutions, starting with ensuring that comrades understand and adhere to the organizational aims and structure of our Party.

Presently we are a Prison Chapter (PC), which means the New Afrikan Black Panther Party's (NABPP) membership is based primarily within the Empire's prisons. So long as we remain a Prison Chapter there are obvious limits on what we can achieve, and on our ability to collectively decide a lot of matters. So, in this respect, we are not able to fully integrate with, and exercise Democratic Centralism within our mass base. Our mass base consists principally of the oppressed urban New Afrikan peoples and those confined within the prisons.

We aspire to advance from a mere PC, to an outside party structure based in the oppressed communities, and ultimately into an international vanguard party of all oppressed and urbanized Afrikan peoples the world over.

To make the transition to the outside requires that cadre trained in our political and ideological lines and committed to our Ten Point Program and Platform, hold a founding Party Congress, elect a free world Central Committee, organize a Politburo and draft a Party program. Developing these cadres is part of our aim in educating and politicizing prisoners, so they can, upon their release, form the nucleus of that outside Party. We are also educating comrades on the outside. Towards developing the International BPP, we look to develop cadre in other countries and all areas where Afrikan people are concentrated to found chapters of the party, and consolidate them into the IBPP.

The White Panther Organization (WPO) and Brown Panther Organization (BPO) are arms of the NABPP (which are also primarily prison-based at present), who carry the line and work of the Panthers into the poor and working-class white, Red, Brown and Yellow communities, to serve these oppressed sectors, and to unite all oppressed peoples into a United Front Against Imperialism. We aim to see these organizations also transition into outside structures based in the oppressed communities of their respective national and "racial" groups, and ultimately into international structures operating under the leadership of the IBPP as a United Panther Movement.

This explains the basic organizational aims of the Party. We now will elaborate the structural outline of the Party.

## Organizational Structure

Structurally, the NABPP-PC breaks down at three levels: National (Chapter), State (Branch), and Local (Unit). The outside NABPP once constituted will also be structured much the same. The IBPP once developed will simply add a fourth level: the International.

## I. Chapter

At the National level is the Chapter. The Chapter is presided over by the Party's highest decision-making body, the Central Committee (CC). The CC oversees, and its decisions are to be obeyed by, the entire Party. The Chairperson is the spokesperson of the CC and the Party, and its highest-ranking member. The Politburo (political bureau) of the CC is composed of the heads of the Party's various ministries. The present ministries within the NABPP-PC consist of the Ministries of:

1. Culture
2. Defense
3. Education
4. Finance
5. Health and Welfare
6. Human Rights
7. Information
8. Justice
9. Labor

The CC will also have a General Secretary. Each arm of the Party (viz., WPO and BPO) will have a national spokesperson, each of whom will also have a seat on the CC. The CC thus consists of the Chairperson, the heads of the Party's Ministries, the General Secretary and the National spokespeople.

CC decisions are reached by means of Democratic Centralism (DC), which we will explain more fully below. But as said, we are not able to fully implement DC due to communication barriers created by our being confined in various prisons across the Empire. CC members are to be elected to their positions by peer vote with input from Party members and the masses at all levels, and may be removed from these positions in the same manner. Election to these positions shall be based upon qualifications, integrity, commitment and work in the struggle proven in practice.

## II. Branch

At the state levels are the Branches. The Branches are the intermediary Party structures beneath the Chapter. Each state will have its own Branch, and each Branch is presided over by a Branch Committee (BC) composed of Party members who reside in the state in which that particular Branch presides. For example, the BC of Connecticut will preside over the entire Connecticut Branch of the NABPP-PC, etc.

The BC operates beneath the CC and works to implement and coordinate CC decisions and goals at the statewide level, and also to implement and coordinate other work at this level consistent with the Party's work, programs and goals.

Each Ministry within the Party will have a Branch level delegate or "deputy," for example: Deputy Minister of Culture, Deputy Minister of Defense, and so on, who together compose the Branch level Politburo. There will also be a Deputy Chairperson, who is the highest ranking member at the Branch level, and a Branch Secretary. Together these Deputies, along with Deputy Spokespersons of the WPO and BPO form the BC.

BC decisions will also be reached by means of DC at the Branch level, and will govern activities of the entire Party Branch in the state in which it presides.

BC members are also appointed or withdrawn by election of members at the Branch level and with input of the masses. Until the Party is fully operational, individual CC members may appoint provisional deputies (for example the Minister of Culture may appoint a provisional deputy to his/her ministry in Branches where there is no functional Party leadership), who may be later confirmed or withdrawn and replaced by vote of Branch members upon that membership's being enlarged and organized.

Deputies answer and report on developments in their area to the Chapter head of the Ministry, Chair, etc. which they belong to. For example the Deputy Ministers of Culture report and answer to the National Minister of Culture, etc.

### III. Unit

At the Local levels are the units. The units are the basic Party structures beneath the branches. Each prison or jail will have its own unit, (as will each city, county or town upon the development of the outside Party). Each unit is presided over by a Unit Committee (UC) composed of Party members who are confined in the prison or jail in which that particular unit presides. For example, the UC of Pelican Bay State Prison (PBSP) will preside over the entire Party within PBSP.

The UC operates beneath the BC of the state in which it exists, (for example, the UC of PBSP operates under the California BC), and works to implement and coordinate BC decisions and goals (and those of the CC directly, in absence of a BC or when otherwise appropriate), and also to carry out other work consistent with the Party's work, programs and goals at the unit level.

Each Ministry within the Party will have a unit level delegate or "Captain," for example: Cultural Captain, Defense Captain, and so on, who together compose the Unit Politburo. There will also be a Chairperson Captain, who is the highest-ranking member at the unit level, also a Secretary Captain. Together these Captains, along with Captains of the WPO and BPO form the UC.

UC decisions will also be reached by means of DC at the unit level, and will govern activities of the entire Party unit within the prison or jail in which it operates.

UC members are also appointed or withdrawn by election of members at the unit level and with input of the masses.

The most basic groups within the Party are collectives or local cells consisting of comrades living or working together within a prison or jail. The unit will be composed of various collectives in the prison headed by a Captain or elected Lieutenant.

At the unit level it will be much easier for comrades to interact regularly and often without intense enemy scrutiny, therefore DC can be most effectively exercised at this level, especially for comrades in the general population settings. We therefore encourage comrades to exercise and become experienced in the practice and application of DC.

Unit Captains answer and report on developments in their prison or jail to the Deputy of the Ministry, Chair, etc. to which they belong and in the state in which they operate. For example, the Cultural Captain for PBSP reports and answers to the Deputy Minister of Culture for the California Branch.

### Reports

The object is to achieve an organizational system of accountability and transmitting ideas and information from the lowest to the highest levels of the Party and vice versa, while allowing comrades flexibility and creativity in applying our line and directives to the particular conditions in their area (state, prison and/or jail).

To this end Party cadre should hold regular meetings when and where they can, to sum up work in their area, and prepare and submit reports up to the next highest body or up to the CC. For example, those presiding over unit groups should prepare and submit reports to their Branch Chairperson. And the Branch should do the same and sum up unit reports to the National Chairperson. In the absence of Branch membership or leaders, unit groups should submit reports directly to the National Chairperson.

### Organizational Principles

The fundamental organizational principle of the party is DC.

At all levels leading bodies within the Party are elected and subject to recall by democratic decision.

Leading bodies within the Party shall regularly report on their work at general membership meetings or to the Chairpersyn, listen and pay heed to the opinions of the masses in and outside the Party and submit to their supervision. All Party members have the right to criticize Party organizations and leading members at all levels and make recommendations to them. If a Party member disagrees concerning decisions or directions of a Party organization, although s/he must abide by those decisions/directions, s/he may reserve her/his views and has the right to bypass the immediate leadership and report directly to higher bodies, up to and including the CC and the CC Chairpersyn. We must maintain a political environment with both centralism and democracy, both unity and struggle, both discipline and freedom, and both collective unity of purpose and individual mental ease, and which is energetic and active. This political climate should exist both within and without of the Party, because without it we will be unable to motivate and inspire cadre to work vigorously and effectively or the masses to take up the struggle.

### Democratic Centralism: The Purpose, The Method

As our central organizational principle it is imperative that all Party members and the people clearly understand what DC is, its purpose and how it works.

DC applies the principles and processes of collective decision-making and conflict resolution practiced by communal societies, and proves to be the most effective and correct method, because it corresponds to the basic needs and principles of social or group psychology. DC understands that within any society or group there will exist different ideas and disagreements amongst its members about important issues and how to address and resolve them. And unless the most correct ideas are brought forward and the group is able to unite in implementing them, then the group will be unable to solve its problems and there will be disharmony. So it is in the interest of the group that its members cooperate towards common goals.

But how does a group resolve incompatible ideas and bring forward the best most correct ones, and unite its members in applying them? This can only be done through methods that promote compromise and mutual concession. DC is the only method that allows this and in a way that enables all members to participate in reaching decisions. For people most willingly embrace decisions that they participate in that gave ear and consideration to their views and concerns, and where all members are invited to contribute and are willing to make concessions and compromises toward reaching and implementing the most correct decisions. People able to contribute to decisions are empowered and are able to feel greater responsibility for and satisfaction with the terms of the decision. This is what DC applies.

### Democracy

DC as its name implies combines both democracy and centralism. The object of genuine democracy is to bring out all ideas. To give everyone, not merely small groups or "special" individuals, the right and opportunity to speak up and express their views, to openly and honestly criticize people and practices high and low that are believed to be in error and harming the interests of the whole. This so that problems may be identified and solved.

In this process various different ideas are allowed to struggle with each other through reasoned debate and discussion, not coercion or violence. And people are allowed to vent anger and frustration but not to spite others. The object is to encourage open speech not to attack people's minor flaws or ridicule them.

DC draws on the collective wisdom of the group and its experiences at all levels. The emphasis of DC is on mass participation and learning their interests, views, needs, and concerns, whether of social conditions or related to the Party and its members. The Party must give the masses our hearts, encouraging them to freely voice their grievances and opinions and speak out. For this is the only way to bring them forward and eagerly into the struggle. When they see we are concerned with, empowered by, and committed to their interests and voice, they will enthusiastically support the Party, join the mass organizations, and take up the struggle alongside us.

But if we attempt to silence them, to make them feel their ideas are of no value, or that we are scorned and offended by their criticisms and refuse to examine and correct our errors and ourselves before them, if we seek to dominate and coerce them, the oppressed masses will not embrace us as *their* Party. They will not feel responsibility for or satisfaction with decisions made or advice given by the Party, and they will not support us. Therefore, we will not be their vanguard.

Without democracy, without allowing Party members and people to express themselves, how can we learn the actual conditions under which we and the masses are struggling? How will we know what works and what doesn't? How will we determine when resources or work needs to be diverted into certain areas or when there is a surplus or extra manpower in another place that can be sent to needy areas? How will we know when the masses are not content with our work or the performance of particular comrades?

We are not talking about that form of so-called democracy that the bourgeoisie uses *against* not *for* the people, where the masses have no say so in decisions that affect them but can only rush to the polls every few years to choose between Tweedledee and Tweedledum, both of whom serve the same corporate masters, and bleed the people to serve their benefit. We're talking about functional participatory mass democracy where the people have a say in every important decision that affects them; and this Party is *their* party not the tool of the capitalist class.

Our inner-Party democracy serves to ensure that upper levels of the Party know, understand and are responsive to what is happening down below. So comrades are able to evaluate things from all sides, and not make evaluations based on one-sided accounts or bits and pieces of information. This way we draw on the collective wisdom of the entire Party and the people in reaching decisions. Only thus can we discuss and unite together to reach correct ideas.

So there must first be open struggle (democratic discussion) of ideas *before* there can be unity (centralism) of ideas—of *all* ideas—within the group or society. These principles—democracy and centralism—go hand-in-hand.

## Centralism

Centralism is what we arrive at when, after broad discussion (the process of democratic struggle), our understanding of things reaches unity. It is the centralization of correct ideas; upon which we can then have unity in understanding policies, plans, organization, command, action, etc. This is called "centralized unification," which cannot be reached if the people and Party are not able to openly express their ideas and concerns, have them seriously considered, and allow them to contribute and participate in developing all-sided views of problems. So the foundation of our centralism is democracy.

Once we reach unity on ideas and there is agreement by majority vote, we all unite to apply the agreed upon policies, plans, etc. Applying the agreed upon ideas then proves or disproves the correctness of our decisions in practice. If proven incorrect, we then return to democratic discussion to reach a new level of unity and revise our plans, then return to practice again.

Essentially centralism means once a decision or course of action has been agreed upon through democratic discussion, debate, and vote, all members must wholeheartedly unite in applying that decision or course of action. Those who disagree with the majority decision must still abide by and apply it, but may reserve their disagreements and appeal them up to higher Party levels or bring them up for discussion and debate again at the next committee session.

## Inner-Party DC

Mao Tse-tung gave an important explanation of inner-Party DC:

> "The Party Committee at various levels is the organ which implements centralized leadership. But the leadership of the Party committees is a collective leadership: matters cannot be decided by the first secretary alone. Within Party committees democratic centralism should be the sole mode of operation. The relationship between the first secretary and the other secretaries and committee members is one of the minority obeying the majority. For example, in the Standing Committee and the Political Bureau situations like this often arise: when I say something, no matter whether it is correct or incorrect, provided that everyone disagrees with me, I will accede to their point of view because they are the majority. I am told that the situation exists within some provincial Party committees, whereby in all matters whatever the first secretary says goes. This is quite wrong. It is nonsense if whatever one person

says goes. I am referring to important matters, not to the routine work which comes in wake of decisions. All important matters must be discussed collectively, different opinions must be listened to seriously, and the complexities of the situation and partial opinions must be analyzed. Account must be taken of various possibilities and estimates made of various aspects of a situation: which are good, which bad, which easy, which difficult, which possible and which impossible. Every effort must be made to be both cautious and thorough. Otherwise you have one-man tyranny. Such first secretaries should be called tyrants and not 'squad leaders' of democratic centralism."

By living among the people, even in times of intense enemy repression and surveillance when open meetings are not feasible we can still exercise DC, by investigating problems through observation and inquiry of the masses, drawing out informal discussions, and keeping our ears close to the ground. What we learn and experience at lower levels should be conveyed to higher levels to inform decisions made there.

Also comrades should not fear, avoid or seek to repress the masses' criticisms of them or their conduct. But they should be humble and willing to examine themselves. The people should be encouraged to speak out as we are committed to truth. Those unable to accept the truth of their own actions and errors being exposed and criticized, are not suited to serve as the people's vanguard leadership, because our commitment is to serve the masses first and foremost. The same holds true for those who cannot stand to hear their ideas contradicted or challenged.

No one is always right or above criticism, even if sometimes we are wrongly criticized. To deal with truth we must be able and willing to be contradicted and disputed. If our views or actions are wrong we must honestly examine and correct them. This is the only way forward. Those unwilling to accept supervision and criticism of the people are not their genuine leaders, but are capable only of oppressing them, of placing individual pride before collective principle. Attitudes of this sort act as a corrosive and undermine unity.

At bottom, inner-Party DC enables the CC to make strategic decisions upon the broadest consideration of all available information. The entire Party is bound by these decisions. At the intermediate and lower levels the Branch and Unit committees are allowed great flexibility and initiative in determining how best to implement those decisions at their levels. In the process of doing so they collectively analyze and sum up their experiences, achievements and failures and report on them to other Party levels, and also share them with comrades in other areas to inform, test and refine theory and practice all round in carrying out the Party's goals. This is how DC works. A process many organizations have claimed to apply but which few even grasped. Indeed most lacked the humility and commitment to the mass line and revolutionary proletarian ideology—and no other—necessary to genuinely implement it.

At times of enemy repression of political activity, greater centralism and restricted democracy applies to protect cadre and our work, however, when conditions are permissive, we should apply democracy arousing and engaging the masses as broadly and openly as possible. Our Party must be adaptable to changing conditions and flexible. Only in this way can we stay ahead of enemy subversion and remain true to the cause of leading the oppressed working people and marginalized poor in struggle to defeat this imperialist system and its puppets.

## The Role of the Party

Our role is not to exercise political or state power over the people, (which is their prerogative), but to influence them, to set positive examples. When our outside structure unfolds and we are able to lead the masses to form their own popular governing bodies such as Community Councils, our cadre will be free to accept election as delegates of these popular political structures: but only as delegates with no greater power than any other delegate. Our leadership role is one voluntarily embraced by the people, based upon our unity and demonstrated ability to lead them in solving difficult problems and winning majority support. This sort of leadership is based on education, reasoned persuasion, and active involvement in the daily lives and struggles of the oppressed peoples.

This will lead to the Party's winning a certain level of prestige among the people we serve, based upon our commitment to them and proving to put forward correct policies that serve their interests. This involves our leading by example, actively participating in all mass organizations, systematically educating the people, and proving our devotion to the people by being the most principled, committed and self-sacrificing.

There will always be those who will find their way into our ranks whose personal qualities and ambitions run counter to the Party's principles. This is another reason DC is important and valuable. It will allow such elements to be examined and exposed by and before the masses. This is why comrades should be upright and sincere, and willing and able to accept the supervision and criticism of the people: because like it or not, the people will expose them. And it explains why organizations that are not genuinely committed to the interests of the oppressed masses cannot and do not integrate with them, and while many have professed to, *very, very few have really practiced DC.*

*Dare to Struggle, Dare to Win! All Power to the People!*

# 16. PANTHER LOVE: ADDRESSING THE SURVIVAL NEEDS OF THE PEOPLE, BUILDING PAN-AFRIKAN UNITY & SOWING THE SEEDS OF WORLD SOCIALIST REVOLUTION 2005

> "International capitalism cannot be destroyed without the extremes of struggle. The entire colonial world is watching the blacks inside the U.S., wondering and waiting for us to come to our senses. Their problems and struggles with the Amerikan monster are much more difficult than they would be if we actively aided them. We are on the inside. We are the only ones (besides the very small white minority left) who can get at the monster's heart without subjecting the world to nuclear fire. We have a momentous historical role to act out if we will. The whole world for all time in the future will love us and remember us as the righteous people who made it possible for the world to live on."
>
> *George Jackson, 1970*

The primary motive of a true revolutionary is love of the people—not just the people in your family, your neighborhood, or your country, but also the people of the whole world, and particularly the generations of people yet unborn. It is the duty of a revolutionary to represent and fight for the future in the struggles of today.

Not everything is possible, but what is possible is for humyn society to, at long last, break free of the Epoch of Exploitation, that has, since the rise of the Patriarchy and the institution of Slavery, chained humyn society to a succession of forms of political economy based upon class exploitation and oppression. It is not just possible ... It is necessary, because unless we do so, the present monopoly capitalist system (imperialism) will be the end of our evolution. It will bring on the extinction of our species, (and all our relations), by its wanton destruction of the ecosystem on which our survival depends, and by the necessity of unending war on which imperialism's existence depends.

The leopard cannot change its spots, and imperialism cannot change its nature. It is driven by only one law, and that is the maximization of the rate of profit on investment of capital. Capital seeks the highest rate of profit like a vampire seeks blood. It cannot change its predatory nature. It can only put on a "humyn face" to conceal its fangs and lull its victims into a false sense of security, but everyone is on the menu. Money is the master, and people are the slaves, even the monopoly capitalists. They are bound by the Law of the Maximization of the Rate of Profit as if by an unbreakable curse, and they will do whatever serves this master regardless of the human cost, even to the point of their own self-destruction.

Money is a humyn invention. It is an abstract idea to represent value created by humyn labor to price commodities in the market of exchange. It is only as real as we agree that it is. Value is created socially by the masses of workers each doing their jobs, extracting wealth from the earth and transforming it by their labor and the application of technology into commodities for consumption. The labor power of the workers is itself a commodity, bought by the capitalists, and is the source of their wealth and power. The difference between the cost of the workers' labor power and the value created by it is the capitalist's profit, (less the cost of materials and overhead), and the rate of profit is the speed at which a profit is turned. Capitalists compete to invest where the rate of profit is highest.

The contradiction between the social nature of production and the private ownership of the means of production, (including the workers' labor power), prevents the social control of production and society and ensures the dictatorship of the monopoly capitalists over the whole of society. The politics of imperialism are dictated by the class interests of the monopoly capitalists. As it is the nature of the rate of profit to fall under conditions of automation, (as production becomes more capital intensive and there are fewer workers to exploit), the monopoly capitalists are driven to seek cheaper labor costs and lower overhead, (cheaper rent on land, cheaper raw materials and energy costs, lower taxes, and less safety and environmental protection regulation), and thus boost their rate of profit. This is the force that drives politics under imperialism and brings on wars as the imperialists contend among themselves to control the underdeveloped countries, (and their natural resources), and keep the people of these countries poor and down-pressed as a reserve of cheap labor.

The vampires seek the freedom to suck the people's blood, and their appetite only grows, it doesn't slacken. The alternative to this "free market" political economy is a "command" economy (socialism), where the people make decisions about what is best for them on a collective basis and decide how to develop their economy. As every movie buff knows, when you've got vampire troubles, it doesn't do any good to try to reason with or make deals with the vampire. You've got to get scientific on its ass. You've got to study and learn all about vampirism, what they can and can't do, what their weaknesses are and how to take them out. They are powerful and scary, but they are not invincible. You just have to go about things the right way, use the right weapons and pick the right time to do battle with them. Meanwhile, you've got to survive while you get your shit together.

Now, everybody knows that the monopoly capitalists hate socialism. They hate the word; hate the merest whisper of it. They hate it like a vampire hates holy water or the light of the sun. Even a little socialism, like nationalization of a country's oil reserves, drives them into a murderous frenzy. They want to privatize everything: That is, they want to own everything, and squeeze a profit out of everything and everybody. They don't want the people to control a thing.

Socialism is more than a brake on the excesses of a free market economy dominated by the interests of global monopoly capitalists. It is the means to escape the Epoch of Exploitation altogether: A means to slay the vampire and end vampirism once and for all, by abolishing the division of society into classes and all forms of exploitation and oppression that go with it. It is the dawning of a New Day.

All societies based upon exploitation are class dictatorships. The ruling class dictates to and oppresses the exploited classes in order to maintain the unequal and exploitative relations that have been created. But under socialism, the working class has seized the power to change these relations.

All governments consist of "special bodies of armed men," (and now wimyn as well), whose job it is to maintain the existing property relations in society. They are the military, secret agents, the police and prison guards and those who command them. After a socialist revolution, the class at the bottom, the workers, create their own state with their own special bodies of armed men and wimyn in order to transform the property relations in society. This is necessarily a protracted process that advances in stages. Step by step, they revolutionize society to uplift and empower the poor and create new social relations based upon serving the people's needs, promoting social justice and the highest interests of humynity, while preventing a capitalist restoration and a return to the old exploitative ways.

At a certain point, society takes a qualitative leap forward, and the need for a state withers away because the basic contradictions and divisions in society have been eliminated. The Epoch of Exploitation will be over, and the new Post-Exploitative Epoch, or Communism, will be a radically different new world, in many ways reminiscent of the Pre-Exploitative Epoch but on a global basis and with a much higher technological base. The operating principle will be: "FROM EACH ACCORDING TO THEIR ABILITY AND TO EACH ACCORDING TO THEIR NEED." Money will be a thing to show the kids in museums.

## Panther Love

When we speak of "Panther Love," we are not just talking about serving the people as a form of charity, but as a means of creating a new social order based upon equality and true freedom. Panther Love is revolutionary love, liberating love, world-changing love. We begin with the people's basic needs, their survival needs, because to make revolution, we must first survive. We are everywhere under the gun, and we are the victims and survivors of genocide.

Afrika is the poorest place on earth: That is, it is, under the guns of imperialism and neo-colonialism. Otherwise, it is the richest place on earth: Richest in natural resources and the cultural legacy of humyn social evolution. Afrika is where it all began. Every person on the planet can trace back their roots to Mother Afrika and to the first man and womyn in the genetic chain that makes us all one humyn family. Nowhere did the Pre-Exploitative Epoch last longer.

Its wealth is its curse. Capitalism emerged sucking the blood of Afrika. European imperialists rose to global domination by colonial domination, slavery and genocide, starting with Afrika. Technological advances in the building of sailing ships gave the European merchants mastery of the seas in the 15th Century. European nobles had gotten a taste for the riches and fine things of Asian craftsmanship during the Crusades. They were hungry for the opulence of silks and jewels, spices and teas, but their conflict with Islam cut them off from the traditional trade routes that connected the Near and Far East, until the Portuguese found an alternative route by sailing around Afrika.

The Spanish then discovered the Western Hemisphere by sailing west to reach the Far East. But even though there was a great market for the goods of China in Europe, there wasn't much of a market for the goods of Europe in China, until the Spanish started sending the silver extracted by Amerindian slave labor from Peru and Mexico. While the China Trade was the top end of mercantilism, the "meat and potatoes" was the "Triangle Trade" between Europe, Afrika and the Amerikas. This was based on transporting Afrikan slaves to the Amerikas (principally to Brazil and the Caribbean) to grow sugar to make rum.

Rum and guns and the goods of European manufacture were traded to the Amerindians of North Amerika in exchange for furs for Europe and China to make hats and warm clothing for the rich, and rum and guns and the goods of European manufacture were traded to the Afrikans to get more slaves. The introduction of tobacco as a commodity on the world market inspired the colonization of North Amerika and the creation of tobacco plantations worked by the forced labor of local Amerindians, the transported poor of England and Ireland and Afrikan slaves.

Eventually, Afrikan slaves were exclusively employed on the southern plantations of British North Amerika. As the genocide and dispossession of the indigenous Amerindian nations opened more land for cultivation, cotton was introduced, and after the invention of the cotton gin, the rate of profit was so great that millions of Black slaves were imported and bred to work these plantations concentrated in the "Black Belt" South. This continued after the Civil War, when former slaves and poor whites were made sharecropping peasants tied to the land by the terror of the KKK and institutionalized racism and enforced illiteracy and poverty. Black people were forged into the New Afrikan Nation under these conditions of internal colonialism.

In Afrika, European colonialism pushed inland, as those fleeing enslavement moved inland, and here too, the European colonial-settlers established plantations and instituted forced labor to grow export crops and work the mines, raping Afrika of its great mineral wealth. The various imperialist powers of Europe carved up the continent into colonies and viciously suppressed resistance with genocidal violence. Countless millions of Afrikans and Amerindians perished in the centuries of primitive accumulation of capital that brought forth the dominance of capitalism in the world's political economy.

White racism emerged as justification for these great crimes against humynity, and Christianity offered its blessing for this "spreading of civilization," and "saving the souls of the heathens." Christian missionaries worked to pacify and control the colonized offering the crumbs of Christian charity and limited educational opportunities to a select class of elite Afrikans groomed in European prejudices and culture to act as go between and front men. But a few of these assimilated Afrikans, men like Patrice Lumumba, Amilcar Cabral and Agostinho Neto, ended up becoming the revolutionary intellectuals and leaders of the anti-colonial struggles that rocked Afrika in the post-WWII period.

In the course of the world wars, and in their wake, great upheavals and revolutions rocked the imperialist world. In 1917, the Russian Revolution brought forth the world's first socialist state. Following WWII, triumphant revolution in China, led by Mao Tse-tung and the Chinese Communist Party, created a socialist people's republic in a formerly colonized Third World country. All across Asia, Afrika and Latin America, anti-imperialist struggles challenged the reactionary dictatorships and colonial administrations with the support of the socialist countries.

Imperialism was seriously threatened, but it reasserted itself, and the U.S. emerged as the sole imperialist super-power. But the high tide of struggle in the 1960s shook up the system within the U.S. as well with the revolt of Blacks and other oppressed people, students, wimyn, and youth in general. The Black Panther Party emerged as the revolutionary

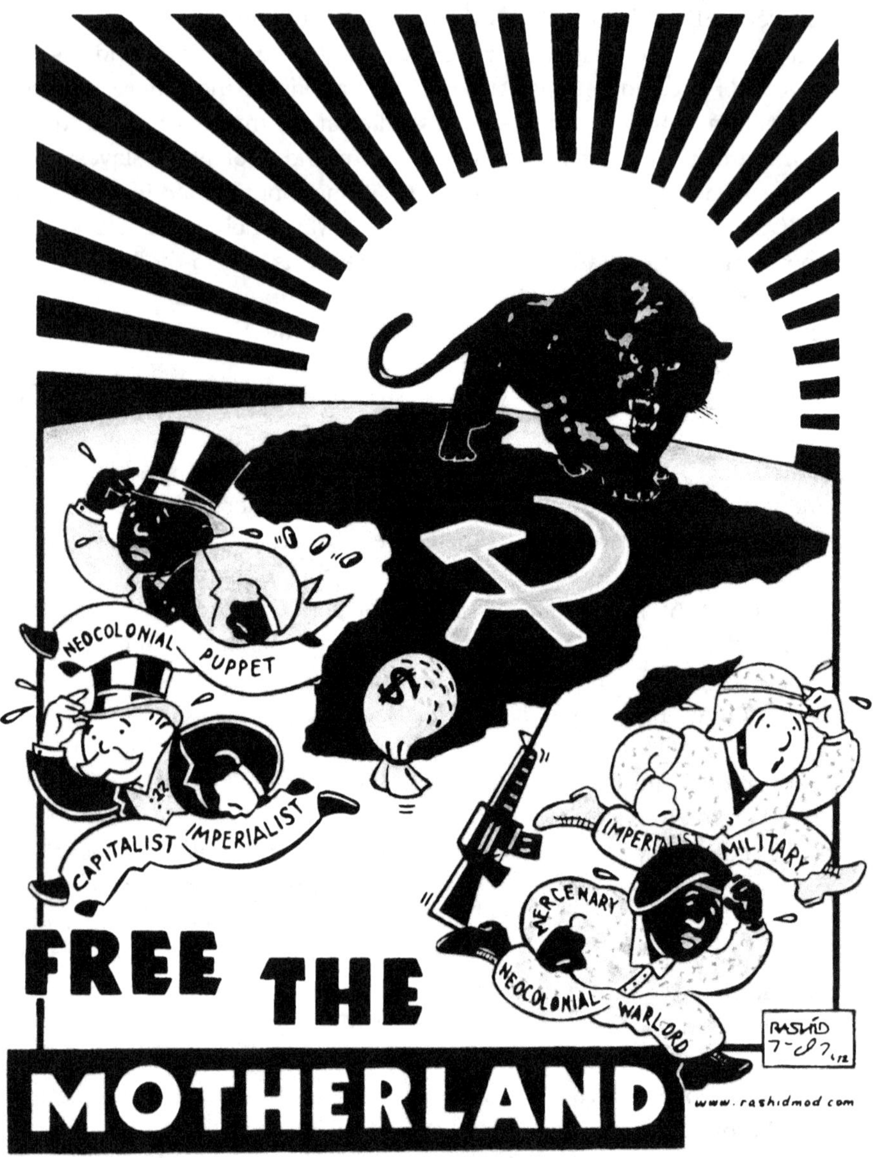


vanguard of this mass upsurge. The Panthers combined vigorous community-based survival programs with revolutionary political education and armed self-defense.

Most successful was the Free Breakfast for Children Program, started by the Seattle Chapter of the BPP in 1968, which by the following year had been replicated by all of the Party's chapters across the country. Getting up early every morning, the young Panthers served a hot breakfast to tens of thousands of poor Black children every day. Mostly, the program was run out of churches and community centers. This demonstrated the Party's love for the people and commitment to the community's health and welfare. Other programs included "Liberation Schools," free clinics, free clothing and shoes, free ambulance services, and other creative applications of the dictum to: SERVE THE PEOPLE!

As Huey P. Newton, the BPP Minister of Defense, pointed out: "Politics are merely the desire of individuals and groups to satisfy first their basic needs—food, shelter and clothing, and security for themselves and their loved ones." Demonstrating that these things could be obtained through self-reliance was the first step in getting the people to see the potentiality of their taking history into their own hands.

## Addressing The People's Survival Needs

We must first of all make a concrete analysis of conditions to assess the most urgent needs of the people in different settings and then organize the appropriate programs, uniting all who can be united and interfacing with existing groups and services as much as possible. Everywhere Black people are concentrated, there are common problems; poverty, hunger, police oppression, illiteracy, unemployment, disease, crime, homelessness, hopelessness, mental illness and fear. Children wake up hungry, the elderly need help to survive, families of prisoners want to see and hear from their loved ones, the homeless seek shelter, and workers want better wages and working conditions. All of these basic needs and more need to be addressed by the Party and the people's mass organizations.

To accomplish this, the Party must initiate and build neighborhood councils composed of the veteran organizers and respected elders of the communities. Programs can be organized under these councils including the employment of people's security forces. These councils would serve as parallel government formations in the oppressed communities and the embryo of people's power.

## Free Breakfast For Children

The Party should set as its goal seeing that every poor Black child on the planet starts the day with a wholesome breakfast. This includes areas of Afrika where famine is raging. It will take an army of workers to achieve this goal, and it is an army we must build. Children are not hungry, even starving, because there is a shortage of food in the world, but because their families cannot afford to buy enough food, and there is no profit in feeding them.

Every basic unit of the Party should maintain a mobile field kitchen and stockpile of powdered eggs and milk and dry goods to make hot cereal and cocoa, so that it can set up to provide emergency breakfasts for masses of children in disaster situations. Party members should be rotated to do service in other regions and countries wherever poor Black people are, and we should be as active in Luanda, Kinshasa, Dar Es Salaam, Cape Town and Port Au Prince, as in Harlem, Detroit, Chicago, Compton and Oakland. This massive undertaking is central to the Party's work, and other programs such as supporting the establishment of grower's co-ops, food co-ops, liberation schools, daycare centers and free clinics should be unfolded around it.

## Combating The Aids Epidemic

AIDS/HIV is an epidemic particularly affecting Black people. AIDS kills some 6,000 people each day in Afrika. 2.2 million of the 3 million people who died from AIDS in 2002 were Afrikans. Almost $^{2}/_{3}$ of those affected by AIDS/HIV are in Afrika, and Black people make up a considerable number of the 9.8 million victims outside of Afrika. 40 million Afrikan AIDS orphans are predicted by 2010. To make matters worse, AIDS relief efforts have been backing off from condom distribution under pressure from the Bush administration in favor of abstinence education and offering bounties to girls who remain virgins.

In response to this problem, the Party should strive to distribute hundreds of millions of condoms with a black panther logo and the words: "SURVIVE AND MAKE REVOLUTION!" in many languages on the packaging. The broadest international support should be sought to fund this effort. A mass publicity campaign involving buttons, posters, billboards, websites, and TV and radio spots should be waged, and in particular, mass youth organizations should be enlisted to help with fundraising and condom distribution.

The issue of finding sponsoring families, (both in-country and internationally), for AIDS and war orphans, should also be addressed by the Party. This is an area where the Party can grandstand, creating media events where planeloads of orphans from Afrika are united with host families in America and Europe. These families can also be enlisted in mass mobilizations to call attention to the issue and the obstructionism of the imperialists.

### Overall Health Care And Public Health

The situation presents a wide range of problems calling for a variety of programs including; free clinics, free pre-natal care and maternity centers, immunizations, sewage treatment and composting, drug and alcohol rehabilitation programs, abuse shelters, hospices, public heath education and free ambulance services. The "barefoot doctor" program developed in People's China can be replicated, training volunteers in traditional herbal medicines so they can go deep into the countryside to provide medical and health services. Well digging crews can address the problem of potable drinking water, particularly in the urban shantytowns and poor villages. Portable public chemical toilets can also be used, swamps can be drained and so forth.

### Assisting Prisoners And Their Families

The Party's work among prisoners revolves around the strategy of; "TURN THE IRON HOUSES OF OPPRESSION INTO SCHOOLS OF LIBERATION, AND THE OPPRESSED COMMUNITIES INTO BASE AREAS OF CULTURAL, SOCIAL AND POLITICAL REVOLUTION!", and the struggle for prisoners' rights and against cruel and unusual punishment, including capital punishment, the sentence of life without parole, and indefinite confinement in SHU (Security Housing Units) without review. We raise the demand: "NO INCARCERATION WITHOUT REPRESENTATION!" and call for amending the 13th Amendment to abolish all slavery. Special humyn rights watchdog committees should be organized to monitor prisons, sentencing and parole proceedings. Legal defense funds should be created for political prisoners and movement lawyers trained and retained to free them.

Free bus rides and overnight accommodations should be organized for the families of prisoners, and they should be organized to press for prison reforms. Mutual aid associations should be formed among these families, and the Party should carry out political education among them. Particular attention should be paid to the welfare of children of prisoners.

### War Refugees

Contention between rival imperialist corporations, (particularly between U.S. and French-based multinationals), and rival factions has led to brutal genocidal wars between tribes and ethnic groups and warlordism, (particularly in the Congo), causing millions of deaths and even more displaced people, who are crowded into refugee camps. These masses, who are the witnesses and survivors of genocide, suffer from malnutrition, shock and often debilitating wounds. Particular attention should be paid to their survival needs.

## Building Pan-Afrikan Unity

In rejecting the narrow nationalism on which the New Black Panther Party was founded and returning to the original Ten Point Program of the BPP, the NABPP-Prison Chapter adopts a broader perspective. We reject hate and playing the racial blame game. The old definitions of "nationalism" no longer apply. The new reality doesn't fit the language. The New Afrikan Nation is no longer a predominantly peasant nation concentrated in the Black Belt South but a dispersed nation of predominantly proletarian composition. We are part of the multinational U.S. working class and the international working class. It is also true that we are part of the Pan-Afrikan *Nation*, and comprise a significant portion of its proletariat. We still suffer national oppression, but not in the same old way.

The emergence of U.S. imperialism as the sole superpower and the headquarters of global imperialism has changed the situation. The principal enemy and oppressor of the people of Guinea-Bissau and the Cape Verde Islands, Angola and Mozambique is no longer Portuguese imperialism, as it was in the '60s and '70s. Throughout Afrika, the rising force and dominant vampire is U.S. imperialism, (along with its pack of junior partners), exercising neo-colonial domination. Many of the forces that resisted direct colonial rule have dropped their Marxist and Afrikan Socialist politics and become eager allies and clients of U.S. imperialism, as if the problem of the fox in the chicken coop was to get a bigger fox.

The same superpower and headquarters of the New World Order is now the principal enemy and neo-colonial slave master of the whole Afrikan Diaspora. European imperialism still exists in Afrika, and it is fighting (by proxy) to retain some measure of its old feeding grounds in Afrika (and elsewhere), but it is the Amerikans who are consolidating their grip. The practicality and desirability of Pan-Afrikan unity is now infinitely greater than ever before. It is based primarily on class interests and anti-imperialism rather than a vague sense of cultural nationalism or desire for racial separatism.

## Intercommunal News Service

It is important to have a regularly published newspaper that is a collective organizer that links up all the fronts on which the Party is active, and that is published in all the necessary languages. This can be accomplished with internet computer technology, and it is also possible to run a news wire on the net to supply raw news to Panther Radio outlets. These local radio shows can also be carried on the internet. Everywhere the Party organizes, it should distribute its newspaper, translated into the local language, with local sections added on. Besides English, the paper should be available, in print and online, in Spanish, Portuguese, French and Arabic and major Afrikan languages.

Afrikan and New Afrikan people share a common history—Slavery and Colonialism—and a common destiny—Liberation! We need a line of communication and education to understand our history, our situation and the collective corrective action to effect our common liberation. Pantherism is the glue to hold together the Pan-Afrikan World. Each country must form its own vanguard party and army of liberation to carry forward New Democratic Revolution and advance to socialism, but it must also be guided towards a Union of Afrikan People's Republics, a union as unbreakable as a bound together bundle of arrows.

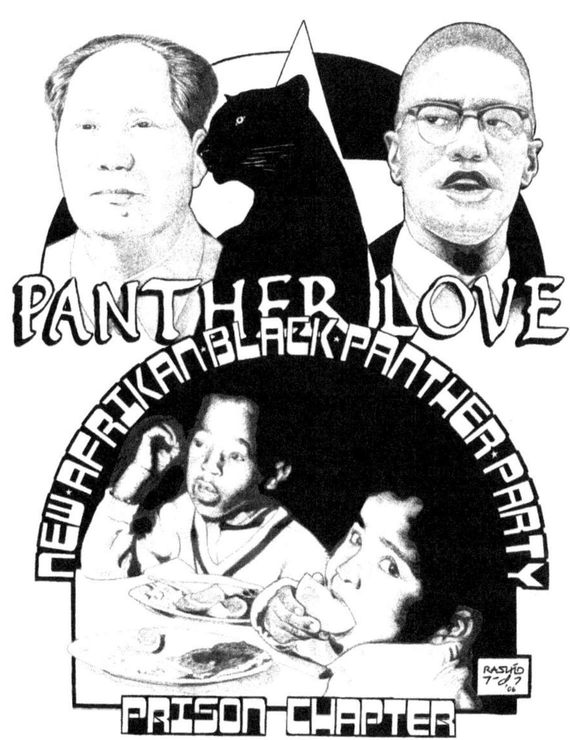

## Sowing The Seeds Of World Socialist Revolution

Understanding the role that the Party must play is also understanding the role others must play and how these roles fit together to serve the highest interests of humynity. The Party cannot be all things. Its special purpose is to represent the future in the movement of the present and illuminate the path forward. It is a Black revolutionary nationalist party that recognizes that class struggle and socialist revolution is the path forward. Black people alone cannot make this revolution, not even all the people of color in Amerika acting together can do that. A significant section of the white workers and people in general must commit themselves to this revolution, and to lead this requires a vanguard party of the whole U.S. proletariat acting as a detachment of the whole world proletariat. What we can, and must, do on our own is use our struggle to create more favorable conditions for this revolution, by liberating, (to the greatest extent possible), the ground under our feet, creating base areas for revolution in our communities and culturally, socially and politically asserting our will and desire for all-the-way revolution.

Too many people have become addicted to the insanity, and pulling a new order out of this chaos is a great challenge, but the struggle is a great teacher. We must use the struggle and let it teach us, sowing the seeds for the ultimate show-down with imperialism, sowing the seeds for the people's victory. Comrade George's words at the top of this essay are more glaringly true today than when he wrote them more than 30 years ago. They call out to us to be the "righteous people … who can get at the monster's heart." To perform this service, we must be worthy. We must kick our addiction to the insanity and purge ourselves of hate. We must nurture and fill our hearts with love, Panther Love!

We must commit ourselves to a long and protracted struggle, one that will test and strengthen us, perfect us, and make us worthy to win the love and respect of the whole world and future generations. We must: "DARE TO STRUGGLE AND DARE TO WIN!"

*Dare to Struggle, Dare to Win!*
*All Power to the People!*

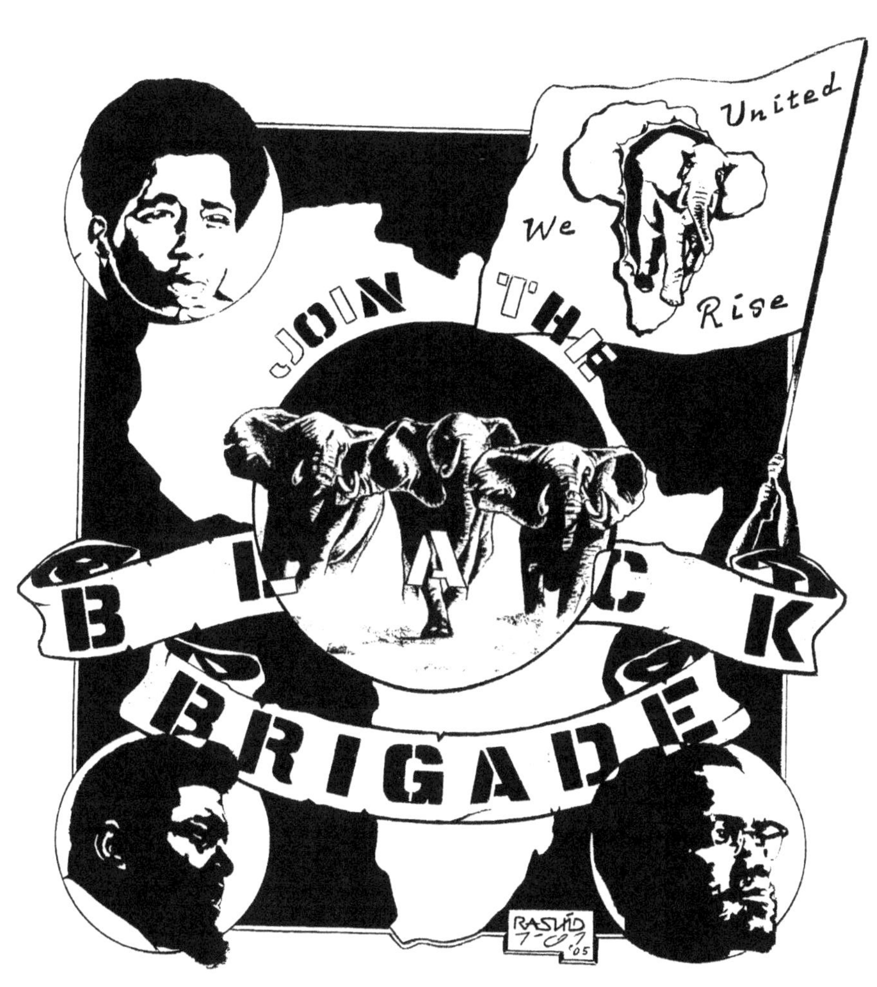

United
We
Rise
JOIN THE
BLACK
BRIGADE
RASHID

# 17. APPLIED PANTHER LOVE: ORGANIZING THE BLACK BRIGADE AND ITS WORK WITHIN THE RAZOR WIRE PLANTATIONS 2005

The Black Brigade is a mass organization, which means that its members are warriors drawn from a variety of political, spiritual and cultural schools of thought. What enables the Brigade's membership to function as a unit in programmatic unity is its core function of rendering service to the Nation of Afrikans in Amerika.

So far, the Brigade has operated in a relatively loose and unaccountable fashion. Its work and organizational structure have not been consolidated nor clearly defined, particularly in relation to serving the needs of the imprisoned New Afrikans. This is natural given the conditions under which it has been founded, but it is time to pull the Brigade together into chapters at the respective prisons where the members are confined and to begin developing concrete programs to serve the people.

In order to do this, the members must develop a clearer understanding of the tasks before us, and the members of the NABPP-PC within the Brigade should play an active and leading role in this process. We are ourselves in process of creation of our organizational structure, and the two tasks are intertwined and dialectically united.

Our people's material needs are food, clothing, medical care, shelter, security (conflict mediation), literacy and education, family-community support and cohesion, spiritual freedom, legal support, safe and healthy working and living conditions and so on. Some of our people need psychiatric care, drug and alcohol addiction counseling, and other specialized rehabilitative services. There are two primary aspects of serving these needs within the razor wire plantations: 1) The first aspect is creating STP (Serve The People) program committees. 2) The second aspect is organizing study and discussion circles to politically and ideologically educate and continually deepen people's understanding. In other words, the Brigade must develop revolutionary practice and revolutionary theory using one to enrich the other.

The Party has the same basic tasks. The difference is that the Party members should be committed revolutionaries in a fuller sense, who are down for the whole thing. Their role is to be the advanced detachment or vanguard. In carrying out the two tasks, we must implement Panther Love, which is the positive commitment to raise the oppressed masses out of their physical and mental enslavement to imperialism, and to pave the way for a better world for future generations through revolutionary struggle.

## Study and Discussion Circles

An enslaved people are brought into and kept in this state by being made to believe that they are physically and mentally incapable of doing for themselves without a slave master. They are conditioned to rely upon their enslaver for motivation and direction and to achieve their survival needs. Fundamental to accomplishing this is to keep the enslaved misinformed and ignorant and living under conditions where they are compelled to seek the necessities for survival from the enslaver.

This is essentially how things worked on the old cotton and tobacco plantations and how they work on today's razor wire plantations. And overall, it is how things are for the New Afrikan Nation within the Amerikan Nation and for the working class under capitalist dictatorship. The imperialist (mis)education system, the (mis)information and entertainment industry, and even the religious indoctrination establishment all work to keep the masses of people numb from the neck up. They fill our heads with false and misleading information about what is going on and how things got to be this way.

They teach us false histories and interpretations of world and domestic affairs, swamp us with mind-numbing entertainments and diversions, and subtly (and not so subtly) infect us with self-hate and contempt for our blackness, keeping us in the dark about our truly remarkable Black heritage. Such positive images and examples empower us and enhance our self-esteem as Black people and give us the confidence that we can not only be independent but contribute in a powerful way to advancing society to a higher level.

As Comrade Russell "Maroon" Shoats pointed out: "When a whole people undergo ... separation from their historical past, they invariably become easy prey to those who want to use them, because not having any historical record to fall back on, they have nothing to compare things to." He further stated that, "Ironically, they are like the circus and zoo lions and elephants raised in captivity. Never having been taught by other lions and elephants in the wild, they don't know how to hunt or forage and survive in their natural habitat. They are pretty easy to control and are pretty harmless to their controllers."

"European slavers and expansionists," he argues, "were well aware of this phenomenon, and they argued and fought with their peers to have strict laws adopted that were designed to eradicate as much past knowledge from their enslaved Afrikans and Amerindians foes as possible; including their traditional spirituality, languages, folklore, hair styles, diets, family patterns, their values and sense of right and wrong, their former group solidarity, and overall, their customs and self-identity."

So it becomes self-evident how valuable correct education is for an oppressed, marginalized and neo-colonized people, like we New Afrikans, and especially in the creation of effective mass organizations. Any organization that is not based on the people and their true history is opposed to them and will treat them as slaves and manipulate them against their true interests. Organizations that are based upon the people's true interests do not fear the truth and encourage their members and the people to study hard and to be critical thinkers.

We do not want to be manipulated and exploited by our own Black bourgeoisie but to free all of humynity. Black liberation can only be accomplished by the overthrow of global imperialism, and we in the Belly of the Beast, the heart of the monopoly capitalist empire, must play the leading and decisive role and deliver the coup de grace, the death blow, to this epoch of exploitation and oppression.

To do this, we must liberate ourselves from the mental, spiritual and ideological shackles of slavery. We must rise above our station as beasts of burden, wage slaves and lumpen proletarians, and become the New Men and Womyn of the Socialist Revolution. The Black Brigade's first duty is developing its member's minds, their knowledge and understanding along with the people so they will not lose confidence in their ability to become the makers of history.

Bravery in the absence of political understanding is only brute courage. The courage we need is conscious and the result of understanding what needs to be done and how to go about doing it. It is what will make us unconquerable. Death comes to all, but like life it can vary in significance. To live a life of purpose, to live and die a revolutionary, is the highest calling there is. To be like Comrade Hasan and fear neither life nor death in the strength of total commitment, that is the ultimate freedom.

To develop this level of political understanding and commitment, the New Afrikan Black Panther Party-Prison Chapter must set the example for the Black Brigade and the masses. We must study the hardest, teach and demonstrate the principle of revolution, and in every way strive to be the people's pride and inspiration. Through the regular practice of organized collective study and discussion and applying the principle of "each one teach one," the Brigade's political and spiritual development will be enhanced and welded more and more into a unified force to serve the people.

### Serve The People Committees

The work of the STP Committees is as the name implies, to develop programs to serve the basic survival needs of the people. By practicing self-reliance, mutual assistance and creativity, we can achieve a measure of self-determination and people's power even under the most oppressive conditions. This is applying Panther love in practice. Those who have particular skills or abilities can apply them to help others. Even the unskilled can donate their time and efforts.

We should strive to be as independent of Empire as we can be and look to our own needs and collective welfare. Of course we will still demand the services the state is obligated to provide, but to the extent we can, we should be self-reliant and not dependent. For example there is a lot we can learn about natural cures, nutritional supplements and health. We can assist each other in legal work and research, in learning languages and dealing with personal issues like anger, grief, addiction or self-discipline. This demands unity in theory and unity in practice, getting past self-centeredness and becoming family and comrades to one another.

The STP Committees should implement survival programs according to conditions within the particular prisons in which they operate. They should make assessments of these conditions and the prisoners' needs and resources. Successes should be shared with others so they can be replicated when applicable.

**Within the razor wire, our survival needs are many:**

**Health**: There should be a public health committee at each prison to address the issues of disease prevention and treatment. HIV/AIDS, Hepatitis A and C, TB and STDs are at epidemic levels in many prisons, yet little is being done on prevention education, testing and treatment. Sanitation, use of disinfectants, healthy diet, exercise, and access to proper medical care and medicines are issues that need to be addressed in an organized way.

**Legal Aid:** Many people would not have to be in prison if they had proper legal advice and assistance. There should be a legal assistance committee to organize the jailhouse lawyers, legal resources, community legal aid and support contacts, and to assist prisoners with legal paperwork, filings and record keeping.

**Literacy and Language:** There should be a committee to help illiterate prisoners learn to read and write and/or to become bilingual.

There are many other potential committees that can be formed to address a whole range of issues from drug and alcohol dependency to rape prevention. These committees should research and hook up with services available on the outside and the inside to obtain and produce educational literature and distribute it.

## Get Organized!

No people have to accept the role of slaves and submit to violations of their humyn rights. Organizations like the Human Rights Coalition (HRC), initiated by Comrade Maroon to mobilize prisoners, their families and supporters in the communities to fight for respect for prisoners' humyn rights, should be spread nationwide with chapters in every state.

We are building a national campaign to amend the 13th Amendment to the U.S. Constitution to strike the clause that perpetuates the status of slave for those convicted of a crime, and along with this to abolish the racist death penalty and other Draconian practices, and to extend universal suffrage to give voting rights to prisoners and others denied this fundamental civil right. Political action committees need to be organized to advance this work.

Within each unit and prison chapter, captains and other officers need to be chosen and organizational structure needs to be developed. This must be done in coordination with the Brigade Commander, Nathaniel Lee, but it must also reflect the will of the people and recognize the natural leaders among us.

The NABPP-PC has a responsibility to be a leadership vanguard, but the Black Brigade is an independent organization with a life of its own and needs to develop its own leadership structure. Not everyone in the Brigade is going to agree with our Party Line in total nor should they be expected to. Our unity is programmatic unity.

Important as our work on the razor wire plantations is, it is mainly to transform them into "Schools of Liberation." Our principal task is to train revolutionary warriors who will in turn transform the oppressed communities into base areas of cultural, social and political revolution. We must always keep this strategic orientation in mind.

Our struggle is for the liberation of our people from centuries old oppression. It happens that our liberation is impossible short of the liberation of mankind from the system of capitalist exploitation that was built on the backs of our ancestors. Though conditioned to think as slaves, we must learn to think as liberators and as leaders of a worldwide struggle.

Indeed he who has been last will later be first, for the times they are a changing!

*Dare to Struggle, Dare to Win!*
*All Power to the People!*

# 18. ADVANCING FROM THE BLACK BRIGADE TO THE NEW AFRIKAN SERVICE ORGANIZATION (NASO): A GREAT LEAP FORWARD! 2007

The Black Brigade was co-founded by two prisoners in Pennsylvania, Nathaniel Lee and Samuel "Angel" Coley. "Angel" was a former member of the original Black Panther Party and a founder of the Philly Panthers' Free Breakfast for Children Program. He was already dying from advanced hepatitis, and he passed over before the first issue of *Leviathan*, the Black Brigade's newsletter was published.

The Brigade was sponsored by the Red Heart Warriors Society (RHWS), an inter-tribal Native American organization centered in the prisons and sponsored by the Traditionalist United Eastern Lenape Nation (TUELN). TUELN is headed by Chief Tom Big Warrior.

The RHWS grew out of the struggle of Native American prisoners seeking to practice their traditional ceremonies and to study the traditional spiritual orientation of warriors—which is to serve the people. The Black Brigade's orientation was to serve the Nation of New Afrikans in Amerika and all oppressed people.

The example of Malcolm X and the original BPP were major influences on the Black Brigade from the start. But there was another influence promoted by Bro. Lee, which was the philosophy of Thomas Hobbes, a 17th century English philosopher, whose major work, *Leviathan*, (published in 1651), was chosen as the name of the Black Brigade's newsletter.

### Struggle Between Two Lines: Hobbesianism vs. Pantherism

The struggle between these two ideological and political worldviews took the form of Bro. Lee's insistence of having complete control as the Brigade's "Commander," though in reality, he was content to let others do the work including raising all the funds to publish the newsletter.

Meanwhile, within the Brigade, various individuals came together to form the New Afrikan Black Panther Party-Prison Chapter (NABPP-PC), with their own newsletter, *Right On!*, and they required prospective members to first join and help build the Black Brigade as a mass organization through which the Party could play its vanguard role.

A lot of prisoners hooked up, expressing a desire to both work with the Brigade and to join the Panther Party. Eventually things came to a head when Commander Lee announced that he wanted to take the

Brigade in a completely different direction and openly attacked the idea of restoring the Black Panther Party and what it stood for.

At this point, it was decided that RHWS would cease to fund the Brigade and would instead support the formation of a new mass organization under the leadership of NABPP-PC. Thus the NASO was conceived. Instead of a "Commander," it will have a National Steering Committee, composed of both Party and non-Party members, and it will have an overall democratic structure.

Even in his own time, Thomas Hobbes was a reactionary philosopher and a proponent of the absolute power of the monarchy over the masses. He put forward the theory that people must give up their liberty to a leviathan (giant) in exchange for security and peace.

Now in his day, bourgeois liberalism was challenging the royalist establishment and overthrowing autocratic rule with the English Revolution, and Hobbes had to flee to France to write his book. But as Cromwell made himself High Protector (dictator) over England, Hobbes was able to return, and his philosophy was used to justify the bourgeois dictatorship.

Ever since, the bourgeoisie have promoted a Hobbesian worldview that the natural state of man is war between every individual, and a powerful state (and Head of State) is required to create law and order. In fact in class society, the state is a dictatorship and everyone is put in competition with everyone else.

In this context, there is a contradiction between Black bourgeois nationalism and revolutionary New Afrikan/Black nationalism. To the latter, revolutionary nationalism is an expression of proletarian internationalism.

Nationalism is by its nature a product of the bourgeois (capitalist) epoch of history. However, under proletarian leadership, national liberation is a step towards socialist revolution and stateless (communist) society. When Huey P. Newton stated, "We are nationalists and internationalists," he was asserting that the Black Panthers, unlike the narrow "pork chop" Black nationalists, rejected a bourgeois conception of nationalism.

Pantherism is part and parcel of the global socialist revolution to transform all of humyn society and move it beyond the epoch of exploitation, war and oppression. It links the struggle for Black liberation with the struggle against class exploitation and all types of oppression. It will not tolerate the substitution of Black capitalist oppression for white capitalist oppression, nor does it seek to gain democratic rights for Black people by taking them away from anyone else. Quite the contrary, it encourages Black people to play a vanguard role in the struggle to build a united front with all other oppressed people against capitalist imperialism and to stand in firm solidarity with each other in the spirit of "Panther Love."

Some folks, including Bro. Lee, would have us believe that Pantherism is "out of date" and no more than nostalgia for a bygone day. But what is "new" in their offering? It's just the same old bourgeois philosophy expounded by Hobbes and others for the past 350 years.

They mistake the ebb and flow of class struggle for "proof" that the proletariat cannot remake the world in its own interest and do away with class society and all oppression. But, what struggle has not gone through stages of internal gains and losses, successes and setbacks, rises and declines?

The ideology of the capitalist imperialists permeates all of this society and is reflected back most strongly from those whose lifestyles mimic their own, such as the criminal element, or as Huey P. Newton characterized them, the "illegitimate capitalists." Their lifestyle, which embraces the core of capitalist values, leads them to the distorted view of humyn nature that Hobbes came up with.

> "Hereby it is manifest that during the time men live without a common power to keep them all in awe, they are in that condition which is called war; and such a war as is of every man against every man. For war consisteth not in battle only, or the act of fighting, but in a tract of time, wherein the will to contend by battle is sufficiently known: and therefore the notion of time is to be considered in the nature of war, as it is in the nature of weather. For as the nature of foul weather lieth not in a shower or two of rain, but in an inclination thereto of many days together: so the nature of war consisteth not in actual fighting, but in the known disposition thereto during all the time there is no assurance to the contrary."
>
> *Leviathan*

Far from war being the natural state of humynity, humyn beings were around for tens of thousands of years and living in community before the first weapons were conceived. Primitive egalitarian societies were characterized by their lack of authoritarian figures and forms of compulsion as well as their customs of sharing and hospitality.

Far from everyone being in a state of war with everyone else, as Hobbes asserts, the normal state of humyn relations was for tens of thousands of years characterized by its lack of conflict and general peace. Conflict arose with the creation of private property and the division of society into exploiting and exploited classes, which brought on violence and war, which has intensified with the development of class society.

Far from standing above society to maintain peace, the sovereign maintains inequality and forces submission of the masses to a privileged class of exploiters. This is civilization.

The proletariat, the class of wage slaves created by capitalism, has the historic destiny of being the gravediggers of the epoch of exploitation and the harbingers of the post-exploitative epoch based upon socialized control over socialized production—creating a society in which each receives according to his or her needs from the collective effort of socialized labor.

Under these conditions, racism, war and all oppression can, and will, be abolished, national boundaries will disappear, and humynity will rise above the struggle for survival to enjoy a degree of liberty and quality of life not previously possible. This is the goal and logical outcome of the class struggle; not simply to make class exploitation and oppression more tolerable but to end it.

The New Afrikan Nation in Amerika has an historic destiny, which is to play a leading, vanguard role in this struggle to create a bright future for all of humynity. As capitalism arose with the enslavement of our ancestors so will it fall through our self-liberation.

The formation of the New Afrikan Service Organization (NASO) is a great leap forward in that it is being conceived as a mass organization that can build the vanguard party to lead the liberation struggle under the most difficult conditions, and continue to rebuild it as necessary, while at the same time uplifting and involving the oppressed Black masses and other oppressed people in day to day struggle to serve the basic survival needs of the people and politically arm them with revolutionary understanding. Our philosophy is: *From the Masses to the Masses.*

Without a revolutionary vanguard party to act as a strategic and tactical headquarters, there can be no successful revolution. Such a party must be built by the masses from the bottom up under centralized leadership in accordance with the principles of democratic centralism.

NASO, which is democratic in character, will be united around the Ten Point Program of the NABPP-PC, (which is part of the legacy of the original Black Panther Party). Chapters of NASO can be established by three or more people in conjunction with the National Steering Committee. Those who demonstrate their dedication and grasp of Pantherism may rise to become members and cadre of NABPP-PC and build the infrastructure of the Party under the leadership of our Central Committee.

NASO is a mass organization that is intermediate between the Party and the people as a whole. It is open to people with a wide range of ideological and political beliefs who are in programmatic unity with the minimum goals and aspirations of the New Afrikan Black Panthers. It is about service to the people.

It is also a "School of Revolution" where those who are inclined can become comrades schooled in revolutionary theory and practice, rise in their level of commitment and understanding, and be entrusted with leadership responsibilities. Revolution is about solving problems, and revolutionaries devote their lives to struggle and service to the people. The minimal program of the Party, which addresses the immediate problems of survival the people face, will also reorient the masses to address the main problem, which is capitalist imperialist rule with the only solution possible—taking history into their own hands.

The New Afrikan Black Panther Party belongs to the people. We will build it in the course of struggle against oppression, drawing into our ranks the best and most dedicated fighters for liberation. The New Afrikan Service Organization will link the Party to the people and people to the Party.

*Dare to Struggle, Dare to Win!*
*All Power to the People!*

# 19. ON THE ROLES AND CHARACTERISTICS OF THE PANTHER VANGUARD PARTY AND MASS ORGANIZATIONS 2006

> "[T]he existence of a political vanguard precedes the existence of any of the other elements of a truly revolutionary culture."
>
> George Jackson, *Blood In My Eye* (1971)

> "A revolutionary party cannot be built on the quicksand of ideological confusion. Obviously there are a lot of people in the Black movement whose political positions are dead wrong, and someone has to have the courage to say it, even if it busts wide open the façade of unity. A political split, like a divorce, is often healthier than trying to live together in the same house when you have fundamental differences ... There are political differences inside the Black Movement representing different socio-economic layers inside the Black community. It is better to start the vanguard party from scratch with the serious few ... than with many assorted persons who are all going in different directions and who are therefore bound to split at the moment of crisis, just when the need is for maximum organizational strength and unity. This does not mean that those who cannot or will not accept the ideology and discipline of the vanguard party cannot play a role in the movement or in concrete struggles for liberation that will culminate in the taking of power. But their place is in the various organizations of mass struggle, not in the vanguard party."
>
> James and Grace Lee Boggs,
> *The Role of the Vanguard Party* (1970)

Recurring criticisms and questions have been raised about the New Afrikan Black Panther Party-Prison Chapter's organizational structure. Most of these criticisms and questions have come from veteran comrades of the original Black Panther Party, (and those they've influenced), whose negative experiences under the leadership of Huey P. Newton, (the BPP's co-founder and Minister of Defense), has led them to reject both the need of a Vanguard Party and the decision-making process of Democratic Centralism (DC), both of which we believe are absolutely essential for the success of any revolutionary struggle. Our purpose here is to answer those criticisms and questions.

In order to address these issues, we must begin with analyzing what type of organization the BPP really was and what sort of decision making process the BPP leadership actually applied.

### Was the BPP a Vanguard Party?

While we believe the BPP contained many genuine vanguard elements, (comrades who had cultivated a revolutionary proletarian outlook), it also contained many elements who maintained and cultivated unremolded lumpen class values and perspectives. In fact, BPP leaders Huey Newton and Eldridge Cleaver in 1970 and George Jackson in 1971 proudly identified the BPP as being a lumpen party. Furthermore, as pointed out by Charles E. Jones and Judson Jeffries in chapter one of *The Black Panther Party Reconsidered* and by Comrade Sundiata Acoli in his *A Brief History of the Black Panther Party*, the class backgrounds of BPP members spanned from petty bourgeoisie, to lumpen proletarian, to pre-class high school and college students and many were in fact employed workers. There was no requirement within the Party that its members commit "class suicide" or otherwise develop proletarian class consciousness, despite the fact that in the Black communities different classes, with various different ideological and political views, were contending to influence the direction of the movement.

Membership in the BPP was generally open to all members of the Black communities. All one had to do was walk into a Party office and sign up. This allowed raw elements to join who were not trained and prepared to lead a revolutionary movement, and offered no protection against infiltration by disruptive elements and enemy agents who would undermine the Party's ability to operate at a high level of ideological, political and practical unity.

So, in essence the BPP, while operating under the banner of a vanguard party, actually combined the features of both a vanguard party and a mass form of organization. This occurred because the BPP's leadership failed to make the distinction between the different natures and roles of a vanguard party versus a mass organization. They thus combined both organizational structures into one with the result of having many different tendencies pulling in different directions inside the Party. So, while a strong sense of cultural unity and collective willpower was able to hold the Party together in many ways, it ultimately blew apart as a result of the pigs' inciting these different internal tendencies into factionalism, competition, envy, paranoia and distrust, à la COINTELPRO. This sort of division would have been much harder to accomplish within a genuine Vanguard Party that practiced DC.

### What is a Vanguard Party? What is a Mass Organization?

In order to understand where the BPP went wrong in its organizational structure, we must examine the difference between the Vanguard and the mass organizations. We must also understand that the kind of organization that an oppressed people needs is determined by what the people are ultimately trying to accomplish. As Chairman Bob Avakian of the RCP USA has stated:

> "If the goal is simply to fan dissent and protest, or to build a movement that may take militantly to the streets around particular outrages, but does not aim to overthrow the system, then one can dispense with revolutionary organization; a vanguard is not necessary, and for that matter there's no need for revolutionary ideology.
>
> "But if the goal is to mobilize the masses to seize power from a murderous ruling class and to establish a new power that enables the masses to run and transform society, then you have to act on the implications of this: a vanguard party becomes essential."

How else can the masses defeat a highly organized oppressive system controlled by a united class enemy? Accomplishing this requires a highly disciplined, organized and united revolutionary party; one that understands the underlying nature of class society and imperialism, and the stages and forms of struggle necessary to overthrow such an enemy order and replace it with a system that genuinely implements the will of the masses. This form of organization is the revolutionary vanguard party.

The vanguard party must consist of the most ideologically and politically united, advanced, disciplined, and dedicated class-conscious elements of a people's revolutionary forces. These elements must have developed the class perspectives of the revolutionary proletariat, and apply the scientific method of *Historical and Dialectical Materialism* to its analyses and practice and to educating and guiding the less-advanced masses in solving socio-economic problems.

The vanguard party must be able to investigate material conditions and social contradictions, taking in a broad view of all relevant factors, drawing their information from *all* areas and sectors of society, high and low, at home and abroad. This data must be analyzed, then synthesized to draw conceptual conclusions and implement programs and policies that organize the masses to solve their own economic and political problems. The vanguard party must be united in theory and practice in the highest sense, and aspire through guiding and educating the masses to raise mass consciousness up to the level of the vanguard elements.

The vanguard party does not seek to be a specialized group operating above and out of reach of the common people, instead it actually lives and struggles alongside the people and educates them in the process of struggle so that they too will become vanguard elements. The ultimate objective is to make the Party and the people one and the same.

Until the masses of people are raised up to the level of the vanguard elements, they are organized into mass organizations. The mass organizations represent and include people of various different political, cultural, ideological and class backgrounds, views, influences and levels of awareness. In the case of New Afrikans, for example, our mass organizations like the New Afrikan Service Organization (NASO) include New Afrikan people of different political, cultural and spiritual persuasions. But they are united by a common objective of carrying out programs that serve the needs and interests of the Nation of Afrikans in Amerika. Many of the members of mass organizations are not even revolutionary minded, but they do recognize a burning need to change and improve the social-economic conditions of Black people.

So, mass organizations will include some open proponents of capitalism, liberals, reformists, activists of various persuasions and everyday apolitical people. But also spread throughout these organizations are cadre of vanguard elements whose role within these organizations is to struggle alongside and learn from the people, to materially serve their needs and interests, to educate, lead and advance their levels of political and ideological consciousness, and to ultimately develop the masses from within these mass structures, to become themselves vanguard elements. As people's consciousness and understanding are raised, and they prove their dedication through their work and study within the mass organizations, they are recruited into the vanguard party where they become fully committed leaders, educators and servants of the People.

The reality is that no people have *ever* made a spontaneous and leaderless revolution. In *every* case where any revolution succeeded (Russia, China, Angola, Mozambique, Guinea-Bissau, Cuba, Vietnam, etc.), there was a party of vanguard elements that led and organized them. It is unrealistic to suppose that a people can spontaneously unite, rise up and overthrow and then themselves replace the institutions of a highly organized economic system and state. Many ultra-leftists theorize about the possibility, but no one has ever achieved it in practice. It is therefore an idealistic and materially unsupportable premise. (Theory, to be accepted as "truth," must be proved in practice.) It is no more realistic than expecting that a person with no mechanical study, training or experience could spontaneously build a modern car engine. To develop such a skill, one must be actively instructed over a period of time through study, practice and guidance by others who *are* advanced in the appropriate technical fields, or they must have had plenty of leisure time, opportunity and hands-on access to the necessary technical information and tools to learn the skills themselves. They must be exposed to or studied in the practice itself to become capable and effective in applying it.

So this is to say that yes, the common persyn definitely can learn to build a car engine, however, they cannot develop the ability instantly and spontaneously without practical exposure or instruction. To claim otherwise would be absurd and we dare say improvable. The same reality exists for a people consciously struggling with a society's highly developed and complex economic, political, military and cultural processes, in pursuit of first seizing power from the bourgeoisie, and then effectively operating these institutions themselves. This is why the masses need a revolutionary party to lead, organize and raise their collective consciousness to achieve and then successfully administer a revolutionary seizure of power.

In this regard, the vanguard party must consist of a hard core of committed revolutionaries who scientifically understand the various economic, political, military, cultural and historical conditions that underlie present society and its various levels of development; who recognize the changes and forms of struggle necessary to overthrow the oppressive system in the ebbs, flows and weaves inherent in the developments of revolutionary struggle; and who have the ability to organize the masses to seize the reins and administer the institutions of the new mass-based society that must smash and build itself upon the ruins of the bourgeois society. As Amilcar Cabral pointed out, while the vanguard party is needed to lead a revolutionary struggle, "our problem is to see who are capable of taking control of the state apparatus when the colonial power is destroyed." This is a key question. The answer, as Cabral observed, is the mass-based revolutionary party.

So, in essence, the vanguard party is the administrative nucleus of the aspiring and rising revolutionary society. When out of power, the Party acts as the political embryo, which guides and organizes the people's struggle to ultimately seize power from their bourgeoisie and imperialist oppressors.

And of course we do not claim that less-advanced elements won't find their way into a vanguard party, because they will. Unity of opposites and uneven development exists within all social phenomena, including a revolutionary party. People are always going to have different levels of understanding of Historical and Dialectical Materialism and how to apply it. What is important is that the center is consolidated while uplifting and educating the cadre and party rank and file in an ongoing way. Envision an escalator where people get on at ground level and go up in stages floor by floor. There will always be new people getting on and therefore unevenness at each successive level of a vanguard party. The deeper understanding will be at a higher level.

These are the distinctive features and functions of the vanguard party versus the mass organizations. The fact that the BPP failed to make these distinctions and organize the Party accordingly, created the internal conditions that allowed the government to destroy it.

Actually, despite his organizational genius, Comrade Amilcar Cabral made a similar error in structuring the vanguard party of Guinea-Bissau, the PAIGC. Too many aspiring bourgeois elements were allowed to enter the leadership levels of the PAIGC. Therefore, all these aspiring capitalist elements had to do was neutralize the advanced class-conscious elements like Amilcar, (through assassinating him in 1973), and his brother Luis Cabral, (through a coup that sent him into exile), and these elements took over the Party and derailed Guinea-Bissau's revolutionary advances.

### Did the BPP Practice Democratic Centralism?

The questions remain whether the BPP applied DC and whether DC is the correct decision-making process of a vanguard party.

> "Every comrade ... should help the masses to organize themselves step by step and on a voluntary basis to unfold gradually struggles that are necessary and permissible under the external and internal conditions obtaining at a particular time and place. Whatever we do, authoritarianism is always erroneous because, as a result of our impetuosity, it makes us go beyond the degree of the masses' awakening and violates the principle of voluntary action on the part of the masses."
>
> *Mao Tse-tung, 1945*

Quite a few BPP veterans, especially those on the East Coast, are still smarting from Huey's unilateral purges of committed Party cadre, beginning in 1970 when the BPP split into the pro-Huey West Coast and pro-Cleaver East Coast factions. Huey had reached an icon status as a result of the massive nation-wide campaign led by BPP cadre (1968–1970) to free him from prison on charges of killing a cop. An unintended consequence of this campaign was a centralization of the Party's decision-making powers in Huey. As some Comrades point out, the BPP became in reality "Huey's Party," instead of the "People's Party." What's worse, is that many of these Comrades mistakenly equate Huey's centralized power as an expression of DC, when in fact the BPP did not practice DC.

Indeed, Huey's purges of BPP cadre occurred because he was unaccustomed to, and unwilling to accept, criticisms from the Party's rank and file. Whereas criticism of this nature is an essential feature of DC. What Huey practiced was a form of Commandism or Authoritarian Centralism, which is the very opposite of DC.

BPP veteran Mumia Abu-Jamal described the process aptly:

> "Despite the ideological claim that the Party functioned under the principle of criticism and self-criticism, the Party hierarchy in fact functioned much like any other group in bourgeois society, that is, according to the principle of power dynamics: those who have power strive mightily to keep it—period.
>
> "So when Huey received letters full of criticism of his leadership, he struck out at those he thought were angling to undermine his rule of the organization. When Eldridge received letters critical of Huey's leadership, he felt a sense of affirmation. Neither apparently questioned the authorship of this critical correspondence.
>
> "Why would they? Why should they?"
>
> *We Want Freedom: A Life in the Black Panther Party* (2004), p. 208

In answer to Brotha Mumia's closing questions, we must point out that *if* the BPP was accustomed to practicing DC, then Party leaders would not have taken offense to criticism nor would they have allowed it to generate factionalism. Indeed, secret criticisms of the sort described by Mumia would not have been tolerated, but the letters would have been turned over to the Party's Chief of Staff (Bobby Seale) for investigation as attempts to incite inner-Party rivalries and factionalism. DC demands that criticisms of Party members be made openly, and assures all Party members at all levels the right to criticize any other member's actions. The very object of DC is to preserve unity and prevent divisiveness and factionalism.

That the BPP did not practice DC is further demonstrated in Huey's belief that he *owned* his leadership position in the Party; that he was not subject to recall or being held accountable for his actions; and that he could unilaterally expel those who criticized or exposed his conduct or failure to meet the obligations of his leadership. Under DC, Party leaders are *elected* to their leading positions and are likewise *subject to recall by vote.*

So that we don't repeat the errors of the past and so that comrades today can dispense with the mistaken view that the BPP practiced DC, it is *essential* that we explain what DC is.

### What Is Democratic Centralism?

The basic principles of DC are expressed in V.I. Lenin's slogan, "freedom to criticize, unity of action." I repeat, *"freedom to criticize,* unity of action." The *Democratic* component of DC means *all* Party members are free to criticize, debate and discuss internal matters of Party decisions, policy and direction in open sessions, and final decisions on such matters are reached by majority vote of all Party members. The *Centralism* component of DC means that once decisions are reached by majority vote, all members must uphold that decision. Those who disagree with the decisions must still abide by them, they must reserve their personal opinions, but they are free at the next session to raise the issues again and struggle to change the Party's views and vote on the matters.

Furthermore, *no* individual Party member has unqualified power. Indeed, all Party members must answer to the Party itself and to the public criticism of the masses.

Many sincere comrades stereotype and reject DC as an organizational fetish of "Leninist" parties, based upon the practices of parties who've *claimed* to practice DC but *actually did not.* Many Leftist parties applied commandism much like Huey did and *called* it DC, leading many to erroneously equate DC with those bourgeois forms of *authoritarian* centralism.

Many on the Left also reject DC as a peculiarly "Leninist" ideology, not realizing that not only did the concept pre-date Lenin, but that DC was an organizational form embraced and practiced by Lenin's opponents such as the bourgeois liberal Mensheviks who adopted it in November 1905, a month *before* Lenin's Bolsheviks adopted it. Indeed, in its 1905 resolution, "On the Organization of the Party," the Mensheviks state that, "the RSDLP must be organized according to the principle of democratic centralism." The Bolsheviks, a month later, elaborated on DC in their resolution, "On Party Organization," and gave a very different picture of DC than what the Left depicts it as today. That resolution states: "Recognizing as indisputable the principle of democratic centralism, the Conference considers the broad implementation of the elective principle necessary; and, while granting elected centers full powers in matters of ideological and practical leadership, they are at the same time subject to recall, their actions are given broad publicity, and they are to be strictly accountable for these activities."

In fact, DC was *never* in dispute between the opposing Bolshevik and Menshevik wings of the RSDLP (Russian Social-Democratic Labor Party), neither in definition nor practice. At a 1906 unity conference both the Bolsheviks and Mensheviks adopted a resolution by vote that stated "All party organizations are built on the principles of democratic centralism." The committee report adopting this resolution was written by a Menshevik, Zagorky-Kokhmal, who stated that all Mensheviks and Bolsheviks accepted this resolution, "unanimously."

In actuality, none of Lenin's contemporaries in the Social Democratic movement criticized DC, not even Rosa Luxemburg, who strongly opposed features of "Leninist" organizations. Features, which her failure to adopt into her German Communist Party, left its entire Left wing—Luxemburg included—open to assassination.

At bottom, corruption and abuses of power are essentially impossible when DC is observed, since all Party members, leaders especially, are subject to criticism, exposure and recall through open democratic processes. Leaders are *elected* to their positions based upon *demonstrated* qualifications and integrity, and are subject to having their powers *revoked* for *failure* to live up to their responsibilities, also by majority vote.

So, in summing up the errors of the BPP's organizational practices, and recognizing the *actual* role of the vanguard party and its appropriate decision making process, we must disagree with those comrades who reject the need of a vanguard party and the role of DC as such a party's correct method of deciding its policies and practices. In actuality, what these comrades oppose from their experiences in the BPP are tendencies that we too oppose, and were not genuine examples of the type of party and practices that we promote as essential for leading an oppressed people in a revolutionary struggle.

This is not to say the BPP got it all wrong, because it didn't. Actually, the Party was right on in much of the mass work it accomplished—in mobilizing the people around their needs and showing them through example and participation that we can solve our own problems, that indeed *we must*. It was just in its internal organizing and in its attempts to perform as both a vanguard party *and* a mass organization that it erred. The Party came into being spontaneously, in response to immediate crisis in the New Afrikan communities, and consisted primarily of youth. It didn't have the time, experience or prior examples to rigorously work out its program and structure, but today we do. And we are determined not to repeat yesterday's mistakes.

### A Consensus on the Need of a Revolutionary Vanguard

The essential need of a Vanguard Party stands above all other organizational forms in revolutionary struggle. This has been acknowledged and proved by the successes of all revolutionary movements.

Lenin recognized it, and committed most of his work to building the revolutionary Party.

What few people realize is that until 1917 Lenin rarely addressed himself to a mass audience, either in writing or speaking, nor appeared on a public platform. Instead, he concentrated his extraordinary abilities and energies on the task which he concluded was decisive to the success of the Russian Revolution: the building of an apparatus of dedicated, disciplined revolutionaries to lead the masses in the struggle for power.

> "For the revolutionary movements developing today in every country, the great contribution of Lenin was the clarity with which he put forward and acted upon his fundamental convictions regarding the vanguard party: 1) that the purpose of a revolutionary party is to take absolute power in order to revolutionize the economic and social systems as the only way of resolving fundamental popular grievances; 2) that it is absolutely essential to build a revolutionary vanguard party if you are not just playing with the phrase; and 3) that a revolutionary party can only be built by *a)* unceasing ideological struggle, *b)* strict discipline, *c)* organized activity of every member, and *d)* merciless self-criticism."
>
> James and Grace Lee Boggs, *The Role of the Vanguard Party*

Lenin's organizing work paid off in dividends enabling his Bolshevik Party to not only seize power in Russia, achieving history's first working-class revolution, but it survived the most extreme repression at the hands of the Czar's secret police, and the world's imperialist powers that promptly invaded Soviet Russia (1918–1920).

> "Why was it that the Bolsheviks (for example) could be so heavily infiltrated, suffer many busts and setbacks of all kinds, and yet remain strong enough—effective enough—to seize power in 1917? There's probably no single or simple answer, but a few things stand out:
>
> "There was a significant level of ideological training and consistency among leadership and cadres, and extensive political education.
>
> "There was a certain type of organizational structure, disciplined practice of principles, methods and style of work.
>
> "There was a relatively secure system of communications.
>
> "There was a mass-based infrastructure, and broad, active connections to the mass movement.
>
> "The party construction began at the center, and spread outward."
>
> *Vita Wa Watu: a New Afrikan Theoretical Journal,*
> Volume 11, p. 30 (1987)

In pursuing the anti-imperialist and New Democratic aims of the Chinese Revolution, Mao Tse-tung acknowledged the essential role of the Vanguard Party.

> "If there is to be a revolution, there must be a revolutionary party. Without a revolutionary party, without a party built on the Marxist-Leninist revolutionary theory and the Marxist-Leninist revolutionary style, it is impossible to lead the working class and the broad masses of the people in defeating imperialism and its running dogs."
>
> "Revolutionary Forces of the World Unite, Fight Against Imperialist Aggression!" (November 1948)

> "A well disciplined Party armed with the theory of Marxism-Leninism, using the method of self-criticism and linked with the masses of the people; an army under the leadership of such a Party; a united front of all revolutionary classes and all revolutionary groups under the leadership of such a Party—these are the three main weapons with which we have defeated the enemy."
>
> "On the People's Democratic Dictatorship" (June 30, 1949)

Mao's vanguard party walked its talk. Not only did it repel a Japanese imperialist invasion, defeat the imperialist-backed puppet bourgeois KMT army and seize power in 1949, empowering and improving the living conditions of China's millions, but with a peasant army—and fresh from a civil war—it repelled the day's most powerful combined military forces, (the U.S. and UN), from its borders in the Korean War (1950–1953).

In Guinea-Bissau's revolutionary struggle for national liberation from Portuguese colonialism, Amilcar Cabral acknowledged the essential role of the vanguard party.

> "[W]e must try and unite everybody in the national liberation struggle against the Portuguese colonialists. It is imperative to organize things so that we always have an instrument available which can solve all the other contradictions. This is what convinced us of the absolute necessity of creating a party during the national liberation struggle."
>
> *The Politics of Struggle* (May 1964)

But as Cabral admitted, "we are not a Marxist-Leninist party." The fact of Cabral's failure to organize the PAIGC as a Marxist-Leninist

Vanguard, left it internally weak and vulnerable to destruction by bourgeois elements as occurred when he and his brother were neutralized by the rightists inside the Party.

George Jackson acknowledged the indispensable role of the vanguard party in any people's revolutionary struggle, and especially the one that must occur here in Amerika. In fact, all of Comrade George's military proposals surrounded protecting the vanguard elements at their work in organizing and educating the masses.

> "Recall: our Mao teaches that when revolution fails it isn't the fault of the people, it's the fault of the vanguard party ... There have never been any spontaneous revolutions. They were all staged, manufactured, by people who went to the head of the masses and directed them.
>
> "The liberalist slogan 'you can't get ahead of the people' is meaningless. From what other position can one lead? From the rear? Rearguard leadership?!! A typical Yankee innovation ... . In all the successful class struggles and colonial wars of liberation, the vanguard elements did get ahead of the people and pull. There is no other way in forward mass movement ... .
>
> "I'm not implying that the vanguard party act out the people's role. I'm not implying a 'society superior to society.' We must never forget that it is the people who change circumstances and that the educator himself needs educating. 'Going among the people, learning from the people, and serving the people' is really stating that we must find out exactly what the people need and organize them around those needs."
>
> George Jackson, *Blood In My Eye* (1971)

The same was acknowledged by the Vietnamese, the Colombians, and every other movement for revolutionary overthrow of oppressive conditions under capitalism and imperialism. And every reverse in the gains of those movements took place because of capitalist elements infiltrating and subverting the vanguard parties, or errors in their internal structures allowed external forces to cause internal destruction. Comrade Mao was the first to point out the importance of waging ongoing struggle *inside* of vanguard parties to prevent their subversion and destruction by bourgeois elements, or bureaucratic errors. The vanguard party is indeed the motor of a people's revolution.

### Is the NABPP-PC a Vanguard Party?

The NABPP-PC was founded under uncommon conditions. Being based as we are amongst prisoners confined across the U.S. Empire, it is difficult, if not impossible, to function as a genuine vanguard party that can lead and organize the masses on society and practice DC. We are not idealists, but dialectical materialists, and therefore do not deceive ourselves and the people about our practical limits.

Because of our material limitations, we exist in reality as only a pre-party formation: the embryo of a genuine revolutionary vanguard. The scope of our work is limited and defined as it should be. As set out in one of our founding position papers, "Our Line," we aspire through our practice and example to develop the actual NABPP on the outside within our oppressed communities, and ultimately into a Vanguard Party of Afrikan people worldwide. Our Party will take root as our cadre re-enter society. As Uncle Ho once wrote in a poem, "what becomes of a Nation when its people come out of confinement? ... when the prison gates open the real dragon will fly out!"

The NABPP won't be real until it can hold a founding Congress, draft a Party Programme, and elect a free world Central Committee and Politburo. Then DC can be fully implemented. At that eventual stage, the Prison Chapter will be one of many Chapters within the Party.

At the present stage, we *are* able to practice limited forms of DC, with our focus on *Transforming the Razor Wire Plantations into Schools of Liberation* and organizing around serving the material and spiritual needs of oppressed people in the inside.

As a pre-Party structure, we are struggling to outline a blueprint of the ideological and organizational basis upon which our broader struggle must be built. Earlier efforts gave us examples and lessons to build on—our object is this time to get it right, and organize to win!

As we've stated before:

> "We who are inside the 'Belly of the Beast,' may perish inside these razor-wire fences and stone walls, but not without first illuminating the path forward for our sisters and brothers, our sons and daughters. If we can offer nothing but our dying breath, it will be to say: 'DARE TO STRUGGLE AND DARE TO WIN!'"

*Dare to Struggle, Dare to Win!*
*All Power to the People!*

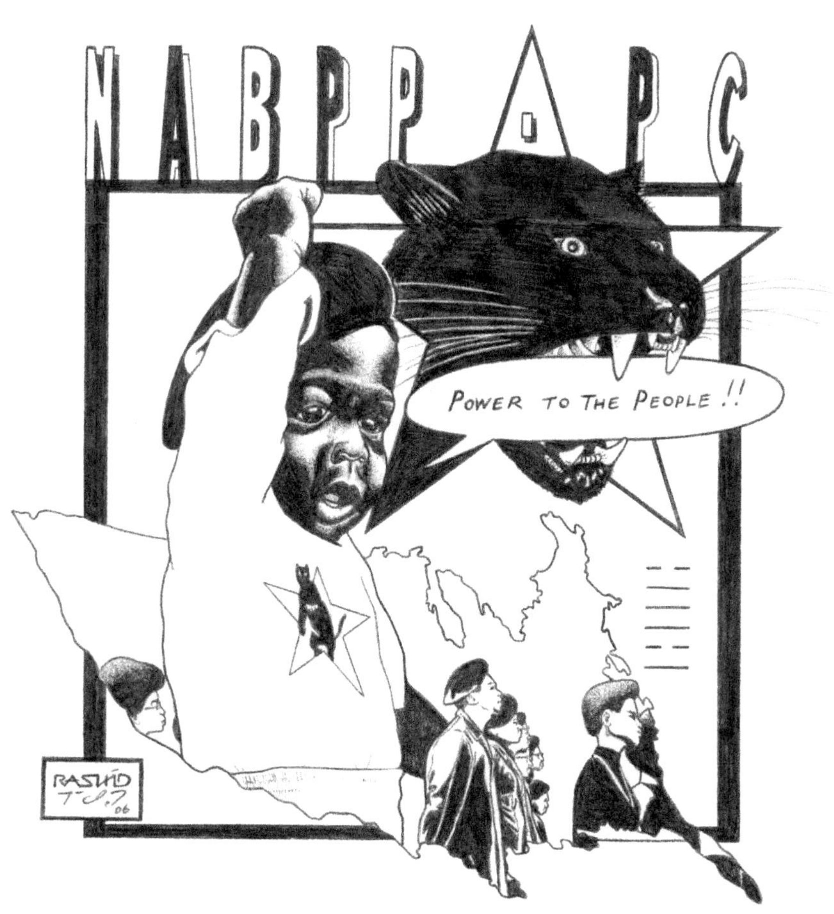
NABPP-PC
POWER TO THE PEOPLE !!
RASHID
06

# 20. UNITY–STRUGGLE–TRANSFORMATION: ON REVOLUTIONARY ORGANIZATION, LEADERSHIP AND CADRE DEVELOPMENT

REVISED 2013

## Introduction

The object of a revolutionary organization is to unite (and unite with), mobilize, organize, and lead masses of oppressed people to achieve fundamental economic, political and social change and collective security. Founded in 2005, the New Afrikan Black Panther Party-Prison Chapter (NABPP-PC) arose within the most oppressed strata of U.S. society, the imprisoned masses, to take up the banner of revolutionary struggle on behalf of New Afrikans and all oppressed and exploited people. We aspire to become, but are not yet, a functional vanguard party of the oppressed.

We will be formally constituted once we transition to the outside, build bases in the oppressed communities, hold a founding convention and elect a free world central committee and an executive committee (politburo). We will be functionally constituted only when the oppressed urban masses embrace us as their revolutionary leadership.

Even while we remain a primarily prison-based organization, we have an important revolutionary role to play which is to transform the razor wire plantations into schools of liberation. This is the first phase of our Party's strategy, along with transforming the oppressed communities into base areas of cultural, social and political revolution in the context of building a worldwide united front against capitalist-imperialism. The two aspects of our strategy are dialectically related and will advance the overall strategy of advancing the World Proletarian Socialist Revolution.

At this point, comrades are learning and struggling for ideological and political clarity on how to build and consolidate the Party's structure and a mass anti-racist, anti-imperialist and revolutionary movement around it. There are issues we need to work out related to organizing on both the inside and outside. There are issues, some of them long-standing, that have been raised by our supporters and detractors we need to address. Some of these people do not understand, or refuse to accept, the need for revolutionary leadership, discipline and organization. There is also the question of who should be in leadership positions and how to achieve a balance between democracy and centralism.

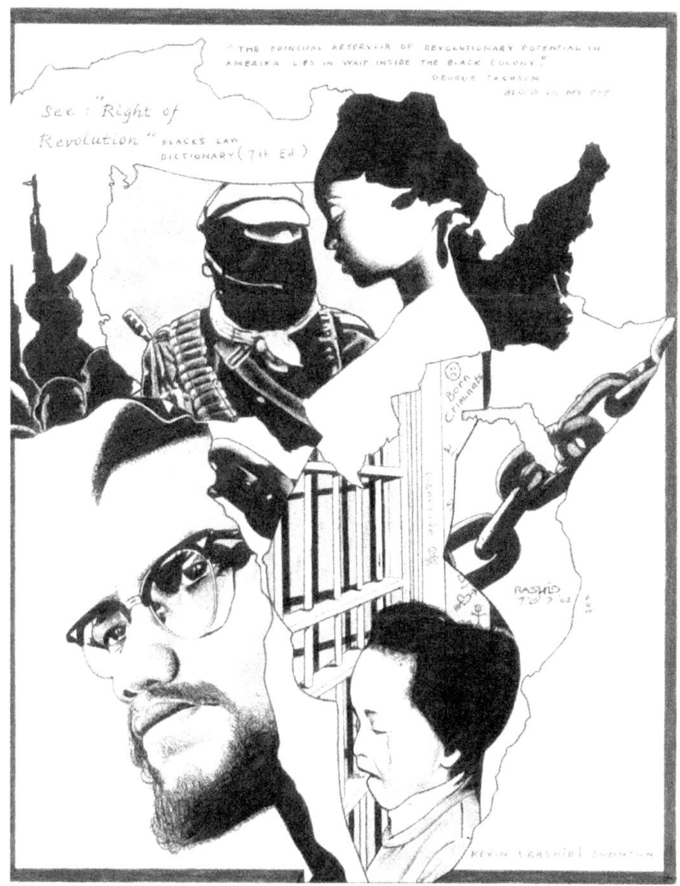


## On Organization and Security

The term "organizing" is often used loosely on the Left, especially by those who oppose forming, joining or subordinating themselves to any sort of disciplined political organization. Although they may exhort the virtues of "solidarity," they actually practice extreme individualism, which runs counter to building a movement for collective social change.

Obviously, one cannot be a political organizer and not be part of a political organization. One implies the other. An organization is a body of people—not one person acting alone—who share common purpose and goals and have an organizational structure. The members must perform certain functions assigned to them that advance the purpose of the organization. This calls for leadership and a degree of discipline or everyone will be acting individually without accountability or responsibility, which is the definition of disorganization, and this leads to the opposite of "solidarity."

Joining and remaining in an organization involves important considerations, such as whether one trusts, believes in, agrees with, and understands the organization's purpose and goals. To the more mature and committed members, these are issues of special concern and determine whether they will whole-heartedly commit themselves on a long-term basis to the organization and its goals and purpose. Transparency is therefore important so people know, understand and trust the organization and what it is about. Without this, the organization cannot have even the foundations for "security."

Comrade Safiya Bukhari, a former BPP and BLA cadre explains:

> "By definition, security means freedom from danger, fear and anxiety. Individual and organizational safety and well-being begin with the knowledge of what you're about, what the organization is about, your limitations, your strengths and the organization's strengths. Knowledge is the key to security. History has shown that the best security depends on the internal strength of the organization and the internal principles of the people who make up the organization."[1]

As an example of solid organizational and individual principles, she points to the creed of the Republic of New Afrika (RNA), which states, "I will steal nothing from a brother or sister, cheat no brother or sister, misuse no brother or sister, inform on no brother or sister and spread no gossip." These principles, she observed, express ...

> "an extremely important component of individual and organizational security. The knowledge that the person next to you—the person working beside you—will not cheat you, lie and spread gossip about you is the basis for your feeling secure in your environment and within your organization. The ability to trust your comrades implicitly and to know with certainty what they will do in any circumstance is the best security.
>
> "The question then, is how do we get to this point? It begins with knowing what you're about—what you want and what you believe and how far you will go to obtain it. The reciprocal reality is knowing what the organization is about. If the purpose and mission of the organization is clear, not subject to interpretation, then people joining will not be able to say that they thought the organization was about one thing when they joined only to find out later it was about something totally different.
>
> "This means that both the individual and the organization must be open and honest."[2]

Our Party's rules embrace standards akin to the RNA creed, which actual and potential members must know and obey. An important criterion of Party recruitment is that one's internal principles be proven to be compatible with the Party's. The comrades also must know, understand, and commit themselves to our Ten Point Program and Platform, which clearly sets out "what we want" and "what we believe." They must also understand and adhere to our ideological philosophy, which is Historical and Dialectical Materialism (HDM) and not some form of subjective idealism, such as dogmatism, sentimentalism, pragmatism or metaphysics.

HDM begins with the premise that objective reality exists independent of our understanding it, and that concrete analysis of concrete conditions—tested in practice—is the only true foundation for political theory. It teaches us that everything is in motion and that quantitative changes give rise to qualitative leaps of development. An historical understanding of a thing's development and understanding the internal contradictions and the effect of things happening in connection to it enables us to see the potentiality to accelerate its development.

All things develop and transform through the struggle between their contradictory aspects. Evolution gives rise to revolution. One divides into two creating a new unity of opposites. Revolution is the main trend in the world.

Prior to recruitment in to the Party, comrades must prove themselves to be serious and dedicated to the struggle. They must stand tall and be willing to stand firm in the face of adversity and repression and be able to withstand isolation and even torture. Their commitment to advancing the struggle to victory must be that of a "professional revolutionary," who carries on when others falter or flee to safety and comfort. Their credo must be "for self nothing, for the masses everything!" Only comrades of this caliber will win the trust of the masses and make our Party the true vanguard of the revolution. The Party has no private agenda to pursue. It exists solely to serve the people. It must never alienate itself from them nor set itself above them but rather seek their supervision and guidance. It is their party, not ours. In all things it must uphold and practice the Mass Line.

This work calls for planning, discipline and accountability. To proceed without a plan, without discipline and order is counter-productive and irresponsible. Our individual moral outrage and our love for the people should be the fuel that powers our actions, but our actual course of action should be based upon a strategic plan and carried out with iron discipline and organizational coordination. All this requires strong organizational leadership.

## On Leadership

No revolutionary movement can hope to succeed without a strong revolutionary leadership, and no one can be permitted to participate in such a movement who is not willing to commit themselves to following the leadership and accepting the discipline required by the struggle. To think otherwise is idealism and opportunism. As already discussed, an organizer belongs and is loyal to an organization. The organization collectively devises ways to achieve certain goals. The organizer is in fact a leader. This is especially true when the work of the organizer is influencing and affecting people outside the organization among the broad masses of the people. So the organizer leads others, whether for good or ill, and regardless of whether or not they admit to being a leader and accept the responsibility that goes with that.

The same truth applies to individuals outside of organizations who seek to inform, motivate and guide the actions of others. They are in fact leaders and bear responsibilities.

But in as much as a revolutionary organization that seeks to lead a mass movement must have leaders, these leaders must win the consent of those who they seek to lead. It must be earned by proven merit and consistent practice. They must listen to and learn from the masses if they seek to teach and be listened to—we must be both teachers and students! As students, we learn from the masses about their conditions, needs and concerns, and being of the oppressed masses ourselves, we share their conditions alongside them on a daily basis. We must attentively listen to their views, learn from their strengths, and remain close to them. If we think they are wrong, we must patiently explain why after hearing them out. But we don't know everything, so we must be good at listening and learning, accept criticism and correcting our mistakes. As teachers, we take the masses' raw and unorganized ideas and by applying HDM and our understanding of this oppressive system as a whole, return their ideas to them in the form of programs, examples and solutions which involve and empower them. This is the essence of the Mass Line!

In this dialectical relationship of student and teacher, leader and masses, we don't quibble over assuming the role of leader because it is inherently impossible to teach and influence people's thoughts and actions without assuming a leadership role. Since we are constantly teaching and learning, we are always giving or accepting leadership. So unlike those "Leftists" who shun the Marxist-Leninist-Maoist revolutionary line, we don't reject the role and responsibility of leaders and leadership. Indeed, we recognize that in class-divided society, the thinking of every person and group reflects the ideas of the dominant class in part or in whole, and as soon as any person or group speaks out or puts pen to paper to influence others they assume the authority of leadership. In as much as their ideas reflect the teaching and indoctrination of the ruling class, they're serving that class in its dictatorship over society.

Conversely, in as much as they have freed their minds of this indoctrination and revolutionized their thinking, their speaking out or putting pen to paper is an act of revolutionary leadership. That's what revolutionary organizers do, they teach about and they learn from the masses how we oppressed people can become our own liberators. Revolutionary leadership is what Panthers are about.

MLM illuminates the revolutionary line of our Party and the United Panther Movement (UPM). MLM scientifically sums up the lessons of the class struggle and the experience of the revolutionary proletariat from the mid-19th Century to the present through the application of HDM by Marx, Engels, Lenin, Stalin, Mao and many other revolutionary thinkers and leaders. Most particularly, our Party's line is illuminated by the work of the original BPP, particularly Huey P. Newton, Fred Hampton and George Jackson, New Afrikan freedom fighters like W.E.B. DuBois, Malcolm X and Walter Rodney, as well as Afrikan revolutionaries such as Amilcar Cabral, Frantz Fanon and Kwame Nkrumah.

Intelligent people who desire to change the world seek to learn from the contributions of others and to illuminate their practice with the most advanced and scientific understanding of revolutionary theory. Who among us who oppose this oppressive system based upon human exploitation do not aspire to influence the ideas, and by extension the actions, of others in relation to this system? Therefore it is deception to claim that we do not aspire to be or approve of leaders. And who would deny that revolution is the ultimate act of authority?

There is actually a class basis for this sort of thinking. Furthermore, consider how absurd it would be for a teacher to challenge and change your beliefs (say about capitalism for example) that affect how you perceive and relate to the world at the most fundamental levels and tell you go forth and apply these teachings to change the world and then deny they were giving you leadership? How much more absurd if they did not plug you into an organization and movement of like-minded people? Leadership and organization go hand in hand.

Here is what distinguishes genuine revolutionary teachers from elitist philosophers: The revolutionary teacher not only consciously teaches what is wrong in the world but they also lead in correcting it, building organization among the masses to create a new reality, teaching by example and participation.

Mao Tse-tung summed up this Marxist line saying: "Marxist philosophy holds that the most important problem does not lie in understanding the laws of the objective world and thus being able to explain it, but in applying these laws actively to change the world … only social practice can be the criterion of truth."

This is where the traditional "Left" falls short. In the manner of petty bourgeois intellectuals, they analyze, criticize, and interpret the world in various ways, but they fail to bring their analysis down to the level of practical application to change the oppressive conditions. At best, they resort to individual counter-cultural or academic rebelliousness which does nothing to organize or empower the masses. It is all about self-validation and feeling good about their radical self-identity.

And why?

Because their class stand prevents it, which is the principal reason why many of them reject the need for and function of a revolutionary leadership. While in fact they act as leaders and teachers of the class stand of those who talk about but don't dare to organize to solve the problems of the oppressed class—namely the petty bourgeoisie, the so-called "middle class." Deep down, many of these "radicals" don't want to change things in any fundamental way because they have privileges and comforts under the status quo and dread of the exercise of power from below.

So while they protest and arouse the discontent of others, they don't want to start something that will empower the poor and go all the way to overthrowing the dictatorship of the rich. They only want to protest the things that oppress and disempower them. This leaves the people without all-the-way leadership, which leads to spontaneous rebellions subject to both co-option and violent suppression, leading to demoralization of the masses and continued business as usual for the exploiting class.

We have seen this cycle repeated over and over in the oppressed communities and prisons. This is why we created the New Afrikan Black Panther Party-Prison Chapter and the United Panther Movement, because we recognized the need for a truly revolutionary vanguard party and movement. Vanguard means "out in front." We saw things were not going to change until people got serious and took on the responsibility to lead the people's struggle to victory.

## On the Practice of Cadres

A revolutionary vanguard is only as strong and solid as its members or cadre, who must be rooted among the masses in struggle. Thus it is vital that the cadre be good at communicating and connecting with other oppressed people. They must be the natural leaders of the people whom others look to and seek the opinions of. Her or his love for the people must run deep. As Che Guevara once said: "Let me say, at the risk of seeming ridiculous, that a true revolutionary is motivated by great feelings of love." However, the work of a revolutionary is not measured by motive alone.

> "How can we tell the good from the bad—by the motive (the subjective intention) or by the effect (social practice)? Idealists stress motive and ignore effect, while mechanical materialists stress effect and ignore motive. In contradiction to both, we dialectical materialists insist on unity of motive and effect. The motive of serving the masses is inseparably linked with winning their approval; the two must be united. The motive of serving the individual or a small clique is not good, nor is it good to have the motive of serving the masses without the effect of winning their approval and benefiting them. In examining the subjective intention of a writer or artist, that is, whether his motive is correct or good, we do not judge by his declarations but by the effects of his actions (mainly his works) on the masses in society. The criteria for judging subjective intention or motive is social practice and its effect."[3]

Of course not everyone among the people will be receptive, interested in intellectual and political growth, or even friendly. We have found, however, that at this time, many prisoners are, but they are hampered by limited access to literature and information and rules that strictly limit what they may receive and how much property they may keep. So collective pooling of materials and cadre-led study circles within the prisons are very important. On the other hand, many do not have a high degree of literacy or think reading is not "cool." So, it is important that we do verbal agitation and organize discussions, particularly on the yard.

Cadre must be patient, sensitive and tolerant, and most important, be good at listening. Some prisoners have been beaten down to where they have withdrawn into themselves and we must reach them before we can teach them. Others are so full of rage that they reject reason and are locked into individualistic and self-destructive behavior.

To serve the people we must take a genuine interest in them and demonstrate Panther Love towards them. Don't just talk at people or expect them to open up to you right away. We must strive to understand where they are at and what their concerns are to build a relationship of camaraderie with them. One can always find some points of common interest. Our politics flow from our love for the people and represent the highest interests of humanity, so they naturally uplift and inspire people once we get their attention.

Most all of our cadre will be capable communicators, although one should struggle to excel in this area. It was actually in prison that Fidel Castro developed his exceptional abilities as a motivational speaker. Fred Hampton, another exceptional communicator, once said: "I listen to anyone who speaks well." It is important that we are able to reach people's deepest feelings and longings.

Whether good speakers or not, all of our cadre will have specific skills that they can work on and develop to serve the struggle and enhance the effectiveness of our Party. As in any organization, everyone has contributions to make and a part to play.

> "No one person can do everything, but every person can do something—and all jobs are more or less equally important. That is, the 'soldier' is no more important (may in fact be less important) than the person putting out the newsletter, or the person organizing the students, or the person agitating on issues such as no-rent housing, or people's control of the air waves ..."[4]

And not all cadre will be equally advanced in applying the principles of HDM to problem-solving. At this point, many cadre have very little or no training or understanding of this revolutionary science, due to our loose organization in the prisons and difficulty in obtaining suitable study materials, which we must resolutely struggle to overcome. Because to apply any method of study other than a correct application of HDM will inevitably lead to the errors of dogmatism or some other form of subjective idealism. Therefore, it is of primary importance that the leading cadre master this method and train others to train others. Like shooting at a target, proper instruction and practice makes all the difference.

It is also imperative for the organizational life of our Party and creating the caliber of leadership that can lead the masses to take history into their hands that we train our cadre to excel at every aspect of party building, mass organization, and the strategy and tactics of creating a worldwide united front against capitalist-imperialism. The Party and mass organizations it creates and builds must be strong structures with strong internal unity and able to withstand overt repression and attempted covert disruption by the agents of repression.

The mass organizations must have a strong democratic character and be rooted in the oppressed communities where our mass work is concentrated. We must be good at bringing people in to participate in our events and programs and at reaching out to all strata and groupings of the people in the communities; in particular the youth, wimyn, veterans and members of lumpen street organizations, families of prisoners, as well as workers old and young. The New Afrikan Black Panther Party must be broadly based in the communities.

All of this is important to do effective organizing, but what is key is revolutionary leadership. Cadre must be thoroughly knowledgeable on many subjects and able to converse intelligently one on one or in front of a group. To enhance our ability to serve, and learn from, the people, cadre must expand their all-around knowledge through study and following the news. In all things we must seek to uncover the truth, which requires investigation.

Collective leadership is key to building a strong party and movement. Collective wisdom brought out through democratic discussion on every level of the Party helps us to uncover the truth and illuminate our practice. An army of "professionals" will try to misdirect and discredit us as they do every liberation movement. This too highlights the importance of collective leadership and inner-party democracy, where we pool our knowledge and experience to collectively arrive at truth and make sound decisions.

We must follow Sun Tzu's direction to "know your enemy and know yourself, and in a hundred battles you will never face defeat." This applies at all levels—strategic and tactical—and on all fronts—cultural, educational, economic, political and military. It is especially important in cadre development. Because to have cadre assigned to roles where their particular strengths are going to apply is conducive to achieving the Party's goals. We must be good at assessing comrades' strengths and weaknesses and at using their strengths to overcome their weaknesses.

By knowing the enemy's strengths and weaknesses, we shall know where to assail and where to avoid him, and we shall not become arrogant after a few successes nor despondent after a few losses. When we are able to remain objective in the face of both victories and defeats and can adjust our tactics accordingly, there is no such thing as an unbeatable foe nor an insurmountable obstacle to victory. The use of wrong tactics is generally caused by failure to objectively analyze conditions in the first place.

We must be mindful not to hold ourselves up as authorities on matters we have not investigated thoroughly. "No investigation, no right to speak," is Mao's famous dictum. When it becomes apparent we lack necessary information to make a good decision, we should seek it out without hesitation.

> "To put forward a correct political line for the new Party, we must have concrete analysis of concrete conditions on the major questions: class struggle, the national question, trade union work, the woman question, the international situation, etc."[5]

### On Cadre Purpose

As already pointed out, cadre are the component parts of the vanguard party and its basic units, which are the Party collectives. Together they form the "nervous system" of the movement, linking the Party's HQ with all its parts.

The cadre must be good at building bases of support for the revolution among the people (winning the masses to the Party's revolutionary line and organizing them into mass organizations that advance the revolutionary struggle), and be prepared to do what the Party requires of them to the best of their abilities. A revolutionary movement can only be as effective as its leadership prepares it to be. As Mao pointed out, "When revolution fails, it is the fault of the vanguard party." Therefore cadre development is crucial.

> "We must purposely train tens of thousands of cadres and leaders versed in Marxism-Leninism, politically far-sighted, competent in work, full of spirit of self-sacrifice, capable of taking problems on their own and devoted to serving the nation, the cadres and the party. It is on these cadres and leaders that the party relies on its links with the membership and the masses, and it is relying on their firm leadership of the masses that the party can succeed in defeating the enemy. Such cadres and leaders must be free from selfishness, from individualistic heroism, ostentation, sloth, passivity, and sectarian arrogance, and they must be selfless, national and class heroes, such are the qualities and style of work demanded by the members, cadres and leaders of our party."
>
> *Mao Tse-tung*

Mao demonstrated the indispensability of good cadre in revolutionary struggle. So too did Amilcar Cabral, Afrika's most outstanding revolutionary leader. As the founder of the revolutionary vanguard party of Guinea-Bissau, the PAIGC,[6] he proved that the development of revolutionary cadre is key to the success of a revolutionary movement. In 1959, oppressed workers in Guinea-Bissau plunged blindly and recklessly into armed revolt against the Portuguese colonialists. This disastrous failure led comrade Cabral to reassess the situation and their tactics. He then spent three years organizing and leading patient political education and doing preparatory work across the country, training a thousand party cadre.

> "We prepared a number of cadre from the group [of pre-classed semi-intellectual urban youth], some from people employed in

> commerce and other wage-earners, and even some peasants, so that they could acquire what you might call a working-class mentality … When these cadre returned to the rural areas they inculcated a certain mentality into the peasants, and it is among these cadre that we have chosen the people who are now leading the struggle."[7]

These PAIGC cadre reignited the struggle in 1963, winning and mobilizing immense and immediate mass support, which quickly liberated vast sections of the country from Portuguese control. By 1969, two-thirds of the countryside was liberated, and only five years later, Portuguese control was completely overthrown, even though Cabral had been assassinated by the Portuguese agents a year before. It was the cadre, trained and prepared by Cabral, that led the people to victory.

As we discussed in a previous article, the original Black Panther Party's efforts to lead the mass struggle here in Amerika met with failure, largely because it neglected to train and root its members in revolutionary proletarian ideology.[8] Instead, its cadre retained and acted upon the values and perspectives of other classes, particularly the lumpen proletariat and urban petty bourgeoisie, and even tried to advance a lumpen (as opposed to proletarian) political theory to validate this.

Failures and reversals of revolutionary mass movements, here and around the world, have resulted, in large part, because of the failure to develop a solid core of revolutionary proletarian leadership. In the past, revolutionary movements have relied upon the petty bourgeoisie to supply the intellectuals for leadership positions and this has proven to be a weakness, as these tend to be vacillating elements prone to right and "left" opportunism and revisionism.

Because of its position in class society, the petty bourgeoisie vacillates between the bourgeoisie and laboring masses in outlook and interests. They have had the advantages of better education and standard of living over the poor and working masses, and though radicalized, they tend to retain bourgeois ideology and prejudices which they bring with them into the workers' movement.

The petty bourgeoisie have produced some fine revolutionary intellectuals and leaders for the revolutionary proletarian movement, such as Marx, Engels, Lenin, Mao, Cabral, Nkrumah and so on, but on the whole, many more have been disappointments. As a class, they are not so ready to commit "class suicide," as Cabral put it, and adopt the revolutionary perspective of the proletariat. Instead, they impose their own perspectives and prejudices on the movement and resist the development of all-the-way revolutionary class struggle and consciousness.

However, the development of the decline of capitalist-imperialism has called forth a strategy of mass incarceration in Amerika, aimed primarily at the New Afrikans and other people of color in the urban communities. Prisons have proven to be powerful settings for the creation of revolutionary intellectuals from the oppressed class, such as: Malcolm X, Eldridge Cleaver, George Jackson, Hasan Shakur and James Yaki Sayles. Malcolm X even dubbed them the "poor man's universities."

Here, poor proletarians have both time to do deep study and to access revolutionary books and literature. This is what the NABPP-PC is tapping into and is the basis for our strategy of "turning the 'razor wire plantations' into 'schools of liberation' … ," which is taking our movement down a different path of development. Our object is not to indoctrinate prisoners with a political line from outside, but to develop the intellectual basis for formulating our own line and training cadre to provide leadership to build the movement on the outside, among the people in the oppressed communities, independent of the petty-bourgeois-dominated Left.

In training cadre, we need to do more than give them materials to read and expect them to spontaneously develop. We need to create Party-led study/discussion circles and an interactive study program as part of our strategy of transforming the prisons into "schools of liberation." We need to train prisoners to be critical and tactical thinkers. Cadre need to be flexible and apply critical analysis to developing and amending tactical plans. We need cadre to be creative and innovative in applying the Party's general line.

We need to encourage cadre to go beyond learning a few basic concepts and develop in-depth understanding of all aspects of the struggle, strategy and tactics, different techniques and methods, and historical applications. Overall intellectual development must be stressed. Intellectual skills, such as doing research, writing and debating must be developed.

The Party should assimilate and circulate good ideas and practices from the cadre. We should develop information sharing through our newsletters and implement new ideas and practices that arise in our organizational work.

Cadre must be good at teaching organizational skills to others. They should also be conscious to set the best possible examples in character and conduct at all times. This is important because our role is not to exercise political power over the masses but to empower them. Our example must be of selfless dedication to the masses and their best interests, helping them to create and build institutions of people's power in the communities and programs to serve their specific survival needs, enabling them to solve problems in their daily lives.

It is also why we must guard against allowing just anyone into the Party or to remain there if they don't have the proper motivation and dedication. Party cadre should be more disciplined and self-sacrificing than ordinary people. People should look to them as role models. People tend to characterize a whole movement by what they observe in its members they have contact with. This places a heavy responsibility on each and every Panther cadre to always represent the Party in the best way.

If we deviate from the Party's principles, discipline and program, people will think our Party is a joke, a sham and a hustle. They will not support our Party or listen to our message. The enemy will use our mistakes and shortcomings to vilify and discredit us in the eyes of the people. Instead of leading we will become another obstacle to the people's liberation.

This too is why the Party must be open to the scrutiny and criticism of the masses, transparent in its relations with them and willing to rectify its errors, humbly and honestly demonstrating that we are servants of the people. As Cabral said, "Hide nothing from the masses of our people. Tell no lies. Expose lies whenever they are told. Mask no difficulties, mistakes or failures. Claim no easy victories."[9]

### Conclusion

Hopefully, this will give Party comrades and supporters a clearer picture of the importance of cadre training and development and the kind of leadership we need to develop. We are serious about revolution, and we see a revolutionary situation developing in the period ahead of us. This is a time of preparation, a time of laying a strong foundation. If you have what it takes, join us!

*Dare to Struggle, Dare to Win!*
*All Power to the People!*

## END NOTES

1. Safiya Bukhari, *The War Before: The True Story of Becoming A Black Panther, Keeping the Faith in Prison & Fighting for Those Left Behind* (NY: The Feminist Press at CUNY, 2010), p. 37.

2. Ibid., p. 37.

3. Mao Tse-tung, *Selected Works*, Vol. III pp. 88–89.

4. James Yaki Sayles, *Meditations on Frantz Fanon's Wretched of the Earth: New Afrikan Revolutionary Writings by James Yaki Sayles* (Montreal: Kersplebedeb/Chicago, Il.: Spear & Shield, 2010), pp. 184–185.

5. V.I. Lenin, *What is to Be Done?*

6. African Independence Party of Guinea and Cape Verde Islands.

7. Amilcar Cabral, *The Politics of Struggle* (1964).

8. Kevin "Rashid" Johnson, "On the Roles and Characteristics of the Panther Vanguard Party and Mass Organizations," *Right On!* Vol. #8 (Summer 2008), also reprinted in *Defying the Tomb, Selected Prison Writings of Kevin "Rashid" Johnson Featuring Exchanges With an Outlaw* (Montreal: Kersplebadeb, 2010) and on pages 278–291 in this volume.

9. Amilcar Cabral, "Directives of PAIGC" (1965) published in Basil Davidson, *The Liberation of Guinea: Aspects of an African Revolution* (Baltimore: Penguin, 1969 ).

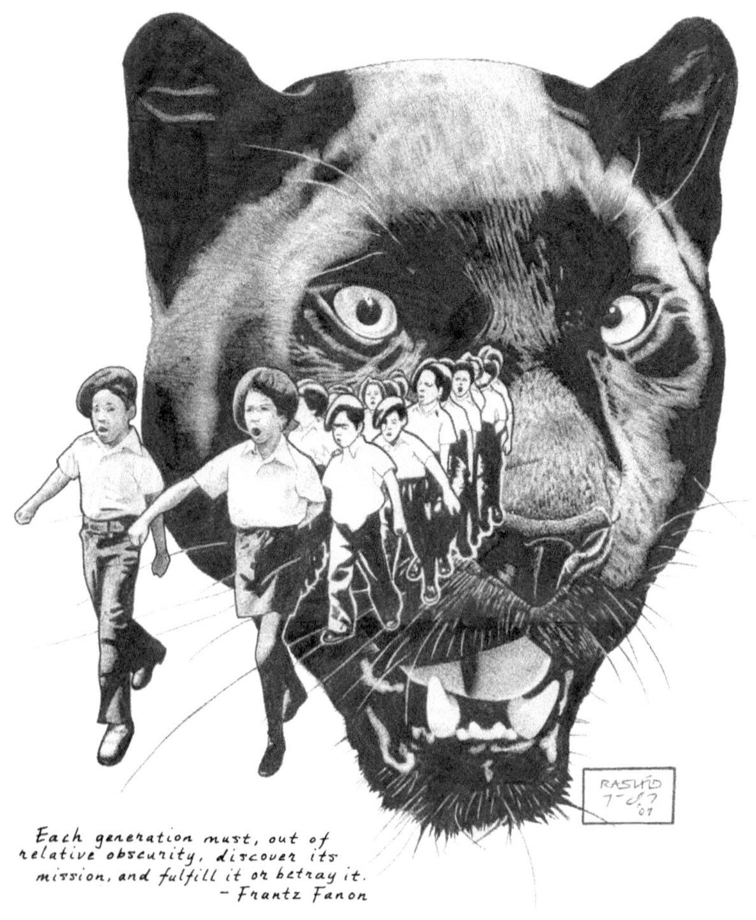

# 21. BLACK CATS HAVE MANY LIVES: REVIVING THE PANTHER VANGUARD AND BUILDING THE UNITED PANTHER MOVEMENT 2014

As convention would have it, the Black Panther Party (BPP)—founded in October 1966 by Huey P. Newton and Bobby Seale—ceased to exist in 1982.[1] Not so.

Although the last of its major community service programs and newspaper, *The Black Panther,* closed down in 1982, the Party's politics, goals, and identity have lived on in the hearts and work of many.

The BPP was a mass-based Party, whose membership and work were rooted within the downtrodden, poor, and oppressed New Afrikan/Black communities. It also developed prison chapters across Amerika, with the first one founded in California by George Jackson.

Although it maintained a highly visible leadership from 1966–1982 in the personages of Huey, Bobby, Kathleen and Eldridge Cleaver, Fred Hampton, Sr., Elaine Brown, David Hilliard and others, its body was composed of a broad base of lesser-recognized everyday urban people. And that body never died. Nor has its struggles to serve the people in our ongoing collective need for a revolutionary leadership and movement for fundamental change.

## Prison Panthers

Even as I've been bounced around the country between prison systems and from prison to prison from 2012 to 2014, I've met numerous comrades who identify as BPP members, who still know and adhere to the BPP's original Ten Point Program and Platform, and who apparently never got the memo that the BPP is supposed to be dead—obviously because it isn't. Rather the Party has lived on in them and in the various programs and initiatives they have continued to carry on as Panthers within the prisons, including teaching prisoners literacy and their legal rights, instructing them in self-defense and physical fitness, defending them against racist violence, passing on Panther history, helping them obtain basic necessities, and so on.

In the Oregon Department of Corrections (ODOC), where I was confined from February 2012 through June 2013, I met several elder comrades who identified as BPP members, and who passed on their teachings to younger comrades.

In the Texas Department of Criminal Justice (TDCJ), where I've remained since June 2013, I've encountered comrades at each TDCJ prison I've been to who identify as BPP Prison Chapter members. As I've politicked with this body of comrades, I've found there are members all over the TDCJ, and there exists a rich history of ongoing political struggle and work by these cadre within TDCJ, continuing from and dating back to the early 1970s.

There is also a TDCJ prison organization known as the Mandingo Warriors (MW) formed in the early 1980s that have a formal alliance with the BPP comrades. MW formed to defend New Afrikan/Black prisoners against a surge of violent attacks and stabbings by white supremacist groups at the behest of TDCJ officials in the wake of Texas federal courts banning the TDCJ's use of violent inmate guards in the early 1980s (known as Building Tenders [BT]), to run the prisons for officials.

BT's were inmates armed by TDCJ officials with street knives, bats, pipes, etc. and allowed through violence, extortion, and rape to terrorize and thereby "control" the prisoner population for officials.[2] In some cases BTs had more power than rank and file guards. TDCJ officials resisted the federal orders to eliminate BTs, and in efforts to bolster their arguments that the BTs were "needed" to control the prisons, officials incited and manipulated outbreaks of prisoner-on-prisoner violence including racial violence against Blacks, this prompting the founding of MW as a Black self-defence group.

In the mid-1980s MW merged with another group that had been influenced by Panther comrades.

A number of the Oregon and Texas BPP Prison Chapter comrades have merged with the New Afrikan Black Panther Party-Prison Chapter, as have various others who've identified as BPP cadre in other prisons across the Empire since we were founded in 2005. Indeed several of these comrades preside on our leading bodies, including Comrade Bobby Dixon, our Minister of Justice.

Although the BPP didn't die, it did go into decline as a result of intense government repression (under its secret war code-named COINTELPRO), unresolved internal contradictions, its lack of a consistently revolutionary ideological and political line and decision-making process, and decline in the 1960s–1970s mass upsurge.

Actually, many parallels exist between the BPP's decline and that of the Russian Bolsheviks which occurred as a result of intense repression by the Czarist government and secret police, line struggle and internal contradictions within the Russian Social Democratic Labour Party (RSDLP), and the attendant ebb in mass upsurge in pre-revolutionary Russia.

Additionally, a key factor that engendered the decline of both Parties was a decisive split between internal factions that represented different class tendencies within these respective Parties. But whereas V.I. Lenin was able to wage a struggle to maintain a correct line upon which to lead the Russian revolution to success under the leadership of his Bolshevik faction, the BPP failed to provide such a leader of Lenin's caliber to wage this internal line struggle. Consequently the decline of the BPP and official containment of the potentially insurgent oppressed masses in Amerika has lasted several decades—far longer than the Russian experience.

An examination of this history and its parallels is illuminating and instructive to our work today. In addition to the fact that we've consistently found active BPP prison cadre, this comparative examination has led us to change our previous acceptance of conventional claims that the BPP has not existed since 1982.

### The Bolsheviks: Birth, Decline, Revival

In Russia, Lenin was the first to meet the previously unresolved challenge of developing an organizational structure, line, and program that could successfully unite, organize, and lead the working class (proletariat) and other exploited and oppressed sectors in struggle to overthrow an oppressive political-economic system, and seize and exercise power themselves. This he did in the thick of bitter struggle against various opponents including the Czarist government.

He began his work within the RSDLP (founded in 1898) wherein he developed his revolutionary program and flexible organizational concepts and tactics. Within the RSDLP Lenin and his comrades ended up splitting with his opponents into Bolshevik (majority) and Menshevik (minority) factions. Leading the Bolsheviks, Lenin struggled to organize the RSDLP around a consistently working class-based revolutionary line as against the reformist and opportunist liberal bourgeois lines of the Mensheviks.

During this period (1900–1904) the membership of the RSDLP consisted primarily of petty bourgeois (middle class) intellectuals. Only a small number of its members were from the working class and poor. The Party also had very weak ties to the working-class masses whom it proposed to give leadership to.

As Lenin struggled to deepen the Party's working-class roots, in 1905 the Russian masses rose up in a mass upsurge against the Czarist regime, which caught both the Bolsheviks and Mensheviks off guard. But, caught up in the high tide of revolutionary enthusiasm of the masses, the factions moved toward reconciliation and together deepened their roots within the working masses.

It wasn't long, however, before the Czar's repressive forces moved in to crush the revolt and violently suppress the political and workers organizations found to be endorsing and leading it. These organizations including the RSDLP were outlawed and driven underground.

This backlash brought the internal contradictions within the RSDLP to a head again, as the factions disagreed on responses to the repression. The Mensheviks sought to pursue lines consistent with the interests of the capitalists to compromise with the Czar, and even to liquidate the Party altogether. The Bolsheviks, however, pursued the interests of the workers in alliance with other oppressed sectors as against the capitalists and Czar, and maintained the essential need of a revolutionary Party to carry the struggle forward to success.

Under the Czar's backlash the RSDLP's membership dissolved and all but disappeared. The Party was claimed to be dead. Lenin, however, held fast to the revolutionary line, rejected claims that the Party was dead, and bitterly criticized those who'd abandoned the Party and retreated into "personal" lives, or the academy as writers or educators, or other careers, etc. As one of Lenin's contemporaries recalled of him:

> "It pained him to see how in the post-1905 era the ranks of the professional revolutionaries began to thin rapidly, especially among the Mensheviks. Everyone was preoccupied with his own affairs, he recalled; revolutionaries were talking about such things as planning marriage and a family, about getting out of the revolutionary movement—temporarily, they claimed—in order to finish school or find a job. Even among the more educated and intelligent workers, precisely those who were the most needed in the movement, there was a tendency to desert the ranks of the proletariat, to take up teaching or some other white-collar job in order to achieve a more promising personal career and life. The intellectuals within the party, too, often turned to more lucrative types of writing and other intellectual pursuits not directly related to the revolutionary movement."[3]

Lenin contended:

> "The flight of some people from the underground could have been the result of their fatigue and dispiritedness. Such individuals may only be pitied: they should be helped because their dispiritedness will pass and there will again appear an urge to get away from philistinism, away from the liberals and the liberal-labor policy, to the working-class underground. But when the fatigued and dispirited

use journalism as their platform and announce that their flight is not a manifestation of fatigue or weakness, or intellectual wooliness, but that it is to their credit and then put the blame on the 'ineffective', 'worthless', 'moribund', etc. underground, these runaways then become disgusting renegades, apostates. These runaways then become the worst advisors for the working-class movement and therefore its dangerous enemies."[4]

Lenin struggled against this tendency to "liquidate" the Party and for a flexible application of both aboveground and underground tactics as circumstances required and allowed.

"Our immediate task is to preserve and consolidate the Russian Social Democratic Labor Party. The very fulfillment of this great task involves one extremely important element: the combating of both varieties of liquidationism—liquidationism on the right and liquidationism on the left. The liquidators on the right said that no illegal RSDLP is needed, that the Social-Democratic activities should be centered exclusively on legal opportunities. The liquidators on the left go to the other extreme: legal avenues of Party work do not exist for them, illegality at any price is their 'be all and end all.' Both in approximately equal degree are liquidators of the RSDLP, for without methodical judicious combination of legal and illegal work in the present situation that history has imposed on us, the 'preservation and consolidation of the RSDLP' is inconceivable ... The Bolshevik section as a definite ideological trend in the Party must exist as before. But one thing must be borne firmly in mind: the responsibility of 'preserving and consolidating' the RSDLP ... now rests primarily, if not entirely, on the Bolshevik section."[5]

In this vein Lenin and his comrades completely split from the Mensheviks and established the Bolsheviks as an independent Party in 1912 and rooted themselves within the workers' movement. This followed his refusal to embrace the Menshevik "liquidationist" position which denounced the Party—because repressed and outlawed by the Czarist state—and declared it dead.

"It was precisely after the Plenum Meeting of 1910 that the ... chief publications of the liquidators, *Nasha Zarya* and *Dyelo Zhizni*, definitively turned to liquidationism all along the line, not only 'belittling the importance of the illegal Party', but openly renouncing it, declaring that the Party was 'extinct', and that the Party was

> already liquidated, that the idea of reviving the illegal Party was a 'reactionary utopia', using the columns of legally published magazines to heap slander and abuse on the illegal Party, calling upon the workers to regard the nuclei of the Party and its hierarchy as 'dead', etc."[6]

Under Lenin's leadership the revolutionary Party was revived with a broad working-class leadership and base. It went on to lead a successful overthrow of the Czar, to defeat the liberal capitalists' subversive schemes, and to seize power for Russia's workers and peasants, establishing the world's first socialist state.

## BPP: Birth and Decline

Similarly the BPP was founded in the thick of a rising popular struggle of urban New Afrikan/Blacks against their oppressed and colonized conditions. Huey, sensitive to the interests and unmet needs of the New Afrikan masses, initially proved a capable organizational and tactical leader. His political line and practice were initially influenced by Marxist-Leninist-Maoist (MLM) theory.

Through Serve the People (STP) community service programs and its newspaper, the BPP was able to inspire the imagination of poor and working-class urban people, teaching them that they could and how to collectively defend their communities against police terror, meet their own basic needs, and become organized into a united force that could break free of their oppressed condition at the bottom of society and beneath the boot heel of imperialism

But the Establishment quickly recognized and responded with repression against the mass upsurge, and the revolutionary challenge and danger of the Party's leadership. In fact the FBI declared that, "the Black Panther Party, without question, represents the greatest threat to the internal security of the country."[7] They especially feared that the Panthers' infectious leadership example was being followed by groups also developing among poor whites, Asians, Mexicans, Puerto Ricans, Natives, and other oppressed sectors (and even in other countries), and these groups were moving toward uniting their people into a common struggle under BPP leadership against the overall U.S.-based imperialist system.

However, just as had occurred with the RSDLP, the government's backlash brought internal contradictions within the BPP to head, and the Party split into factions—one led by Huey Newton and the other by Eldridge Cleaver.

What the Panthers lacked, however, was a theoretical leader like Lenin who was rooted in and able to wage the decisive struggle to keep a genuinely revolutionary proletarian line in command of its ideology and work. Therefore, this split saw both factions follow the same flawed "liquidationist" lines that Lenin had struggled against—namely one of rightist reformism and legalism (Huey's faction) and the other of ultra-left militarism (Cleaver's faction).

Despite losing its revolutionary edge, the BPP's work as a community service mass organization continued, because its rank and file membership consisted largely of the working-class and poor people who lived in the oppressed communities where its programs were based and sorely needed.

When finally its last community-based STP program and newspaper went under in 1982, many declared the Party dead, rejecting efforts to revive it as wasted energy and mere nostalgia for a movement and organization whose time had passed. Many under the influence of this modern liquidationist line that met with no decisive ideological resistance, rejected the role and need of a revolutionary Party altogether.

The NABPP-PC now rises to the occasion of combating this trend, contending that the BPP is not dead nor is its needed role as a genuinely revolutionary mass-based vanguard. And we firmly root our political and ideological lines in the revolutionary science of MLM, which is Dialectical and Historical Materialism as applied to the struggle against 21st century capitalist-imperialism. While conditions have changed, fundamental principles have not.

And just as occurred in Lenin's day, official repression has led to many fleeing the struggle, retreating into "family" life, the academy, careers in journalism, integrating into the system, and so on. Others still have turned to peddling their past BPP memberships and Party history for personal profit and to achieve celebrity statuses; exposing themselves as capitalist renegades, opportunists, and traitors of the revolutionary cause to which many of our best committed and gave up their lives. But pockets of Panther cadre and those still "ready for revolution" have kept up good work.

Still, the Party went into decline and has remained so for several decades.

But as former Panther Mumia Abu-Jamal observed, the BPP made a deep and lasting impact on the consciousness of the people, and—despite its decline—many have emulated the Party, even if only in name, so that many Panther formations have since emerged.[8] Meanwhile, as already noted, a rank and file BPP membership within the Empire's prisons has continued in the Party's work and ideals despite standard claims that the Party, and by extension they, are no more.

## Reviving the Party

At present NABPP-PC comrades and allies are leading a United Panther Study Group (UPSG) which aims to bring together today's various Panther formations, allies, and BPP alumni and members to impart the history and lessons of the BPP, and correct ideological and political lines with which to revive the revolutionary Panther vanguard and carry forward our ongoing struggle to success. We aim to rebuild the Panther movement and vanguard from the grassroots.

As Comrade Tom Big Warrior posted to the study group,

> "Rebuilding the Panther Movement from the grassroots up requires comrades in every oppressed community to take up the initiative to form collectives and imitate 'Serve the People' (STP) survival programs, to create community newsletters and organize campaigns against police murder and oppression in the communities. Before we can come together nationally and internationally, we must build our movement locally and sink roots among the people in the oppressed communities of every ethnic composition. Pantherism is applied revolutionary science to the concrete conditions of declining capitalist-imperialism in the 21st century.
>
> "We must think in threes, not just ones and twos. Not just the alliance of workers and peasants, but of the great surplus army of the unemployed proletarians, the marginalized poor, the street people and shantytown people, the people in the projects and living in abandoned buildings and houses, the prison slaves and brothers and sisters on the block. It is a reality that declining capitalism cannot profitably exploit a majority of the people needing to work to survive and that the majority of this excluded and oppressed section of the people are people of color, though the number of poor whites in this underclass is growing as the downward spiral of capitalism-imperialism continues.
>
> "We must think in threes in terms of Black Panthers, Brown Panthers, and White Panthers in organizing all poor and oppressed people in our communities and building revolutionary class consciousness and a worldwide United Front Against Capitalist-Imperialism, Racism, and Repression!"

In this post-industrial era the Panther exists as a servant and organization of the vast numbers of urban and marginalized poor and imprisoned, who number in the billions. The vast majority of New Afrikans/Blacks in the U.S. live in urban areas. The vast body of oppressed peoples exists largely outside the system of production and contain large numbers of lumpen proletarians or are influenced by lumpen culture and infused with lumpen values.

This is a new world social dynamic and one that must be turned to the favor of winning proletarian power the world over. Because if we don't win these elements over to the cause of world revolution, they will, as Lenin, Mao Tse-Tung, Frantz Fanon and others recognized, be used by the imperialists against the revolution. This is the necessity of building the Panther movement.

We must create a broad-based United Panther Movement in alliance with revolutionary proletarian Parties (the RCP's), which includes forces in the communities based upon programmatic unity ("The Elephant"[9]), while at the same time pulling together a hard core of vanguard ("the Panther") consisting of the most advanced elements that come forward.

When we have many consolidated collectives in various communities and regions, it will be possible to call together a founding Party congress on the outside, and based upon the principles of Democratic Centralism create a Party center and function as a genuine Vanguard Party.

We will find the cadre to build this Party from within the masses engaged in mass struggle. Among examples today are the Black Riders Liberation Party, Panther Liberation Organization and others. There are also Panther formations in other countries such as Sweden.

As Fred Hampton once said, the struggle continues so long as the people's beat goes on; a beat that won't stop until we've buried this imperialist system once and for all and ended all oppression. Until then, even though mortally wounded time and again, the people will breathe new life into their Panther, which itself symbolizes the many lives of their struggle to be free until victory is won!

*Dare to Struggle, Dare to Win!*
*All Power to the People!*

## END NOTES

1. Various writers on BPP history put forward the position that the closing down of the last of the Panthers' community service programs and its newspaper in 1982 marked the end of the Party. See, e.g., Joshua Bloom, et al., *Black Against Empire: The History and Politics of the Black Panther Party* (Berkeley and Los Angeles, California: University of California Press, 2013), p. 3; Charles E. Jones, ed., *The Black Panther Party: Reconsidered* (Baltimore, Md.: Black Classic Press, 1998), p. 10.; Mumia Abu-Jamal, *We Want Freedom: A Life in the Black Panther Party* (Boston, Ma.: South End Press, 2004), pp. 232–33); etc.

2. For the lengthy federal decision discussing the TDCJ's use of BT's see Ruiz v. Estelle, 503 F. Supp. 1265 (S.D. Tex. 1980) .

3. K.D. Kristof Ladis, "B.I. Nicolaevky: The Formative Years," in Alexander and Janet Rabinowitch, et al., eds. *Revolution and Politics in Russia: Essays in Memory of B.I. Nicolaevky* (Bloomington, Ind.: Indiana University Press, 1971), pp. 28–29.

4. V.I. Lenin, *Collected Works*, Vol. 19. (Moscow: Progress Publishers, 1960–1970), p. 398.

5. V.I. Lenin, *Collected Works*, Vol. 15., pp. 432–33.

6. Tony Cliff, *Lenin. Volume 1: Building the Party* (London: Pluto Press, 1975), pp. 309–310; Lenin: *Collected Works*, Vol. 7, p. 481 (Moscow: Progress Publishers, 1960–1970).

7. *Newsweek*, February 1969.

8. Mumia Abu Jamal, *We Want Freedom*, pp. 229–245.

9. For an elaboration on "the Elephant" as our mass form of organization, see Kevin "Rashid" Johnson, "The Panther and the Elephant" (2005) (pp. 237–244 in this volume).

# 22. NABPP-PC RULES OF DISCIPLINE

2005

Unity, discipline, coordination and commitment are essential requirements of Party membership. And they are essential for accomplishing the Party's objective of uniting the New Afrikan Nation here in Amerika and all Afrikans in an organized and determined struggle for liberation from imperialist and neo-colonial domination. In pursuit of achieving these aims, Party members must adhere to basic Party discipline, namely:

### Principles of Subordination

1. Individuals are subordinated to the collective.
2. The minority is subordinated to the majority.
3. The lower level is subordinated to the higher level.
4. The entire membership is subordinated to the Central Committee.

### Points of Discipline

1. We shall not steal from the people, bully them, take liberties with them, nor disrespect them, nor use Party membership or rank to gain personal advantages or benefits from Party members or the people.
2. We will practice and promote respect for the rights of individuals, oppressed nations and peoples, including the disabled, wimyn, children, elderly, gay/lesbian, all ethnic and racial groups, and especially the working classes of all nations and nationalities.
3. We will practice and defend the "Right of Free Speech," and to assemble and protest.
4. We will fearlessly speak the truth and expose lies and corruption.
5. We will treat the false beliefs and prejudices of others as "loads upon their backs" and endeavor to enlighten and uplift them.
6. We will strive to set the best example for the people through upright conduct and honesty, leading and educating by example.
7. We will not be used to spy upon the people nor reveal their secrets to their enemies.

8. We will serve the people "heart and soul" to the best of our abilities.
9. We will conduct ourselves with honor and strive to be the people's pride.
10. We will not practice discrimination within the Party's ranks based upon gender or sexual orientation. All ranks and leadership positions within the Party will be equally available to men and wimyn, with their qualifications being determined by their proven abilities and commitment, and they will be equally respected and obeyed by lower ranks.
11. We will practice criticism and self-criticism.

Violations of party rules and discipline are disruptive of party unity. Of primary importance in preserving party unity is to educate all rank and file members of the party in its rules of discipline and the general directives of the party. It is also important that they hold the party's leadership to account, whether deliberately or by error, for deviations from these principles.

## THE GENERAL DIRECTIVES

At this early stage of organizing our party, our energy must be focused upon forging our cadre into a tightly knit organization capable of building and rebuilding itself and ultimately leading the Afrikan and New Afrikan masses on many fronts in a successful struggle to achieve liberation from imperialism and neo-colonialism, to reclaim our independent history and identity as a people, and to ally our forces with other revolutionary peoples to deal monopoly capitalism the *coup de grace.*

The party's main developmental goal is to perfect its line by promoting and adhering to the most scientific method to find correct solutions to the problems of Afrikan and New Afrikan people suffering under imperialist oppression and exploitation. The spirit of our ideology is making concrete analysis of objective conditions. We are not an idealist, adventurist, or opportunist organization. Our Party must be fresh and on time, knowing the actual problems of our people and finding the correct solutions. We must honor and pay tribute to our leaders and fighters of yesterday, while advancing, developing and correcting their analysis and praxis in solving the problems of today.

In building a tightly knit organization of cadre, we must commit ourselves to relentless study, of our history, of various revolutionary theorists and practice, and also, we must advance that history, and the methods we adopt, in the process of developing our own revolutionary practice. And we must continually educate and uplift the Party members and the masses.

The New Afrikan Black Panther Party-Prison Chapter is open to all loyal and sincere members of the Afrikan and New Afrikan working class and radical students, intellectuals, peasants and lumpen who have developed clear working-class consciousness and discipline, while we must remain unceasingly vigilant in preventing infiltration by enemy agents, whose aim will be to disrupt the Party and undermine our struggle. Our goal is to expand the Party, drawing in the best fighters from the masses, while maintaining its integrity.

The Party is the key to our liberation struggle, and all external influences must be subordinated to our loyalty to the Party as our unifying political force. Therefore, we must not allow ourselves to become provoked, baited or taunted by opportunist, ultra-leftist or enemy forces into premature, adventuristic actions and practices. As the leading element in organizing the Afrikan and New Afrikan masses, the Party must remain clear-headed, well-informed, and honest with the people in its analysis, decisions and actions.

Political work must lead over all other Party endeavors. Towards this end, frequent meetings must be held, political education must be stressed, and serious political commitment must be demanded of all members. Party members and leading cadre must dedicate themselves to serious study of all root problems and issues that affect the lives and welfare of our Afrikan and New Afrikan people.

We must be good at learning and never cease learning—from our people and their experiences, from books and from our own life experiences and those of our Party. We must continually educate ourselves and the people, going into questions deeply and using dialectical and historical materialism, which does not teach us what to think, per se, but how to think. We must observe the dictum: "KNOW THE ENEMY AND KNOW THYSELF."

We must struggle against all forms of negative thinking which undermines the Party's and the people's morale and confidence, spreading fear, confusion, mistrust and defeatism. We must resist tendencies towards individualism, commandism, gossip, slander, bullying and towards either overestimating or underestimating ourselves or the enemy.

The comrades and the people must understand that the enemy will employ dual tactics, offering reforms with one hand and coming down with repression with the other, employing both deception and force. The people must be made to understand that no oppressor can indefinitely continue to oppress the people when faced with their determined and organized resistance.

The people must cease to view the enemy with awe and believe in their invulnerability or god-like omnipotence. Ultimately, it is the people who are really powerful and who, when united, cannot be defeated. Inspiring fear, self-doubt, disunity, and slavish passivity are the oppressors' tactics. They rely upon ignorance, alienation, apathy, cynicism and lack of leadership to maintain control.

Our political education work must penetrate everywhere, including within the enemy's ranks. We must write leaflets, letters, essays, pamphlets, books, plays and poetry, draw graphics and cartoons, compose posters, songs and slogans, and spread them far and wide. We must struggle to win over all whom we can to join the struggle.

In every respect and every aspect of our work, we must practice revolutionary responsibility, carry out tasks to completion and to the best of our abilities. We must respect the opinions and work of others and strive to be open-minded and fair. We must not pick fights or hold grudges. The solution to almost every problem is to rely on our comrades and to rely on the people.

We must hide nothing from our Party comrades and from the masses of our people, tell no lies, expose lies whenever they are told and conceal nothing. We must not factionalize nor let others factionalize with us. All should be open and aboveboard, and we should follow the principle of: UNITE DON'T SPLIT!

## CRITICISM AND SELF-CRITICISM

Criticism, in the positive usage, is the examination, analysis and evaluation of the comparative worth of the ideas, actions, policies, prejudices and practices of others. Self-criticism is, of course, this same principle applied to oneself. But it also applies as the method of critically examining our line and practice and openly admitting when we have made mistakes, including to the people, whose criticism we must welcome.

Criticism and self-criticism are wholly necessary to human progress and to the building of a genuinely revolutionary movement. Revolutionary nationalism elevates criticism and self-criticism to a conscious principle and incorporates it into the day-to-day functioning of the Party. In its positive usage, it helps us to correct what is wrong, make adjustments and resolve differences between individuals and groups. In the words of Frantz Fanon, "Self-criticism has been much talked about of late, but few people realize that it is an AFRIKAN INSTITUTION."

## DEMOCRATIC CENTRALISM (Operating with a Central Committee)

Too often the comrades have an incomplete or incorrect idea about what democratic centralism is all about. It is exceedingly important that this aspect of our organizational structure be understood by all the members. Democratic centralism, and its key feature—the Central Committee—are scientific organizational concepts formulated by V.I. Lenin, which enable a vanguard party (and the mass organizations it provides leadership to or influences) to function with the unity and impact of a clenched fist, as well as be able to perform many separate tasks independently with the desired coordinated effect.

Democratic centralism combines aspects of inner-party democracy with a centralized command structure in conformity with the objective and subjective conditions the Party must face, balancing the objective needs of the actual concrete conditions and the need for a unified and coordinated Party with the subjective need of the individual members to participate fully in the decision-making process and have their opinions respected. We recognize the need and primacy of having centralized authority; to steer the Party and hold the members to binding discipline—on penalty of punishment or expulsion. But we also recognize the need for drawing on the collective wisdom of the whole party and the importance of inner-party discussion and struggle to sum up practice and arrive at correct decisions regarding political line and practice.

By absorbing the democratic discussion and input of the whole Party, (both majority and minority opinions), the Central Committee can best arrive at decisions and programs to be implemented by the whole Party. The principle of: CRITICIZE UP AND IMPLEMENT DOWN, best describes this process. Once a decision is reached, the minority has the right to reserve their opinions (until the next discussion), but the whole Party must unite to carry out the decisions of the Central Committee. Party members must not publicly criticize the Party or its leadership outside the channels of inner-party discussion nor reveal inner-party business to anyone outside the Party. This is factionalization, as is attempting to form rival headquarters to the CC within the Party.

The Central Committee is the highest body of the Party, except for a Party Congress composed of elected representatives of the whole Party. The Chairman is the spokesperson of the CC and the Party and its highest-ranking member. The CC will also have a General Secretary and a standing Political Bureau (Politburo) composed of the heads of the various "Ministries" (such as the Ministry of Defense, Ministry of Information, and so on) and other key members of the CC.

As the Party expands, so will its organizational structure, but the principles of democratic centralism will remain the same. Lower bodies will be subordinated to higher ones and the minority will be subordinated to the majority. The "Basic Unit" of the Party will be the "Collective" or local cell composed of comrades living and/or working together. Chapters will be composed of various collectives and be headed by a "Captain."

The basic guiding principle is to keep it simple and practical and to afford the comrades engaged in particular work the greatest latitude to be creative in the application of the Party's line and directives. All work and meetings should be summed up and reports made to the next highest body on up to the CC. Comrades have the right to appeal up to the CC if they believe they have been wrongly treated by their superiors in a serious matter.

## AN OBJECT LESSON FROM THE PAST

One of the successful tactics used in the FBI's COINTELPRO program of disruption of the old Black Panther Party was its use of "Brown Mail," private correspondence purported to be from leading or rank and file Party members or supporters authored by FBI agents imitating the handwriting of those people and mailed form the appropriate city. In particular, the feds set out to drive a wedge between two of the Party's leading members, the Minister of Defense, Huey P. Newton, and the Minister of Information, Eldridge Cleaver, (who was then in exile in Algeria).

Instead of turning this mail over to the Party's chairman, Bobby Seale, for internal investigation of apparent attempts at factionalization, and to check out the allegations they contained, these leaders kept the "Brown Mail" secret, believing the lies contained, and began conspiring against one another. The Party was eventually split apart as each carried their line differences to extremes instead of struggling for reconciliation through inner-party democracy.

Other members were summarily expelled and declared "Enemies of the People," based upon "Brown Mail" they knew nothing about, as "Commandism" replaced democratic centralism. Alliances were sabotaged, and masses of Party members and supporters quit in confusion and disgust at the bitter infighting and paranoia generated.

We must not underestimate the skill, (born from long experience), that the political police have acquired at sowing disruption and division. Nor should we ignore the summed up experience of the people's revolutionary forces at combating this by developing protocols designed to combat it, such as democratic centralism.

Another important protocol is to refuse to talk to the police or FBI beyond stating your name and address (or prison number). Fools who ignore this rule are often suckered in and turned to become informers or agent provocateurs. Some brag and show off to people (particularly of the opposite sex) about things that should not be talked about, when they don't even really know who they are talking to, or if their phone is tapped, or whatever.

Another thing we must avoid is falling into the trap of "Legalism," and believing that just because our actions are legal that the enemy won't break the law to set us up on bogus charges, violate our rights, or commit illegal acts, including murder, to silence us. This *is* a fascist dictatorship! The window dressing of "Legality" and "Democracy" cannot be taken for reality.

The necessity of doing legal, aboveground work makes us vulnerable, and retaliation only plays into the state's hands and allows them to brand us as "terrorists" and escalate their attacks. There is no safety in being a revolutionary, even in a non-revolutionary situation, and we have to accept that. We also have to minimize the danger by relying on the masses to defend us, by exposing the true nature of the beast, and by making the enemy pay a high price in exposure when they commit crimes to attack us.

Millions of people get screwed by the system, get railroaded into jail or prison, or murdered by the police, just because they are Black, Mexican, Indian or Puerto Rican. These are not revolutionaries, but this *is* a class dictatorship! Even poor and working-class whites, who may have voted for Bush, get screwed every day. This class dictatorship is a criminal enterprise through and through, and that is why we need to make a revolution.

We have to steel ourselves for struggle and be strong, have courage, and do what must be done. If we worry too much about what they might do to us, they will automatically win, because we will be distracted from what must be done.

### BECOME FAMILIAR WITH THESE TERMS

THE LEFT: The more vehemently a person or party advocates revolution, socialism, etc., the farther to the left he, she or they are said to be. The Left includes Communists, Anarchists, Revolutionary Socialists, Revolutionary Nationalists and others who hold that significant change can only come about through the overthrow of monopoly capitalism. These schools of thought differ on issues, but are firmly anti-imperialist.

THE LEFT OF CENTER: These folks would earnestly like to reform the system, and may advocate socialism (even communism), but they balk at revolution and cling to the capitalist system and the illusions of "Legalism" and "Democracy." The Left-Center includes civil rights organizations like the NAACP, radical trade unionists, radical feminists, anti-war activists, libertarians, and radicals in general with a reformist agenda. Generally speaking, these forces tend to align together in the left-wing of the Democratic Party in the U.S. and in social-democratic parties elsewhere.

THE CENTER: This shrinking category includes the "Old Guard Liberals" who believe in capitalism but think it can be modified to preserve concessions won by the people and that the worst excesses of imperialism can be curbed by legislation. They look backwards to the "New Deal" era and the Kennedy-Johnson "Cold War Liberalism." They defend the status quo.

THE RIGHT OF CENTER: These folks espouse concern for the people, but really they are subservient to the monopoly capitalists. The more the Right attacks the Center, the further right they creep. They are the Moderate Democrats and Liberal Republicans.

THE RIGHT: The more vehemently a person or party advocates keeping the people down and giving more power to the monopoly capitalists the farther to the Right he, she or they are said to be. The Neo-Liberals and Neo-Cons differ only on the pace at which they think the move toward the right should be done. On major issues like NAFTA, the WTO, the increase of the prison population and the invasion of Afghanistan and Iraq, they agree completely. They are both fascist in essence. The extreme Christo-Fascists, allied with the Neo-Cons, want to create a Christian theocracy.

## THE CENTER IS UNDER ATTACK BY THE RIGHT

What most characterizes this time period politically is the swing toward the Right and that the most reactionary forces, the Neo-Cons and Christo-Fascists, centered in the Bush administration, want to make a radical rupture, not only with "Cold War Liberalism" but with the whole trend of liberal democracy going back to the Enlightenment. Ideologically, they oppose any constraints on monopoly capitalism and envision a theocratic dictatorship where fundamentalist Christianity, the state and U.S.-based multinational corporate interest are merged to suppress all dissent and opposition. The material basis for this is that the interests of monopoly capital are so at odds with the interests of humanity as a whole that only the fundamentalist Christian belief in the "End times" fits their agenda.

The Left presents the only positive alternative, but it has yet to recover from the setbacks at the end of the Cold War, and what is left of the Left is groping for reorientation and fresh leadership. The Center will not hold, and ready or not, the Left will be forced to confront the Right in an all-out struggle that will determine not only which class will rule in the future, but if there will be a future for the human race.

It is this all-out struggle that we must prepare for. We who are inside the "belly of the Beast," may perish inside these razor-wire fences and stone walls, but not without first illuminating the path forward for our sisters and brothers, our sons and our daughters. If we can offer nothing but our dying breath, it will be to say: "DARE TO STRUGGLE AND DARE TO WIN!"

ALL POWER TO THE PEOPLE!

## CLASS AND THE INDIVIDUAL

> "The function of a class analysis is to enable a revolutionary to examine large segments of society and draw generalizations about those segments' reaction to historical, economic, and social trends, and those segments' role in social struggle. Another function of class analysis is to provide a tool for analyzing ideology from the standpoint of what class of society that ideology represents and serves."
>
> Judah Hill

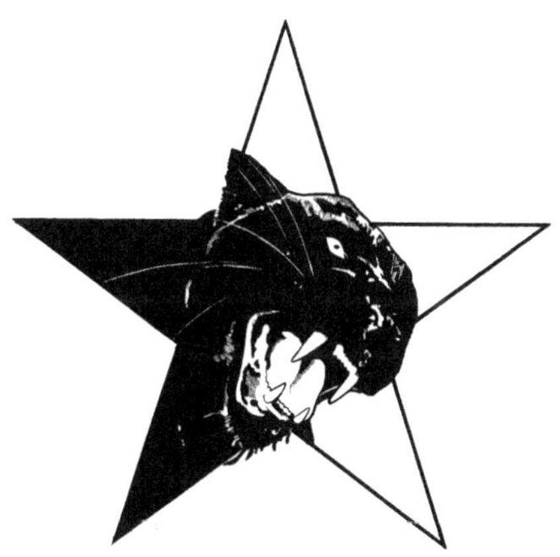

# THE TEN POINT PROGRAM AND PLATFORM

## NEW AFRIKAN BLACK PANTHER PARTY-PRISON CHAPTER

1. **WE WANT FREEDOM. WE WANT POWER TO DETERMINE THE DESTINY OF OUR BLACK AND OPPRESSED COMMUNITIES.**
   We believe that Black and oppressed people will not be free until we are able to determine our destinies in our own communities ourselves, by fully controlling all the institutions which exist in our communities.

2. **WE WANT FULL EMPLOYMENT FOR OUR PEOPLE.**
   We believe that the federal government is responsible and obligated to give every person employment or a guaranteed income. We believe that if the Amerikan businessmen will not give full employment, then the technology and means of production should be taken from the businessmen and placed in the community so that the people of the community can organize and employ all of its people and give a high standard of living.

3. **WE WANT AN END TO THE ROBBERY BY THE CAPITALISTS OF OUR BLACK AND OPPRESSED COMMUNITIES.**
   We believe that this racist government has robbed us and now we are demanding the overdue debt of forty acres and two mules. Forty acres and two mules were promised 100 years ago as restitution for slave labor and mass murder of Black people. We will accept the payment in currency which will be distributed to our many communities. The Amerikan racist has taken part in the slaughter of our fifty million Black people. Therefore, we feel this is a modest demand that we make.

4. **WE WANT DECENT HOUSING, FIT FOR THE SHELTER OF HUMAN BEINGS.**
   We believe that if the landlords will not give decent housing to our Black and oppressed communities, then housing and the land should be made into cooperatives so that the people in our communities, with government aid, can build and make decent housing for the people.

5. **WE WANT DECENT EDUCATION FOR OUR PEOPLE THAT EXPOSES THE TRUE NATURE OF THIS DECADENT AMERICAN SOCIETY. WE WANT EDUCATION THAT TEACHES US OUR TRUE HISTORY AND OUR ROLE IN THE PRESENT-DAY SOCIETY.**
   We believe in an educational system that will give to our people a knowledge of the self. If you do not have knowledge of yourself and your

position in the society and in the world, then you will have little chance to know anything else.

**6. WE WANT COMPLETELY FREE HEALTH CARE FOR ALL BLACK AND OPPRESSED PEOPLE.**

We believe that the government must provide, free of charge, for the people, health facilities which will not only treat our illnesses, most of which have come about as a result of our oppression, but which will also develop preventive medical programs to guarantee our future survival. We believe that mass health education and research programs must be developed to give all Black and oppressed people access to advanced scientific and medical information, so we may provide ourselves with proper medical attention and care.

**7. WE WANT AN IMMEDIATE END TO POLICE BRUTALITY AND MURDER OF BLACK PEOPLE, OTHER PEOPLE OF COLOR, ALL OPPRESSED PEOPLE INSIDE THE UNITED STATES.**

We believe that the racist and fascist government of the United States uses its domestic enforcement agencies to carry out its program of oppression against Black people, other people of color and poor people inside the United States. We believe it is our right, therefore, to defend ourselves against such armed forces and that all Black and oppressed people should be armed for self-defense of our homes and communities against these fascist police forces.

**8. WE WANT AN IMMEDIATE END TO ALL WARS OF AGGRESSION.**

We believe that the various conflicts which exist around the world stem directly from the aggressive desire of the United States ruling circle and government to force its domination upon the oppressed people of the world. We believe that if the United States government or its lackeys do not cease these aggressive wars it is the right of the people to defend themselves by any means necessary against their aggressors.

**9. WE WANT FREEDOM FOR ALL BLACK AND OPPRESSED PEOPLE NOW HELD IN U.S. FEDERAL, STATE, COUNTY, CITY AND MILITARY PRISONS AND JAILS. WE WANT TRIALS BY A JURY OF PEERS FOR ALL PERSONS CHARGED WITH SO-CALLED CRIMES UNDER THE LAWS OF THIS COUNTRY.**

We believe that the many Black and poor oppressed people now held in United States prisons and jails have not received fair and impartial trials under a racist and fascist judicial system and should be free from incarceration. We believe in the ultimate elimination of all wretched, inhuman penal institutions, because the masses of men and women imprisoned inside the United States or by the United States military are the victims of oppressive conditions which are the real cause of their imprisonment. We believe that when persons are brought to trial they must be guaranteed, by the United States, juries of their peers, attorneys of their choice and freedom from imprisonment while awaiting trial.

**10. WE WANT LAND, BREAD, HOUSING, EDUCATION, CLOTHING, JUSTICE, PEACE AND PEOPLE'S COMMUNITY CONTROL OF MODERN TECHNOLOGY.**

When, in the course of human events, it becomes necessary for one people to dissolve the political bonds which have connected them with another, and to assume, among the powers of the earth, the separate and equal station to which the laws of nature and nature's god entitle them, a decent respect to the opinions of mankind requires that they should declare the causes which impel them to the separation.

We hold these truths to be self-evident, that all men are created equal; that they are endowed by their Creator with certain unalienable rights; that among these are life, liberty, and the pursuit of happiness. That to secure these rights, governments are instituted among men, deriving their just powers from the consent of the governed; that, whenever any form of government becomes destructive of these ends, it is the right of the people to alter or to abolish it, and to institute a new government, laying its foundation on such principles, and organizing its powers in such form as to them shall seem most likely to effect their safety and happiness. Prudence, indeed, will dictate that governments long established should not be changed for light and transient causes; and, accordingly, all experience hath shown that mankind are most disposed to suffer, while evils are sufferable, than to right themselves by abolishing the forms to which they are accustomed. But, when a long train of abuses and usurpation, pursuing invariably the same object, evinces a design to reduce them under absolute despotism, it is their right, it is their duty, to throw off such government, and to provide new guards for their future security.

All members and potential members must study and memorize our Ten Point Program and Platform.

*ALL POWER TO THE PEOPLE!*

# 23. NEW RULES OF CONDUCT OF THE NABPP-PC JANUARY 1, 2012

All functional members of the NABPP-PC shall obey these rules and the founding "Rules of Discipline and General Directives." All leading cadre and formations of the Party shall uphold and enforce these rules, and report any serious violations of these rules to the Ministry of Justice of the Party and all responsible comrades and higher bodies within the Party. Responsible comrades shall conduct fact-finding investigations to determine guilt or innocence and recommend a method of correction with input from other comrades. The method of correction shall be appropriate to the seriousness of the violation.

Each Party member is responsible to know and abide by these rules and to report any violations.

### The Rules:

1. This is a Party of struggle and you must strive to develop your knowledge and leadership abilities and your integrity and commitment to serve the people and conduct yourself so as to win the trust, respect and confidence of the people.
2. Know and understand the Party's Ten Point Program, its history and its significance at this point in history and be able to explain and defend it to others.
3. Read at least two hours a day to develop your knowledge and keep abreast of what is going on in the world.
4. Develop your understanding of Historical and Dialectical Materialism, which is the philosophical basis of our party's ideological and political line, and apply it in your political work and analysis.
5. Show Panther Love to your comrades and strive to encourage and uplift them, recognize and praise their contributions, be open and above board, practice criticism and self-criticism and do not be liberal.
6. Maintain a regimen of healthy physical exercise and diet and keep yourself fit for duty as best you can. Don't abuse your health with excessive drinking or drugs.
7. Be reliable, punctual and good to your word. Carry out your assigned tasks responsibly, effectively, to the best of your ability and with a good attitude.
8. Practice collective leadership and not commandism.

9. Hold and attend regular meetings, at least weekly or bi-weekly, discuss things thoroughly and practice mutual criticism in a comradely way. Strive to reach consensus. Uphold decision by the majority.
10. If arrested or interrogated by the authorities, give your name and ID only. Make no statements without an attorney being present.
11. Do not discuss Party business or comrades with any law enforcement officer, agent or informer.
12. Know your legal first aid.
13. Attend and conduct political education classes, forums and study circles.
14. Familiarize yourself with martial arts and techniques of self-defense. Do not use violence except in the extremity of self-defense.
15. Know your medical first aid.
16. Do not allow anyone to put a "gang" or "terrorist" label on the Party or United Panther Movement, or by word or action give support to such slanders.
17. Support the Party with the regular donations.
18. Do not take or borrow anything from the people without permission or misuse funds entrusted to you.

### Eight points of attention

1. Speak politely
2. Pay fairly for what you buy
3. Return everything you borrow
4. Pay for anything you damage
5. Do not hit or swear at people
6. Do not damage the crops or property of the poor oppressed masses
7. Do not take liberties with wimyn
8. If we ever take captives, do not ill treat them

### The three main rules of discipline

1. Obey orders in all your actions
2. Do not take a single needle or piece of thread from the poor and oppressed masses
3. Turn in everything captured from the attacking enemy

# PART V

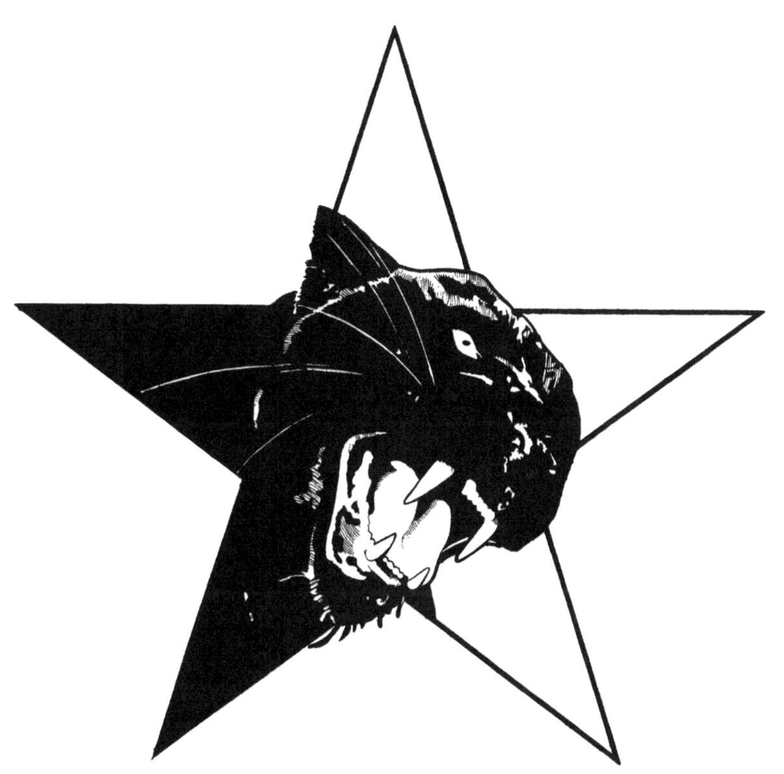

# ARTICLES & ANALYSES

*Rereading these articles that were originally printed in the newsletters published by Rising Sun Press and passed from prisoner to prisoner in the "Slave Pens of Oppression," I am struck by how correct the analysis has proved to be. Like the original BPP, the NABPP-PC has been continually evolving and becoming more international in its perspective—Comrade Rashid most of all!*

*The 2005 uprising of Arab and Afrikan youth that began in Clichy-sous-Bois, France and spread to oppressed communities all over Europe, was something the ghetto-bred comrades of the NABPP-PC could readily identify with. Nine years later, we see the effect of the rising of people in Ferguson, MO against the police murder of an unarmed youth is having around the country and the world. As Empire sinks its claws deeper into Afrika via USAFRICOM, we see a new generation discovering the example set by comrades like Patrice Lumumba, Kwame Nkrumah, Frantz Fanon, Thomas Sankara, Steve Biko and Amilcar Cabral. Cabral, who led the independence struggle in Guinea-Bissau and Cape Verde Islands, made a particular effort to hook up with the comrades of the Black liberation struggle in the U.S. and deepen their understanding of global imperialism and neo-colonialism.*

*I am reminded of the courage and dedication of our dear comrade Hasan Shakur, the NABPP-PC's Minister of Human Rights, who joined the Party from "Death Row" in Texas and was executed in August of 2006. Hasan was a much loved comrade whose unbreakable spirit and tireless work for prisoners' human rights impressed the other comrades, leading to him being the first to be drafted to serve on NABPP-PC's Central Committee. I will never forget his phone call on the day of his execution and the pride he felt that was going to die as a Black Panther. "Watch what I do now!" he said to me. He knew he was setting an example for comrades that would follow in his footsteps.*

*A critical aspect of building the United Panther Movement is understanding and applying the Mass Line. As Jalil Muntaqim put it in* We Are Our Own Liberators*: "This is a lesson revolutionaries need to relearn in terms of the working formula developed by the former Black Panther Party. The strength of the BPP was its ability to speak to the need of the people as the people in the various communities identified them. The BPP was then able to develop programs that serve to relieve some of the conditions of disenfranchisement and impoverishment the* *people suffered. By doing so, the people rallied to the Party and began to accept the Party-line as their own."*

*It was also essential for the NABPP-PC to formulate a correct understanding of fascism and how it applies to our contemporary situation. We needed a better working definition than was commonly accepted in Amerika. It doesn't necessarily have to involve goose-stepping parades, a single party, or a leader cult. It is much more effective to have a two-party dictatorship and the trappings of a democratic process. What is essential is the merger of corporate and state power and the subordination of the state to corporate interests. At this stage, the primary tactic of Empire is diversion. Instead of using its state power to smash the Left and drive it underground, it diverts it with false ideas and ideologies to misdirect those who seek to oppose the system.*

*As fascism is adaptable to any group, it is particularly useful to Empire. For example, as Jewish nationalism, or Zionism, it has been quite useful in establishing a foothold for imperialism in the Middle East, diverting the Jewish masses away from the Left and pushing them into genocidal conflict with the Palestinian people. But it has also been successful at promoting Islamic nationalism, or Salafism (Wahhabism), as exemplified by al Qaeda, or more recently ISIS (ISIL), both as a proxy force (for false flag operations) and as a "threat" to justify the "War on Terror."*

*Championed by the Kingdom of Saudi Arabia and the other feudal Gulf regimes where the sect is the dominant minority, and covertly backed by Israel and Empire, the Islamic fascists provide a useful proxy force for destabilizing secular republics with plausible deniability and an excuse for Empire's aggression. Having credited al Qaeda with the attacks on 911, and used them to justify the U.S./NATO invasions of Afghanistan and Iraq, it became an embarrassment to be seen again using them as a proxy force in Libya and Syria, so it was convenient to morph al Qaeda into a new incarnation as ISIS.*

*Meanwhile, in the Ukraine, we see the U.S./NATO forces openly allied with neo-Nazis and other fascists to force another "regime change" to put pressure on the Russian oligarchy to submit to Empire's global hegemony. In India, we see the alliance of Hindu nationalism with western neo-liberalism. And at home we see the fanning of racial tensions by the unjustifiable murder of Black youth, like Trayvon Martin and Mike Brown, being defended by white nationalists and exploited by Black nationalists seeking to divert and racialize the growing struggle against what is in essence class oppression.*

*All of this points to the need for a revolutionary vanguard to lead a Worldwide United Front Against Capitalist-Imperialism, Racism and Police State Repression, and ultimately World Proletarian Socialist Revolution to create a Worldwide Dictatorship of the Proletariat. We need a political compass to point us in the right direction. We need to distinguish Left from Right, and resist misdirection. We need to defend our leaders and build revolutionary infrastructure and community-based people's power and organization. We need to "Red Up!" ourselves, our communities, our ideology and political line, and our global struggle!*

*Tom Watts*

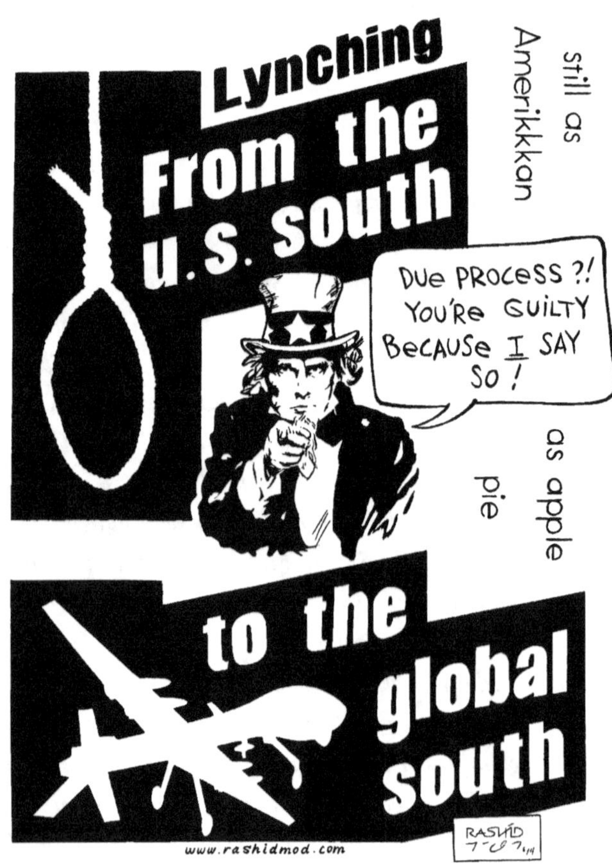

# 24. UNCLE SAM IN BLACKFACE: BARACK OBAMA AND THE DESIGNS OF U.S. IMPERIALISM 2009

## Destroying and Replacing our Leaders

When contradictions between Blacks/New Afrikans and the imperialist interests of Amerika sharpened in the 1960s, independent leaders emerged to guide our struggle. Under their direction we advanced towards seizing control of our history, destiny and identity, and organizing to break free of our oppressed conditions.

In response, the U.S. government moved to destroy and replace these leaders with ones who'd keep us in line as its continued dependents and victims. In advancing this plan FBI assistant director William C. Sullivan stated in 1964:

> "When this is done, and it can and will be done, obviously much confusion will reign, particularly among the Negro people ... The Negroes will be left without a national leader of sufficiently compelling personality to steer them in the proper direction."

Under these designs Malcolm X and Dr. Martin Luther King, Jr., the two most influential independent Black leaders of that era, were both targeted and murdered. But it was Malcolm's image and example that resonated most deeply with the urban concentrations of New Afrikans—especially the youth.

## A Resurgent Leadership

The plan to destroy the movement by targeting its leadership did not initially succeed. Instead of demoralizing the movement and severing its head, Malcolm's assassination inspired a new mass-based leadership to assume the front and with a clearer plan.

Inspired by Malcolm's ideas and unfulfilled aspirations, Huey P. Newton and Bobby Seale co-founded the Black Panther Party (for Self-Defense) the year after his death. In fact, Malcolm's murder so enraged Bobby Seale that he vowed, "I'll make my own self into a motherfucking Malcolm X, and if they want to kill me, they'll have to kill me!" Huey went on to explain:

> "We read also the works of the freedom fighters who had done so much for Black communities in the United States. Bobby had collected all of Malcolm X's speeches and ideas from papers like *The Militant* and *Muhammad Speaks*. These we studied carefully. Although Malcolm's program for the Organization for Afro-American Unity was never put into operation, he had made it clear that Blacks ought to arm. Malcolm's influence was ever present. We continue to believe that the Black Panther Party exists in the spirit of Malcolm. Often it is difficult to say exactly how an action or program has been determined or influenced in a spiritual way. Such intangibles are hard to describe, although they can be more significant than any precise influence. Therefore, the words on the page cannot convey the effect that Malcolm has had on the Black Panther Party although, as far as I am concerned, the Party is a living testament to his life work. I do not claim that the Party has done what Malcolm would have done. We do not say this, but Malcolm's spirit is in us."

The Panthers also drew insight from the principles and methodology of Mao Tse-tung in China. The Party developed, expanded and refined programs for Black community control based upon the model Huey witnessed among national minorities in China under the Maoist revolution.

The Party's achievements as a successful and uncompromising revolutionary Black leadership and an infectious example to not only other oppressed but even privileged peoples across Amerika quickly marked it for destruction by the U.S. government, under a secret war led by the FBI code-named COINTELPRO (COunter INTELligence PROgram).

The major problem that the Establishment had with the BPP was not only that it spoke to the needs of the most oppressed U.S. sectors, but that it was leading and teaching them and others by example how to (and that they could) meet their own needs and solve their own problems, free of dependence on the power structure. And that it was that very power structure at the source of many of their problems and a deliberate obstacle to their solutions.

## Leading by Example—Serving the People

The earliest example of the BPP to the poor of their ability to meet their own needs was set in a New Afrikan community where several children were run over and killed by cars at an unregulated intersection. Parents and other community members had gone repeatedly to the local government pleading for a solution to the problem. The officials put them off each time with promises to look into the matter. No help ever came.

Huey and Bobby resolved the problem by simply finding and posting a stop sign at the intersection themselves, as residents observed. No more children were run over. Other communities with the same problem followed the Panthers' example, with the same successful results, and came to realize that by simply relying on their own efforts and resources, instead of blindly depending on the system, they could themselves have protected their children all along.

Likewise, the BPP led and set the example of community self-reliance through socialist community service (Serve the People) programs, which independently pooled and organized the resources and labor power of the poor communities to feed their own hungry children; organize against police brutality and murders of Black youth; operate liberation schools, health clinics, clothing, shoe and grocery distribution, senior citizen services, busing to prisons, sickle cell anemia testing and research, pest control, maintenance, day care, ambulance, news services, etc.

## The Empire Strikes Back

The greatest fear of an enslaver is that his victims might realize that they can live free of dependence on his system, that he lives at their expense and needs them to survive, and not vice versa. This because he knows once the enslaved people realize this they will naturally struggle to break free of his illegitimate power and take control of their own destiny.

This was the infectious example set by the Panthers, as Party chapters sprang up to replicate Serve the People programs in poor Black communities across Amerika, and similar organizations followed their example in poor Mexican, Puerto Rican, Asian, white, and other communities. Panther formations also arose in England, Australia, Bermuda, and Israel.

But as a young organization, inexperienced and untrained in the methods of (and countering) government subversion, and not even aware of official designs to crush them, the Panthers were viciously slandered, attacked, and ultimately destroyed. And our marginalized urban masses have since been left confused and divided, just as the FBI predicted would occur in the absence of our own authentic liberationist leadership.

In the wake of its destruction of the BPP, the U.S. government implemented a policy in 1978—National Security Council Memorandum #46

(NSC-46)—calculated to keep our oppressed communities in leaderless chaos, and to prevent our learning from and joining forces with the liberation struggles fighting across Afrika against apartheid, and U.S. and European imperialist domination, and their theft of Afrika's natural resources and wealth.

NSC-46 proposed, among other things, to exploit every option to prevent any independent leadership from ever emerging again that could unite our communities; to eliminate all desire among us to establish our own independent political party; to incorporate more Blacks into high U.S. political offices where their activities and images could be controlled and molded by the system, and then used to mislead and misdirect us into supporting and remaining dependent upon and loyal to the Establishment; and to create a broader Black middle class and more Black business leaders who would serve as tokens and "success" stories to inspire false hope of, and false aspirations toward, Black "achievement" within the imperialist slave system, instead of fighting to break free of and destroy that system.

### Fear of a Reawakened Dragon

Over the following decades our suffering continued and intensified: police brutality and murders of our youth, violent occupation of our communities by militarized police, increased poverty and social deterioration, medical neglect, polarization of society along racial lines exemplified in Jena 6, mass imprisonment of our youth, general government neglect of our basic needs and security, massive gentrification, forced depopulation and displacement of Black communities (ethnic cleansing), the abandonment and subsequent declaration of war against desperate poor victims of natural disasters (for example during the Hurricane Katrina crisis), flooding our communities with narcotics and inciting gang wars, etc. These conditions continued to reawaken and heighten our disaffection with the power structure and its endless stream of false promises, lies and empty rhetorical claims to respect for human and civil rights, racial and cultural diversity, democracy, the rule of law, and so on.

Just beneath the surface lay the real danger of a resurgent Black/New Afrikan liberation struggle of the sort that inspired the movements that shook the very foundations of the U.S. imperialist empire in the 1960s and '70s. And the powers that be knew this.

## Obama—the Trojan Horse

Yesterday, the answer to this insurgent threat proposed by the FBI was to create a Black liberationist leadership vacuum and fill the void with a Black corporate lawyer groomed by the system—Samuel Pierce. Today the void is being filled by a pro-capitalist ex-Harvard law professor also groomed by the system—Barack Obama.

But the game, although the same, runs a bit deeper.

Obama was pushed forward not merely to subvert and misdirect the initiatives of the disaffected Blacks here in Amerika, but also to woo the Afrikan nations in particular. Remember, Obama is not only half Black, he is also half Afrikan.

As the U.S. economy spirals towards acute depression, as it struggles to maintain hegemony over world oil supplies, and as its efforts to secure control over Middle Eastern oil reserves become more remote—in Iran in particular—its interest in Afrika's largely untapped oil wealth increases by the day. The U.S. imperialists have long aspired to dominate world petroleum supplies and access. As the State Department expressed in an April 11, 1944, memorandum:

> "United States policy should in general aim to assure to this country, in the interests of security, a substantial and geographically diversified holding of foreign petroleum resources in the hands of the United States nationals. This would involve the preservation of the absolute position presently obtaining, and therefore vigilant protection of existing concessions in United States hands coupled with insistence upon the Open Door principle of equal opportunity for United States companies in new areas."

As Nigeria's president expressed a few years ago, a new "Scramble for Africa" is underway, with the U.S. and other imperialist countries maneuvering for control over Afrika's oil. Having an Afrikan-born father and Amerikan-born mother, Obama is the perfect front man to promote U.S./Afrikan ties toward achieving U.S. control of the continent and its oil.

In July 2007 the African Union held a conference to discuss a proposal to federate the 53 Afrikan nations into a United States of Afrika. The year before, the U.S. Defense Department formed a planning team to establish an Amerikan United Military Command for the Afrikan continent (USAFRICOM). On December 15, 2006, USAFRICOM was approved and established by President George W. Bush.

USAFRICOM will set up, control and coordinate U.S. military operations within all 53 Afrikan nations, except Egypt which is already under

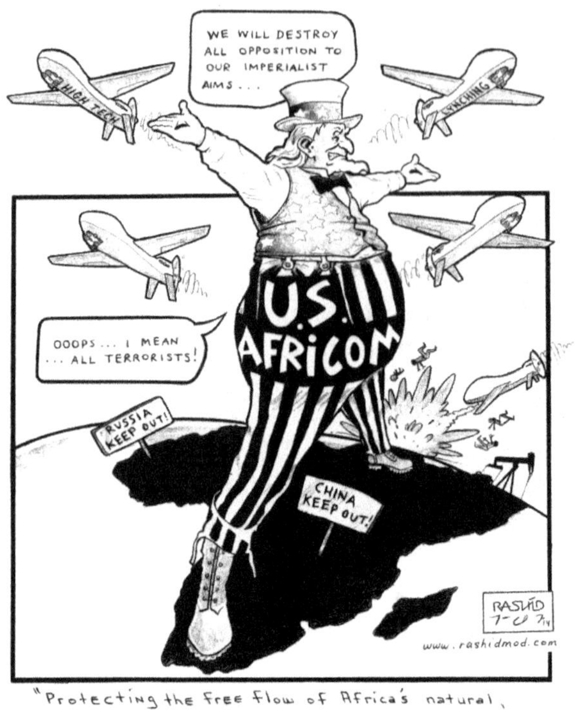


"Protecting the free flow of Africa's natural, resources to the global market is one of AFRICOM's guiding principles"
Robert Moeller, Dep Comm. AFRICOM '08

U.S. control and has since the 1970s been the world's second largest recipient (next to Israel) of U.S. military and economic "aid." In fact, the role of Egypt alongside Israel has been to protect U.S. oil interest and allies in the Middle East (especially Saudi Arabia) from hostile neighbors. These are clearly the first steps towards consolidating U.S. neo-colonial domination across Afrika, to control its vast natural resources and squeeze out China, who is Amerika's main rival in the region. In turn, China recently hosted the Afrikan heads of state in a counter-attempt to coax them into its own camp.

Also, China has been promoting itself as a kinder and gentler imperialist lite, by promoting humanitarian aid, debt forgiveness and low interest loans to Afrikan countries. But don't they wish they had an Obama!

With Obama as President, and the U.S. government's operating its centralized military command across Afrika, he'll be overseeing the killing of kids and common people from Tripoli to Johannesburg, and giving protesters a taste of U.S. military crowd control for which it has won infamy across Iraq. All to ensure U.S. domination over and the "safe" extraction and removal of Afrika's natural resources and wealth.

In February 2008, Robert Moeller, the first deputy to the Commander for Military Operations of AFRICOM stated that, "protecting the free flow of natural resources from Africa to the global market is one of Africom's guiding principles." On the other hand, the U.S. public will hear only of fighting terrorism (which means violent repression of those who oppose imperialist designs in Afrika) and U.S. Marines on peacekeeping humanitarian missions, with staged filmings of troops passing out chocolate bars and bottled water.

## Racism at Home Undermines U.S. Interests in Afrika

U.S. interests to control Afrika and its vast natural resources are not new. Neither are its schemes to try and woo Afrikan political leaders to achieve this end. Using Obama as a frontman is just the latest scheme.

As the Afrikans across the continent began struggling for independence from European colonialism in the 1950s, it became apparent to U.S. officials that Europe would not be able to maintain its valuable Afrikan colonies. With its eyes set on Afrika's wealth, the U.S. began maneuvering to take over in the region by promoting decolonization and coaxing Afrika's new and aspiring heads of state. As Vice President Richard Nixon declared to the U.S. Senate Foreign Relations Committee in 1957:

> "American interests in the future are so great as to justify us in not hesitating even to assist the departure of the colonial powers from Africa. If we can win native opinion in the process, the future of America in Africa will be assured."

This scheme in part involved the State Department inviting Afrikan leaders and diplomats to visit Amerika intending to give them the red carpet treatment. This effort backfired in many cases, because these Afrikans came face-to-face with Jim Crow segregationist policies that barred them from eating in restaurants, staying in exclusive hotels and visiting establishments from which Amerikan Blacks were barred.

Even in cases where the State Department was able to make special accommodations, the Afrikans saw how other Blacks were treated and excluded from these places. They were not fooled. In general the Afrikan ambassadors suffered the same humiliations and abuses as U.S. Blacks. In the face of the prevailing discriminations against these Afrikans, and its negative impact on U.S. plans in Afrika, Secretary of State Dean Rusk testified before a Senate committee on July 10, 1963, as reported the next day in the *New York Times*:

> "As matters stand racial discrimination here at home has important effects on our foreign relations ... I now turn to a special concern of the Department of State: the treatment of nonwhite diplomats and visitors to the United States. We cannot expect the friendship and respect of nonwhite nations if we humiliate their representatives by denying them, say, services in a highway restaurant or city café.
>
> "Yet within the last two years, scores of incidents of racial discrimination involving foreign diplomats accredited to this country have come to the attention of the Department of State. These incidents have occurred in all sections of the United States."

Rusk also observed that racial oppression of U.S. Blacks was pushing Afrikan leaders to side with Black/New Afrikan resistance leaders in Amerika against the U.S. government.

During the same period Amerika's main rival—the Soviet Union—was exposing the reality of U.S. race relations to the Third World through its international media. U.S. Blacks and opposition leaders visiting and emigrating to the Soviet Union were also vocal about the stark contrast between racial equality in the S.U. versus the discrimination, segregation, lynching, and general violence against Blacks in Amerika. Also the majority of the nations within the newly created United Nations were non-white. And within the UN, the S.U. consistently took the side of the dark Third World peoples and thus undermined Amerika's efforts to win their opinion to its side. Not to mention that the violent resistance of whites and government officials in the U.S. South to desegregation was being graphically exposed in the world media.

It was in efforts to counter the negative impact of racism on its international economic schemes, that the federal government moved to break down, with much fanfare, legalized segregation beginning in 1954 with the Supreme Court's ruling in Brown v. Board of Education of Topeka, Kansas, which ordered that segregation in public institutions be dismantled "with all deliberate speed."

### Paul Robeson: A Fly in the Ointment

U.S. efforts to curry favor with Afrikan leaders were also counteracted by such outspoken Blacks as Paul Robeson (one of Malcolm X's early heroes), who traveled around the world exposing the truth of racial oppression in the U.S., and revealing to Afrikans that our suffering in Amerika was much the same as their own suffering under European colonialism.

In return, the State Department revoked Robeson's passport in 1950, and the FBI denounced his international activities as a "threat to national security" and instituted a manhunt to capture him to prevent his leaving the country. The following year the State Department sent Adam Clayton Powell, Jr., its lackey in blackface, to tour Afrika on a "goodwill" mission to repair Robeson's damaging exposures. The U.S. government denied Robeson's revelations as lies and "Communist propaganda."

The height of U.S. embarrassment came when later that year, Robeson filed a petition with the UN on behalf of "fifteen million black Americans" charging the U.S. with "genocide."

In return for his efforts on behalf of his oppressed people and to expose the true face of the U.S. power structure on others it was scheming to also prey upon, the government destroyed Robeson's career as one of Amerika's most accomplished Black entertainers. However, Robeson was honored in Afrika and the Soviet Union, and in December 1952 he was awarded the International Stalin Peace Prize.

### Malcolm X Takes up the Torch

A decade and a half later Malcolm X took up Robeson's torch. He traveled Afrika exposing U.S. imperialist designs abroad, denouncing its treatment of Blacks in Amerika, and promoting our right to political independence just as Afrikans were fighting for across the continent. He sought to link our struggle up with that of Afrika against European colonialism and Amerikan imperialism.

In return Malcolm too was hounded and persecuted, and countermeasures were taken at high levels of the government to silence him and subvert his efforts. At a 1964 summit of the Organization of African Unity, he pronounced:

> "In order to keep the Organization of Afro-American Unity [which he founded that year] from gaining the interest, sympathy and support of the independent African states in our effort to bring the miserable plight of the 22 million Afro-Americans before the UN, the racist element in the State Department very shrewdly gave maximum worldwide publicity to the recent passage of the Civil Rights Bill …
>
> "The racist element in the State Department realizes that if any intelligent, really militant Afro-American is ever permitted to come before the United Nations to testify on behalf of the 22 million mistreated Afro-Americans, our dark-skinned brothers and sisters

> in Africa, Asia, and Latin America, would then see America as a 'Brute Beast' even more cruel and vulturuous than the colonial powers of Europe and South Africa combined."

Several attempts were made on his life as he moved to lodge a petition with the UN similar to the one Robeson pursued just over a decade earlier. The U.S. government was outspoken in its opposition because of the loss of credibility and international embarrassment it would suffer before the dark nations of the world at the UN. The media was used to demonize Malcolm, and just a week before he was to attend a special Afrikan-Asian conference in Algeria, where he was to introduce his proposed UN petition, he was silenced by assassins' bullets under designs of the CIA.

So today in continuing its decades-long designs to hide its racist and imperialist face, and to portray itself as a friend of Afrika in order to gain control over her natural wealth (oil in particular), the U.S. Establishment has promoted the half-Afrikan Obama as its front man and Trojan Horse. And he will be used to develop friendly ties with the heads of state across the continent and to oust "unfriendly" ones, thereby choosing governments that will bow to U.S. interests via "regime change." Such imperialist designs will be called "spreading democracy."

Obama has never had the interests of Black people nor any others of the oppressed at heart. His own campaign strategy demonstrated this.

## The Obama Electoral Strategy

Before going into the particulars of Obama's electoral strategy it is important that we understand that he is a tool of the faction of wealthy U.S. interests represented by the opportunistic Democratic Party. A party that until the 1960s was a rabid opponent of racial integration and granting Blacks voting and civil rights.

The Democrats in Washington only became pretended supporters of the interests of Blacks when in 1963 a march of millions of Blacks on Washington was planned. This "March on Washington" was originally planned at the grassroots by poor Blacks, millions of whom intended to converge on, lay siege to, and shut down all government and commercial operations in the U.S. capital, and not leave until the government resolved the problems of systemic poverty, racial oppression, and government abuse and neglect of Blacks.

Such a movement would have driven the nail in the coffin for Amerika's designs to win over the dark nations, particularly where Dean Rusk had, just the month before the planned Black siege on Washington, spoken to the need to rein in discrimination against Blacks because of its negative effects on U.S. relations with those nations.

It was in response to the situation that President John F. Kennedy suddenly presented the Democratic Party as a champion of integration and Black civil and voting rights. Kennedy's corporate backers then funded the financially strapped Dr. Martin Luther King, Jr. and used the mainstream media to make King the leader and voice of the planned march. King was thereby used to convert the march from an angry militant siege into a one-day peaceful rally where a few "authorized" speeches would be made, Blacks would sing and cry out their frustrations alongside a few white sympathizers, and everyone would be out of town by sundown.

Malcolm X witnessed the entire scam and bitterly criticized King and his circle in his autobiography, and in his speech entitled "Message to the Grassroots."

And here we should keep in mind that Obama is being used as the frontman by and of the same Democratic Party.

To win broad electoral support in his presidential bid, Obama replicated the electoral "Accommodation" strategy used successfully by other Black Judases like David Dinkins in his bid for New York mayor, and Douglas Wilder in his 1989 campaign for governor of Virginia; which were rhetorically portrayed, like Obama's election, as triumphs over racism in Amerika.

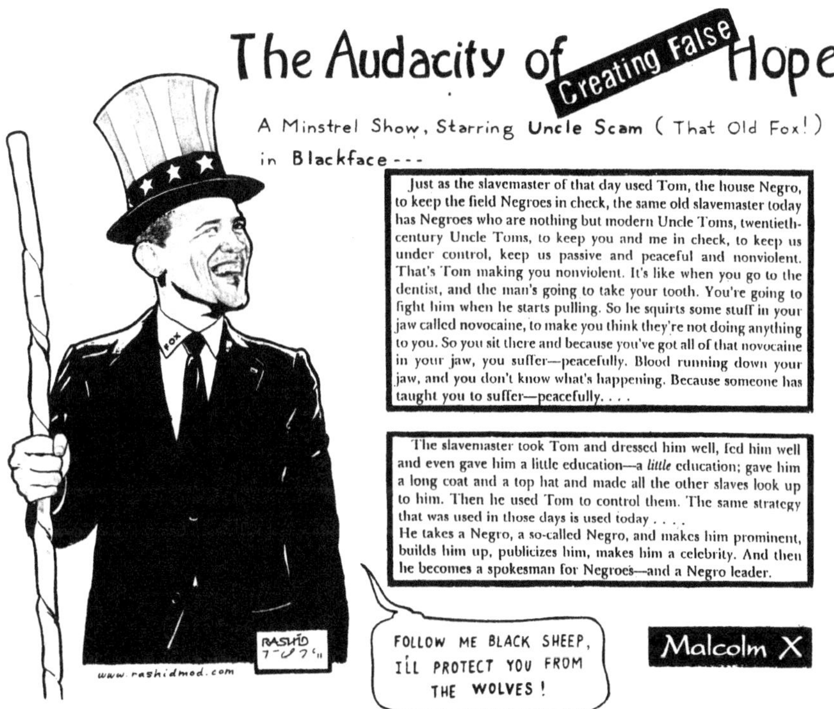

Just as Obama has done, both Wilder and Dinkins took advantage of an atmosphere of broad social disaffection with government policies implemented over several prior administrations. They ran moderate campaigns which appealed to a broad and diverse electoral base recognizing that the Black vote alone was too small to win their bids for office.

Wilder promoted himself as a pro-corporate, anti-crime conservative, using a carefully crafted political image instead of his skin, to cross the color line and win broad white voter support. He avoided addressing the cause or needs of deteriorating conditions for Blacks/New Afrikans. Like Obama, Dinkins and Wilder ran mainstream oriented campaigns, and avoided building coalitions specifically oriented towards Blacks, Latin@s, "Leftists" and workers. When both won their elections, neither provided any genuine advances for Blacks, workers or the poor, nor advanced policies to benefit the needy.

As Wilder stated in 1989, comparing his campaign strategy with the failed 1985 and 1989 presidential campaigns of Jesse Jackson, Sr., "Jesse runs to inspire. I run to win." Meaning Wilder, like Obama, opportunistically said all the right things to win over the necessary sectors of a broad and diverse voter base to win his campaign.

### False Leadership Generates False Hope

Today many Blacks and poor people are taken in by Obama's rhetoric that his win will mean a positive "change" for the common people, such as economic improvement and expanded services for the needy. Nothing could be farther from the truth, which was proven by events that occurred when Bill Clinton took office in 1993, after running a campaign upon promises to improve conditions for Amerika's needy and resolve the "debt crisis" generated from 1981 to 1993 under Ronald Reagan's and George H.W. Bush's "Reaganite" policies.

As past White House advisor Daniel Patrick Moynihan stated in a July 21, 1985, *New York Times* op-ed piece:

> "[The Reagan administration made a] deliberate decision to create deficits for strategic, political purposes ... The Reagan Administration came to office with, at most, a marginal interest in balancing the budget—but with a very real interest in dismantling a fair amount of the social legislation of the preceding 50 years. The strategy was to induce a deficit and use that as grounds for dismantling."

When Clinton took office the U.S. national debt was at an all-time high. Reaganite policies had transformed the U.S. into the world's largest debtor nation by 1987, after 70 years as a creditor nation.

Right after Clinton won the presidential election a front page *New York Times* article of November 6, 1992, made clear that the wealthy corporate powers that control the U.S. economy would defeat any attempts by Clinton to implement or revive social reform programs. As Moynihan admitted, Reaganite policies like those of Bush, Jr. today, were designed to create such immense U.S. debt that the social spending programs and laws passed in the 1960s and '70s to appease the protest and resistance movements of Blacks and other marginalized groups would have to be dismantled, and government spending could be increasingly shifted to the wealthy corporate sector.

The deliberate creation of massive debt under Reaganite policy was accomplished by the U.S. Treasury Department's selling hundreds of billions of dollars in securities—U.S. Treasury notes, bonds, etc.—to wealthy investors to be traded on the securities market. With this immense share of the U.S. debt in the hands of private investors, any efforts to shift government spending away from the corporate sector and back towards social needs would be quickly upset by investors selling off just a tiny amount of Treasury bonds, which would instantly increase the interest rate and U.S. deficit by tens of billions of dollars.

Investors warned Clinton that if he attempted to live up to his campaign rhetoric of social reform, which he had no intentions of fulfilling anyway, he'd find his administration in a worse economic predicament than the one that cost Bush Sr. his second presidential bid. Clinton not only toed the line but increased government spending with private corporations.

He did also balance the budget, however, but only by cutting social spending to the bone through such methods as demonizing the poor (especially Blacks) and kicking millions of poor Black children—average age of 7 years old—off welfare, under the Welfare Reform Act of 1996, plunging urban Black Amerika deeper into the morass of poverty. In turn he expanded the police and prison systems beyond anything done by prior administrations to brutalize and confine the victims of his policies who'd be unable to find "legitimate" work in the steadily shrinking U.S. job market, especially in and around urban areas.

Yet all the while Clinton portrayed himself as a hero and champion of New Afrikans, whom Toni Morrison rhetorically called "the first Black president."

Obama serves the same corporate forces, whose interests he will also prioritize over that of the common people. He will also face the same sort of corporate resistance if he attempted to implement social reforms: his empty campaign promise to institute "change" if elected is nothing more than seeds of false hope. And it is a dangerous thing to give oppressed people false hope.

Clinton did cure the immense national debt generated by Reaganite policies, but he did so at the expense of Amerika's poor and working-class—with Blacks suffering the worst of it. At that time there were remnants of a social safety net from which government funds could be diverted to "service" the debt. But thanks to the last four administrations up to Bush Jr., that safety net has been rent to shreds.

Indeed Bush Jr. has plunged the economy into its worst deficit to date in financing his War (for oil) on Terror and corporate spending, which debt he hasn't even put a dent in with his attendant cuts in social spending and privatization of public services. Obama has inherited an economy in a state of acute crisis of the sort that brought on the Great Depression of the 1930s.

There now remain no non-essential areas of the economy from which Obama as president could service the unprecedented debt created by Bush Jr. Any further cuts in spending not directed at corporate interests would only amount to the government cannibalizing itself and its own labor force. So his promises to cure the present economic and military crises haven't a leg to stand on. A major economic downturn is at hand.

What we can expect is greater social instability, a greater militarization of domestic Amerika, and enhancement of its surveillance and police state features. As the December 17, 2008, *Phoenix Business Journal* reported, the U.S. Army War College has police departments on alert that anticipated economic crisis may lead to civil unrest requiring martial law (military intervention), with the general public the targeted "enemy." Lest we forget, in 2007 the Bush Jr. Administration "revised" federal law to allow the U.S. president to occupy Amerikan cities with the military. The military occupation of New Orleans following Hurricane Katrina in 2005 was only a trial run.

### Exploiting our Desperation

Many of us are so desperate for the slightest show of recognition from the Establishment that seeing someone of darker skin on pedestals of power traditionally reserved for the wealthy white male causes us to throw sanity and the lessons of history to the wind. As the Black Martinique revolutionary Frantz Fanon once observed, an oppressed and colonized people tend to feel a sense of blind over-appreciation for any crumbs and tokens thrown to them by the racist status quo. This is the euphoria we see across Black Amerika in blind reaction to seeing a Black face seated as U.S. President.

Most of Afrika's 53 nations are headed today by Black presidents and prime ministers. Yet their people remain victims of desperate poverty, government neglect and exploitation, and massive unemployment because those "leaders" are but puppets of European imperialist countries and corporations who continue to rob them of their natural resources. And it has been so since Afrikans won their claimed independence. Quislings and Uncle Toms are nothing new. Dark faces in high places do not equal genuine liberation. Under imperialist power it only means the continuation and often intensification of their suffering, only with a dark face at the wheel (neo-colonialism).

## We Need Panther Power

As our social deterioration and attendant crises accelerate, we need now more than ever Panther Power. We need to develop programs to serve the people and build self-sufficiency and self-reliance with a greater awareness of addressing also our security needs, under the leadership of an independent mass-based Panther vanguard party. There are no individual heroes in this struggle—it is the masses through collective struggle, guided by correct and competent leadership, that make and change history.

Barack Obama, as Uncle Sam in black face, cannot and will not meet our needs, nor win us the freedom we've aspired toward against centuries of oppression and exploitation. His black skin serves only as a token of false hope, to pull us back into support for and dependence upon this imperialist slave system. A system that was built by the labor and blood of our ancestors. A system that has never once met our needs, but has only devised to keep us under its thumb by destroying and replacing our genuine leaders, and subverting our every effort to break free and rise above our debased conditions, claim our own history and identity, and take our place in history as a leading force of change here and abroad.

Obama can and will serve no interests but those of the obscenely wealthy 1% who own and control the economic, political, military, cultural and ideological institutions of this U.S. imperialist system.

The people don't need an imperialist wolf dressed in a black sheep's clothing. We need freedom. Which means rebuilding our Panther vanguard into an international and intercommunal force, to unite our oppressed people everywhere into an allied struggle against imperialist domination and for Pan-Afrikan socialist unity.

*Dare to Struggle, Dare to Win!*
*All Power to the People!*

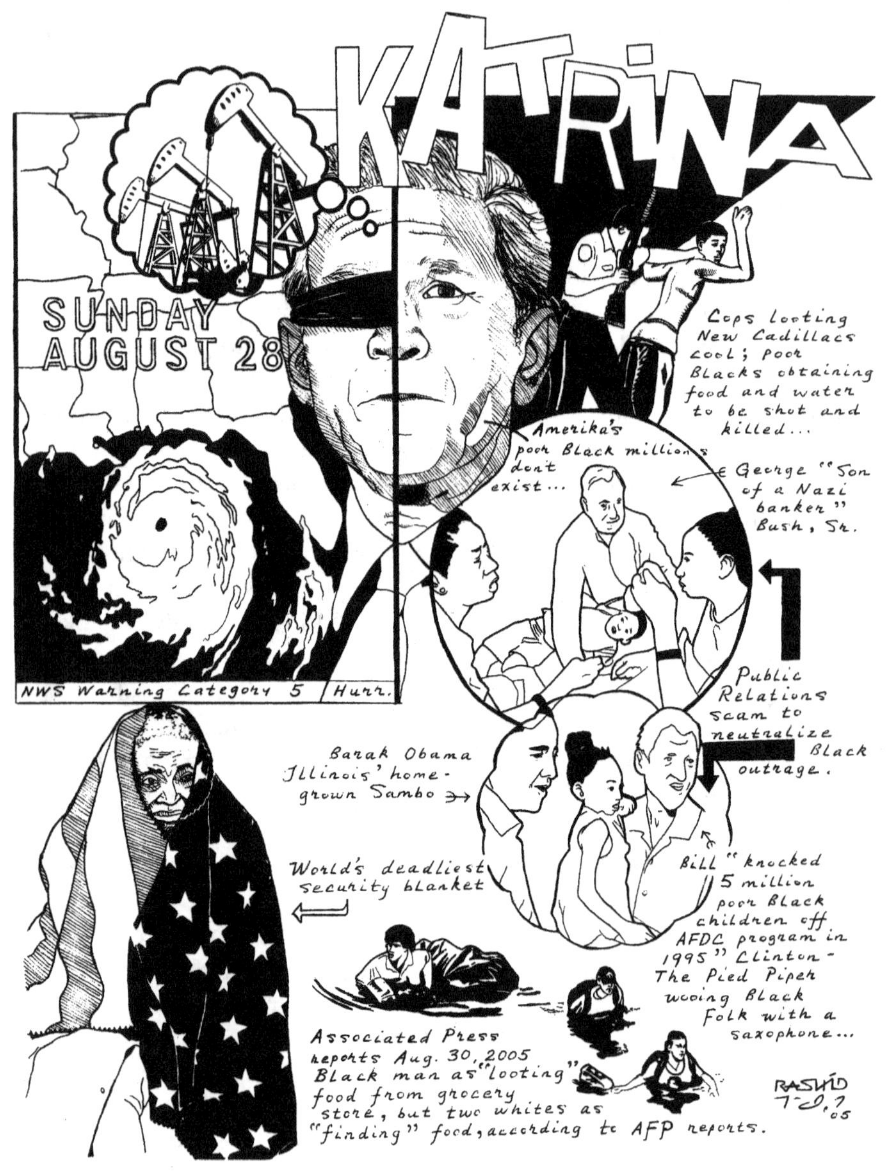
KATRINA
SUNDAY AUGUST 28
NWS Warning Category 5 Hurr.
Cops looting New Cadillacs cool; poor Blacks obtaining food and water to be shot and killed...
Amerika's poor Black millions don't exist...
George "Son of a Nazi banker" Bush, Sr.
Public Relations scam to neutralize Black outrage.
Barak Obama Illinois' home-grown Sambo
Bill "knocked 5 million poor Black children off AFDC program in 1995" Clinton - The Pied Piper wooing Black Folk with a saxophone...
World's deadliest security blanket
Associated Press reports Aug. 30, 2005 Black man as "looting" food from grocery store, but two whites as "finding" food, according to AFP reports.
RASHID 7-27-05

# 25. KATRINA; CAPITALISM AND CONTINUING BLACK CRISIS IN AMERIKA 2005

Hurricane Katrina brought the twisted illogic of capitalist imperialism to the surface; exposing that corporate profits take precedence over environmental and humyn needs. Disregard for and exploitation of the poor and people of color by the government at every level, the big corporations and even the wealthy minority "Uncle Toms" in their response to (and lack of response in) this crisis, and the suffering of the poor Black and white people left to fend for themselves, played out in front of a shocked nation and world.

On August 28, 2005, the National Weather Service warned that vast structural damage would be inflicted to the Gulf Coast region by Hurricane Katrina, and that many homes and other buildings would be destroyed. Three days earlier, the Governor of Louisiana gave emergency warnings. But no provisions were made to evacuate the poor of New Orleans. When the hurricane hit on August 29th, these people suffered devastation that those in power knew would occur. They knew that the levies could not withstand a level three, let alone a level five, storm, and that the city, being below sea level, would be flooded.

Typically, the masses of poor people in Amerika are ignored by the media and hidden from sight. If they are shown it is to heap blame and ridicule on them for being poor, such as in 1996, when Bill Clinton was pushing through the welfare "reform" laws. Welfare recipients were portrayed as driving Cadillacs and exploiting the system. But the flooding of New Orleans showed the extent of real poverty in Amerika. In fact the main reason so many poor Black wimyn and children died in New Orleans was because they had no cars or money to flee the city on their own.

In a pretence of offering the unevacuated citizens "hurricane relief," the city government told them to go to the Convention Center and the Superdome. Thousands of mostly Black residents walked or waded to these locations from miles away expecting to find help, food, water and medical care. What they found instead was cruel indifference, unpreparedness and chaos. Surrounded by disease contaminated water, there was nothing to drink and no food as they were jammed into these darkened arenas without sanitary toilet facilities.

When the desperate, abandoned people began to obtain basic necessities from abandoned stores, (certainly doing no worse than the Cadillac-stealing police), orders came down to "shoot to kill looters." The mainstream media blatantly described whites and police as "finding" food and water from abandoned stores but Blacks as "looting" these things. Martial law was declared, and the actual relief and rescue operations being organized by the people were shut down by armed mercenaries (hired by FEMA) and the military and police.

Brigadier General Gary Jones, commander of the Louisiana National Guard Joint Task Force, compared the operation to the U.S. invasion of Somalia in 1993. According to reports aired on *Democracy Now!*, private mercenaries admitted to shooting up a group of young Blacks on a New Orleans overpass. The media reported it as a group of "snipers" killed by the military who they had fired upon. A *Miami Herald* article on July 5, 1987, reported that former FEMA director Louis Giuffrida's deputy, John Brinkerhoff, handled the martial law planning of FEMA, and that it was similar to a plan Giuffida had developed earlier at the Army War College to confine "at least 21 million American negroes [in] assembly centers or relocation camps."

FEMA has built and staffs such camps spread out all over the U.S., and it is now part of the Department of Homeland Security. From the moment FEMA appeared on the scene in New Orleans, it made matters worse not better. FEMA cut civilian communication lines to the outside, flew in the infamous Blackwater mercenaries from Iraq, blocked and delayed assistance coming from other cities and countries (including Cuba) from reaching the hurricane victims, and it channelled massive amounts of funding donated to help the Katrina victims to right-wing Christian groups like Pat Robertson's Operation Second Blessing, to mention just a few of the outrageous things it did.

While Robertson was getting windfall subsidy from FEMA, he used his TV ministry show to degrade the Black hurricane victims and depicted items left behind in the city as "voodoo" paraphernalia. Operation Second Blessing had previously been exposed for exploiting Black people in the Congo, where it turned out that Robertson invested the funds collected for disaster relief in a Congo diamond mine. Robertson was exonerated by former VA Attorney General Mark Earley, whom Robertson had gifted with a $30,000 campaign contribution. Previously, Robertson pulled a similar scam in Liberia, where he invested in a gold mine.

I could go on and on about the dirt that has come to the surface already regarding this disaster and the lies told by the government. The lesson we must learn from all this is the need to organize ourselves to deal with our security and welfare issues and to create people's power in our communities. The government won't help us, and we shouldn't waste our time trying to get it to. It's not our government! It belongs to the rich white ruling class of Amerika who got rich by exploiting us. We need to rely on ourselves.

*Dare to Struggle, Dare to Win! All Power to the People!!*

# 26. FROM BENTON HARBOR, MICHIGAN TO CLICHY-SOUS-BOIS, FRANCE: THE INTERNATIONAL OPPRESSION OF YOUTH OF COLOR

2005

As a policy of atomizing the Nation of Afrikans in Amerika, the U.S ruling class has cultivated a sense of isolation from the rest of the Afrikan world. The reason behind this policy is to keep us from seeing ourselves as part of Afrika's people around the world, a common people suffering common conditions of oppression and exploitation at the hands of a single system of imperialism.

Close scrutiny of the recent revolt of Afrikan and Arab youth in Clichy-sous-Bois, and across Europe, demonstrates the reality of a common condition of oppression in Europe and the U.S. for people of color. The conditions that sparked the youth uprising in France mirror those that we face in Amerika, an example being those that sparked the 2002 Black uprising in Benton Harbor, Michigan.

Benton Harbor is a small, Black, working-class town with a history of racist oppression by the local police and judicial system. Police chases, beatings, shootings and false arrests in Benton Harbor had taken their toll on its population, where Black children and youth were regularly killed by the police at a rate 14 to 28 percent higher than the national average.

Benton Harbor had gone from a town with a vibrant economy to one of dire poverty in just a few short decades. This was caused by its relationship with the predominantly white town of Saint Joseph's across the river. Most of the property in Benton Harbor is owned by residents of St. Joseph's, and most of the major job and revenue generating opportunities were taken out of Benton Harbor and moved to St. Joseph's, (the hospital, courthouse, water department, etc.), leaving the Black town without jobs or basic infrastructure and its people owning nothing.

The police department, (located in St. Joseph's), is 99% white. The jail is situated so that it is the first building you see upon crossing the river from Benton Harbor into St. Joseph's.

The routine brutality suffered by the Black residents of Benton Harbor psychologically conditioned them to fear police stops. It was the death of a fleeing young Black motorcyclist named Terrance Shurn, during a police chase, which ignited the uprising in Benton Harbor. Eyewitnesses reported seeing one police car driving closely behind Shurn and bumping into his bike's tires, while another police car drove him off the road and into an abandoned house. The next day, police attempted to break up a vigil being held by the youth's family, which incited anger and the ensuing two days and nights of street battles with the police.

Much like Benton Harbor, and the U.S. inner cities in general, Clichy-sous-Bois, France, (where the youth uprising that spread to over 400 European cities and towns in less than two weeks began), is a small working-class ghetto of single family public housing units isolated from France's metropolitan areas. The ghetto's residents are mostly Afrikans and Arabs lacking regular jobs and forced to pay high rents, which leaves them in a cycle of poverty. The town doesn't even have a cinema or library.

For Clichy's youth, police brutality, harassment and humiliation are routine. Many abuses occur during the frequent raids of homes as police claim to be looking for "illegal immigrant" squatters to deport. Carloads of police suddenly swarm young men out walking, under the pretext of making "identity checks." As in Benton Harbor, Clichy's youth have a reasonable fear of police stops. The French Interior Minister, Nicolas Sarkozy, publicly described the residents of these ethnic working-class ghettos as "scum" and "filth" to be "scoured with industrial cleaner."

The uprising, which began on October 27, 2005, was sparked by the deaths of two teenage boys resulting from their fleeing from and being chased by the police. The two teens, Buena Traore and Zyed Benna, fled from police who chased them into an electric power substation, where they were electrocuted to death. Weary of the repression by the French police, who were in Sarkozy's words, "waging a war without mercy" against the "riffraff" of the public housing ghettos, the Afrikan and Arab youth rose up.

The youth revolt took the form of burning thousands of cars, including police cars, and spread to other cities where poor Afrikan and Arab people are concentrated and oppressed, including in Germany and Belgium. These disempowered youth, like those in the Amerikan cities, have endured the humiliation of poverty, racism, and official oppression all their young lives. But inside there is a burning desire for liberation.

The mainstream imperialist media, as in all cases of such uprisings of the oppressed, have attempted to conceal, misrepresent and minimalize the real causes of the uprising and vilify the participants. The same demonizations were used to discredit the urban Black uprisings that swept across the U.S. from 1964 to 1968 in response to poverty, racism and police brutality. In the wake of the 1960s rebellions, multitudes of government-funded studies were conducted which demonized our people and proposed to respond with a war against youth of color under which the prison-industrial complex was born as a mechanism to "restore order" and deplete and contain the Black Nation within Amerika.

As H.R. Haldeman, Nixon's top aide, noted in 1969 in his now published diary: "Nixon emphasized that you have to face the fact that the problem is really the blacks. The key is to devise a system that recognizes this while not appearing to."

However, white riots against Blacks in Amerika have never been depicted as depraved in the same way that Black riots against racist oppression and systematic—indeed government sanctioned—discrimination, repression and abuse have been. In fact, government and police officials often incited and participated in these riots in which Black communities were overrun by rampaging mobs of armed whites who indiscriminately beat up, maimed and killed innocent Black men, wimyn and children, such as the 1863 NYC Draft Riot, the New York Riot of 1900, the 26 white riots that occurred during the "Red Summer" of 1919, and the innumerable lynchings that took place throughout the 19th and most of the 20th centuries in Amerika.

Because the oppression and super-exploitation of people of color is the norm in the imperialist countries, and the youth are particularly targeted for police repression, we must recognize the need for intercommunal (multi-ethnic) and Pan-Afrikan unity to resist this oppression and to struggle to put an end to the imperialist (monopoly capitalist) system and replace it with People's Power.

The New Afrikan Black Panther Party-Prison Chapter (NABPP-PC) supports the righteous rebellion of the Afrikan and Arab youth in Europe against their oppression, and we call upon them to do more than vent their anger. We call upon them to form mass organizations to serve their people and defend their communities and to take up the principles of "Pantherism" to form a vanguard party to lead their struggle and link it to that of the New Afrikan and oppressed people of color around the world.

We understand that monopoly capitalism, which thrives upon the super-exploitation of Third World people, both inside the imperialist countries and the neo-colonial countries of the Third World, cannot meet the needs or provide for the security of our people. We must do this ourselves by creating community-based People's Power. We must organize ourselves and link our struggles with those of the advanced detachments of the international proletariat IN ALL COUNTRIES to form a revolutionary United Front Against Imperialism.

*Dare to Struggle, Dare to Win!*
*All Power to the People!*

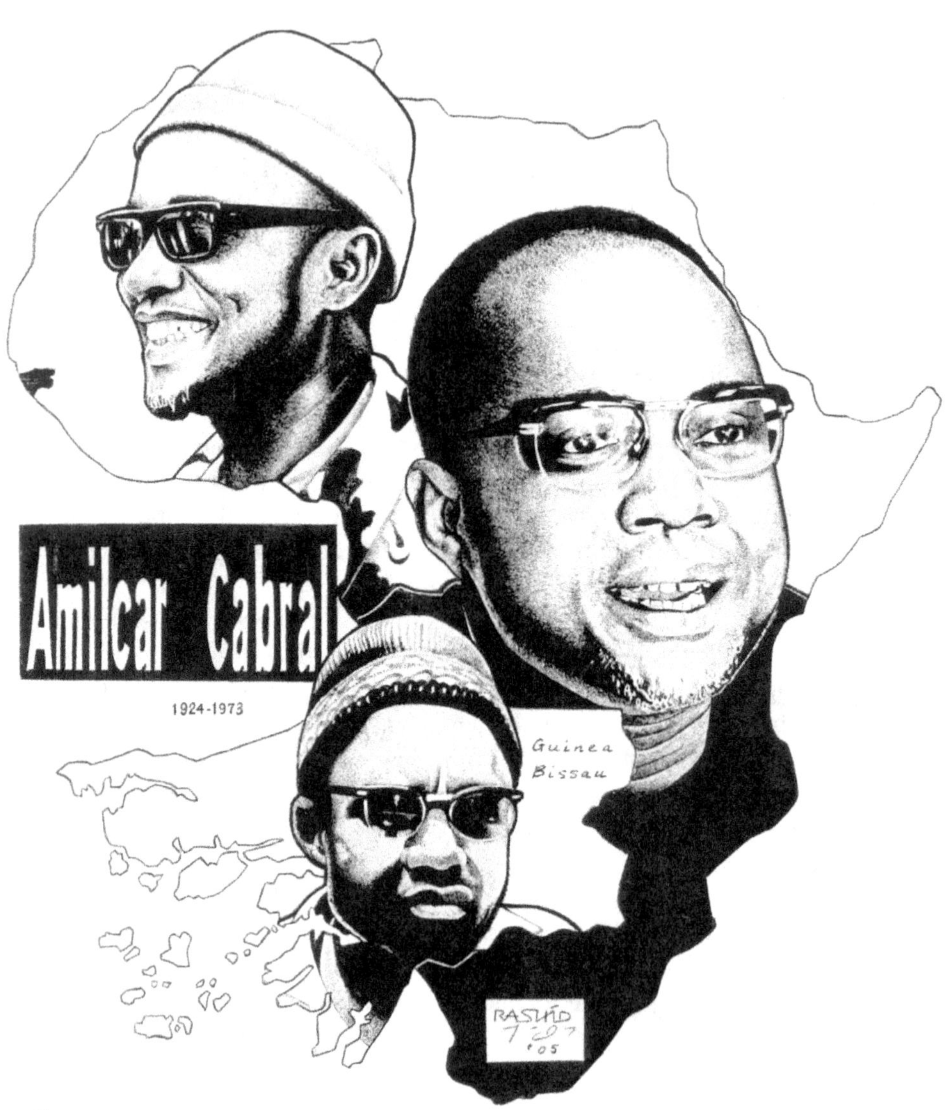


"By far the sharpest fighting ideologue
in Portugese Africa - and indeed in the
whole continent - is Amilcar Cabral...."
John Gerassi

# 27. PERSPECTIVES ON COMRADE AMILCAR CABRAL: AFRIKAN REVOLUTIONARY EXTRAORDINAIRE 2005

Comrade Amilcar Cabral led one of the most successful Afrikan national independence struggles of the 20th Century, in Guinea-Bissau and the Cape Verde Islands. Cabral was Afrika's foremost revolutionary theorist and practitioner of his time. In my opinion, his contributions to the question of national and colonial liberation rank him with such renowned revolutionary thinkers as V.I. Lenin, Mao Tse-tung, Frantz Fanon and Che Guevara.

One of Cabral's greatest strengths was his recognition that while valuable lessons can be learned from other's struggles, each movement must develop and apply methods suited specifically to their material conditions and people. Cabral was able to make a clear and correct analysis of his country's objective conditions and organize appropriate and successful resistance to Portuguese colonial rule based upon this analysis.

Cabral organized and led the African Independence Party of Guinea and the Cape Verde Islands (PAIGC), which was formed in 1956 to resist the brutal colonial occupation by the Portuguese. Cabral followed a plan that advanced in three-year increments. He committed the first three years to the internal organization of the PAIGC (1956–59), the next three years to educating and organizing the masses for waging armed struggle (1959–62), and then waging revolutionary war until independence, which was won in 1974.

Cabral understood that the working class was the only class capable of leading all the way revolution and not settling for a new accommodation with the imperialists that puts black faces in high places but left the masses poor and exploited. He recognized that all power and control had to be placed with the working masses.

Recognizing that his country had virtually no industrial proletariat, he saw that the intellectuals leading the PAIGC, such as himself, must cultivate a working-class outlook and proletarian consciousness to lead the struggle.

By 1969, the PAIGC had liberated two-thirds of Guinea-Bissau and begun educating the 98% illiterate population that had long been oppressed by Portuguese colonialism. Armed by the United States, the Portuguese Army launched repeated military assaults that were repulsed by the fighters of the PAIGC.

The imperialists concentrated more firepower and military manpower against the Guineans than the Vietnamese. But all the government controlled was a few fortified cities.

During his last visit to the U.S. (1972), Cabral called an informal meeting with various leaders of the Black organizations here, and he extended the support and familial bond of solidarity of the people of Guinea-Bissau. He encouraged Amerikan Blacks to come visit in his country, to learn from their struggle, but to keep in mind that we must make our revolution in Amerika based upon the concrete conditions that are here.

Cabral struggled unceasingly to prevent the armed struggle from degenerating into racial or tribal war, as happened elsewhere in Afrika with the sponsorship of the colonists and imperialists. He also made it clear that his fight was not with the people of Portugal.

"We do not confuse exploitation or exploiters with the color of people's skin," Cabral stated in March, 1968, at the release of several Portuguese prisoners of war; "we do not want any exploitation in our countries, not even by Black people."

"We are not fighting against the Portuguese people, against individual Portuguese or Portuguese families ... we have been forced to take up arms in order to extirpate from the soil of our African fatherland, the shameful Portuguese colonial domination."

Unfortunately, shortly after his visit to the U.S., Amilcar Cabral was assassinated by Portuguese secret agents who had infiltrated the PAIGC. They incited anti-white and anti-mulatto hatred against Cabral, who was half Black and half Portuguese. Upon his death, his brother, Louis, took over leadership, and the struggle continued to surge forward. In April of 1974, a revolutionary coup brought down the government in Portugal and ended the occupation of Guinea-Bissau and the Cape Verde Islands.

But the greatest struggles came after liberation, when the people had to struggle to keep the initiative in their hands and smash all remnants of elitism and colonial rule. Shortly before his death, Cabral stated that accomplishing this, "was the most important problem in the liberation movement." He observed that, "the nature of the state created after independence is perhaps the secret of the failure of African independence."

Under the PAIGC, led by Louis Cabral, the country made several substantial gains in economic and political development. However, in 1980, Louis was driven into exile in Cuba, and he was replaced by the former PAIGC guerrilla commander and minister of defense, Joao Vieira, who played the "race card" against Louis Cabral, promoting Black racialism.

Instead of the PAIGC commanding the gun, the gun came to command PAIGC leading to privilege, corruption and arbitrary rule by a new elite. Amilcar Cabral called for Power to the People and for the people to "return to the source" of their tribal cooperative heritage.

*Dare to Struggle, Dare to Win! All Power to the People!*

# 28. THE REAL FACE OF U.S. CAPITAL PUNISHMENT 2006

## An Appeal on Behalf of Comrade Hasan Shakur and All Death Row Inmates

When Amerika's ruling elite wish to rationalize their violent schemes against other nations, (predominantly those of people of color), they manipulate and then cite "world opinion" as supporting their positions. By "world opinion," they generally mean the opinion of the rulers of other imperialist countries. They never consider the opinions of the REAL WORLD, which includes the people of color and the poor and working people generally, (who end up as the victims of their violent schemes), nor even of the Amerikan people as a whole.

This is because their intentions are typically self-serving and exploitative. In truest fascist form, the U.S. and European-based multinational corporations, which are the source of their wealth and power, serve only their interests, and the same is true of the political parties and governments they control.

Oddly however, when it comes to capital punishment, which is the most irrational form of state violence, they ignore the opinion of their European brethren who have long since abolished the practice. For many years now, the U.S. has been cited and criticized for violating international treaties and norms by continuing with this barbaric form of punishment.

That it is meted out predominantly and discriminatorily against people of color cannot be concealed, and it exposes the real white supremacist and racist core values behind the facade of democratic and multiculturist propaganda the U.S. rulers promote to the world and claim to represent. Actions speak louder than words.

On Human Rights Day 2005, The European Union issued a formal declaration asking Amerika's rulers to end capital punishment. With what our rulers consider to be "world opinion" ringing in their ears, and opposing capital punishment, one must wonder—why then does the Amerikan ruling class persist with this practice? It can only be explained in the context of the racial practices and policies that have always been at the core of Amerikan politics and social control.

European societies are particularly sensitized to institutionalized state killing of their own citizens due to the not so distant experience of Nazi and overt fascist rule and its continuing reminders. The "ethnic cleansing" of Jews, Gypsies, Poles, Slavs and others prior to and during World War II, and the more recent "ethnic cleansing" in the former

Yugoslavia, were carried out by white people against white people. And this struck close to home.

However, European and Euro-Amerikan imperialism was built upon genocidal practices and enslavement of indigenous people of color from Afrika to the Amerikas and Asia, and the massive wealth accumulated by the ruling elites of the imperialist countries is the basis of their power and their ability to continue to exploit the majority of the people of the world and steal their national resources. They have no qualms about murder on a grand scale of either white or people of color as exemplified by the imperialist wars they have caused and continue to perpetuate.

In Europe, the killing of white-skinned people was recognized as "genocide." In Amerika, which was founded on genocide, the killing of dark-skinned people is, as Comrade Imam Jamil Al-Amin (H. Rap Brown) once put it, "... as Amerikan as cherry pie!"

As Dhoruba Bin Wahad stated in his recent comments on the execution of Stanley "Tookie" Williams in California: "The death penalty in Amerika has always operated as a legal instrument of racial terror. The death penalty evolved from, and assumed the psychological role of lynching. Lest we forget, every Black man lynched was 'guilty of a crime'! ... [T]here is not one legal or 'Constitutional' right Afrikan people have in Amerika that white folks don't have the veto over, or not subject to judicial review, including the right to life. A Black man's life is subject to termination by a cop or agent of the state at any given moment—without recourse to appeal."

So in reality, all of us in Amerika who wear dark skins entered into this life with a state-imposed death sentence. The U.S. Declaration of Independence declares that the enjoyment of life is an inalienable right, but poor people of color were not included within that body of "We The People" on whose behalf that founding document was written—and we still aren't today. Therefore, we remain targets of oppression, repression and genocide. This is the design of the U.S. ruling class, and they could care less about "world opinion" regarding the death penalty.

In Texas—where they legally murdered Comrade Shaka Sankofa—Amerika's Kapital Punishment Kapital—our New Afrikan Black Panther Party-Prison Chapter's Minister of Human Rights has been scheduled to die on April 27. Hasan Shakur is a comrade who even before being recruited into our Party has struggled tirelessly over the years to bring a voice to the oppressed millions of poor and people of color locked away in cages in Amerika, and he has championed the humyn rights of the thousands sentenced to die by "legal execution."

Hasan Shakur (s/n Derrick Frazier) is not guilty of murdering anyone. The cops who arrested him, denied him his right to legal counsel and coerced a false confession from him, knew that. The judge who allowed this illegal "evidence" to be used against him in court, knew that. The all white jury who heard the case had to know it. And the appeals courts who upheld his illegal conviction based solely on this illegal "evidence" definitely know it.

The point being that racial terror and tradition demands that two Black men must die, even if one is innocent, for the murder of two white people in rural Texas. This is the logic of lynching. It is as Amerikan as cherry pie! Since we are deemed to have no rights, (really). We were born guilty. Therefore we're already sentenced to be marginalized, exploited and condemned in a thousand ways. So there is no appeal (really).

Nonetheless, we must continue to resist and struggle for liberation, for Comrade Hasan, for all the condemned, for ourselves and future generations! We salute you Comrade! All Power to the People!

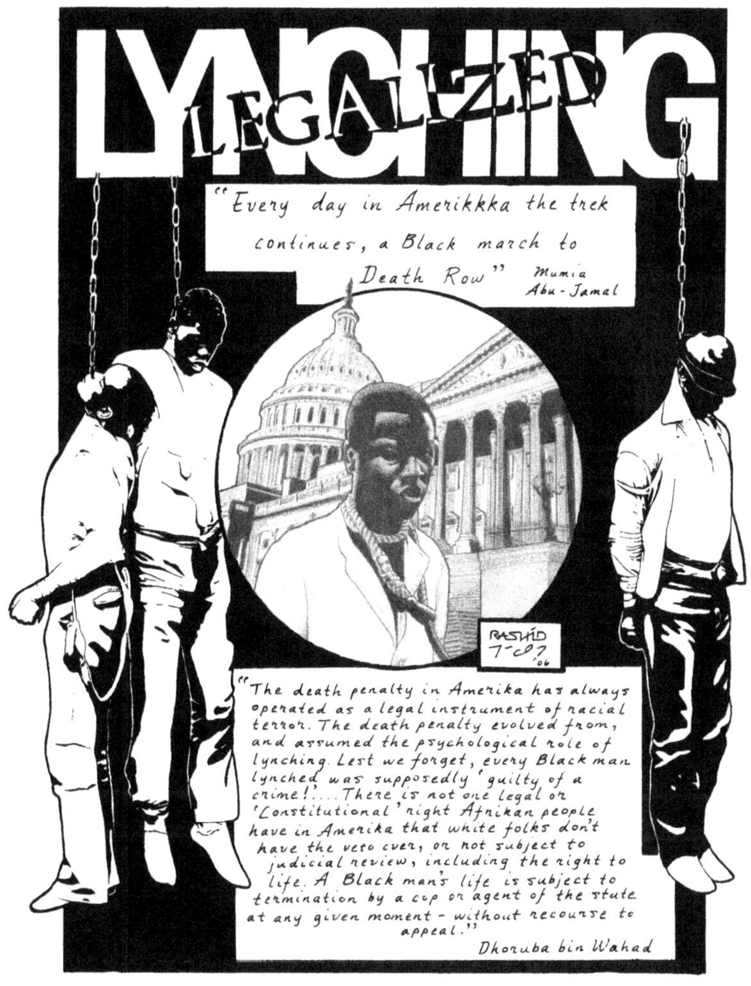

# 29. IN MEMORY OF OUR SLAIN COMRADE HASAN SHAKUR 2006

> "Know that I stood committed to not only die for the people but to live for them as well, for that is the real challenge!"
>
> March 2, 2006, letter from Hasan Shakur to the author

Following the founding of the New Afrikan Black Panther Party-Prison Chapter (NABPP-PC), [formerly the New Black Panther Party-Prison Chapter (NBPP-PC)], in July 2005, Comrade Hasan Shakur was recommended to us, and was quickly recruited as the 3rd member of our Central Committee. Hasan had demonstrated through various initiatives he'd headed, despite facing a sentence of death, his dedicated work in service to the people. He was appointed to be our Minister of Human Rights.

Hasan brought his infectious energy and commitment into the Party and immediately set to work developing the Party and its work. He did this as if he was totally unfazed by designs to take his life within weeks or months. Although this reality seemed not to burden Hasan, it had a definite effect on me. As a persyn conditioned to action and made very uncomfortable with being unable to help a friend and comrade in need, I'd expressed in one of my last letters to Hasan my frustration in knowing that the very same forces that have prematurely destroyed so many promising Black lives were devising to take his life, while I could take no decisive action to help him or to stop them.

Hasan assured me that I had not failed him. He stated in reply:

> "We all have a certain level of limitation. We can attempt to surpass it, but there will be boundaries in place that we just cannot surpass. But what we must do is turn that frustration into fuel—fuel that will be used to push you in several other areas. I have a problem with patience. Yet, I must refocus that extra energy to push other agendas, like building bridges, building the Party, and building the Human Rights Ministry as well.
>
> "Do me a favor. Hold your hand—right hand—out with fingers extended. Your individual fingers aren't very effective weapons for punching through obstacles are they? Now, when I call out a letter, drop a finger, starting with your pinky. 'P!—O!—W!—E!—R! What have you got? Now punch through that adversity and continue to lead by example!"

Comrade Hasan's level of intelligent fortitude in the face of death reflects a conviction that only a revolutionary awakening brings. It reflects a firm love-inspired confidence in the cause he lived for and the masses of people he sought to serve and lead by example. On this point he wrote to me:

> "Brotha, a true servant of the people NEVER forgets his/her role, even in times of need and despair. For me it is natural. I do what I do 'cause I have a sincere love for what I do. I have faith in self, the Creator, and no doubt, my People! Therefore, my blessings will became the People's blessings as well. You should see the brothas I have had DIRECT influence on—they have the same personality!"

Hasan clearly led by example. And it was his ability to reproduce his own revolutionary fervor in others that tipped the scales of reaction against preserving his life a moment longer. Despite admitted fundamental errors in the proceedings that landed him on death row, the courts refused him the usually granted delay in execution, and the racist, fascist death machine in Texas murdered him on Black August 31st, 2006.

Hasan stood as a shining example that struggle on the road to revolution can awaken, redeem, heal and transform people. Especially those people whom the Establishment claims are unredeemable and beyond healing. He was a living contradiction of this decadent and rotten capitalist system, a cancerous, gangster system that breeds sicknesses which it makes no attempt to cure—because it cannot! Only a revolutionary remolding of our values away from being property-centered and toward becoming people-centered, and struggling to develop similar values within the broad masses can effect the necessary healing process.

This is a process that the imperialists cannot tolerate. For imperialism to reign, the people must be kept divided by fear, hatred and suspicion. Because if they unite and become a common force recognizing the common cause of their poverty and oppression, the common source of their alienation and division, as being a predatory, greed-driven minority; and they realize that through their united action they can liberate themselves from this ruling elite class, then people's power will reign supreme.

It is because of this reality that the imperialist capitalist class recognizes that people who love people above property and profit constitute a threat to their empire. People who struggle to uproot racism and national oppression, sexism, poverty and inequality and every form of oppression generated by the imperialist capitalist system are bad for business. Comrade Hasan embodied the true spirit of anti-imperialism and the highest aspirations of the New Afrikan Liberation Movement.

Hasan was the third member of our Central Committee, our first recruit and first martyr. Just as Lil' Bobby Hutton, who was murdered by police on April 6th, 1968, was the first recruit and first martyr of the original Black Panther Party. Lil' Bobby's sacrifice inspired many more recruits to step forward to join the Party and became an impetus and inspiration to the work of the original BPP. So too will Hasan's sacrifice and memory inspire our New Afrikan Black Panther Party and push our work forward.

The forces of reaction can kill a revolutionary—but they can't kill the revolution. They can imprison our bodies—but they can't imprison our spirit. They can't take away our love for our Comrade and the Panther Love he gave to us! The Struggle continues! Panther Love to the memory and example of Comrade Hasan Shakur! Let 1,000 fighters arise to fill his place!

*ALL POWER TO THE PEOPLE!*

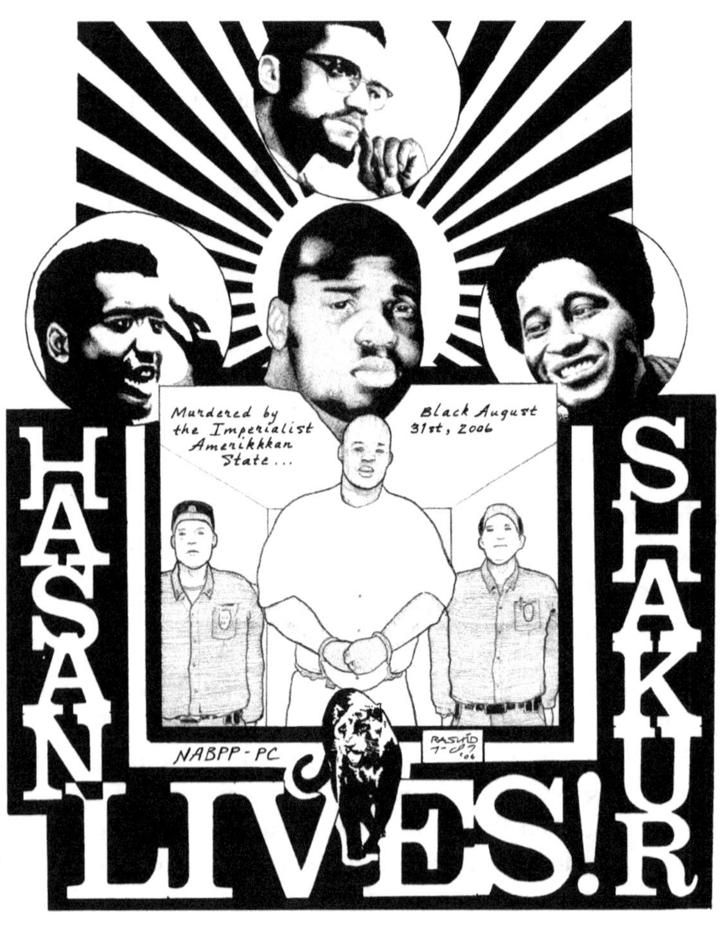

# 30. PROTECT OUR LEADERS, DEFEND OUR PEOPLE! 2007

On January 23, 2007, nine men were charged in what is being called a campaign of "chaos and terror" that saw at least three police killed from 1968 to 1973. Emphasis is being placed on official claims that most of these men were members of the Black Liberation Army (BLA) when the police killings occurred. Eight of them were charged with the August 29, 1971, shotgun slaying of San Francisco police sergeant, John Young.

Is it coincidence that the killings of a handful of police over 30 years ago have suddenly become a major concern to the Establishment? Whereas, typical of this very same Establishment is a blatant disinterest in pursuing and prosecuting the legions of police (state and federal) who've wantonly murdered multitudes of New Afrikans across Amerika from that time period till today. Indeed, during those same years of targeted BLA activities (1968–1973), the U.S. government, in collaboration with local "law enforcement" agencies, was involved in the murders of prominent Black political leaders like Martin Luther King, Jr. (1968), Fred Hampton and Mark Clark (1969), George Jackson (1971), and others. In each of these cases, the government's role in orchestrating, executing and covering up these assassinations has been exposed with unimpeachable proof. I'll elaborate later.

In fact it was in response to this climate of raw fear, violence and murder of Blacks, that the BLA arose as a defensive arm of the New Afrikan communities. The BLA warriors had summed up from our historical experiences at the hands of slave patrols, vigilantes, lynch mobs and police that the official "enforcers" of the law could not be looked to for protection of Black lives. Instead, they were, for us, a principal source of violence, death and terror. Many of the BLA's members were victims of such official violence and assassination attempts, often carried out as part of government efforts to destroy the Black Panther Party (BPP), which arose in 1966 to serve our poor, urban communities in areas of survival and basic needs that the Establishment could not and would not.

During that era, there was little "sugar-coating" the raw terror suffered by communities of color living under police occupation, and especially prominent was the open police violence displayed against leading political organizations like the Black Panther Party (BPP), who struggled to serve these communities. John Gerassi, a white journalist and author who lived in that era, witnessed this reality with his own eyes:

> "[R]epression in the United States is worse than ever before and much, much harsher than the world—or most Americans, for that matter—is aware or told. In New Mexico, for example, the Alianza, led by Reies Tijerina, has been hounded relentlessly since 1966; its offices have been dynamited (by policemen at that), its leaders shot, its members jailed on such flagrantly outrageous charges that few Americans would believe—even today—the strictly factual story. At the time of writing, Tijerina himself was locked up for years and his Alianza was flagging. As for the Blacks, their repression is not less brutal, just more widespread. The whole primary and secondary leadership of the Black Panther Party has been jailed on obvious frame-ups. They have been beaten, tortured and murdered. Twice in Oakland, I saw with my own eyes, policemen in official cars zoom by a group of Panthers talking peacefully on a street and open fire at them. Three times I witnessed policemen arrest Panthers, handcuff them, and then pistol-whip them. In over a dozen cases, after seeing Panthers arrested, I have gone to see them in jail and found them bloodied from having 'fallen down the stairs' or from having 'assaulted a policeman.' And the whole world knows—for this time it was reported in the press—that on-duty Chicago policemen murdered Panthers Fred Hampton and Mark Clark in their sleep. By the end of 1969, not a single policeman had been brought to justice for these acts of violence. On the other hand, all of white America's law enforcement agents, including federal marshals and the FBI, have gone out of their way—and, often, out of their jurisdiction—to arrest Panthers, without having warrants. Federal marshals have even refused to honor a court order not to remove Chairman Bobby Seale from California (which, legally, made the marshals kidnappers). By 1970, twenty-eight Black Panthers had been murdered by the police, some beaten to death after arrest (Charles Cox in Chicago), some in unprovoked police assaults, (seventeen-year-old Bobby Hutton in Oakland, Hampton and Clark in Chicago), most in front of scores of witnesses, who could never testify, as the policemen were never charged. It is little wonder, then, that the Browns and Blacks consider themselves colonized and imperialized, part of the same dominated world as Latin Americans, the Vietnamese, and the Congolese."
>
> John Gerassi, *The Coming of the New International: A Revolutionary Anthology* (NY: World Publishing Co., 1971)

The BPP's deadly experiences were also witnessed by the New Afrikan communities, and reported first hand by the Party itself. These experiences served to solidify the communities, raise the consciousness of Black people, and expose the true function of the police as violent oppressors of the poor and protectors of the wealthy ruling class. In the Harris Survey Yearbook of Public Opinion (1970), it was found that 66% of Blacks took pride in the BPP and its strong example in supporting Blacks' basic rights and needs. But more telling is that 86% of Blacks in that survey answered "yes" to the question: "Even if you disagree with the views of the Panthers, has the violence against them led you to believe that Black people must stand together to protect themselves?" So there was an overwhelming consensus in the Black communities that Blacks must unite to resist violent police oppression. It was during the very same year that the Harris Survey was taken, that many of the most trusted and committed BPP members were pushed out of the Party and went underground to join the BLA.

Every honest witness to and participant of that period acknowledges that the BLA was forced into existence in response to the brutal police murders and attacks on Black political organizations, leaders, and everyday people. But today, after decades of the corporate entertainment media's romanticizing the roles of police, the image of these occupying forces has been given something of a face-lift to all except the youth of urban communities of color, who still see the same oppressive face of policemen as did our communities of the 1960s and '70s. As Comrade Sundiata Acoli has pointed out, this ongoing media effort to clean up the police image was a product of the BPP's exposing to New Afrikans across Amerika the real face of our occupiers:

> "One singular indication, although there are others, of the effectiveness of BPP propaganda techniques is that even today, over a decade later, a large part of the programs shown on TV are still 'police stories' and many of the roles available to Black actors are limited to police roles. A lot of this has to do with the overall process of still trying to rehabilitate the image of police from its devastating exposure during the Panthers era, and to prevent the true role of the police in this society from being exposed again."
>
> Sundiata Acoli, *A Brief History of the Black Panther Party and its Place in the Black Liberation Movement*

But let me return to my original question, whether the recent charges against those nine men are coincidence. I think not. First, let's consider the timing, which is interesting.

Only once a year is there an official commemoration of any Black personality in Amerika. That would be January 21st, Martin Luther King's birthday. Those charges were issued two days after the King holiday. Then, there's only one time of year that Black history is even acknowledged in Amerika—although not "officially" recognized. That would be Black History Month. The charges issued just a week before the commencement of Black History Month. Hmmm ...

In the context of Black History Month, no honest account of Amerika can avoid the fact that ours has been a history of continued suffering and resistance. And the Amerikan Establishment has been both at the root of our suffering and a fierce opponent of our resistance. The latter is demonstrated in its trumping up charges nearly 40 years old to vilify the BLA and its symbol of resistance against brutal national oppression of New Afrikans. This is political persecution plain and simple.

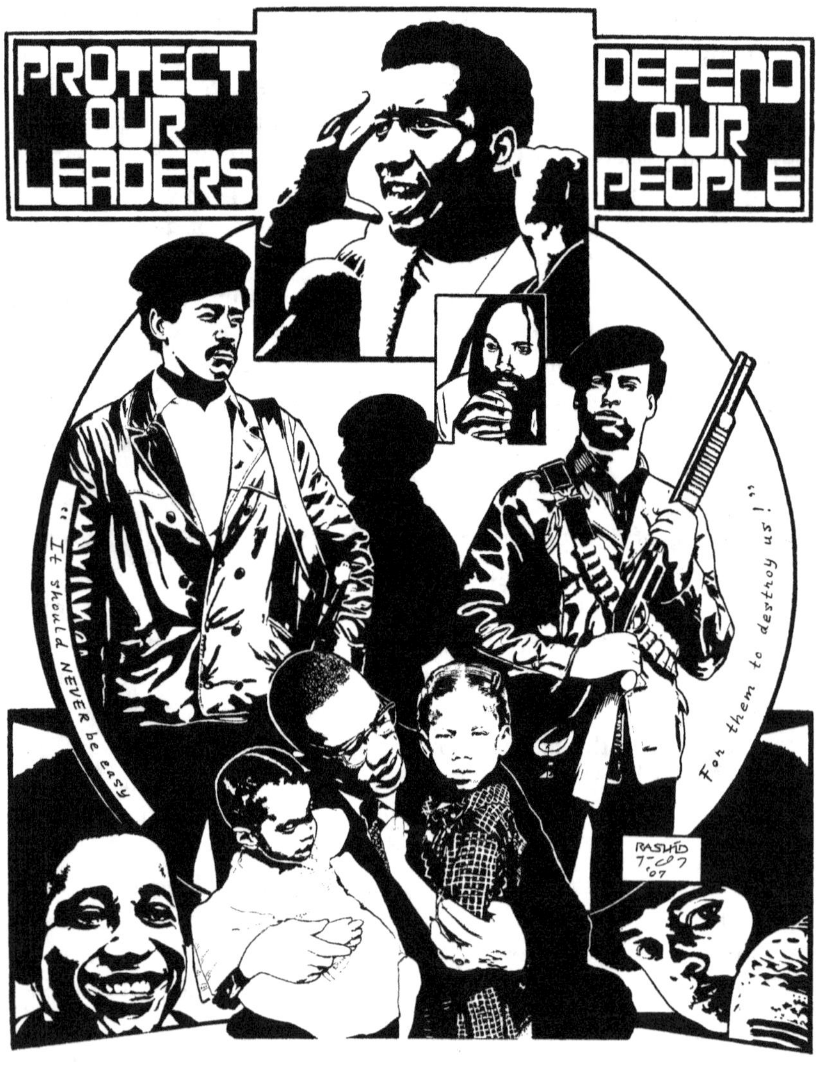

And what of Martin Luther King? Our brotha who was also murdered by government forces, the very same government that was venomously opposed to making his birthday a national holiday. These facts are now beyond dispute, although the mainstream media refuses to report them. Like the BPP, King was a target of the vicious government covert action program called COINTELPRO (the FBI's Counter Intelligence Program). This program, as described in an internal FBI memorandum dated August 25, 1967, was calculated:

> "... to expose, disrupt, misdirect, discredit, or otherwise neutralize the activities of black nationalist, hate-type organizations and groupings, their leadership, spokesmen, membership, and supporters, and to counter their propensity for violence and civil disorder.
>
> "The pernicious background of such groups, their duplicity, and such publicity will have a neutralizing effect. Efforts of the various groups to consolidate their forces or to recruit new or youthful adherents must be frustrated. No opportunity should be missed to exploit through counterintelligence techniques the organizational and personal conflicts of the leadership of the groups and where possible an effort should be made to capitalize upon existing conflicts between competing black nationalist organizations. When an opportunity is apparent to disrupt or neutralize black nationalist, hate-type organizations through the cooperation of established local news media contacts or through such contact with sources available to the Seat of Government, in every instance careful attention must be given to the proposal to insure the targeted group is disrupted, ridiculed, or discredited through the publicity and not merely publicized.
>
> "Intensified attention under this program should be afforded to the activities of such groups as the Student Nonviolent Coordinating Committee, the Southern Christian Leadership Conference, Revolutionary Action Movement, the Deacons for Defense and Justice, Congress of Racial Equality, and the Nation of Islam. Particular emphasis should be given to extremists who direct the activities and policies of revolutionary or militant groups such as Stokley Carmichael, H. 'Rap' Brown, Elijah Muhammad, and Maxwell Stanford."

Another internal FBI memorandum dated March 9, 1968, made clear the Bureau's meaning and intentions in proposing to "neutralize" those who promoted fundamental changes in the living conditions of the poor and oppressed nationalities. It urged that, "the Negro youths and moderates must be made to understand that if they succumb to revolutionary teaching, they will be dead revolutionaries."

Before his assassination, King was a major target of subversion at the hands of the FBI and other U.S. intelligence agencies, including Military Intelligence Groups. FBI memoranda show orders given to "neutralize" King as late as one month before his death. A lengthy discussion of some of the many illegal actions against King can be found in the Church Committee's Congressional Report of 1976, entitled *Intelligence Activities and the Rights of Americans*, Books II and III, especially Book III, pp. 79–184. The report points out that:

> "[T]he 'neutralization' program continued until Dr. King's death. As late as March 1968, FBI agents were being instructed to neutralize Dr. King because he might become a 'messiah' who could 'unify, and electrify the militant black nationalist movement, if he were to abandon his supposed "obedience" to "white liberal doctrines" (nonviolence) and embrace black nationalism.' Steps were taken to subvert the 'Poor People's Campaign' which, Dr. King was planning to lead in the spring of 1968. Even after King's death, agents in the field were proposing methods for harassing his widow, and Bureau officials were trying to prevent his birthday from becoming a national holiday."

King was indeed questioning his earlier assumptions and moving towards a more radical perspective:

> "By 1964, King was not only firmly established as a preeminent civil rights leader, but was beginning to show signs of pursuing a more fundamental structural agenda of social change. Correspondingly ... the [FBI]'s intent had crystallized into an unvarnished intervention into the domestic political process, with the goal of bringing about King's replacement with someone 'acceptable' to the FBI."
>
> Ward Churchill, et al., *The COINTELPRO Papers: Documents from the FBI's Secret Wars Against Dissent in the United States* (Boston: South End, 1990), p. 97

Military surveillance of King began far earlier than the FBI operations against him:

> "The government's interest in Dr. King went considerably beyond 'snooping,' however, to constitute one of the most prolonged surveillances of any family in American history. In the early years of

the [20th] century, Lieut. Col. Ralph Van Deman created an Army Intelligence network targeting four prime foes: the Industrial Workers of the World, opponents of the draft, Socialists and 'Negro unrest.' ... Van Deman was much preoccupied with the role of black churches as possible centers of sedition.

"By the end of 1917, the War Department's Military Intelligence Division had opened a file on Martin Luther King, Jr.'s maternal grandfather, the Rev. A.D. Williams, pastor of Ebenezer Baptist Church and first president of the Atlanta NAACP. King's father, Martin Sr., Williams' successor at Ebenezer Baptist, also entered the army files. Martin Jr. first shows up in these files, (kept by the 111th Military Intelligence Group at Fort McPherson in Atlanta), in 1947, when he attended Dorothy Lilley's Intercollegiate school; the army suspected Lilley of having ties to the Communist Party.

"Army intelligence officers became convinced of Martin Luther King, Jr.'s own Communist ties when he spoke in 1950 at the 25th anniversary of the integrated Highlander Folk School in Monteagle, Tennessee. Ten years earlier, an army intelligence officer had reported to his superiors that the Highlander school was teaching a course of instruction to develop Negro organizers in the Southern cotton states.

"By 1963, so Tennessee journalist Stephen Tompkins reported in the Memphis *Commercial Appeal*, U-2 planes were photographing disturbances in Birmingham, Alabama, capping a multilayered spy system that by 1968 included 304 intelligence offices across the country, 'subversive national security dossiers' on 80,731 Americans, plus 19 million personal dossiers lodged at the Defense Department's Central Index of Investigations.

"A more sinister thread derives from the anger and fear with which the army high command greeted King's denunciation of the Vietnam War at Riverside Church in 1967. Army spies recorded Stokely Carmichael telling King, 'the man don't care you call ghettoes concentration camps, but when you tell him his war machine is nothing but hired killers you got trouble.'

"After the 1967 Detroit riots, 496 black men under arrest were interviewed by agents of the army's psychological operations group, dressed as civilians. It turned out King was by far the most popular black leader. That same year Maj. Gen William Yarborough, assistant chief of staff for intelligence, observing the great antiwar march on Washington from the roof of the Pentagon, concluded that the empire was coming apart at the seams. There were,

Yarborough reckoned, too few reliable troops to fight in Vietnam and hold the line at home.

"In response, the army increased its surveillance of King. Green Berets and other Special Forces veterans from Vietnam began making street maps and identifying landing zones and potential sniper sites in major U.S. cities. The Ku Klux Klan was recruited by the 20th Special Forces Group, headquartered in Alabama as a subsidiary intelligence network. The army began offering 30.06 sniper rifles to police departments, including that of Memphis.

"In his fine investigation, Tompkins detailed the increasing hysteria of Army Intelligence chiefs over the threat they considered King to pose to national security. The FBI's J. Edgar Hoover was similarly obsessed, and King was dogged by spy units through early 1967. A Green Beret special unit was operating in Memphis on the day he was shot. He died from a bullet from a 30.06 rifle purchased in a Memphis store, a murder for which James Earl Ray was given a 99-year sentence in a Tennessee prison. A court-ordered test of James Earl Ray's rifle raised questions whether it in fact had fired the bullet that killed King."

Alexander Cockburn et al.,
*Whiteout: The CIA, Drugs and the Press* (NY: Verso, 1999)

But more revealing of the government's role in King's murder are the findings of attorney William F. Pepper, based on his 25-year extensive investigation of King's death and the government cover-ups that followed. His findings and the results of a wrongful death lawsuit he filed and won in 1999 on behalf of the King family concerning Martin Luther King, Jr.'s assassination are exhaustively reported in his 2003 book *An Act of State: The Execution of Martin Luther King.* King's wife, the late Coretta Scott King, had this to say about Pepper's book:

"For a quarter of a century, Bill Pepper conducted an independent investigation of the assassination of Martin Luther King, Jr. He opened his files to our family, encouraged us to speak with the witnesses and represented our family in the civil trial against the conspirators. The jury affirmed his findings, providing our family with a long-sought sense of closure and peace, which had been denied by official disinformation and cover-ups. Now the findings of his exhaustive investigation and additional revelations from the trial are presented in the pages of this important book. We recommend it highly to everyone who seeks the truth about Dr. King's assassination."

From the jacket of the book comes this summary of its contents:

"On the evening of April 4, 1968, Martin Luther King was in Memphis supporting a worker's strike. By the end of the day, top-level army snipers were in position to knock him out if ordered. Two military officers were in place on the roof of a fire station near the Lorraine Motel, to photograph the events. Two black firemen had been ordered not to report to duty that day and a black Memphis Police Department detective on surveillance duty in the fire station was physically removed from his post and taken home. Dr. King's room at the motel was changed from a secluded, ground-floor room to number 306 on the balcony. Lloyd Jowers, owner of Jim's Grill, which backed onto the motel from the other side of the street had already received $100,000 in cash for his agreement to participate in the assassination. He was to go out into the brush area behind the grill with the shooter and take possession of the gun immediately after the fatal shot was fired. When the dust settled, King had been hit, and a clean-up procedure was immediately set in motion. James Earl Ray was effectively framed, the snipers dispersed, and witnesses who could not be controlled were killed, and the crime scene was destroyed.

"William Pepper, attorney and friend of Dr. King and the King family, became convinced after years of investigation that not only was Ray not the shooter, but that King had been targeted as part of a larger conspiracy to stop the anti-war movement, and to prevent King from gaining momentum in his promising Poor People's Campaign. Ten years into his investigation, in 1988, Pepper agreed to represent Ray. While he was never able to successfully appeal the sentence before Ray's death, he was able to build an airtight case against the real perpetrators. In 1999, Lloyd Jowers and co-conspirators were brought to trial in a wrongful death civil action suit on behalf of the King family. Seventy witnesses set out the details of a conspiracy in a plot to murder King that involved J. Edgar Hoover and the FBI, Richard Helms and the CIA, the military, the local Memphis police, and organized crime figures from New Orleans and Memphis. The evidence was unimpeachable. The jury took an hour to find for the King family. But the silence following these shocking revelations was deafening. Like the pattern during all the investigations of the assassination throughout the years, no major media outlet would cover the story. It was effectively buried.

"Until now, the details, evidence, and personalities of all these nefarious characters have gone unreported. In *An Act of State*, you

> finally have the truth before you—how the United States government effectively shut down one of the most galvanizing movements for social change by stopping its leader dead in his tracks."

The very government that is concerned today with prosecuting the killings of a few anonymous policemen, is the same one that continues to effectively whitewash its own role in the assassination of one of Amerika's most well known Black political and religious leaders, and whose memory it pretends to respect and promote. But the sad irony and bitter contradiction in the entire King affair is toward the end of his life, King acknowledged that, "the greatest purveyor of violence on earth is my own government." Yet, while denouncing Black self-defense such as that symbolized by the efforts of the BLA, he looked to the very same violent government—indeed the very government that killed him—to defend him against its own violence. So, no, it is no coincidence that just as New Afrikans are commemorating and remembering the birthday of this slain Black civil rights leader and our rich history of struggle and resistance against institutionalized oppression, that the government has instituted show trial proceedings to vilify and persecute the example of New Afrikans who took courage in hand and rose to the challenge of defending us against the "greatest purveyor of violence" against people of color.

And what about the murders of Fred Hampton and Mark Clark in 1969? Hampton, the charismatic chairman of the Illinois chapter of the BPP and Mark Clark, Defense Captain of the Peoria Chapter of the BPP were both assassinated on December 4, 1969, by Chicago police in cooperation with the FBI. Both Comrades Hampton and Clark had been drugged by FBI agent provocateur and informant William O'Neal and were, as a result, asleep in bed when police shot them at point blank range. Both Illinois state Attorney General Edward Hanrahan and David Goth, the cop who led the raid, were exposed as having given false statements to the media about the raid. A civil suit was filed and won on behalf of the Hampton and Clark families, but none of the involved federal agents and police were ever punished. Yet, today the FBI is heading a witch-hunt against former BLA members.

And what about Comrade George L. Jackson, murdered by San Quentin prison guards in August 1971, which triggered prison uprisings around the country culminating in the Attica rebellion? The facts of the government plot to kill him are set out in the investigative study by Eric Mann in *Comrade George: An Investigation into the Official Story of His Assassination* (1972). Again no prosecutions are being pursued.

Then there's the tragedy of the MOVE family, whose Philadelphia, PA headquarters was bombed on May 13, 1985, by police, who also fired over 10,000 rounds into the MOVE house. As a result, six adults and five children were murdered. Those who attempted to flee the fire were shot at and only two MOVE members escaped the blaze. Again no police were charged or convicted, however, Ramona Africa, the only adult who survived the fire, was charged and convicted of riot and conspiracy, and was imprisoned for seven years. Upon her release she filed and won a lawsuit against the city of Philadelphia. But no amount of money recovered from litigation can replace the lives of our slain leaders and comrades.

The pattern is unmistakable ...

It has always been the case in Amerika, (since racial divisions were first created in the 1600s by the wealthy ruling class to divide poor white against poor Black, and to empower the whites to violently repress Blacks and other peoples of color), that the lives of poor Blacks have no value in the eyes of those who hold power. From the white slave

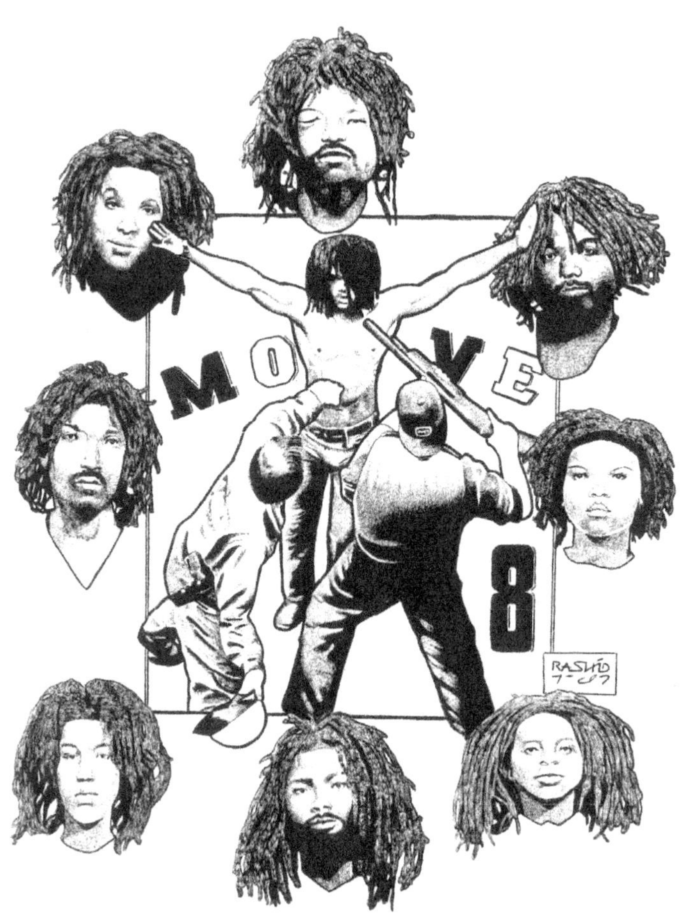

patrols, to the Klan, to the modern police and even military; deadly violence against the dark faces at the hands of the armed thugs of the ruling class is part and parcel of the U.S. social contract. However, counter-violence against the same forces in defense of the lives of their Black victims is unacceptable. Just as the routine rape of Black wimyn by white men in the South throughout U.S. history was the expected norm, against which Blacks were forbidden to resist. It took a nationwide campaign to win the acquittal of Joann Little who was charged with murder, for killing a white Washington, NC sheriff deputy in August 1974, who entered her jail cell and attempted to rape her at knife point.

This completely lopsided power dynamic and the resultant police violence and injustice against Black life, provoked most every major urban Black uprising in Amerika. Many of the major revolts of 1964 through 1968 were provoked by incidents of police violence against or murders of Blacks. Major uprisings followed the assassinations of Dr. King and Malcolm X.

Malcolm X was another of our leaders murdered with government complicity and even now the government refuses to release most of its over 50,000 pages of intelligence files on Malcolm. The 1991 uprisings in Los Angeles and other cities were incited by the videotaped brutal beatings of Black motorist Rodney King by police. The 2002 uprising in Benton Harbor, Michigan was triggered by the police killing of Black motorcyclist Terrance Shurn. The 2005 uprising in Toledo, Ohio was triggered by the earlier murder of a Black man by police electrocuting him nine times with a taser and the subsequent violent protection by police of a Nazi demonstration, and so on. The cycle repeats, the power imbalance continues, and Black self-defense is vilified and criminalized.

Many of us choose to ignore or forget, some of us simply don't know and most have been wooed by shows like *Cops, CSI, America's Most Wanted,* and so on, into denying the real role that the political police have played in and against the New Afrikan nation in Amerika. They have had a hand in persecuting all of our genuine leaders and in the murders of each one who's died a violent death; they've created and continue the infrastructural deterioration and internal implosion of our communities with narcotics infestations, and they've instigated armed violence amongst our youth. With minimal success, Black congressperson Maxine Waters has been trying for years, from within established channels, to expose and compel action against the CIA's role in creating and continuing the urban crack cocaine epidemic, and arming and instigating major armed gang violence beginning in the early 1980s; they're the enforcers of the genocidal policy of depopulating our communities, through arrests and imprisonments, of massive numbers of Black males, thereby undercutting our ability to reproduce, and removing Black fathers and role models from Black social life; they've operated inside our communities as an occupying army with their training, postures and methods becoming more and more militaristic every year; and they murder, beat, brutalize and slander us with impunity and total immunity from "legal" challenge. Essentially, they are the hired guns of the wealthy ruling class whose function is that of repressing and containing the poor, marginalized and oppressed lower class sectors.

But nowhere was the repressive function of the police, and U.S. military, shown more blatantly within Amerika, in modern times, than in the neglect and violence against stranded, sick, hungry, dehydrating and terrified poor Blacks in the Gulf Coast following Hurricane Katrina. Outrage over those events spanned the globe. Even the usually apolitical Black entertainers, (who otherwise know enough to keep their mouths closed about Amerika's duplicitous politics on race, poverty and the brutality of Black life in Amerika), spoke out. In the context of New Afrikan struggle and resistance, that situation is worthy of close scrutiny.

For those that recall, the Louisiana governor Kathleen Blanco declared a "shoot to kill" martial law in New Orleans, upon claims that looting and violence were sweeping the city. Blacks were "looting," but whites doing the same were simply "finding" food and basic needs for survival. Specifically referred to—as the final incident that triggered the need for martial intervention—were claims that some "black gang bangers" on an overpass had fired on the U.S. Army Corps of Engineers while busy doing repair work. The army supposedly returned fire, killing several of these youths. Images of these dead youth were beamed into homes across Amerika by the corporate news media. It was declared that under these dangerous circumstances, "rescue and relief" operations, (which the police—federal and state—were not much involved in anyway), would be terminated and martial law declared to restore order against the unruly Black population.

In the words of Brig. Gen. Gary Jones, commander of the Louisiana National Guard's Joint Task Force, as quoted by the *Army Times*, "this place is going to look like Little Somalia, we're going to go out and take this city back. This will be a combat operation to get this city under control."

This call to official violence against a desperate, hungry, sick and already officially neglected population is problematic. Not because it departs from the way Black folk in Amerika are already treated, but because of the level of violence called forth and the fabricated justifications made for declaring martial law. First let's look at the justifications.

Reporter Jeremy Scahill gives a very different account of what happened on that overpass near the Ninth Ward. According to his report, private mercenaries from the Alabama-based company, Bodyguard and

Tactical Services (BATS) killed those youth and then casually told both U.S. Army forces and state police, who showed up later, what they'd done. No reports were filed, no questions asked, the army and troopers went their way as did the BATS mercenaries. No one cared that the mercs could've been lying about why they shot those Black youth. And it seems the U.S. Army decided later to take responsibility. Someone would have to explain the bodies of several Black youth riddled with .223 rounds, which is the standard caliber bullet of U.S. military assault rifles. Scahill's report, entitled "Blackwater Down," was printed in the October 10, 2005, issue of *The Nation*.

This account of the mercs' conduct and the subsequent military bailout, is consistent with the observations of the behaviors of such mercs made by Brig. Gen. Karl Horst, deputy commander of the 3rd Infantry Division in charge of security in Baghdad. He stated in September 2005 of such mercenaries operating in Iraq: "These guys run loose in this country and do stupid stuff. There's no authority over them, so you can't come down on them hard when they escalate force … They shoot people, and someone else has to deal with the aftermath. It happens all over the place."

And what about Brig. Gen. Gary Jones' remarks that New Orleans would be turned into a "Little Somalia," that martial law meant not policing the city, but a "military operation"? of course we know that Somalia is an Afrikan country, so Jones' point of comparison between Somalia and the stranded Black New Orleans population in this regard is obvious. But let's look at Somalia. What was it that the U.S. military did in Somalia during the 1992 U.S./UN invasion that he was saying would be repeated in New Orleans?

> "There were times when [U.S. troops] shot at everything that moved, took hostages, gunned their way through crowds of men and women, finished off any wounded who were showing signs of life. Many people died in their homes, their tin roofs ripped to shreds by high-velocity bullets and rockets. Accounts of the fighting frequently contain such statements as this: 'One moment there was a crowd, and the next instant it was just a bleeding heap of dead and injured.' Even with a degree of restraint on the part of the gunners, the technology deployed by the U.S. Army was such that carnage was inevitable."
>
> Alex de Waal, "U.S. War Crimes in Somalia," *New Left Review*, No. 230, July/August 1998, p. 143

A December 8, 1993, *New York Times* article reported that the U.S. government estimated "6,000 to 10,000 Somali casualties in four months last summer" alone, with "two-thirds" of these being women and children, compared to 26 U.S. soldiers killed. Also, a July 1993 report *Somalia: Human Rights Abuses* by the United Nations Forces reported atrocities committed by U.S. and UN soldiers, including shooting into crowds of protesters, attacking a hospital and bombarding political meetings.

To present date, no one knows what the joint martial forces did in New Orleans under martial law. There were reports of combat raids and explosions, but reporters were kept out and recording equipment was often confiscated and smashed by soldiers and mercs. No account has been given or even sought of the total death toll in the Gulf region, nor the causes of these deaths (whether a result of drowning, illness, dehydration, or official violence). I suspect that autopsies would find many Black bodies riddled with shrapnel and .223 rounds. But, of course, no investigations or inquiries are being made. Yet, the FBI, in collaboration with various local police departments, is pursuing criminal proceedings of alleged BLA activities from over 30 years ago.

Scahill's report closed with a warning quote from one of the mercs in New Orleans, stating, "This is a trend. You're going to see a lot more guys like us in these situations."

This reality is even more ominous when we look at who most of these mercs are; that is, where they come from. The vast majority of these paramilitaries are past members of the U.S. military's special operations units, like army Rangers (Green Berets), Delta Force, Navy Seals, Force Recon, etc. These units are largely manned by a closed society of white supremacist and racist white Anglo-Saxon Protestants (WASPs).

Stan Goff, a retired career Special Operations soldier, spanning from the Vietnam era through the 1990s, describes the special brand of anti-Black racism that pervades this community of Amerika's most highly trained ground combat forces:

> "In the world of Military Special Operations, I have seen Anti-Africanism function as the litmus test for assimilation of non-WASP soldiers. Asians, Europeans, Jews, American Indians, Polynesians, Latinos, all can be legitimized in the eyes of their peers by sharing in the Special Ops contempt for African Americans (sic). This is my experience. Black people have a special place in Special Operations—the bottom."
>
> Stan Goff, *Hideous Dreams: A Soldier's Memoir of the U.S. Invasion of Haiti* (Canada: Soft Skull, 2000)

Goff pointed out how (and why) Blacks are systematically and quite deliberately weeded out of the elite Special Operations community, and increasingly reduced in the less combat capable conventional ground forces. Goff's observations bear quoting at length:

> "When I was in Vietnam, I never saw two Black soldiers greet each other without givin' up dap. White officers were clearly uncomfortable with it, and some Black NCOs were pressured to put a stop to these elaborate improvisational handshakes.
>
> "It never worked. Dap was as much a part of Black GI culture as Motown.
>
> "And make no mistake. It was oppositional culture. White officers were right to feel uncomfortable with it. It was an open display of Black solidarity by Negroes with guns. When African American (sic) GIs spoke with one another, they referred to one another as 'Black' with the same frequency guys call each other 'man' (another vestige of Black oppositional culture, as opposed to 'black ops').
>
> "This new, super-elite, 'black ops' unit's 'operators' will have hardly a Black face to be seen. In the U.S., 'black ops' is always done by white operators. No one is going to teach large numbers of African Americans (sic) these clandestine skills.
>
> "Every time in the history of the United States that Black soldiers have fought in wars, there has been an outbreak of Black resistance afterward. Surely this is no surprise.
>
> "I referred earlier to Odoacer, a mercenary in the service of Rome, leader of the Germanic soldiers in the Roman army, who deposed the western Roman emperor, Romulus Augustus, in 476 AD, and thereby terminated the Western Roman Empire.
>
> "There is a limit to how much an oppressed people within a state will take. Rumsfeld and his ilk know this. You can bank on it.
>
> "When the Bush regime made the claim that the U.S. was attacked by people who hate freedom and democracy, the irony was not likely lost on African Americans (sic) or any other oppressed nationality.
>
> "I stress African Americans (sic) here because Black people are the very embodiment of white ruling class fear, especially in the military. Three out of ten soldiers in the Army today are African American (sic), as is one out of ten officers. Until you look at Special Operations.
>
> "Negrophobia, and not generalized racism, is characteristic of

special ops units, and the more rarefied the unit, the whiter it gets—with a few honorary Aryans from Hispano-Latina and Pacific Islander ranks. There are special places for Black Soldiers in Special Operations: kitchens, supply rooms, personnel offices, and motor pools.

"This lack of 'minority' participation as 'operators' in Special Operations began to leak some years ago. In 1999, the Rand Corporation released a report that attempted to describe Barriers to Minority Participation in Special Operations Forces (SOF), which attempts to put an empirical mask over SOF racial exclusion, even repeating many of the urban myths within SOF about why Black soldiers are so vastly under-represented there. 'They can't swim,' and so forth.

"Horse shit.

"When we put two and two together, we will likely end up with four. I saw Special Operations schools' cadre use every available opportunity, particularly those numerous aspects of periodic evaluations that are subjective, to weed out Black soldiers. Not all of the cadre did it, but there were enough spread out over the process to ensure the 'correct' result.

"Conventional ground forces were to be held back for any but the most banal military tasks: mop-up and guard duty. The new emphasis on using SOF for any decisive ground combat tasks is partly predicated on the Powell Doctrine fear of U.S. casualties. Interestingly enough, in an article for the Spring 2003 *Color Lines*, Glen Ford, a veteran of the Vietnam era 82nd Airborne Division, showed how conventional combat arms units are now being systematically loaded up with southern whites and Latinos, and lowering Black participation. No reason to take any chances.

"The secret fear is BPCSSD. Black post-combat social stress disorder. Not to be confused with PTSD, post-traumatic stress disorder.

"Black troops who go to war, especially if they are required to fight become restive and uncooperative when they get home. They ask embarrassing questions, like, 'where's ours?' BPCSSD.

"Let there be no doubt that the American white terror of Black rebellion still haunts the psyches of our pale ruling class. The U.S. Army has a disproportionate number of Black troops. Having too many of them crossing the psychological barrier against squeezing triggers on human targets can't strike the Man as a very good idea

"Vietnam taught the white supremacist U.S. ruling class a lot of lessons about the military. One was that it's not wise to maintain a large military conscript force of many oppressed nationalities, while simultaneously exposing them to combat for colonial objectives, when their lives at home mirror the conditions against which their ostensible enemy is fighting.

"Open and violent rebellion in the form of armed confrontations and fraggings by Black soldiers were common in Vietnam.

"By 1973, as U.S. forces were well along in a phased withdrawal from Vietnam, the U.S. Armed Forces were dumping the draft.

"They didn't want citizen-soldiers any more. They wanted mercenaries. Do what you're told and collect your check.

"And now, with the immense expense of the new higher-tech War Department, whose cost will tear the frayed carpet from under the U.S. working class, with workers of oppressed nationalities hitting bottom first, they sure don't want a bunch of Negroes with guns coming home with role conflicts.

"They don't need any BPCSSD. In Iraq today, against all Rumsfeld's calculations, there are thousands of Black folk doing Uncle Sam's wet work, even as Rumsfeld's military is attempting to minimize their numbers in combat arms. As they are obliged to occupy Iraq, many come from communities that are occupied by the police at home. BPCSSD will be returning from Iraq, soon, at a station near you."

Stan Goff, *Full Spectrum Disorder: The Military in the New American Century* (NY: Soft Skull, 2004)

Taken together, the foregoing should be unsettling in the extreme to any Black in Amerika with even a fraction of common sense. Let's summarize what we have to consider.

- New Afrikans in Amerika have suffered and continue to suffer brutal political, economic, social and cultural oppression at the hands of the Establishment.
- The Establishment's political police operate as the most direct violent oppressors of New Afrikans.
- Every genuine effort of New Afrikan leaders and common people to speak out against and challenge our oppressor, and to seek the most basic respect of our humyn rights and improvement of our political and economic conditions, has been met with official persecution, violence and murder. The

Establishment then replaces our slain leaders with ones it deems "acceptable."

- While the Establishment has wantonly murdered New Afrikans and our genuine leaders, it criminalizes and vilifies our efforts to defend our people and selves against its murderous violence.
- At the same time that the Establishment is stepping up its militaristic posture and preparedness against New Afrikan communities, it is decreasing the presence of Blacks in its military ground combat forces, excluding us from any operational training in the combat skills of its most elite ground combat forces, and nourishing the spread of anti-Black racist sentiment within its military combat rank and file.
- The role of mercenaries who harbor anti-Black sentiments is expected to see increased involvement in "control" of urban unrest—the same sort of "unrest" which is repeatedly provoked by police abuse and murder of Blacks.
- The Establishment's police forces do not act in the interest of Black people, nor does it effect any positive changes in our communities in relation to "crime control" or "narcotics control," nor social stability in general. The police operate instead as an occupying army in our communities and facilitate the spread of crime and dope to keep our communities divided and unstable and thus unable to unite and organize.
- The Establishment can and will manufacture false justifications for declaring open war (namely martial law) against New Afrikan communities, and setting loose mercenaries and soldiers who nurture desires to engage Blacks in a genocidal race war.

COINTELPRO is alive and well. The political police are as active as ever in repressing dissent and the liberation struggles of oppressed nationalities within Amerika. Puerto Rican independista leader Filiberto Ojeda Rios was assassinated on September 23, 2005, by FBI snipers, provoking outrage across Puerto Rico. Last year, FBI director, Robert Mueller, appeared before a senate subcommittee to announce the FBI's "threat assessment" program; a modern COINTELPRO focusing on subverting the political education of U.S. prisoners, under the pretext of protecting Amerika from possible violent acts of radical prisoners returning to society. This is the very same FBI that targeted Martin Luther King, an avowed pacifist, with the claimed motive of preventing his potential violence. Our political leaders continue to be persecuted. Indeed one of the men charged on January 23, 2007, for alleged BLA actions against police, is our New Afrikan comrade and political prisoner Jalil

Muntaqim (aka Anthony Bottom) who recently authored a book on New Afrikan liberation, *We Are Our Own Liberators*.

We must pay close heed to the words of comrade George Jackson, which are as vital to our survival today as when he first wrote them over 35 years ago:

> "[I]t should never be easy for them to destroy us. If you start with Malcolm X and count all of the brothers who have died or been captured since, you will find that not even one of them was really prepared for a fight. No imagination or fighting style was evident in any one of the incidents. But each one that died professed to know the nature of our enemies. It should never be easy for them. Do you understand what I'm saying? Edward V. Hanrahan, Illinois State Attorney General, sent fifteen pigs to raid the Panther headquarters and murder Hampton and Clark. Do you have any idea what would have happened to those fifteen pigs if they had run into as many Viet Cong as there were Panthers in that building. The VC are all little people with less general education than we have. The argument that they have been doing it longer has no validity at all, because they were doing it just as well when they started as they are now. It's very contradictory for a man to teach about the murder in corporate capitalism, to isolate and expose the murderers behind it, to instruct that these madmen are completely without stops, are licentious, totally depraved—and then not to make adequate preparations to defend himself from the madman's attack. Either they don't really believe their own spiel or they harbor some sort of subconscious death wish."

Any questions why we need our own independent Community Security Forces and a New Afrikan National Guard? BPCSSD.

*Dare to Struggle, Dare to Win!*
*All Power to the People!*

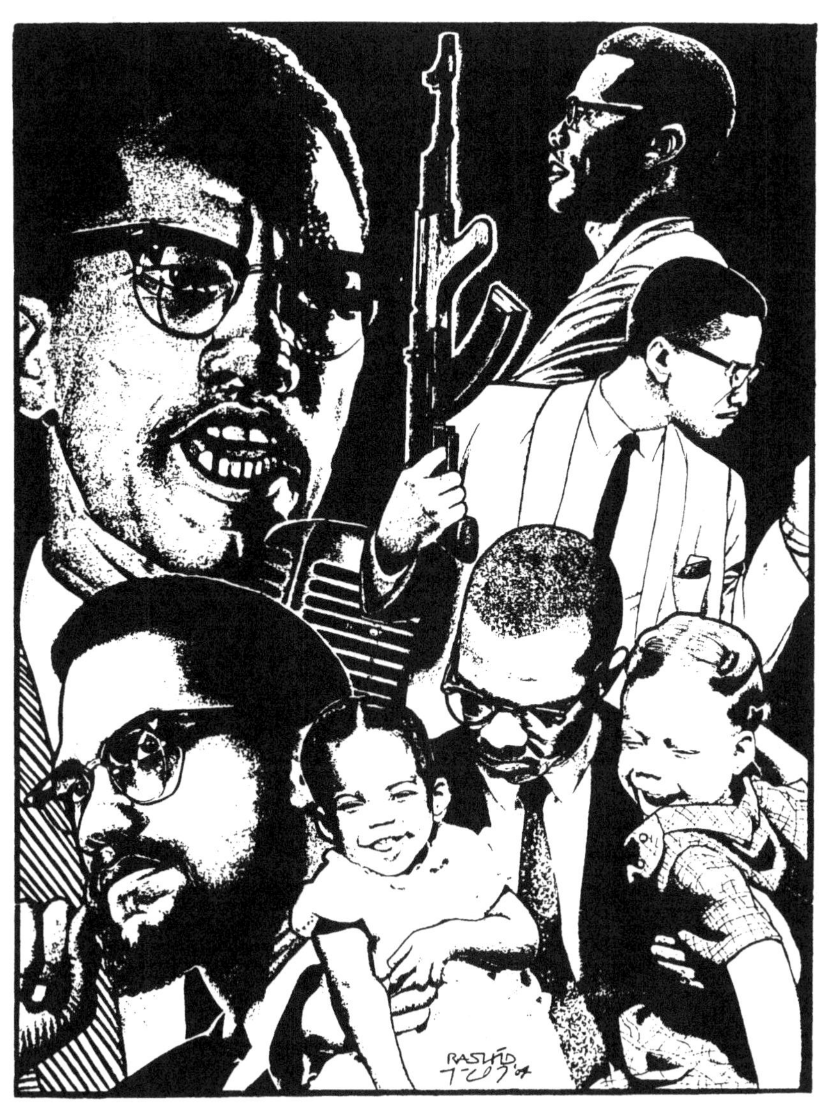
RASHID

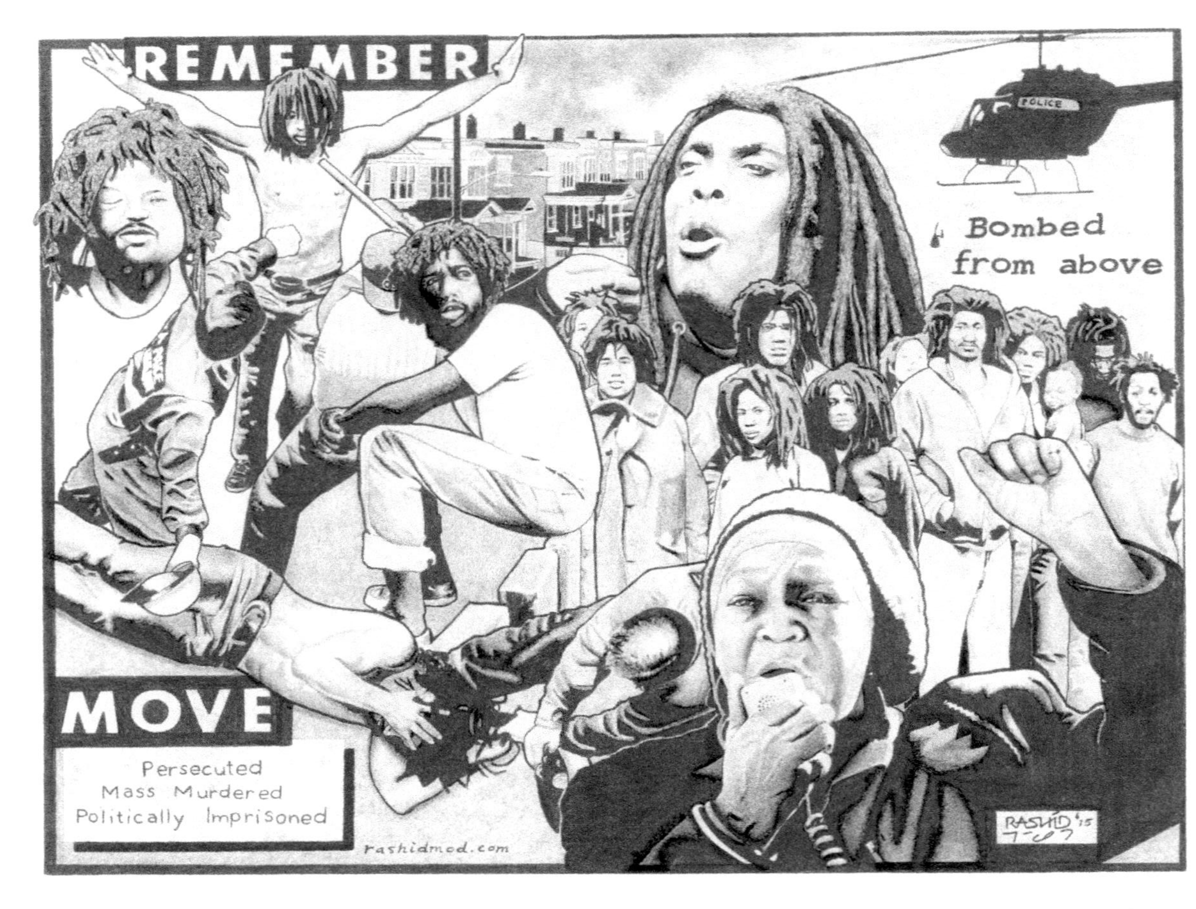
REMEMBER
POLICE
Bombed
from above
MOVE
Persecuted
Mass Murdered
Politically Imprisoned
rashidmod.com
RASHID '15

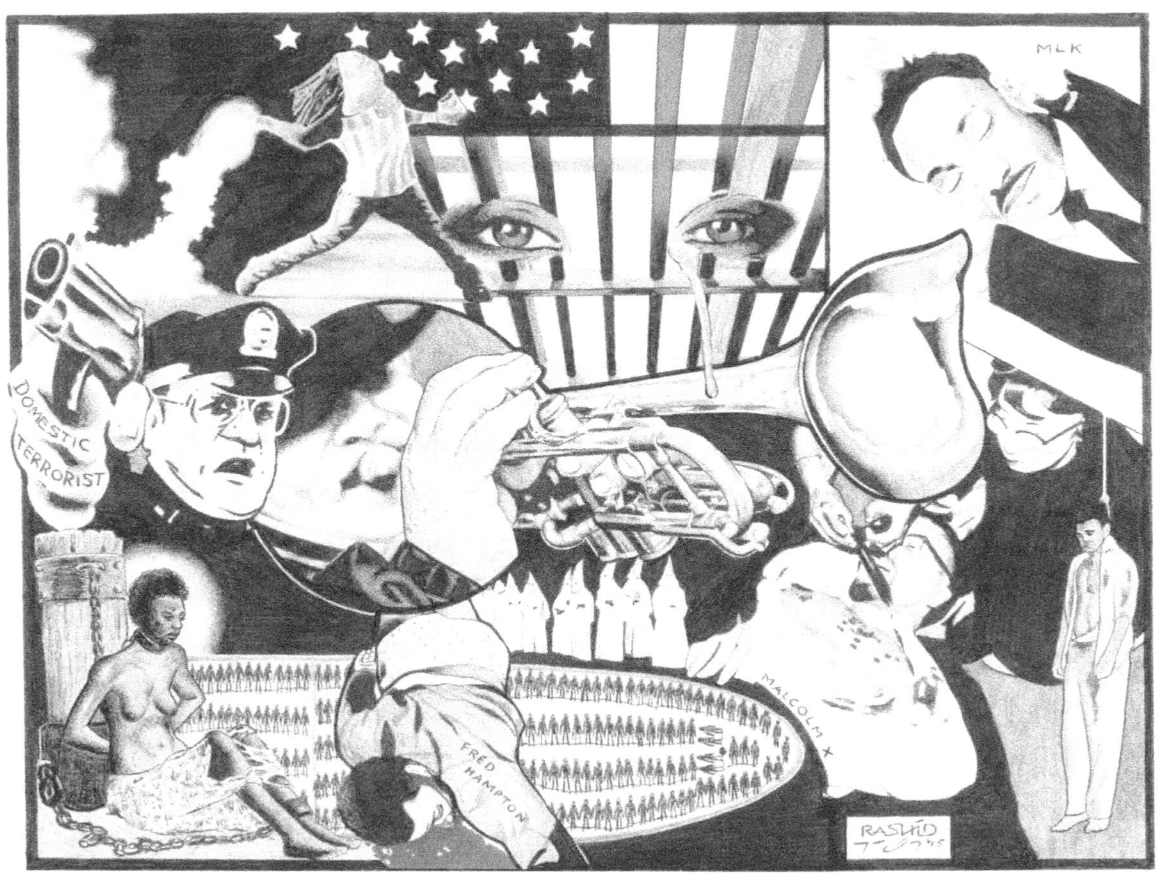
MLK
DOMESTIC TERRORIST
MALCOLM X
FRED HAMPTON
RASHID

# 31. LETTER ENTITLED "RACIAL AND POLITICAL PERSECUTION OF GRASSROOTS BLACK POLITICAL LEADERS AND ACTIVISTS" 2008

**To:** Director, Department of Homeland Security and Staff;
Director, Office of National Intelligence and Staff;
Director, Central Intelligence Agency and Staff;
Director, Federal Bureau of Investigation and Staff;
Commonwealth Attorney Adrian Collins, Wise County, VA;
Virginia Department of Corrections,
Director and Deputy Director,
Inspector General and Staff,
Publication Review Committee;
Red Onion State Prison,
Warden and Assistant Warden,
Investigator and Intelligence Office Staff,
Security Chief,
Mailroom Staff;
Virginia Attorney General and Staff.

From: Kevin "Rashid" Johnson, Minister of Defense,
New Afrikan Black Panther Party/White Panther Organization

**Date:** June 3, 2008

**Re:** Racial and Political Persecution of Grassroots Black Political Leaders and Activists.

As many of you are certainly aware, Amerika's "intelligence" and executive policing agencies (federal, state and local) have a sordid legacy of persecuting and targeting grassroots Black political leaders and activists for destruction. The spectrum of methods applied have ranged from slander (false character and image depictions and attacks) spread through and by government agents and friendly media "assets," to false and malicious criminal arrests and prosecutions, to violence and outright murder.

Such designs come as no surprise in a country that was built upon history's first race-based and most brutal system of enslavement and native genocide and land-theft. The very place where the false concept of race and attendant racism (white racial supremacy) were created.[1]

Since chattel slavery, when Amerikan society was artificially divided along *politically created* racial lines, it has been a central policy to prevent Blacks from organizing independent political institutions and parties. Until just a few decades ago, this policy included our systematic exclusion from participating as genuine citizens in electoral politics. Indeed, Amerika's "dual party" system evolved from the struggle to keep Blacks enslaved and out of the political sphere—contrary to deceptive official claims that this system arose as an expression of respect for diverse political views and representatives.[2]

It is also telling that many of the historical figures projected today as Amerikan heroes and "founding fathers" embraced bigoted views and practiced genocidal and criminal policies that would have made even the most vicious German Nazi blush.[27] Let's not forget that the Central Intelligence Agency, in its formative years, absorbed and employed many of the Nazis' worst war criminals as agents, assets and advisors.[3] Indeed, president George W. Bush's grandfather was Hitler's chief Amerikan financer during World War II, and ended in having his Union Banking Corporation confiscated under the Trading with the Enemies Act in October 1942 by the Roosevelt administration.[4]

Since U.S. executive policies of targeting "non-imbedded" Black politicos for destruction were exposed in the 1970s, culminating in several Congressional investigations and reports,[5] efforts have been made to gloss over this history and to rehabilitate the images of these agencies, particularly through glamorized images and cultural fantasies projected of Amerikan police and intelligence agencies, via the vast entertainment/information media. However, behind this iron curtain of deception, official designs have not changed. A fact that I bear witness to, because I have been and am a target of them, which is the basis of this letter.

I have been incarcerated since 1990, and have experienced first-hand the brutal reality of Amerikan prisons. A system that, as the American Civil Liberties Union has acknowledged, is more and more "dedicated to the African American (sic) community,"[6] and the underlying anti-Black orientation of this system, which cannot be honestly denied.[7]

For many years I have been reporting and pursuing public exposure and redress of the brutality, torture, and abuses occurring inside these institutions, and have supported and co-founded several groups and organizations that also pursue these ends.

In 2005 I co-founded the New Afrikan Black Panther Party/White Panther Organization, a non-violent, legal and above-ground party whose focus is on promoting the interests and humyn rights, in strictly legal forms, of sectors of the U.S. population whose needs and interests are ignored, and who are not represented, by the "established" political-economic system—especially poor, working-class and imprisoned Blacks.

The NABPP/WPO specifically opposes criminal activities, "street gang" mentalities and behaviors, violence (except in the extremes of self-defense), all forms of discrimination (racial, ethnic, gender, sexual orientation, national, etc.), and all forms of oppression. We also promote the right to free, open and honest speech. Our orientation, ideologies, and views have been and are elaborated in our various periodicals and publications, many of them I authored.[8]

Because U.S. social policies are not oriented towards serving or promoting the needs, interests, rights and benefits of poor, working-class and ethnic people, while our Party's orientation specifically is, we are likely viewed as promoting views unpopular with and to the status quo. As a result of this in general, and my role in these efforts in particular, I have been and am targeted with those repressive methods reserved in Amerika for independent Black leaders and activists.

One typical form that this targeting has taken is my being falsely profiled by this prison as the leader of a criminal street gang or Security Threat Group (STG), namely the NABPP/WPO. This tactic of stigmatizing and consequently repressing Black political groups is certainly not new or unique, and harkens back to policies applied by U.S. officials during periods when official racism was less veiled.[9] As Associate U.S. Supreme Court Justice, Hugo Black pointed out:

> "History should teach us ... that ... minority parties and groups which advocate extremely unpopular social or governmental innovations will always be typed as criminal gangs and attempts will always be made to drive them out."
>
> Barenblatt v. U.S., 360 U.S. 109, 150 (1959) (dissenting opinion).

So much for the facial validity of STG profilings.

I have persisted in seeking an explanation from this prison's and prison system's administration as to what the NABPP/WPO has done or promotes that qualifies us for STG classification, besides the obvious reasons of their own racial and political intolerance. To date my inquiries have been evaded and I am told that I cannot formally grieve the matter through the established grievance procedures.

It is of course a crime to be a member of, to recruit for, or to act in furtherance of the goals of a criminal street gang. The criteria of what constitutes a criminal street gang is defined by law.[10] Incidentally, I might add, "street gang" implies groupings of people of color, since it is generally recognized that, since the 1970s, "urban" is basically synonymous in Amerika with the Black population, over 90% of which lives in urban communities. Yet another "legal" embodiment of the race factor, targeted at people of color selectively.

Moreover, to falsely impute criminal activities to one not duly convicted is per se defamation and slander[11]—and one is presumed innocent of crimes that they have not been thus convicted of.

This entire gang profiling of me and the NABPP/WPO here has been at the instigation of this prison's near-exclusively white staff and investigator, (and admittedly conveyed to federal intelligence agencies), who come from local, rural, race-segregated communities of mountainous south-western Virginia and eastern Kentucky and Tennessee, who harbor socially conditioned and culturally ingrained insensitivities towards, and genuine ignorance of the views, values, history and culture of urban people of color.

Typical of the tendency of racists to stereotype groups of people, these officials make no distinctions between Black political organizations, and indeed declare that "all Black groups that promote dissent" fit their criteria of a gang or STG, as does any group or organization that criticizes government and prison practices and policies.

Further, they lump together every group that has ever used the "Black Panther" name, (characterizing them all as generically, the "Black Panther group", or "Black Panther gang"). Although, there have been a great number of different organizations that have used the "Black Panther" name or logo; none of which is the NABPP/WPO affiliated with. In fact, initially they claimed the NABPP/WPO and the New Black Panther Party, which is led today by D.C.-based attorney Malik Zulu Shabazz, were one and the same organization, whereas these two organizations have no connection. Interestingly, however, they have stated in writing that Mr. Shabazz—a federal lawyer—is the leader of a criminal gang also, namely the NBPP.

Many of the organizations that have used the Black Panther name in fact no longer exist, and had very different ideologies, agendas and views.[12] Indeed, the NBPP is a quasi-religious group connected to the Nation of Islam, whose racial, political and economic views the NABPP/WPO do not share. Fundamentally, this prison designated the NABPP/WPO a gang and STG before even knowing what our views and interests are, and subsequently have ignored them in order to preserve this false criminal profile.

And using the generic, all-inclusive "Black Panther" designation, they systematically bar any and all information on any BP organization, past and present, from possession by any prisoner, although most Black history reference books and general encyclopedias have entries on the original Black Panther Party and its leaders. So in essence, the policy here is to censor Black history while promoting the history and memory of white Amerikan figures and political leaders who exterminated Indians, and enslaved, brutalized and raped Blacks as an accepted political norm.[27] Racial discrimination.

But of course this repression is not without precedent.

The original BPP, which was founded in Oakland, California in 1966 by Huey P. Newton and Bobby Seale, and destroyed by the U.S. government, met with similar persecution. Indeed, its treatment by the U.S. government, the Federal Bureau of Investigation in particular, set the standard on official hatred and smear-mongering against groups bearing the BP name.

The original BPP was founded as a legal above-ground Black political party that promoted the rights of urban Blacks to defend their communities against crime and violence,[13] and promoted community service programs to meet the economic needs of desperately poor urban Blacks that the government ignored: such as free breakfast programs for children (this was before food stamps and free school meals were widely available—in fact the government expanded food stamps and school meals as counter to the Panther's programs), petition drives against police brutality, free schools, free health clinics, free clothing and shoe programs, free busing to prisons, free senior citizen service programs, free sickle-cell-anemia research and testing, free pest control, plumbing and maintenance, ambulance, day-care, and news service programs.[14]

Various surveys found the vast majority of the urban Black population supported the BPP. The BPP was so popular that similar BP formations sprang up in England, Israel, Bermuda, Australia and India. It also aided in forming similar groups among whites (the White Panther Party and Young Patriot Party, the latter being a formation of Appalachian whites), the Mexicans (Brown Berets), Puerto Rico (Young Lords Party), and white college student groups, which it worked closely with as allies. As Todd Gitlin of the Students for a Democratic Society noted, "At a time when most other black [groups] donned dashikis and glowered at whites, they [Panthers] welcomed white allies." Eldridge Cleaver, the BPP's Minister of Information pointed out:

> "[I]n reality there is no such thing as a black movement and a white movement in the United States. These are merely categories of thought that only have reality in terms of the lines that the ruling class itself has drawn and is implementing amongst the people. The United States is controlled by one ruling class."

Solely because of its orientation toward uplifting and serving communities, the BPP was viciously slandered and attacked by the government.

Violence prone street gangs were incited by the FBI and police to attack and kill BPP leaders and members;[15] racial and anti-white stereotypes were played up via the media; bogus letters were written by the FBI agents and sent to BPP members, the public, landlords, employers, spouses, supporters, religious leaders, etc. to play the Black community, Panthers and other Black groups against each other; assassination raids were conducted by FBI and police to murder Panthers; false arrests and prosecutions of Panthers were conducted to stigmatize them as criminally inclined and to harass them and deplete Party funds and resources on defending members against false criminal charges, and much more. All orchestrated by the FBI's covert action program, COINTELPRO (COunter INTELligence PROram).[16]

The derogatory and violence-prone image of the BPP was solely the creation of a then openly racist and sexist FBI,[16] led by J. Edgar Hoover,[17] and other agencies, at a period when Blacks and women were refused employment with the FBI, and it was openly operating as an agency opposed to Blacks and Black communities.[18] The concededly illegal and criminal methods used by the FBI against the BPP were exposed and denounced by the U.S. Congress in 1976,[5] and several in-depth studies have been written on the FBI's anti-BPP and anti-Black crusade.[19]

While the FBI claimed, in the face of its exposure in the 1970s, that it would end or limit future COINTELPROs (although it has not), the false images it portrayed of the BPP continue and live on in the white Amerikan public mind.[20] Hence, the very mention of the name BP today evokes images of a gun-toting Black version of the Ku Klux Klan.

But let there be no mistake about it, the BPP was not an exception to the rule in the application of these methods against Black political activists and leaders. As the Church Committee Congressional investigations of U.S. intelligence agencies exposed, all Black leaders and groups were targeted, even such groups and leaders as the Southern Christian Leadership Conference and Martin Luther King, Jr., all under FBI labels of their being "violence prone" "Black Nationalist Hate Groups."[9] Just like the criminal gang label is thrown around today.

As a recent in-depth exposé by attorney William F. Pepper, and a wrongful death lawsuit he successfully prosecuted on behalf of the King family in 1999 revealed the FBI, in collaboration with other U.S. civil and military intelligence agencies, were King's actual killers.[21]

King's widow, the late Coretta Scott King, had this to say about Pepper's book:

> "For a quarter of a century, Bill Pepper conducted an independent investigation of the assassination of Martin Luther King, Jr. He opened his files to our family, encouraged us to speak with the

witnesses, and represented our family in the civil trial against the conspirators. The jury affirmed his findings, providing our family with a long-sought sense of closure and peace, which had been denied by official disinformation and cover-ups. Now the findings of his exhaustive investigation and additional revelations from the trial are presented in the pages of this important book. We recommend it highly to everyone who seeks the truth about Dr. King's assassination."

Yet today, the U.S. government pretends to respect the memory and work of this man that it murdered, with a national holiday.[22]

The object, then as today, is to destroy independent and influential Black political leaders and replace them with ones "approved" by U.S. officials to mislead us.[23] To continue the oppressive and steadily deteriorating conditions within, and to divide the U.S. Black communities.

As the Church Committee report revealed, assistant FBI director William C. Sullivan promoted a COINTELPRO in which the FBI would hand-pick a "new national leader," once King was eliminated.[24] Sullivan's overall strategy, which he wrote in 1964, was to simultaneously destroy Dr. King, Malcolm X and Elijah Muhammad. He wrote:

> "... when this is done, and it can and will be done, obviously much confusion will reign, particularly among the negro people ... The negroes will be left without a national leader of sufficiently compelling personality to steer them in the proper direction ..." [25]

Sullivan recommended Black corporate lawyer Samuel R. Pierce, Jr. as King's replacement.

Yesterday it was a corporate lawyer, today it is an ex-law professor—Barack Obama.

We of course know that COINTELPRO is alive and well. The repressions I face are classic COINTELPRO methods. Also, three years ago FBI director Robert Mueller announced before a Senate subcommittee the implementation of a new "Threat Assessment Program" (TAPS). A modern COINTELPRO targeted specifically at U.S. prisoners who are politically active, under the cover, as always, of professing to prevent potential violence. The same self-serving rationale used to justify the ongoing persecution and ultimate murder of Dr. King, and targeting all other Black political groups, leaders and activists.[26] TAPS involves the FBI, along with Homeland Security and other agencies, working in collaboration with various prisons and prison systems nationwide to identify, profile, disrupt, repress, and neutralize prisoner activists (groups and individuals), being mindful that several influential Black political leaders like Malcolm X and George Jackson developed inside of prison. I have been informed that I have been and am a target of TAPS.

Methods that I have been targeted with include the following:

- Frequent interception and destruction of my mail;
- Systematic obstruction of all articles I write or artwork I create from coming into the prisons;
- Obstructions of my ability to collaborate with outside editors and contacts to have my articles and a book I wrote published;
- Blocking nearly all of my periodicals from reaching me;
- Repeated targetings with trumped-up disciplinary reports;
- Repeated indictments on trumped-up violent crimes that have been each dismissed in turn—the last one with prejudice where I conducted my defense pro se (abuse of process);
- Habitually disappearing my incoming mail or rejecting it as in violation of prison policy without explanation;
- Barring my contacts with various attorneys who have attempted to assist me;
- Rejecting, opening and delaying my legal mail—even from the ACLU—outside my presence;
- Hampering my contacts with the courts in anticipated and pending litigations;
- Frequent destructions and thefts of my legal property which I have had to obtain court orders to have returned;
- Barring my visitors and telephone use and blocking the telephone numbers of loved ones and others;
- Targeting me with threats, attempts and actual acts of violence by guards and their white supremacist inmate lackeys; etc.

I should add that further conditions exist at this prison, and within this prison system, which are openly race-motivated and otherwise unlawful, e.g. the censorship of Black- and Brown-oriented cultural, political and historical publications as STG materials; while no such measures are applied to mainstream and white publications and media; censorship of all media and publications that in any way critique U.S. government, prison and economic policies and practices; censorship of publications and media by or about grassroots Black historical figures and leaders such as Huey P. Newton and Harry Haywood, while publications about racist, murderous and criminally oppressive white historical figures like Adolf Hitler, George Washington, Thomas Jefferson, Christopher Columbus,[27] etc., etc. are stocked in the prison library and accessible to all prisoners; promoting, protecting and hiring of staff at the prison who are members and affiliates of white supremacist groups and gangs; repression of prisoners who are "documented members" of actual Black and Brown street gangs, while officials protect and give free rein to members of white supremacist gangs and use them as hit men against disliked prisoners of color,[28] removing all television stations from the prison's closed circuit television system that aired Black programs; harassing local radio stations and programs that play Black music and allow call-ins to prisoners from friends, family and supporters; subjecting Black and Brown prisoners to the harshest and highest security levels and conditions while maintaining white prisoners in minimum security with extensive privileges and benefits making security level classifications along blatantly racial lines; frequent targetings of Black and Brown prisoners with abuse, violence, denied meals, etc.; deliberately engineering and facilitating violent conflicts between and against prisoners of color, particularly between prisoners documented as members of rival Black and Brown street gangs,[29] populating these remote prisons that are staffed nearly-exclusively by rural whites with predominantly non-white prisoners, etc., etc.

That the FBI and other intelligence and executive agencies are more racially diverse today than during the 1960s and '70s in no way invalidates their anti-Black policies. Indeed it was a Black Chicago policeman—Gloves Davis—that shot two sleeping BPP leaders, Fred Hampton and Mark Clark, in their heads at point-blank range in December 1969, in an FBI orchestrated assassination raid. It was today's FBI that assassinated Puerto Rican grassroots leader Filiberto Ojeda Rios in September 2005 sparking protests across Puerto Rico, which spanned everyday civilians to government leaders.[30] Also, the most brutal violence against South Afrikan Blacks during openly racist apartheid was often carried out by Black soldiers and police.[31] We see Black and Brown police involved as viciously as white ones in unprovoked and unjustified violence and murders of urban youth of color today in Amerika.

Furthermore, the National Security Council (NSC), which is chaired by the U.S. president, and whose enforcement arm is the CIA, implemented NSC memorandum #46 in 1978, the stated goals of which were/are to ensure the permanent demise and destruction of the U.S. Black liberation and civil rights movements.[32] In its own words the NSC-46 devised to ensure that there would never evolve another independent Black leader or organization that could unite the U.S. Black population; to play white working-class people against Blacks; to divide the Black community and political groups; to bring more Blacks into established political institutions so they could be controlled and used to mislead the Black population; and to destroy all aspirations then prevailing among Blacks to develop an independent Black political party.

So we see an overall historical continuum till today of targeting Black leaders and activists for destruction who are not "approved" by the Establishment, and deliberately maintaining the urban Black communities in crisis. And the same old tactics are being used.

Officials at this prison have conceded working with the FBI and DHS in "intelligence sharing"—government speak for interagency repressive covert actions against targeted individuals and groups.

Of course, none of what I've touched on herein related to the history and designs of this country's intelligence and policing agencies is unknown to the various recipients of this letter, it's your M.O. and S.O.P. It's the general public that's kept oblivious of it. Moreover, I've only skimmed the surface, just enough to place my issues in their proper context, and to satisfy my burden of placing each of you on notice of my issues before pursuing redress in other forums, and to afford you the opportunity to address/redress these matters.

I am therefore presenting this letter of complaint to all named agencies and officials, requesting that such racially and politically-motivated persecution and abuses cease, that the false gang/STG profiling of me and the NABPP/WPO at this prison and anywhere else be rescinded with an apology for this defamation, and that all the illegal, discriminatory and retaliatory treatments and conditions mentioned herein be abolished. If I hear nothing from you all within 20 days, I will proceed to seek both public and judicial exposure and redress of these and other practices against those officials hereby notified, via copy of this letter.

Sincerely,
Kevin "Rashid" Johnson, No. 185492

## END NOTES

1. See, e.g., Theodore Allen, *The Invention of the White Race: Vol. II* (NY: Verso, 1997); Steve Martinot, *The Rule of Racialization* (Philadelphia: Temple University Press, 2003).

In 1676 Afrikan and English slaves and indentured servants, who enjoyed equal statuses and conditions of brutality and abuse, came together under a rebellious young planter, Nathaniel Bacon in a united revolt that overthrew the colonial government in Virginia and burned down the capitol at Jamestown (Bacon's Rebellion). Six months into the revolt Bacon died of influenza, and without its leader the revolt was defeated by colonial forces. Subsequently, the colonial government instituted a policy designed to prevent any similar revolt from occurring again, by dividing the society of poor workers against each other along racial lines. In 1682 laws were passed creating the "Negro" and "White" races and making slavery an hereditary and permanent status for Afrikans. (See, William W. Hening, *Statutes at Large: The Laws of Virginia* [Richmond, 1809], pp. 492ff). In

1705 the "race" line was further clarified by laws that defined as "negro" anyone having "one drop" of Afrikan blood. Slavery and servitude of whites was phased out, and they were brought together under the concept of being a "superior" race, religiously ordained to enslave Blacks under the Biblical "curse of Canaan." The entire white society was mobilized as a united force (slave patrols) to police and brutally repress Blacks, whom they were indoctrinated to hate and fear. This politically manufactured system gave birth to white racism, that persists till today, and was exported from the Virginian colonies to all areas where Europeans came into contact with and sought to conquer the lands and seize the wealth and labor power of people of color and is preserved in multitudes of ways by today's capitalist political-economic systems, which deliberately pit Whites, Blacks and other "races" against each other.

2. "The purity of democratic institutions was, in the historical debates around Manifest Destiny, an extension of the purity concept of whiteness. And in the evolution of the two-party system, a further extension of the structure of racialization expressing itself. The force driving U.S. political process toward a two-party system historically was none other than the question of slavery and the disenfranchisement of the black voter …

> "The disenfranchisement of the black voter has been a major issue throughout U.S. history. It was hotly debated right after the Revolution, imposed in most states before the Civil War, imposed by means of paramilitary operations during and after Reconstruction, and flaunted in the face of Constitutional guarantees of the right to vote until the Voting Rights Act of 1965. The drive to disenfranchise black people continues today through massive felony incarceration for misdemeanors and victimless crimes, from which they lose suffrage. According to Paul Haygood, more than 13% of potential black voters are currently disenfranchised. (Ryan Paul Haygood, *Black Commentator,* June 10, 2004. According to Maygood, of the 4.7 million people disenfranchised by felony conviction in the U.S., 1.4 million are black males, or 13% of the adult black population. This does not count black females.)"
>
> Steve Martinot, "Mexico, Iraq, and the Two-Party System: Studies in White Supremacy," *Socialism and Democracy,* Vol. 19, No. 1, March 2005, pp. 129–130

3. Exposés on the protection and employment of Nazi war criminals by the U.S. and British governments are legion. See for example, Christopher Simpson, *Blowback: America's Recruitment of Nazis and its Effects on the Cold War* (New York: Weidenfeld & Nicolson, 1988). (On Rauff, the inventor and administrator of the gas truck execution program which murdered approximately 250,000 people, see pp. 92–94; on Gehlen, Hitler's most senior intelligence officer on the brutal Eastern Front, see pp. 40–72, 248–263, 279–283; on Barbie, the Gestapo's "Butcher of Lyons," see pp. 185–195); see also, Mary Ellen Reese, *General Reinhard Gehlen: The C.I.A. Connection* (Fairfax, Va: George Mason University Press, 1990); Erhard Dubringhaus, *Klaus Barbie: The Shocking Story of How the U.S. Used This Nazi War Criminal As An Intelligence Agent—A First Hand Account* (Washington: Acropolis, 1984); John Loftus, *The Belarus Secret* (New York: Knopf, 1982) ch. 5; Tom Bower,

*Klaus Barbie: The "Butcher of Lyons"* (New York: Pantheon, 1984); Kai Hermann, "A Killer's Career," *Stern* (Germany), May 10 and following, 1984 (six part series based upon declassified U.S. government documents and interviews conducted in Bolivia); Linda Hunt, *Secret Agenda: The United States Government, Nazi Scientists, and Project Paperclip, 1945–1990* (New York: St. Martin's, 1991); Alexander Cockburn, et al., *Whiteout: The C.I.A., Drugs and the Press* (London: Verso, 1998), chs. 6 and 7; Eugene J. Kolb, (former U.S. counterintelligence corps officer and chief of operations in the Augsburg region of Germany), "Army Counterintelligence's Dealings with Klaus Barbie," Letter, *New York Times*, July 26, 1983, p. A20 (defending the employment of Barbie); Michael McClintock, *Instruments of Statecraft: U.S. Guerrilla Warfare Counter-Insurgency and Counter-Terrorism, 1940–1990* (New York: Pantheon, 1992), especially ch. 3 (important study of U.S. intelligence's absorption of Nazi methods and practitioners into U.S. special warfare doctrine after World War II).

4. Charles Higham, *Trading with the Enemy: An Exposé of the Nazi-American Money Plot* (New York: Delacorte, 1983). George Bush is certainly not an exception among prominent U.S. government officials with direct lines of descent from major Nazis. Karl Rove's grandfather helped run the Nazi Party and build the Birkenau Death Camp, and California governor Arnold Schwarzenegger's Austrian father was a Nazi SA volunteer and became a ranking officer. See, *The Free Press*, October 6, 2003.

5. See, Church Committee, *U.S. Congressional Report: Intelligence Activities and the Rights of Americans*, 94th Congress, 2nd session, report no. 94–755 (Washington: U.S. Government Printing Offices, 1976), Books II and III.

6. ACLU, *Cracks in the System: Twenty Years of the Unjust Federal Crack Cocaine Law* (October, 2006).

7. *Harvard Law Review*, "Developments in the Law—Race and the Criminal Process," vol. 101, no. 7, May 198, pp. 1473–1641 (comprehensive dissection of racial discrimination in the "criminal justice" system, determining that discrimination exists at every stage of the "criminal justice" process); Steven R. Donziger, ed., *The Real War on Crime: The Report of the National Criminal Justice Commission* (New York: Harper Collins, 1996), especially ch. 4. Michael Tonry, *Malign Neglect—Race, Crime, and Punishment in America* (New York: Oxford University Press, 1995).

8. Kevin "Rashid" Johnson, "The Don't Shank The Guards Handbook: Legal Recourse to Guards' Brutality, Harassment and Rape" (2005); "On The Questions of Race and Racism" (2006) (pp. 64–96 in this volume), "Wimyn Hold Up Half the Sky" (2008) (pp. 137–181 in this volume), etc.

9. Op. cit., note 5, Book III p. 4. (The FBI's "covert action" programs were generally targeted at any Black political and other groups. "The Black Nationalist program, according to its supervisor included 'a great number of organizations that you might not today characterize as black nationalist but which were in fact primarily black.' Indeed, the nonviolent Southern Christian Leadership Conference was labeled as a Black Nationalist 'Hate Group.'")

10. In Virginia where I am incarcerated for example, the criminal laws defining and governing "Criminal Street Gangs," are set out under Va. Code, Sections 18.2—46.1:3, which parallel similar Federal criminal laws under Titles 18 of the U.S. Code.

11. For defamation law in Virginia governing false imputations of crime, see for example, Zayre of VA., Inc. v. Gowdy, 207 Va. 47, 147 S. E. 2d 710 (1966); Shupe v. Rose's Stores, Inc., 213 Va. 374, 192 S. E. 2d 766 (1972). But see especially, Schnupp v. Smith, 249 Va. 353, 457 S. E. 2nd 42 (1995). (Words that impute the commission of a crime that is punishable by imprisonment in a state or federal institution are actionable defamation and slander per se). Accord Va. Code Section 8.01–45.

12. The various Black organizations that have used the Black Panther name, past and present, include, The original Black Panther Party (U.S. 1966–1982), the Black Panther Movement (England), The Black Panther Party of Israel (Israel), Black Panther Party (Australia), Dalit Panthers (India), New Black Panther Party (U.S., 1990—present), Black Panther Collective (U.S. 1994-present), the National Alliance of Black Panthers (U.S.), Anarchist Black Panthers (U.S.), the NABPP/WPO (U.S., 2005–present), etc.

13. As Huey Newton pointed out in a February 11, 1973, interview with William Buckley, on Public Television's *Firing Line*, "we were very careful to follow city ordinances, gun regulations, state law, and our constitutional rights."

14. Charles E. Jones, et al., "Don't Believe the Hype: Debunking the Panther Mythology," *The Black Panther Party Reconsidered* (Baltimore, MD: Black Classic Press, 1998), pp. 29–31.

15. Op. cit., note 5, Book III, p. 42, one of many examples was where the FBI sent "[a]n anonymous letter … to the leader of the Blackstone Rangers, a Chicago gang 'to whom violent type activity, shooting, and the like, are second nature,' advising them that 'the brothers that run the Panthers blame you for blocking their thing and there's supposed to be a hit out for you.' The letter was intended to 'intensify the degree of animosity between the two groups' and cause 'retaliatory action which could disrupt the BPP or lead to reprisals against its leadership'."

16. Op. cit., note 5, Book III, pp. 185–225, section titled "The FBI's Covert Action Program to Destroy the Black Panther Party":

> "[R]ecently a reporter's Freedom of Information Act investigation into COINTELPRO files found that the American government had done everything possible to infiltrate the Black Panthers and other lesser-known activist groups, then had its 'agents lead the groups into violent gestures that would divide them, undermine their credibility and bring down the full weight of the state' on the leaders' heads."
>
> William Hinton, *Through A Glass Darkly*
> (New York: Monthly Review, 2006).

> "[R]epression in the United States is worse than ever before and much, much harsher than the world—or most Americans for that matter—is aware or told. In New Mexico, for example, the Alianza led by Reies Tijerina, has been hounded relentlessly since 1966; its offices have been dynamited (by police at that), its leaders shot, its members jailed on such flagrantly outrageous charges that few Americans would believe—even today—the strictly factual story. At the time of writing, Tijerina himself was locked up for years and his

Alianza was flagging. As for Blacks, their repression is not less brutal, just more widespread. The whole primary and secondary leadership of the Black Panther Party has been jailed on obvious frame-ups. They have been beaten, tortured and murdered. Twice in Oakland, I saw with my own eyes, police in official cars zoom by a group of Panthers talking peacefully on a street and open fire at them. Three times I witnessed police arrest Panthers, handcuff them, and then pistol-whip them. In over a dozen cases, after seeing Panthers arrested, I have gone to see them in jail and found them bloodied from having 'fallen down the stairs' or from having 'assaulted a policeman.' And the whole world knows—for this time it was reported in the press—that on-duty Chicago policemen murdered Panthers Fred Hampton and Mark Clark in their sleep. By the end of 1969, not a single policeman had been brought to justice for these acts of violence. On the other hand, all of white America's law enforcement agents, including federal marshals and the FBI, have gone out of their way—and, often, out of their jurisdiction—to arrest Panthers, without having warrants. Federal marshals have even refused to honor a court order not to remove Chairman Bobby Seale from California (which, legally, made the marshals kidnappers). By 1970, twenty-eight Black Panthers had been murdered by the police, some beaten to death after arrest (Charles Cox in Chicago), some in unprovoked assaults (seventeen year-old Bobby Hutton in Oakland, Hampton and Clark in Chicago), most in front of scores of witnesses, who could never testify, as the police were never charged."

John Gerassi, *The Coming of the New International* (World Publishing Co., 1971), pp. 552–553

17. See, Curt Gentry, *J. Edgar Hoover: The Man and His Secrets* (New York: W.W. Norton & Co., 1991).

18. Kenneth O'Reilly, *"Racial Matters": The FBI's Secret File on Black America, 1960–1972* (New York: Free Press, 1989).

19. Ibid.; Ward Churchill et al., *Agents of Repression: The FBI's Secret Wars on the Black Panther Party and the American Indian Movement* (Boston: South End, 1988); etc.

20. "The FBI has attempted covertly to influence the public's perception of persons and organizations by disseminating derogatory information to the press, either anonymously or through 'friendly' contacts." Joy James, *Shadow Boxing* (New York: St. Martin's Press, 1999), p. 112; see also op. cit., note 5.

21. William F. Pepper, *An Act of State: The Execution of Martin Luther King* (London: Verso, 2003).

22. "Even after King's death, [FBI] agents in the field were proposing methods for harassing his widow, and Bureau officials were trying to prevent his birthday from becoming a national holiday." Op. cit., note 5, book II, p. 223.

23. Ward Churchill, et. al., *The COINTELPRO Papers: Documents from the FBI's Secret Wars Against Dissent in America* (Boston: South End, 1990), p. 97.

24. Op. cit., note 5, Book III, p. 136.

25. Ibid.

26. The Church Committee summed up the limits on law enforcement agencies' methods of "preventing violence":

> "The prevention of violence is clearly not, in itself, an improper purpose, preventing violence is the ultimate goal of most law enforcement. Prosecution and sentencing are intended to deter future criminal behavior, not only of the subject but also of others who might break the law. In that sense, law enforcement legitimately attempts the indirect prevention of possible violence and, if the methods used are proper, raises no constitutional issues. When the government goes beyond traditional law enforcement methods, however, and attacks group membership and advocacy, it treads on ground forbidden to it by the Constitution. In Brandenburg v. Ohio, 395 U.S. 444 (1969), the Supreme Court held that the government is not permitted to 'forbid or proscribe advocacy of the use of force or law violation except where such advocacy is directed toward inciting or producing imminent lawless action and is likely to incite or produce such action.' In the absence of such clear and present danger, the government cannot act against speech nor, presumably against association." (Op. cit., note 5, Book III, p. 6.)

27. David E. Stannard, *American Holocaust: Columbus and the Conquest of the New World* (New York: Oxford University Press, 1992). An excerpt, p. 120:

> "[T]he surviving Indians later referred to [President George] Washington by the name 'Town Destroyer,' for it was under his direct orders that at least 28 of the 30 Seneca towns from Lake Erie to the Mohawk River had been totally obliterated in a period of less than five years, as had all the towns and villages of the Mohawk, the Onendaga, and the Cayuga. As one Iroquois told Washington to his face in 1792: 'To this day, when that name is heard, our woman folk look behind them and turn pale, and our children cling close to the necks of their mothers.'
>
> "[President Thomas] Jefferson ... in 1807 instructed his Secretary of War that any Indians who resisted American expansion into their lands must be met with 'the hatchet.' 'And ... if ever we are constrained to lift the hatchet against any tribe,' he wrote, 'we will never lay it down till that tribe is exterminated, or is driven beyond the Mississippi,' continuing: 'in war, they will kill some of us; we shall destroy all of them.' Indeed, Jefferson's writings on Indians are filled with the straightforward assertion that the natives are to be given a simple choice—to be 'extirpate[d] from the earth' or to remove themselves out of the Amerikans' way. Had these same words been enunciated by a German leader in 1939, and directed at European Jews, they would be engraved in modern memory."

In fact Hitler based his genocidal methods on study of the U.S. treatment of Native Americans. See, John Toland, *Adolf Hitler* (New York: Doubleday, 1976), p. 702. ("Hitler's concept of concentration camps as well as the practicability of genocide owed much, so he claimed, to his studies of English and United States history. He admired the camps for Boer prisoners in South Africa and for the Indians in the Wild West, and often praised to his inner circle the efficiency of America's extermination—by starvation and uneven combat—of the red savages who could not be tamed by captivity."); Joachim C. Fest, *Hitler* (New York: Harcourt Brace, 1973), p. 214 (Hitler's "continental war of conquest" was modeled "with explicit reference to the United States."); Richard Rubenstein, "Afterword: Genocide and Civilization," Isidor Wallimann, eds., et. al. *Genocide and the Modern Age: Etiology and Case Studies of Mass Death* (Westport, Ct: Greenwood, 1987), p. 288 ("Hitler saw the settlement of the New World and the concomitant elimination of North America's Indian population by white European settlers as a model to be followed by Germany on the European continent.")

On Columbus, see Samuel Eliot Morison, *Christopher Columbus, Mariner* (Boston: Little, Brown, 1955), p. 129:

> "By 1508 a census showed 60,000 of the estimated 1492 population of 250,000 [on Hispaniola] still alive, although the Bahamas and Cuba had been raided to obtain more slaves. Fifty years later, not 500 remained. The cruel policy initiated by Columbus and pursued by his successors resulted in complete genocide."

Furthermore, Washington and Jefferson were two of the largest slave-owners of their day. Jefferson, himself a pedophile, in fact, raped and ultimately sired children by a 14-year-old slave girl, Sally Hemings.

28. Prison officials' inciting and facilitating violent conflicts and "gladiator fights" between rival racial groups of prisoners is a common trend in U.S. prisons, as the 1997 documentary exposé film *Maximum Security University* revealed.

29. Ibid.

30. *The Nation*, "The Killing of Filiberto Ojeda Rios," October 7, 2005. http://www.thenation.com/doc/20051024/jimenez

31. Kurt Campbell, "Marching for Pretoria," *Boston Globe Magazine*, March 1, 1987, pp. 16f.

32. The National Security Act of July 26, 1947, which created the NSC and CIA, limits the powers of these agencies to political and military matters outside the U.S.

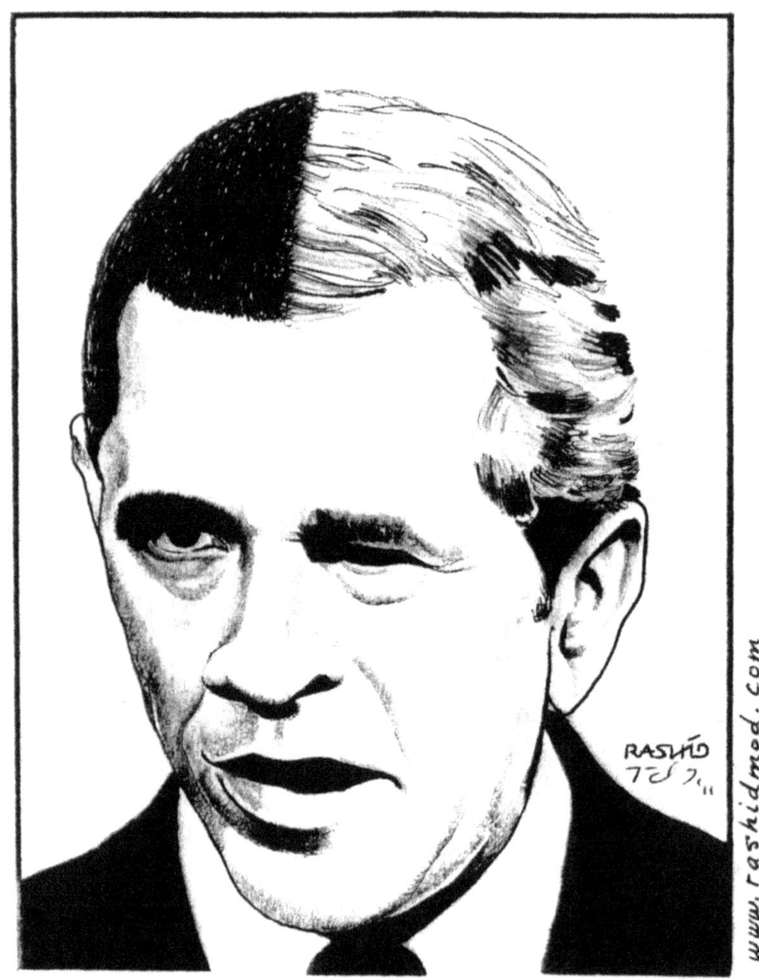


It's not as though Democrat and Republican are substantially different. They merely represent the two faces of fascism, one with a smile (Democrats) the other a sneer (Republican), the liberal and conservative. As Malcolm X described them: The fox and the wolf.

# 32. SOME THOUGHTS ON AMERIKAN FASCISM AND OUR CONTEMPORARY SITUATION 2006

"The Fascist State organizes the nation, but it leaves sufficient scope to individuals; it has limited useless or harmful liberties and has preserved those that are essential. It cannot be the individual who decides in this matter, but only the State."

*Benito Mussolini, 1922*

"Fascism is capitalism in decline."

*V.I. Lenin*

In the late 19th Century, banking and industrial capital merged to form finance capital and ushered in the Age of Proletarian Revolution. V.I. Lenin pointed this out in *Imperialism, the Highest Stage of Capitalism.* However, Lenin by no means meant that Imperialism (monopoly capitalism) would not itself continue to evolve until it was overthrown. In fact, he emphasized that we must define imperialism "as capitalism in transition, or, more precisely as moribund capitalism," or capitalism in decay, capitalism rotten ripe for revolution.

He emphasized that this decay was by no means negated by the rapidity of its growth, that the accelerated growth rate was symptomatic of its rottenness and parasitism. And that this decay manifested itself most profoundly in the countries richest in capital. Since Lenin's time, we have seen the evolution of Fascism as an even more virulent form of imperialism.

Lenin also recognized that in whatever stage of its evolution, capitalism balances two approaches to maintaining its power and control over the working masses: 1) The Carrot—bribery and liberal concessions, and 2) The Stick—violence and repression. In Lenin's words:

"The receipt of high monopoly profits by the capitalists in one of the numerous branches of industry, in one of the numerous countries, etc., makes it economically possible for them to bribe certain sections of the workers, and for a time a fairly considerable minority of them, and win them to the side of the bourgeoisie of a given industry or given nation against all the others. The intensification of antagonisms between imperialist nations for the division of the world increases this striving. And so there is created that bond

> between imperialism and opportunism, which revealed itself first and most clearly in England, owing to the fact that certain features of imperialist development were observable there much earlier than in other countries."

Fascism emerged in Italy and spread to Germany and other countries which did not have the colonial base to extract super-profits from to compete with the Western Democracies in the employment of bribery for the workers. Thus they employed "the stick." Ironically, Fascism, founded in 1919 by Benito Mussolini, should come from the name of a bundle of sticks. The Italian name of the movement, fascismo, is derived from fascio, "bundle, (political) group," but also refers to the movement's emblem, the fasces, a bundle of rods (sticks) bound around a projecting axe-head that was carried before an ancient Roman magistrate by an attendant as a symbol of authority and power. In Mussolini's words:

> "... For Fascism, the growth of empire, that is to say the expansion of the nation, is an essential manifestation of vitality, and its opposite a sign of decadence. Peoples which are rising, or rising again after a period of decadence, are always imperialist; and renunciation is a sign of decay and of death. Fascism is the doctrine best adapted to represent the tendencies and the aspirations of a people, like the people of Italy, who are rising again after many centuries of abasement and foreign servitude. But empire demands discipline, the coordination of all forces and a deeply felt sense of duty and sacrifice: this fact explains many aspects of the practical working of the regime, the character of many forces in the State, and the necessarily severe measures which must be taken against those who would oppose this spontaneous and inevitable movement of Italy in the twentieth century, and would oppose it by recalling the outworn ideology of the nineteenth century—repudiated wheresoever there has been the courage to undertake great experiments of social and political transformation; for never before has the nation stood more in need of authority, of direction and order. If every age has its own characteristic doctrine, there are a thousand signs which point to Fascism as the characteristic doctrine of our time. For if a doctrine must be a living thing, this is proved by the fact that Fascism has created a living faith; and that this faith is very powerful in the minds of men is demonstrated by those who have suffered and died for it."

Dr. Lawrence Britt has examined the fascist regimes of Hitler (Germany), Mussolini (Italy), Franco (Spain), Suharto (Indonesia) and several Latin American regimes. Britt found 14 defining characteristics common to each:

"1. Powerful and Continuing Nationalism: Fascist regimes tend to make constant use of patriotic mottos, slogans, symbols, songs and other paraphernalia. Flags are seen everywhere, as are flag symbols on clothing and in public displays.

"2. Disdain for the Recognition of Human Rights: Because of fear of enemies and the need for security, the people in fascist regimes are persuaded that human rights can be ignored in certain cases because of 'need.' The people tend to look the other way or even approve of torture, summary executions, assassinations, long incarcerations of prisoners, etc.

"3. Identification of Enemies/Scapegoats as a Unifying Cause: The people are rallied into a unifying patriotic frenzy over the need to eliminate a perceived common threat or foe: racial, ethnic, or religious minorities; liberals; communists; socialists; terrorists, etc.

"4. Supremacy of the Military: Even when there are widespread domestic problems, the military is given a disproportionate amount of government funding, and the domestic agenda is neglected. Soldiers and military service are glamorized.

"5. Rampant Sexism: The governments of fascist nations tend to be almost exclusively male-dominated. Under fascist regimes, traditional gender roles are made more rigid. Divorce, abortion and homosexuality are suppressed and the state is represented as the ultimate guardian of the family institution.

"6. Controlled Mass Media: Sometimes the media is directly controlled by the government, but in other cases, the media is indirectly controlled by government regulation, or sympathetic media spokespeople and executives. Censorship, especially in war time, is very common.

"7. Obsession with National Security: Fear is used as a motivational tool by the government over the masses.

"8. Religion and Government are Intertwined: Governments in fascist nations tend to use the most common religion in the nation as a tool to manipulate public opinion. Religious rhetoric and terminology is common from government leaders, even when the major tenets of the religion are diametrically opposed to the government's policies or actions.

"9. Corporate Power is Protected: The industrial and business aristocracy of a fascist nation often are the ones who put the government leaders into power, creating a mutually beneficial business/government relationship and power elite.

"10. Labor Power is Suppressed: Because the organizing power of labor is the only real threat to a fascist government, labor unions are either eliminated entirely, or are severely suppressed.

"11. Disdain for Intellectuals and the Arts: Fascist nations tend to promote and tolerate open hostility to higher education, and academia. It is not uncommon for professors and other academics to be censored or even arrested. Free expression in the arts and letters is openly attacked.

"12. Obsession with Crime and Punishment: Under fascist regimes, the police are given almost limitless power to enforce laws. The people are often willing to overlook police abuses and even forego civil liberties in the name patriotism. There is often a national police force with virtually unlimited power in fascist nations.

"13. Rampant Cronyism and Corruption: Fascist regimes almost always are governed by groups of friends and associates who appoint each other to government positions and use governmental power and authority to protect their friends from accountability. It is not uncommon in fascist regimes for national resources and even treasures to be appropriated or even outright stolen by government leaders.

"14. Fraudulent Elections: Sometimes elections in fascist nations are a complete sham. Other times elections are manipulated by smear campaigns against or even assassination of opposition candidates, use of legislation to control voting numbers or political district boundaries, and manipulation of the media. Fascist nations also typically use their judiciaries to manipulate or control elections."

"Fascism Anybody?" *Free Inquiry,* Spring 2003, p. 20

George Jackson pointed out in his essay "Classes at War: Mobilization and Contra-Mobilization," that at home Amerika's liberal fascist mode took on the form of liberal democracy in the "New Deal," and after WWII as Cold War liberalism—which applied neocolonialism in the 3rd World (namely replacing European colonial administrations with overtly fascist ones under the pretense of promoting "democracy.") While at home, Cold War liberalism combined intense anti-Communist propaganda and McCarthyism with liberal concessions promoting opportunism in the trade unions and the Civil Rights movement.

The super profits generated from super-exploitation in the 3rd World financed the bribery of a section of the industrial working class to the point where some unionized workers were actually being paid more than the value of their labor. This served the dual purpose of both winning the unions away from the "reds" and "radicals" who had built them and enabling the large multinational-based corporations to squeeze out and absorb the smaller national-based companies, who could not pay the higher wags and compete, allowing the monopoly capitalists to consolidate their control over the U.S. economy.

WWII had pulled the U.S. economy out of the "Great Depression." As Richard B. DuBoff pointed out in *Accumulation and Power: An Economic History of the United States*:

> "Only the second world war ended the Great Depression. 'Rearmament' commenced in 1940, and over the next year, before the Japanese attack on Pearl Harbor, military spending jumped more than six-fold, to 11 percent of the GNP. It rose to 42 percent of the GNP in 1943–44. Under this immense stimulus, real national product increased 65 percent from 1940 through 1944, industrial production by 90 percent ... What had really happened between 1929 and 1933 is that the institutions of the nineteenth-century free market growth broke down, beyond repair ... The tumultuous passage from the depression of the 1930s to the total economic mobilization of the 1940s was the watershed in twentieth century capitalism. After that nothing would ever be the same; there was no going back to the days of a pure, practically unregulated capitalist economic order."

The merger of corporate and state interests was a reality. As Fred J. Borch, the president of G.E., put it in a speech before the Economic Club of New York on November 9, 1964: "Overriding both the common and cross-purposes of business and government, there is a broad pattern—a consensus if you will, where public and private interests come together, cooperate, interact, and become the national interest."

Mussolini would have applauded loudly.

Let us return again to Lenin for it is impossible to really grasp what fascism is without firmly grasping what imperialism as the highest stage of capitalism is all about, for it is the economic essence that drives fascism and determines the form it will take:

> "We have seen that in its economic essence imperialism is monopoly capitalism. This in itself determines its place in history, for

monopoly that grows out of the soil of free competition, and precisely out of free competition, is the transition from the capitalist system to a higher socio-economic order. We must take special note of the four principal types of monopoly, or principal manifestations of monopoly capitalism, which are characteristic of the epoch we are examining.

"Firstly, monopoly arose out of the concentration of production at a very high stage. This refers to the monopolist capitalist associations, cartels, syndicates, and trusts. We have seen the important part these play in present-day economic life. At the beginning of the twentieth century, monopolies had acquired complete supremacy in the advanced countries, and although the first steps towards the formation of the cartels were taken by countries enjoying the protection of high tariffs (Germany, America), Great Britain, with her system of free trade, revealed the same basic phenomenon, only a little later, namely, the birth of monopoly out of the concentration of production.

"Secondly, monopolies have stimulated the seizure of the most important sources of raw materials, especially for the basic and most highly cartelized industries in capitalist society: the coal and iron industries. The monopoly of the most important sources of raw materials has enormously increased the power of big capital, and has sharpened the antagonism between cartelized and non-cartelized industry.

"Thirdly, monopoly has sprung from the banks. The banks have developed from modest middleman enterprises into the monopolists of finance capital. Some three to five of the biggest banks in each of the foremost capitalist countries have achieved the 'personal link-up' between industrial and bank capital, and have concentrated in their hands the control of thousands upon thousands of millions which form the greater part of the capital and income of entire countries. A financial oligarchy, which throws a close network of dependence relationships over all the economic and political institutions of present-day bourgeois society without exception—such is the most striking manifestation of this monopoly.

"Fourthly, monopoly has grown out of colonial policy. To the numerous 'old' motives of colonial policy, finance capital has added the struggle for the sources of raw materials, for the export of capital, for spheres of influence, i.e., for spheres for profitable deals, concessions, monopoly profits and so on, economic territory in general. When the colonies of the European powers, for instance, comprised only one-tenth of the territory of Africa (as was the case in 1876), colonial policy was able to develop—by methods other than those of monopoly—by the 'free grabbing' of territories, so to speak. But when nine-tenths of Africa had been seized (by 1900), when the whole world had been divided up, there was inevitably ushered in the era of monopoly possession of colonies and, consequently, of particularly intense struggle for the division and the redivision of the world.

"The extent to which monopolist capital has intensified all the contradictions of capitalism is generally known. It is sufficient to mention the high cost of living and the tyranny of the cartels. This intensification of contradictions constitutes the most powerful driving force of the transitional period of history, which began from the time of the final victory of world finance capital.

"Monopolies, oligarchy, the striving for domination and not for freedom, the exploitation of an increasing number of small or weak nations by a handful of the richest or most powerful nations—all these have given birth to those distinctive characteristics of imperialism which compel us to define it as parasitic or decaying capitalism. More and more prominently there emerges, as one of the tendencies of imperialism, the creation of the 'rentier state', the usurer state, in which the bourgeoisie to an ever-increasing degree lives on the proceeds of capital exports and by 'clipping coupons'. It would be a mistake to believe that this tendency to decay precludes the rapid growth of capitalism. It does not. In the epoch of imperialism, certain branches of industry, certain strata of the bourgeoisie and certain countries betray, to a greater or lesser degree, now one and now another of these tendencies. On the whole, capitalism is growing far more rapidly than before; but this growth is not only becoming more and more uneven in general, its unevenness also manifests itself, in particular, in the decay of the countries which are richest in capital (England)."

In the space between WWI and WWII, monopoly capitalism plunged the world into the Great Depression, with the exception of the then socialist Soviet Union. The overtly fascist Axis powers (led by Germany, Italy and Japan) formed a bloc to challenge the Western European imperialists and the U.S. for a redivision of the world's spheres of influence and domination. (After the Spanish Civil War, fascist Spain and Portugal remained "neutral.") There were strong movements towards overt fascism in the West, most notably in France, but also in England with the National Front, and in the U.S., where the KKK reached its peak

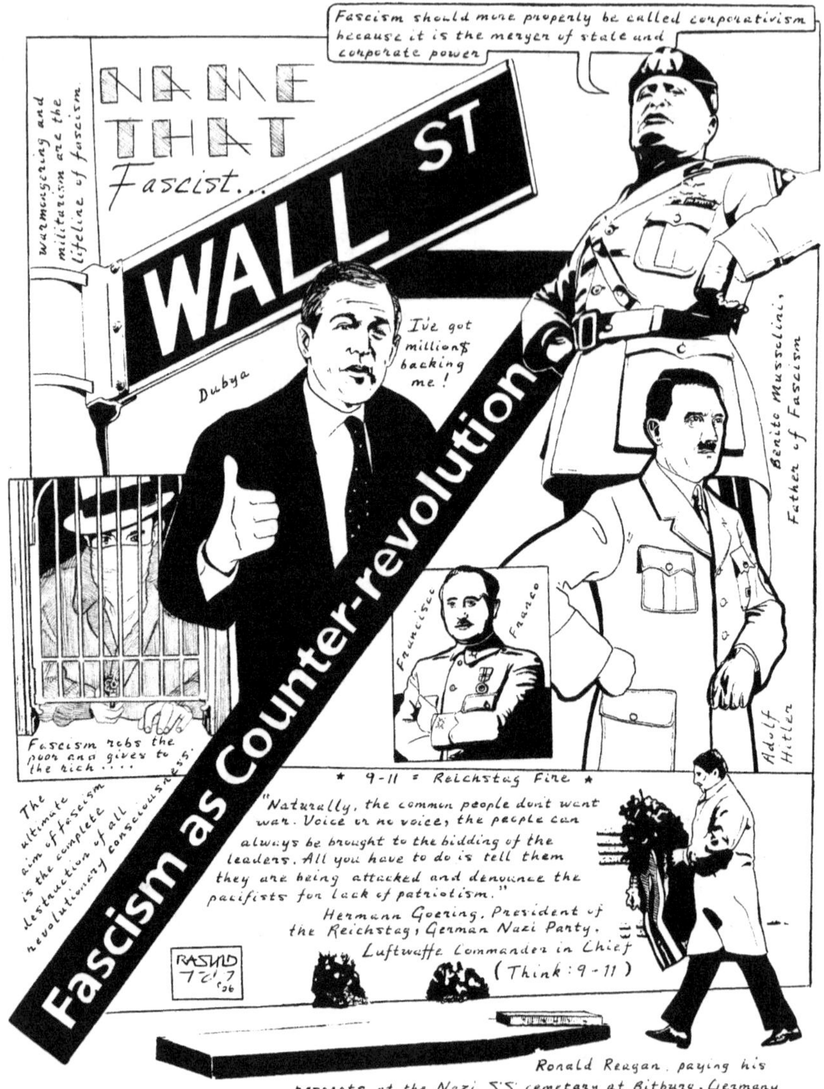


strength in the 1920s and the American Nazi party (and others of their ilk) held mass rallies. A significant section of the bankers, (including Prescott Bush, George W. Bush's grandfather, who was Hitler's banker in New York), and industrialists, like Henry Ford (who was awarded the Iron Cross by Hitler), openly called for overt fascism in America. *Time Magazine* even made Mussolini its "Man of the Year."

While FDR and his "New Deal" did not pull the U.S. economy out of the Great Depression, it did stave off overt fascism and succeeded in pulling a significant section of the rising Left into the opportunist belief that socialism could be achieved through liberal democratic reform rather than revolution. Few identified the "New Deal" as a covert form of fascism.

When the Axis Powers made their bid to conquer Europe and grab up their rivals' colonial possessions, and at the same time to invade and attempt to conquer the Soviet Union, the Left jumped to unite with their own bourgeoisie, forgetting the class struggle in the name of a United Front against Fascism.

The Left had a hard time coming to grips with the rise of fascism and flip-flopped on how to respond to it. At first it was seen as no big threat. Many former socialists and anarchists were recruited into its ranks during fascism's "left" phase, when it was out of power. Mussolini had himself been kicked out of the Socialist Party, and Hitler had been a police spy within the socialist movement. So they were familiar with how to conduct propaganda to appeal to sections of the working masses. After gaining power, the fascists moved against the Left with a vengeance. This too was hard for the Left to gauge and the tendency was to only recognize fascism in its overt form and see it as wholly outside the framework of bourgeois democracy.

## The Class Character of Fascism

> "Comrades, fascism in power was correctly described by the Thirteenth Plenum of the Executive Committee of the Communist International as the open terrorist dictatorship of the most reactionary, most chauvinistic and most imperialist elements of finance capital.
>
> "The most reactionary variety of fascism is the German type of fascism. It has the effrontery to call itself National Socialism, though it has nothing in common with socialism. German fascism is not only bourgeois nationalism, it is fiendish chauvinism. It is a government system of political gangsterism, a system of provocation and torture practiced upon the working class and the revolutionary elements of the peasantry, the petty bourgeoisie and the intelligentsia. It is medieval barbarity and bestiality, it is unbridled aggression in relation to other nations.
>
> "German fascism is acting as the spearhead of international counter-revolution, as the chief instigator of imperialist war, as the initiator of a crusade against the Soviet Union, the great fatherland of the working people of the whole world.
>
> "Fascism is not a form of state power 'standing above both classes—the proletariat and the bourgeoisie,' as Otto Bauer, for instance, has

asserted. It is not 'the revolt of the petty bourgeoisie which has captured the machinery of the state,' as the British Socialist Brailsford declares. No, fascism is not a power standing above class, nor government of the petty bourgeoisie or the lumpen proletariat over finance capital. Fascism is the power of finance capital itself. It is the organization of terrorist vengeance against the working class and the revolutionary section of the peasantry and intelligentsia. In foreign policy, fascism is jingoism in its most brutal form, fomenting bestial hatred of other nations.

"This, the true character of fascism, must be particularly stressed because in a number of countries, under cover of social demagogy, fascism has managed to gain the following of the mass of the petty bourgeoisie that has been dislocated by the crisis, and even of certain sections of the most backward strata of the proletariat. These would never have supported fascism if they had understood its real character and its true nature.

"The development of fascism, and the fascist dictatorship itself, assume different forms in different countries, according to historical, social and economic conditions and to the national peculiarities, and the international position of the given country. In certain countries, principally those in which fascism has no broad mass basis and in which the struggle of the various groups within the camp of the fascist bourgeoisie itself is rather acute, fascism does not immediately venture to abolish parliament, but allows the other bourgeois parties, as well as the Social-Democratic Parties, to retain a modicum of legality. In other countries, where the ruling bourgeoisie fears an early outbreak of revolution, fascism establishes its unrestricted political monopoly, either immediately or by intensifying its reign of terror against and persecution of all rival parties and groups. This does not prevent fascism, when its position becomes particularly acute, from trying to extend its basis and, without altering its class nature, trying to combine open terrorist dictatorship with a crude sham of parliamentarism ..."

Georgi Dimitrov, "The Fascist Offensive and the Tasks of the Communist International in the Struggle of the Working Class against Fascism," Main Report delivered at the Seventh World Congress of the Communist International.

It is a big mistake to view overt fascism as stronger and more dangerous than covert fascism. Rather it is an expression of weakness and desperation. So long as they can, the monopoly capitalists will mask their dictatorship and maintain the illusion of liberal democracy.

Dimitrov had this backwards. The Axis Powers were from the start weaker than the more established Western imperialists, and they were doomed from the start to lose their bid for world domination, but few in the Communist movement, other than Mao Tse-tung, could see this. When ordered to subordinate the Chinese Red Army to the nationalist KMT, he only changed the Army's name. He never surrendered control of it nor the liberated base areas it controlled to the KMT, whom he recognized as being fascist to the core. He never gave up the initiative of the Chinese Communist Party and its revolutionary orientation to the United Front against Fascism.

Unfortunately, this was not the case elsewhere. Even the Communist International was disbanded in the interest of building closer ties with the Western "democracies." In Amerika, the CPUSA completely let down its guard and abandoned the class struggle, and it deluded itself with the illusion of postwar cooperation between the U.S. and the USSR and was completely taken by surprise when the U.S. initiated the Cold War. So were the CPs of Western Europe and the leadership of the Soviet Union.

Instead of rallying the workers and masses to resist McCarthyism, the Party ordered its cadre who were hauled before the House Un-American Activities Committee to plead the Fifth like criminals and meekly accept being blacklisted. It liquidated the party in the South without discussion, and it ordered half its cadre to go underground and await the onset of "fascism" and left them there. When the revolutionary upsurge came in the '60s, there was no communist vanguard party to give it leadership. It had thrown itself on its sword in the '50s. It was up to the revolutionary masses to create their own vanguard party.

America is moving towards overt fascism, because of weakness:

> "As in Italy and Germany in the '20s and '30s, business associations clamour for more deregulation and deeper tax cuts. The gradual erosion of antitrust legislation, especially in the United States, has encouraged consolidation in many sectors of the economy by way of mergers and acquisitions. The North American economy has become more monopolistic than at any time in the post-WWII period.
>
> "U.S. census data from 1997 shows that the largest four companies in the food, motor vehicle and aerospace industries control 53.4, 87.3 and 55.6 per cent of their respective markets. Over 20 per cent of commercial banking in the U.S. is controlled by the four largest financial institutions, with the largest 50 controlling over 60 per cent. Even these numbers underestimate the scope of concentration, since they do not account for the myriad interconnections

between firms by means of debt instruments and multiple directorships, which further reduce the extent of competition.

"Actual levels of U.S. commercial concentration have been difficult to measure since the 1970s, when strong corporate opposition put an end to the Federal Trade Commission's efforts to collect the necessary information.

"Fewer, larger competitors dominate all economic activity, and their political will is expressed with the millions of dollars they spend lobbying politicians and funding policy formulation in the many right-wing institutes that now limit public discourse to the question of how best to serve the interests of business.

"The consolidation of the economy and the resulting perversion of public policy are themselves fascistic. I am certain, however, that former president Bill Clinton was not worried about fascism when he repealed federal antitrust laws that had been enacted in the 1930s."

Paul Bigioni, "Fascism Then, Fascism Now?"
*Toronto Star*, November 27, 2005

The monopoly capitalist class is in trouble. Not because the left is so strong, but because imperialism is moribund capitalism, and it is in decay from within.

*Dare to Struggle, Dare to Win!*
*All Power to the People!*

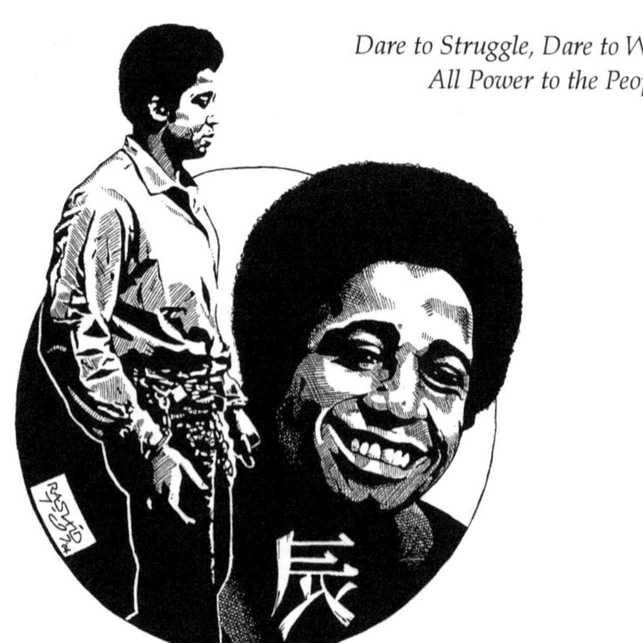

# 33. THANKSGIVING: CELEBRATING GENOCIDE AND U.S. IMPERIALIST LIES 2010

It's interesting how history is whitewashed. Many of it's most horrendous crimes are not just concealed, but often repackaged as benevolent and honorable deeds to be commemorated and celebrated. Thanksgiving is an example.

The true history of Thanksgiving is very different from the false story we're taught in American schools and through mainstream channels. The first unofficial Thanksgiving occurred in 1621 following the pilgrims' surviving their first harsh winter in Plymouth, thanks to Indian advice and help. There was no big loving relationship between the pilgrims and the Narragansett, Pequot and Wampanoag Indians. Not on the pilgrims' part anyway. The pilgrims had actually built an eleven foot high wall around the Plymouth settlement to keep the Indians out. And just a few days before the feast, Miles Standish, one of the leading pilgrims, led a group of pilgrims on an expedition to kill a local Indian chief. The Indians who were on hand during that first unofficial Thanksgiving were actually neither invited nor welcomed.

Thanksgiving as an official holiday came into being sixteen years later in 1637. And again, it wasn't a holiday to celebrate any loving

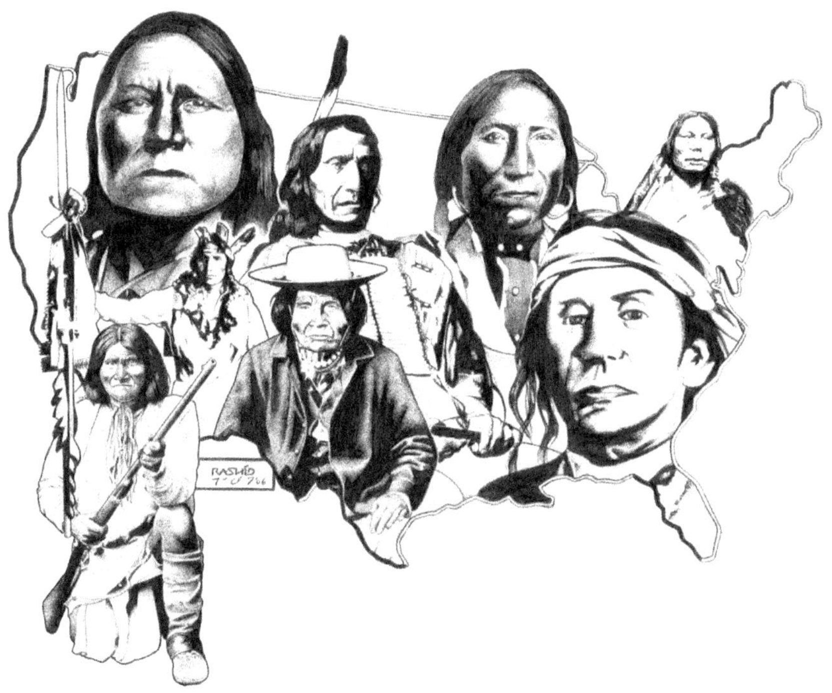

relationship between the European settlers and the Indians who'd done so much to help them survive in rugged North Amerika. This first official Thanksgiving Day was declared by John Winthrop, governor of Massachusetts Bay colony, to celebrate the return of the colony's men from an expedition in which they participated in the massacre of over 700 Pequot children, wimyn and men, in what is now Mystic, Connecticut. Winthrop officially declared and dedicated this holiday to give thanks for this so-called victory in mass-murdering a defenceless Indian community.

Glamorizing these sorts of crimes by distorting and erasing their true histories, set the stage for whitewashing and erasing from modern memory two of history's greatest crimes. Crimes that created these United States and its monopoly capitalist political economy. The first being the deliberate genocidal murders of over a hundred million Native Americans, destruction of their cultures and lifestyles, the early enslavement of many, and the continued forced confinement for over a century of those who sought to hold onto their heritage and cultures in concentration camps, euphemistically called reservations. The Natives confined to these concentration camps are left to a slow deterioration with casinos and alcohol supplied to aid in their distraction and destruction.

Likewise, the second greatest whitewashed crime of Amerika was the murders of over fifty million Afrikans in our brutal forced transport away from our native lands and to the Amerikas, to serve as slave laborers that cultivated, enriched and indeed built Amerika on this stolen land; the destruction of our cultures, heritage and histories; the systematic rapes of the Black femyl slaves and domestic servants (wimyn and girls); and our subsequent forced migrations into urban refugee camps to serve as super-cheap laborers, where we remain confined, euphemistically called the "hood." The Blacks/New Afrikans who are today concentrated in the urban centers are, like the reservation Indians, left to a slow deterioration, but instead with the club and dope to aid our distraction and destruction.

Before there was an Underground Railroad, freedom for many enslaved Afrikans was found within the Indian and Mexican nations. The struggles and history of suffering of Amerika's Native and Afrikan peoples was a common one and continues to be. And many poor whites rejected the lies of white supremacy and joined with the Natives and New Afrikans in our struggles against national, racial and class oppression and exploitation at the hands of Amerikan imperialism and capitalism. It has been the system of imperialism and capitalism that has designs to keep us divided and ruled.

It is in the spirit of these unified struggles of the oppressed against this ongoing oppressive system, that the New Afrikan Black Panther

Party-Prison Chapter joins with the Red Heart Warriors Society, the White Panther Organization, the Brown Panther Organization, the New Afrikan Service Organization and all other revolutionaries and progressive groups and peoples in exposing truth and struggling to raise the banner of genuine independence, self-determination and revolutionary people's power for all oppressed peoples.

So we say New Afrikan Power to New Afrikan People! Native Power to Native People! Latin@ power to Latin@ people! Mexican power to Mexican People! And Panther Love to all who stand firmly opposed to imperialism and the lies that sustain imperialism.

*Dare to Struggle, Dare to Win!*
*All Power to the People!*

# 34. ON THE LYNCHING OF TROY DAVIS

## 2011

On September 21st Troy Davis was lynched for the 1989 death of a Savannah, Georgia policeman, of which he was known to be innocent. When I heard of his murder at the hands of Georgia representatives, my mind traveled back in time; to lynchings no less sinister, carried out by the "good" citizenry of Georgia against innocent Black life.

I thought of Mary Turner. Not because her lynching back in 1918 was any more depraved than Troy Davis' in 2011. But because both are a measure of the value of Black life in Amerika. That the more things change, the more they stay the same. They also reflect the sickness that underlies this rotten capitalist system, which can bring people to rationalize and glory in sadistic destruction of innocent life, devalued because of its color and class.

Mary Turner was gruesomely murdered by a jubilant white mob on May 18, 1918, in Valdosta, Georgia. A white man had been killed. The suspected killer, a Black man, was found and lynched. But so too were several other New Afrikan men, including Mary Turner's husband—all known to be innocent of the white man's death. But just like Troy Davis' killers, the mob didn't care. Passions raged, seeking an outlet. So mob mayhem was incited, with local government officials in the vanguard.

Eight months pregnant and in a wife's anguish, Mary cried out for justice. The mob heard her cry, and came for her too.

As reported in the May 18 *New York Times*, she was dragged down an abandoned road, hanged upside down from a tree, doused with gasoline and oil, and, still alive, had her clothes burned off. Her belly was cut open and her premature baby fell to the ground, when it cried out weakly its head was smashed beneath the boot heel of one of the mob's members. Mary was then shot hundreds of times.

Heinous as it was, this 1918 lynching reflected the typical conduct of "respectable" citizens who often celebrated their deeds, posing for group photos and keeping body parts for souvenirs. None feared prosecution, since the laws have always served to persecute not protect us. It also reflected, as does the lynching of Troy Davis today, that innocence means nothing when the hypocritical hounds of American "law and order" come for sport and vengeance against poor Black life.

All of us, poor, urban Black and Brown know this like second nature. It was known a century ago, like it's known today ... We are all Troy Davis.

*Dare to Struggle, Dare to Win! All Power to the People!*

# 35. IT'S RAINING PIGS, RATS AND MOLES! VERMIN CULTURE, "GOOD COP" BRAINWASH, AND NATIONAL OPPRESSION IN AMERIKA

2012

### The "Good Cop" Brainwash

In Amerika, government-empowered forces (military, police, spy agencies, jailers and their proxies) have been *the* key forces of persecution and violence against minority nationalities and people of color. Whether the military, slave patrols, slave drivers and overseers, or lynch mobs and racist paramilitary groups; whether COINTELPROs and urban police or the Prison-Industrial Complex; whether the Wars on Drugs, Crime and Gangs in pretended response to the U.S. government itself flooding the ghettos and barrios with narcotics, military grade firearms, and inciting gang wars, or the blatant multi-agency *declaration of war* (Martial Law) against Louisiana's desperate, stranded and officially abandoned Black Hurricane Katrina victims and subsequent policy of ethnic cleansing in New Orleans, etc. Executive forces have been *anything* but our servants and protectors.

Yet the entertainment media (the *real* CBS: Central Brainwash System) is infested with fantasy images of romanticized vermin (pigs, moles and rats): hero cops, and military action figures, spy agent intrigue and shifty informants. But nowhere do they show the *actual* violence, oppression and terror these vermin inflict on poor people of color every day across Amerika. And what's worse is the conscious effort to cast these good cop images in Blackface.

From Ice Cube (of "Fuck Tha Police" rap fame) as a cop in *All About the Benjamins*, to Ice T (who back in the day also spit anti-police rhymes like "Cop Killer") starring in *Law and Order* as a cop and as a snitch in *Boyz in the Hood*; even activist actor Danny Glover as a cop in the *Lethal Weapon* series; Will Smith as an urban cop alongside Martin Lawrence in the *Bad Boys* series, as an Air Force pilot in *Independence Day* (commemorating July 4th, a holiday celebrating a war fought in large part to keep Black folks in slavery and exterminate Natives), and as a futuristic cop in *I-Robot*; Samuel L. Jackson, in *The Negotiator*, who only as a cop could rise above the law and resort to "crime" (taking hostages and multiple shoot-outs with other cops) to clear himself of being framed by cops with killing another cop [!?]; Martin Lawrence, again as a cop (impersonator) in *Blue Streaks*. Then there's Chris Tucker alongside Jackie Chan in the *Rush Hour* series, and Jamie Foxx in *Miami Vice* and *Stealth*, Denzel Washington in *Training Day* and as a rogue spy in *Safe House*, DMX in *Exit Wounds*, Morgan Freeman in *Kiss the Girls*, *Along Came a Spider* and so on *ad nauseam*. In most all other roles Blacks are cast as criminals and villains.

It's "Good Cop Brainwash" and criminal stereotyping projected in modern minstrel shows, which the system finds necessary to gloss over the continued growth in size and violence of *Pigs in the Hood*, and to perpetuate a criminalized image of the poor urban people of color that they brutally occupy.

Indeed, in the era of the War on Drugs (on government-supplied drugs that is), heavily-armored paramilitary SWAT teams have become everyday parts of oppressive urban policing, while TV gives a totally distorted portrayal of their role. As one critical race writer, Steve Martinot, observed, "Swat team operations are presented on TV cop shows as well-choreographed high-tech raids in dangerous situations. But 80% of their 'raids' are to serve warrants on people of color for non-violent crimes."[1]

Prominent critical intellectual Noam Chomsky revealed:

> "Recently there've been some very interesting studies of urban police behavior done at George Washington University, by a rather well-known criminologist named William Chambliss. For the last couple of years he's been running projects in cooperation with the Washington, D.C. police, in which he has law students and sociology students ride with the police in their patrol cars to take transcripts of what happens. I mean, you've got to read this stuff: it is targeted against Black and Hispanic populations almost entirely. And they are not treated like a criminal population, because criminals have constitutional rights—they're treated like a population under military occupation. So the effective laws are: the police go to somebody's house, they smash in the door, they beat the people up, they grab some kid they want, and they throw him in jail."[2]

Cops don't make our communities safer, nor do they positively impact the people's security needs, nor reduce "crime," nor the drug plagues. Even Malcolm X recognized, decades ago, that when the police presence increases yet community problems only worsen, the police are obviously a big part of the problem. Steve Martinot gave a vivid example of this in the tragic story of Adam Hakim, a Black New York youth who was the victim of a massive "search and kill" police manhunt, which concluded in his being beaten and paralyzed by guards, because he refused to sell drugs for local cops in his neighborhood.[3]

I've previously written in some detail about the well-documented practice and designs of U.S. police in persecuting, murdering, then attempting to replace popular independent New Afrikan political leaders like prominent Black Panther Party members, Malcolm X, Dr. Martin Luther King, Jr. and others.[4] Also, their roles in facilitating crimes, violence, gang wars and the drug plagues in our oppressed communities, then in turn expanding the police presence and violence, and mass imprisoning us where we cannot reproduce and fathers are torn away from our families and communities—also well documented.[5]

So, the media image projected of the pig establishment is a far cry from, indeed the very opposite of, reality. Their role has been to make war on, contain, criminalize and cripple our communities, which the drug plague plays a key role in.

> "The presence of drugs gets people fighting among themselves over the money generated by trafficking. Massive drug presence in a community produces a strung-out and desperate populous, increasing petty crime and gang warfare over control of the trade. A tide of actual criminality emerges, feeding stereotypes that have criminalized those communities before the fact. Ostensibly to stem this tide, police departments demand bigger appropriations from state legislatures. They expand to become very powerful political forces in urban areas, which they manifest through increased militarization and aggressiveness. That power is now nationally coordinated and centralized through the Law Enforcement Assistance Act passed under Nixon."[6]

## Why the "Good Cop" Brainwash?

Why indeed is there the perpetual onslaught of Good Cop brainwash?

*First* off, glamorizing pigs and generating preoccupation with crime and punishment are essential elements of fascism. Dr. Lawrence Britt observed this in his comparative study of various fascist regimes of Hitler (Germany), Mussolini (Italy), Franco (Spain), Suharto (Indonesia) and several in Latin America. Among 14 common features of fascism, Britt listed:

Obsession with crime and punishment: under fascist regimes, the police are given almost limitless power to enforce laws. The people are often willing to overlook police abuses and even forego civil liberties in the name of patriotism. There is often a national police force with virtually unlimited power in fascist nations.

Supremacy of the Military: Even when there are widespread domestic problems, the military is given a disproportionate amount of government funding, and the domestic agenda is neglected. Soldiers and military service are glamorized.

Other features common to fascist systems relevant to this discussion are:

Controlled Mass Media: Sometimes the media is directly controlled by the government, but in other cases, the media is indirectly controlled by government regulation, or sympathetic media spokespeople and executives. Censorship, especially in wartime, is very common.[7]

*Second*, as the U.S. economy slips further towards acute depression, the line dividing the haves (the capitalist imperialists) and their vermin gunslingers, and the have-nots (the working-class and the poor) is being drawn more sharply. With economic want and instability comes doubt and distrust of the masses in those in power. In turn society becomes increasingly polarized between those who conform and those who oppose the *status quo*. As resistance increases the vermin become more extreme in repressing and villainizing it. These are the dynamics, the dialectics that generate mass revolutionary struggle to overthrow oppressive and exploitative systems, like we live under. Thus conformity versus resistance must be cast in a "law abiding" versus "criminal" light, placing malcontents on one side, with the ruling class and their vermin and conformists on the other. The masses are driven to choose sides. Indeed for oppressed community youth, the only options presented to them, early on, by the system are to become either "criminal" or "cop."[8] Hence the media glorification of the Black soldier/cop role and preoccupation with "crime and punishment."

*Third*, up to and during the 1960s–'70s high tide of revolutionary struggle in Amerika, the blatant official violence against people of color here and abroad, and open persecution and government-orchestrated murders of popular independent New Afrikan leaders and activists, exposed the *real* oppressive character of the pigs and U.S. vermin culture, driving mass resistance against the system. In "Protect Our Leaders Defend Our People," I pointed out that a 1970 survey found that brutal police violence against the Black Panthers led some 80% of urban Blacks "to believe that Black people must stand together to protect themselves" *against* the police, who were certainly not seen nor embraced as our heroes or helpers. I quoted comrade Sundiata Acoli's observation that the increasing role of Black cops in the media was a conscious effort to repair the pigs' image and conceal their real function:

> "... a large part of the programs on TV are still 'police stories' and many of the roles available to Black actors are limited to police roles. A lot of this has to do with the overall process of still trying

> to rehabilitate the image of police from its devastating exposure during the Panther era, and to prevent the true role of the police in this society from being exposed again."[9]

To achieve this effect today, and counter Black opposition to pig oppression, popular Black entertainers with independent street credibility (rap artists, comedians, etc.) are "turned" and *used* to popularize and glamorize pigs and vermin culture to the very people they oppress, and to project criminal stereotypes of their own people, culture and communities. Note too that the vermin are *always* portrayed as wealthy or upper middle class, and possessing the material trappings of Amerikan "success": large homes, flashy cars and clothes, beautiful women, etc. And they are literally above the law, with the power to execute or set-up and thereby dispose of opponents and exact revenge, usually without consequences to themselves.

*Fourth*, by casting vermin as the only legitimate models of social heroes and objects of achievable power and respect to be held in awe and sympathy by the oppressed, the system teaches aspirations toward and conformity to pig "authority," and counters a possible resurgent revolutionary mass culture which would instead promote the masses of people as the real heroes, and the only *legitimate* power holders who should *and can* take control of their own communities' security needs. This is also why the common people are always portrayed in these dramas as helpless, especially in response to "corrupt" pigs. Vermin culture projects pigs as invulnerable and imperious to challenge by the common people, who must suffer passively and hope some hero good cops will rescue them. However, the oppressed communities *can* rid themselves of death dealing dope peddlers and their pig supply lines, and gangsters who prey on the people, and resist killer cops and paramilitary goons like the KKK. If the people come to see themselves as the true heroes and agents of real change, as capable of being organized and united to meet their own economic, political, cultural and security needs, this would eliminate their conditioned belief that we need to turn to the pigs and system to solve our problems, which they have never done anyway!

Allowing such ideas to take root and spread is intolerable to any enslaver, since it reveals to the enslaved whom he profits off and rules by force and fraud that they don't need him, and they can seize and exercise their own formal *independence*. This would deprive the enslaver of the very source of his wealth and power. Namely us. This is what the Black Panther Party was teaching urban New Afrikans and other oppressed people through its "Serve the People" community survival programs. For pigs to be able to function or even exist in our communities requires our cooperation and communication with them. Recall the instant media and industry backlash to suppress the popular grassroots

"Stop Snitching" movement a few years back? Now all one sees are pig dramas where if folks aren't joining forces with the pigs, copping out to them or snitching on themselves, they're informing on everyone and his grandma. The pigs took similar measures when the FBI tried to prevent the release of *Uptight*, a 1970s Blacksploitation era movie starring Julian Mayfield with the theme that snitching has bad consequences.

How easily the system and its racist mass imprisonment practices could be frustrated by folks simply refusing to talk to the cops, period. In fact, the vast majority of those warehoused in these razor wire plantations plea-bargained, were informed on, or told on themselves.[10]

Without our most basic cooperation the pigs are powerless. Our communities must provide for their own security.

## Pig-In-Chief

In several articles I've discussed U.S. government policy, beginning with Assistant FBI Director William C. Sullivan in 1964, and formalized in 1978 in National Security Council Memorandum #46, to destroy and repress popular independent leadership, and then replace it with misleaders groomed and "approved" by the system. As Sullivan predicted,

> "When this is done, and it can and will be done, obviously much confusion will reign, particularly among the Negro people ... The Negroes will be left without a national leader of sufficiently compelling personality to steer them in the proper direction ..."[11]

Actually, planting U.S.-trained "dark faces in high places" is how Amerika subverted all the revolutionary socialist national liberation struggles across Afrika and Asia during the 20th century, and maintained Western imperialist control over their natural resources and economies.

So it is no real accomplishment or surprise that a man of color was implanted as Commander-in-Chief of the U.S. executive branch in 2008—i.e. Barack Obama. In fact, it can be clearly seen as a tactical move in large part to counter and contain growing Black unrest.

Obama's role as Amerika's highest-ranking cop served to redeem the legitimacy of pig authority to Black Amerika right in the midst of our growing disaffection and outrage with the U.S. government. How many of us went from raging against the pig machine (in response to our treatment during Hurricane Katrina, Jena 6, the increasing scourge of cops killing and brutalizing our youth, gentrification, mass displacements and breaking up of Black communities, cutting already substandard and inadequate social services, massive imprisonment, police racial profiling, etc.) to rallying in support of it, solely because of Obama's presidential campaign and victory? His nomination and victory sent waves of euphoria bordering on mass hysteria through our communities.

## We Instantly Forgot Reality

All it took to defer our reviving dreams of struggle for real power and change was to plant a dark skinned prostitute in a suit in the Oval Office, a prostitute beholden to the same corporate powers as the 43 white ones that preceded him. Mere color don't make a brother.

And what is Obama but an entertainer—a play actor? A role-playing politician whose business is to woo and inspire false hope in desperate people with slick sounding rhetoric, clever sounding turns of phrases, and empty promises totally unrelated to reality. The real litmus test for us is to question what substantial positive changes have taken place in the oppressed communities since his election? The answer: Absolutely none!

The dope-dealing CIA, that operates *right out of the White House*, still floods our communities with narcotics and the attendant social chaos. The government is *still* enlarging its militaristic posture and aggressiveness against us while keeping us under increasingly closer surveillance. We are *still* murdered, brutalized, race-profiled and railroaded *en masse* into prison by the cops, then consequently disenfranchised and stripped of access to public housing and social "benefits"! Our Third World level infant mortality and child hunger rates *continue* to rise, while the availability and quality of already substandard health care and social services for us continues to fall in the face of our steadily rising health needs and problems and the HIV/AIDS/HCV pandemics we face. Our poverty and depression level unemployment rates *continue to grow*. Our community, family and individual security needs *remain unmet*. Basic humyn and civil rights don't exist for us. In fact, the court system remains inaccessible and financially out of reach for purposes of litigating to enforce our interests and basic rights. Indeed, our plight has deteriorated markedly under the Obama administration. We remain victims of a system of racial and national oppression, economic exploitation, neocolonialism, imprisonment, impoverishment and police impunity, and all-round insecurity and desperation.

But, emotionally, we can tolerate it all a little better when a Black cop is the U.S. Pig-In-Chief. The Good Cop Brainwash has worked like a charm.

### Who Controls the Brainwash System?

Now let's look at the broader picture and explore who controls the Brainwash system, how and why it works to control the People's thinking.

The Central Brainwash System (CBS) operates on two levels. The first is the elite media that indoctrinates the upper "educated" sector of the population. The second is the mass media that indoctrinates and distracts the general public so they don't understand or interfere with the decision making power in society. The media is a cultural weapon of mass influence and control.

The "educated" sector who participate in society's decision making processes are indoctrinated through corporate controlled school curricula (of "higher" learning), and such "high level" media as *The Wall Street Journal, The Washington Post, The New York Times*, etc.

For the general masses (the other 80–90% of the population) there's football (and other spectator sports) and violence and sex themes to excite and stimulate the lower passions and inhibit critical thinking. The mass entertainment media portrays the most sordid, animalistic and cynical characters or emphasizes escapism and fantasy. Just like on the old slave plantations, the common people are kept preoccupied in their leisure time with irrelevance and "fun" to distract and discourage them from knowing how the world works, and learning of their actual power to impact and change its conditions. The news (info-tainment) media also works to distort and conceal reality. In a speech given at CIA headquarters, *Washington Post* publisher, Katherine Graham, stated:

> "There are some things the general public does not need to know and shouldn't. I believe democracy flourishes when the government can take legitimate steps to keep its secrets and when the press can decide whether to print what it knows."[12]

On this point I refer the reader back to Dr. Britt's observation that just such "controlled mass media" is a common feature of fascist systems. We can also see how independent media and whistleblowers that critically expose the true oppressive face of the pigs are persecuted, villainized and suppressed, like Wikileaks founder Julian Assange and PFC Chelsea Manning today.

Also, I refer the reader to the fact, pointed out in *Kill Yourself*[13] that the government and media jointly concealed that, beginning in the early 1980s, the CIA with the U.S. Justice Department's "okay," began dumping tons of crack cocaine and guns into Black ghettos and inciting gang wars over drug turf. Over a decade later journalist Gary Webb broke the story. The CIA then destroyed his career, and he ultimately was found dead from gunshots to the face, which was dismissed as a suicide.

So the common people face, not only indoctrination and deception, but effective depoliticization, to prevent their developing a mass culture based upon critical popular media that acquaints them with the real world, with what's going on, and why and how they can change it in profound ways. It was in this light that Afrikan revolutionary, Comrade Amilcar Cabral, observed in the context of leading a mass movement for Guinea-Bissau's national independence:

> "When Goebbels, the brain behind Nazi propaganda, heard culture being discussed, he brought out his revolver. That shows that the Nazis—who were and are the most tragic expression of imperialism and of its thirst for domination—even if they were all degenerates like Hitler, had a clear idea of the value of culture as a factor of resistance to foreign domination."[14]

It's important to remember the U.S. government adopted Nazi methods into its propaganda, military and intelligence systems.[15]

Which brings us to the really important question of who controls society—who has the real power? In the U.S., it's not those with government authority who are the real power holders. Those vermin are merely the servants and protectors of those in power. So the pigs *do* actually serve and protect ... just not you and me. Instead, they serve the owners of society, the super rich 1% who hoard social wealth and are the big business interests behind Wall Street and the multinational corporations. And it is the common people, the masses of working-class and poor, the pigs serve and protect the wealthy *against.*

The established media is the tool of the wealthy. It serves them and exists by their design. The system and process breaks down very simply.

Big media exists and survives because big business pays for it through advertisements. Without advertisements the mainstream media would collapse or remain very small and weak.[16] Because the wealthy keep big media in business, these outlets air only programming and information that serves and promotes the interests and values of big business, which is to indoctrinate the educated elite, distract and depoliticize the poor and working-class, and glorify the wealthy to all.

An example of how a popular media is crippled without the support of big business occurred in England with such labor newspapers as *The News Chronicle* and *The Daily Herald*, which reported world conditions and events to working-class people from a perspective that opposed big business. Although both papers had a very wide readership, they went out of circulation for lack of funds. Subscription fees alone are never sufficient to maintain media.[17]

Here in Amerika, many examples present themselves as well. For example, the wealthy promote media that report business and investment trends, stocks, etc. to middle and upper level investors and corporate shareholders. Therefore, they invest and advertise extensively in media that carry such "news." In turn, these media outlets act as virtual mouthpieces of the business communities and appeal especially to the elite educated sector.

Similarly, they invest and advertise in and promote "dumbed down" entertainment media that distracts, misinforms and depoliticizes the general masses, and indoctrinates them with pro-business values to "spend, spend, spend" and "buy, buy, buy," chasing sensory gratification, high-tech toys, gizmos and trinkets, meaningless status symbols, and ever-changing fads that are advertised for mass consumption, day in and day out, via multi-million dollar ads and commercials. Sponsoring and promoting entertainers, music, art, etc. works the same way. Big business creates the market then supplies it, and advertises to "tell" the people what to believe and want, what to like, what to buy, while using the labor power of the same working-class people, entertainers, artists, musicians, etc. to produce the goods, services and materials they advertise—which always conforms to the values and interests of the wealthy.[18]

One can routinely hear rap artists explain that they rap about *what the industry promotes* (which are irrelevant and degenerate themes), and not about "conscious" issues or reality *because the industry won't promote that.* This was a major topic of discussion in recent years, debating whether "Hip hop is dead." Likewise, actors find themselves playing roles or in movies and TV shows that the industry (and not them) promotes and makes available. A principled actor just won't have a lucrative career. If it isn't about sex, pimping, murder, money, cops and crime, fantasy or escapism, the big producers, recording labels, promoters, or advertisers won't back it. And by being bombarded with such asinine themes, we generally can't and don't think outside the box of degenerate topics, irrelevance and worshipping materialism. It's a process of mass brainwash, indoctrination and miseducation imposed on us by outside forces that replace our self-defining and authentic culture and identity. The U.S. government is now even promoting programs of sending rap artists, sports entertainers and others abroad to influence people in other countries with U.S. values.

And it's *not* that people don't want "conscious," authentic music, art, movies, etc., but that industry executives realize such music, art, etc. runs counter to their brainwash. That it may get people thinking the wrong things. Like how the wealthy leech off the working-class and poor, or that the system is the cause of urban poverty and crisis, or that we can collectively change things for the better on our own, or that the pigs are our oppressors, not our heroes. So they don't promote it. And neither will the so-called "independent" music labels that expect to compete in the industry for market sales.

Thus "conscious" musicians, like independent media, must operate "underground" with very limited resources, few advertising options, and a small "fan" base. Otherwise, they must sell their souls and "cross over" to the mainstream and promote the values, images and messages desired by big business, which is why so many rappers who yesterday were authentic voices of the oppressed and expressed their displeasure with the pigs now promote pig culture and lifestyles of the rich and famous in Blackface.

Remember, the pigs are the protectors of the powerful, and exist to keep the powerless in line. And, it's the *Central Brainwash System* that has us infatuated with sex, money, murder, and now pigs.

## Conclusion

In this light we can clearly see that not only does big business and government go hand-in-hand, but that glamorizing vermin culture—especially to the most oppressed, and therefore most potentially revolutionary, sectors of the population—is essential to maintaining the power of the bloodsuckers who own society and the stability of their system. It was Benito Mussolini, the man credited as the creator and founder of fascism, who defined it very simply as the merger of the interests of private corporations and the state. So now you know. And knowing is half the struggle. The other half is applying this knowledge to actively change the world in favor of the oppressed.

*Dare to Struggle, Dare to Win!*
*All Power to the People!*

## END NOTES

1. Steve Martinot, "The Question of Fascism in America," *Socialism and Democracy*, Vol. 22, no. 2 (July 2008), p. 18, n. 3.

2. Noam Chomsky, *Understanding Power: The Indispensible Chomsky* (NY: The New Press, 2002), p. 373.

3. Op. cit. note 1

4. Kevin "Rashid" Johnson, "Protect Our Leaders, Defend Our People" (2007), pp. 365–384 in this volume.

5. Kevin "Rashid" Johnson, "Kill Yourself or Liberate Yourself: The Real U.S. Imperialist Policy on Gang Violence versus the Revolutionary Alternative" (2008), see pp. 97–131 in this volume.

6. Op. cit. note 1, p. 29. See also Michelle Alexander, "The New Jim Crow: How the War on Drugs Gave Birth to a Permanent American Under Caste." *Socialist Viewpoint*, Vol. 12, No. 3 (May/June 2012), p. 24:

> "The drug war has been brutal—complete with SWAT teams, tanks, bazookas, grenade launchers, and sweeps of entire neighborhoods—but those who live in white communities have little clue to the devastation wrought. This war has been waged almost exclusively in poor communities of color, even though studies consistently show that people of all colors use and sell illegal drugs at remarkably similar rates. In fact some studies indicate that white youth are significantly more likely to engage in illegal drug dealing than Black youth. Any notion that drug use among African Americans (sic) is more severe or dangerous is belied by the data. White youth, for example, have about three times the number of drug-related visits to the emergency room as their African American (sic) counterparts.
>
> "That is not what you would guess, though, when entering our nation's prisons and jails, overflowing as they are with Black and brown drug offenders. In some states, African Americans (sic) comprise 80 percent–90 percent of all drug offenders sent to prison."

7. Dr. Lawrence Britt, "Fascism Anyone?" *Free Inquiry* (Spring 2003), p. 20.

8. See, Kenneth Saltman, *Education as Enforcement: The Militarization and Corporatization of Schools* (NY: Routledge, 2003):

> "Military generals running schools, students in uniforms, metal detectors, police presence, high-tech ID cards, dog tags, real-time internet-based surveillance cameras, security consultants, chain link fences, surprise searches—are all part of the investment the military industrial complex is embedding in U.S. public schools as they increasingly resemble the military and prisons. Militarism and the promotion of violence as virtue pervade foreign and domestic policy, popular culture, educational discourse and language. In addition to promoting recruitment, military education plays a central role in fostering a social focus on discipline. In short, to speak of militarized schooling in the United States context is inadequate to identify the ways that schools increasingly resemble the military and prisons. This phenomenon needs to be understood as part of the militarization of civil society exemplified by the rise of militarized policing, increased police powers for search and seizure, anti-public gathering laws, 'zero tolerance' policies and the transformation of welfare into punishing workfare programs."

9. Op. cit. note 5, quoting Sundiata Acoli, "A Brief History of the Black Panther Party and Its Place in the Black Liberation Movement" (1985).

10. 96.4% of all criminal cases (97% of all federal and 94% of all state criminal cases) end in plea bargains. *New York Times*, March 20, 2012.

11. Quoted in Church Committee, *U.S. Congressional Report: Intelligence Activities and the Rights of Americans.* 94th Congress, 2nd Session, report no. 94–755 (Washington: U.S. Government Printing Office, 1976), Book III, p. 136.

12. *Regardie's Magazine*, Vol. 10, No. 5, January 1990, pp. 90f.

13. Op. cit. note 5

14. Amilcar Cabral, *National Liberation and Culture* (1970).

15. Michael McClintock, *Instruments of Statecraft: U.S. Guerrilla Warfare, Counterinsurgency and Counter-Terrorism 1940–1990* (NY: Pantheon, 1992).

16. See, for example, Martin A. Lee and Norman Solomon, *Unreliable Sources: A Guide to Detecting Bias in the News Media* (NY: Lyle Stuart, 1990), p. 59 ("TV and radio get nearly 100 percent of their income from advertisers, newspapers, 75 percent, and magazines about 50 percent ... Between 60 and 70 percent of newspaper space is reserved for ads, while 22 percent of TV time is filled with commercials."); Erik Barnouw, *The Sponsor: Notes on a Modern Potentate* (NY: Oxford University Press, 1978), on the influence advertising has on media content; Ben H. Bagdikian, *The Media Monopoly*, 5th ed. (Boston: Beacon Press, 1997), esp. chps. 6–9; James Curran et al., *Power without Responsibility: The Press and Broadcasting in Britain* (London: Routledge, 1981), pp. 118–132; Alfred M. Lee, *The Daily Newspaper in America: The Evolution of a Social Instrument* (NY: MacMillan, 1937).

17. Although the readership of the workers' press in Britain surpassed the readership of the combined business papers, the workers' press was destroyed by lack of sufficient advertising. James Curran, "Advertising in the Press," in James Curran, ed., *The British Press: A Manifesto* (London: MacMillan, 1978), pp. 229–267.

18. An outstanding analysis and exposé of the mass media is Noam Chomsky and Edward S. Herman, *Manufacturing Consent* (NY: Pantheon, 1988), where they elaborate a "Propaganda Model," summarized thus:

> "A propaganda model focuses on [the] inequality of wealth and power and its multilevel effects on mass-media interests and choices. It traces the routes by which money and power are able to filter out the news fit to print, marginalize dissent, and allow the government and dominant private interests to get their messages across to the public. The essential ingredients of our propaganda model, or set of news 'filters,' fall under the following headings: (1) the size, concentrated ownership, owner wealth, and profit orientation of the dominant mass-media firms; (2) advertising as the primary income source of mass media; (3) the reliance of the media on information provided by government business, and 'experts' funded and approved by these primary sources and agents of power; (4) 'flak' as a means of disciplining the media; and (5) 'anti-communism' [today it's anti-terrorism] as a national religion and control mechanism.
>
> "These elements interact with and reinforce one another. The raw material of news must pass through successive filters, leaving only the cleansed residue fit to print. They fix the premises of discourse and interpretation, and the definition of what is newsworthy in the first place, and they explain the basis and operations of what amount to propaganda campaigns."

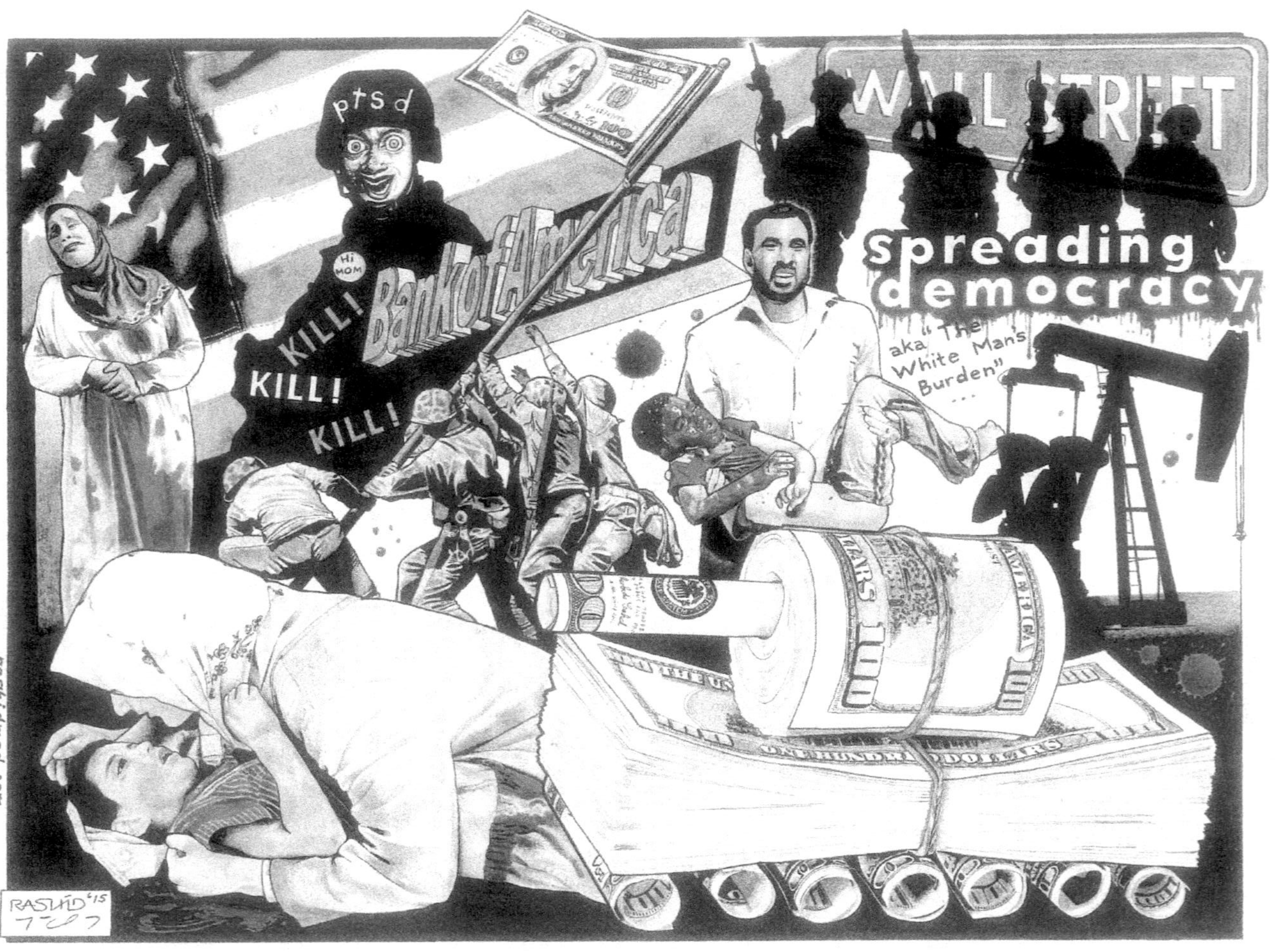
WALL STREET
spreading democracy
aka "The White Man's Burden" ...
ptsd
Hi MOM
Bank of America
KILL!
KILL!
KILL!
RASHID '15
rashidmod.com

The black cop could be a large factor in preventing our genocide. But no help can be expected from that quarter. The same stupidity and desperation that brought him to the gates prevents him from interceding.... Often he feels compelled to prove that he is loyal to the force, prove that he is not prejudiced in favor of us. The black pig is afraid, too unsure of his position.... This same fear will cause him to show more zeal in the "club therapy" sessions than even the whites manage. If the victim is black, he's going to get so mad the white pigs will have to stand back and let him swing. If they don't have murder planned for that session, they'll have to pull that nigger off you. George Jackson

a PIG is a PIG!

RASHID '15
7-07

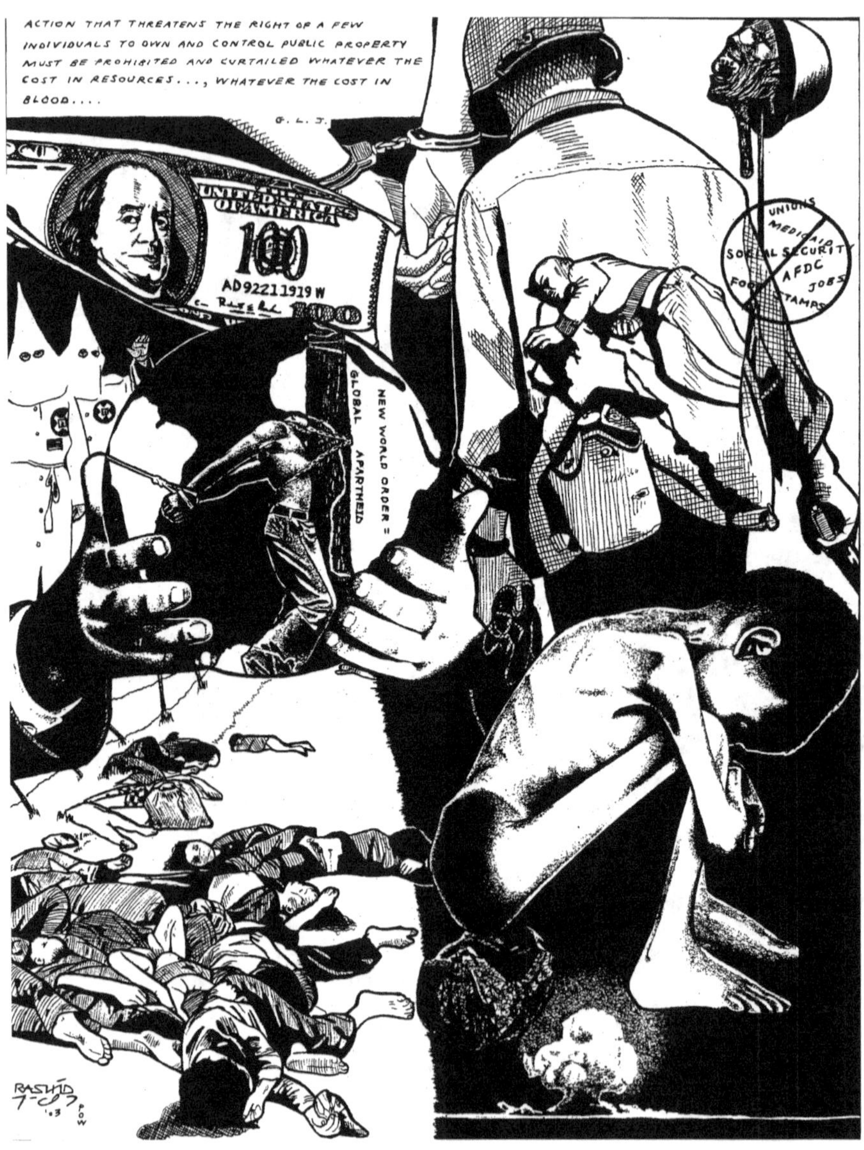
ACTION THAT THREATENS THE RIGHT OF A FEW INDIVIDUALS TO OWN AND CONTROL PUBLIC PROPERTY MUST BE PROHIBITED AND CURTAILED WHATEVER THE COST IN RESOURCES..., WHATEVER THE COST IN BLOOD....
G. L. J.
UNITED STATES OF AMERICA
100
AD92211919 W
NEW WORLD ORDER =
GLOBAL APARTHEID
UNIONS
MEDICAID
AFDC
JOBS
RASHID
7-03

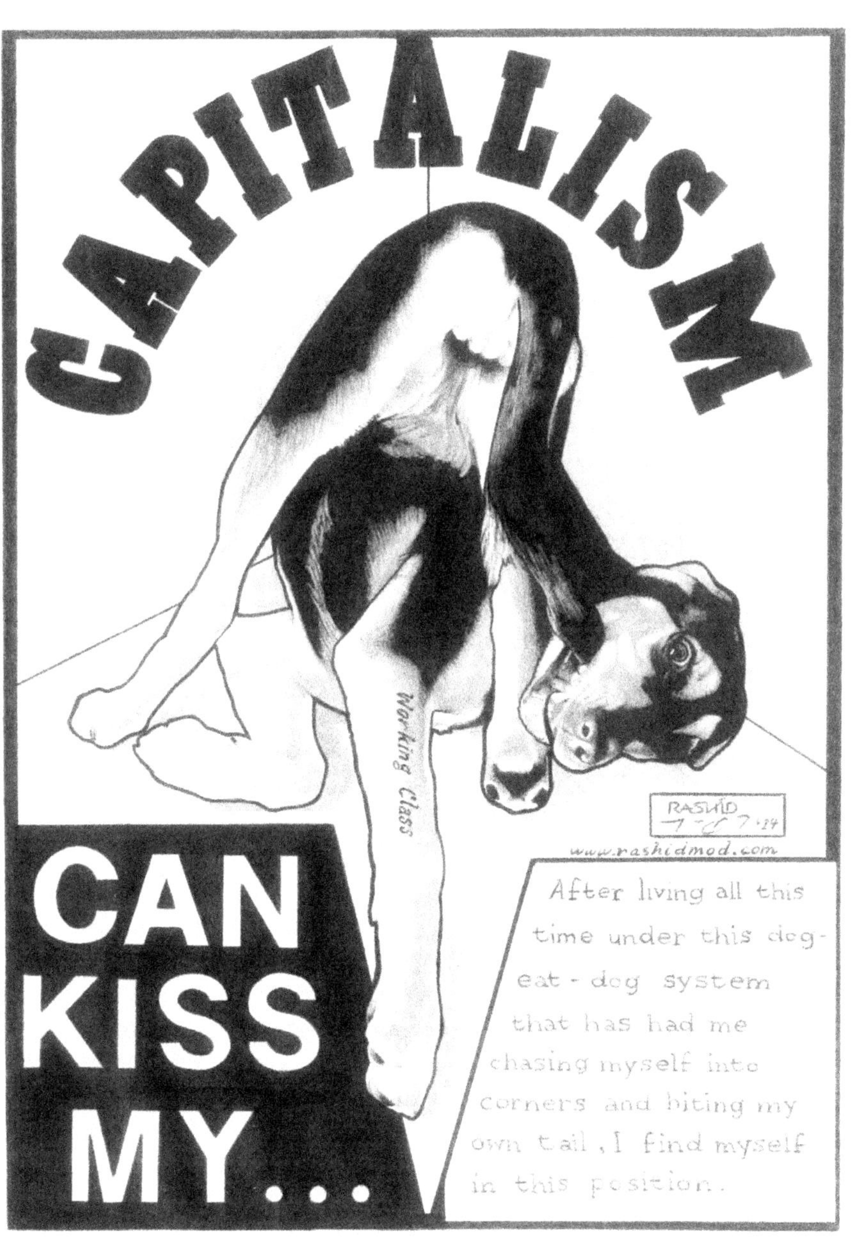
CAPITALISM
Working Class
RASHID
7-7-14
www.rashidmod.com
CAN KISS MY...
After living all this time under this dog-eat-dog system that has had me chasing myself into corners and biting my own tail, I find myself in this position.

# 36. AGAINST CAPITALISM: TO EXIST WE MUST RESIST 2012

## Capitalism's Insane Logic

Capitalist logic proclaims no one has the right to exist, to be here, except the wealthy. This illogic inheres in the very system itself.

Early capitalist economists like Thomas Malthus and David Ricardo expressed it without shame. They explained, in a world ruled by capitalism only the rich have rights. Everyone else exists solely to serve them; to enhance their wealth. Those of no profitable use should receive nothing. For sharing their wealth would only lead to the wealthy's own impoverishment; making them equals of the common people, which was unthinkable.

Therefore, according to Malthus, those sad unprofitable souls, whom he deemed a surplus population, should just "go somewhere else."[1] Like to a prison labor camp or to some distant land. Ricardo explained that these are unalterable capitalist principles, "the principle of gravitation,"[2] as he called it. For those unable to "go somewhere else," it was proposed that they be disposed of by artificially created plagues, wars, and famines.

## Capitalism goes viral

In those early days of capitalist development, Europe was sending expeditionary forces throughout the non-European, non-capitalist world searching out new bases to set up shop and newer sources of wealth, profit, and plunder. These were found in the Amerikas, Afrika, Asia, Australia, and so on. This expansion called for conquering the indigenous peoples of these "new" lands, subduing and putting them and their lands to profitable uses; requiring that some millions be displaced here, and that other millions be corralled there, that some millions be enslaved in other places, and other millions be outright exterminated. All carried out with the utmost brutality.

Clearing those lands of their native peoples in turn provided that "somewhere else" for Europe's unprofitable poor to go. But these lands were quickly overrun and subjugated by the invading hordes of Europe's poor, and those who overflowed her prisons, along with her freebooters, mercenaries, missionaries, merchants, aspiring wealthy, and, of course, many who were already accomplished in wealth and privilege. And soon, capitalism cast its grisly shadow across the globe: expanding into imperialism.

Its victims resisted the forced implantation of a system that put profiteering for a few over the needs of the many. But with the combined power of the world's stolen wealth and technologies, a mass of European invaders united under a manufactured "master race" philosophy, and driven by an insatiable and compassionless greed, the predatory capitalist system won out; and its insane logic took hold everywhere.

And as in Europe, the unprofitable "surpluses" of native peoples were repeatedly driven "somewhere else", until with capitalism spreading like a plague, they were cornered with nowhere else left to go. So wars, plagues, and famines were generated while multitudes were exterminated or corralled into prisons and economically unviable urban enclaves (ghettos and shantytowns). Reservations continued, negating the right of the common people to exist. While running its course, capitalism overran, polluted, degraded and razed the land, also negating the right of the natural world to exist.

### Capitalism's Chickens Come Home to Roost

But today we approach the endgame. The deadly cycle has spiralled continuously until now everyone's existence (including that of the foolishly self-centered wealthy), and the balance of nature are compromised. Capitalism's chickens are definitely coming home to roost. Yet, the harebrained capitalists still persist.

For those whose forefathers encroached upon, and who today have inherited from the land, wealth, labor, and destroyed civilizations and lives of billions; for those who yesterday participated or were silent and tacitly acquiesced when in the name of expanding profits and seeking out wealth in new lands, whole societies were crushed and the land defiled; today fate is coming full circle. You now stand to suffer loss of your own prized civilizations and cherished lives, but on a vastly greater scale, since now nature itself is resisting the excesses of capitalism. And nature has the decided advantage, since she is the very source of *all* our existence.

And unlike people, she doesn't discriminate. She sees neither skin color, nationality, nor social status. She's ruthlessly indifferent to age, gender, sexual preference, and such. She crushes, burns, freezes, and sweeps away whatever—and whoever—stands in the way of her restoring the natural balance she evolved over billions of years, which we as tools of fools have upset in only a few centuries; more so in just the last hundred years. And because the damage we've caused and the system we've implanted is global in proportions, today we don't have the option to "go somewhere else". We're painted into a corner. But there *is* a choice.

## Us Against Them or Nature Against Us All

Collectively and of our free will we can choose to put down this predacious system of a few profiting *at all our expense,* and build in its place a new mass-oriented socialist system of mutual cooperation, fair and equal distribution, and respect for nature, *to all our benefit. Or* we can continue being fools' agents, and stand by idly and ostrich-like (with our heads in the sand) as many did yesterday, while this system continues devouring, defiling and wasting land, resources, people, and the planet.

But in either case, capitalism's day of reckoning is coming. And if we *don't* act, we will share that fate alongside the greed-driven idiots who created this havoc. Remember the billions who've already suffered horribly and died—and continue to—at the designs of these madmen. Now think of our children who will thank us for an inheritance of bones and ashes, of massive die-offs and unimaginable crises.

The intensifying economic troubles, plagues, resource depletions, wars, unparalleled environmental and natural disasters we're witnessing today, are but early warning signs of what's to come. The planet is on an independent course of exercising its own right to exist. And the wealthy know worse is yet to come. They know too that we have the collective power not only to stop them and right their wrongs, but to restore the balance between humyn society, and nature.

But to do this compels stripping away their power, wealth, prestige, and influence. They know this too. And would rather watch the world suffer and die than give up what was never rightfully theirs to begin with. So they stand indifferent as always to the devastating effects of *their* system, driving us all "full speed ahead and damn the torpedoes", while spreading conspiracy theories and apocalyptic culture to have us believing that the doom they're driving us towards is really the work of secret societies, aliens, or supernatural forces beyond our power to challenge, change, or correct.

Secret and supernatural have nothing to do with it! There's a *very* natural, very open, and very *humyn* cause of our problems. And one we *can* challenge, change, and correct. But there is also a time factor. It will take our collective effort, to first snatch these fools out of the saddle who dare hoard wealth, power and desperately needed resources without performing a day's labor, and then smash their system, and rebuild an entire new one oriented towards meeting the needs of working people, the poor, and our environment. Otherwise we and our progeny *will* go "somewhere else", only it won't be on *this* planet or in *this* world.

### The People's Endgame

As a Party of struggle, the New Afrikan Black Panther Party-PC is rooted in revolutionary optimism. We not only *believe* that a bright future is possible, but we're committed to the united struggle to *make it happen*. So we join with and aspire to arouse and organize *all* the world's oppressed—and *especially* unprofitable—people to *stay right where you are*, to liberate the ground under your feet, and join together in consolidating it into a collective base of worldwide revolutionary resistance against capitalism and imperialism in the name of the people's and the planet's right to exist.

*Dare to Struggle, Dare to Win!*
*All Power to the people!*

## END NOTES

1. See: Patricia James, ed., Thomas R. Malthus, *An Essay on the Principle of Population* (Cambridge, UK: Cambridge University Press, 1989) (based on Malthus's 1803 edition), vol. II, ch. 6, pp. 127–28.

2. David Ricardo, *The Principles of Political Economy and Taxation,* (NY: E.P. Dutton, 1911) (Original 1817-1821) ch. 5, p. 23.

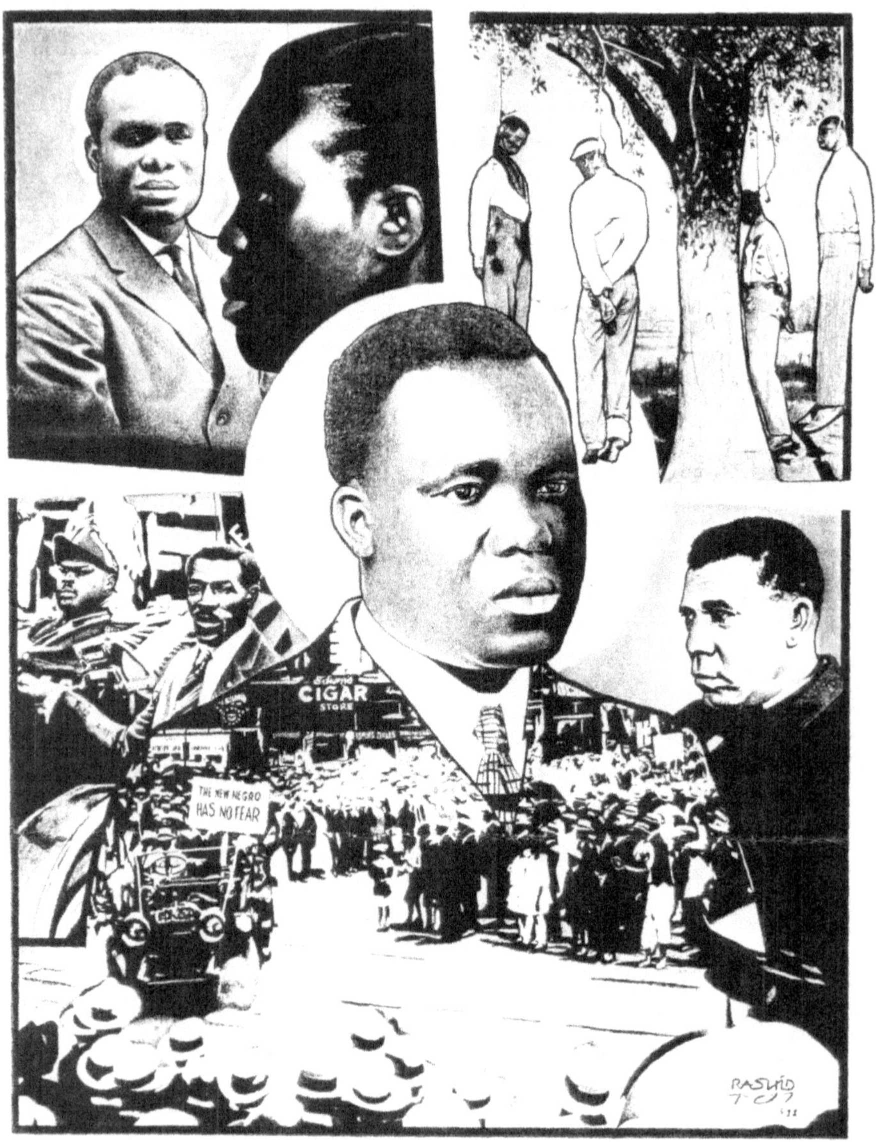
CIGAR
STORE
THE NEW NEGRO
HAS NO FEAR
RASHID
www.rashidmod.com

# 37. RESTORING THE PAST TO SERVE THE FUTURE 2013

Some Comments in Review of *A Hubert Harrison Reader,* ed. and intro. by Jeffrey B. Perry (Middletown, CT: Wesleyan University Press, 2001) and Jeffrey B. Perry, *Hubert Harrison: The Voice of Harlem Radicalism, 1883–1918* (New York: Columbia University Press, 2008)

"Those who do not learn from history are bound to repeat it."

*George Santayana*

To advance correctly, an oppressed people must be correctly oriented in today's and tomorrow's struggles. To do this they must get the history right.

The masses of New Afrikan/Black People have long suffered a condition of historical amnesia, which has stagnated our development economically, politically, culturally and in matters of our collective security. This has allowed those who have kept and mean to keep us in a state of subjugation and repression, the power to mold and manipulate our every thought and belief. And as Carter G. Woodson once stated, when you control a people's thinking you control them. You don't have to tell them to use the back door; they will do it automatically. And when there is no back door they will cut one for the purpose.

The cause of our amnesia is a lack of historical continuity. We've forgotten—and by design—where we came from, where we've been, how we got where we are, and the obstacles we met along the way. Our body is covered with scars that we don't remember how we got. In fact many of us don't recognize ourselves as an organic part of a common body.

Therefore, every few generations we find ourselves repeating the same processes, treading the same paths, falling over the same obstacles, and suffering the same injuries in our quest for liberation. In fact, we keep struggling with the same questions, including trying to determine what liberation actually is. So we don't even know what we are struggling for, nor who our true enemies and friends are, with the result that many of us exhaust ourselves reacting blindly and thrashing around, while many others don't struggle at all beyond treading water and floating with the current. But even treading water becomes exhausting too … so we drown.

Jeffrey Perry's labors in excavating the history of the work of Hubert Harrison represent an important step towards restoring our collective memory. One need make but a cursory study of Hubert Harrison's life and work to recognize his invaluable contribution to the struggle for New Afrikans/Blacks—in particular as we developed from the stifled conditions of a rural peasantry (sharecropping, peonage, etc.) into the worldly conscious urban proletariat.

Hubert Harrison's was a great critical mind—perhaps one of our greatest—that pondered and sought out practical solutions to all aspects and troubles of the New Afrikan/Black experience at a critical stage of our awakening and development. And he pulled no punches. He questioned, challenged and sought to organize us and against not only the external forces that oppressed his people, but also the opportunists amongst us who for personal gain played on the People's desperation, insecurities and need of genuine liberatory leadership. He even challenged the most influential institution of New Afrikan/Black society, namely the church.

Like those genuine popular-based leaders and organizations that came after him, such as Malcolm X, Mao Tse-tung, Amilcar Cabral, the Black Panther Party, etc., Hubert Harrison was a teacher, leader and organizer who based himself among the people and committed his work and energy to serving them. He used his mind not for personal gain, but to serve and uplift the downtrodden, the poor and the oppressed. He was a true working-class intellectual, and like many of our great independent New Afrikan/Black leaders (e.g. Huey P. Newton, Malcolm X, George Jackson, James Yaki Sayles aka Atiba Shanna, etc.), he was self-educated.

Hubert Harrison was the founder of the "New Negro Movement," the "Black Power Movement" of the early 1900s, and influenced every radical current in what was the greatest period and place of our cultural awakening—the Harlem Renaissance. Indeed, he was called the "Father of Harlem Radicalism." And no one contributed more than he to the development of the New Afrikan/Black press during that era, which in 1926 was called "the greatest single power in the Negro race."[1]

He was among the first New Afrikans/Blacks: to recognize that we constitute not merely a race but a distinct historically developed nationality of people and preceded the Comintern in calling for an "independent Negro nation" in the U.S.; to advance our right to organize armed self-defense against lynching and racial violence, and lead the fight for federal anti-lynching laws; to lead the fight for New Afrikan/Black voting rights; to develop a left orientation on Pan-Afrikan unity and struggle; to see our condition in America as connected to that of other peoples across the world oppressed by capitalist imperialism. It was his work and mass-based approach to teaching that made Marcus Garvey's UNIA-ACL the single largest New Afrikan/Black organization to date. He was among the first to recognize white racism as the principal obstacle to revolutionary class struggle in Amerika, and he struggled with both the white Left and amongst his own People to counter this impediment. And consistent with this important realization, Jeffrey Perry has linked excavating Hubert Harrison's work with also advancing that of Theodore Allen, who has given greater and clearer historical and political study, analysis, and insight to racism as a capitalist divide and conquer strategy, that has been used and refined with the greatest effect since the latter 1600s to prevent united struggle of the laboring and oppressed classes.[2]

In many respects, Hubert Harrison was more comprehensive and advanced than most radical leaders we've had to date, many of whom would undoubtedly have avoided and conquered many of the obstacles that have thwarted our struggles, had they been exposed to and built upon his contributions. Indeed, his was such a powerful, controversial and uncompromising beacon that, from his day until now, those who serve as the historical and cultural gatekeepers of the imperialist system and other institutions of exploitation, consciously wrote him out of history.

By reviving the life and work of this monumental leader, Jeffrey Perry is restoring to us and all suffering people a large chunk of forgotten history, from one of the most important stages of New Afrikan/Black development with which we can today discover who we are, where we've been, how we got here, and what obstacles to avoid and how, in our ongoing struggle for genuine liberation. In fact we can begin to answer and understand collectively what liberation really means.

We can't overstate the importance of Hubert Harrison's work and life, nor the service Jeffrey Perry is rendering to a long oppressed people, in restoring this missing link to our collective memory.

*Dare to Struggle, Dare to Win!*
*All Power to the People!*

## END NOTES

1. Edwin Mims, *Advancing South: Stories of Progress and Reaction* (Garden City: Doubleday, Page & Co., 1926), p. 262.

2. Jeffrey B. Perry, "In Memoriam: Theodore W. Allen," *Cultural Logic*, Vol. 8 (2005); Jeffrey B. Perry, "Introduction," in Theodore W. Allen, *Class Struggle and the Origin of Racial Slavery: The Invention of the White Race* (Stony Brook: The Center for the Study of Working Class Life, SUNY, 2006) in *Cultural Logic*, Vol. 9 (2006); see also Jeffrey B. Perry, "Introduction," *The Invention of the White Race, Vol. I: Racial Oppression and Social Control*, (New York: Verso, 2012) and Vol. II: *The Origin of Racial Oppression in Anglo-America* (New York: Verso, 2012); Jeffrey B. Perry, "The Developing Conjuncture and Some Insights from Hubert Harrison and Theodore W. Allen on the Centrality of the Fight Against White Supremacy," *Cultural Logic* (2010).

# 38. THE CONCURRENT TRAGEDY OF THE TRAYVON MARTIN CASE AND OUR POLITICAL CONFUSIONS 2013

## Who's to Blame?

Following what could only be called a high ratings show trial, Latino neighborhood watchman George Zimmerman was acquitted by an all-female jury in the killing of unarmed New Afrikan/Black teenager Trayvon Martin. Almost instantly, masses of outraged Black people and sympathizers took to the streets in protest. All felt "betrayed" by a so-called justice system that has never served them to begin with.

What they didn't understand is, from the beginning, the establishment's entire response to Trayvon's killing was a staged performance aimed to contain and "channel" public anger, to deflect the system's own responsibility in manufacturing the very culture that led to Trayvon's murder and that of multitudes of our youth at the hands of cops and vigilantes, and to protect the status quo.

Trayvon, like many of our youth, was targeted and killed based upon prevailing slanders and criminal stereotypes of young New Afrikan males, projected by the government working hand-in-hand with the mainstream entertainment and "news" media: outlets which the masses of New Afrikan and common people neither own nor control.

Zimmerman, without doubt under such influences, felt an overzealous urge to "protect" his gated community from the menace of a hooded young Black male walking about, who was likely (in Zimmerman's media-hyped mind) up to some criminal mischief. Trayvon (thus racially profiled), had to be "kept in his place," which, in the minds of folks of elevated social status, means out of their living space. So Zimmerman ended up pushing Trayvon out of this life altogether.

Trayvon's death triggered waves of protest from a long-suffering people, enraged at yet another example of poor Black life being of no value and persecuted in Amerika. Where yet another of our youth was profiled and gunned down in cold blood by cops and their imitators. Justice was demanded *against* the system, which has always dealt us injustice and which by criminalizing our youth to the broader public was rightly to blame for Trayvon's death.

## The Troupe Comes to Town

In stepped career camera shark and Black capitalist windbag Al Sharpton, who, loyal to the system as ever, moved to contain mass protest and steer it into the system's own "safe" channels of resolution: the courts. Thus was applied the same tried and true tactic a panicked John F. Kennedy implemented in 1963 against an unwitting Dr. Martin Luther King, Jr., to gain official control of the March on Washington, which was originally organized by masses of poor Blacks who planned to lay siege on the U.S. capital *and not leave*, in protest against the same sorts of abuses, including widespread murders of Black youth by police and vigilantes, from which we are *still* suffering today.

True to his politics, Sharpton weaseled his way into becoming the spokesman for Trayvon's distraught family, and through the all-too-accommodating mainstream media, counseled the riled-up masses to look to the courts for justice. The same courts that alongside the murderous police are disposing of masses of our young males in the world's largest, brutal, and profit-oriented prison system … a system widely recognized as the "New Jim Crow."[1]

Recall it was against the "old" Jim Crow system that the old Civil Rights Movement was fought. Indeed, the U.S. government killed King because he woke up and realized that it was the system itself at the source of everyone's suffering, and he thus broke with the old Civil Rights program of looking to the same system as a savior.[2] This is why types like Sharpton, who remain loyal to the old pro-capitalist Civil Rights program, have us seeking justice from the forces of government behind today's Jim Crow.

Only a terribly confused people would fall for such a trick as this (again!), which is like directing a coop of chickens to put their fate into the hands of a den of foxes.

Then, right on cue, the system trotted out from backstage yet another insider and token dark face (the Florida Attorney General), who promised to deliver just the sort of justice that ol' Uncle (Tom) Al was crowing for. But of course it was all a show, an old script with actors new and old played out to yet again lasso and hogtie public outrage and protest in the face of yet another Black tragedy until things simmered down, so the system could go on about its usual business—until the next tragedy provoked another round of angry mass protest.

### Be Careful What You Ask For

So after much hemming and hawing, the next scene was staged: criminal charges were issued against Zimmerman and a show trial was underway.

But as Mumia Abu-Jamal observed in his July 8th commentary predicting, "The Coming Acquittal," each of the prosecution's witnesses were "flipped," becoming witnesses for Zimmerman, as the prosecuting attorney himself proved completely incompetent in handling the case and definitely unsuited to win a conviction.

### Stage Trial, Y'All

And so, with the cast of actors having played their designated roles, Zimmerman was acquitted … and folks were riled up again. But this time the system had a ready retort designed to make further protest look absurd. It responded, "But we gave you and Trayvon's family what you asked for—a criminal prosecution. It's not *our* fault that a jury of *your* peers acquitted. That's the system of justice at work!" So rather than recognizing the entire farce for what it was, folks felt deflated and moped about in disbelief that "the jury really let him off!"

### Redirecting the Rage—to Divide and Rule

Alongside all this was also the divide, agitate, and rule tactic, where the system—in ways open and subtle—played up Black versus Latino antagonisms to channel much of the mass anger away from itself and play the oppressed masses against themselves. Because we don't understand that the capitalist system and its political conniving are at the root of all our mounting tragedies and suffering, many fall victim to its using tragedies like Trayvon's killing and Zimmerman's acquittal to drive a wedge between its victims, like New Afrikans and Latin@s. Groups that it is rightly terrified of uniting as politically conscious allies in struggle to tear down this rotten system, to empower *all* working-class, poor, and others who are disadvantaged, oppressed, and exploited by this system and its super-rich owners. We must not allow such divide and conquer schemes to work.

As George Jackson once observed, it is the system itself that manufactures a thousand different categories of contradictions and divisions among the people, so that its small group of wealthy owners can continue to rule. Our ignorance is their weapon against us.

Zimmerman wanted to be a cop because that's the role of "heroes" glamorized by the status quo since the pigs are their protectors, not ours. He felt a need to keep poor Black people in line because that is one of the principal functions of the pigs in service to the status quo. And he killed Trayvon because violent terror is how the pigs keep the oppressed masses at the lowest levels in line. And this system of terror is justified and projected as the inalienable and unchallengeable right and entitlement of pigs to use, by the criminalization of the oppressed.

So we see routine pig murders of our youth dismissed by the system as "justifiable homicide." And this is why Zimmerman had to be protected from punishment by that very system (since he was playing the role of a cop as against the member of a criminalized group who was *in the wrong place*). But Zimmerman had to be protected indirectly and in such a way as to pretend that the system was responsive to the people's cry for justice for the murder of yet another innocent New Afrikan by a cop (or a cop wanna-be).

They couldn't just ignore irate Black folks taking to the streets, since they remember—even if we don't—that almost every major urban uprising of New Afrikans was provoked by incidents of police murders or beatings of our people, from the 1960s urban revolts, to the uprising in Los Angeles in the early 1990s, from the 2002 revolt in Benton Harbor, Michigan to the 2005 Toledo, Ohio uprising, etc. And in the wake of many of these revolts came conscious political awakening and organizing that genuinely threatened the system from below.

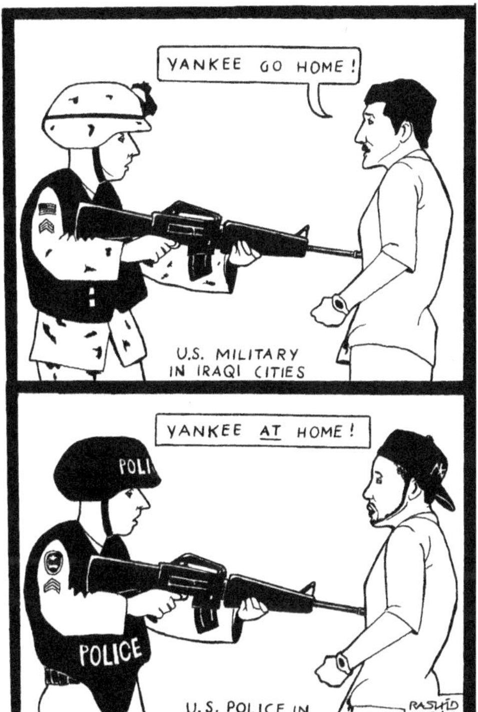

*Occupation starts at home... and spreads abroad*

So, as they say in litigation, the end result was "a convenient convergent of outcomes" that were win-win for the establishment and lose-lose for the People.

We lost in that yet another of our innocent young lives was stolen through the institutionalized and culturally rationalized terror of the system used to keep us in check since slavery days, and in that we not only won no justice yet again, but we also still have not learned the lesson that this system cannot be "fixed" and it means us no good. The system won in that it quelled and diverted our outrage into nonthreatening (to itself) channels including against other sectors of the oppressed, and it continues with its usual business of playing and profiting off us all.

### The Capitalist System is the Enemy

The system is the problem. Black cops brutalize and murder Black youth just as viciously as any white cop. As do Latin@s. In fact, under the openly racist system of South Afrikan Apartheid, it was commonly Afrikan soldiers and police who, working for the racist regime, committed many of the most brutal atrocities against their own people. Divide and conquer. Capitalism survives by playing Black against Black, against white, against Latin@, etc.; women against men, old against young, ad nauseam—it's the same old Willie Lynch game of dividing the oppressed against themselves that insulates the wealthy oppressors from the united resistance of their victims.

It works only because we are politically confused, and therefore believe such political tricks as the system's placing a few token dark faces in high places is a real gain for the masses of oppressed nationalities and people of color. We don't see the reality that these are instead old and well-established political tactics of mass control.

Until we wake up and recognize that this capitalist imperialist system is at the root of *all* our problems, we'll keep suffering tragic losses and being manipulated by political opportunists and their sleight of hand and empty rhetoric. We must recognize and remedy the fact that the greatest weapon the system has against us is our own ignorance.

*Dare to Struggle, Dare to Win!*
*All Power to the People!*

## END NOTES

1. Michelle Alexander, *The New Jim Crow: Mass Incarceration in the Age of Colorblindness* (New York: The New Press, 2010/2013).

2. William F. Pepper, *An Act of State: The Execution of Martin Luther King,* London: Verso, 203).

# 39. WHY NO INDICTMENT WAS ISSUED AGAINST THE COP WHO KILLED MICHAEL BROWN: THE PROBLEM AND ANSWER 2015

### "No Indictment"—I Already Knew

It's easy to say, after the fact, that I knew there would be no grand jury indictment against Darren Wilson, the white Missouri cop who killed New African/Black teenager Michael Brown in cold blood on August 9, 2014. But, truth be told, I *did* know it. And you'll recognize how obvious the game was too, once I explain.

I recognized the game not just because the Amerikan criminal (in)justice and (selective) law enforcement systems work hand-in-hand against (not in favor of) people of color and the poor, but because of two major deviations from established grand jury procedure that were made by the St. Louis prosecuting attorney, Robert McCulloch, who was supposedly seeking the indictment against Wilson.

The red flags were the massive amount of "evidence" presented to the grand jury, but more specifically, that Wilson was allowed to testify before the grand jury. This *never* happens.

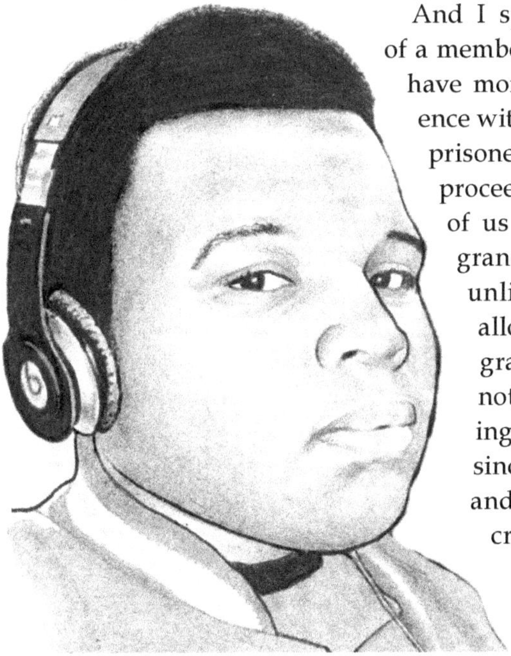

And I speak with the experience of a member of a class of people who have more than just a little experience with indictments, namely, U.S. prisoners. Most all of the criminal proceedings that landed each of us in prison were based on grand jury indictments, but, unlike Wilson, we were never allowed to testify before those grand juries. Why? Cuz that's not how grand jury proceedings work. And I should know since over the years I've fought and beat some 16 indicted crimes representing myself. So I have a legal understanding of the process as well. But don't just take my word for it, ask any attorney with experience in criminal law. S/he might do a bit of hemming and hawing and trying to rationalize what was done, but in the end they'll admit it's almost unheard of for a prosecutor to call the subject of a grand jury proceeding to testify before the jury.

### The Prosecutor's Game

Unlike a trial, a grand jury proceeding is not adversarial. Meaning it doesn't function to have the jury consider both sides of a case. It is a *summary* proceeding that exists solely to hear a sample of what evidence the prosecution has collected which tends to show a crime occurred, without any consideration of the potential defendant's side of the story, and thereupon determine if the prosecutor has enough evidence to show probable cause to believe the subject committed a potential crime. That's it. The prosecutor presents only the most basic incriminatory evidence and never puts the potential defendant on, because unless the prosecutor is in effect using the potential defendant as her/his own witness (which is exactly what McCulloch did with Wilson), to do so would transform the grand jury proceeding into an actual trial which would compel a wide range of procedures and rights of the potential defendant to come into play.[1]

This is why McCulloch dispensed with another common procedure in such cases, namely, he never had Wilson charged and arrested on a warrant prior to supposedly seeking an indictment. Because, the moment Wilson was arrested, McCulloch would become his adversary (and could not advocate for him as he did in calling Wilson as his own witness to give his side of the story to make it conform to other evidence in a way that would exonerate Wilson). As Wilson's adversary, McCulloch could only present such "evidence" as would paint Wilson's actions in a criminal light to the grand jury. And if he were to call Wilson as a witness under these circumstances, Wilson would have to have his own attorney present to ensure he didn't say or do anything to incriminate himself or sabotage his own defense. So he most likely would have been instructed by his attorney to say nothing by invoking his 5th Amendment privilege against self-incrimination.

So McCulloch took very deliberate tactical steps to ensure that he could advocate for Wilson rather than function as his adversary to the end of ensuring that no indictment would be issued.

And these *major* departures from established grand jury practice were made by a white prosecutor whose own father was not only himself a cop, but a cop who was allegedly killed by a Black man. So he had not just a professional bias in Wilson's favor, but a personal one as well. So, when I heard on the news a few days before the verdict not to indict was announced, that Wilson had been allowed to testify before the grand jury, I knew, just like with the trial of George Zimmerman for the murder of Trayvon Martin, that the prosecutor was deliberately sabotaging the proceeding to ensure an outcome in favor of the cop (or cop wanna-be, as in Zimmerman's case).

And you can bet every legal "expert" in Amerika recognized it too, including past Harvard law professor, Barack "uncle scam in Blackface" Obama, who implored everyone to accept the verdict cuz the rule of law had prevailed and the grand jury rendered a decision that it was its duty to make. Sadly, many of us oppressed people of color can't get past our skin worship of Obama and recognize him for the imperialist running dog (a wolf in black sheep's clothing) that he really is.

As for the grand jury's duty, these bodies are actually the tools of prosecuting attorneys, who have almost absolute control over both the conduct of grand jury proceedings and over influencing these juries. This is why New York State Judge Sol Wachtler once admitted, "it's so easy to get a grand jury to indict, they'd indict a ham sandwich if that's what the prosecutor wanted."

Then there's the fact that grand jury proceedings lasted from August 20th to November 24th. As noted, prosecutors typically put only a small bit of evidence before grand juries, and only that which incriminates the potential defendant. Even University of Missouri Law Professor, Ben Trachtenberg, admits that McCulloch, "put on a much greater amount of evidence than we're used to," producing 24 volumes of evidence which included 5,000 pages of testimony from 60 witnesses (100 pages of which was Wilson's testimony). In the "normal" proceeding, Trachtenberg said, "the grand jury can see evidence *in a few minutes* and take a vote." As various legal experts concede, McCulloch's method was to inundate the grand jury with so much information that it was overwhelmed and confused.[2] I too recognized this, since, in a grand jury proceeding the jury is not guided by adversarial attorneys to pay attention to certain evidence and the implications of it as would occur in a trial.

So that now, Wilson's testimony, which was not subject to cross examination to expose obvious lies and inconsistencies (such as his claim the he used his gun because he had no non-lethal options, which he obviously did—such as use of mace—which McCulloch never brought up), now stands as the official version of what happened when he killed Michael Brown. As the late Johnnie Cochran pointed out and most criminal defendants know, cops almost instinctively lie in court. They do it because they feel compelled to validate their arrests and actions, and make them fit with the law to support the desired outcome. And they're "comfortable lying in a courtroom because the system always tolerated [their] lying; judges look the other way and jurors [are] supposed to accept it."[3] And jurors *do* accept it, because the typical overwhelmingly white jury just doesn't believe cops do bad things and are in almost visceral denial of prevailing institutionalized racism in Amerika, even as they entertain racist stereotypes, fears and caricatures of people of color. White Amerika has a very different experience with cops than people of color. Blacks and Browns especially. Indeed, Black parents across Amerika must take special pains to teach their sons to show special deference and passive body language when confronted by cops to avoid being beaten or killed, just as Blacks had to be trained to act when in company of whites during chattel slavery and open Jim Crow, also to avoid beatings and lynching.

In essence, the entire grand jury proceeding was staged to produce the very outcome that resulted, and in a society racially divided by policy, practice and design of those in power.

## Towards a Real Solution

How absurd is it anyway to look for a savior in the very courts that we know and see every day railroading people of color into prison at such astronomical rates, that they are recognized to be a continuation of both slavery and Jim Crow?[4]

Yet this is exactly what our frustrated youth are being misled to do (while being left in the crosshairs) by an old guard aspiring bourgeois civil rights misleadership, who can do nothing more than continue engaging in empty moralizing and playing bargaining games with the very forces that are murdering our youth and bent on our suffering and destruction.

Indeed, every time I hear of these civil-rightists raising a hue and cry against yet another government outrage, I'm reminded of the words of Anthony Asadullah Samad, criticizing the ineffective civil rights advocacy tactics in the *Black Commentator* some years back:

> "Whether it's protest, negotiation, boycott or voter revolt (the latter two of which we rarely, if ever, use), watching Black advocacy is like watching re-runs of *Sanford and Son*; you know what's about to come next—and what the line is going to be when Redd Foxx grabs his chest ... Okay, this is where they march in. Now, they're about to holler and scream, and give long speeches, watch 'em. Here is where they put the community mothers up to cry, sigh, ain't it sad?

Now this is the part where they march out singing 'we shall overcome,' then they'll go home and be quiet until the next time we get caught violating them or their interests. But the response will be the same."

And we should remember that while these old tactics proved effective in dismantling the old Jim Crow laws of the rural South, they failed miserably in changing the oppressed conditions, including police murders and brutality in the urban communities of color. Indeed, these stark failures led to the demise and discrediting of the civil rights movement in the urban areas, which gave rise to youth-based, Black and Brown liberation movements, and struggles for socialism in Amerika in the 1960s–70s.

It was the ineffectiveness and failures of the civil rights movement to address urban suffering that resulted in the mass urban uprisings of 1964–1968. And each of those uprisings was triggered by police murders or beatings of urban Blacks, exactly as continues to occur today in the face of these fruitless civil rights tactics.

It was in response to just such conditions that the Black Panther Party took root and won broad support as a community-based revolutionary organization that brought real solutions to the oppressed communities and real challenge to the murderous police. It was actually in their response to a police killing of a Black male, Denzil Dowell on April 1, 1967 (a murder not very different from Michael Brown's), that the Panthers brought an effective model of leadership and resistance to urban people. And one that also pointed out the futility of spontaneous mass uprisings. As Panther co-founder and Defense Minister Huey Newton pointed out:

> "We are continuing to function in petty, futile ways, divided, confused, fighting among ourselves, we are still in the elementary stage of throwing rocks, sticks, empty wine bottle and beer cans at racist cops who lie in wait to murder unarmed Black people. The racist cops have worked out a system for suppressing these spontaneous rebellions that flare up from the anger, frustration and desperation of the masses of Black People. We can no longer afford the dubious luxury of the terrible casualties wantonly inflicted upon us by the cops during these spontaneous rebellions ... There is a world of difference between 30 million unarmed, submissive Black people and 30 million Black people armed with freedom and defense guns and the strategic methods of liberation."[5]

The Panthers instantly struck fear in the hearts of the murderous police and the centers of capitalist power in the U.S., and won allies across all exploited sectors of U.S. society: poor white hillbillies and working-class whites and students, Mexicans/Chicanos, Puerto Ricans, Natives, anti-war activists, youth gangs, etc. But as an inexperienced youth organization, they were ill-equipped to contend with or even recognize the dirty counter-intelligence tactics of the police, led and organized by the Federal government, which had coopted and infiltrated the civil rights movement. The government's anti-Panther crusade applied devious no-holds-barred methods developed and refined from use in war and peacetime against foreign "enemies" and political movements.

As a result, the BPP ended up internally split along antagonistic lines and critically wounded. But it gave us, by far, the best example and lessons of organized tactical resistance to the oppressive U.S. system, which we can continue to learn from and build on, and this is the basis of the work of the New African Black Panther Party-Prison Chapter.

The same mass ferment and anger of our youth is evident and cries out for real solutions as it was during the old Panther era. And without a genuine revolutionary organization and leadership it will be coopted and converted into a tool of the old conformist collaborationist civil rights agenda, that has us looking to our oppressors to be our savior instead of ourselves, or it will explode into destructive spontaneous uprisings which the pigs actually want, because it polarizes New Afrikan/Black and white society instead of allying us, and gives them grounds to justify their murderous and militaristic practices that we are rising against.

*Dare to Struggle, Dare to Win!*
*All Power to the People!*

## END NOTES

1. Now, if the prosecutor knows or believes no crime was committed, then there exists no basis at all to present a case to a grand jury. To do so would be an illegal misuse of the grand jury process and to convert the process into something other than its intended purpose.

2. See Marisol Bello et al., "Grand Jury Charges Easy, Except Against Police: Prosecutor Piled on Members An Extreme Amount of Info," *USA Today*, p. 3A, November 26, 2014.

3. Johnnie Cochran, *A Lawyer's Life*, p. 111.

4. See Michelle Alexander, *The New Jim Crow: Mass Incarceration in the Age of Colorblindness*, (NY: The New Press, 2010/2013).

5. Huey P. Newton, "In Defense of Self Defense," *Black Panther*, June 20, 1967, pp. 3–4.

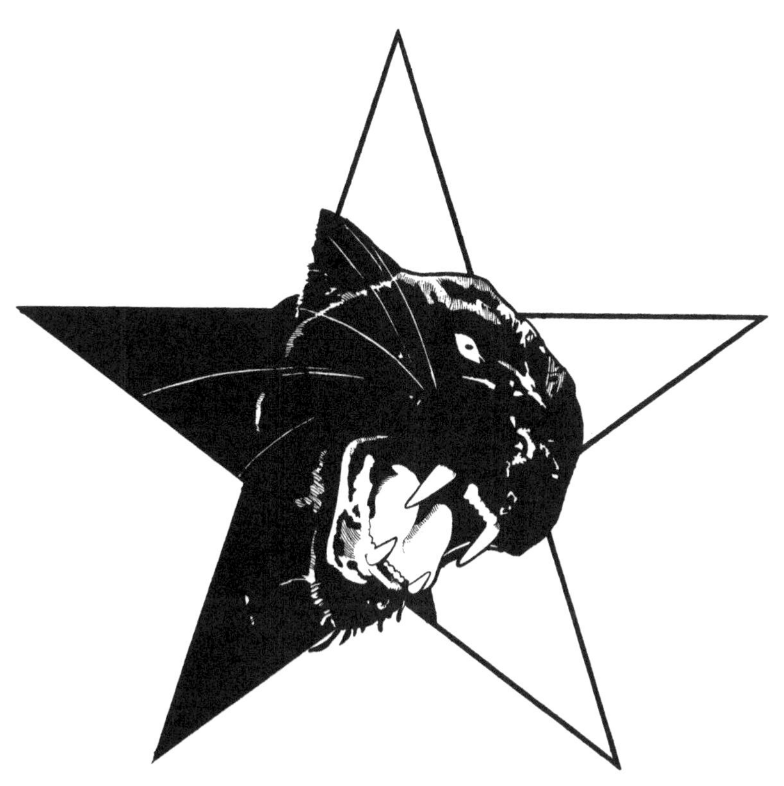

"When the prison doors are opened, the real dragons will fly out."
*Ho Chi Minh*

From the dungeons of Amerika, where silence and isolation are daily enforced, Rashid Johnson's voice rings out with unmistakable clarity. His call for revolution of the global capitalist system could not be more unequivocal. The clarity of his analysis unmasks the violence faced by prisoners—a fact of daily life for more than two million inmates in the USA (a higher proportion of prisoners to population than in North Korea). In the name of human rights, Amerika has murdered millions of innocent civilians since World War 2, from Korea to Vietnam and more recently in Iraq and Afghanistan. While much the rest of the world abhors capital punishment and lifetime imprisonment, Amerikan judicial practice is little more than a contemporary form of slavery. The masters get away with murder while those at the bottom of the hierarchy face deprivation and hardship.

Even captured North Korean infiltrators who spent decades in prison have been released by South Korea, white Weatherpeople were declared immune from prosecution, and many captured RAF prisoners were released by German authorities. Yet dozens of Afrikan-Amerikan freedom fighters languish behind bars, with no prospects for liberation from confinement. In Amerika's gulags, how many thousands have abandoned hope of ever again being free?

Rather than considering themselves simply as victims of the prison-industrial complex, however, Rashid and the New Afrikan Black Panther Party-Prison Chapter (NABPP-PC) carry forward the struggle for freedom from one generation to the next. Within the belly of the beast, their determination and energy proudly claims the tradition of the original Black Panther Party founded in 1966. Rashid and the NABPP-PC boldly speak truth to power. They fight racism with solidarity and stand up to injustice in their daily lives. Inspired by his intelligence and determination, the new Panthers for whom he speaks are organized among the most oppressed within the USA. The threat they pose to the powers-that-be stands in direct proportion to the brutality meted out to them.

Years of sadistic violence aimed at quelling Rashid's indomitable spirit have only further radicalized him. His treatment at the hands of malevolent guards has been exceptional. Sentenced in Virginia to life in prison, he was named that state's "most dangerous inmate," after which he was regularly confronted with violence from guards and denied basic rights such as proper health care, family visits and letters from friends (among whom I am proud to count myself). Transferred overnight and without notice 3,000 miles away to Oregon, Rashid was suddenly immersed in a prison system with a majority white population where white supremacists openly paraded. Within a few months, he had forged interracial alliances that threatened the system's divide and rule strategy. Without warning, he was transferred to Texas just as suddenly as he had been expelled from Virginia. Once again he was accosted with the violence of miscreant jailers.

More than forty years ago, prison writings such as George Jackson's *Soledad Brother* and *Blood in My Eye* played significant roles in inspiring us. George's trenchant exposé in theory and practice of how rule by force rather than consent dominated our lives resulted in his murder in 1971. As society becomes more like a prison under the surveillance state, his insights—like those of Rashid—become even more perceptive. As Amerika moves toward a system of total control by a secret government, our lives on the outside increasingly resemble the conditions under which prisoners live. In clear prose, Rashid unmasks such lies as that the 1960s civil rights movement ended racism, corporate capitalism works for the benefit of the majority, and prisoners for life have lost their humanity. His loving faith in people is revealed in the precise strokes of his artwork, strikingly realistic images crafted with ordinary pen and paper.

Although I have never met Rashid in person, I have felt the glow of his gentle love. In 2012, after my comrade-soulmate suddenly passed, I was as low as one can get in this life. Within days, Rashid embraced me with a loving drawing he sent, a pen and ink piece that was one of the first pieces of mail I received after Shin Eun-jung had left me to my isolation. He enclosed a letter explaining how his need for love, for a partner with whom he could live and work, would never be fulfilled. By sharing his sorrow with me in my moment of loss and desperation, we touched souls. Our common ground strengthened the bond we felt as revolutionaries in the center of imperialism.

You—reader—you will feel Rashid's love in the pages here. These are organizational documents, which if written by any normal bureaucrat, progressive or not, would put even the most ardent true believer to sleep. Yet, as you absorb Rashid's passion and intelligence in these pages, you will discover a deep humanity. Many of you, I suspect, will be unable to sleep after reading Rashid's prose—neither to sleep that evening nor to return to the deep sleep that might have overtaken you.

But it is not merely personal feelings that compel me to work with Rashid to finish his book. Indeed, as he (and anyone who has read my work) knows well, we have many political differences. Why then have I spent dozens of hours helping bring his book to print? My political sense is that revolutionary solidarity across ideological barriers could be a key factor in determining the difference between our movement's future victory and defeat. How often have I pondered the question: If only Russian and Chinese Communists had united against the USA, how different might the outcome of the 20th century have been?

Because I reject the state's censorship of Rashid's ideas, I work to break the chains engulfing him within Amerika's gulags. I also reject the kind of Left sectarianism that has brought murder, mayhem and isolation into liberation movements the world over. Real solidarity demands that all of us support the movement's political prisoners, even if we have disagreements with their actions or perspectives.

As an intellectual, I feel a responsibility to help give voice to insurgencies. By facilitating the publication of Rashid's book, I assist propagating his unique clarity of mind as he cuts through obfuscations and hesitations to expose the violent reality he knows only too well. Within the prison-industrial complex, Rashid's ideas build resistance and solidarity—no small feat under his circumstances.

When Rashid and I first got to know each other, I wondered: what could I possibly offer him? After some thought, I decided that the best possible means of showing my solidarity would be to send him the most trenchant critique of his writing I could muster—and I did. After we exchanged two letters, however, the state intervened, blocking my letters from delivery, cutting off further discussion. Permit me here to elaborate.

In this book, Rashid lays out his organizational blueprint for building a revolutionary party modeled on that of Lenin and Mao Zedong—and continuing the struggles of the original Black Panthers. In my view, the Leninist party is an outmoded organizational form developed more than a century ago under very different conditions than those we face in 2014. Moreover, the very democratic centralism that Rashid embraces was a key reason for the BPP's demise.

The historical specificity of successful organizations, the suitability of the Bolsheviks to 1917 Russia, of Mao's Communist Party to 1949 China, is proven by their seizures of power. Similarly, the place in history of the IWW, SDS and the Panthers correlate with the massive popular resonance each of these formations enjoyed. For whatever reason, each of these organizations has been reincarnated decades after they all but disappeared along with the vital popular movements that spawned them. Without the innovative energy of their initial emergence, inherited organizational forms can inhibit as much as they inspire and activate.

Precisely because the New Afrikan Black Panther Party-Prison Chapter continues the original mission of the Black Panther Party and takes it organizational form from them, it is important to consider the role of democratic centralism in the dissolution of the Panthers in the early 1970s. Was too much power in the hands of one person—or two people—regardless of how we understand the factions inside the organization that fought for control of the Party? Should multi-dimensional tendencies have been encouraged, not repressed?

I agree with Rashid that, "What the Panthers lacked, however, was a theoretical leader like Lenin who was rooted in and able to wage the decisive struggle to keep a genuinely revolutionary proletarian line in command of its ideology and work. Therefore, this split saw both factions follow the same flawed 'liquidationist' lines that Lenin had struggled against—namely one of rightist reformism and legalism (Huey's faction) and the other of ultra left militarism (Cleaver's faction)."

At the same time that the Panthers split, the mass movement was growing by leaps and bounds. As police and FBI infiltrated, attacked, and assassinated members of the BPP, the Party had to close itself off for its own survival. Its relationship with the popular movement became strained. The growing gap between the BPP and the movement it led was most visible at the 1970 Revolutionary Peoples' Constitutional Convention—the high point of the 1960s in the USA, when more than ten thousand of us gathered in Philadelphia at the invitation of the BPP to write a new constitution for the USA. Revealed in reports written by decentralized workshops, the popular movement's aspirations were far ahead of the BPP's positions. And with the split in the Party, Huey decided to liquidate all chapters outside Oakland, where he hoped to build an exemplary commune as the basis for revolutionary intercommunalism. Facilitated by "democratic centralism," Huey unilaterally expelled dozens of comrades, left others to face decades of prison, and liquidated dissident voices within the Party as he shut it down as a national organization.

Hindsight allows us today to look back with greater clarity than was possible in 1970. Yet even then, some among us sought to revolutionize the revolution. Herbert Marcuse understood we needed a "new, very flexible kind of organization, one that does not impose rigorous principles, one that allows for movement and initiative. An organization without the 'bosses' of the old parties or political groups. This point is very important. The leaders of today are the products of publicity. In the actual movement there are no leaders as there were in the Bolshevik Revolution, for example."

From the dungeons of Pennsylvania, Russell "Maroon" Shoatz has already articulated criticisms that Marxist-Leninist parties that have "... gained power using DC have always ended up using it to defeat the aspirations of the workers and the oppressed, and to install themselves as the new ruling class." His point should give pause to notions of simply adopting that DC organizational form in the future. Furthermore, while parties aligned with the 3rd International led successful takeovers of power in Russia, China, Vietnam, and North Korea, "Leninist" parties in the core of capitalism in the 20th century betrayed or opposed revolutionary movements in France in 1968 and Italy in 1977. Rashid would rightly say that neither of these latter two were Maoist parties—but then, I must ask: What about the Khmer Rouge's killing of more than 1 million Cambodians after power fell into their hands with the defeat of U.S. imperialism in Indochina in 1975?

In tying together the 1960s Panthers with 21st century social movements, isn't it possible that revolutionary organizations might break with inherited organizational forms? Clearly leadership by the most oppressed—as the Panthers were for the vibrant Rainbow Coalition that emerged in the 1960s—remains historically necessary. Might future Panthers have a participatory democratic structure? Can a revolutionary party celebrate differences, while uniting the many to defeat the few? Certainly not with a single central committee thinking for the whole movement—let alone one that kidnaps and kills leading activists who disagree with them—as tragically befell thousands of comrades in Russia and Spain, to say nothing of many others killed by Stalinist violence.

Democratic centralism with people like Rashid would be a pleasure, but in the real world of male competitive power politics, it means sectarianism, hierarchy—or worse, far worse. I do not doubt that Rashid would be diligent and flexible, that, he would do as he says—to "discuss things thoroughly and practice mutual criticism in a comradely way. Strive to reach consensus. Uphold decisions by the majority." The tendency that is encouraged within organizations founded on democratic centralism, however, is to elevate leadership above general members, to insulate the elite from criticisms, and to punish dissident voices.

Very often, anyone in such formations who is bold enough to offer a different view than what comes down from leadership is automatically written off as "petty bourgeois"—at best or, in less familiar moments, "racist" or "sexist" (when those they criticize are different in race or gender)—or even traitorous. Regarding "non-proletarian" insights as less worthy, a judgment is routinely made that marginalizes the "petty bourgeois"—as well as the lumpenproletariat. No matter how reactionary they were found to be by Marx in 19th century Paris, the lumpen have been a central constituency for the Panthers and many other movements. We should therefore be cautious with completely negative evaluations of "non-proletarian" constituencies. Rashid takes a step in that direction: "The petty bourgeoisie have produced some fine revolutionary intellectuals and leaders for the revolutionary proletarian movement, such as Marx, Engels, Lenin, Mao, Cabral, Nkrumah and so on, but on the whole, many more have been disappointments."

Clearly, Rashid believes that the M-L party is a product of "proletarian" thinking. In his article, "On the Vanguard Party, Once Again," Rashid writes:

> "But the critical problem which opponents of the vanguard party have never answered in over 100 years of debate is the theoretical and practical question of how to unify the broad and fragmented working class into a united movement wherein it is conscious of itself (and its interests) as a class."

This is a critical point of departure for I believe that the answer is that workers—and the vast majority of society—must do this for themselves if genuine freedom (a socialism worthy of the name) is to exist. The difference between heteronomously imposed and autonomously determined unity is crucial.

Every genuine revolution develops its own theory in accordance with local conditions. In China, Mao insisted upon a break with the Russian Revolution's strategy of seizing power through urban insurrections after mechanical imitations cost the movement tens of thousands of lives. For his critique, he was expelled from the party. In Vietnam, Ho and Giap insisted upon a break with Chinese human wave assaults prior to victory at Dien Bien Phu. They instead ordered trenches to be dug increasingly closer to enemy positions, saving many lives in the process. Rashid does not simply take as ready-made the original Panther form. By including White Panthers and Brown Panthers within the NABPP-PC as well as forging an alliance with the Red Heart Warrior Society, he adapts his vision to contemporary conditions.

As Marx famously said, we do not make history under conditions we select, "but under circumstances existing already, given and transmitted from the past." It is no accident, therefore, that at the same time as Huey P. Newton articulated his vision of "revolutionary intercommunalism," anarchist thinker Murray Bookchin arrived at a similar conclusion—although he named it "libertarian municipalism." Historical conditions have created the possibility of reduced governmental powers and increased power to the people. In the 21st century, as we move in the direction of revolutionary intercommunal struggles, wouldn't that involve communes in different parts of the world forming from below and entering into alliances with each other? We already see emergent communal forms in the Gwangju Uprising of 1980, in the seizure of Taksim and Tahrir Squares. The task of revolutionary organization would be to stabilize the participatory character of decision-making in communes in every region while lubricating connections from the grassroots nationally and internationally. At each of these levels, many formations and types of organizations will be involved. There will be no single vanguard party leading the way forward, but many vanguards, such as Zapatistas, Occupy Wall Streeters, Indignados, the Greek anarchists and Tunisian actor-activists.

Despite all differences, Rashid has much to teach all of us—and not only those enrolled in "poor man's universities." He and his comrades in the NABPP-PC continue the Panthers' glorious tradition. They refuse to submit to authoritarian control no matter what the cost. Their solution to the problem faced by all of us today is not simply to reform the existing system. They speak for the most oppressed within the global imperialist system. All revolutionaries should offer them support and respect.

*Panther Love!*
*All Power to the People!*

George Katsiaficas
Santiago, Chile
November 23, 2014

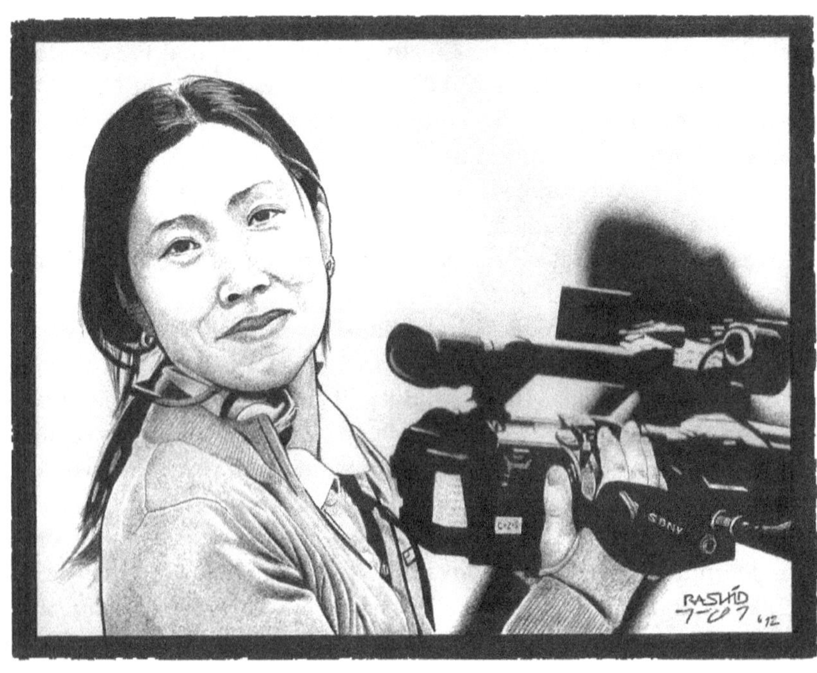

Comrade Rashid has asked me to respond to Comrade George Katsiaficas' Afterword, which is appropriate, I think, because his criticisms reflect those of many who oppose capitalist-imperialism, yet hold back from becoming "all-the-way revolutionary." As Panthers and revolutionary communists, we firmly believe in combining unity and struggle and treating people's incorrect ideas as "loads upon their backs," and in a comradely manner, we seek to help them get rid of this unnecessary baggage. Overall, a person's social being determines their consciousness, but it is possible for people to "commit class suicide" and through study, struggle and social practice to remold their worldview and adopt that of the revolutionary proletariat.

So, with "Panther Love," I will attempt to point out some of the fuzzy thinking and incorrect ideas Comrade George has expressed in hope this will promote greater clarity on these questions from a revolutionary proletarian perspective. But first we must ask: "Why does the petty bourgeoisie vacillate so much?" The answer is because they are the "middle class," (really not a true class at all), in a world that is polarizing between the two real classes, the bourgeoisie (capitalist class) and the proletariat (working class), and they vacillate between allying with one class or the other depending on circumstances and self-identity.

The proletariat is destined to be "The Last Class in History," and it is the first "All-The-Way Revolutionary" class in History. This is because we are at the end of one epoch of History and the beginning of another. The "Epoch of Exploitation" is in its final stage—capitalist-imperialism (or capitalist neo-liberalism)—and the new epoch—Communism—is in birth. Indeed, the World Proletarian Socialist Revolution is in its 167th year, if we take the *Communist Manifesto* as its starting point.

The proletariat can only liberate itself from its exploitation and oppression by liberating all of humanity and ending the system of class exploitation altogether. It must revolutionize all of society and all human relations, overthrowing all outmoded ideas and conventions and uprooting that which regenerates exploitation and perpetuates the inequality of class society. The proletariat is destined to remake the world on new foundations of equality and social justice for all, to remake the world in its own interest and image, which is a world without borders or wars in which each contributes according to one's abilities and receives according to one's needs, for the resolution of the class struggle can only be the elimination of classes.

The petty bourgeoisie, on the other hand, have no future at all, except as future proletarians, a future even now being forced upon them by the bourgeoisie, as the concentration of wealth into ever fewer hands pushes them back down the ladder of upward mobility. Historically, they are caught between the dictatorship of the bourgeoisie and the dictatorship of the proletariat, and so they vacillate and have pipe dreams of a "Third Way" that secures their position without the necessity of committing "class suicide," (and keeps the wage slaves and the poor in their place at the bottom).

Now, Comrade George ponders the question: "If only Russian and Chinese Communists had united against the USA, how different might the outcome of the 20th century have been?" well, we must point out that they were united, as Mao expressed in his "The East Wind is Prevailing Over the West Wind" speech he delivered in Moscow in 1957, when delegates from 64 communist and workers' parties gathered to celebrate the 40th anniversary of the Great October Socialist Revolution.

This great unity had been forged under Comrade Stalin's leadership of the World Communist Movement. But what happened? Modern revisionism, led by Nikita Khrushchev, swept through the Socialist Bloc and World Communist Movement like food poisoning at a fireman's picnic. Of the socialist countries, only People's China and Albania stood firmly against this revisionist coup, while others vacillated or capitulated. Was this "Left Sectarianism"?

If so, we must accuse Lenin of "Left Sectarianism" when he stood firm against the revisionist capitulation of the Second International during World War I, when the various "Socialists" retreated to their "National Tents" to unite with "their own" bourgeoisie. And was Marx being "Sectarian" when he stood firm for "Scientific Socialism" against the Utopians and Anarchists who split the First International? If we are going to sum up the 20th century correctly, the great advances of the World Proletarian Socialist Revolution must be credited to the leadership of Lenin, Stalin and Mao, and the great setbacks to Kautsky, Khrushchev and Deng (and other revisionists of their ilk).

The question is one of revolutionary science vs. revisionism, and yes, the 20th century would have ended differently if revolutionary science had defeated revisionism, instead of the other way around. And who was the real winner? U.S. imperialism!

The world certainly has changed a great deal since the time of Lenin, and even of Mao, but Leninism and Maoism are based on applications of the "Science of Revolution" with one built on the foundation of the other and both further enriching Marxism. The Panthers, and especially Huey P. Newton, enriched it further, and NABPP-PC is building on this. Leninism is Marxism in the period of imperialism, and we are still in that period, but imperialism has itself evolved, and we must use the science of revolution to make fresh analysis of this new period of U.S. global hegemony and world revolution.

Now to the question of "Democratic Centralism:" What is it and why do we need it to properly apply the science of revolution? It is not very complicated, really, it is about combining the greatest degree of inner-party democracy with unity of action once a decision has been made. Now we should all be able to agree that it is dysfunctional to have a breakdown in either area. But evidently not! There are those who oppose inner party democracy and those who oppose centralism. Without broad inner-party democracy, the center is blind and cannot reap the benefits of learning from the masses, and without a strong center, the inner-party democracy falls apart and there is no unity in action.

There are those who want ultra-democracy and unlimited debate and discussion without ever coming to unity, and those who want to practice commandism and to order the comrades around without accountability. Neither of these tendencies is democratic centralism and both reflect petty-bourgeois idealism and individualism. Once a vote is taken, those who are in the minority must subordinate their views and carry out the decision of the majority, or else quit the party. Now some complain that this violates their individual rights, but to be in the party you have to stand with the party. If you try to sabotage the party's work, you violate the discipline that makes the party work, and you deserve to be disciplined or expelled. In some case you may be treated as a criminal, as if you took a bribe to betray the party and the people.

That said, it is still a Marxist-Leninist principle to swim against the tide and stand firm against revisionism. It is true that Mao got kicked off the Central Committee of the Chinese Communist Party, (I believe twice), for opposing incorrect strategic decisions, but when the majority summed up that he had been right, he was not only voted back but made Chairman over those who had knocked him down. Isn't this how democratic centralism is supposed to work?

What was actually going on in 1970? Briefly, the Central Committee of the BPP was attempting to make the qualitative leap from revolutionary nationalism to Marxism-Leninism, but more than that, they were applying revolutionary science to making a fresh analysis of the world situation and the prospects for revolution. It is precisely at such moments that the vanguard is apt to get isolated and the comrades are likely to retreat.

What Huey and the CC uncovered was that the World Proletarian Socialist Revolution was entering a new period, which Huey's "Theory of Revolutionary Intercommunalism" was intended to define and address. His "Speech at Boston College" in 1970 introduced some radical new concepts. The "growing gap" between the BPP and the radical movement that was evident at the People's Constitutional Convention that year was not because the more than 10,000 of us in attendance were "far ahead" of the BPP's positions—we weren't even on the same page. In fact, the idea of writing a new constitution for the U.S. was pretty "retro" considering that the BPP had summed up that the U.S. had ceased to be a nation and had become a world dominating empire in which socialist revolution was impossible outside the context of the World Proletarian Socialist Revolution, and we needed to be preparing for a world dictatorship of the proletariat.

The BPP went into a nose-dive after the first meeting of the People's Constitutional Convention in Philadelphia. Faced not only with COINTELPRO and their cultural Black nationalist proxies, by internal factionalization and now rejection by their "New Left" allies, Huey and the CC "circled their wagons," risking everything on Bobby Seale's run for mayor of Oakland. Trying to distance themselves from the "Left" adventurists, they swung too far to the right and into the arms of the Democratic Party.

It was not democratic-centralism but the lack of it that was a contributing factor to the split in the BPP, a weakness the FBI COINTELPRO agents could exploit. The CC did not first win the whole party to Huey's theory before going public with it, it came down as a booklet of his Boston College speech entitled "Long Live the Invincible Thoughts of Huey P. Newton." The mostly white radicals summoned to the People's Constitutional Convention had not been won to the line change in the BPP prior to the event, nor had thought been given to holding a very different kind of People's Convention, one that would have been a "Clarion Call" to the world's oppressed to build a Worldwide United Front Against Capitalist-Imperialism.

Now if Huey's theory had been as "Off The Wall" as the "New Left" proclaimed it to be, it would hold little relevance today, except as a footnote to History. But 45 years later it rings with relevance, and it is the "New Left's" analysis that stinks of rank idealism. We can truly say that in "The Movement" of today there are no leaders as there were in the Bolshevik Revolution, but is this a good thing? What we have is a lot of mediocrity and amateurishness raised to a principle. Even the forces of repression do not regard this "Left" as a threat or more than petty-bourgeois intellectual posturing divorced from the masses of oppressed people.

Comrade Maroon puts the question backwards. It is not "Leninist" parties that have historically sold out the workers and oppressed people, but formerly "Leninist" parties that have turned revisionist and "The (white Petty-Bourgeois) Movement" in general. Where are the "Marxist" parties (that are not "Leninist") that haven't built careers out of selling out the workers and oppressed people? If you get married, you might end up divorced and single, but marriage isn't the cause of being single. Parties can go rotten (just like individuals). There is no magic to democratic centralism that prevents a revisionist takeover, but without it, the proletariat doesn't have a chance to defeat revisionism.

Spontaneously, the working class remains stuck in trade unionism and accommodation to wage slavery. It needs the science of revolution to get beyond this, which means it needs the help of revolutionary intellectuals. But in capitalist society, the proletarian wage slaves are excluded from higher education by the cost. The petty bourgeoisie, who have the access to academia, are groomed to accept a bourgeois worldview and regard the dictatorship of the proletariat with dread.

Even among "Leftists," they all too often approach the science of revolution as an intellectual game of self-validation, not as a real struggle for power—not as "Class War." They often play a game of "bait and switch"—"Want revolution? Cool, I can hook you up—Here try Occupy, Arab Spring or EZLN instead!" But where is the revolution? Where is the overthrow of one class by another? How can you have "many vanguards" unless people are going in many different directions at once? In other words; unless you are substituting disunity for unity and diversion for revolution!

The comrades of NABPP-PC and the United Panther Movement know they are condemned men. Almost all are condemned to spend their lives locked away in solitary confinement, tormented (even tortured) by racist guards and will probably die in captivity like Comrade Hasan Shakur or Comrade Samuel "Angel" Coley. So why do they refuse to be counted among the "broken men"? Why have they raised the banner of Pantherism, except to illuminate the path forward for the rest of us? Many had to begin by learning basic literacy before they could study and master the science of revolution. Some teach by reading aloud into a ventilation duct or passing of handwritten notes from hand to hand.

Younger comrades, like Rashid, learned from older, original Panthers, still locked down for daring to aspire to be "all-the-way revolutionary." Many were formerly members of lumpen street organizations who were tricked into fratricidal gang wars by the strategy of mass criminalization and mass incarceration of the poor that targets Black youth in particular. Even if they never held a straight job on the outside, they learn they can adopt the worldview of the revolutionary proletariat. Unlike the lumpen proletariat of Marx's time, they are products of the surplus of labor power that marks capitalist-imperialism in decline.

In Today's World, the peasantry and industrial proletariat are in decline as they are displaced by automation and mechanized, capitalist agribusiness. The only growing "class" is the lumpen proletariat, who are forced to face day to day survival "by any means necessary." In every urban center of the world, their ranks are legion. Around the world, more than half the people are struggling to survive on $2.50 a day or less. They have already come to the "Dead End" that is at the bottom of the downward spiral of capitalist-imperialism. They cannot on their own overthrow the system, but they can serve as a catalyst to inspire the rest of the proletariat and masses of people to rise up and seize the power with their own hands.

For the lumpen proletarians, revolutionary theory is not an academic exercise. Like the petty bourgeoisie, they must "commit class suicide" to become "all-the-way revolutionary." They have to remold their world outlook and "proleterianize" themselves. This is a struggle the comrades inside the razor wire are well familiar with, where becoming a revolutionary intellectual marks you for "special treatment" in the "special housing units" where every cruel trick is employed to break a human being's spirit. "Half-way revolutionary ideology" is just not good enough!

Surely it is true that: "When the prison doors are opened, the real dragons will come out!" The strategy of the NABPP-PC, and the United Panther Movement it leads in the prisons, is to transform the "Slave Pens of Oppression" into "Schools of Liberation" in the context of building a "Worldwide United Front Against Capitalist-Imperialism, Racism and Police State Repression." It is not a "Security Threat Group" but a serious political party dedicated to the propagation of revolutionary science among the most oppressed of the oppressed and creating revolutionary intellectuals. Not that we do not welcome comrades from the more privileged strata to join us in the struggle; comrades like Lenin and Che, who become "all-the-way revolutionary" and take the stand of the oppressed class, but on the whole, we must be our own liberators.

We recognize that there is a dialectic between the oppressed masses and their leaders, and we must create great leaders who have been forged and tempered in struggle, and who are motivated by great love of the people. Leaders like: Malcolm X, "Bunchy" Carter, George Jackson and Kevin "Rashid" Johnson. We further recognize that leadership is primarily a question of ideological and political line. Correct ideas always develop in struggle and contradiction with incorrect ones. We must be fearless and welcome hardships. The most worthy comrades will always be found where the struggle is hardest and sacrifices are demanded.

As one young imprisoned comrade wrote to me: "If I was willing to kill or be killed for a corner that in no way would ever really belong to me, now that I am politically conscious, what wouldn't I be willing to do or to give up to liberate the whole world?"

I hope this book will inspire many new comrades to join the struggle and to become "Real Dragons." I hope too that it will inspire more intellectuals like Comrade George to ally with the Panthers of this generation, to open their minds and allow themselves to learn from the oppressed masses, throwing unnecessary baggage by the roadside and picking up the banner of "All-The-Way Revolution"!

*Dare to Struggle, Dare to Win!*
*All Power to the People!*

# ABOUT THE CONTRIBUTORS

A longtime activist for peace and justice, **George Katsiaficas** has written books on the global uprising of 1968 and European autonomous movements, in which he developed the concept of the eros effect to explain the sudden emergence of internationally synchronized insurgencies. Together with Kathleen Cleaver, he co-edited *Liberation, Imagination and the Black Panther Party.* His latest book is *Asia's Unknown Uprisings,* an analysis of the Asian wave from 1980–1992 that overthrew 8 dictatorships in 9 places. He is based in Gwangju, South Korea, where is International Coordinator of the May 18 Institute. His web site is http://www.eroseffect.com

**Jared A. Ball** is a father and husband. After that he is a multimedia host, producer, journalist and educator. Ball is also a founder of "mixtape radio" and "mixtape journalism" about which he wrote *I MiX What I Like: A MiXtape Manifesto* (AK Press, 2011) and is co-editor of *A Lie of Reinvention: Correcting Manning Marable's Malcolm X* (Black Classic Press, 2012). Ball is an associate professor of communication studies at Morgan State University in Baltimore, MD. and can be found online at IMIXWHATILIKE.ORG.

**Jalil Muntaqim** is is a former member of the Black Panther Party and the Black Liberation Army. For the past 42 years, Jalil has been a political prisoner, and one of the New York Three (NY3), in retaliation for his activism in the 1960s and early 1970s. Jalil has had published a compilation of some of his prison writings, *We Are Our Own Liberators* (Arissa Media Group). His essays have been published in such anthologies as *The New Abolitionists: (Neo) Slave Narratives and Contemporary Prison Writings,* ed. Joy James (2005); *Schooling a Generation,* ed. Chinsole (2002); *This Country Must Change,* ed Craig Rosebraugh (2009). Jalil's articles have appeared in NYC's *Amsterdam News,* the *BayView* newspaper from San Francisco, and many other progressive publications. He has also completed a novel and a teleplay, seeking publication. Many of his poems have appeared in *Olive Trees Literary Magazine,* and a collection of his poetry *Escaping the Prism ... Fade to Black* was published by Kersplebedeb in 2015.

Over the years, **Tom "Big Warrior" Watts** has been involved in many struggles as a workers and social activist, and also as a member of the United Eastern Lenape Nation. For more on his biography, see page vii.

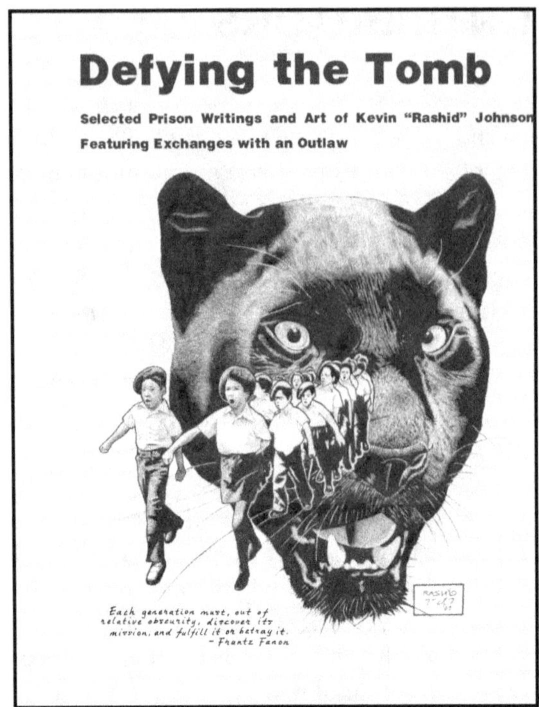


FOREWORD BY
RUSSELL "MAROON" SHOATS

INTRODUCTION BY
TOM BIG WARRIOR

AFTERWORD BY
SUNDIATA ACOLI

CO-PUBLISHED IN 2010
BY KERSPLEBEDEB

ISBN 978-1-894946-39-1

PAPERBACK

386 PAGES

$20.00

"Kevin 'Rashid' Johnson has put together an outstanding compendium of political essays and letters that addresses many of the critical issues of today. His intra-prison correspondences with his comrade, Outlaw, is a rewarding study in the determined and ingenious maneuvers that prisoners have to go through to politically educate and organize themselves—and others around them. As a result, just reading the book itself provides one with the basic foundation of a political education."

*—from the Afterword by Sundiata Acoli,*
*New Afrikan political prisoner of war*

"Your mission (should you decide to accept it) is to buy multiple copies of this book, read it carefully, and then get it into the hands of as many prisoners as possible. I am aware of no prisoner-written book more important than this one, at least not since George Jackson's *Blood In My Eye*. Revolutionaries and those considering the path of progress will find Kevin 'Rashid' Johnson's *Defying The Tomb* an important contribution to their political development."

*—Ed Mead, former political prisoner, George Jackson Brigade*


KERSPLEBEDEB, CP 63560, CCCP VAN HORNE, MONTREAL, QC, CANADA H3W 3H8
EMAIL: INFO@KERSPLEBEDEB.COM WEB: WWW.KERSPLEBEDEB.COM

www.ingramcontent.com/pod-product-compliance
Lightning Source LLC
LaVergne TN
LVHW020039110826
845155LV00029B/555

* 9 7 8 1 8 9 4 9 4 6 7 6 6 *